THE MARTIAL ARTS OF RENAISSANCE EUROPE

THE MARTIAL ARTS OF RENAISSANCE EUROPE

Sydney Anglo

Yale University Press
New Haven and London

Endpapers: detail from Johann Jacobi von Wallhausen, *Künstliche Piquen Handlung* (1617), figs 102–22. See also fig. 40 below.

Set in Garamond 3 by Best-set Typesetter Ltd., Hong Kong
Printed and bound by C.S. Graphics Pte Ltd., Singapore

Library of Congress Cataloging-in-Publication Data

Anglo, Sydney.
    The martial arts of Renaissance Europe / Sydney Anglo.
       p.   cm.
    Includes bibliographical references and index.
    ISBN 0-300-08352-1 (alk. paper)
    1. Martial arts – Europe – History – To 1500.   2. Martial arts – Europe – History – 16th
century.   3. Renaissance.   4. Europe – Social life and customs.   5. Europe – Social life and
customs – 16th century.   I. Title.
    U167.5.H3 A6395   2000
    796.8'094'09031 – dc21

                                                                        99-089407

A catalogue record for this book is available from the British Library.
10 9 8 7 6 5 4 3 2 1

Contents

Abbreviations

For full details see Bibliography.

Dall'Agocchie (1572)	Giovanni dall'Agocchie, *Dell'arte di scrimia* (Venice, 1572).
Agrippa (1553)	Camillo Agrippa, *Trattato di scientia d'arme* (Rome, 1553).
Auerswald (1539)	Fabian von Auerswald, *Ringer Kunst* (Wittenberg, 1539).
Capoferro (1610)	Ridolfo Capoferro, *Gran simulacro* (Siena, 1610).
Carranza (1582)	Geronimo Sánchez de Carranza, *Libro que trata de la philosophía de las armas* (Lisbon, 1582).
Castle (1885)	Egerton Castle, *Schools and Masters of Fence* (1885, reprinted 1969).
Dancie (1623)	François Dancie, *L'Espée de combat* (Tulle, 1623).
Docciolini (1601)	Marco Docciolini, *Trattato in materia di scherma* (Florence, 1601).
Fabris (1606)	Salvator Fabris, *Scienza e pratica d'arme* (Copenhagen, 1606).
Falloppia (1584)	Alfonso Falloppia, *Nuovo et brieve modo di schermire* (Bergamo, 1584).
Fiore, ed. Novati (1902)	Fiore de' Liberi da Premariacco, *Flos duellatorum*, ed. Francesco Novati (Bergamo, 1902).
Fiore (Getty MS)	Fiore de' Liberi da Premariacco, *Flos duellatorum*, Getty Museum, MS Ludwig XV, 13.
Gaiani (1619)	Giovan' Battista Gaiani, *Arte di maneggiar la spada* (Loano, 1619).
Gelli, *L'arte* (1906)	Jacopo Gelli, *L'arte dell'armi in Italia* (Bergamo, 1906).
Ghisliero (1587)	Federico Ghisliero, *Regole di molti cavagliereschi essercitii* (Parma, 1587).
Giganti (1606)	Nicoletto Giganti, *Scola overo teatro* (Venice, 1606).
Di Grassi (1570)	Giacomo di Grassi, *Ragione di adoprar sicuramente l'arme* (Venice, 1570).
Di Grassi (1594 edn.)	*Giacomo di Grassi, his True Arte of Defence, etc* (1594).
Hils (1985)	Hans-Peter Hils, *Meister Johann Liechtenauers Kunst* (Frankfurt, 1985).

La Touche (1670)   Philibert de la Touche, *Les Vrayes Principes de l'espée seule* (Paris, 1670).

Leguina, *Bibliografía* (1904)   Enrique de Leguina, *Bibliografía de la esgrima española* (Madrid, 1904).

Leguina, *Glosario* (1912)   Enrique de Leguina, *Glosario de voces de armería* (Madrid, 1912).

Liancour (1686)   André Wernesson de Liancour, *Le Maistre d'armes* (Paris, 1686).

Manciolino (1531)   Antonio Manciolino, *Opera nova* (Venice, 1531).

Marcelli (1686)   Francesco Antonio Marcelli, *Regole della scherma* (Rome, 1686).

Marozzo (1536)   Achille Marozzo, *Opera nova* (Modena, 1536).

Meyer (1570)   Joachim Meyer, *Gründtliche Beschreibung der kunst des Fechtens* (Strasbourg, 1570).

Monte (1509)   Pietro Monte, *Exercitiorum, atque artis militaris collectanea* (Milan, 1509).

Narváez (1600)   Luis Pacheco de Narváez, *Libro de las grandezas de la espada* (Madrid, 1600).

Pallavicini (1670)   Giuseppe Morsicato Pallavicini, *La scherma illustrata* (Palermo, 1670).

Pallavicini (1673)   Giuseppe Morsicato Pallavicini, *La seconda parte* (Palermo, 1673).

Pauernfeindt (1516)   Andre Pauernfeindt, *Ritterlicher kunst der Fechterey* (Vienna, 1516).

Sainct Didier (1573)   Henri de Sainct Didier, *Traicté contenant les secrets du premier livre de l'espée seule* (Paris, 1573).

Saviolo (1595)   Vincentio Saviolo, *Saviolo his Practise* (1595).

Silver (1599)   George Silver, *Paradoxes of Defence* (1599).

Swetnam (1617)   Joseph Swetnam, *The Schoole of the Noble and Worthy Science of Defence* (1617).

Talhoffer (1443)   Hans Talhoffer, *Fechtbuch aus dem Jahre 1443*, ed. G. Hergsell (Prague, 1889).

Talhoffer (1459)   Hans Talhoffer, *Fechtbuch aus dem Jahre 1459*, ed. G. Hergsell (Prague, 1889).

Talhoffer (1467)   Hans Talhoffer, *Fechtbuch aus dem Jahre 1467*, ed. G. Hergsell (Prague, 1887).

Thibault (1630)   Girard Thibault, *Académie de l'espée* (Leyden, 1630).

Viggiani (1575)   Angelo Viggiani, *Lo schermo* (Venice, 1575).

Wierschin (1965)   Martin Wierschin, *Meister Johann Liechtenauers Kunst des Fechtens* (Munich, 1965).

Photographic Acknowledgements

Illustrations 17, 60–1, 81–2, 92, 98, 102, 105, 114, 140, are from the Corble Collection of the Catholic University of Leuven and are reproduced by kind permission of the Librarian and Curator.

Colour plates IV–X, and illustrations 108–9 are from the Collection of the Royal Armouries and reproduced by kind permission of the Trustees of the Armouries.

Illustrations 107, 162, 167–8, 218 are reproduced by kind permission of the Bibliothèque Nationale in Paris.

Illustrations 113, 122–6 are reproduced by kind permission of the Getty Museum.

Colour plates III, XI–XIV, XXII–XXIV and illustration 20 are reproduced by kind permission of the Kunsthistorisches Museum of Vienna.

All other illustrations are from books and manuscripts in the R.L. Scott Collection and reproduced by kind permission of the Glasgow Art Gallery and Museum, Kelvinside.

To Nick Norman and Claude Blair

Preface

The seventeenth-century French fencing master, Philibert de la Touche, begins the preface to his treatise, *Les Vrais Principes de l'espée seule*, by affirming that, although he knows that most people do not read prefaces, he feels obliged to write one because there are important matters which he has been unable to fit into the body of the book. None the less, he assures his readers, 'I have made my preface so short that those who take the trouble to read it cannot be bored with it'.

I recognize, from my own bad practices, that La Touche was right. Prefaces are more often passed over than perused so that, to encourage the reader, it is necessary to keep them as short as possible. This preface, therefore, is confined to two important subjects: acknowledgement of help that I have received in the course of writing this book; and some words about the R.L. Scott Library in Glasgow which has so enormously facilitated both my research and the practical preparation of my work.

I have been particularly fortunate in my choice of friends. Indeed, had I realized that so many of them would prove useful, I would have tried to make more. Some, like Ronald Taylor, Pamela Waley, Raymond Jenkinson, Nosniknej Dnomyar, and Graham Gibbs, have given generously of their time and skill to help me out of some very knotty linguistic difficulties; others, like S. Matthew Galas and Noel Fallows, have kindly supplied information and copies of their own work relevant to my enquiries. The two great arms and armour experts to whom this book is dedicated – Claude Blair and the late Nick Norman – gave unremitting encouragement and constant advice on every kind of technical matter and, although it is true that they both helped swell my telephone bill to monstrous proportions, they were worth every penny of it. And finally I owe a special debt of gratitude to Bob Woosnam-Savage who was, for most of the time that this book has been in preparation, curator in charge of the R.L. Scott Collection in the Glasgow Museum and Art Gallery. When I was working on the collection, he used to share his office with me; he was tireless in locating items which had got themselves misplaced; and he organized all the photography from Scott's books and manuscripts which provide the major proportion of the illustrations in this present work. Had he not engaged me in so much conversation and community singing, I might have got through my work marginally quicker. But I happily forgive him.

My research was greatly helped by a generous award from the British Academy which enabled me not only to visit Glasgow but also to work in the Corble Collection at Leuven where the curator, Dr Coppens, and his assistant Guido Cloet gave me every assistance, and at the Kunsthistorische Museum in Vienna where Christian Beaufort Spontin and

Matthias Pfaffenbichler were enormously welcoming and helpful. A further visit to Glasgow to check references was aided by a small travel grant from the Society of Antiquaries of London. But, with regard to institutions, my greatest debt is to the Glasgow Museum and Art Gallery where the R.L. Scott Collection is preserved. The shipping magnate, Robert Lyons Scott, built up a remarkable collection of European arms and armour which, augmented by other materials at Kelvingrove, constitute one of the finest in Britain, although it is still relatively unappreciated except by a small band of specialists. More remarkable still – and scarcely known even to specialists – is the library assembled by Scott and bequeathed with his arms and armour to the city of Glasgow.[1] Scott began his acquisition of books and manuscripts with material relating to the history of swordsmanship but then expanded his horizons to cover every aspect of western military science: weaponry and defensive armour, chivalry, tournaments, duels, the art of war in general, artillery, cavalry, military medicine, physical training and military gymnastics. Moreover, he grasped the importance of buying variant versions and editions of primary texts so that, by the time of his death in 1939, his library had become perhaps the most comprehensive collection of its kind in the world and, thanks to his bequest, it retains this position. Earlier major fencing libraries such as those of José Ramón Garcia Donnell and Cyril Matthey were not kept intact and, indeed, Scott bought a considerable number of items from their sales. Alfred Hutton's books, now preserved at the Victoria and Albert Museum, are a valuable resource but total barely a twentieth part of Scott's library. Perhaps the only comparable accumulation is the Corble Collection put together by Scott's friendly rival Archibald Corble who bequeathed his magnificent library to the Catholic University of Leuven:[2] but Corble concentrated almost exclusively on fencing materials whereas Scott's interests embraced almost the entire field of western martial arts and warfare up to the mid-nineteenth century. Given the relatively scanty holdings of the Bibliothèque Nationale in non-French fencing books, and the fact that a significant part of the outstanding collection of fencing and duelling books in the British Library was destroyed in the Second World War, then the importance of R.L. Scott's library becomes all the greater. It is sad that, currently, the Scott Collection is not available for consultation and one can only hope that it will soon be possible to rectify this.

Introduction

> Let us suppose one man endued with an excellent naturall use and dexterity in handling
> his armes; and another to have added to that dexterity, an acquired Science, of where he
> can offend, or be offended by his adversarie, in every possible posture or guard: the ability
> of the former would be to the ability of the latter, as Prudence to Sapience; both usefull;
> but the latter infallible.

IT WAS WITH this martial example that Thomas Hobbes, in his *Leviathan* of 1651, sought
to clarify what he saw as the essential difference between *Prudentia* and *Sapientia* – that
is between wisdom acquired on the one hand by experience and, on the other, by
science. Given that Hobbes is England's mightiest political philosopher, the distinction is
not well made because he has, in fact, endowed his second fencer with both practical and
theoretical skill. This is weak enough, but his development of the figure is even worse
because he goes on to say that those who 'trusting onely to the authority of books, follow
the blind blindly, are like him that trusting to the false rules of a master of fence, ventures
praesumptuously upon an adversary that either kills or disgraces him'. Hobbes is here
begging the question. Are the rules prescribed by masters of fence necessarily false? And
did masters of fence ever advocate total reliance either on book learning or on physical
practice?[1]

The issue was much better handled by a writer active more than 150 years earlier who,
though vastly inferior to Hobbes as a philosopher, certainly knew much more about fencing
and about how to teach the martial arts. Pietro (or Pero) Monte (or Monti) was a late
fifteenth-century Spanish master of arms whose career was mainly pursued in Italy; and he
has been remembered by posterity solely because he figures in Baldassare Castiglione's *Libro
del Cortegiano* as the man who instructed the famous Galeazzo da Sanseverino in wrestling,
vaulting and handling various types of weapon. Monte is lauded by Castiglione as the 'true
and only master of every form of cultivated strength and agility'; and that he was well
known to his contemporaries is clear because Leonardo da Vinci, when puzzling over problems posed by the trajectory of javelins hurled from a sling, had scribbled himself a note
to talk about this with 'Pietro Monti'.[2]

What has generally been overlooked about Monte is the fact that he wrote and published
a great deal, including an elaborate treatise on physical exercise, the martial arts, and the
art of war – the *Exercitiorum atque artis militaris collectanea* (1509) – which includes a succinct statement on the problem which had so entangled Thomas Hobbes. We do not, Monte
insists, learn mechanical or manual skills by word alone. Speech must be accompanied by

practical demonstration. The limbs need some settled order of learning, in exactly the same way as does the intellect. One may, for instance, understand the meaning of words, yet find great difficulty in translating them into action; or, as in the case of mathematics, we may not fully grasp the significance of a set of symbols until our teacher actually demonstrates it to us. Thus, while he has himself embarked upon an explanation and description of corporal exercises, Monte insists that his lessons will be more readily grasped if there is a master to show how they should be done – although, he warns, the physical action will not immediately be performed as correctly by the pupil as by the teacher.[3] Many masters of arms shared this view of the intimate interrelation between theory and practice; and it is largely because of their endeavours to give some sort of permanence to their ideas that we are able to attempt a reconstruction of a very important but relatively little-studied subject in the history of ideas – the martial arts of renaissance Europe.

Both the significance of these arts, and the fact that they have been largely ignored by historians, are easily established. While nobody has ever doubted the importance of expertise in the handling of weapons to the knightly classes of medieval Europe, our knowledge of what these skills were and how they were acquired remains generalized and inexact. More remarkably, the same holds true of the Renaissance when, despite the constant reiteration by humanist educational theorists of the value of training the body as well as the mind, we still know next to nothing about the practice of physical education and the provision of combat training for youths.

Our understanding is no greater when we move from the schoolroom to the battlefield or duelling ground. Medieval and renaissance warfare have long been under academic scrutiny, and historians have much to say about the evolution of military organization, weaponry, and communications; about finance and logistics; and about the social and political consequences of warfare. The one thing they scarcely ever mention is hand-to-hand combat and the ways in which soldiers might have been prepared for it. Nor are writers less squeamish when dealing with the tournament where they largely content themselves with questions of chronology, pageantry, expenditure, and social hierarchy and only occasionally offer perfunctory remarks about what knights actually did to each other. Even the rapidly expanding modern literature on duelling has managed to ignore fighting altogether. This may seem remarkably perverse, but recent scholars – abandoning the anecdotal, moralistic or legalistic approaches to the duel, favoured by earlier generations – have come to regard ritualized personal conflict as a symptom of some pyscho-sociological malaise afflicting the elite; as a manifestation of something called a 'crisis' of the aristocracy; or as a gesture of defiance against increasing centralization and bureaucratization of government. The psychological implications of social alienation have been duly pondered. The relevance of systematic personal combat training, wholly aggressive and homicidal in purpose, has not even been recognized let alone studied. The intellectual atmosphere has become so rarified that nobody asks how duellists studied the arts of killing, who taught them, and where.

In this last respect we are no better informed about European rulers. For several centuries, it was rare for a monarch not to take pride in his martial skills, especially when the element of personal rivalry entered into the reckoning. Renaissance monarchs such as Maximilian I, James IV, Henry VIII, François I, and Charles V, were noted for their prowess with lance and sword; and some also fancied themselves as wrestlers. We know about their tilts, tourneys, and barrier combats – what they wore, whom they fought, and how they fared. What, in the majority of cases, we do not know is how they acquired their skills and who taught them. Furthermore, the techniques of personal violence were studied not only by emperors, kings, and princes, but also by their most humble subjects. The carrying and the use of lethal weapons was normal throughout the social hierarchy. Yet, although social historians are remarkably keen on violence (especially in book titles) and have provided all sorts of ingenious analyses of the brutality endemic in the Middle Ages and Renaissance, their pages will be searched in vain for mention either of the men who taught the martial arts, their principles, or their methods of instruction.

Whatever the reasons, personal violence has been avoided by scholars working in the very areas where one might legitimately expect to discover something about it. It is, therefore, hardly surprising that students of the fine arts have also been reluctant to delve into such brutalities; and, as a consequence, they have ignored one of the most striking and continuous series of illustrated books in western graphic art. From the late thirteenth to the mid-nineteenth centuries, artists worked with masters of arms trying to record the techniques of personal combat. As is the case with every genre, the quality of such illustration ranges from the abysmal to the highly accomplished: but, because their real purpose is to notate movement, they are all of interest to the historian of ideas and some, perhaps, are worth the attention of historians of art.

Admittedly, many of the relevant questions are difficult to answer (indeed some cannot be satisfactorily answered at all). Nor can all the gaps in our knowledge be filled. But their neglect still constitutes an historiographical curiosity. The only serious treatment of these matters has been by historians of fencing, by students of arms and armour and, more recently, by re-enactors and enthusiasts for historical modes of combat. Unfortunately, historians of fencing were at their most active a century ago when they confined themselves principally to tracing the evolution of swordsmanship towards a wholly notional ideal constituted by their own practice; while, in any case, sword play was only one part of the many activities which together constituted the martial arts of the Renaissance. Specialists in arms and armour have carried out much meticulous research but, in their case, the centre of interest has inevitably been more with artefacts than activities. Serious modern re-enactors, on the other hand, while frequently aware of a far wider range of combat techniques than the old fencing historians and far more pragmatic in their approach to physical action than the armour specialists, still tend to base their reconstructions upon a limited number of primary sources – although this situation is changing rapidly.[4] All these approaches have provided valuable insights into practical issues which, as Monte pointed out, are difficult to grasp solely on the basis of a theoretical exposition. But it is still necessary to establish the martial arts within the broader contexts of intellectual, military and art history while establishing more precisely what these activities were, and how they were systematized.

My purpose in this book is to attempt these tasks and to provide at least some answers to the problems I have suggested. In the first chapter I discuss the role of physical education, and more especially martial education, in the Renaissance; the status of professional masters of arms and the kind of men they were; the various sources available to us, their strengths and limitations; and the general methods whereby the masters sought to bring their skills to a wider audience.

Chapter 2, dealing with the problem of recording series of movements and of conveying information to readers not actually present, focuses principally on the evolution of systems of movement notation and illustration. Chapters 3, 4 and 5 are concerned with the ways in which language was used to convey information about a wide range of foot combats where the principal division was between the single sword (either alone or in combination with such aids as dagger, cloak, or buckler) and two-handed weapons such as the two-hand sword, hand-and-a-half sword, polaxe and various other staff weapons. A great many problems are involved here: the influence of historical, military and civil fashion; the definition of what precisely constitutes fencing; and debate concerning the use of point and edge, general principles of fighting, the mechanics of movement, and the psychology of combat.

Chapter 6 is devoted to wrestling and deals not only with the various traditions of holds and throws – that is with the art of killing or disabling an enemy with one's bare hands – but also with the ways in which wrestling was used in combination with sword fighting and dagger combat.

Chapter 7 concerns the arms and armour used in some of the martial arts of medieval and renaissance Europe. Monte included such material in his own *Collectanea* and my purpose here is not descriptive but rather to see what sort of knowledge an outstanding master like Monte judged to be necessary to a fighting man at the turn of the fifteenth and sixteenth centuries and to consider why other masters did not pursue this approach. This section also constitutes a bridge between combat fought on foot, generally (though not always) without defensive armour, and Chapters 8 and 9 which reconstruct the techniques of combat on horseback (jousting and mounted fencing) in which armour was usually worn. In conclusion I briefly consider the relationship (or irrelation) between the techniques of personal combat – as taught by medieval and renaissance European masters – and real fighting either on the battlefield, the duelling field, or in streets and taverns.

Since an introduction affords opportunity not only to advise readers on what they may expect to find but also to alert them to idiosyncrasies and limitations, I must enter here a couple of caveats. In the first place, the licence with which I interpret the 'renaissance Europe' of my title requires, perhaps, a word of explanation. Although the bulk of the material in this book derives from late fifteenth- to early seventeenth-century sources, I believe that in the history of ideas there are few precise cut-off dates and I have, accordingly, pushed as far back as the thirteenth century and as far forward as the eighteenth (occasionally even to the twentieth) century simply because the sense of the material demands it. In those earliest treatises there are techniques of exposition, as well as descriptions of modes of combat, which were to be repeated and developed by the masters of the sixteenth century and later. Conversely, when considering, for example, methods of notating movement in fencing, it would be arbitrary not to pursue the subject as far as Rada (1705) who represents the idea's most elaborate development. Similarly, some combat techniques receive their most sophisticated exposition in later works which I use to throw a retrospective light on texts which are otherwise obscure, while it has also seemed worthwhile, from time to time, to demonstrate essential continuities. No master of arms woke up one morning to find that his teaching had been rendered obsolete overnight because the Middle Ages had suddenly ended or that he had just missed the Renaissance by a few minutes.

Finally, I must point out that, although there is an abundance of cold steel and manual violence in this book, there is very little gunpowder. This is because none of the masters whose writings provide the basis of this study ever mentioned arms other than swords, daggers, staff weapons, or bare hands; and the new technology, designed originally for unskilled killing *en masse*, was unattractive to specialists in close combat. Whatever use may have been made of the pistol in street and tavern brawls, the handling of such crude weapons offered masters nothing worthy of systematic analysis and, until the latter half of the seventeenth century, the personal duel remained essentially the province of swordsmen.[5] Similarly, despite the steadily increasing significance of firearms on the field of battle, the group drill necessary for troops using handguns was not the kind of thing that interested masters of arms.

My concern throughout is with what the masters thought they were doing when they wrote their treatises, and with the methods whereby they sought to systematize the activities pursued in their schools in order to convey essential information to absent third parties – that is their readers. Some tackled this daunting task with heroic incompetence; others were remarkably intelligent, ingenious and effective. All merit serious attention.

This book is, in many ways, an experimental essay: and I do not say this as a Castiglionesque disclaimer: 'because it imprinteth in the minds of the lookers on, an opinion that who so can so slightly do well hath a great deal more knowledge than in deed he hath'. I am making a simple statement of fact. At almost every turn I have been confronted with a mass of unsorted evidence. Bibliographical aids though helpful are, with honourable exceptions, incomplete and inaccurate; the availability of primary sources is subject to many restrictions; and few serious critical works exist. There are, for example, editions of only a tiny fraction of the immense corpus of German manuscripts, and only a few monographic studies of that tradition; while with regard to Iberian sources the situation is, if anything, even worse. Renaissance Spanish texts on the martial arts pose technical problems which have scarcely been addressed by modern scholars: and, when one adds to this the fact that, even for France and Italy, analytical (as opposed to bibliographical and descriptive) treatments are extremely rare, then the difficulties of writing in a single volume anything more than an 'experimental essay' must be evident.

I

Violence in the classroom:
medieval and renaissance masters of arms

IN 1220 A certain Walter de Stewton was charged with complicity in an especially nasty pickaxe murder and, as a result, was incarcerated in the Tower of London to await trial by combat. Whether or not Walter had himself delivered any of the fatal strokes, little martial expertise had been involved in the crime for the victim had been in bed, blind drunk. Skill in weaponry was only acquired later when Walter was released on bail so that he could learn fencing (*et discere eskirmire*) in readiness for the combat which, in the event, he won.[1] This arrangement, generous as it seems, was not unusual. About twelve years earlier at Winchester, Sir Jordan de Bianney had been allowed out of custody at least twice a day to receive similar instruction;[2] and it is clear from surviving contracts that some-times even when a professional champion was hired there might also be provision for his *magister*. In 1287, two bruisers – Roger the Clerk and his trainer – were entertained by their employer, the Abbot of St Edmunds in Suffolk, for more than six months while they prepared for the big fight. In this case the money was not well spent. Roger lost his life and the abbot lost his suit.[3] We do not know who provided the lessons, in what kind of environment they took place, or how they were conducted; but the very fact that they were available and were considered helpful to a man preparing for judicial combat suggests the existence both of professional masters and of some sort of acknowledged expertise.[4] It also represents remarkable double-thinking on the part of established authority in London, since the maintenance of fencing schools had been officially prohibited in the City from at least as early as 1189.[5]

THE MASTERS

Throughout the Middle Ages and the Renaissance masters of arms enjoyed an equivocal position in European society. Their skills were recognized and utilized, but the kind of reckless violence engendered in many pupils by their teaching earned them an unsavoury reputation. Street brawling and, later on, duelling were alike laid at their door, and the more literate masters of the Renaissance often felt obliged to defend themselves from such imputations. It must also have been galling for teachers of the martial arts to see officialdom happy enough to utilize their skills while simultaneously penalizing them.[6] This was espe-cially marked in the case of men who served as professional champions in trials by combat during the long period when such battles were common throughout Europe. Fighting in the lists as a proxy was a doubly dangerous activity, for the champions were exposed not only to the hazards of mortal combat but also to the rigours of the law, even when successful.[7] The men who undertook this strange profession were not necessarily teachers of the martial arts but Elias Piggun, who gave lessons in sword play, found his expertise a distinct disadvantage. In 1220 Elias was a champion involved in a case concerning a stolen mare but, when revealed to be a professional teacher of sword fighting who had perjured himself for lucre, he was promptly found guilty of fraud and sentenced to the loss of a foot.[8] With that lightness of touch so characteristic of legal humour, it has been written that his amputated foot bestowed immortality on poor Piggun, 'for Bracton has nailed it up for ever as a practical illustration of English law'.[9] Piggun's foot may also be seen as emblematic of a distrust founded, perhaps, on unfortunate experiences with the masters' over-enthusiastic pupils. 'Bruisers' and 'misdoers walking by night' were a nuisance in many medieval cities. The records of the City of London are dotted about with examples of sword and buckler bullies and with repeated prohibitions against the fencing schools which were thought to encourage them. In 1285, the authorities were driven to reiterate penalties already more than a century old: 'As fools who delight in their folly do learn to fence with buckler, and thereby are encouraged in their follies, it is provided that none shall keep school for, nor teach the art of fence within the City of London under pain of imprisonment for forty days.' This failed to deter Master Roger le Skirmisour who maintained a fencing school until the authorities caught up with him in 1311 and sent him to prison for 'enticing thither the sons of respectable persons, so as to waste and spend the property of their fathers and mothers upon bad practices: the result being that they themselves became bad men'.[10]

The prohibition on schools of arms was enshrined in the customs of the City of London, yet professional masters continued to sell their skills and to take the attendant risks. In the fifteenth century experts in the martial arts made sporadic appearances as coaches to litigants preparing for trial by combat – the best-known instance being the activities of the fencing fishmonger, Philip Treher, who was involved in at least three such cases between 1446 and 1453.[11] Yet, in 1496, both jousting and playing with the sword and buckler were still declared illegal without royal licence; while, in 1530, a certain William Smith was held to have committed a presentable nuisance when he upset the righteous citizens of the parish of Dowgate by keeping a 'sworde pleying house' whither divers apprentices congregated at 'unlawful hours, namely at night time and at time of Divine service' in order to practise the art.[12] Much later, around 1572, when Humphrey Gilbert was proposing an academy for London – where noble youths were to be instructed, amongst much else, in the martial arts by a 'master of defence' – he still found it necessary to stipulate that the teacher should have a 'dispensation against the Statute of Roages'.[13] On the other hand it is clear that, already in the reign of Henry VIII, these martial experts were organized into something resembling a craft guild which received at least tacit recognition when, in a signed bill of 1540, the king established a commission to investigate widespread malpractice by fencing masters operating 'without any sufficient lycence or lawfull auctoryte'.[14]

Elsewhere in Europe there were, from time to time, similar objections to the moral and social threat posed by the martial artists. In 1386, barely a year after the founding of the University of Heidelberg, its students were already being forbidden to disrupt their studies by attending the local schools of arms – a prohibition which seemingly had little lasting effect since it was repeated by the Rector in 1415. Similarly, the eagerness with which sixteenth-century Parisian students cut classes at the university to haunt the schools of 'maistres escrimeurs et joueurs d'espée' caused so much concern that, in 1554, an Ordonnance of the Parlement sought to banish these masters from the entire area and in 1575 this prohibition, too, was repeated.[15] In general, though, compared with England, masters of arms enjoyed greater esteem and were able to ply their skills more openly and more systematically on the Continent where confraternities of fencers certainly existed in Germany and Italy from the late thirteenth century; and where official recognition, according some of these groups craft status, is documented for Germany, Spain and France (though not Italy) around the closing decades of the fifteenth century. The first known imperial privilege to a fighting fraternity was granted by the Emperor Frederick III on 10 August 1487 to the masters of Nuremberg.[16] There is a royal licence dated 24 June 1478 at Saragossa to Gómez Dorado as 'maestro mayor' to examine masters of arms; and a month later at Cordoba there is recorded a royal act fixing the number of masters to be examined, and granting the company of *Esgrimidores* a shield of arms.[17]

The public examination of aspirants to membership or to promotion in these organizations is well attested in all those countries where a licensing system was firmly in place, allowing successful candidates to teach and forbidding the unqualified.[18] The system, which was essentially that of a craft guild with clearly defined levels of achievement and length of apprenticeship in the various grades of expertise, was much the same everywhere with the aspirants proceeding from the rank of scholar, through that of provost, and on to master – the *lanista seu magister in usu palestrinae* as he is referred to in early sixteenth-century Spanish diplomas.[19] The Spanish system, which endured longer than those anywhere else in Europe, was widespread and solemn. The examinations were public occasions and took place before the masters, provosts and scholars, together with a large lay audience. The master who had taught the candidate presented him to the other masters; the tests with various weapons followed; and then, if successful, the candidate's new grade was publicly proclaimed and he took a solemn oath to observe all the rules appertaining to his art.[20]

In Italy, too, where documentary evidence on this point is curiously lacking, there was evidently some kind of examining and ratifying process. In 1536 Marozzo asserts that this had indeed been so, and he contrasts the unregulated teaching of his own time with earlier practice, when only 'authenticated masters' who had been duly 'granted their licence by other masters' were allowed to take students.[21] The same point is made at greater length by a later Bolognese master, Giovanni dall'Agocchie, who concentrates less upon practical achievement than upon the purely pedagogical skills of anyone trying to instruct others in the art of swordsmanship. He regrets the incompetence of current teaching which arises solely because 'the old custom of the creation of masters has fallen into oblivion'. Not all that long ago, says dall'Agocchie, if anyone wished to achieve the excellent rank of a doctorate his wisdom would first be diligently examined. And the same procedure had applied to Masters of Fencing. Anyone intending to teach the art had first to demonstrate his knowledge of fencing theory before being confronted with a bad student – whose performance he had to criticize and correct – and then with various able students. The whole procedure was assessed by established masters who only granted a privilege when satisfied as to the candidate's competence: an excellent custom, says the author, but sadly corrupted partly by time and partly by the negligence of the masters themselves.[22] As in Marozzo, the date of the good old custom is unspecified and it remained so when Gaiani sighed nostalgically for the same better regulated times in his *Arte di maneggiar la spada* (1619). Here the master is asked by a pupil to explain what he means by *un Maestro approvato*; and he begins with the familiar expression of regret. Formerly, in Italy, no one could be accepted as a master of arms without first satisfying the senior masters (*i Maestri vecchi*) and then receiving his privilege. This system, he says, still operates in Spain, Brussels, and Paris, but in Italy 'this good custom has been lost'. Now anyone who knows how to strike four blows is immediately made a master – 'like a cobbler' – and besides spoiling the profession it brings dishonour upon the art.[23]

In France there is plentiful, if scattered, evidence about the care with which the examination and licensing process was supervised. In 1455 at Paris, for example, Jehan Taillecourt, *maistre joueur de l'espée à deux mains et du boucler*, acting on a report by Jehan Perchel *prévost des ditz jeux*, issued an authorization to a certain Jehan Baugranz to be granted the rank of *prévost* and be allowed to hold a school in the said arms in all places throughout the realm; and in 1489 there exists a process concerning the public examination of a *prévôt d'armes* at Aubenas.[24] This candidate was put through his paces by a master, assisted by other experts, and had to demonstrate proficiency in the two-hand sword and the small sword with both shield and buckler. Then, after satisfying his examiners, he took an oath to live an honest life, to be loyal to his colleagues, and to teach pupils to the best of his ability. The Statutes of the Parisian *Maistres Joueurs et Escrimeurs d'espée* were confirmed – despite the anxieties of the university – by Charles IX in 1567 and included strangely rudimentary provision for apprenticeship and examination, which was expanded in the reign of Henri III with provisions against unlicensed masters, and then further elaborated and strengthened under Louis XIII and Louis XIV.[25]

Even in England, despite the long-standing legal restrictions, public examination of candidates by their superiors was well established at least by the reign of Henry VIII, and it was being taken as seriously as elsewhere in Europe. The main complaint against unlicensed fencing teachers, in the bill of 1540, was not so much that they were violating the solemn oath to their masters 'at theyr fyrst entryng to lerne theyr said science', but that, having set up schools throughout the country, 'frome Towne to Towne and place to place', they were doing their job so badly that it amounted to fraud. They had been taking

> great sommes of money for theyr labours, and yet Nevertheles have untrowly and Insufficiently Instructed and tawght their scollers wherby the same scollers have been and are Illuded and deceyved, To the sclaunder and hynderaunce of the masters and provosts of the said Scyence of defence and to the utter subversion and dystruccion of the same, and the good and lawdable orders and Rules of the same Science.[26]

Obviously, it was one thing to institute a licensing system and quite another to implement it. The kind of discontent demonstrated by the Henrician Bill was still being forcibly expressed by late Elizabethan and Jacobean critics and concerned the incapacity of officially approved masters as well as the practices of illicit teachers. In Spain, the masters, not content with serving as a butt for literary ridicule, further tarnished their reputation when the imperious Narváez fought a running battle not only with the satirist Quevedo but also with the disciples of Carranza.[27] Nor was the situation more happy in France where, in 1623, the Limousin authority François Dancie considered that things had so far deteriorated that it was very rare to find a good master anywhere in the realm; and he complains about

> a rabble of pub-crawlers (*un taz de coureurs*) who, professing mastership in this trade, are nothing but ignoramuses deserving to be called smatterers of arms (*Clercs d'Armes*), if not something worse. For, besides doing wrong to men of honour who *do* understand it [the trade], they bring the whole profession into disrepute by their incapacity. Moreover, they lead a debauched life and fence with knives in taverns and ale-houses, showing that they

perform better with a glass than with a sword. Add to this that they seem to have an understanding with Messieurs the Surgeons to give them practice: for they teach their scholars so badly that they learn how to receive more blows than they give. And they abuse them sottishly, and lead them to vicious acts by their evil examples, and to fight with neither foundation nor reason, whence they verify the common saying, *like master, like pupil*.[28]

Good, bad and indifferent – societies and schools of instruction devoted to the martial arts were evidently a common feature of medieval and renaissance city life. Moreover, the public examination of candidates became an important popular entertainment despite the obstacles which city authorities, nervous about law and order, threw in their way. In London, for example, where there was constant difficulty over the granting of licences, 'playing for prizes' still managed to attract crowds of fight enthusiasts – partly, perhaps, because entrance was free and rewarding the contestants entirely voluntary.[29] On the Continent, on the other hand, similar spectacles were run on a more solid commercial basis and when, in 1580, during his visit to Augsburg, Michel de Montaigne went to see a display of fighting with poniard, two-hand sword, quarter staff and braquemart, he noted that 'after dinner we went to see the fencing in a public salon where there was a great crowd; and one payed on entry – as for mountebanks – and, on top of this, for one's seats on the benches'.[30]

Yet, for all this activity, the vast majority of the masters remain totally unknown or survive as mere names which only briefly emerge from darkness through some quirk of fate. Elias Piggun's foot marches on. Bertolfe Vander Eme's thumb has rescued its owner from oblivion by getting itself wounded during long-sword practice with King Henry IV of England.[31] The Italian masters Pompée and Sylvie are known only because they allowed themselves to be defeated, in a demonstration of sycophantic swordsmanship, by their youthful pupils, the future kings of France, Charles IX and Henri III.[32] A more effective means of entering the record – for swordsmen, as for the general public – was anti-social or criminal behaviour. Nicholas Chezault, fencing master of Dijon, has his memorial in the obscure pages of an old learned monograph because he offered a prize of taffeta scarves and a gilded dagger to anyone who could defeat his champion in a public match and, when his man was run through by 'un simple vigneron', promptly absconded with the prizes and entrance money.[33]

The Portuguese mulatto master Jorge Fernandes made his mark as a public nuisance in Setúbal where his brawling career culminated in ten years of exile to Brazil for murdering an unarmed man. Another Portuguese swordfighter commemorated by criminal proceedings was Antonio Mourão of Lisbon who regularly fell foul of the authorities: for carrying a sword which was not only too long but also had a spun silk handle; for wearing silk in violation of the sumptuary laws; and for getting in some illicit practice on a passing breeches-maker whose hat he cut in two.[34]

Others, like the Portuguese Manuel Fernandes or the Englishman John Turner, achieved notoriety by poking out opponent's eyes during friendly bouts in the schools.[35] Turner achieved this dubious distinction on two or three occasions, 'which bred an admiration in the ignorant and vulgare sort' but aroused the wrath of one noble victim – Robert Crichton, Baron of Sanquhar – who nursed a grudge for seven years and eventually hired a pair of assassins to gain his revenge.[36] The blustering Jacobean blade Joseph Swetnam was not impressed by Turner's skill for, 'if a man choppe a thruste at the face' he may not hit the eye, 'but with proffering many, by chance he may'. As is only to be expected, swordfighters who lived blameless lives have scarcely been remembered even when they left richer records than their peccant brethren; and it is significant that a master such as John Blinkinsop (or Blenkinsopps) is known not because his career can be traced from free scholar to provost and finally to master, but merely because Ben Jonson refers to him in passing as 'Blinkinsopps the Bold'.[37]

There are any number of these aggressive meteorites shooting across the historic firmament. One of the earliest names recorded is a 'maestro Goffredo schermitore' who appears as a witness to a notarial act in Cividale on 31 July 1259; but both he and a certain 'maestro Arnaldo scharmitor', whose name is documented at the beginning of the fourteenth century, are otherwise obscure.[38] Nor, apart from their addresses, are we better informed about the seven 'escrimeurs' living in Paris in 1292 – Guillaume, Richart, Sanse, Jacques, Thomas, Nicolas and Phelippe – although, on the basis of no evidence whatsoever, the fencing historian Japoco Gelli asserted that three were Italian emigrés who, unable to find employment amidst the keen competition in their native land, set up schools in Paris.[39]

The German masters emerge from the shadows with the advent of Johann Liechtenauer and his disciples towards the end of the fourteenth century, and thereafter many German masters not only cease to be anonymous but have even gained a measure of immortality through the survival of their combat manuals.[40] In France, Spain and Portugal we start to find such men recorded towards the end of the fifteenth century and from then onwards, right through to modern times, the civic archives yield the names of scores of French and Iberian masters.[41]

In medieval England, by contrast, apart from a number of professional champions whose skills are known from their participation (actual or anticipated) in judicial combat, we have little information until the fortuitous survival of a single manuscript (together with the commission of 1540 and another of 1605) provides a tolerably complete list of all those officially involved with the Tudor Masters of Defence of London from the third decade of the sixteenth century to the early seventeenth century. We do not lack names. Sadly, for the most part, these references remain skeletal and apart from the few who have left some written record of their art, there is little flesh on the bones. Merely heaping them together tells us nothing substantive about the masters' deeds, attitudes and purposes.[42]

The schools of arms are even more obscure than the men who taught in them. Not only do we lack documentary evidence about the day-to-day running of these establishments, we do not even know what they looked like. There are literally thousands of illustrations in combat treatises (German, Italian, Spanish and French) but, since all these pictures are designed to show fighting postures not to set a scene, the space surrounding the combatants is generally ignored. Sometimes, as in Talhoffer, the warriors dance about on surfaces seemingly situated nowhere. Marozzo provides a floor ruled with squares in perspective; Agrippa a simple horizon line; di Grassi a few scattered mounds of earth; Sainct Didier, tufts of grass along with triangles, quadrilaterals and numbered footprints; and, as in Ghisliero and an anonymous German *Fechtbuch*, landscapes and townscapes are occasionally sketched in.

The point is this. Not one of these masters, who generally supervised the illustrations to their own work, has envisaged the combats as taking place within a school or even within any sort of pedagogical context. The problem comes sharply into focus if we look at Joachim Meyer's treatise of 1570 and consider the woodcuts executed for him by Tobias Stimmer. Here the fencers (under the eye and baton of their instructors) wage furious battle with swords, daggers, halberds and staves. They do so, moreover, within a three-dimensional

1. A fantasy school in Meyer. 1600, Book I, fol. 39.

2. One of Thibault's surreal halls. 1630, II, Tabula vi.

3. School and bath-house as depicted by the Master of the Banderoles. Engraving, *c.* 1464.

architectural space. These illustrations have often been taken as representations of contemporary German fencing schools: but, in fact, they are fantasies and no more represent reality than do the surreal halls later to be seen in Girard Thibault's *Académie de l'espée* (figs 1,2).

It is rare to find early representations of schools of arms which encourage confidence: but one which does seem realistic is an engraving by the 'Meister mit den Bandrollen'. This is a two-part scene – a dubious bath-house *cum* brothel on the right and, on the left, a school of arms with men lifting weights, practising contortions, wielding the two-hand sword, and perilously holding a target while someone takes aim with a primitive handgun (fig. 3).[43] The implications of the scene are clear: attendance at a school of arms is, like public bathing and fornication, a form of moral depravity; and those who taught or studied there are as contemptible as the fool whose genitalia are being critically evaluated by three nude lady bathers. One has only to compare this with an engraving by Willem Swanenburgh, at the end of the sixteenth century, to see the vast alteration which had taken place in the status of continental masters in the course of the Renaissance (fig. 4). Again the view combines firearms and edged weapons (with vaulting on the horse added for good measure), but now it is all very decorous. The floor is marked out with an elaborate geometrical design to facilitate correct foot movements: rapiers are carefully buttoned; the two-hand swords are posed rather than swung; and all this activity now takes place in a room devoted to the martial arts at the University of Leiden.

We have moved from a house of ill-repute to an academic community.[44] What was once a naughty activity forbidden to students has become an accepted part of their normal curriculum. This change is, in some ways, even more marked in a series of illustrations cele-

DELINEATIO LVDI PVBLICI GLADIATORI VRBIS ET ACADEMIÆ LVGDVNENSIS APVD BATAVOS.

4. Swanenburgh's view of the fencing school (with geometric ground plan) at the University of Leyden. Engraving, end of sixteenth century.

brating life at the University of Tübingen early in the seventeenth century. We are shown the college courtyard, dining hall, a lecture theatre, library, and a view over the gardens. We also see the fencing school with students practising at rapiers, two-handed swords, staves, and Düsacks; a tennis court with a game in progress; the *sphaeromachus* or football match; tilting at the ring; an arquebus shooting range; a contest at the archery butts; and finally a combat at the barriers with the contestants clad in half armour. In other words, out of a total of twelve engravings, only two depict intellectual activity. Two show ball games, while five are concerned with various military skills – including sword play.[45]

The orderliness of Swanenburgh's scene was probably typical of academic schools of instruction, and later examples are often similar if less detailed. The frontispiece to Johann Andreas Schmidt's *Fecht-Kunst* of 1713 shows vaulting, rapier play and wrestling. The grandiose title page of Alexander Doyle's *Fecht und Schirm-Kunst* suggests, within its triumphal arch, a simple fencing room hung with weapons. The master, in the title page to

5. Frontispiece of Schmidt's *Fecht-Kunst* (1713) showing his fencing school.

7. Title page of Blackwell's *The Art of Defence* (n.d.) with Blackwell about to be crowned by the Gods while his students perform.

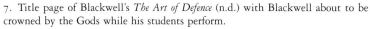

6. Title page of Doyle's *Fecht und Schirm-Kunst* (1715) with his triumphal arch and fencing school beyond.

8. Marozzo's geometric ground plan for fencing students. 1536, fol. 47v.

9. Meyer's wall diagram for teaching the attacks with a düsack. 1600, Book II, fol. 3. (Cf. fig. 27).

Blackwell's *Art of Defence*, is about to be crowned by Minerva and Mercury while his pupils perform within a heavily draped amphitheatre. And Belfin's treatise on *L'Exercice des armes* (1767) depicts his fencing school as a veritable theatre filled with swordsmen going at it hammer and tongs (figs 5–7 and plate I).[46] All these establishments have some family resemblance in that they are the resort of gentlemen and even of the Olympian gods and are, therefore, obviously respectable. But I suspect that only the fifteenth-century scene reflects the style of most plebeian schools of arms in the Middle Ages and Renaissance: plain, violent and dissolute.

Surviving descriptions of such schools in action are even rarer than illustrations, although Achille Marozzo's *Opera nova* provides a rudimentary account of how the novice is to be treated when beginning instruction; and he also suggests the use of visual aids in the classroom. When dealing with foot movements he provides an illustration of two swordsmen taking up positions on a geometric ground plan ('placing the feet on these lines which cross the circles') which is a simple version of that shown by Willem Swanenburgh; and then, in the following chapter, he explains how to teach beginners the entire range of strokes by having an appropriate life-size figure drawn upon a wall (figs 8, 94).[47] Since the use of wall diagrams is also illustrated in Meyer's work, it is likely that this kind of thing was usual: but we cannot tell (fig. 9).

Even apparently detailed written accounts tend to convey more social than gladiatorial information – as when the fiery English fencer, George Silver, sneers at the portentous surroundings within which the Italian, Rocco Bonnetti, taught 'Noblemen and gentlemen of the Court'. Rocco had acquired a fine house in Warwick Lane 'which he called his Colledge, for he thought it great disgrace for him to keepe a Fence-schoole'. The walls of the school room were adorned with the arms of his noble pupils and their rapiers, daggers and 'gloves of male and gantlets'. Around the floor were seats for the gentlemen to watch the lessons. A large, beautifully appointed square table was provided, with 'inke, pens, pin-dust, and sealing waxe, and quiers of verie excellent fine paper gilded' ready for Rocco's patrons to write their letters and dispatch them while still watching the fights – in much the same way as a modern gymnasium might supply a fax machine and the Internet. 'And to know how the time passed, he had in one corner of his schoole a Clocke, with a verie faire large Diall'. More significantly, however, 'he had within that schoole, a roome the which was called his privie schoole, with manie weapons therein, where he did teach his schollers his secret fight, after he had perfectly taught them their rules'.[48]

Apart from the fact that Rocco made some of his pupils 'weare leaden soales in their shoes, the better to bring them to nimblnesse of feet in their fight', Silver tells us nothing about the master's teaching method.[49] Nothing, that is, except his tantalizing reference to Rocco's 'secret fight' – a reminder that, throughout our period, the notion of secret strokes was an obsession with continental fencers. Brantôme tells of masters who refused to allow anybody other than specially favoured (and wealthy) pupils into their chambers; and even then they would look everywhere, even under the beds; and would examine the walls to discover any cracks or holes through which their rivals might spy on them.[50] Naturally, with such precautions, all these secret strokes and devices have tended to remain very secret indeed. Dall'Agocchie scoffs at the very idea that there are such secret blows which cannot be withstood, for 'every blow has its parry'; and the seventeenth-century master, Philibert de la Touche, who devotes a chapter of his own treatise to 'Des bottes secrettes' – those 'marvellous blows by means of which one kills one's adversary indubitably and without any peril' – does so only to demonstrate that they are the knaveries of charlatans who prey upon the weakness of ignorant and lazy scholars who hope to gain success without taking the trouble necessary to master the science.[51]

None the less, there was a practical reason for secrecy which was better understood by contemporary oriental masters who knew that a warrior's life might depend upon his opponent's not knowing his special technique.[52] This is something which the Tudor masters of defence seemed not to appreciate, and George Hale's most passionate criticism of contemporary English professional masters is precisely that 'They will suffer their Schollers to see one another's practise, and likewise they themselves will discover every mans play to any man'. This, says Hale, gives a great advantage to the spectator and is 'much prejudiciall unto him whose practise is seene: and most murtherous and damnable in the Teacher to betray their owne Schollers to deth'.[53] Unfortunately, we remain as much in the dark about these open demonstrations of English skills as about the secret lessons of the continental masters and must turn elsewhere for enlightenment.

Although we know relatively little about the masters and their schools (relative, that is, to the total number which must certainly have existed), we do know a great deal about the content and purpose of their teaching which we may reconstruct from two principal types of source material. One, of only limited usefulness, consists of narratives and descriptions of personal combat. The other, of infinitely greater value, comprises technical treatises – generally, though not invariably, well illustrated – designed to record systems of combat and to provide instruction in them.

NARRATIVE SOURCES AND THEIR LIMITATIONS

Chronicles and other narrative sources furnish numerous accounts of physical combat, ranging from the conflict of armies on the battlefield, the encounter of knights in the mêlée and joust, to the struggles of individuals in judicial combat, duel and, occasionally, in personal affray. Close examination, unfortunately, reveals them to be patchy, inadequate and unreliable. From the thirteenth to early fifteenth centuries it is virtually impossible to reconstruct, from such material, the techniques of personal combat anywhere in Europe. The situation improves in the fifteenth century when a number of chroniclers – especially those recording Burgundian and French material – offer not only more detail but information of a kind suggesting at least some knowledge of the activities they describe. Elsewhere in Europe, however, there is little useful evidence. English sources are poor, and Italian writers, while offering saturation information on dress and emblematic devices, have little to say about actual combat. Moreover, despite the multiplication of printed narratives in the sixteenth century, the later sources are, if anything, even less helpful.

The limitations of narrative sources for the reconstruction of the martial arts in renaissance Europe may be illustrated by studying occasions where there survive several independent, and apparently circumstantial, first-hand accounts. Two examples are especially revealing. When, in the summer of 1467, Anthony Woodville (Lord Scales) met the Bastard of Burgundy in a chivalric contest at West Smithfield, four eye-witnesses – two English and two Burgundian – recorded the events. One of the Englishmen was the herald who had been concerned with the organization of the challenge and was certainly on duty within the lists at the time of the encounter; and the other was Robert Fabyan, an experienced and well-known London chronicler. Of the Burgundians, one remains anonymous: but his minutely detailed narrative indicates that he was a member of the Bastard's entourage and accustomed to witnessing and participating in court spectacle. The other Burgundian was the famous Olivier de la Marche – most prominent of all contemporary chroniclers, Master of Ceremonies of the Burgundian household and a writer skilled, above all else, in recording the details of court festivals and chivalric combats within the lists. Indeed, his special expertise in the last matter was singled out for praise by Michel de Montaigne in a note he appended to his copy of Olivier's *Mémoires*.[54] Yet, even with this array of experienced observers, it is impossible to reconstruct the fighting. Indeed, some of the discrepancies between the accounts are so extraordinary that they defy understanding. With regard to the mounted tourney with swords, on the one hand we are told that the Bastard's horse was blind and died from a blow up the nostrils administered by an iron spike on Lord Scale's horse; on the other we are assured that there was no such spike. One observer declares that the horse dropped dead instantly; another, that it staggered about a bit and survived until the following day. The Bastard is said, by some, to have wished to fight on but was refused royal permission; by others, that he himself refused the offer of a fresh mount. Concerning the foot combat with polaxes, which took place the day after the chaotic tourney, one observer cannot even make up his own mind as to whether the action was brief and inconclusive, or whether it was stopped because Lord Scales had the advantage. Elsewhere we are told that the fight waxed long and fierce before being stopped with Lord Scales in a favourable position; that it was the longest and fiercest ever, but inconclusive; and finally that it was, indeed, the longest and fiercest ever, but ended as the Bastard was gaining the upper hand. There was, in fact, almost total confusion as to what happened. That this should be the case with regard to the force of the blows is understandable; but it is incomprehensible that the witnesses do not agree as to whether a horse dropped dead on the spot or was able to get to its feet again, and whether a combat was stopped after a few blows or continued for an unusually long time.[55]

Contradiction is similarly the most striking historiographical feature of the celebrated duel between Bayard and the Spaniard Alonzo de Sotomayore late in 1503. This deadly encounter was reported by three eye witnesses whose reports are especially discrepant where it matters most. The fighting was certainly on foot. But that is the only significant point of contact between the sources. The so-called 'Loyal Serviteur' tells us that the warriors were 'armez de gorgerin et secrete' (that is with protection for throat and head) and that the weapons of choice were an *estoc* and a *poignart*. These sound like a thrusting sword and a stabbing dagger and seem simple enough until one tries to establish precisely what these weapons may have looked like and to trace the history of the use of such a combination in single combat.[56] Then, when describing the fighting, the 'Loyal Serviteur' points out that each knight began with 'ung merveilleux coup d'estoc' – which may mean a thrust, or it may indicate a blow with the *estoc*. He also notes that the Spaniard had a habit of guarding his face after delivering a blow, so that Bayard resorted to a ruse. He waited for his adversary to raise his arm to deliver a stroke, raised his own simultaneously but held his *estoc* 'in the air, without throwing his blow'. Then, when Sotomayore's blade had passed and left him momentarily exposed, Bayard delivered 'so marvellous a blow to the throat' that, despite the quality of the throat defence, the *estoc* penetrated 'a good four fingers' and could not be withdrawn.

The chronicler, Jean d'Auton, gives a different and more minute account of the fight. For one thing, he says that the knights were armed 'de toutes pièces' but with their faces bare. Bayard had his *estoc* in his right hand and his *poignart* in the left, whereas Sotomayore had *estoc* in hand but *poignart* at his belt. The combat opened with both adversaries seeking to deliver 'grans estocz' to the exposed face while Sotomayore watched for an opportunity to get to grips with Bayard and seize him, 'and for this reason kept his left hand free'. Eventually Bayard, dodging a blow, was able to land a mighty thrust to the face; and the Spaniard, bending his head back, received the point on his gorget but with such force that the mail was penetrated and the blade entered his throat 'more than four fingers'. When the *estoc* was withdrawn, the wound gushed with blood although Sotomayore continued his attempt to get to grips. At last, however, Bayard suddenly thrust the dagger, which he held in his left hand, into the Spaniard's face, between the left eye and the end of the nose. Such was the force of this blow that the dagger was driven in up to the handle and penetrated the brain.

All that could hardly be more circumstantial, yet it differs from another report – this time by the famous physician, Symphorien Champier who should have known a wound when he saw one. Champier does not tell us what armour was worn but reports that, early in the combat, Bayard delivered so mighty a thrust to the visor with his short dagger that the Spaniard's blood ran on the ground. Later in the combat Bayard struck again with 'a marvellous thrust to the mid-oesophagus, striking below the right side of the windpipe towards the lung'. We may admire Champier's medical precision but we are left to guess at the weapon which inflicted the final wound. Was it again the short dagger as declared by d'Auton? Or was it the *estoc*, as stated specifically by the 'Loyal Serviteur'. There is simply no way of knowing. Nevertheless, although the question may have been irrelevant to the doomed Sotomayore, anyone interested in the history of fencing would like to know which weapons were used and in what combination.[57]

These two combats are exceptional in that they are carefully described by several, independent, highly qualified observers. Yet they are discrepant and report only selected episodes of what actually took place. They tell us nothing precise about the weapons used and say nothing about how the combatants held them. We learn nothing from them about movement either of body or foot; about the relative and changing positions of the antagonists; or about the force of the blows, their speed and angle of delivery. We cannot even tell how many blows were delivered, or how long the fighting lasted even though, in both cases, the combats were waged according to strict conventions.

Since narratives prove unsatisfactory in situations where conditions for accurate observation were entirely favourable, it is obvious that reports of a street or tavern brawl must be less reliable still. This is true even when the reporter is an expert doubly armed with fighting skill and a gift for words.[58] The xenophobic swordsman, George Silver, described several affrays involving the Italian masters in London, though it is not evident that he witnessed any of them.[59] He informs us that Rocco Bonnetti had angered a certain Austen Bagger, 'a verie tall gentleman of his handes, not standing much upon his skill, but carrying the valiant hart of an Englishman'. Bagger, armed with sword and buckler, stood outside the Italian's house and taunted him until Rocco rushed out with his two-hand sword and 'let flie' at the Englishman who bravely defended himself 'and presently closed with him, and stroke up his heeles, and cut him over the breech, and trode upon him, and most grievously hurt him under his feet'.

This is lively reading but no more precise than the story Silver tells of Vincentio Saviolo's misadventure in a tavern at Wells. The local master, Bartholomew Bramble, invited Saviolo to visit his school of defence to 'play at the rapier and dagger'; but the offer was refused in so insulting a fashion that Bramble 'up with his great English fist, and stroke maister *Vincentio* such a boxe on the eare that he fell over and over'. The conflict came to an inglorious conclusion when Bramble poured the contents of a great black jack over his enemy and left him foaming with ale and anger. The third encounter described by Silver involved Jeronimo who was called out to fight on the highway by 'one *Cheese*, a verie tall man, in his fight naturall English, for he fought with his Sword and Dagger, and in Rapier-fight had no skill at all'. Jeronimo drew his rapier and dagger and

> put himself into his best ward or *Stocata* which ward was taught by himselfe and *Vincentio*, and by them best allowed of, to be the best ward to stand upon in fight for life, either to assault the enemie, or stand and watch his comming, which ward it should seeme he ventured his life upon, but howsoever with all his fine Italienated skill *Jeronimo* had, *Cheese* with his Sword within two thrustes ran him into his bodie and slue him.

Again, the narration cannot be faulted for vivacity: but how could the *stoccata* (a thrust under the oncoming sword) have been used by Jeronimo as his best *ward* or guard? Who delivered the 'two thrusts'? Did Jeronimo stand stock still while being run through? Did Cheese move his feet? Did he thrust Jeronimo through the heart, the lungs, or the abdomen, and did he himself have to parry an attack first? What was the length and weight of each of the four weapons used in the fracas? Silver's story provides no information concerning these technical matters.

For the vast majority of combats, the surviving witnesses have far less expertise than those who described the encounters between Lord Scales and the Bastard of Burgundy, between Bayard and Sotomayore, and between the English and Italian masters. Moreover, they are rarely supported by collateral evidence. If, to these limitations, we add that most narratives are not by eye witnesses or experts, and that they are frequently not even by contemporaries of the events described, then it becomes clear that they can only be used with extreme caution. They are often informative about attitudes towards personal violence. They may say something about the conditions within which such violence occurred; and they are frequently evocative of mood. What they rarely provide is a reliable account of what actually happened. And they never explain how.

TREATISES

Much more profitable than narrative descriptions are analytical studies of combat technique, statements of general principles and purpose, ordered rules and procedures, and experimental schemes to record and notate movement and to systematize fighting according to the personal practice of individual masters. Fortunately, a great many texts of this nature survive, and we owe their existence to a perversity of human nature, noted and exemplified by Isaak Walton. In the epistle with which Walton introduced his *Compleat Angler* he confessed that 'to make a man that was none to be an Angler by a book' is a harder task than that undertaken by Mr Hale

> a most valiant and excellent fencer, who in a printed book called *A private School of Defence*, undertook to teach that art or science, and was laughed at for his labour. Not but that many useful things might be learned by that book, but he was laughed at, because that art was not to be taught by words, but practice: and so must Angling.

Yet Walton still took the trouble to write a book on angling. The jeer of the smart, shallow character-writer, Sir Thomas Overbury – that fencers 'care not if all the world were ignorant of mere letters then onely to read their patent' – may largely have been true of his contemporaries in England, but elsewhere many masters felt a strange compulsion to perpetuate their methods in treatises on personal combat, even in face of the obvious difficulties inherent in the task, and despite the possible betrayal of trade secrets.[60]

Up to the mid-fifteenth century such texts are extremely rare but thereafter the number increases and production accelerates throughout the period with which we are concerned. Apart from two notable exceptions (by an Italian master and a Portuguese monarch), the earliest manuscripts are German; but from the late fifteenth century there are also isolated texts in Italian, English and French. The advent of printing brought about an increase in the number of treatises on combat manuals as on every other technical subject although, unfortunately, the two fencing books (both of them Spanish) which are said to have been the earliest into print do not survive.[61]

German texts, both in print and manuscript, continued to appear throughout the sixteenth century though these were primarily adaptations of, and commentaries upon, earlier works and were, in any case, soon overtaken both in number and sophistication by the publications of Italian masters or, as in the case of Pietro Monte, of a Spanish master practising his skills in Italy. Apart from a single translation *cum* paraphrase of an early German treatise, France was notably unproductive until the publication of Sainct Didier's *Traicté* in 1573, while England was equally barren until a little flurry of activity at the very end of the sixteenth century.

In Spain, with the exception of a fencing manual by Francisco Román (which certainly existed but has not been located),[62] publications were more concerned with mounted combat and horsemanship, and it is not until Carranza's *Philosofía de las armas* (1582) that there is a significant Spanish contribution to the art of the sword. The early seventeenth century witnessed a rapid growth in this literature. Original treatises on personal combat on foot and on horseback, along with translations or adaptations of important texts, were issued throughout Europe and the flood continued into the latter part of the nineteenth century, albeit with an increasing concentration on the art of fencing.[63]

The earliest systematic treatment of swordsmanship so far discovered is German in origin and has been dated as either late thirteenth or early fourteenth century.[64] It deals with sword-and-buckler fencing, and all movements are demonstrated by a master to his pupil in short sequences of words and pictures. The master is a priest (*sacerdos*), and this poses a problem for we know nothing about the manuscript prior to 1579 when, in a short history of swordsmanship by Heinrich von Gunterrodt, it is referred to as a very ancient work recently discovered in a Franconian monastery. Gunterrodt postulates that it was the work of some noble warrior who had turned to the monastic life in his old age while retaining an interest in the martial arts.[65] This explanation is plausible, but it has some drawbacks. In the first place, sword and buckler play was more the preoccupation of the common man and city dweller than of the knightly classes so that a concern with that particular technique is not the first thing one would associate with a retired nobleman. Second, is the difficulty of relating the fighting *sacerdos* to any subsequent monastic tradition. Allusions, mostly hostile, to priests going about armed are not uncommon throughout medieval Europe: but that is a different matter from providing systematic instruction to pupils. Only two famous figures in early German *Fechtbuch* literature, Hanko Döbringer and Johannes Lecküchner, were also priests; while even more unusual is a reference to the sixteenth-century duellist, the Baron des Guerres, who is said to have been instructed by a priest who was 'a very fine master' of the hand-and-a-half (or bastard) sword.[66]

Monks enjoyed greater fame (or notoriety) as wrestlers; and the same Baron Des Guerres, when his combat with Fendilles was going badly for him, decided to resort to wrestling in 'which he had been very well trained by a little Breton priest who used to be almoner of the Cardinal de Lenoncourt'. In Anthoine de La Sale's *Jehan de Saintré*, when a worldly abbot challenges the hero to a wrestling contest, Jehan tries to avoid it on the grounds that 'these worthy monks be masters thereof, likewise of playing at tennis, of tossing bars, stones, and iron weights, and all manner of exercises'. In the event, Jehan cannot dodge the fight, and the abbot throws him about with ease.[67] La Sale's work is fiction, but the activities he describes are generally based on current mid-fifteenth-century realities and, with regard to wrestling, this is partially confirmed by a contemporary account of holds, throws, and locks employed in an allegorical wrestling match between Poverty and Fortune which occurs in the *Arçipreste de Talavera* by the Spanish priest, Alfonso Martínez de Toledo. Alfonso certainly does know what he is talking about.[68] On the other hand, his expertise is again in unarmed combat, and there is little evidence to suggest that swordsmanship was widely accepted as a monkish accomplishment, and – despite the evidence of the *sacerdos* in the sword and buckler manuscript, and of Döbringer, Lecküchner and Des Guerres's unknown teacher – not enough to establish a tradition of monastic (or priestly) masters of arms.

It is also impossible to establish any direct connection between this early manual and later manuals of the martial arts. This becomes clear when we consider the content of these works. Manuscript I. 33 is atypical in its concentration upon sword and buckler combat. The next approximately datable text, Johann Liechtenauer's didactic poem on the use of the long sword, not only includes brief comments on other kinds of fighting but is also known first in a manuscript of 1389, where it is collected with diverse material including information on various fencing systems, sword and buckler play, and Liechtenauer's wrestling notes.[69]

What was to become the norm up to at least the early seventeenth century may be exemplified by an Italian treatise which dates from the turn of the fourteenth and fifteenth centuries but deals with an already firmly established tradition – the fruit, as its author declares, of some fifty years' study. This is the *Flos duellatorum*, by Fiore de' Liberi, a native of the village of Premariacco near Cividale in the northernmost part of Italy. Fiore did not commit his ideas to paper until comparatively late in a career which had taken him not only to many parts of Italy but also to Germany where he studied with Johann the Swabian who was himself a pupil of Niklaus of Toblem from the diocese of Metz.[70] Fiore's work demonstrates the varied matters with which the professional master of arms was concerned: wrestling both with and without a dagger; handling an armed assailant while being oneself unarmed; fencing with single-handed sword; foot combat with axes or other staff weapons; handling a light lance on horseback; combat with two-hand swords; dealing with more than one adversary at a time; mounted fencing; and even mounted wrestling. This wide range of activities recurs in numerous other works on the martial arts and must have been typical of what went on in the schools of arms, which rarely concentrated solely on sword and buckler fighting. The powerful Germanic tradition (where certain authoritative texts, such as Liechtenauer's treatise on the long sword, were commented upon, copied, recopied, augmented from other sources, and further enlarged by personal contributions) has resulted in a corpus of more than sixty surviving manuscripts embracing the wrestling system of the Jewish master Ott, the short sword technique of Martin Hundfeld, the Jewish master Lew's fencing on horseback, the all-in fighting of Lecküchner and Peter Falkner, and the

10. Lofty claims in Agrippa's frontispiece (1553).

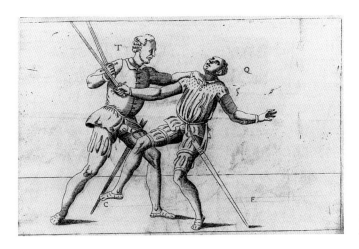

11. Wrestling and grappling in Agrippa. 1553, fol. 56.

exhaustive studies of hand-to-hand combat (wrestling, use of knife, dagger and different types of sword) by artists such as Albrecht Dürer, Gregor Erhart and Jörg Breu the Younger.

The mid-fifteenth-century German master, Hans Talhoffer, is especially noteworthy because, like one or two later masters, he himself posed for the illustrations in his *Fechtbuch* of 1459, as we are told by the man who wrote out the text – a certain Michael Rotwyler.[71] The contents of Talhoffer's compilations are much the same as in Fiore but the range is even wider, and the illustrations cover most kinds of combat which might theoretically have been encountered at the time: two-hand sword fighting; combat within the lists in full armour and using short thrusting spear and two-hand sword; fighting with various weapons (polaxe, large spiked shield and mace, similar shields with single-handed sword, the shield on its own); dagger technique and unarmed combat; the use of the short sword (messer) on its own, with a small buckler, and with buckler against two assailants; judicial combat between a man and woman; sword fighting on horseback; mounted wrestling; and finally mounted combat with lance against sword, or lance against arbalest.

This repertoire, with variations and limitations, was to remain typical of personal combat in western Europe well into the seventeenth century and its remnants may still be found in sophisticated and well-informed treatises of the late seventeenth century.[72] The whole question of the content of so-called 'fencing books' requires reassessment. In the Middle Ages and Renaissance, the great majority of these books were not concerned solely with fencing and it is reasonable, therefore, to doubt whether the masters of arms themselves were. Consider Camillo Agrippa's *Trattato* of 1553, which has been seized upon by most historians as the first scientific work on fencing. Certainly Agrippa, who was not a professional master of arms at all, himself adopted a particularly elevated stance (fig. 10). In the frontispiece to the *Trattato*, we see him seated at a table holding a pair of dividers and an armillary sphere, while his left foot rests on a terrestrial globe. The atmosphere is that of an academic dispute: but Agrippa is girded with a sheathed sword; two naked daggers are on the table before him; an armoured gauntlet lies on the floor; and just in front of it is another sword with its blade partly obscured by a polyhedron. The meaning is clear. The author – a distinguished mathematician and engineer – is using both pure and applied mathematics to place personal combat upon a scientific basis. Yet even Agrippa still considers it worthwhile to touch upon sword and buckler play, the handling of the halberd and two-hand sword, tourneying on horseback, and the use of wrestling tricks (fig. 11). He

25

even devotes a chapter to fighting with two swords, one in each hand (the 'case of rapiers', as it was called in England) which, though cumbersome, was used by some duellists and continued to attract occasional attention amidst the heterogeneous skills professed by later masters (fig. 12).[73] It remained unusual for a master to declare, as did Alfonso Falloppia in 1584, that since he was writing an 'operetta cavalieresca' he would exclude such outlandish instruments of assassination as the rotella, targe, buckler, two-hand sword, and staff weapons, but would concentrate only on those weapons which a gentleman would carry every day: sword, dagger, glove and cape.[74] Most experts thought, fought, and taught differently.

The merest glance at the principal treatises on the martial arts published in the sixteenth century shows the extent to which the 'scientific' Agrippa was typical in his coverage of more than sword fighting alone. Leaving aside the few works devoted solely to mounted combat, most authors felt obliged to expatiate upon several types of fighting. In this respect, no master was more comprehensive than Pietro Monte in 1509. He not only deals with wrestling, dagger fighting, the use of long and short lance, two-hand sword and the single sword on its own or in combination with various types of shield and buckler or cape; he also discusses the handling of various types of pole arm such as the partisan, the ronca, spetum, and halberd. He examines in detail fencing and wrestling on horseback, along with various types of mounted lance combat; treats physical exercises such as running, jumping and vaulting; provides a little encyclopaedia of contemporary arms and armour; and finally places the entire corpus of material within a broader context of the art of war. Set beside this bellicose thesaurus, the claims of Giacomo di Grassi seem almost modest. When he caused himself to be depicted at the head of his treatise on offence and defence he was surrounded by a veritable arsenal: rapier, dagger, two-hander, polaxe, roncone and bill; rondella, square and round target, large buckler and small. The picture also includes an hour glass for timing lessons, and a pair of dividers to show that, like Agrippa, di Grassi knows his mathematics (fig. 13).

There are other sources, besides technical treatises, to demonstrate the varied skills professed by the masters and practised by their pupils even at the highest levels of society; and there is no more striking evidence of this variety than in the *Freydal*, designed as a sumptuous illustrated record of the chivalric pastimes of Monte's exalted contemporary, the Emperor Maximilian I. The manuscript includes a complete series of the different types of mounted combat with sword, lance, club and mace in which the emperor himself participated, and provides a similarly detailed record of his foot combats embracing not only all the weapons already alluded to but also the short hammer, ahlspiess, flail, mace and scimitar.[75]

The versatility of the masters appears also in the gruelling examinations to which they were subjected by their peers in order to qualify for promotion in their career. When, for example, Pedro Forno was examined at Perpignan in 1519, to achieve the rank of provost he had to prove his skill with eleven weapons or combinations: sword and small buckler, two-hand sword, staff, demi-lance, poignard, short dagger, sword and large buckler, sword and dagger, sword and rondella, sword and cape, and finally sword alone. Moreover, he was expected to cope with all the masters, each wielding one of these arms, delivering a single blow simultaneously (*simul et semel*). When Gabriel de Contreras was registered as master in June 1528 in Seville, he had satisfied his examiners at two-hand sword, sword and small buckler, sword and large buckler, sword and rondella, sword alone, dagger, and quarter staff. Nearly sixty years later, Juan de Morales was examined at Madrid in the use of sword alone, sword with dagger, buckler, or rondella, and finally with the broadsword (*montante*).[76] Right through the sixteenth century, English masters were publicly tested for their competence in a wide variety of weapons, most of which were exhibited in a challenge played before Queen Elizabeth I at Whitehall in February 1561.[77] And when, around 1572, Humphrey Gilbert drafted a scheme for an academy in London 'for education of her Majesties Wardes and others the youth of nobility and gentlemen', he envisaged more than a wide-ranging academic programme. He also intended that physical education would be fully catered for, with a riding master, a soldier to teach military science, and a 'Master of Defence, who shalbe principally expert in the Rapier and dagger, the Sworde and tergat, the gripe of the dagger, the battaile axe and the pike, and shall theare publiquely teach'.[78]

LAWYERS, HUMANISTS AND THE MARTIAL ARTS

Gilbert's academy was a remarkable conception. Had the scheme come to fruition it would have established an environment in which arms, letters and public utility might have flourished to their mutual benefit. Gilbert's dream never materialized until, at a later period, a purely military education developed in European academies but, throughout the Middle Ages and Renaissance, exercising in the martial arts had raised legal, moral and social problems which learned men addressed in their usual well-intentioned fashion.[79]

All the current combat techniques were potentially lethal in application and dangerous

27

even in training: so how was the law to regard deaths arising from exercise? Barthélemi de Chasseneux's authoritative *Catalogus gloriae mundi* stated explicitly that such cases were exempt from the punishment meted out for homicide on the grounds that martial exercises are permitted as useful to the state – a view later cited by the Sicilian jurist Mario Muta. Later still the whole passage from Muta was adopted by the Sicilian master swordsman, Morsicato Pallavicini, who explained that the fundamental reason for immunity from punishment is that fencing is 'good, licit, honest, useful and delightful', whereas any death which may result from practising it is adventitious and unintentional. Hence arises the antiquity, necessity, nobility, goodness and utility of fencing and of its 'experienced masters who with their art maintain the state, preserve life, and augment the valour of the people'.[80]

In England, a fatality resulting from a bout of friendly wrestling would generally be adjudged misadventure; and, early in the fifteenth century, even when death resulted from play with staves or swords, there was still an inclination to consider this a misadventure because 'such martial acts are good to be used for the defence of the realm'. A century later English lawyers expressed anxiety about the prohibition of dangerous martial exercises on account of their potential utility to the realm; and a distinction was made between unlawful acts committed without profit to the common weal and acts (such as slaying a man in 'play with sword and buckler') which were 'lawful and for the common good at the beginning'. The situation was summarized in elegant law French: 'si un wrestyller jua id est luder all dagger ou pollax et tiels sembles et tua un, ceo nest felonie . . . silles sont myxtez oue malise ou violence cest felonie'. It is difficult, though, to see how two-handed swords, polaxes and the like could be used – even in training – without at least a modicum of violence. Just as it is difficult to see how a state, which needed able-bodied and expert fighters, logically could suppress those who taught the relevant skills.[81]

The question of the relationship between training with weapons and the common weal was implicit in the whole organization of feudal warfare, though it was never subjected to theoretical analysis or to systematic, practical organization. Members of the knightly class were expected to acquire their skills under the tutelage of their elders. When anybody did ponder the training necessary for rank and file recruits the best that could be done – whether by a medieval authority such as Christine de Pisan or by a renaissance luminary such as Machiavelli ('the first modern military thinker', so-called)[82] – was to paraphrase Vegetius's general principles and his account of Roman military training and exercises. Intrinsically, there was nothing wrong with this procedure except that no one yet knew how to put it into practice, as Florence discovered to its cost when its militia experiment proved disastrous.[83] There is no evidence that anyone tried to apply these ideas to the feudal levies beyond instructing men to bring along the arms deemed appropriate to their social standing and, in England especially, enjoining the yeomanry to practise archery.[84]

The civic benefits to be derived from military training did, however, greatly concern humanist educationalists and the issue came into prominence early in the fifteenth century when Pierpaolo Vergerio composed his treatise 'On noble customs and liberal studies of youth', one of the most influential works on education in renaissance Europe. The treatise was addressed to Ubertino da Carrara, a member of the ruling family in Padua, but it became a theoretical model for the training of all citizens. While Vergerio's primary concern was with academic matters, he devoted some space to bodily exercise and especially to training in the art of war which he considered essential for good citizenship. Just as the Romans had insisted on 'systematic and scientific training in arms' so, too, should contemporary youth 'learn the art of the sword, the cut, the thrust and the parry; the use of shield, of the spear, of the club, training either hand to wield the weapon'. Vergerio also advocated a more general programme of physical training for the soldier who must be fit and strong. He recognized that the arms and methods of war change from age to age, but

> Whatever the method or the weapon of the time, let there be ample practice for our youth, with as great variety of exercises as can be devised, so that they may be ready for combat hand to hand or in troop, in the headlong charge or in skirmish. We cannot forestall the reality of war, its sudden emergencies, or its vivid terrors, but by training and practice we can at least provide such preparation as the case admits.[85]

Vergerio's treatise became immensely popular in the fifteenth century, and the notion that skill in arms was somehow conducive to good citizenship became a pedagogic commonplace. One author after another dutifully declared the social and political importance of such training and the theme continued through the sixteenth century. Even Luther approved of physical exercise though, in his case, it was less for military advantage than for counteracting the common rabble's propensity for falling into 'rioting, vice, gluttony, drunkenness and gaming', and he recommended jousting, fencing, and wrestling to promote good health. Another reformer, Ulrich Zwingli, similarly favoured a martial training – 'Corpus exercebant, cursus, saltus, discus, palaestra, lucta' – a passage which, in the Tudor translation of his Christian education of the young, reads more invitingly as 'the body shalbe exercised with running, leapyng, coyting, the exercyse of weapons, and wrestling'.[86]

Educationalists, almost without fail, recommended some form of physical training. What they never explained was how instruction in the handling of weapons should be given and by whom. The problem evidently did occur to Vergerio who came up with the example of Publius Rutilius who, according to Valerius Maximus, had been the first person to institute regular lessons for the Roman soldiery on the handling of arms by calling together the 'Teachers of the Gladiators' to demonstrate 'the way of shunning and giving blows, according to the reasons of Art'.[87] Vergerio approved the story but did not explain how those who instructed Roman gladiators were going to serve within the context of a fifteenth-century school for young boys.

The most extended of all renaissance discussions of physical exercise and sport within an academic context was provided in 1581 by the English pedagogue Richard Mulcaster who, amongst much else, recommended wrestling and fencing.[88] The former is 'good for the head ache, sharpneth the senses, is an enemie to melancholie, and whetteth the stomacke being troubled with any cold distemperature'. The latter, that is fencing, is even more useful. The art had been practised by the ancients in three different ways: against a real opponent; against a stake or pillar 'as a counterfet adversarie'; or against an imaginary person, 'a fight against a shadow'. All are beneficial, 'both for the health of our bodies, and the helpe of our countries'; but the most effective method is against a real adversary, because it soon 'canvasses out a coward, that will neither defend his freinde, nor offend his foe: the cheife frute that should follow fensing'. Alone among pedagogues, Mulcaster devotes a long chapter to the 'training master'. But it is an immense disappointment to anyone seeking information on the practicalities of physical education. Moralistic and flatulent, it merely argues the inseparable nature of soul and body and recommends that the trainer of the one should also be the trainer of the other. Such universally gifted men may have existed (another Alberti, Leonardo, or even Pietro Monte might have filled the vacancy) but hardly in sufficient numbers to make Mulcaster's suggestion a practical proposition.

29

There was a complete mismatch between social and educational theorists and the masters of arms who, in a sense, took matters into their own hands. They started to write books of their own, thereby making a reality out of the ideal union between arms and letters, although the putative benefit to the common weal was not the principal purpose of their labours.

THE REAL PURPOSE OF THE MASTERS OF ARMS

'It is said the warrior's is the twofold Way of pen and sword, and he should have a taste for both Ways'. This was the belief and practice of the seventeenth-century Japanese virtuoso of swordsmanship, Miyamoto Musashi.[89] A significant number of his European colleagues shared this attitude and developed literary as well as martial techniques. Fiore de' Liberi's *Prologo* provides the kind of justification which would have answered Izaak Walton's doubts about trying to teach practical skills through books. Fiore asserted the importance of providing a written systematic study of combat techniques which, he said, 'without books and writing can only be badly retained in the mind', adding that 'there will never be a good scholar without books'.[90] Two centuries later, Salvator Fabris was to tell his readers not to marvel that a man of the sword should presume to write a book, or that the 'practical knowledge of the sword' should be reduced to rules and precepts for, just as the learned have transferred their theoretical arts into practice, so the 'armigero' converts his practice into a 'vera theorica'.[91] It was at about the same time that George Hale took on his unlettered English colleagues by asserting that 'The Science of Defence, not unworthily stiled Noble . . . was never before in any Language brought to any Method. The Professors thereof being so ignorant, that they could rather doe, than make demonstration, or reduce their doing to any certaintie of principle.' The attitude of those masters who took pains to write about their art was distilled into a punning aphorism by Morsicato Pallavicini, perhaps the most historically conscious of all the great fencers. 'Chi non legge non può dar legge', he wrote. 'He who does not read cannot lay down laws.'[92]

While it was increasingly common for masters to put their ideas into print, it was extremely rare for any of them to claim that written words would, of themselves, suffice to make a student proficient in the martial arts. As Jean-Baptiste Le Perche explained: 'in all those arts where one has need to use the hand, it is not enough to have knowledge of the principles, it is also necessary to join with it a long experience'; and he added that, without the help of an excellent master, no one could learn how to use weapons just by reading his book written only 'to aid the memory and ease the master's burden'.[93] This was the generally accepted position, and at least one apparent claim to the autonomy of the text turns out to be no more than an advertising puff. Blazoned forth on the title page of the English version of Giacomo di Grassi's treatise is the following bold statement:

> Di Grassi his true Arte of Defence, plainlie teaching by infallible Demonstrations, apt Figures and perfect Rules the manner and forme how a man without other Teacher or Master may safelie handle all sortes of Weapons aswell offensive as defensive (1594).

The original Italian text had made no such boast but included 'un modo di essercitarsi da se stesso, per acquistare forza, giudicio, & prestezza' – a course of free-standing exercises and weight training to strengthen the fighter's arms, legs, body and stamina, and to develop

La suma de lo que contiene efte libro hallaras
en la hoja antes del fol.1.

14. Pacheco de Narváez: portrait of another mathematical master. 1600, frontispiece.

15. Narváez's complexities and ambiguities. 1600,
p. 202.

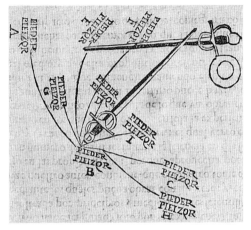

judgement and speed. This is very important, but was not intended to teach combat techniques. There is, however, a slight ambiguity in di Grassi's discussion of the handling of
the pike. He stresses that his advice should be verified in deeds not words, and that every
man who wished to practise this art should first diligently learn the principles and 'afterwards by exercise of the weapon to attain to the most subtil and delicate knowledge of the
times' – but he does not stipulate that the exercise must be carried out with a master. A
similar ambiguity occurs in the *Advertisement to the Reader* preceding the English edition,
where the writer praises both author and translator for making available a treatise from
which any 'wise man of an unpartiall judgement' might learn not only through reading
and remembering 'to furnish his minde with resolute instructions' but also through practice and exercise 'gallantly to perfourme any conceited enterprise with a discreete and
orderly carriage of his bodie'.

   An author who did make a bold claim for his clarity of exposition was the Spanish master
Don Luis Pacheco de Narváez who, in 1600, declared that he would expound many secrets
'with which everyone will be able to teach himself to learn without the necessity of a master
to direct him' (fig. 14).[94] He may even have believed this himself, but it would require the
skills of a cryptographer to translate his mathematical diagrams into physical action (fig.
15). More judiciously, in a treatise on pike exercise published in 1668, Marin Bresciani
pondered on the 'difference between the practical and the speculative'. He recognized 'that
a sublime and perspicacious intellect, with its own elevated judgement as its only guide'
might well be able to understand fully what he sets forth. Yet, without actually seeing the
activity in practice, that 'sublime intellect' would not be able to do it 'since there is a great

16. Bresciani's unambiguous instruction on how to trail the pike when retreating. 1668, plate for chapter 27.

17. Professor Gioberti's fencing machine for practising without a master. Viti, *Taccometro* (n.p., n.d.), fig. 1.

discrepancy between seeing the ways in which a sport (*Giuoco*) is actually practised and reading about the rules which one ought to observe' (fig. 16).[95]

The necessity of practice with a master was rarely in doubt. Even when, late in the nineteenth century, fencing enthusiasts devised mechanical methods for practising without the aid of an opponent, they still assumed some preliminary knowledge and skill on the part of their readers. They were at pains to point out that teaching was indispensable and that the systems they offered were merely to facilitate practice when no master or opponent was available. Thus 'Le Commandant E.T.', in his *Escrime de chambre* recommends an articulated and adjustable arm attached to the wall, which would enable the keen fencer to practise in his own room first thing in the morning, 'or to relax from study, or when the weather is bad and does not allow him to venture out' and, while not replacing the instruction of a master, would provide excellent practice and physical exercise.[96] Similarly circumspect is the study by J.B. Viti, recommending Professor Gioberti's fencing machine, the Taccometro – a name derived from 'Tocos vitesse et Metron mètre'. Viti prefaced his account by recalling the hostility first encountered by Watt's steam engine and Arkwright's spinning jenny, and he hastens to assure any Luddite fencing masters that Gioberti's machine is designed solely to lighten their labours by eliminating the need for personal involvement in boring and time-consuming repetition of movements with each individual student. It will save everybody an immense amount of trouble, but 'it does not free anyone from the instruction of the master' – something readily apparent from the illustrations which accompany Viti's encomium (fig. 17).[97]

Like these nineteenth-century enthusiasts for mechanical contrivances, the early masters were convinced that even the most assiduous reader would still require practical instruction. As Hanko Döbringer had remarked in 1389, qualifying his own attempt to set down a combat system, a reader 'should know that one cannot speak or write about fighting as clearly as one can show and demonstrate with the hand; therefore use your common sense and reflect on things further'.[98] The difficult relationship between teaching, comprehension and practice was clearly set out in the first significant combat manual ever to be printed

– Pietro Monte's *Collectanea* – where the author clarified his own position as both theoretician and teacher of the martial arts and insisted that words must be accompanied by practical demonstration.

Lessons in practical arts demand the presence and help of a master.[99] This point was also well grasped by Saviolo who stressed not only that words were inadequate to convey the intricacies of movement but that even seeing an action performed is insufficient without first-hand instruction by a master taking his pupil through the whole process. 'And that this is so many Gentlemen can witnes who although they have seene me doo, yet coulde neither understand nor practise them untill that I shewed them the waie, and then with much adoo and very hardly'.[100] Even then mere understanding is not enough. If the pupil has not mastered the moves by constant exercise ('as in all other artes the speculation without practise is imperfect'), when he comes to performance 'hee shall perceive his want, and put his life in hazard and jeopardie'.

This was the crucial issue. The masters were concerned with matters of life and death, not with sport. This is why, when, towards the middle of the sixteenth century, the question of sword practice was discussed by the Bolognese master, Angelo Viggiani, he strongly warned against exercising with rebated weapons.[101] As so often in renaissance treatises, Viggiani's work is cast in the form of a conversation, but there is no doubt as to who is giving and who receiving instruction. The pupil, on being told to take up his sword ready for a lesson, rather nervously asks whether it would not be better to arm himself with a sword *da giuoco* (that is without edge or point).[102] He is promptly rebuked for such pusillanimity. Without the real thing, it is neither possible to acquire courage and spirit nor to learn *uno schermo perfetto*. Surely, the pupil protests, one can practise all the strokes just as well with a rebated weapon as with a sword *da filo* (that is with a sharp edge)? But the master flatly denies this, pointing out that although the movements might well be similar, their execution will be imperfect with a rebated sword because – secure in the knowledge that the opposing blade will not inflict much damage even should you fail to parry it adequately – you simply do not need to use the same force, pressure and speed as when fighting with real swords. Reluctantly the pupil agrees, although still grumbling that with a sharp weapon even a slight error can result in serious injury.

What is at issue here is the psychology of combat, and this is as crucial to our own historical understanding of the purpose of these martial arts as it was to the safety of Viggiani's contemporaries.[103] The modern sport of fencing has rationalized the distinction between sharp and rebated weapons. Egerton Castle – whose primary interest lay in the evolution of swordsmanship towards the sport of his own day and who was, therefore, critical of renaissance technique – nevertheless recognized that 'things are done with the foil which would never be attempted in earnest with a sword' and accepted that modern play is artificial and that 'foil practice may in fact be looked upon as "diagrammatic" fencing, freed from most extraneous, disturbing elements'.[104]

Unfortunately, it was precisely those 'extraneous, disturbing elements' which really mattered to men who habitually carried bladed weapons and knew that it might, at almost any time, be necessary to wield them. Armed brawling was commonplace everywhere in Europe and the punctilios of the formal duel, designed to give some semblance of structure to personal violence, were more frequently violated than observed. In an attack on duelling, published in 1560, Sebastiano Fausto had pointed out that while the sword, when used for a good cause, is the arm of justice, it is also the arm of the killer and ruffian; and his contemporary Bernardo Sacco lamented that nowadays duellists sought only to slay one another.[105] The Elizabethan Italian, Saviolo, advised his students that, when a man takes his sword in hand against you (even if you have hitherto regarded him as your friend), you must remember that he intends to kill you. 'Wherefore if he be your friend go not with him into the field; but if you go, do your best, because it seemeth childish to say, I will go and fight, but I will spare and favour him.' As for any man prepared to fight you, says Saviolo, 'well you may be his friend, but you shall finde him to be your enemie'. Therefore 'whensoever you see anie man drawe upon you, staie not untill hee doo his pleasure, and trust him not, for hee hath not his weapon drawn to no purpose'.[106] The only rule that mattered was self-preservation. A man had to be ready to kill his adversary as quickly and efficiently as possible.

Courtesies and generosity were a costly luxury when the price was your own life. Brantôme, writing at about the turn of the sixteenth and seventeenth centuries, was explicit on this when commenting on the duel which had taken place in 1503 between Bayard and the Spaniard, Sotomayore. The latter had chosen to fight on foot thinking that this would give him the advantage over his opponent who had been weakened by an ague. In the event Bayard was victorious but, says Brantôme, this does not alter the fact that Sotomayore was correct in trying to take advantage of the situation, for no man should ever 'concede any point of courtesy to his enemy while he has arms in his hand, until one sees him below one and at one's feet'.[107] The Jacobean master, George Hale, was similarly forthright. The 'Science of Defence', he asserts, is a 'remedie to an unavoyded Disease, in opposing sodaine assaults' and is tolerated both by God and Nature 'since Innocence is no protection against murtherous intents'. The fact is that 'Accidentall quarrels' greatly outnumber 'occasions for the field' and it is, therefore, important to learn how to cope with unfavourable odds when a man may be faced with 'sodaine on-sets' and have to defend himself with his 'wearing weapons, being for the most part, a single rapier or short sword'.[108]

The question of 'wearing weapons' – that is weapons carried as part of one's everyday dress – is very important in the history of personal combat, and it is worth comparing Hale's remarks with two apparently similar but, in fact, very different Italian statements on the same theme. Roughly contemporaneous with Hale is the combat treatise by Giovan' Battista Gaiani who maintained that there was nothing more useful than knowing how to defend oneself. No one, he said, could deny that the art of using sword and dagger, 'armi da Cavalliere', was worthy of great honour. It is vain to carry a sword and not know how to attack your enemy or how to defend yourself against him. Nearly a century earlier, Baldassare Castiglione had declared that the perfect courtier must be able to handle every kind of weapon and be especially skilful with those normally used among gentlemen. 'For beside the use that he shall have of them in war, where peradventure needeth no great cunning, there happen oftentimes variances between one gentleman and another, whereupon ensueth a combat'. In such circumstances it will frequently be necessary 'to use the weapon that he hath at that instant by his side, wherefore it is safest to know how to use it'.[109] The difference between these various observations is that whereas the two Italians assume that it is only courtiers or gentlemen who will carry sword and dagger, Hale suggests that everybody will be so armed.

The available evidence supports Hale's view of an England where personal violence was endemic. Men seemed prepared to thrust and slash at each other anywhere and at any time. 'Divers naughty and insolent persons', a proclamation of 1557 complains, have recently 'attempted to make quarrels, riots, and frays as well in churches and churchyards as in sundry other places, cities, towns, and markets; and for the accomplishment of their naughty purposes and quarrels have caused swords and rapiers to be made of much greater length than heretofore hath been accustomed or is decent to use and wear.' Another proclamation in 1562 laments that a habit had crept in of wearing long swords and rapiers, 'sharpened in such sort as may appear the usage of them can not tend to defence, which ought to be the very meaning of wearing of weapons in times of peace, but to murder and evident death, when the same shall be occupied'.[110] In William Harrison's *Description of England* (1577), there is a well-known lamentation on this contemporary fashion for carrying weapons.

> Seldom shall you see any of my countrymen above eighteen or twenty years old to go about without a dagger at the least at his back or by his side, although they be aged burgesses or magistrates of any city who in appearance are most exempt from brabling and contention. Our nobility wear commonly swords or rapiers with their daggers, as doth every common serving-man also that followeth his lord and master. Some desperate cutters we have in like sort, which carry two daggers or two rapiers in a sheath always about them, wherewith in every drunken fray they are known to work much mischief.

Harrison goes on to complain about the excessive length of these swords and daggers, 'longer than the like used in any other country, whereby each one pretendeth to have the more advantage of his enemy', and he points out that, despite repeated official attempts to curb this abuse, nothing has been achieved. He adds that many wayfarers also carry 'excessive staves' some of which are 'twelve or thirteen feet long, beside the pike of twelve inches'. Honest men suspect these fellows of being thieves and robbers and are thus themselves compelled to travel about with 'a case of dags' at their saddle-bows or 'with some pretty short snapper' in order to deal with the villains before they get near with their weapons. In conclusion he remarks that 'no man travelleth by the way without his sword, or some such weapon, with us, except the minister, who commonly weareth none at all, unless it be a dagger or hanger by his side'.[111]

This is the context within which George Hale was explaining the importance of being able to use a sword but, elsewhere in Europe, the carrying of weapons and the easy transition from quarrel to deadly conflict was at least as common, if not more so. In Valencia, for example, during the closing decades of the sixteenth century and well beyond, public proclamations against the carrying of firearms and a whole armoury of swords, knives and daggers were a regular feature of civic life – so regular, indeed, as to make it obvious that, despite the threat of heavy fines and slavery in the galleys, the Valencians continued not only to carry all manner of offensive weapons (especially long and narrow-bladed thrusting swords) but constantly used them 'to inflict injuries and murders on their neighbours'.[112]

There is no reason to suppose that the violence of Valencia was in any way untypical of life in contemporary Spain. The duelling craze in renaissance France is copiously documented but has been too frequently studied to require further comment here. And in Italy, where a labyrinthine code of honour was designed to stifle the formal duel, armed affrays were commonplace. Where, asked the Bolognese soldier, Federico Ghisliero, would a man use his sword? His answer is short but revealing for, like George Hale, he stresses that most brawls and duels take place in the public streets. In such circumstances – due to rain, mud and general unevenness – we may have to fight on an extremely dangerous surface. It is essential, therefore, for men to adapt themselves to every sort of site.[113] The likelihood of having to defend oneself at virtually any place and at any time underlies the exposition of combat by di Grassi who points out that these perils arise so suddenly, and in so many different ways, that mastery merely of a few strokes of point and edge is quite inadequate. It is impossible, he says, to take instant decisions without a thorough grasp of the underlying rules and principles of both attack and defence, with or without a weapon, for a man may be attacked when he is himself without arms and is 'constrained to defend himself with a peece of wood from a javelin, with a stool or fourme from a sworde, or with a cloake from a dagger'.[114]

Any master of arms worth the price of his lessons would have known what his pupils, whether soldiers or civilians, really needed. Historians have tended neither to understand what they did nor why they did it. The few scholars who have attempted to deal with medieval and renaissance fighting masters have shied away from the brutality of the truth. They have not merely concentrated their attention almost exclusively on swordsmanship but have, even within that limited sphere, singled out only those elements which can be related to the evolution of modern fencing and its obsession with the thrust. One might say sylleptically that, by concentrating on the point, the historians of personal combat have missed it completely. It is not enlightening to be told, in effect, that the early masters failed to understand modern play with foil, épée and sabre. We might as well criticize them for not taking advantage of electronic scoring. In much the same way, recent studies of duelling concentrate almost exclusively upon the stratification and fragmentation of social codes and ignore the fact that, however widely spread the duelling craze may have become, the habit of carrying arms and of being trained in the arts of killing did not merely induce men to duel. Such training also informed their behaviour outside the formal structures of challenge and reply, and of rules seeking to impose equality on the combatants. There were many upper-class fools prepared to observe the niceties, but there must have been a far greater number of belligerents sufficiently intelligent to ensure that violence was, as far as possible, weighted in their favour – whether this meant knifing an enemy in the back, blinding him with a handful of grit, or throwing a tankard of ale in his face before kicking him in the testicles.[115]

The masters taught everything that pertained to physical violence in times of peace and of war. They dealt with every weapon and with every trick of unarmed combat. We should not be surprised that, in the land of the landsknecht, masters were devoted to such 'outlandish' instruments of destruction as the 'long sword' and a variety of staff weapons. Staff weapons as a genre have taken a very long time to disappear from the battlefield. The fixed bayonet has seen plenty of action throughout the twentieth century and what is it, after all, but a staff weapon. The same may be said of medieval and renaissance techniques for knife combat and all-in fighting whose relevance for modern warfare is made abundantly clear by the merest glance at any commando training manual. It is true that the rapier would have been useless in the crush of battle at any time and not especially effective when brawling in a narrow alley. This is why George Silver deemed it an 'imperfect' weapon and was so scathing about its 'inconvenient length and unweildinesse'. But it was designed for quite another purpose and was deadly in formal single combat between men *en chemise* – or *en* rather less (fig. 18). The business of the master of arms was to prepare his pupils for all eventualities; and there is no more succinct description of what this involved than that given by Hale's contemporary, George Silver. Silver has no time for the fancy posturing of the Italian masters with their unrealistic rules and regulations and their concentration upon Terpsichorean grace. Real fighting is an all-in affair and so brutal that, 'as long as we barre anie maner of play in schoole, we shall hardly make a good scholler'. For Silver, the old ways were best and it is clear not only that the violent pages of Talhoffer would have

18. L'Ange demonstrates fencing in its bare essentials. 1664, plate 49.

delighted him but that they must have been very close to earlier English traditions of
personal combat. Nothing, he says, compares to the 'ancient teaching':

> that is, first their quarters, then their wardes, blowes, thrusts, and breaking of thrusts,
> then their Closes and Gripes, striking with the hilts, Daggers, Bucklers, Wrastlings,
> striking with the foote or knee in the Coddes, and all these are safely defended in
> learning perfectly of the Gripes. And this is the ancient teaching, the perfectest and most
> best teaching; and without this teaching, there shall never scholler be made able, doe his
> uttermost, nor fight safe.

For many centuries, the fighting taught by professional masters was relevant either on
the battlefield, in the formal duel or in a brawl. The space given to the different skills
required in each case varied from author to author, place to place, and (certainly) from time
to time. There were changes of emphasis related to changes in weaponry, warfare and social
habits; and, until a number of useful conventions became generally accepted, the authors
of treatises on the martial arts each had to find his own way to explicate his ideas. To achieve
clarity was extremely difficult. Even face to face in the schools of arms it was not always
possible to teach effectively for, as is the case with all executive skills, the greatest performers were not necessarily gifted teachers. Marozzo pointed this out. He complained that,
among his own contemporaries, there were valiant and experienced men, 'good and expert
swordsmen' who had nevertheless not been adequately prepared by their own teachers to
be able to give instruction to others.[116]

Nearly 150 years later, Morsicato Pallavicini attacked men who, calling themselves
Schermitori, would open a school of fencing and teach their pupils how to 'hasten with the
greatest speed to the grave'. Pallavicini recognized that, where teaching is concerned,
fencing was as much an intellectual as a practical matter. An understanding of mathematics
and geometry was essential, not to execute moves correctly but in order to have a grasp of
fundamental principles and vocabulary. It is only such intellectual mastery which enables
teachers to *explain* physical actions rationally and lucidly. This is why Pallavicini makes
such a sharp distinction between the 'Maestro d'Armi' and the mere 'Schermitore'.

The Master of Arms is one who wisely instructs his pupils in true rules not false; demonstrating, with authority of reading, all his reasons to the fencer or scholar so that he too, properly instructed, may obtain the honourable title of Master of Arms. But he who, without knowing how to read, nor count, nor calculate, wishes to call himself Master of Arms, or Master of Fencing, and wishes to pass himself off as such, ought to be punished for his presumption.

The qualities requisite for the successful master constitute a formidable list. He must have a good physique, neither too big nor too small; must be well read; and have strength, dexterity, knowledge, judgement, practical skill and long experience. 'Without doubt, he who with the tongue sets forth, and with the hand executes, is to be regarded as a true Master.'[117]

It is not surprising that masters, faced not with live students but with an invisible audience of readers, found it difficult to convey the knowledge they wished to impart. Many failed to achieve any clarity at all. Others, however, devised sophisticated systems of varying efficacy to meet their needs which — apart from the fundamental problem of finding some acceptable and readily grasped general principles — were twofold: first, to develop an analytical, descriptive vocabulary; second, to devise visual aids to augment a reader's understanding of the words. Not all masters consciously recognized that these difficulties existed, and the resulting farrago could be totally incomprehensible to anyone not already familiar with the master's system — as was the case with some late fifteenth-century English treatises on the two-handed sword.[118] One of the few masters who specifically dealt with the problem of language was, curiously, the first to survive in print. Pietro Monte's *Collectanea* begins with a *Vocabulorum expositio* which defines technical terms in modern languages as well as in Latin, and explains why many of these derive from Spanish, the language in which the book was originally written. Especially interesting is the way Monte insists that he has found it necessary to invent new words in order to be properly understood. He then works his way through a great variety of terms relating to wrestling, weaponry, and defensive armour although, in all these cases, and especially with regard to fencing and mounted combat, he defers the bulk of the vocabulary to the appropriate chapters.[119]

Following Monte's example, I, too, shall deal with technical vocabulary in connection with individual modes of combat. However, the other difficulty — of devising pictorial or diagrammatic aids to explicate movement — was not confronted by Monte who might, in an ideal world, have enlisted the help of his gifted acquaintance Leonardo da Vinci to solve it for him.[120] Many authors, however, did grapple with the problem; and it is to these, and to their various devices, that I next turn.

II

The notation and illustration
of movement in combat manuals

In 1653, Sebastiano Sardi of Padua printed *Lo spadone*, a treatise on two-handed sword play by the celebrated local master of arms, Francesco Ferdinando Alfieri. The text was enhanced by six plates of mediocre quality, and readers must have been confused by the fact that these six plates were repeated, where space allowed, and with a cheerful disregard of context, to provide a total of seventeen illustrations. None of this is remarkable. Books were frequently published with irrelevant plates. But it is curious that earlier works by Alfieri, also printed by Sardi, had been illustrated profusely, accurately and according to a more sophisticated notational system. The title page of *Lo spadone* proclaimed that the use of the weapon would be demonstrated 'per via di figure'; and, in his first chapter, Alfieri declared that whoever so desired might achieve perfection by studying the accompanying illustrations which were intended to make clear those particularities 'which with difficulty can be declared with words'. Unfortunately, the pictures did nothing of the kind.[1]

Images could be more trouble than they were worth, and some writers on fencing dispensed with them altogether. The Florentine master Francesco Altoni, writing around the middle of the sixteenth century, asserted that, even though readers might desire illustrations, he was deliberately avoiding them. In the first place, he considered that they were unreliable and that it was impossible for any picture to explain human actions completely. Furthermore, when a book was printed more than once, it was impossible to avoid some variation in the plates, as had happened in the case of Galen's *Libro delle logationi*. The kind of variations which occur even in architectural drawings with pen and pencil happen much more easily in print, not only in the illustrations but also in letters, syllables and words: 'as they know who, in order to correct authors, return to the oldest volumes nearest to their origin'. As far as Altoni is concerned, figures are merely for show. They are more hindrance than help.[2]

Visual aids were even more summarily dismissed by Alfonso Falloppia who, in 1584, considered his system so simple and rational, and his explication so clear, that it could be easily understood 'without figures'.[3] The Limoges master, François Dancie, considered illustrations to be quite useless since one would need 'as many postures in a book as there are words'.[4] And a number of later writers, particularly in England, professed to share this view. In 1711, the English master Zachary Wylde omitted 'Cuts of the Postures' because, he said belligerently, 'several Books of this kind hath done it before, tho' in my Opinion, to little or no Purpose, for where I give an Explanation of the Postures, I think it is sufficient to satisfie the Curiosity of any one, and to save an unnecessary Expence.'

Similarly, in 1771, it was expense which deterred Lonnergan who made a virtue of necessity by arguing that words were superior to pictures in such matters.

> I have also avoided the expense of copper plates, judging them to be more amusing than instructive, as not one in a thousand is finished according to truth: it must also be generally granted, that the pen can much better describe any kind of motion than the pencil; for were all variations of this art to be expressed even to the strictest nicety by the latter; a figure, or representation, should then become necessary for almost every word produced by the former.

Finally, Joseph Roland, another master active in late eighteenth-century England, also considered his explanations to be adequate without 'perplexing reference to plates'. The 'intelligent young amateur' for whom he was writing would already be familiar with the principal fencing postures, and, more significantly, Roland felt that readers tended to adhere too closely to illustrations, and thereby contracted 'an exceeding stiff and awkward manner' – a pedagogical consideration unique in the annals of fencing literature.[5]

Despite their speciousness, none of these arguments won general acceptance and, throughout the long history of combat manuals, most masters of arms have considered it advantageous to supplement their words with pictures even though, as in Alfieri's case, the results might be variable.[6] My purpose in this chapter is to examine the problems confronting such masters. Physical combat is dynamic; its patterns are kaleidoscopic, and, in the case of fencing, not only the opponents' hands, feet and body, but also their swords, are in more or less constant motion and in constantly changing relationships. How far could any of this be adequately expressed in pictorial form? What kinds of solution were adopted? And what were their successes and failures?

Annotating one of his drawings of the anatomy of the heart, Leonardo da Vinci asks, 'How in *words* can you describe this heart without filling a whole book? Yet the more you write concerning it the more you will confuse the mind of the hearer.'[7] This is a genius's gloss on a medieval and renaissance commonplace, that a well-executed picture may be more eloquent than pages of text, and not only artists and fencing masters but also theologians recognized the ease with which an image can convey ideas and information.[8] The question is, how far can it convey ideas and information about movement?

Strictly speaking, a picture can barely convey even an illusion of movement, or at least it can do this only in the non-representational trickery of 'op art', or in isolated, stroboscopic effects such as the revolution of a spinning wheel in Velázquez's *Hilanderas*.[9] As far as human motion is concerned, a single picture may, at best, suggest that some movement has already started and would continue in another picture, were the artist to execute it. Moreover, such potential movement can usually be completed only in the mind of a viewer already familiar with the story depicted. The paratactical illustrations of medieval hagiography would, for example, make little sense without prior knowledge. Otto Pächt made this point by alluding to a drawing in the Caedmon Manuscript, illustrating an episode from the 'Life of St Cuthbert' (when the saint prophesies that an eagle will provide him with food during a journey). An uninformed beholder, says Pächt, would think that it represented the 'story of one monk, two boys, two eagles, and one fish'. Yet anybody familiar with the legend would immediately realize that both boy and bird occur twice within the same picture and, once it is understood that two separate figures are meant to be one and the same person, the mind solves the puzzle by 'interpolating a passage of time between the two occurrences'.[10]

The difficulty is that the information provided by most pictures is so ambiguous that the mind can provide far too many hypotheses about what has happened before the moment illustrated, and what may happen afterwards. As a record of real movement their usefulness is severely limited, and modern attempts to treat isolated works of art (such as paintings, drawings, sculptures, or reliefs) as though they were intended as a form of dance notation, are mere academic games – something which can be demonstrated easily enough by a glance at the figures in Fabritio Caroso's *Nobiltà di dame* (1600). These allegedly depict the 'correct' opening position for a number of dances described in the text. Yet, even with the descriptions, it has proved impossible to reconstruct the steps in a way satisfactory to all scholars. Without them, we would not know that the people involved were meant to be dancing at all.[11]

The problem, in Caroso, arises from attempting to record something as complicated as a dance (which is a series of movements) merely by summarizing everything within a single picture. The difficulties become less intractable when the converse is attempted, that is, when a single movement is depicted by a series of pictures. In the latter case, each illustration can show a different stage of development providing, in effect, a series of parataxes, like staging posts for the mind. This is a technique with which we are all familiar, and simple pictorial instructions on how to fasten an aircraft seat belt, put someone's arm in a sling, tie a bow tie, assemble a flat-packed piece of furniture, or operate a fire extinguisher, spring to mind.[12] More pertinent examples of this method are pictorial drill manuals of which perhaps the earliest example is Jacob de Gheyn's *The Exercise of Armes* (1607). This takes its reader through every stage of carrying, loading and preparing the caliver for firing, in a carefully drawn series of forty-two plates; repeats the process for the musket in forty-three plates, including one amusing gesture, when the injunction 'Balance your musket in the rest with your left hand, leaving the right hand free' is illustrated by the musketeer doffing his bonnet; and concludes with thirty-two plates devoted to the pike drill. The pictures in de Gheyn, and in the many drill manuals which followed, are effective both as a record of a specific activity and as a guide for anyone wishing to reproduce the whole process himself. Without doubt, movement has been notated here. But it is movement of a very limited nature, and the sequence of gestures is immutable.[13]

Drilling of the kind recorded by de Gheyn is a completely closed activity, whereas many dances and all serious sword fights are open activities with no fixed conclusion and with multifarious, interrelated sequences of movement, susceptible to immense and ceaseless permutation. To what extent was it possible to evolve, for such complexities, a notation analogous to that used in music, something which would enable skilled interpreters both to duplicate and to interpret a score in different places, at different times, and in different circumstances?

A few years ago, when dealing with the theory of symbols, Nelson Goodman assessed conflicting arguments about the feasibility of developing a notation for the dance, and observed that, 'because the dance is visual like painting, which has no notation, and yet transient and temporal like music, which has a highly developed standard notation, the answer is not altogether obvious'. Some people deny the possibility because dancing involves 'the infinitely subtle and varied expressions and three-dimensional motions of one or more highly complex organisms', and is, therefore, far too complicated to be captured by any notation. But, as Goodman remarks:

a score need not capture all the subtlety and complexity of a performance. That would

19. Austin's oratorical
gestures. 1806, plate I.

be hopeless even in the comparatively simpler art of music, and would always be point-less. The function of a score is to specify the essential properties a performance must have to belong to the work; the stipulations are only of certain aspects and only within certain degrees. All other variations are permitted; and the differences among performances of the same work, even in music, are enormous.[14]

A somewhat similar position had been adopted in 1806 by the Reverend Gilbert Austin whose *Treatise on Rhetorical Delivery* clearly expresses the assumptions underlying all attempts at movement notation. Although, says Austin, the variety of human gesture and movement may seem almost infinite, there is 'a similarity and relation among many ges-tures, which afford opportunity for classification and nomenclature: so that however unat-tempted hitherto in this view, the art of gesture and its notation (that is the representation of any gesture by appropriate symbols) seems capable of being reduced to a regular system.' This 'regular system' uses symbolic letters: for hand gestures, for the elevation, transverse positions, motion and force of the arm, for the behaviour of breast, chin, eyes, forehead, lips and nose, and for the movement of the feet. All these are combined with expression marks or, as Austin puts it, 'symbols for noting the force and rapidity or interruption of the voice in delivery'. And the whole notation is then combined in elaborate figures which enable the orator to give a performance which may then be repeated either by himself or by another orator in a regular, controlled and essentially similar manner (fig. 19).[15]

Despite Austin's pioneering work on gesture, and a long list of subsequent treatises on rhetorical delivery, the history of movement notation has been principally the province of dance historians for whom sources abound from the end of the seventeenth century onwards, with the development of many sophisticated and complex choreographic systems.[16] For earlier periods there is considerably less material to work on – an unfortunate circumstance which has deterred nobody. Of the principal sources for renaissance dance theory, only two have anything like a symbolic notation and both of these remained in manuscript until modern times, but, from our point of view, it is a printed book of 1588, Arbeau's *Orchésographie*, which is especially noteworthy because the principles underlying its method (that is, the definition, naming and illustrating of certain key postures which may then be grouped in various sequences and at different tempi) are very similar to what had already evolved, more than fifty years earlier, for fencing.[17] 'Do not', says Arbeau's pupil, Capriol, 'be sparing with pictures because I find them very useful in following your explanation and fixing it in my memory.'[18] Especially revealing is Arbeau's application of his pedagogical technique to the Pyrrhic, or sword dance which he illustrates with a group of six woodcuts depicting the 'Feincte', 'Estocade', 'Taille haulte', 'Revers hault', 'Taille basse' and 'Revers bas', which are worth comparing, both for style and content, with the cuts in Sainct Didier's fencing treatise which antedates the *Orchésographie* by fifteen years. 'Besides these', Arbeau continues, 'there are several other body movements but it seems to me it will suffice for you to have them in writing without necessitating pictures.' His pupil replies that fencing has already acquainted him with all these gestures and, in the accompanying illustration, the requisite movements are geared to their musical expression.

Certainly, by Arbeau's time illustrated fencing books already had a long, indeed an ancient, history. The earliest attempts at a systematic depiction of sequences of individual movements are associated with various types of personal physical combat; and from the beginning, these were more didactic than commemorative; and, as might be expected, pictorial (or pictorial and verbal), rather than diagrammatic or symbolic. It was only possible, therefore, to indicate movement by multiplying the images of figures in series of related postures in much the same way as in seventeenth-century drill manuals. And, despite the sophistication of several of the diagrammatic experiments which shall be discussed later, it is a fact that, throughout the long history of didactic combat illustration, this representational approach, despite its obvious limitations, has always predominated.

THE EVOLUTION OF PERSONAL COMBAT ILLUSTRATION

The most ancient examples of systematic combat illustrations are Egyptian reliefs of wrestling couples shown in long sequences (59 in one instance, 122 in another, and as many as 219 in a third) showing different stages of fighting or different styles. The wrestlers from the tomb in Beni Hasan about 2050 BC are deservedly famous, and the care with which holds are depicted and differentiated, and the fact that, in some cases, the wrestlers are drawn in contrasting colours to clarify the positions of the intertwined limbs, suggest that these sequences were intended to instruct the onlooker.[19]

Medieval pictures of combat styles were rarely as accomplished, although the earliest fencing book thus far known to us, the German manuscript already referred to (Royal Armouries MS.I.33), reveals that the anonymous author and his artist had worked out an intelligent if imperfect notational system, the details of which shall be discussed in a later chapter. This treatise consists of thirty-two leaves, with each page divided into two scenes

20. A dance from *Freydal*. (Vienna, Kunsthistorisches Museum), plate 127.

illustrating sword and buckler fighting as demonstrated by a priest and his pupil. Most of the illustrations are accompanied by a short observation written in Latin, and the combat technique has been broken down into a visual repertoire of standardized postures (or rather frozen movements) which are constantly reproduced, almost as if from templets, and are shuffled about into various permutations to clarify the written commentary which, in its turn, repeatedly refers the reader to the images. A further refinement is achieved by arranging the postures into short sequences, with each new group indicated and marked off by a cross. The presentation of the material has been carefully thought out and the purpose of the volume is plainly didactic. Yet, although the handling of the weapons, including the position of the fingers on the grip, is well indicated, leg and foot positions are wholly stylized: and this, together with the stereotyping of the postures, their ambiguity with regard to the direction of the blows, and the inadequacies of the verbal commentary, makes it difficult to reconstruct more than a general notion of the combat techniques depicted.[20] (See plates IV–X)

From the late fourteenth century onwards, several masters tried to perpetuate their skills by using a similar combination of words and pictures. The best known of these is Fiore de' Liberi da Premariacco's *Flos duellatorum* which survives in a number of variant manuscript versions, all of which combine good illustrations with short descriptive verse captions. Masters are distinguished from their pupils by the simple expedient of wearing a crown, although this scheme is not carried out as consistently as in MS I.33 where the monk's tonsure is never omitted. The various hand positions are generally well indicated. Leg movements and foot positions are unambiguous and, as in MS I.33, there is a serious attempt to arrange each group of postures relating to some particular type of combat in a logical sequence.[21] (See illustrations in Chapters IV and V.) There are still vast gaps between what is depicted and what would have to be done in order to move from one posture to another: but it is worth making the general point here that a single picture of fencing or of wrestling usually conveys more information than an illustration of dancing. This is easily demonstrated by the Emperor Maximilian's *Freydal*, where the isolated fighting postures are far more suggestive than any of the same manuscript's dancing scenes. In fencing, the weapon itself sets limits to the possible permutations of movement, while wrestling, to a large extent, depends upon specific holds, locks and throws (fig. 20 and plate III).[22]

There was, for a long time, no significant improvement on these early methods of conveying information.[23] The works of the followers of Fiore's contemporary, Johann Liechtenauer, in the long sequence of illustrated *Fechtbücher* by fifteenth- and sixteenth-century German masters, are beset by much the same limitations as the *Flos duellatorum*.[24] On the other hand, the increased number of illustrations in many of these German manuscripts, and the precision with which they are often drawn, help ease the problems of reconstruction. It is a pity that the relationship between author and artist is rarely as clear as one would like. Sometimes a master of the sword had sufficient skill with the pen to illustrate his own text as did, for example, Gregor Erhart in 1533 and Francisco Antonio de Ettenhard in 1675 [25] and at least one great artist was sufficiently interested in combat techniques to prepare his own *Fechtbuch*. In 1512, Albrecht Dürer prepared a series of 123 carefully annotated drawings explaining wrestling holds and throws, to which he added another fifty-eight drawings, without accompanying text, of hand-to-hand fighting with swords, staff weapons and daggers. As one would expect, his work is superior in exactitude to anything which had preceded it, but it is based upon an earlier manuscript and introduced no new method of notation.[26]

Much the same holds true for the manuals which now began to appear from the German presses, except that the availability of woodcuts facilitated the pictographic method used in MS I.33. A rudimentary use of this technique may be seen in the first known fencing book to be printed with illustrations, the *Ritterlicher kunst der Fechterey* by the master of arms, Andre Pauernfeindt, published at Vienna in 1516 and re-issued in a French version with copies of the woodcuts in 1538.[27] The most substantial section of the book concerns combat with the long sword, and is illustrated by pairs of combatants, each picture being composed of two separate blocks printed opposite each other. There are twenty-one of these blocks which are arranged and rearranged to comprise twenty-two separate encounters,[28] and the very first block is repeated later in the section on fighting with the Düsack to illustrate a combat between that single-handed weapon and an opponent wielding a long sword.[29] In both the German and the French edition the stances are sharply differentiated, and the positions of hands, feet and sword blades are clear. The blocks, however, are crude in execution and far surpassed in quality by the woodcuts in *Der Alten Fechter*, a textbook on various modes of personal combat, which was issued in four editions between 1531 and 1558 by the Frankfurt printer, Christian Egenolff.[30] The Strasbourg artist, Hans Weiditz, who prepared these illustrations, also took advantage of the pictographic method, was extremely careful to indicate the hand positions for fencing and dagger fighting, and was especially effective at depicting wrestling techniques (figs 21–2).[31] Furthermore, the provision of an alphabetically arranged *Register* enables a reader to look under such headings as 'Gurgle' or 'Armbrechen' if a quick refresher on strangling or arm snapping is desired; while, if throws are sought, three may be found listed under 'Werffen'. This is a decided convenience but, on the debit side, it is still not easy to relate pictures to text and, in this

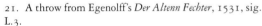

21. A throw from Egenolff's *Der Altenn Fechter*, 1531, sig. L.3.

22. Egenolff's one-handed strangle-hold. 1531, sig. L.4v.

respect, there is an improvement in the eighty-nine woodcuts by Lucas Cranach the Younger for Fabian von Auerswald's *Ringer Kunst* (1539) which are meticulously executed and are of great clarity.[32] On the other hand, these, too, with their isolated and unrelated poses and short descriptive captions, remain firmly within the tradition established by the fifteenth-century German masters, as can be seen by comparing some of them with similar postures in Talhoffer. (See illustrations in Chapter VI.)

In the history of printed fencing illustration there is one notable lacuna which, being a lacuna, is of an importance impossible to estimate. In 1532 Bartolomé Pérez printed a *Tratado de la esgrima con figuras* by an illustrious contemporary Seville master, Francisco Román.[33] It is frequently mentioned by later writers and is actually quoted by Pacheco de Narváez, but no copy of this book has yet been discovered so that, as far as surviving evidence is concerned, the first significant development in conveying technical information about fencing came in 1536 with the publication of the *Opera nova* by the Bolognese master, Achille Marozzo. As is claimed on the title page, this book discusses single combat, both offensive and defensive, with every kind of weapon, 'with figures which show, with the arms in hand, all the effects and guards which can be made'. These 'figures' are eighty-two simple but clear woodcuts of the postures adopted by combatants fighting with swords, staff weapons, or daggers, all of which are closely and intelligently allied to verbal descriptions far longer and much more systematic than in any preceding manual. Most of these illustrations are signed with the monogram .b. and, in one case, .b.R. and have been attributed conjecturally either to Francesco Barattini or Giovanni Britto, though neither attribution has won acceptance.[34] The artist, whoever he may have been, renders the text as faithfully as his modest talent allows. Body postures and foot positions are unambiguous and, while the artist is not always successful in drawing fingers, his scrupulous intentions are exemplified in Marozzo's fifth book dealing with twenty-two ways in which an unarmed man can overcome an opponent who is wielding a dagger. The holds are fully described by Marozzo who explains, in each case, whether the dagger is being held *sopra mano* or *sotto mano*, that is with the blade stabbing downwards from above, or thrust from below, and these distinctions are, without fail, accurately recorded in the woodcuts. (See illustrations in Chapters V and VI.)

Marozzo's *Opera nova* had an instant and sustained success. It was reissued in 1550, revised and printed with new and inferior plates by Giulio Fontana in 1568, and again issued in Fontana's version in 1615. Its fencing method and didactic technique were widely influential throughout Europe, and some of its illustrations were still being plagiarized in the eighteenth century.[35] From a purely notational point of view Marozzo is important not merely for defining, naming and depicting individual strokes and postures (a process familiar to all fencing masters) but rather for his method of using that nomenclature as a kind of shorthand to summarize a whole complex of linked movements, a technique akin both to the dance notation used many years later by Arbeau and to the illustrative conventions followed in most modern fencing manuals.

Nevertheless, despite Marozzo's historical importance, a far greater range of possibilities was opened up in 1553 when the first edition of Camillo Agrippa's *Trattato di scientia d'arme* was printed by Antonio Blado at Rome. Although enjoying something of a reputation as a brawler, ruffian and friend of Michelangelo, Agrippa was not a master of arms but was, in fact, a noted mathematician, architect and engineer who applied his technical knowledge not only to the problems posed by armed combat but also to the ways in which these might be elucidated. Thus, while his illustrations still show a series of set postures, they are now placed within a self-consciously theoretical framework, alluded to in the official licence which says that the *Trattato* discusses the 'science and art of arms', with 'mathematical demonstrations and many other proofs, and engravings'. The author, as we have seen, even went so far as to have himself depicted on the engraved frontispiece, demonstrating some mathematical nicety of fencing with a pair of compasses. Agrippa was interested in the engineering principles underlying the movements of the human body when engaged in fencing, and he examines these both to rationalize such movements and to clarify the style of combat he envisages. How far any of Agrippa's mathematical demonstrations were really significant in the development of the art of fencing remains matter for dispute because, while it has been usual to regard them as epoch-making – he was 'the most expert of all those of this profession' wrote André Desbordes in 1610; 'he was the first who published on lines, angles, diameters etc.' wrote Morsicato Pallavicini in 1670 – some authorities have dismissed them as largely irrelevant.[36] He wrote, sneered the French master François Dancie, 'to show that he was both geometrician and philosopher, rather than a great swordsman'.[37] None the less, his work does mark the beginning of two distinct approaches to the problem of notation. One was to encourage the application of geometrical figures and symbols, an approach which shall be discussed later in this chapter. The other was to suggest various experiments in, and improvements to, the purely representational recording of movement.

One simple but very effective device introduced by Agrippa was to label each human figure in his illustrations with a letter, or letters, of the alphabet which could then be referred to in the text. This serves, of course, to identify any particular fencer under discussion but, much more significantly, each letter indicates a different guard, posture, movement or blow, and the idea, however obvious it may now seem, was recognized by Agrippa himself as a novelty.[38] He identifies four principal guards which, he says, will be labelled 'A', 'B', 'C', and 'D' respectively. Then, deriving from these four guards are other related postures and attacks which are similarly allotted letters, running through the alphabet as far as 'T'. Using these letters Agrippa is thus freed not only from the necessity of repeat-

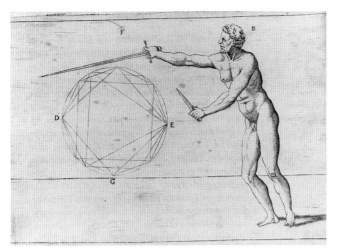

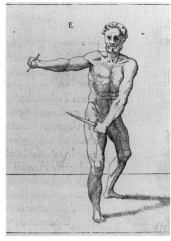

23. Agrippa's 'Seconda per B'. 1553, fol. 11.

24. Agrippa's 'Seconda per E'. 1553, fol. 17.

ing lengthy verbal descriptions of his principal moves every time they occur, but also from the bewilderingly profuse nomenclature which had bedevilled Marozzo's attempts at clarity. Each chapter of Agrippa's book has its own illustration which is precisely related to the discussion in the text. Pictures and words are completely integrated while, further to facilitate reference, Agrippa supplies a 'Tavola' in which he lists the contents of his treatise not simply seriatim, but according to the occurrence of the different fencing procedures. Thus, if we look up his 'Prima guardia segnata per A', we first find it fully described and illustrated in a three-quarter frontal view (Part I, iv) and then later discussed and illustrated with a three-quarter back view (I, xx). Alternatively, we can locate the normal 'Second Guard indicated by B' (I, v) in its basic form, but can also find the same guard with the arm held wide, 'indicated by E' (I, ix), and illustrated by a perspective view. The close collaboration of author and illustrator is evident here because Agrippa points out to his readers that they will not actually see the sword held in the fencer's right hand 'because it is in perspective', and this is, in fact, the case (figs 23–4).

Another novelty introduced by Agrippa was the technique of using composite, or multiple, postures in one picture to suggest the unfolding of a single movement. He uses this method in his depiction of the natural progression from first to fourth guard (fig. 25). And the same technique (combining postures already defined, and individually designated by a letter, in Part I) is used to produce action sequences in Part II (fig. 26).

Agrippa brought an original and inventive mind to the problems of movement notation, and he was fortunate in his illustrator (as yet unidentified) who shows body postures, foot positions and such details as finger holds with admirable exactitude.[39] He was, however, less fortunate in his printer, Antonio Blado, whose execution of Agrippa's ideas was seriously flawed. The principal weakness was in the location of the plates, a difficulty which has, to the present day, plagued authors and editors of illustrated books. In the 'Prima Parte' of the *Trattato*, for example, the letterpress of the first chapter (dealing with the four principal guards) ends with a typographical diminuendo at the foot of fol. 2v. The relevant plate then appears at the top of the next folio immediately above the second chapter, 'Concerning a geometrical figure', to which it has every appearance of belonging. And much the same

25. Agrippa's sequence of four guards. 1553, fol. 3.

26. A combat sequence from Agrippa. 1553, fol. 47.

thing happens throughout the rest of this part of the book, that is for another twenty-eight chapters and their accompanying illustrations. In the 'Seconda Parte' of the *Trattato*, however, the situation is reversed. Now each illustration comes before its related chapter, often at the foot of a preceding page, and generally looking as though it refers back, not forward. If one takes the trouble to read the text, there is no ambiguity about any of this. The figures are all clearly labelled alphabetically and these letters are referred to in the discussion. Problems arise only when a reader chooses to skim through the work, ignoring Agrippa's careful system of reference, and relying solely on the apparent logic of the page layout. This is why Jacopo Gelli provided wrong captions when he reproduced plates from Agrippa.[40]

When, in 1568, the Venetian publisher Antonio Pinargenti decided that the time was ripe for a second edition of the *Trattato*, the brothers Giulio and Giovanni Battista Fontana, who were supplying fresh engravings for this work as also for Marozzo, hit upon the idea of grouping several of the illustrations together in fewer plates, and clarifying the author's intentions by labelling each posture with its appropriate chapter reference.[41] The intention was good, though, unfortunately, Giulio Fontana failed to recognize the misleading layout of the 1553 edition and so got many of his captions wrong. On the evidence of his plates, it is unlikely that he had read Agrippa's text. Certainly he did not understand it. Indeed he did not even understand fencing, as is apparent from the way in which he fudges the delineation of hand positions and of hilts even though such details are of crucial importance and are always indicated precisely throughout the first edition. Furthermore, when Fontana does try to indicate the position of fingers, he gets it wrong even to the extent at one point (the illustration for Chapter 3), of showing the sword held in the left hand. The obfuscation was compounded by the printer who introduced some bad misnumbering of chapters in the second part of the *Trattato*. Agrippa himself had clearly been worried that readers might be confused by his new illustrative techniques, and had taken particular care to warn them against misinterpreting the plates showing multiple figures.[42] It was all to no avail, and even the nineteenth-century authority, Jacopo Gelli – whose views on Italian fencing history are still, mistakenly, cited as authoritative – thought that the second part of the *Trattato* dealt with 'various combats of two against two, and three against two'.[43] If the proof of a good system of explication is the ease with which it is understood by its readers, then, it has to be said, Agrippa's method was not an unqualified success.

The idea of multiple postures, despite some obvious advantages, did not impress many other authors. One treatise which has the appearance of using the technique was the comprehensive *Gründtliche Beschreibung* by the Strasbourg master Joachim Meyer. Published in 1570, this ambitious volume was copiously illustrated by Tobias Stimmer with woodcuts showing large clusters of frenetically active warriors wielding every kind of weapon – polaxes, rapiers, two-handed swords, düsacks, fists, elbows and feet – within elaborately decorated palaces beyond whose pillars, arches and patterned floors various fantastic townscapes appear in remarkable perspectives. The individual postures of the fighters are admirably rendered and the woodcuts are of a considerable, indeed luxuriant, virtuosity: but they dazzle the eye and, in some ways, obscure the sense of the treatise. The fighting figures, upon close analysis, can be seen sometimes to represent different phases of a movement. But they are extremely difficult to read as a sequence. The eye obstinately sees them as unrelated groups so that, in the end, they fail to convey more information about the activities depicted than any other conventional series of isolated postures. Indeed, because of their multilinear fussiness and lack of order, they convey rather less, and it is not

27. Verolini *Künstliche Fechter*, 1679. Meyer's düsack practice simplified. Plate opp. p. 8.

surprising that two seventeenth-century German plagiarists of Meyer, Jacob Sutor and Theodor Verolini, simplified the reader's task by picking out only the principal pair of figures in each illustration and omitting all the supplementary postures and architectural backgrounds (fig. 27).[44]

Thereafter, apart from Morsicato Pallavicini, who used a ghostly dotted figure in just one plate to illustrate the lunge, none of the great seventeenth-century Italian and German masters adopted the technique of multiple postures (fig. 28). In fact, this kind of imagery was seriously exploited by only two authors, Federico Ghisliero in 1587, and Girard Thibault in 1628, both of whom will be discussed later in connection with the application of geometry to fencing notation. Most authors, and the artists who worked for them, concentrated on a more simple figurative technique, and their books are filled with pairs of fencers or wrestlers still battling it out as in days of yore, prodding holes in each other, breaking arms and backs, throttling, gouging, stabbing and cutting. Yet even within this circumscribed tradition, some experimentation and variation remained possible.

29. (*facing page*) Fabris's 'Prima guardia' shown simultaneously from both sides. 1606, p. 28.

28. A ghostly lunge in Pallavicini, 1670, p. 33.

For the masters who came after Agrippa, visual aids were almost obligatory. Of some fifteen major combat texts issued in Italy between 1570 and 1640, all but three were illustrated, and of nine German works between 1570 and 1630, all but one.[45] Even in bibliographically backward England, when the fencing master Vincentio Saviolo introduced his treatise on the use of the rapier and dagger in 1595, he claimed to have 'endevoured to expresse in this discourse, and to make plain by pictures all the skill and knowledge which I have in this art'. It is to be hoped that this last statement was not literally true, because the six woodcuts which disfigure his text are execrable and notationally useless.[46] On the continent, by contrast, many authors secured the services of excellent graphic artists whose work in this genre — whatever their fame in other spheres — has been curiously neglected by art historians.

In 1606, for example, Nicoletto Giganti's important treatise on swordsmanship boasted forty-two copperplates by the young Bolognese pupil of Tintoretto, Odoardo Fialetti who evidently threw himself into the task with fervour. The fencers' lean, powerful musculature ripples, and their blood spurts out liberally in all directions in plates which are executed not only with immense panache, but also with due attention to the sense of the text.[47] Plumper but no less gory are the 190 spirited pairs of fencers illustrating Salvator Fabris's *Scienza e pratica d'arme* which was first published in 1606 and went on to be re-edited or copied until well into the eighteenth century. These engravings were principally the work of Jan van Halbeeck and Francesco Valesio, and all students of fencing history are familiar with the contorted postures of the combatants who fight from the exaggerated crouch recommended by Fabris and which anticipates the boxing stance adopted by the early twentieth-century heavyweight champion, Jim Jeffries. What commentators have not noticed is the way in which Fabris and his artists develop a technique first introduced on a modest scale by Camillo Agrippa who had illustrated certain postures viewed from different angles. Agrippa never combined such views within a single plate, but, in Fabris, the great majority of his pairs of combatants are depicted as viewed from the right- and left-

30. Ridolfo Capoferro: portrait of the master. 1610, frontispiece.

hand sides, confronting each other in an identical pose.[48] The difficulty with these pictures is that Fabris's fencing system advocates the use of the *contra postura* – that is the adoption by one swordsman of the posture taken up by his adversary – so that it is easy to interpret what is often simply an illustrative convention as a fencing technique. Yet Fabris himself was at pains to advise his readers not to be astonished if they see two figures in one place, both demonstrating the same position, because this is done in order to represent both sides of the body simultaneously (fig. 29).[49]

Until Crispin van de Pass and his team of engravers, working on Thibault's *Académie de l'espée*, smashed all records for size, complexity, and technical dexterity, the most imposing fencing illustrations were those prepared for Ridolfo Capoferro's *Gran simulacro* which first appeared in 1610 (fig. 30).[50] In terms of combat technique, this work is one of the most influential in the history of swordsmanship, and Capoferro's method has been lauded by authorities as bitterly incompatible as Jacopo Gelli and Egerton Castle. The book's forty-three copperplates were executed by Raffaello Schiaminossi and, while as violent and vigorous as those in Giganti and Fabris, they have a uniquely dark and menacing quality, enhanced by the settings within which the fencers go about their murderous business.[51]

Although most earlier fencing books had ignored the space surrounding their human figures, other conventions are suggested by the architectural and landscape backgrounds in Franz Brun's single-sheet combat etchings of the mid-sixteenth century, and by the highly wrought landscapes shown behind warriors fighting with the two-hand sword in an early sixteenth-century German manuscript of which only photographs have so far been located (figs 31–2).[52] Landscapes and townscapes were also sketched in by the artists who provided manuscript illustrations for Ghisliero. (See figs 53–4.) However, in printed fencing books, only Tobias Stimmer had bothered to put his fencers into three-dimensional space when he littered Meyer's treatise with architectural fantasies. Then along came Schiaminossi.

The surfaces upon which the figures in the *Gran simulacro* move, are unremarkable. They are ruled with a few horizontal parallel lines but are otherwise plain, and, in every case,

31. Two-hand sword combat with landscape. Anonymous sixteenth-century German manuscript. Scott Library.

32. Getting to grips and using the pommel. Anonymous sixteenth-century German manuscript. Scott Library.

33. Capoferro, 1610, plate 2. First and Fourth Guard as depicted in the first edition before Adam and Eve complicated the issue. Cf. fig. 35.

there is a decisively drawn horizon, roughly level with the fencers' ankles or calves. It is above that horizon line that things happen. Schiaminossi depicts landscapes with woods, hills, distant towns and fortresses – all deftly etched, but conceived like theatre backdrops rather than real scenes. These engravings are highly successful both as a rendering of Capoferro's text and as dramatic works in their own right. Yet when, in 1629, the Sienese printer, Ercole Gori, decided to reissue the *Gran simulacro*, many of the original plates were tampered with.[53] In twenty-seven illustrations, the ruled horizonal lines are changed into the perspective squares once favoured by Marozzo: but incomparably more bizarre are the transformations wrought on eight of the plates where the lines and contours of the backgrounds have been so drastically reworked that they are totally absorbed into new designs. The landscapes have disappeared, and the fencers now literally perform on a stage in front of backdrops filled with preposterous allegorical scenes. In one, we see a town, probably Troy, under siege and largely ablaze. Troops batter at the walls with a ram or scale assault ladders while, on the ramparts, defenders prepare to hurl rocks down at the attackers. In the middle distance, a woman flees from a rapist soldier; while in the foreground Venus is seen stepping out of the sea, and Cupid lies on the shore fast asleep, with his quiver beside him. The next plate is more surreal. It displays a vision of the prelapsarian Garden of Eden filled with all sorts of birds and beasts living, it appears, in perfect harmony. Yet all is not well. In the centre of the backdrop stands a great apple tree complete with a serpent, half snake and half boy. This monstrosity has just handed Eve an apple, while Adam sits on a hillock pondering the event. Adam and Eve are on the backdrop: yet they encroach upon reality by standing, like the fencers, on the stage itself; and the tail feathers of a painted peacock similarly intrude into the fencing scene (figs 33, 35). There is no other instance of this Escher-like wandering from one dimension to another. Cain slays Abel, Noahs' ark floats above storm-tossed oceans, Constantinople is besieged, galleys and sailing ships ply between towns, the Tower of Babel is built, and a mariner (possibly Jonah) is flung from a boat sailing on another ocean: but all remain firmly upon the backdrop. What was intended by making the sense of theatre so explicit in these plates, I cannot say. Artistically, the

56

34. Capoferro, 1629, plate 1. Putting one's hand to the sword.

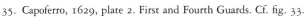

35. Capoferro, 1629, plate 2. First and Fourth Guards. Cf. fig. 33.

36. Liancour's fencers fight unconcernedly while a naval battle rages. 1686, plate 24.

alterations to Schiaminossi's work are intriguing: but the scenographical conceit does nothing to enhance the clarity of Capoferro's exposition and – apart from Thibault's *Académie de l'espée* (1630) which is entirely *sui generis* – the only major fencing books to adopt similar settings were those by the late seventeenth-century masters La Touche and Liancour (fig. 36).

The bibliographical metamorphosis of Ridolfo Capoferro was even now not complete. In 1632, convinced that demand for the *Gran simulacro* remained greater than supply, the Sienese engraver, Bernardino Capitelli hit upon the idea of preparing a smaller and more handy version. Accordingly, he set about re-engraving the entire series of Schiaminossi illustrations, reducing the originals to roughly half size (from 23 cm by 14 cm down to 10.1 cm by 5.6 cm). All forty-three postures of the 1610 edition are reproduced but, as well as being smaller, they are sketchier and without backgrounds (figs 37–8).[54] Such a procedure is, I believe, very unusual for any printed book in the Renaissance and no other major fencing text was accorded similar treatment until the illustrations in Angelo's *École des armes* (1763) were engraved in a reduced format for inclusion in Diderot and d'Alembert's *Encyclopédie*. Capitelli omits all Capoferro's preliminary discussion of the art of fence and his own letterpress is curious, not only because it is engraved to resemble handwriting, but also because it reproduces only so much of the original text relating to each illustration as fits comfortably onto the page.

There is no need to say much more here about the purely figurative tradition because, while many seventeenth-century combat manuals are profusely illustrated with realistic figures, few break new ground in terms of notational technique. One work, the *Fechtkunst* (1620) of Hans Wilhelm Schöffer, merits recognition solely for its bulk – 672 badly executed plates of different fencing postures, all copiously annotated, though otherwise unremarkable.[55] But a later German master, Johann Georg Pascha, did find a way to make traditional figures more informative about movement. Between 1661 and 1683, Pascha produced a series of elaborate volumes on fencing, wrestling, vaulting and flag-waving, each adorned with numerous copperplates.[56] With regard to sword combat, Pascha almost

37. Capitelli's pocket edition of Capoferro. Capitelli, 1632, plate 1. Cf. fig. 34.

38. Capitelli, 1632, plate 2. Cf. fig. 35.

pag: 8   no.   12

13

14

15

39. One of Johann Georg Pascha's fencing strips. 1664, p. 8.

40. Wallhausen offers a cinematographic view of pike and sword. 1617, figs. 102–22.

reverses Capitelli's treatment of Capoferro. In 1661 his *Kurze Anleitung des Fechtens* has a series of 117 postures arranged horizontally either two or three to each page. But, when he prepared another edition in 1664, his figures are about four times larger, much more numerous, and (as in Dürer's *Fechtbuch*) the combatants are arranged vertically down the page, generally in series of four. They are numbered consecutively throughout (169 postures for fencing, 130 for wrestling) and each move is briefly discussed in the text. The postures of the wrestlers are discrete, as in the manuscript tradition of Liechtenauer and Talhoffer; but, for his fencing book, Pascha has adapted the systematic sequentiality of the drill manuals in such a way that his vertical strips can be read almost as though they were freeze frames in cinematography (fig. 39). The purely representational tradition could hardly advance further although Wallhausen, in his manual on the use of the pike, had also come very close to achieving a cinematographic effect horizontally (fig. 40).[57]

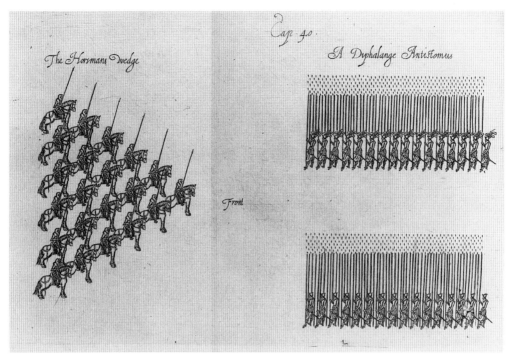

41. Bingham brings an ancient diagram up to date. 1616, between pp. 144 and 145.

DIAGRAMS, MATHEMATICS AND GEOMETRY

When Leonardo da Vinci recommended that artists should make studies of natural actions in the streets, piazze and fields, he suggested that they should only briefly indicate the forms – using an O for the head, and a bent line for arms, legs, body, and so forth.[58] Leonardo was thinking here only of capturing fugitive moments 'of natural action', but, clearly, in order to progress beyond the recording of movement by isolated and naturalistic illustrations, some more systematic diagrammatic shorthand was necessary.

Diagrams were commonly associated with the various branches of mathematics, and had been since classical antiquity. But, throughout the Middle Ages, the most familiar symbolic notations were those used for music and (even more widespread, though perhaps less immediately obvious to the modern reader) for heraldry which had developed as a kind of diagrammatic genealogy. However, the earliest examples of diagrams representing human activity were related to the art of war, notably in Asclepiodotus's *Outline of Tactics* (first century BC) and Aelian's *Tactics* (late first century AD). These diagrams survive only in excessively rare manuscripts, and Asclepiodotus remained unedited until the mid-nineteenth century. Aelian's work, on the other hand, gained currency with the invention of printing which ensured its transmission and adaptation throughout renaissance Europe, and, indeed, Arbeau refers to it when discussing military music and the use of drum beats for regulating marching soldiers.[59] The accompanying illustration shows the simultaneous combination of diagrammatic and representational ways of rendering information which was a common feature of military illustration (fig. 41).

The *Tactica* remained familiar to military scholars into the seventeenth century and beyond, but the possibility of elucidating military formations by means of diagrams was even more widely advertised by two independent military treatises, both first published in 1521 and both frequently reissued, translated and adapted thereafter: Giovanni Battista della Valle's *Vallo* which was printed in Naples in June, and Machiavelli's *Arte della guerra* which was issued in Florence just two months later.[60] In neither case is the handling of diagrammatic form satisfactory. Della Valle is the more successful in relating diagrams to text, but Machiavelli compensates for this by offering readers a key to his symbols (using Greek letters), and a general explanation of the technique:

> To the intent that such as read this book may without difficulty understand the order of the battles, or bands of men, and of the armies, and lodgings in the camp, according as they in the description of them are appointed, I think it necessary to show you the figure of every one of them: wherefore it is requisite first, to declare unto you, by what points and letters, the footmen, the horsemen, and every other particular member are set forth.[61]

Initially, diagrams of this sort indicated static, idealized massed groups and formations rather than movements; or, more precisely, they might be described as pre-movement in that they showed formations of troops about to march or about to go into battle. The complete history of military diagrams has yet to be written. Aelian himself asserted that they were intended to 'lend the mind the assistance of the eye'. But, as far as the earliest experiments are concerned, it is impossible to gainsay Sir John Hale's keen observation that they were designed to 'divert and amuse the eye rather than guide the mind'.[62] Nevertheless, later military writers used diagrams with greater discrimination and precision, not only to elucidate their theories but also to analyse the different stages of particular historic battles.

The earliest known published example of the latter genre is a series of three woodcuts in William Patten's *The Expedition into Scotland* printed by Richard Grafton in 1548. Patten has provided them to make all things 'as easy to the sense of the reader' as he possibly could. 'And forasmuch as the assault, especially of our horsemen at the first; their retire again; and our last onset, pursuit, and slaughter of the enemy cannot all be showed well in one plot; I have devised and drawn, according to my cunning, three several views of them, placed in their order, as follow in the battle.' He has also included such towns and places as he could remember; and, while admitting that his efforts constitute 'no fine portraiture indeed, nor yet any exquisite observance of geometrical dimension', he does believe that they are 'yet neither so gross nor far from the truth, I trust, but they may serve for some ease of understanding'. Further to reduce congestion on his drawings and to aid comprehension, Patten has supplied a key which is considerably more elaborate than the illustrations themselves. He uses up the entire alphabet to indicate places and different groups of troop formations, both English and Scottish; and then lists eight more signs each denoting either a footman, horseman, 'Hackbutter a foot', 'Hackbutter on horse', archer, 'a Footmen slain', 'a Horsemen slain', and 'the fallow field whereon their army stood'.[63] Patten's illustrations, despite their crudity, were immensely ambitious and prophetic; and his approach was developed (independently, no doubt) by many later military historians. Reconstructions of battles became ever larger, more panoramic, and elaborate. The plates are sometimes of enormous dimensions; yet, in a curiously retrogressive fashion, many artists preferred to use straightforward pictorial representations of infantry, cavalry, artillery and fortifications rather than signs and letters.[64]

Despite the importance and wide currency of military diagrams, the most serious renais-

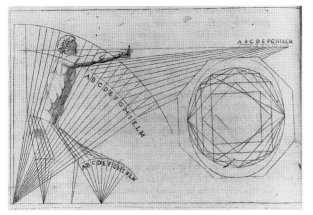 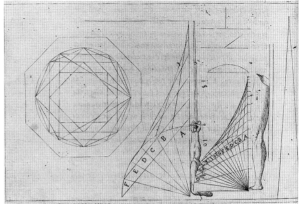

42. The geometry of arm movement in Agrippa. 1553, fol. 4v. 43. The geometry of leg movement in Agrippa. 1553, fol. 5v.

sance experimentation in the diagrammatic notation of movement took place in relation to the art of fencing: although it is a strange fact that Francesco Altoni, one of the earliest writers to apply geometry to swordsmanship, was entirely hostile to the use of illustrations. His *Trattato dell'armi intitolato monomachia* has never been printed – retribution perhaps for his dismissive view of the press – and his interest in the relationship of body movement to the proportions of the circle bore no fruit.[65] Marozzo, on the other hand, who did believe in the value of pictorial aids and who anticipated many developments in the enunciation of technical matters, had not been concerned with the mathematics of fencing; and, in his *Opera nova*, the only plate with a geometrical ground plan relates to the chapter on passing, and illustrates a simple teaching device in which concentric circles are divided by a segmental pattern showing where the student is to place his feet. The little diagram was pregnant with possibilities but, as yet, they remained unrealized. (See Chapter I, fig. 8.)

Unlike Marozzo, Camillo Agrippa regarded geometry as fundamentally important for the understanding, and thus rationalizing, of fencing postures and action, and he devoted two chapters to explaining the angles and length of thrust to be achieved by holding the arm in different positions and by bending the leg to a greater or lesser extent. These observations are illustrated by geometrical figures and by polyhedrons as irrelevant as they are complex: but Agrippa never went on to apply his mathematical skills to devising a movement notation (figs 42–3). The rest of his plates are neither diagrammatic nor geometrical; and this gulf, between the theory of fencing and the practice of fencing illustration, is evident in later treatises. Fabris, for example, despite informing his readers that geometry was the principal foundation of swordsmanship, deliberately avoided the use of 'geometrical words', in order to keep his explanations more natural and easily understood; and the illustrations in his book are wholly naturalistic.[66] Similarly, the editor of Giganti's *Scola* felt that, because the illustrious master had not declared fencing to be a science, it was necessary to explain that it *was* – 'This science of the sword, or of arms, is a speculative science, essentially mathematical, of geometry and arithmetic' – and depended upon the movements of the body and the sword 'which consist entirely in circles, angles, lines, surfaces, measure, and numbers'. All these matters could be read 'in Camillo Agrippa, and in many other professors of this science': but not, as a matter of fact, in Giganti himself whose text, like Fabris's, is as devoid of geometrical terms as of mathematical symbolism.[67]

The Modenese master Giacomo di Grassi was similarly not greatly given to geometrical

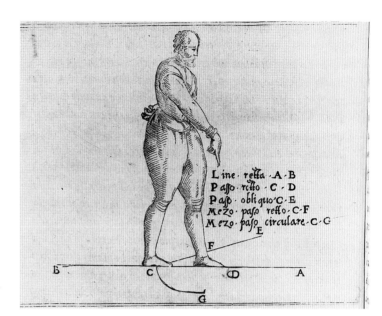

Line. retta. A·B
Passo. retto. C·D
Paso. obliquo. C·E
Mezo. paso. retto. C·F
Mezo. paso. circulare. C·G

44. Di Grassi's geometry of the foot. 1570, p. 14.

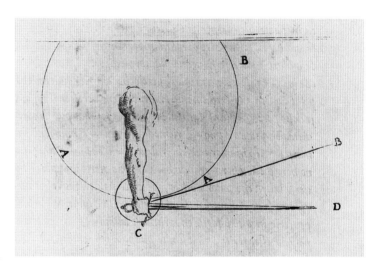

45. Di Grassi's geometry of the hand. 1570, p. 11.

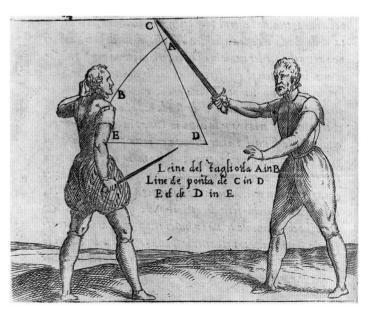

Line del taglio da A in B
Line de ponta de C in D
E ef de D in E

46. Di Grassi's geometry of the sword. 1570, p. 24.

47. Sainct Didier. The combat begins. 1573, fol. 21v.

language, although he used circles and angles to good effect in clarifying the fundamental movements of sword, arm, and foot (figs 44–6).[68] But it was the French master, Henri de Sainct Didier who, in 1573, took the illustration of fencing technique further along the road merely suggested by Agrippa and later ignored by the great early seventeenth-century Italian authorities. In terms of his fencing system, it has been customary among historians to dismiss Sainct Didier as decidedly archaic or, at best, as a mere adaptor of di Grassi. This view, though cogently disputed by Dubois[69] as long ago as 1918, has persisted but – whatever the truth of that argument – Sainct Didier certainly differed from his predecessors by instituting geometrical ground plans and numbered footprints to indicate the correct sequence of movements. It has sometimes been maintained that Meyer's *Gründtliche Beschreibung* had already used such ground plans and footprints: but, while it is true that the floors in Tobias Stimmer's woodcuts for Meyer are covered with elaborate patterns, and that there is an occasional footprint marked here and there, they are of no notational significance.

Sainct Didier's woodcuts, on the other hand, though inferior in quality, are executed according to a coherent plan designed to elucidate, and not merely to illustrate, the text. Perhaps influenced by the confusion which had resulted from the arrangement of Agrippa's plates, Sainct Didier literally spells out the relationship between his words and pictures. He illustrates every guard and movement discussed in the text in terms of the same two adversaries, always appropriately labelled ('Le Lieutenant' on the left and 'Le Prévost' on the right), who are shown confronting each other in every plate. Then he ensures that these two characters are numbered consecutively throughout, either as odd or even; so that 'Le Lieutenant' is 1, 3, 5 and so on up to his final appearance as 127; while 'Le Prévost' is numbered from 2 to 128. These numbers are invariably cited in descriptions of the postures, and even their precise position is given lest any reader should go astray: 'behind the hat', 'behind the neck', 'behind the cap', 'at the top of the head', 'behind the top of the head', 'beside the feather of his cap'.

Finally, Sainct Didier sometimes uses simple geometrical ground plans and numbered footprints arranged in squares or triangles, as is set out in his very first posture (fig. 47). The method, though rudimentary, is intelligently conceived: but it is not carried through consistently. Only twenty-six of the postures are explicated in this way and in several of

48. Sainct Didier. How to complete the quadrangle. 1573, fol. 59v.

these (although the triangles and footprints are shown in the woodcut and are specifically referred to in the text) the numbers are actually missing.[70] Sometimes, though, the whole system is fully operational as we can see in the plate illustrating this description (fig. 48).

> In order to accomplish this quadrangle well it is necessary that the said Lieutenant (having his right foot on the footprint numbered 4, and his left foot on the footprint numbered 3) *desrobera* his sword under the guard of the Provost's sword and gives him a *maindroit* or thrust; the Lieutenant holding his sword hand with the nails facing down, and his left hand close to his face, as is shown to us here below in his portraiture, numbered 75.

Sainct Didier is the forerunner of several centuries of increasingly labyrinthine patterns of interwoven footprints charting the ground plan of complex series of movements, culminating in such foot-twisting complexities as the 'Tango argentino' from Francesco Giovannini's *Il ballo d'oggi* of 1914 (fig. 49). But, as far as fencing is concerned, this approach reached its zenith in the artificial style which developed in Spain from the late sixteenth century, when the kinship between fencing and dancing was readily apparent to any critical observer. As George Silver wrote in 1599: 'This is the maner of Spanish fight, they stand as brave as they can with their bodies straight vpright, narrow spaced, with their feet continually moving, as if they were in a dance.'[71]

The Spanish masters, unlike those who had preceded them in the search for a successful notation of their art, were anxious to work out a symbolic notation rather than one which relied principally on a realistic representation of fencers. And the key to this quest was their obsession with the interrelationship between mathematics and sword play. This belief,

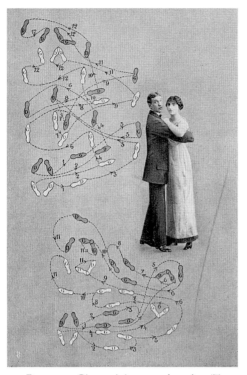

49. Francesco Giovannini untangles the 'Tango Argentino'. 1914, p. 103.

50. Carranza, master of the Spanish masters. 1582, frontispiece.

merely adumbrated by Agrippa, was stated much more elaborately, if less plausibly, by Carranza whose treatise on *La philosophía de las armas* (Lisbon, 1582) influenced the theory of Iberian fencing well into the eighteenth century (fig. 50).[72] Carranza assumed that, in order to achieve mastery of the sword, it was necessary to understand primary causes. Unfortunately, since he considered almost every kind of knowledge (mathematics, perspective, anatomy, medicine, astronomy and music) relevant to fencing, it was inevitable that his book should grow into a vast, rambling and, ultimately, rather crazy edifice.

For Carranza, the first foundation of the art of fencing is the human body itself.[73] He believes that nothing can be achieved without understanding its proportions and their relationship to those of an opposing body; and he likens the movement of the feet, and the subsequent effect on the fencer's posture, to the opening of a pair of compasses. His enthusiasm for geometry knows no bounds. Fencing, he argues, concerns the angles and lines which relate 'one foot and the other of the same man', and between the feet of two opposing fencers. It also concerns the distance between the swords, between the nearest and furthest points of the two swordmen's bodies, and the space between arm and body. A fencer must seek 'the perfection of the angles and knowledge of the quantities of the movements', and the art of fencing is thus subordinate to geometry which is concerned with the 'particularities of point, line, surface, body, angle, triangle, circle, centre, and proportions'.[74]

Carranza also applies the mathematics of perspective to a swordsman's vision, together with a Euclidean exegesis on sight lines ('los ángulos visuales' and 'los rayos visuales'). He explains the best fencing posture with a 'Demonstración Mathematica' also based upon Euclid, and provides a geometrical ground plan, demonstrating foot positions for dagger

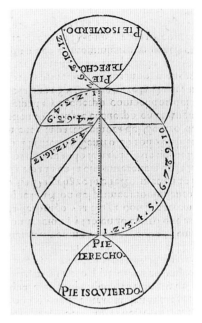

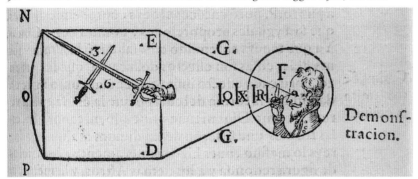

fighting. This diagram is wholly original and represents the first tentative step towards a truly symbolic notation of fencing movement. Yet there are no other devices of this kind in the book, and Carranza's *La philosophía* is unusual amongst illustrated fencing books in having no combat pictures whatsoever (figs 51–2).

Even more peculiar, at least from a bibliographical point of view, is the work of an Italian writer who fell under the influence of Carranza but was far too intelligent to copy him uncritically. In 1587, Erasmo Viotto of Parma printed a treatise on combat techniques by a young soldier, Federico Ghisliero. Entitled *Regole di molti cavagliereschi essercitii*, it is one of the strangest fencing books ever printed.[75] In the course of his technical discussion of combat, Ghisliero refers specifically and minutely to thirty illustrations and eleven textual diagrams. Yet the book was issued with the thirty relevant pages left blank (apart from the running heads), and with little gaps in the letter-press for the diagrams. Obviously it had been intended to complete the impression with engravings, and it is difficult to account for their omission unless the author was having the work printed at his own expense and ran out of money. Whatever the reason, at some time (probably not long after the printing), there was an attempt to supply the missing illustrations with pen and wash drawings. Two of the surviving copies of Ghisliero's book have complete sets which, though by different hands, are so close to each other and to the written text that they are clearly based upon a master copy supervised by the author himself. The *Regole* is particularly interesting for the historian of fencing illustration because, while Ghisliero agreed with Carranza on the geometrical basis of sword play, he did not choose to follow the Spanish master's brief hint at a symbolic notation. Instead, he had his fencers depicted naturalistically but situated within a consistent geometrical ground plan; used lines to indicate both sword movement and angles of vision; and combined all this with a systematic adaptation of the multiple postures first introduced by Camillo Agrippa.

The first part of the *Regole*, which is entitled 'Della theorica', has a concise introduction

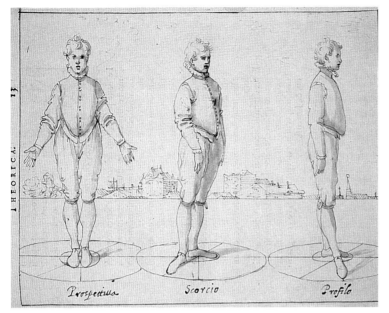 

dealing with the elements, humours and temperaments before getting down to serious business with the fundamental principles of the art of fencing: and it is significant that Ghisliero calls these principles, 'Theoremi'. Like Carranza, he accepts the commonplace notion that the circle is the perfect figure and, citing the third book of Vitruvius, declares that a man with his arms outstretched, and with his navel as the centre, may be inscribed within a circle. He then discusses the three proportions of man *prospettiva*, *scurzo*, and *profilo* (fig. 53) and the three types of motion involving the whole body, arms, or legs. There are eight modes of body movement; three sorts of leg movement; and, while the space between the legs can in theory be divided infinitely, only four divisions are required in practice (half pace, pace, pace and a half, and two paces). Even when stationary, the legs may be disposed in five ways: in equilibrium; with the weight on one leg; at rest in one pace; when, during a pace and a half, the body forms an equilateral triangle; and, finally, with the completion of two paces. The body is thus at the centre of a series of imaginary concentric circles each relating to the length of pace; and this is the fundamental assumption both in Ghisliero's fencing theory and in the method he adopts for illustrating it (fig. 54).

The method is made even clearer when Ghisliero devotes two chapters to various 'principii Geometrici'. He discusses how the movement of the sword describes various types of imaginary line and – combining this notion with the concentric circles produced by 'opening the compass' of the legs (as in Carranza) – he evolves a geometry of fencing which is further complicated by the way in which leg movements may divide the imaginary circles into imaginary triangles (figs 55–6). Like all the other illustrations in the *Regole*, these highlight an essential difference between Ghisliero's fencing which is radial, with all developments along the radius of imaginary concentric circles, and Carranza's system which is circumferential, with both opponents moving around the exterior of the same circle.[76]

The second book of the *Regole* ('Della prattica') deals with various modes of attack, and the accompanying illustrations use the system of concentric circles and radii already set out

55. Ghisliero's geometry of fencing. 1587, p. 39.

56. Ghisliero's circles and triangles of foot movement. 1587, p. 58.

57. Ghisliero combines
lines of vision, angles
of attack and (in the
background) a left hand
parry. 1587, p. 113.

earlier, but augment the information on movement by using both multiple postures and, sometimes, composite scenes. A good example of these techniques (and one which also shows the scrupulousness with which the artists have rendered the text) is in the chapter on how to deal with an enemy who stands in third or fourth guard. Ghisliero asks for several things to be demonstrated in one illustration. The first concerns how the fencer's left hand may be used to ward off a thrust. This, says Ghisliero, is shown by the two little figures 'which are in this first demonstration which follows below' – and these are duly depicted in the middle distance. The foreground figures represent Ghisliero's description of a composite movement beginning with the fencer's left foot well back on the circumference of the imaginary circle while he advances along the diameter. His line of vision, passing through the *forte* of his dagger, is directed to the *debole* of the opposing sword. And he ends the movement with a thrust through the enemy's right side, 'as signifies this figure which follows' (fig. 57).

In the *Regole*, all basic fencing postures are clearly delineated: foot placements, leg movements and hand positions are unambiguous; and the relationship between sword blades is clarified in the vertical plane, though not indicated for the horizontal. The text and illustrations embody a simple, effective and largely original system of movement notation, and it is a matter for regret that excessive rarity prevented their having much impact. Apart from Ghisliero, fencing masters outside the Iberian peninsula were disinclined to spend much space on mathematical speculation, and were even less interested in any kind of geometrical notation.[77] They were prepared to accept that geometrical relationships underlay the movements of fencers, but did not feel that this facilitated either explanation or comprehension. One curious exception was the Florentine master Marco Docciolini whose movement notation is perhaps the most economical on record. He uses a single, simple geometrical figure consisting of two concentric circles, a diameter, two radii and seven letters, and on that basis explains, with great ingenuity, his entire system of fencing.[78]

In Spain, however, Carranza had given a lead which was not ignored and it was Luis Pacheco de Narváez's *Libro de las grandezas de la espada* (Madrid, 1600) which changed, and then to a large extent fossilized, Spanish attitudes.[79] Here, at last, was a fully diagrammatic representation of movement. 'Don Lewis of Madrid' was celebrated by Ben Jonson's Sir Glorious Tipto as 'the sole master now in the world', just as Euclid was the 'only fencer of name, now in Elysium'; and, certainly, Narváez was completely besotted with mathematics. Throughout his life, he continued to publish treatises filled with geometrical and philosophical speculation, though without the diagrams which feature in the *Libro de las grandezas de la espada*, and it is significant that, apart from the ancients, the only foreign authors whom he mentions in his works are Camillo Agrippa, the duelling engineer, and Federico Ghisliero whose own system was based upon circles, tangents and angles.[80]

Narváez explains how his book will enable anyone 'to teach himself, and learn without the necessity of a master to direct him'. And, in order to achieve this, he provides 157 woodcuts in which the sword combats are viewed as though from above, with the relative position of the blades at the final moment of any particular move figured by two swords crossed at various angles, either piercing, or tangential to, small circles (representing the fencer's head and body) according to whether the blow is a thrust or a cut. These symbolic representations are further enhanced by directional lines, key letters and labels to help relate them to a full textual description of each movement. The diagrams enable Narváez to clarify foot placements, body movement and the horizontal relationship between opposing blades. However, since they convey no information about posture, hand positions, or the vertical

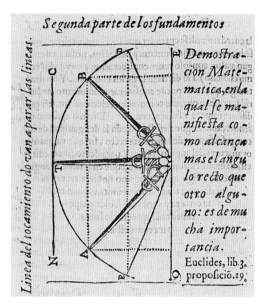

58. A Euclidian demonstration in Narváez, 1600, p. 75.

59. Defence against cuts mathematically demonstrated by Marcelli. 1686, p. 157.

interplay of swords, it has to be admitted that, as a notational system, Narváez's symbols pose as many problems as they solve and they are, at once, more obscure and less efficient than the system devised by Ghisliero (fig. 58).[81]

This concern with the mathematics of fencing, as we have already seen, did not originate in Spain, nor was its development confined to the Iberian peninsula. Geometrical devices were used by later masters, such as the Roman swordsman Francesco Antonio Marcelli, to enhance a mainly figurative approach to fencing illustration, (fig. 59) and everywhere they produced curious pictorial results as we may see in an illustration from Bondi di Mazo's *La spada maestra* which has every appearance of recording late seventeenth-century bicycle fencing.[82] It is scarcely surprising that such mathematical masters were sometimes ridiculed. Quevedo, who was a lifelong enemy of Narváez, pilloried him in his popular novel *El buscón*.[83] The hero, Don Pablo, travelling on the road to Rejas, encounters a strange figure who is simultaneously studying a book, drawing lines on the ground, measuring them with a pair of compasses and skipping about from side to side with the most extravagant motions. This eccentric gentleman explains that he has just thought up a new thrust and is 'reducing it to mathematical rules'. Pablo, curious as to whether mathematics is really relevant to fencing, receives an answer straight out of Carranza – 'not only mathematics, but divinity, philosophy, music, and physic' – and the master then goes on to expound his theories. Pablo understands not a single word but is assured: 'here you have them in this book, which is called, *The Wonders of the Sword*. It is an excellent one, and contains prodigious things; and to convince you of it, at Rejas, where we shall lie tonight, you shall see me perform wonders with two spits; and you need not question but that whosoever reads this book, will kill as many as he pleases.'[84] Even when they arrive at their destination and Pablo is alighting from his horse, the master calls out to him to be sure first to form an obtuse angle with his legs, and then, reducing them to parallel lines, to come perpendicularly to the ground. However, that a more empirical fighting tradition existed in Spain is made abun-

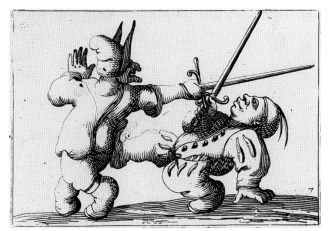

60. Lucini illustrates some fancy footwork. 1627, plate 7.

61. Lucini's exposition of the geometry of fencing and farting. 1627, plate 14.

dantly clear by the lamentable failure of this mathematical swordsman against a mulatto fencing master who says that, although he knows 'neither who is angle nor who is obtuse', he has every intention of cutting his opponent into pieces with his dagger.

At about the same time as Quevedo was poking fun at Narváez and his followers, geometrical fencing follies were even more cruelly pilloried by a young Florentine engraver, Antonio Francesco Lucini in his *Compendio dell'armi de Caramogi* (1627).[85] In fact, this rare set of twenty-four etchings, obviously inspired by the grotesqueries of Jacques Callot, brilliantly parodies the whole range of combat illustration: the spurting gore as throats are slit, and eyes skewered; the devastating blows of the two-handed sword; and the extravagantly fancy footwork (fig. 60).[86] But its surreal high point is reached when tangents, angles and sight-lines are transformed into a spider's web, cat's cradle, fan, and the alternative radial paths of an emergent fart (fig. 61).

Despite such gibes, geometry continued to fascinate the Spanish theorists whose enthusiasm even stirred a reciprocal admiration in the heart of at least one professional mathematician when Don Juan de la Rocha, 'Maestro mayor de Mathemática' to the King of Spain's pages, was moved to write a short treatise on the nobility, antiquity and necessity of fencing – tracing the art back to the very creation of the world and to the combat between the good and bad angels. The superiority of fencing to all other arts is demonstrated by the fact that it is the means whereby cities and kingdoms are kept secure; and La Rocha makes evident the measure of its greatness by surveying the peaks of erudition and human accomplishment. Philosophy has its Plato and Aristotle and geometry its Euclid, Apollonius Pergaeus and Archimedes. Astronomy and geography have their Ptolemy; arithmetic, Euclid and Diophantus; and architecture, Vitruvius. Medicine has Hippocrates and Galen; and rhetoric, Cicero and Demosthenes. But what of 'la destreza de las armas'? Well, La Rocha has already demonstrated that the art of fencing is superior to all other arts; and it comes as no surprise that its greatest luminaries are 'Geronimo de Carrança y Don Luis Pacheco de Narváez con grande aprovación'.[87]

It is impossible to imagine a more exalted view of the Spanish masters than this tribute from their compatriot mathematician; yet, curiously enough, their system received its most magnificent expression in the work of a non-Iberian master. In 1620, Louis XIII granted a

ACADEMIE de

L'ESPÉE
de
GIRARD THIBAULT
d'Anvers:
ou se demonstrent
PAR
REIGLES MATHEMATIQUES
SUR
le fondement d'un
CERCLE MYSTERIEUX
LA THEORIE ET PRATIQUE
des vrais et iusqu'a present
incognus secrets
DU MANIEMENT
DES ARMES
A PIED ET A CHEVAL
M. IDC. XXVIII.

62. Thibault's *Academie de l'espée*. The magnificent title page of the most magnificent of all fencing books. Unfortunately, the author never did write the promised section on cavalry. 1630.

63. Thibault, the master of the mysterious circle. 1630, frontispiece.

privilege to Girard Thibault of Antwerp for his work (already several years in progress) entitled the *Académie de l'espée*; but another decade was to pass before the book was completed by the Elzeviers of Leiden. Although bearing the date 1628, it was not published until 1630, a year after the author's death, and it remains – from a purely bibliographical or, rather, bibliophilic point of view – the supreme masterpiece among fencing books and, indeed, one of the greatest illustrated books in the history of printing (figs 62–3).[88] The vast letterpress is itself a triumph of the typesetter's art: but even more startling are the illustrations, one single page and forty-five double-page copperplates (measuring 48.2 cm by 69.3 cm), drawn and engraved by a team of seventeen distinguished graphic artists led by Crispin van de Pass the Younger.[89] The two Crispins van de Pass, father and son, had already been involved in providing the plates for another prestigious publishing venture, Pluvinel's *Le Maneige royal* which first appeared in 1623.[90] Yet, fine as the Pluvinel plates are, they pale into insignificance before the stupendous, multidimensional virtuosity of the Thibault.

So physically immense is this volume, so labyrinthine are its plates, so mercilessly meticulous and comprehensive are Thibault's verbal descriptions, and so totally committed was the author to the Spanish swordsmanship which was irrevocably falling out of favour elsewhere in Europe, that it has become commonplace in historical surveys of fencing to ridicule the *Académie*. Certainly it is bizarre, full of artifice, and a stiff test for any reader's powers of endurance: but to dismiss it impatiently, as an 'enormous volume of nonsense', is unhistorical and clear evidence of a failure to study the text with care.[91] Thibault's Spanish sympathies were, after all, something he shared with countless other masters and their pupils; and the fact that, on the whole, fencing evolved in quite another direction does not mean that Thibault and those who thought like him were either mad or stupid. Indeed, many years later, the Dutch master Johannes Bruchius considered Thibault's work to be praiseworthy and suggested that the reason for its 'manner of fighting-in-a-circle' having become outmoded was 'on account of its inherently difficult nature' and because modern fencers were not prepared to devote the time necessary for mastering its intricacies.[92] The *Académie* remains impressive in more than mere physical appearance. It is a deeply pondered book which proceeds systematically and is based upon a number of perfectly reasonable assumptions, as well as upon others less plausible and certainly no longer tenable. As will be suggested later, the system of fencing of which it is a gigantic celebration may have been effective for reasons extraneous to its underlying philosophy: but one could say the same about the martial arts of the Samurai. With hindsight, we may well regard Thibault's work as a failure: but it is, none the less, an heroic failure, epic both in conception and execution.

Thibault is particularly concerned to point out that, having practised the art of fence for a good many years in various countries, he has encountered various 'grands amateurs'. Some of these favoured the French style of fencing and others the Italian: but, in every case, they adopted strange postures, with bodies twisted, feet and legs disjointed out of all natural proportion, and in positions wholly repugnant to the normal fashion used either when walking or standing still. By contrast, whereas such methods achieve nothing beyond weakening the fencer's 'propres forces', Thibault believes that all the arts must follow Nature and never contradict her. He has, accordingly, taken his own exercise to the school of 'this Sovereign Mistress of good inventions', and all his measures and examples (which form the foundation of everything that follows) proceed from the proportion of the human body. Without this it is impossible either to understand the art of fencing or to practise it with assurance. As Thibault remarks later in the *Académie*, with Nature as his guide, he rejects all the violent movements and extreme postures which have been employed in the past by those who profess arms.[93] And it is understandable that he devotes an entire plate and its accompanying chapter 'Against the postures of Salvator Fabris'.

Like Carranza, Thibault regards human proportions as fundamental to his system. Indeed, they are so fundamental that he is at great pains to establish his principles on the best authorities available to him – a point which escaped Egerton Castle who assumed that the physiological foundation of the *Académie* was merely an arbitrary hotchpotch invented by its author.[94] In fact, Thibault is acutely aware that some readers might believe that, rather than simply following natural truth, he had selectively arranged his evidence and accommodated his circle to the human figure according to his own fantasy. He has, therefore, decided to offer proofs by applying his circle

> to the portrait of a human figure taken from the Book of the Proportions of Man, written more than a hundred years earlier by the great painter and geometrician Albert Dürer, applying to the said personage our Circle with all its lines and appurtenances: in that the navel is taken for the centre, the sole of the foot rests on the circumference, and the top of the head reaches exactly to the last intersection of the diameter at the letter *V*, all exactly as it is shown in our figure.

This figure is indeed an exact copy, including all indications of mathematical proportions, of the male body in Dürer's *Vier Bücher von menschlicher Proportion* which had been first published in 1528 (fig. 64).[95] Of course, admits Thibault, one could base other circles on human proportions as, for example, placing the centre on the 'parties honteuses', with the cir-

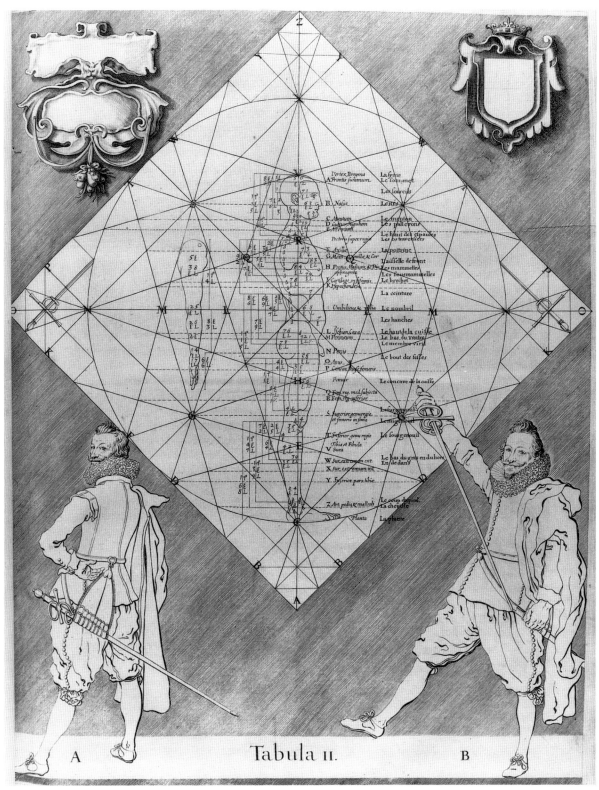

Tabula II.

A   B

64. Thibault. The human body depicted after Dürer; while the master himself draws his sword. 1630, book I, tabula 2.

cumference running through the top of the head and the soles of the feet. One's mind boggles at the kind of notation Thibault might have devised on that basis: but, as he points out, it is the arm which must be extended in order to practise the art of fencing.

In the *Académie de l'espée*, according to the proud announcement on its title page, are 'plainly shewed by mathematical rules, on the foundation of a mysterious circle, the theory and practice of the true and hitherto unknown secrets of the handling of arms'. Egerton Castle was unimpressed by this puff and remarked that, in the plates, 'nothing is represented but an artistic illustration of the Spanish system set forth at such length by Don Luis P. de Narváez'.[96] This is only partially true and, in any case, misses an important point. Thibault was claiming far too much when he wrote of 'hitherto unknown secrets'. But he was rightly convinced that his notation was a novel departure even if, as we now know, it never arrived anywhere; and even if, as must also be admitted, the various elements of his notational system had already been suggested by others. Multiple postures had appeared in Agrippa and Ghisliero. Consistent geometrical ground plans had been the basis of Ghisliero's illustrations and, less effectively, of Sainct Didier's. The horizontal relationship between opposing sword blades had been indicated diagrammatically by Narváez, while, in so far as Thibault's plates show human fencers rather than symbols, they may be regarded as falling within the purely representational tradition. On the other hand, the elaboration of Thibault's method for showing the development of each movement went far beyond the scope of any earlier text, just as his geometrical delineation of foot movements is of an unprecedented precision.

He himself was worried that anyone looking at the pictures would find it strange that so many of his images were not situated in the familiar fixed plane, and he explains at the outset that the reader must imagine that they are painted on the walls or on sheets of paper, or (as in his Plate 19) woven into an arras: 'for the more commodious representation of the science, and for the more ready comprehension of the ordinary person who does not understand perspectives'.[97] Not only do these various illustrations demonstrate the position and movement of the bodies, but in addition, 'one finds an accord of the blades, made at the base of the circle, by which the judgement of the movements of the swords which the figures hold in their hands, is rendered very easy'. In other words, Thibault's plates indicate several things simultaneously, in different ways, and in different planes. The series of realistic representations of the fencers show their postures and hand movements at various stages of each development: the circles, with their lines and letters, indicate the sequence of foot movements; and the swords' shadows, delineated at the fencers' feet, represent the engagement of the blades as they would be seen from above, in the manner of Narváez (fig. 65).

The fundamental principles of Thibault's notational system are illustrated in his first plate (figs 66–7), an engraving of immense complexity, requiring approximately 19,000 words of explication at the end of which he remarks:

It is true that we have been somewhat exact in the research in some parts of this treatise, as in the deduction of the points, graduations, and proportions of the body, and in several other matters which we have calculated with sufficient exactitude. Nevertheless, it is not necessary that those who have no familiarity with Mathematics should, on that account, lose heart. For that which we have done has been rather for the satisfaction of those who wish closely to examine our Theory, than for its being of itself necessary in Practice. Besides which, we have attempted to set the whole in good order, so that everyone will be able to distinguish therein the things necessary for the Theoricke, if so be that he reads our text with attention.[98]

65. Thibault. The horizontal relationship of swords and dagger indicated by shadows on the floor. 1630, book II, tabula 6, detail.

66. Thibault's entire system delineated. 1630, book I, tabula 1.

67. A detail of fig. 66.

This may seem a strange claim to anyone first encountering the thesaurus of riddles posed by the *Académie*'s illustrations. The book had been designed exclusively for that select group of reigning European princes who had subscribed to the cost of production and whose expectations demanded satisfaction. Accordingly, Thibault and his artists used every conceivable technique to delight the eyes and divert the minds of their powerful readers. The entire range of contemporary visual reference was deployed. The main figures fence silently and without passion in lofty schools of arms, or in the courtyards or gardens of strange palaces, amidst mysterious perspectives of arched colonnades, antique statuary, plinths, pyramids, obelisks, turrets, triumphal arches and pagodas. Behind them, above them, and alongside them, pairs of smaller figures are exhibited on every conceivable imaginary surface: painted on walls, woven into tapestries, incised into marble blocks, running along friezes, or fluttering aloft on banners held by winged figures. Yet – despite the myriad images, lines, letters, perspectives and optical illusions – the whole paraphernalia resolves itself merely into multiple postures, a tracking system, and a diagrammatic, overhead view of the swords. It is only necessary to read the letterpress diligently, study the circles in the order prescribed, and follow the ground plans precisely as indicated. Thibault's instructions are almost disconcertingly easy to decode (figs 68–9).

68. An example of
Thibault's combination of
multiple postures. 1630,
book I, tabula 30.

69. A detail of fig. 68.

One other feature of Thibault's system which demands attention is that it was not conceived solely as an illustrative technique for clarifying a written text. As he explains in detail, his geometric patterns are also to be used as a practical aid for teaching. He advises that a place should be chosen with a level floor, whereupon you should begin by marking the centre of a circle with chalk wherever seems most suitable. That done, you must take a sword which is a half diameter in length – in other words when the point is placed on the ground between the feet, 'les branches de la garde' come exactly level with the navel. Then, placing one of the 'branches' on this central chalk mark, you must use it to trace out the circumference. Having done this, you then proceed by taking a twisted string rubbed with chalk, 'after the fashion of carpenters', marking out the diameter and extending it by two feet beyond the circumference, and continue using the sword and its point as a rule and measure until the circle is intersected by lines and tangents, which are themselves linked so that the whole figure is included within a square as shown in the first plate. Finally, all points are labelled with letters.

This application of Thibault's mathematical fencing has generally gone unnoticed, but it is especially suggestive in view of the evidence of Willem Swanenburgh's late sixteenth-century engraving of the fencing room of the University of Leiden. (See Chapter I, fig. 4.) The main feature of interest is in the centre of the floor where, inlaid into the surface, is a circle inscribed within a square, enclosing another square and divided into triangles and segments by radii and intersecting lines. Whatever we may think about Thibault's mysterious circle, it was not a figment of his disordered imagination but had been used to facilitate teaching even before he began work on the *Académie*.

Thibault's *Académie de l'espée* is quite the most sumptuous fencing book ever published, and it incorporates what is, from a purely artistic point of view, the most elaborate notational method in the history of swordsmanship. It would, therefore, be a good place to finish this chapter. However, the story does not really end there because Spanish authors continued their quest for a notation more akin to the purely symbolic method of music: and Pacheco de Narváez, as well as Thibault, pointed the way. Several masters followed hard in Pacheco's footsteps, and often quite literally. In the year 1675 alone there were three examples of this kind of fencing book: one by Gaspar Agustín de Lara who set out his 'necessary geometry' in the *Cornucopia numerosa* (which, as he says, is gathered from the works of Don Luis Pacheco de Narváez, 'the prince of the science of arms'); another by Miguel Mendoza y Quixada whose engraver Marcus Orozco was obliged to compress vast amounts of information into a single folding plate; and a third by Francisco Antonio Ettenhard, a Madrid master of German extraction, who displayed the 'mathematical evidence' for his own system of fencing. Ettenhard was a particularly interesting figure in that he was not only a soldier and swordsman but also a noted painter and engraver who, in fact, engraved the plates for his own books (figs 70–2).[99]

However, none of these – not even the great pioneer, Narváez himself – could bear comparison with the Herculean mathematical labours of Francisco Lorenz de Rada who, at the end of the seventeenth and beginning of the eighteenth centuries, published copiously on the 'art, science, and experience' of swordsmanship.[100] In 1695 he was experimenting with a more sophisticated version of Narváez's fencing notation, in which the combats are again viewed from above, but intermixed with mathematical projections of traditional figures (figs 73–4). But it was in his three-volume *Nobleza de la espada* of 1705 that he finally worked this up into a fully fledged method of movement analysis. Here, Spanish belief in the absolute relationship between geometry and fencing reaches its apogee and the entire

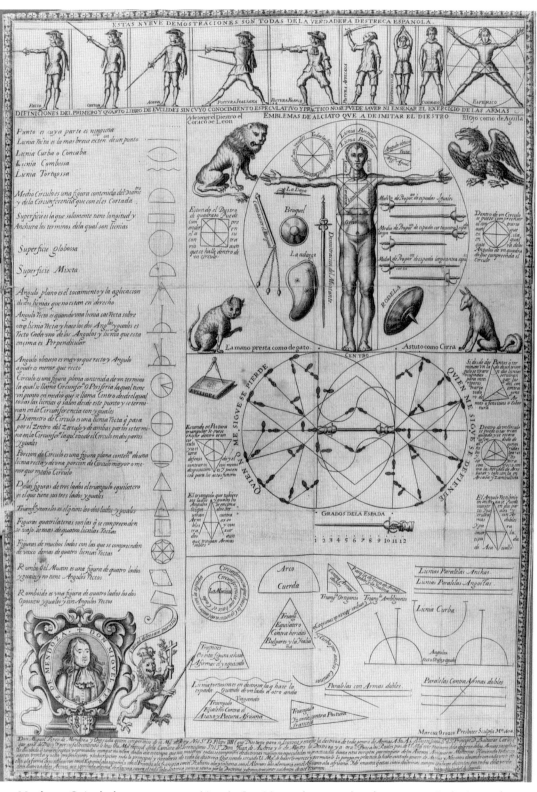

70. Mendoza y Quixada demonstrates everything the Spanish swordsman needs to know – on a single sheet. 1675, plate between pp. 68 and 69.

de especial conocimiento
del Punto.A.Linea en comun.
Linea recta.B.y despues de esto
la Curva.C.Flexua,ò Tortuosa.D.
Perpendicular.F.y luego
la Diagonal.G.Diametral.H.
que es la que demedia el Centro:
De el Circulo entero,plano.I.
de el Semicirculo,ò Medio.L.
de el Quarto.M.y de la Porcion.N.
como fuere,mas ò menos;
De el Equilatero quadro.O.
Quadrangulo,ò Paralelo.P.
de el Triangulo.Q.de el Angulo
principal,que llaman Recto.R.
De el Obtuso.S.de el Agudo.T.
de el Curbelino.V.el compuesto
de dos lineas Curva,y recta.X.
que es Misto su nombre mesmo.
La Superficie,en comun,
considerada en el Cuerpo
de el Hombre,quando se miran
de dos lineas los estremos;
De la Plana.Y.la Convexa.Z.
la Concava.K.que es el hueco
que haze vna figura curva,

y

y la Convexa,lo opuesto.
EL Hombre,se considera
Circular,quadrado entero;
y assi mismo cada parte
considerarla deuemos,
particularmente el Rostro,
y aquel espacio que vemos
desde los Ombros al talle,
que llaman de el tocamento.
Vna linea se imagina
Diametral,que diuidiendo
perpendicular el Rostro
cae al touillo siniestro;A.

*Cuerpo de
el Hombre,
y sus plan-
tas.*

E

qua-

71. Lara's simple geometrical figures for fencers. 1675, pp. 4–5.

structure of the vast treatise is erected upon this premise (fig. 75). The fundamental argument is explained in a long introduction (by far the most intelligent part of the book) providing a plausible justification for the application of a three-dimensional Euclidian geometry to fencing. The whole point of the exercise upon which Rada is engaged is to enable us to comprehend movements too rapid for the human eye.[101]

Rada is well aware that there had been many before him who had made the connection between mathematics and fencing. The inventors of any science, he says, are followed by disciples who develop and systematize the original discoveries, reducing everything to order – just as Plato followed Socrates and was, in his turn, succeeded by Aristotle and that long line of philosophers which culminated in Averroes and St Thomas Aquinas. Mathematics is especially important for Rada because it incorporates everything (geometry, arithmetic, astronomy and music) he deems relevant to the mensuration of movement and, therefore, to a whole variety of applied sciences. Among these subordinate activities are mechanics, military science and, of course, the art of fighting with all weapons, especially the sword, which Rada regards as the 'Queen of them all', and the 'ornament, strength, and defence of man, used and esteemed both by ancient and modern'.

He observes that, just as in philosophy, science and the arts, men have gained immortality through their writings, so there are many who have achieved similar distinction by bringing to light the philosophy and skill of swordsmanship. However, in the brief resumé of the history of fencing literature which follows, he cites only four names – Carranza, Viggiani, Narváez and Thibault – and, although the first two merit praise for their attempts to analyse fencing movements by applying a personal version of the Platonic method, their writings were obscure, and it was left to Narváez, 'como Aristoteles a Platon', to give greater precision and clarity to the subject and to earn esteem throughout Europe. Of the many

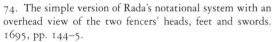

72. Ettenhard delineates all the angles created by a pair of swordsmen. 1675, plate IX.

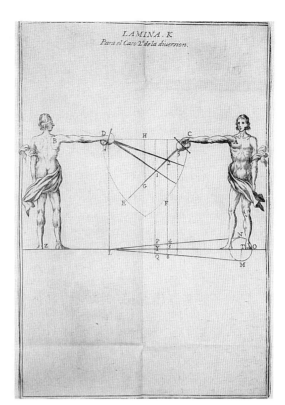

73. Rada explains the movement of fencers' swords and feet. 1695, pp. 140–1.

74. The simple version of Rada's notational system with an overhead view of the two fencers' heads, feet and swords. 1695, pp. 144–5.

75. Rada's weapons: pen, sword, dagger and compasses. 1705, frontispiece.

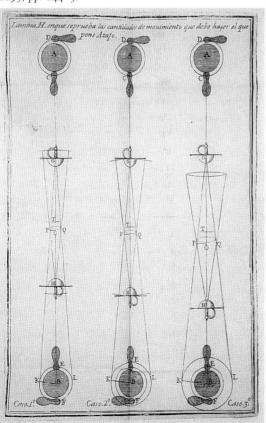

others who had subsequently written on fencing, Rada contents himself with singling out only 'Gerardo Tibaut, moderno Autor, natural de Amberes', whose text was accompanied by especially magnificent plates. This matter is not discussed further but, since Rada had devised his own fencing notation combining representations of swordsmen with diagrams of their actions, it is not difficult to see why Thibault interested him.

Fencing is not only a demonstrable science it is also, in Rada's view, the most noble because its subject is 'man with sword in hand', and because it has a 'certain method of proof which is mathematical'. The art functions by means of straight and curved movements of the body, arm, and sword, which cannot be formed without involving quantity, line, angle, surface and body. The bases of both geometry and fencing are clearly identical and it follows, therefore, that the methods of proof in both sciences must also be identical: 'Geometry and fencing admit of one demonstrable and certain means: and if in Geometry it is infallible, so also it is in fencing'.

All of this was commonplace. Where Rada moves beyond his predecessors is in his awareness that geometry functions in three, rather than two, dimensions; and in his perception of the way in which such a geometry may be used to supply a visual, and therefore comprehensible, record of motion. One cannot, he repeats, make the movements of fencing with the body, arm and sword without thereby causing some type of quantity. This is evident because whichever part is moved, it forms the trace of its movement. For example, the extremity or point of the sword, being moved in a straight or curved line, will necessarily form its trace according to the type of motion. That trace will consist of mathematical lines, surfaces, or solids: although none of this will be perceptible to the sight because the movement merely 'scratches the air' (*que solo rasga el ayre*). Were the same movements performed in some more dense material, they would then be physical and perceptible. If the edge of the sword is moved, it necessarily causes a flat or curved plane, according to the nature and trace of its particular motion; while, if the surface is moved, it forms the body of one or many surfaces, according to the termination of the movement. This, Rada points out, is demonstrable from the definitions of the cylinder and right cone given by Euclid – which he proceeds to cite in full. In Rada's opinion, nothing is more pertinent and more necessary for comprehending sword play than these geometric solids: 'of which no authority in this science of the sword has written apart from Don Luis in folio 26, line 6, of his *New Science*, where he names cylinders and pyramids etc., without applying them in all his works'.[102] Narváez excepted, the fundamental importance of these mathematical principles in fencing has been ignored despite the fact that, unless they are taken into account, it is quite impossible to understand the art.

To clarify the problems of recording movement (and their solution), Rada adopts an Aristotelian stance, citing the 'common maxim of Philosophy' which maintains that our comprehension of any subject comes either through the organs of the senses, or by some analogy which enables us to visualize an idea.[103] Since fencing, by its very nature and particularly in the accelerated movements of a combat, is especially difficult to comprehend because its complex movements are of such velocity that the eye simply cannot follow the trace (*vestigio*) of the sword, it is necessary somehow for the action to be 'translated to the understanding'. And this process of translation is precisely what Rada's notation is intended to accomplish. Comprehension, while inaccessible in the physical sphere, may be supplied

by means of the metaphysical imagination, through the similitude of the pyramidal, cylindrical, and spherical figures, or their parts. For, by the likeness they have with their own appropriate movements and their opposites (however violent and accelerated they may be), understanding is facilitated by mathematical demonstrations which make a physical representation perceptible by the sight.

Thus geometrical figures, intelligently devised, can provide a visual method, enabling us to understand the different movements made by the sword. It will also, in Rada's view, enable us to regulate more perfectly the technique of defence and offence in man, 'which is the purpose of this science'.

Like so many Spanish masters, Rada cannot resist discoursing upon other arts which have a mathematical basis. Perspective and cosmography are duly cited: but music is especially attractive because the relationship between its theory and practice suggests to Rada a powerful analogy. Just as 'la Musica especulativa' provides the mind with an understanding of harmonic proportions and gives rise to the practical art of playing an instrument, so in swordsmanship there is a 'certain type of harmony in the movements, reduced to rhythm and proportionality'. Granted this, and granted also that fencing is subordinate to mathematics, it is possible to construct a speculative and practical science in the regulation of arm and sword movements as they pass through the air in straight lines, curved lines, circles, surfaces, and spherical, cylindrical and pyramidal solids; and to regulate 'the postures, dispositions, movements and operations of the body in the horizontal planes over which it may move, or subsist'.

Regulating the art of fencing is also likened to navigating a ship upon the mighty ocean. The subject may seem almost beyond comprehension: but Rada intends to reduce its vast potentialities, as far as possible, to determinate acts and to do this, moreover, with such brevity and clarity that his method 'neither obscures the memory, nor disturbs the understanding'. He will thus provide the means whereby a student of average intelligence and agility may recognize and attain 'that which with many years of study, experiments, exercise, and communications' he has himself accumulated in order to form this work with 'complete perfection'. He proceeds by principles, arguments and demonstrations from the universal to the particular, erecting his edifice upon a firm basis of the accepted philosophical and mathematical definitions, petitions, axioms, hypotheses and modes of analysis. All these he then applies to the principles of fencing, scrupulously confining himself within the terms most generally accepted in the sciences and arts in order to achieve the greatest clarity:

> in which I am particularly careful, desiring to be understood and to make myself understood, excluding all affectation of phrases and exquisite expressions, because the essential meaning does not reside in the sound of words and the phrases themselves, but rather in the substance explicated by pure, chaste, and appropriate language which philosophy teaches.

This peroration derives almost word for word from the introduction to Isocrates's *Ad Nicoclem* which had also been used by Machiavelli in the dedication of *Il principe* – a work in which that author's muscular and economical prose style had fully justified the claim. Rada, unfortunately, was unable to match such masterly concision, and his enunciation of mathematical fencing occupies 1,156 pages of closely printed letterpress. It also requires ninety-eight imposing but perplexing plates. As in earlier works within the mathematical tradition, Rada starts readers off gently enough with geometrical terms. One cannot go far wrong with the 'point' as defined by Euclid. Ghisliero, too, had started with the point but

facing page
77. (*left*) Three dimensions and increased fantastication. Rada, 1705, book II, fig. 21.

78. An even more mysterious circle. Rada, 1705, book III, fig. 12.

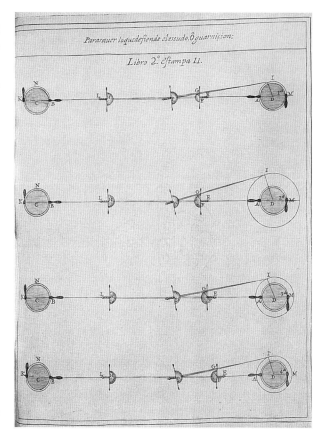

Parasauer loquedefiende elescudo,ỏguarniçion:

Libro 2.º eſtampa LI.

76. The vertical engagements of blades. Rada, 1705, book II, fig. 11.

had thereafter contented himself with a few lines, angles and parts of the circle. Rada, however, provides more than seventy diagrams, culminating in various forms of cone and pyramid, together with a relentless series of definitions. He also demonstrates that Quevedo's satire had been in vain by explaining how the compass is indispensable in the construction of figures relevant to fencing, and develops an analogy between fortification and swordsmanship similar to one previously suggested by Ghisliero in 1587, though much more far-fetched and illustrated by a figure of almost surreal extravagance.[104] He then moves on to the circular 'jurisdiction' of the body; foot movements as shown by footprints on circular and diametrical tracks; linear motion through the air of both sword and arm whose invisible tracks are likened to those of the celestial bodies used for navigation; circular sword movements and their imaginary conic projections; and diagrammatic representations of the vertical engagement of opposing blades along with accompanying footsteps.[105] Eventually, the whole gamut of devices is deployed in plates showing the figures of swordsmen projected downwards into three-dimensional geometrical structures: their foot movements depicted in tracks; and the engagement of blades shown from above (as in Narváez), but arranged down the page in sequences intended to be read rather like lute tablature (fig. 76). The fencers are told where to put their feet and how to place their swords in much the same way as the lutenist is shown where to position his fingers. A vast amount of information is provided; but it is immensely difficult to interpret; and, as an explication of practical fencing technique, it is quite useless (figs 77–8).

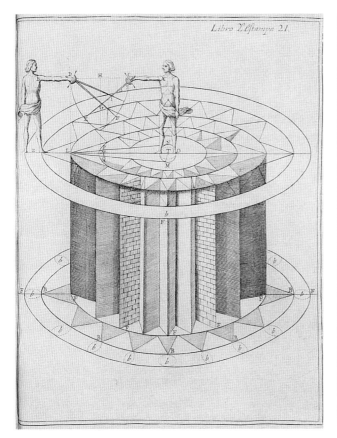
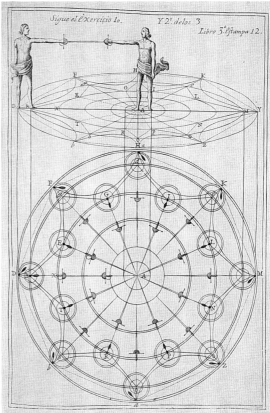

At about the same time as Rada was evolving his system, Beauchamp, Feuillet, Siris, Pecour and others were developing a symbolic notation for dancing. But, whereas dancers and choreographers continued to work with Feuillet's system, or went on to develop new and even more elaborate notational methods, Rada's method was stifled by its own complexities, by the inherent impossibility of the task it was confronting, and by the irrelevance of its purpose. Even in Spain the artificial rapier style was falling out of favour; and with it went its symbolic notation. Everywhere, fencing manuals preferred the simpler, more rational technique of isolating and illustrating key postures – relying on the reader's memory and imagination to fill in the inevitable gaps.[106] Rada's *Nobleza de la espada* remains the nearest thing to a dance notation that the art of fencing has ever managed to achieve: but it was a monumental dead end.

There can be no doubt that the application of mathematics and engineering knowledge could facilitate the abstract analysis of movement: but, when applied to fencing practice, such analysis degenerated into an *amplificatio ad absurdum*. All these mathematical approaches to fencing were based upon three serious fallacies. In the first place, they assumed that the analysis of movement is identical with its notation: whereas analysis follows rather than precedes an activity. Second, they assumed that, in order to perform any movement effectively, it is necessary to understand the scientific principles underlying it: whereas it is obvious that a ponderous, slow-moving fencer with dull reflexes – whatever his grasp of theoretical issues – will always fall victim to an agile adversary blessed with quick reflexes rather than intellectual grasp. Third, they completely misunderstood the real nature of the movements they sought to notate. They regarded fencing as a kind of dance, whereas it is something fundamentally different. In a dance, movements are at least susceptible to planning; and, when a group of dancers perform, they may reasonably expect collaboration from their colleagues rather than opposition and trickery. Fencers, by contrast, seek to deceive and surprise each other. The one thing they do not want is to collaborate with the opponent or do anything which might be anticipated. The basic positions and movements of swordsmanship can certainly be described in words and illustrated by figures but, once the action goes beyond these, the permutations become almost infinite; and, while a notation of sufficient complexity and sophistication might conceivably explicate a combat which has already taken place, it could never prognosticate the movements of a combat yet to be.[107] Historians are, of course, fortunate that, for several generations, fencing masters failed to grasp this fact.

III

Foot combat with swords: myths and realities

The sword is the most noble of all arms, and is used by knights, by learned men, and by the armigerous; whence they make nature marvel that, with a piece of steel, a man may defend his person from any blow which might be aimed at him, either with the point or the edge, with the formation of angles, lines, circles, and with time and measure.[1]

GIUSEPPE MORSICATO PALLAVICINI wrote this concise eulogy of the sword in 1670, and most masters of arms would have agreed with him because – while many of them provided instruction in unarmed combat, knife fighting and the use of various types of staff weapon – their fame or notoriety depended more on their skill as teachers of swordsmanship or, as it came to be known, the art of fencing. Of all the martial arts practised in medieval and renaissance Europe, sword fighting produced by far the greatest literature in quality, volume and the claims it made for itself; and, perhaps as a consequence of this, it has also been the area of personal combat most studied by scholars. Yet this richness of material poses problems for anyone attempting an ordered exposition of the subject. There were many different types of sword, and they were not all handled in the same way. There were many different masters, and – however much they travelled about to gain experience, copied each other, or developed similar solutions to similar questions – they each had their own ideas about how to do things. It is true that much of the vocabulary of sword fighting permeated Europe and became a kind of fencer's lingua franca: but much of it did not, and not all masters were equally gifted at explication. In short, the history of fencing is a good deal less straightforward than was at one time supposed.

THE EARLIEST HISTORIANS OF FENCING

The fact that sword fighting must have had a past as well as a present was rarely commented upon by medieval and renaissance authors.[2] One of the few references to such a pre-history was made by Liechtenauer's disciple, Hanko Döbringer who in 1389 pointed out that, although the art of the sword had been perfected by Master Liechtenauer whose pursuit of martial knowledge had taken him to various lands, it had nevertheless been 'founded and invented many hundred years ago'.[3] Döbringer was aware of antecedents but obviously had no source material relating to them. Nearly two centuries later another German author, Heinrich von Gunterrodt, in his short treatise on the true origins of the art of fencing, confidently pushes the story far back into the ancient world, quoting Galen, Heraclides, Pliny, Strabo, Ovid, Plutarch, Sophocles and others, to demonstrate the longevity of sword play as physical exercise, gladiatorial display and military necessity. He is well over half way through his work before he suddenly leaps from the ancients – via an anecdote in which the medieval Danish hero Starcatherus cut Hama the Saxon in half – to his own time, offering some desultory comments on the two principal German fencing confederations.[4] One of these, comprising men such as 'furriers and other artisans' (who, by imperial privilege, displayed their skills at the Frankfurt fairs), is obviously the *Marxbrüder* for whom Gunterrodt had little admiration. The other, composed of members practising 'less sordid crafts', must be the *Federfechter* who – having been incorporated by the Duke of Mecklenburg, dedicatee of Gunterrodt's treatise – naturally excites greater enthusiasm. He also alludes to Joachim Meyer 'who tried to describe firm rules, and also produced a great book concerning this very art in the German language', but does not consider that it satisfactorily demonstrated the requisite fundamentals. Gunterrodt believes that, for the true origins, one must look at an ancient book recently found in a monastery; and his brief description of this manuscript proves it to have been the very sword and buckler manual which, to this day, remains the earliest fencing treatise thus far discovered.[5] He also gives a summary of the various types of combat taught currently, providing useful glosses for Latin and German terms. But he has nothing else to say about the history of personal combat, and mentions only one other important figure, Fabian von Auerswald who was, as we know, famous for wrestling not swordsmanship.

The first master to show a truly historical turn of mind was the Spaniard, Pacheco de Narváez who constantly referred to the work of his Italian and Spanish predecessors from the late fifteenth century.[6] Spanish followers of Narváez tended to annotate their observations in a similar fashion, but neither they nor their master wrote an ordered narrative;[7] and it was not until Pallavicini devoted several chapters of his *La scherma illustrata* to the origins of swords and swordsmanship that there was any serious attempt to list the evidence available and to explain the gaps in our knowledge. Pallavicini was a very erudite fencer, well read not only in early fencing literature but also in law, history, mathematics and lexicography, widely travelled and – like Liechtenauer, Fiore, Meyer and Capoferro before him – experienced in several practical schools of arms. It must be admitted that his introductory etymological study is unsatisfactory because it throws no light on the word *scherma* itself but his general historical framework is worth studying.

His first concern is to establish the antiquity of fencing which he traces back to Ninus, King of Assyria, the first ruler to use professional fencing masters to instruct his troops. Since that remote period, the sword has remained of fundamental importance in battle despite the 'pernicious use of warlike powder, and of artillery, muskets, bombs, grenades, mines and other firearms, which incinerate the world, and obscure the virtue of the combatants'. Indeed, in Pallavicini's view, the stability of the great empires – as their power translated from Assyria, Persia, Macedon and Greece, to Italy and Rome – was dependent upon the art of the sword which, in his own time, is taught all over the world in schools and academies.[8] Everywhere one sees the flourishing state of this 'celebrated profession' without which it would be impossible to live in safety, since the ploughshare is useless without the sword.

Inventors of arms also interest Pallavicini who notes the conflicting opinions of many scholars and argues that it is unreasonable to seek a specific origin for each type of sword. It is evident from experience that, even within a single city, men might use many types, even those of different nations; and it is recognition of this fact 'which will serve to reconcile the various opinions of ancient and modern scholars'.[9]

After a brief excursus on the nobility of fencing, Pallavicini addresses himself to the 'Famous Masters in this Science or Art'. Observing that the passage of time has left us with little knowledge of the earliest masters (such as the Assyrians, Persians and Greeks), he believes that the first definite information is Valerius Maximus's report on the training of Roman soldiers, as established by the Consul Publius Rutilius who sought out the leading gladiators from the school of Gaius Aurelius Scaurus to devise and teach a system for both defence and attack. It is this dual capacity that has made the sword as famous as the lance of Achilles which had simultaneously inflicted wounds and cured them. The only difference is that, whereas Achilles's lance was a 'ridiculous fable', the efficacy of the sword has been proven in military action.

Pallavicini recognizes that 'there have been many master fencers outstanding in this profession, who (because they have not written about our science) have been buried in oblivion', and he can only write about those whom he has been able 'to fish up from the deep sea of antiquity'. The first authors yielded by this process are 'Giaime Ponz di Perpignano' who, in 1474, 'printed his book' (*il quale impresse il suo libro*) which was highly esteemed; and Pietro de la Torre, 'di Natione Spagnola' whose book was 'printed in the same year' (*stampato il suo libro nel medesimo anno del 1474*). Modern scholars have puzzled over these works and wondered whether, despite Pallavicini's choice of the words *impresse* and *stampato*, they were manuscripts.[10] It would certainly be extraordinary had any books on fencing been printed in Spain at such an early date: but they must have existed in some form because Pallavicini, like Narváez before him, cites them with precision. Yet there is a gap of more than thirty years before another manual was printed, this time by 'Pietro Moncio Italiano' in 1509, followed by the Spaniard, Francisco Román, in 1532.[11] The Bolognese master, Achille Marozzo was next in 1536, writing 'so learnedly that he merited the title of Master General'; but it is odd that Pallavicini, who otherwise orders his material chronologically, should have bracketed Marozzo with Marco Docciolini the Florentine who published in 1601. The sequence continues with Camillo Agrippa, wrongly assigned to 1536 instead of 1553, but recognized as 'the first who published concerning lines, angles, diameters and so forth'; the German Joachim Meyer under 1568 instead of 1570; Giacomo di Grassi of Modena under 1570; and Giovanni dall'Agocchie of Bologna under 1572. A paragraph on the Spanish masters records that 'Il Commendatore Geronimo Sances de Carranza Sivigliano' had written 'with much erudition in 1582', and had been followed by Pacheco da Narváez, 'Maestro Maggiore' of his Majesty Philip III, with the *Grandezza della spada* in 1600, the *Inganno e disganno della destrezza della spada* in 1635, and the *Modo fácil y nuevo para examinarse los maestros en la destreza de las armas* in 1643. Then Pallavicini mentions Salvator Fabris, Master of the King of Denmark, under 1601 instead of 1606; Ridolfo Capoferro da Cagli under 1610; the Roman, Antonio Marchini under 1612; and finally Alessandro Senesio of Bologna under 1660.[12] There were, he concludes, many other learned writers whom he has passed over for the sake of brevity; and he stresses once again that, before the period under discussion and prior to printing, the science must have been promulgated in manuscripts.

Pallavicini's account is suggestive. He recognizes that the art of swordsmanship had a long history prior to the invention of printing and that manuscript treatises must have existed; but clearly he does not know of any and is as ignorant of Italian manuscripts as of the immense German tradition deriving from Liechtenauer. Thus, like most subsequent students of swordsmanship, he is obliged to equate the history of fencing with the history of printed fencing books. His coverage of sixteenth-century treatises is a little untidy. He omits several minor texts but – apart from Manciolino and Viggiani – few major authors. He is well informed on Spanish material; but mentions no German master other than Meyer and ignores Sainct Didier. He refers to, and subsequently cites, a number of writers whose works have since been lost – Pons, de la Torre, Román and Marchini – but is surprisingly weak on seventeenth-century sources, even in the analytical chapters of his treatise where he uses only three authors beyond those listed in his historical survey.[13] For Pallavicini, the recoverable history of fencing extended back only to the late fifteenth century. It is also possible that he did not feel compelled to cite texts from the early seventeenth century to his own day because he genuinely felt a greater admiration for the 'good and ancient authors'; and at one point he even declares that he has found nothing worthwhile in those modern authors who sneer at old books merely because they *are* old books.

Pallavicini was also less interested in contemporary authors because he could acquire the techniques of their swordsmanship from his own practical experience. He was still participating in a living tradition. Nowadays, that option is no longer available to us. Despite rapidly expanding modern interest in the martial arts of medieval and renaissance Europe, and the sometimes heroic efforts of historically minded practitioners, no authentic schools survive where one might perfect combat technique under the guidance of teachers whose pedagogic pedigree extends back to a Liechtenauer, a Marozzo, or any other occidental past master. Students of oriental martial arts claim that there is at least one Japanese school which has maintained an unbroken tradition from the fifteenth century: though no one suggests that its combat system has remained wholly unchanged throughout its history.[14] But not even a pretence of continuity exists in the West. The martial activities with which this book is concerned were central to the life of Europe for several centuries, yet all that remains to us is a tiny proportion of the weapons which once existed and a selection of treatises. We know many more texts than were available to Pallavicini: but those he mentions are still important for anyone seeking to reconstruct the technique and philosophy of renaissance swordsmanship.

The task of reconstruction is inherently difficult and is made even more so by some firmly entrenched but erroneous orthodoxies of which perhaps the most misleading is the assertion that systematic swordsmanship only started to develop during the Renaissance and had been wholly unknown to the medieval masters. This unwarranted assumption made by nineteenth-century historians of fencing might have expired were it not for the artificial respiration applied by more recent scholars who have argued that the sword was not a normal part of civilian dress until the late fifteenth century and that, as a result, lighter and more nimble blades were produced which, in turn, led to the art of fencing.[15] This terrain is tempting but treacherous. In the first place, there has never been a single style of fencing, but always a multiplicity. Second, the history of civilian sword-carrying in medieval Europe is something which can only be inferred from piecemeal pictorial evidence which may be countered by citing other sources. There is a good deal of scattered documentation suggesting that many civilians, including clerics, carried bladed weapons – especially the sword with buckler – long before the hypothetical change of fashion; and the fact that prohibitions against carrying swords were commonplace from the thirteenth century onwards also suggests that many men were going about armed in this way.[16] Similarly, early masters not only maintained schools of swordsmanship which attracted a large clientele but they were also employed repeatedly as trainers for champions fighting in duels and it is unlikely that anybody would have sought their advice unless they had some special skill to offer and were deemed capable of imparting it. But far more decisive than such inferences is an easily verifiable fact. A large number of manuals survive from the period when sword fighting is said to have been unscientific; and it is obvious from these that many early masters had a profound knowledge of the principles of personal combat and had evolved sophisticated methods for translating them into practice. It is true that their techniques were often very brutal and were mainly intended to kill or maim an opponent: but in this they did not differ significantly from their renaissance successors; and their systems were no less rationally conceived.

THE MASTERS AND THEIR SWORDS

The terminology of the sword is a labyrinth of confusion, despite various scholarly attempts at establishing some acceptable typology to facilitate academic discourse.[17] The problem arises principally from the fact that medieval and renaissance masters were completely indifferent to the needs of modern scholars. They rarely defined their terms and, when they did, were even more rarely explicit.

Monte, who is a mine of information on arms and armour in general, confines himself to only a few words about the 'hilts or crosses of the sword' (*De hielzis aut crucibus*) – by which he means the quillons. He thinks that these ought to be long in order to protect virtually the whole arm, it being understood 'that a man should have the skill to keep sword and arm in a straight line'. Since they cannot be broken other than by accident, these quillons should not be so huge and heavy that they weigh down the sword. Monte does, however, advise that they should be thickened gradually towards the tang hole (*preter cassiam vel apperturam per quam spica ensis ingreditur*) because there is no risk of their breaking in any other place.[18] When, some forty years later, the Bolognese master Viggiani commented briefly on the history and construction of the sword, he similarly neglected to say anything about its dimensions; but he stressed that – although there have been those who favoured swords sharpened on only one side of the blade – modern usage has rediscovered (*ritrovato*) that attacks are much more effective when both sides have a cutting edge from hilt to point. Anxious to establish the antiquity of this type of blade, he adduces Psalm 149 where David says that 'the greatness of God is in their mouth and the two-edged sword in their hand, to take vengeance on the heathens'. Indeed, Viggiani deems this so important that he has even consulted a Hebrew friend in Mantua to verify that 'in the Hebrew tongue it is written just as I have said'. Whether or not the sword should have a *costa* – that is a fuller or groove running along the blade – concerns him less, and he dismisses the matter summarily (and erroneously) as a recent and inessential invention. But another question raised by Viggiani's interlocutor does engage his attention. Did the ancients use hilts and grips similar to those of his own day? 'Certainly they used them,' he replies, 'except that there has been added all that garnishment which you see from the pommel to the quillons and which makes a wonderful defence for the hand.' Happily, it seems, 'one always finds some improvement by the moderns'.[19]

Ghisliero, whose geometrical obsessions naturally encouraged speculation on sword length, says that it should be proportionate to a man's stature and recommends a blade of two arms' length which, together with the man's outstretched arm, gives an overall reach of three arms' length.[20] His opinion is clarified in an illustration where the pommel of the

79. Ghisliero's swordsman with the length of sword depised by George Silver. 1587, p. 18.

upright sword is shown almost level with the swordsman's armpit – the length later recommended by Capoferro and condemned by Thibault (fig. 79). George Silver would certainly have disapproved of Ghisliero's recommendation. The xenophobic English master despised the inordinate length of blade favoured by the Italianate fencers of Elizabethan England, considering them to be almost six inches beyond the best length, which he regarded as 'a yard and an inch for meane statures, and for men of tall statures, a yard and three or foure inches, and no more'. Two short chapters of his *Paradoxes of Defence* are devoted to the 'length of weapons, and how everie man may fit himself in the perfect length of his weapon, according to his own stature'. Here Silver advises the swordsman to stand with left foot forward and left hand (that is 'the dagger arme') extended straight out in front of him. The right arm, holding the sword, is then to be drawn as far back as 'conveniently you can, not opening the elbow joynt of your sword arme'. In this position, what you can draw within the length of your dagger, 'is the just length of your sword, to be made according to your owne stature'.[21] The practical advantages of the 'short sword', as opposed to the rapier, were especially evident when 'men are clustering and hurling together' in a real battle. A short, sharp, light sword, says Silver, is easy to carry and to draw; it is 'nimble' for both cutting and thrusting; its 'single hilt' affords excellent protection for the hand against the blows of other swords and even against staff weapons; and, because of its comparative shortness, it is possible to use it in the press of battle to deliver violent downward thrusts at the enemies' faces and bodies. 'One valiant man with a Sword in his hand', he asserts, 'will doe better service, then ten Italians, or Italienated with the Rapiers.'[22]

Another enduring problem is raised by Silver when he comments on the 'perfect length of your two hand sword'. The blade of such a weapon, he says, 'is to be the length of the blade of your single sword'.[23] In other words, for Silver, the difference between two-hander and single-hander lies solely in the length of the handle which, in turn, means that his 'two hand sword' is what is now known as the hand-and-a-half or bastard sword – not one of those immense, cumbrous monstrosities which fill the modern viewer with both awe and some doubt as to their efficacy. The masters, as usual, only illuminate this subject sporadically. The late fifteenth-century swordsman Filippo Vadi has a few observations on the *justa misura* of such a weapon – the pommel of which, he says, should reach to just below the armpit although, in an accompanying illustration showing a man standing with his sword reversed (that is with the pommel at his feet), the point of the blade comes up to his chin. According to Vadi, the size of the pommel should be such that it may be held in the fist; the grip or handle should be equal to the full span of the swordsman's hand; and the *elza* (by which he means the quillons) should be as long as the handle and pommel combined. He also recommends that the *elza* should be strong and square in section, as appears in his illustration; and that the sword's blade (*la ferruzza*) should be wide and tapered to a point, suitable for both striking and cutting.[24] In the illustration to Camillo Agrippa's tiny chapter on the *spadone*, the overall length of the weapon is only slightly less than that of the man posing with it; and the seventeenth-century Spanish manuscript, 'El discípulo instruido', stipulates that the two-hand sword should be 'the same length as the height of a man of good stature'.[25]

Recently, a distinction has been made between two-hand swords, long bastard swords, and bastard or hand-and-a-half swords which helps to clarify not only the weapons themselves but, by implication, also the manner of using them.[26] All were designed to be used with both hands, but were of markedly different length and weight. Unfortunately, few early writers systematically differentiated between them, and Fiore de'Liberi even reversed what one might now expect. Fiore uses the word *spada* to indicate both the two-hand sword (shown as a weapon almost as tall as the man who wields it) and the single-hander, but illustrates the *spadone* as a bastard sword. There is, however, a hint of clarity in *La noble science des joueurs despée* (1538) which is a translation, with some omissions, of the combat manual of Andre Pauernfeindt (1516). Paurnfeindt's first chapter deals with how a man may use various types of *langen schwerdt* which are 'employed with both hands'; and later he has a section devoted to the *Kurczen Swert* which, as is clear from his text, is certainly not a 'short sword' but is still used with both hands. The French version distinguishes here between 'lespée à deux mains' and 'la courte espée à deux mains', which is at least an improvement.[27] Later in the sixteenth century, Giovanni Antonio Lovino also sharply distinguishes *una spada di una mano et meza* (which is shown as having a blade scarcely longer than that of his single sword) from *una spada da due mani* which has a markedly longer blade, ricasso (the unsharpened part of the blade just below the hilt) and lugs.[28] Lovino's weapons are, it must be said, all rather dainty. The true two-hand sword may have a blade of four feet or more, and a grip of well over one foot; can weigh about six pounds; and is precisely what its name implies – a weapon designed principally for huge, swinging, two-handed, cutting strokes although it could be shortened and used for thrusting like a spear, by moving one hand to the ricasso.[29]

With regard to the single sword, by far the most elaborate discussion of its dimensions and parts is provided by Girard Thibault who, like Silver, warns against extravagantly long blades.[30] The sword, he says, must be proportionate to all the movements of the body – something so fundamental that he finds it extraordinary how, among those who have made a lifelong profession of arms and who have published writings on the subject throughout the world, so little attention has been paid to the matter. The sword on its own can do everything both for attack and defence, whence 'it necessarily follows that if the size and reach (*la mesure et la portée*) are unknown, all operations become uncertain and hazardous'. Thibault scorns certain unnamed authorities who smack of cowardice, since they are pleased to recommend weapons of extreme length and prefer to remain always at a distance rather than to demonstrate true science.

> And such is the opinion of those who wish the blades to be equal to two full arms' length so that, the point being placed on the ground beside the man, the pommel of the hilt comes up to his armpit, which is rather the length of a two-hand sword (*espadon*) than a sword. Besides this, it would necessarily be as unseemly and inconvenient for carrying at one's side and drawing from the scabbard, as dangerous and scarcely manageable in use.

It is unlikely that even well-informed readers would have remembered Ghisliero: but any fencing *aficionado* would have known that the illustrious Capoferro had recommended the use of a sword which was two arms' length reaching, as he said, 'from the sole of my foot to the armpit'.[31] For Thibault, the practical problem is that, since there are occasions when one is served best by a longer sword and others by a shorter, some sort of compromise is required; and the key, as always in his work, lies in the relationship between the human body and the imaginary circle which may be drawn with the navel as its centre. The length of the blade from point to quillon block should, therefore, be equal to the half-diameter of that circle: 'that is to say that the point being placed on the ground between his two feet, the quillons of the guard come precisely up to his navel'. The other half diameter would extend from the navel to the fingertips of the arm held vertical above the head. (See Chapter II, figs 66 and 67). Thibault then elaborates the several advantages of his recommended proportion in a series of accompanying figures – explaining, for example, that it does not cause a nuisance when one is in conversation with people, in a crowd, or walking through narrow passages 'where one is usually embarrassed by the arms one carries'; and stressing the even more important point that this length of sword is ideal for drawing from its sheath. He also considers the proportions of the guard, grip and pommel of the sword, along with suggestions for the best kind of girdle and hanger for the scabbard – assuring his readers that he introduces no changes without good reasons.[32] The quillons should be equal in length to the sole of the foot and should not be too extravagant. For recent developments regarding the guard, Thibault has some harsh words. Every day, he complains, there are new inventions without any rational foundation, as though the guard 'is only to serve as a simple ornament for one's person rather than as something to be used in time of necessity'.

> Some make the branches twisted upwards or downwards, or curved; the pommels big, round, and flattened at the top; others fashion the hilt like baskets around the grip; all to make I know not what show of courage, or rather of cowardice, according to the Spanish proverb which says *Cargado de hierro, cargado de miedo* [weighed down with iron, weighed down with fear]. The form which we give it is simple and honest, even in civil conversation, yet remains sufficient for defence.

The quillons must be of the correct size otherwise they will fail in their principal purpose which is to surprise, strike and force the opposing blade to make big movements and great circles about the guard. Thibault likens their function to the ramparts of a fortified town which are designed not merely to hinder assaults by the 'interposition of their corpulence', but much more for 'offensive defences' which can repel the enemy and hurl them to the ground. Similarly the guard, 'which is the rampart of the person', relies on the quillons to 'countermine' the adversary as well as being a simple defence in the form of a shield which can cover the body.

Thibault is never economical with words or illustrations. But he has many virtues. He is both colourful and informative; he understands what is required of a master teaching through the medium of a printed book; and his system (however convoluted it may appear) is both logical and lucid.

WHAT WAS A RAPIER?

Logic and lucidity have not always distinguished subsequent discussions of the sword. The central issue for nineteenth-century historians and their followers was the development of the rapier – a notion which they used to denigrate the medieval masters and, indeed, most swordsmanship prior to the seventeenth century. Nowadays the word rapier conjures up visions of a long, thin-bladed, sharp-pointed weapon capable of being wielded with virtuosic speed and dexterity to delude and, ultimately, to run through an opponent. But were rapiers ever like that? Were they ever one kind of sword at all? For, as was recently discovered by those who sought to legislate against knife-carrying, it is hard to define something which comes in many shapes and sizes. Modern scholars often disagree about the nomenclature of bladed weapons even when dealing with their own tongue; the polyglot nature of fencing literature further complicates matters; and, for anyone interested in how people used swords for fighting, curatorial concerns (more with hilts than with blades) are of limited value.[33] It is self-evident that, in order to understand sword play, one must understand the types of sword used. But this is not wholly unproblematic even with regard to weapons which have strongly marked characteristics such as the two-hand sword, bastard sword, Düsack, falchion, and scimitar all of which, though traditionally considered to be cutting weapons, were also used for thrusting. The ambiguities of the rapier are, however, in a class of their own. As A.V.B. Norman puts it, with masterly understatement: 'the evidence for what was meant by the word rapier at a particular period is very confused'.[34] This would matter little had historians of fencing not tended to equate scientific swordsmanship with the Renaissance, and renaissance swordsmanship with the rapier; and had they not glossed over the fact that, for most of the period with which we are concerned, cutting was as important as thrusting.

There never was any general agreement as to what a rapier might be. It was only in England and Germany, around the middle decades of the sixteenth century, that *rapier* came to be used to denote a long sword which, though designed both for cutting and thrusting, placed emphasis on the use of the point rather than the edge: and in neither country has it been possible to establish a convincing etymology.[35] As far as I am aware, no German master described such a weapon or even used the word until 1542 when Paulus Hector Mair – illustrating fighting with a comparatively light thrusting sword – referred to it as both *rapir* and as the *ensis hispanicus*,[36] while, just a few years earlier, in a Franco-English glossary, *la rapière* had been defined as 'the spannysshe sworde'.[37] Yet the word was uncommon in France and unknown in Spain.

Nor was it used in Italy: which posed a problem neatly encapsulated in 'An Advertisement to the curteous reader' prefixed to the *True Arte of Defence* (1594), an English

99

translation of di Grassi's treatise which had originally appeared more than twenty years earlier. The difficulty is diagnosed thus: 'in some places of the book by reason of the aequi-vocation of certaine Italian wordes, the weapons may doubtfully be construed in English'. Despite the fact, continues the writer, that the word 'Sworde' is generally used by the Italian author, it would have been better translated as 'Rapier' which is 'a weapon more usuall for Gentlemens wearing, and fittest for causes of offence and defence'; furthermore, in Italy, 'where Rapier and Dagger is commonly worne and used, the Sworde (if it be not an arming Sworde) is not spoken of'. This is the crux of the matter. Like all his compatriots, di Grassi never referred to the rapier but consistently used the word *spada* which could only be ren-dered literally as 'sword' even if, in the Elizabethan commentator's view, it really meant 'rapier'. The same holds true for the French and Spanish masters who never used the terms *espée rapière* or *espada ropera*, although these do occasionally occur in early inventories.[38] Italian, French and Spanish authors had several words indicating different types of sword: but *rapier* was not one of them.

One of the rare occurrences of the word *rapière* in renaissance France occurs in an account of the combat between Bayard and Azevedo in Brantôme's *Discours sur les duels*. Brantôme writes that the protagonists wore protection for the head and were armed with two keen-edged rapiers – 'deux rapières bien tranchantes' – adding that he is using these old con-temporary terms 'in order to follow the text and better to honour antiquity'. This passage is curious indeed. Brantôme clearly believes the rapiers to have been cutting swords, hence his remark on their keen edge; but in the contemporary sources, upon which his account is based, the swords were referred to as *estocs* and the word *rapière* does not appear at all.[39] In Spain, the lack of a specific word to define civilian thrusting swords is highlighted by a series of proclamations concerning public peace, issued at Valencia in the decades around the turn of the sixteenth and seventeenth centuries.[40] These documents repeatedly prohib-ited the making, garnishing, carrying, or even storing at home, of 'long and narrow swords which might more properly be called spears' (*espases llargues y estretes que més propriamente se dir asts*) and which have been the cause of many disorders and murders. Specifically con-demned are all long, narrow swords with a quadrate section (*la punta quadrada*) instead of the customary flat blade; and it appears that swords were only acceptable if their blades were broad (*amples*) and did not exceed the length of four palms and seven fingers (*més de quatre pams y set dits de fulla*). This I take to be about forty-three inches and slightly longer than the 'yard and a half-quarter' limit stipulated in Tudor proclamations.[41] Associated with such swords were various kinds of knives and daggers (*terciados, ganivets, punyals de Chelva*), and poniards 'with point of grain of barley, or with point of diamond' (*grano de ordio, o cevada, a de punta de diamante*) – that is with a point long, thin and needle-sharp, or else diamond in section.[42] All these unusually acute weapons were regarded as new inventions designed solely for the injury and slaying of one's neighbours, and it is significant that they are condemned as being useless for war (*inutiles para la guerra*). Apart from the local dagger, the *punyal de Chelva*, the only weapon given a specific name was the *estoque* which is famil-iar enough to students of arms, but occurs only twice in the Valencia documents to indi-cate one of a number of long, sharp, narrow-bladed thrusting swords which English contemporaries would doubtless have called tucks (and perhaps even rapiers or 'spannysshe swordes') but which had no distinctive appellation in Spain.[43]

The full extent of the confusion surrounding the rapier may be gauged by glancing at some contemporary dictionaries. The Italian-English lexicon, *Queen Anna's New World of Words* (1611), was compiled by John Florio who was not merely an expert linguist but also a friend of the Elizabethan fencing master, Vincentio Saviolo. It is even likely that he worked with Saviolo, rendering that master's treatise into English; and we might, on that account, expect him to know how to distinguish one blade from another.[44] Certainly the word 'rapier' is used throughout *Vincentio Saviolo his Practise*. Nevertheless, in his massive dictionary, Florio is regrettably imprecise. He defines *Verdugo* as 'a Rapier, a Tucke, a little Sword', although contemporary English soldiers and modern commentators alike have differentiated sharply between *rapier* and *tuck*, and nobody has ever thought of either as a 'little Sword'. He scarcely does better with *Stocco* which he interprets as 'a short or arming-sword, a tuck'; *Spada* which is 'a Sword, a rapier, a glaive, a blade'; and *Spadetta* and *Spadina* which are both defined as 'a little sword or rapier'.

In the same year as Florio's dictionary appeared, Randle Cotgrave published his *Dictionarie of the French and English Tongues*. It is based largely upon Jean Nicot's *Thrésor de la langue françoyse*: but Cotgrave's definitions often have immense dash and, like Florio, he is one of the most famous names in bilingual lexicography. However, when it came to swords, he did even worse than his Italian contemporary. In view of the vagueness of the word *espée*, it was not unreasonable to define it as 'A Swoorde, Rapier, Tucke, a Glaive, Cuttelasse, Faucheon, Hanger, Blade'.[45] But elsewhere Cotgrave's ambiguities and eccentricities are less excusable. *Espée espagnole* he gives as 'A Rapier or Tucke'; *Estoc* as 'a Rapier, or tucke'; and *Verdun* as 'the little Rapier, called a Tucke'; and, although he includes *Rapière*, he inexplicably translates it as 'an old rustie rapier'. His main source, Nicot's *Thrésor*, had appeared five years earlier and had defined French words in Latin augmented by other languages. Nicot was better informed than Cotgrave though he, too, was evidently puzzled by *une rapière*. That he lists the word at all shows that he must have come across it somewhere, but he provides no Latin equivalent because he could think of none. On the other hand, he has more to say about *Estoc*, defining it as 'une espée longue, estroicte, et roide de poincte' with which combatants give more thrusts than 'de maindroicts ou de revers ou fendants' which are all cutting blows. He also comments on the *Estoc d'armes*, recognizing it as a cavalry sword, and observing that neither Spaniards nor Italians use the qualification *d'armes* but simply refer to *estoque* or *stocco*. His discussion under *Espée* is very full, distinguishing between the *ensis* and *spatha* (from which derive the Spanish *espada* and Italian *spada*) and the *romphea* which, he says, is a long sword called *verdun* in some parts of France, and *estoc* in others.[46] He explains that these latter swords are designed specifically for thrusting rather than cutting and are used in war because, 'as Vegetius says, the thrust is more deadly than the edge stroke' – a classical dictum which has had considerable repercussions in the historiography of fencing.[47]

In view of the general confusion of documentary sources, it is useful, when interpreting treatises by the masters of the late Middle Ages and Renaissance, to augment information based on surviving swords and inventories with the evidence which abounds in the illustrations to combat manuals. Usually these illustrations were supervised, or at least approved, by the masters concerned. In many cases they are by artists of a competence sufficient to justify our confidence; and even when, as in Sainct Didier, the woodcuts are crude (or, as in the Elizabethan and Jacobean English texts, dreadful) weapons are still shown realistically rather than schematically. In the German manuscript treatises, the *langen Schwert* is the principal bladed weapon. Wielded generally with two hands, it is, in fact, the hand-and-a-half sword with a long handle, simple straight quillons and wide blade tapering to a very sharp point.

For one-handed fighting, the weapon favoured by Talhoffer and his colleagues was the

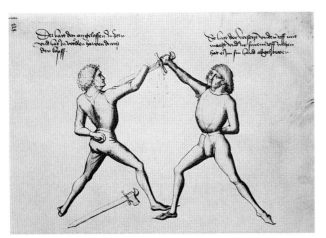

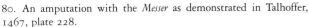

80. An amputation with the *Messer* as demonstrated in Talhoffer, 1467, plate 228.

81. Lucini does better. A double amputation with the two-hand sword. 1627, plate 8.

Messer – a heavy, short and very sharp sword capable of completely severing a hand (fig. 80). In many illustrations, it is shown with a broad blade similar in shape to a falchion, but sometimes the blade just tapers to a point. It has a simple crossguard but, in Talhoffer, this is provided with a lug (a short flat metal tongue) protruding horizontally from the joint between quillons and grip. The blades of the single-hand sword shown in Marozzo's *Opera nova* are all fairly wide at the hilt and generally provided with a side ring and finger ring, while the edges, although not completely parallel, are more or less straight until they suddenly taper to a point. Agrippa's hilts are fitted with finger rings only, and the blades taper continuously from hilt to point; di Grassi's sword is similar though rather wider towards the grip, as is Viggiani's although, in his illustrations, the hilt is somewhat more developed. In Sainct Didier, the swords are wide at the hilt and taper continuously to a point, and their hilts have straight quillons and a simple knuckleguard. At least two different types of *rappier* are depicted in Joachim Meyer's treatise, but both are fitted with long, straight quillons, knuckleguard and side rings, and both are moderately broad-bladed and as suitable for cutting as for thrusting.[48] It is only with Ghisliero that the emphasis changes and blades become narrower, longer and more obviously designed for thrusting alone – a tendency further developed in Capoferro, Giganti and Fabris. With these last three masters, we have already entered the seventeenth century; but there was still no uniformity. For example, in Capitelli's version of Capoferro in 1633 the swords are appreciably wider; Heussler's *rappier* of 1630 is broad bladed; and even as a late as 1686 Marcelli's *spada* has every appearance of being suitable for both cut and thrust.

EDGE AND POINT – CUT AND THRUST

The superiority of point over edge was an article of faith with the major nineteenth-century fencing historians whose views have shaped or, it would be better to say, distorted the attitude of subsequent scholars. Both Egerton Castle and his most hostile critic, Jacopo Gelli, were agreed that the turning point in the art of fencing came with Camillo Agrippa – the man who, they believed, first realized that too little use was made of the point 'notwithstanding the fact that less exertion and less time is requisite for the thrust, which is also more difficult to parry'.[49] Castle argued that most weapons initially suggest a 'round' hit; and, he added:

> Even in mere pugilism an untutored man will strike in that way, and uses his fist as a club. A straight hit along the shortest way, and with the body's weight in its direct prolongation, is the result of both theory and practice. The cut is the more natural, that is, the easiest action; the thrust is the result of a complicated and carefully regulated combination of movements. This fact alone shows why the thrust belongs to a more advanced stage of the art.

This passage is based on a misapprehension natural enough in an author writing prior to the publications of Schaer and Novati on medieval combat, to Hergsell's editions of Talhoffer, and to the critical comments of Wassmansdorff. Even if it were true that the thrust must belong to a more 'advanced stage of the art', Castle was unaware that the medieval masters recognized many occasions when the point was more advantageous than the edge; that they taught how to use it; and that they had distinguished between several different types of thrust long before these were analysed in printed treatises of the late sixteenth century.[50] In any case, why is it that, 'even in mere pugilism', a short hook or well-delivered uppercut can be potent? Why do the Queensberry rules forbid blows delivered with the inside or butt of the hand, along with pivot blows and rabbit punches? None of these is a straight hit, yet all are potentially so dangerous that they are regarded as fouls. And why, in the more serious business of unarmed combat in time of war, are chopping blows (delivered with the edge of the hand) recognized as a better option for most situations than a straight punch?

Obviously, a thrust with a bladed weapon (or indeed with a stick) can be devastating.[51] But Castle's notion that it is *inevitably* superior to the cut was based upon several further misconceptions which, while perfectly understandable, have unduly constricted our general perception of the history of swordsmanship. The first of these was an uncritical confidence in the style of swordsmanship which had developed in western Europe with the advent of the small-sword in the latter half of the seventeenth century. This system was deemed to have reached perfection two hundred years later in Castle's own time so that it was natural to look at the history of fencing solely to discover how the style had evolved. Yet Castle himself recognized the irony of the fact that this perfection had been attained only when the sword was no longer of practical value in civil society; while, as a distinguished fencer and student of swords, he was aware that many of the weapons in general use up to the mid-seventeenth century were heavy and unsuited to quick wrist or finger movement. This was especially true of the *rapier* which was often uncomfortably long and ponderous. Castle further acknowledged that the contemporary sport of fencing which he so admired was wholly artificial, but he still wrote of early swordsmanship as though the combatants would have been competing on level ground and according to generally accepted conventions.[52] In fact, the fighting taught by masters of arms was primarily a matter of how best to survive sudden affrays in environments unhelpful to fancy footwork.

Furthermore, the post-renaissance western tradition of small-sword fencing was not, and is not, the only way to fight with a bladed weapon. There are other traditions which work differently and at least as effectively. The hypothetical outcome of a fight between a renaissance rapier fencer and a Japanese Samurai has long fascinated martial artists and was perhaps first considered by Captain Brinkley who, having concluded that 'a Japanese swordsman could not protect himself successfully against a skilfully wielded rapier', promptly confused the issue by adding that, for anyone using a rapier, 'it would be very difficult to check the onset of a Japanese swordsman' who would 'probably accomplish his cut, in spite of his adversary's parry or point'.[53] He might have added that the speed with which the Bushi drew their swords (the art of Iaijutsu) and delivered a cut would probably have been decisive since rapiers with blades of anything up to four feet in length were not easy to get into action.[54]

The early masters sometimes posed other, and potentially more interesting, hypothetical questions concerning combat between disparate weapons. George Silver, pondering the comparative merits of the English sword and Italian rapier, not only theorized upon the subject but attempted to prove his case by citing the occasion when the sword and dagger of the Englishman Cheese prevailed over the rapier and dagger of the Italian master Jeronimo. Diametrically opposed to Silver was his younger English contemporary Joseph Swetnam who also had no doubts about the issue. He considers that discussing the short sword and dagger is 'time ill spent' because it is very inferior to the rapier. 'In a word', he concludes, 'a short sword and dagger to encounter against a skilfull man with a rapier and dagger is little better then a tobacco pipe, or a foxe tayle.' The short sword, he allows, is effective against another short sword or against a man 'unweaponed', and is even good in the wars both on horse and on foot,

> yet a Rapier will doe as good service in the wars as a short sword, if a skilfull man have him in hand: we have divers examples of those which come out of the field sore wounded, and they will say it was because the enemy had a handfull or a foot ods in length of weapon upon them: wherefor I say one inch is great ods and enough to kill a man, if they both have skill alike, and doe observe a true distance.

Common sense cautions us against the enthusiasms of a man like Swetnam who declares that the 'reasonable length' of his rapier blade should be 'foure foote at the least'! He also suggests that it be accompanied by a dagger two foot long and hard rather than soft because 'I have often knowen a soft dagger cut in twaine with a Rapier'.[55] Here, *en passant*, it is worth remarking that, unless it had a keen cutting edge, no rapier would have been able to hack through any dagger, hard or soft (fig. 82).

Another question – concerning the possible outcome of a combat between rapier and two-hand sword – intrigued Thibault who argued that the single sword, on its own, would prevail against *l'espée a deux-mains*: although, as he reminded his readers, it is important not to meet the huge blows of this powerful weapon with a straightforward parry.[56] Any swordsman attempting that foolhardy move would find 'in his hands, a dagger in lieu of a sword' (figs 83–4). Thibault's discussion, as is clear from the accompanying illustrations, was concerned literally with the two-hand sword – a weapon whose blade alone, according to the author, would reach from the ground to a man's armpit – but it would have been more interesting had he considered another hypothetical confrontation.

What would Thibault's swordsman have made of Liechtenauer's *'langen Schwert'*? This hand-and-a-half sword, generally some two to three pounds lighter than the two-hander was in some ways comparable to the Japanese *katana*.[57] It could be wielded effectively with only one hand but was designed principally for use with two – either both on the grip, or with one on the grip and the other holding the blade. The *halb-Schwert* method was as effective for short jabs of great velocity as for warding blows in the manner of quarter staff play and it facilitated rapid change of direction, and considerable dexterity. The long sword of

82. Lucini's two-hand sword with a remarkable cutting-edge. 1627, plate 24.

83. Thibault shows the inefficacy of the two-hand sword against the rapier. 1630, book II, tabula 11.

84. Detail of fig. 83.

85. Giganti, the great rapier master, poses with a bastard sword. 1606, frontispiece.

the German masters was a cut-and-thrust weapon of deadly efficacy and, had he taken this into account, Thibault might have been less certain about the triumph of his single-hander.[58] Finally, within this context of the efficacy of different kinds of sword, there is one especially curious point worth noting. For Egerton Castle and Gelli alike, Nicoletto Giganti was one of the great heroes of rapier fencing. Yet, in the frontispiece to his famous *Scola*, which deals exclusively with the rapier, Giganti is shown proudly posing with a bastard sword (fig. 85). I do not know why he chose to be so commemorated. But it cannot be because he despised the weapon.

Another weakness of nineteenth-century fencing historiography is its underlying assumption that swordsmanship somehow evolved throughout the Middle Ages and Renaissance – that it advanced on a regular, direct path from primitive concentration on cutting with the edge to thrusting with the point, via an experimental combination of both modes. This, too, is false. George Silver's grumbles about the rapier are well known, but still worth remarking. He had no patience with the fashionable fencers of his own day who forbade the thrust 'at the single Sword, Sword and Dagger, and Sword and Buckler' and similarly forbade the cut at the 'single Rapier, and Rapier and Dagger'. To Silver this made no sense. Either the combination of both cut and thrust is best, or one or the other on its own. 'But knowing by the Art of Armes, that no fight is perfect without both blow and thrust, why do we not use and teach both blow and thrust?'[59] The trouble with Silver is not that he admired an old-fashioned fighting system, but rather that his xenophobia has to a large extent masked the fact that the weapons used by many of the seventeenth-century masters were still designed both for thrusting and cutting. Castle knew this perfectly well but was irresistibly attracted by the glaring contrast which Silver drew between cutters and thrusters at the end of the sixteenth century.[60]

In fact, the debate over edge and point began long before Silver's day and continued long after it. The *locus classicus* (in all senses of the term) is the brief summary of Roman military training in Vegetius's *De re militari* – although it is a dubious text and would not be much esteemed were ancient sources on swordsmanship less exiguous.[61] As Vegetius himself admits, he is writing about unspecified 'ancients' on the basis of unspecified 'books', and he explains that their method of training recruits in sword fighting was to make them exercise at the *palum*, a stout wooden post planted in the ground by each man. Armed with a heavy wooden sword and basketwork shield, the recruit then attacked every part of his post as though aiming at an opponent's head, face, sides and legs; and the exercise included cutting to the back of the lower part of the post in order to facilitate severing a real opponent's hamstrings (a stroke later to be celebrated as the *Coup de Jarnac*). In short, the recruits were expected to apply 'every kind of attack and every art of combat'.[62] (See Chapter X, fig. 189.) This suggests that there was a recognized system involved, and Vegetius specifically associates the *palum* with both 'the arena and the field of battle' – that is with professional gladiators fighting in single combat and with soldiers fighting as a group. This account of the *palum* is immediately followed by what has become the most famous dictum in the history of swordsmanship. The Roman recruits, Vegetius continues, were taught to strike with the point, not the edge; for the Romans easily defeated opponents who relied on edge strokes and, indeed, mocked them because a cut, whatever its force, is seldom fatal since it has to cleave through armour and bone whereas a stab, even if it penetrates only two inches, is deadly. Furthermore, delivering a cut exposes the right arm and side, whereas, in thrusting, the body remains covered and 'that is why, it is agreed, the Romans used chiefly this method of fighting'. This assertion of the superiority of point over edge has become canonical, but Vegetius does not say (and his commentators have never asked) why, in that case, the Roman soldiers devoted so much time to practising cuts at the wooden post, an exercise without which no man ever became 'invincible in armed combat'.

The most revealing account of a battle in which the Roman forces actually deployed the skills acquired by such exercises is in the *Roman Antiquities* of Dionysius of Halicarnassus who describes the campaign against the Gauls in 367 BC. The Roman dictator Camillus encouraged his troops by stressing their superior physical condition and discipline; and, in the event, his confidence was justified. The Gauls, 'quite lacking in military science', fought erratically, either smiting mightily from aloft or throwing 'crosswise blows aimed at no target'. The highly disciplined Roman troops, on the other hand, dodged and ducked under these vain assaults 'which were aimed too high', and

> holding their swords straight out, they would strike their opponents in the groin, pierce their sides, and drive their blows through their breasts into their vitals. And if they saw any of them keeping these parts of the body protected, they would cut the tendons of their knees or ankles and topple them to the ground roaring and biting their shields and uttering cries resembling the howling of wild beasts.[63]

In other words, the Roman soldiers at this period used both point and edge – including the hamstringing learnt at the *palum* – which is what one would expect of experienced, practical fighters on the battlefield, just as it would be expected of professional gladiators fighting to the death in the arena. Yet, despite much historical ingenuity, we still know little about the swordsmanship of the ancients because none of their masters of arms bothered to write about it.

By contrast, the medieval German masters were compulsive compilers of combat manuals, and their works show how keenly they appreciated the use of both edge and point. Their manuscripts constantly illustrate encounters where the fighters thrust at each other – as much with the two-handed sword and polaxe as with shorter bladed weapons. The sword and buckler fighting depicted in MS I.33 shows both types of attack used in roughly equal measure. More particularly with regard to the long sword, we are told by Liechtenauer's pupil Hanko Döbringer in 1389 that the art had been 'perfected and completed' by his master, and that it goes 'simply and directly along the shortest path to the nearest target; so that when one cuts or thrusts at another, it is as if someone ties a string or line to the point or edge of his sword, leading or pulling his point or edge to that opening at which he should cut or thrust, along the closest, shortest and most decisive way possible.' A little later Döbringer describes the nature of the sword in a thoroughly holistic manner. 'No part of the sword', he exclaims, 'was invented in vain', and a fighter should use 'the point, both edges, hilts, pommel and all other parts of the sword, according to the particular rules that apply to each in the art of fighting'.[64] Two centuries later, Lovino, despite the daintier weapon with which he is dealing, shared this view and, in addition to a wide variety of balletic postures, happily advocated smashing in an opponent's teeth with his own hilt or the pommel of one's sword.[65]

Most sixteenth-century masters taught both cut and thrust. Monte's whole system was built on combination attacks where cuts opened the way for the decisive use of the point; Agrippa regarded the cut as a necessary preliminary to the thrust; and, as we have seen, having two sharp edges to the blade was considered to be such a necessity by Viggiani that he had recourse to the Scriptures and Hebraic scholarship to establish its ancient pedigree. It is, none the less, true that by the closing decades of the century, despite the amount of space still devoted to edge strokes, the general opinion – especially in Italy – was that stated by Ghisliero in 1587. Summarizing the characteristics of both forms of attack, Ghisliero admitted that the cut had certain advantages: it came more naturally to a swordsman than the point because human movements are circular; it threatened a greater portion of an opponent's body; by being more obvious it induced fear; and it could strike at whichever area one wished. On the other hand, it had several imperfections. It exposed the right side of the body and the right arm; it was likely not to prove mortal when encountering the resistance of bone and armour; it was likely to encounter wind/air resistance, due to the sword's flat section; and it was likely to cause the sword to break. By contrast, the point might be used while keeping the body covered; it would reach its objective faster than the cut; its movement was less; and, because the section of a thrusting sword was wedge-shaped, the point struck home more securely and more fatally.[66] Continental masters were increasingly coming to share this view. Yet the consensus should not blind us to two significant facts which render untenable the evolutionary theory of fencing as a simple development from cutting to thrusting: first, that Silver was by no means alone in condemning too great a reliance on the thrust; and secondly, even a century later, some important masters were still keeping an open mind on the subject.

In the reign of the French King Henri III (1574–89) the use of the cut was discussed by Giovanni Antonio Lovino, an Italian master resident in France. Lovino's unpublished *Ragionamento* on the science of arms includes a section in which, amongst much else, the master answers his interlocutor who has asked why some swordsmen condemn frequent use of the cut.[67] The master begins with the most fundamental consideration – the nature of the sword itself. The sword, he says, was not made by chance but 'with order and measure', and it has two edges and a point, all made to strike and to parry. Therefore, no man can consider himself perfect in the science of arms unless 'he knows how to cut well with every kind of edge stroke, as opportunity presents itself against his enemy'. The swordsman must practise all the cuts, long and short, complex and simple, so that he knows both how to execute them with 'just measure' and how to parry them when used against him. After mastering the use of the edge, he must then work through the corresponding varieties of thrust so that, in the end, he can avail himself of whatever is required. The science of arms resides precisely in such a mixture. All the means must be mastered and it is important to know when to use any particular technique: 'the fencer must keep his eyes well open to recognize the place, the time, and the truly advantageous method of attack', whether it be with edge or point. This is very much Silver's position: but what makes Lovino's view remarkable is that, in the beautifully executed illustrations which serve as the basis for his text, the swords are wholly untypical of their period. For the most part, sixteenth-century masters used cut-and-thrust blades; and later, when swords appear sufficiently narrow bladed to be regarded solely as a thrusting weapon (as in Giganti and Capoferro), they are still very long. But in Lovino's manuscript all the illustrations show a surprisingly short and narrow-bladed weapon which more closely resembles the eighteenth-century small sword than any of its sixteenth-century contemporaries.[68]

It is worth comparing Lovino's view of swordsmanship with the observations of later masters. Capoferro, for example, sees no merit whatever in the cut apart from its use in mounted fencing where he deems it superior to the thrust whereas Gaiani in 1619 considers that the virtual abandonment of cutting in contemporary swordsmanship has been a mixed blessing.[69] Thibault, too, while adopting the arguments in favour of the point already familiar to us, is undogmatic. It is true, he says, that the edge tends to inflict exterior wounds only, and that its use requires the fencer to make much greater movements which are more easily read by an opponent. It is equally true that the point travels more swiftly, pursues much the shorter route to its target, and does much greater damage by penetration to the vital parts. However, Thibault is judicious:

> Our scholar must not hold cuts with the edge in slight esteem, because there are occasions which render the one as necessary as the other. Also, if he does not know how to counter it correctly, the edge stroke used aptly in the right circumstances may throw him into disorder just as much as the thrust. For, by it, the adversary will gain the time to pursue his advantage.[70]

Thibault, contrary to yet another of Castle's authoritative errors, was not a crazy rhapsodist. He was a pragmatic teacher who fully understood the difference between theory and practice. And this is true of two other masters – one French, the other Italian – who, in 1670, independently discussed the whole matter of edge and point. Even at that late date, Philibert de la Touche and Morsicato Pallavicini came to conclusions very similar to those of Lovino and Thibault, and very different from those promoted by nineteenth-century fencing historians.

La Touche's *Vrais Principes* includes a chapter on the *estramaçon* which he defines as an action whereby one seeks to attack any exposed part of the enemy with the cutting edge of one's sword which is turned and drawn back in a circle. Like his sixteenth-century predecessors, he recommends drawing the cut to achieve maximum penetration – a far better technique, in his opinion, than the downright blows formerly used by the old gendarmerie but no longer practicable. They were good enough in earlier times when one had to break open a helmet or hack through metal armour but they are useless now when defensive armour consists of buff coats or garments more easily opened up by cutting – 'because the sword strikes home along almost the entire length of the blade'. La Touche recognizes that, in treating the cut, he is unusual among contemporary masters. Indeed, he laments that France has for a long time so badly neglected the art of cutting with the sword 'that few people have any knowledge of it'. Certainly no one now teaches it in the salles d'armes. Yet, intermixed with estocades (thrusts), it offers great advantages to the swordsman fighting on foot; while, for mounted combat, it is indispensable. In some circumstances, when it is impossible to use the point, one may still hit the opponent with a cut and 'assuredly, a man who can use the cut always has a big advantage against his adversary both for surprising and striking him, or for feints and parries'. For these reasons, says La Touche, he does not wish his treatise to lack matter of such importance.[71]

The erudite Morsicato Pallavicini hailed from Palermo where, he says, there had always been many schools of fencing; and he proudly invokes the name of his own master, a certain Matteo Galici, who was obviously of more than local fame. According to his own testimony, Pallavicini had himself travelled about a good deal to gain experience of Italian, Spanish and French fencing techniques, so that his views on the qualities and use of different swords were based upon wide practical experience. This, and the late date of his treatise, make it all the more significant that, with regard to the use of the sword edge, he should be so much in accord with Lovino and George Silver who wrote towards the end of the previous century. The good master, says Pallavicini, will first teach his student theory and then practice, and will begin by putting a sword into his hand and explaining thus:

> Fencing is a skilful science for defending one's own life. This is a sword suitable for attack, and composed of two edges and one point, or rather of two *cutting* edges and one point; wherefore Matteo Galici my Master used to say that a cutting sword has three mouths for attack and defence; but in the case of thrusting swords (*Verdughi, ò vero Stocchi*) they have nothing other than a single point, and in the middle it is like a stick. Thus it is better to carry an edged sword than these *Stocchi, ò vero Verdughi* for there is no better defence than attack.[72]

Questions concerning the relative merits of edge and point, and when and where they were used, have continued to intrigue historians. In Scandinavia during the Second World War, when one might think that there were more pressing matters to worry about, scholars engaged in a heated battle about whether Bronze Age swords had been intended for cutting or thrusting and, after many thousands of words and much acrimony, the consensus was that probably both techniques had been favoured by Bronze Age warriors rather than merely one or the other.[73] Historians of Classical swordsmanship, confronting similar questions, have rummaged through their limited sources and the usual piles of pots and poetry to furnish unconvincing answers. It is, of course, possible to hypothesize about fighting on the basis of the shape and quality of surviving weapons: but only a pedant would worry about the impropriety of thrusting with a blunt point or slashing with a blunt edge. Warriors know, either through instruction or from painful experience, that opportunities must be taken however they present themselves. This is not to deny that certain weapons have been designed for, and lend themselves to, one mode of handling rather than another; but most bladed weapons can be used in more than one way, as is obvious from Japanese swordsmanship which, although based on the *katana* (the cutting instrument *par excellence*), still recognizes the use of point as well as edge.

The notion that swordsmen, prior to renaissance theoreticians, were ignorant about the use of the point is simply a myth. What really distinguishes the sixteenth-century masters from most of their predecessors was less their use of the point than their fondness for the pen, their appetite for explication, and the existence of the printing press. Mass production proved decisive for it ensured that their analyses of movement were both public and self-conscious – factors which inevitably resulted in detailed theoretical statements concerning the relative merits of thrust and cut.

One more example must suffice. Di Grassi is certain that the thrust is preferable to the edge-blow 'as well because it striketh in lesse time, as also for that in the saide time, it doth more hurt'. This view he regards as incontrovertible because the Romans, 'who were victorious in all enterprises', taught their legions to thrust only 'Alleaging for their reason, that the blowes of the edge, though they were great, yet they are verie fewe that are deadly, and that thrustes, though litle and weake, when they enter but iij. fingers into the bodie, are wont to kill.'[74]

This axiom is, of course, straight out of Vegetius and had been cited dutifully in military writings throughout the Middle Ages.[75] What always went unnoticed is the fact that Vegetius does not say that Roman soldiers never used the edge; that his description of the *palum* makes it clear that cuts were an integral part of Roman swordsmanship; and that the short thrusting sword was used by the Romans to facilitate battle in close order rather than for fencing. Di Grassi explains that, because of the general superiority of the point, he intends to concentrate upon its use although, as a practical man of the sword, he is prepared to deal with edge strokes 'where it shalbe commodious to strike therewith'. Everything depends on time, 'the shortnes whereof is so to be esteemed above all other things in this Arte'. The thrust is quicker when the point is in a straight line because the blow is then performed 'in one time'. If, however, the point has got out of the straight line – either to the left, to the right, or 'aloft' – then it 'shalbe verie commodious rather to strik with the edg'. This is especially effective when an enemy is so occupied with beating your sword to one side that he will not expect it to strike again so quickly from the side to which it was beaten. With regard to point and edge, di Grassi has two important general words of advice: the point must always be given in such a way that the swordsman has no need to draw back his arm before thrusting which is a sure way to signal his intention and waste time; while edge blows should be drawn 'or slyded' because, without that drawing motion, however much force is used, 'they cause but small hurt'.[76] And the object of using the slide was to do as much damage as possible.

ATTACK AND DEFENCE

The dominant philosophy of sword fighting throughout medieval and renaissance Europe was offensive (fig. 86). For many masters attack was the key to success, and defence was often regarded as effective only if it enabled the defender to regain the initiative by counter-attacking his opponent. A similar attitude remained the hallmark of Japanese sword-fighting and was enshrined in Miyamoto Musashi's *Book of Five Rings* where the famous warrior declares unequivocally that once you take a sword into your hands, even when parrying or touching the opponent's blade, your sole aim is to cut him 'in the same movement' and 'more than anything you must be thinking of carrying your movement through to cutting him'.[77] Liechtenauer's approach to combat with the long sword and with other

86. A vignette from Tavernier, showing the primacy of attack. 1886, p. 61.

weapons is a perfect instance of such a spirit. The basis of his teaching was encapsulated in the dual principle of 'Before and after' (*Vor und nach*) – attack and defence – and it is of the utmost significance that attack comes first. To seize the initiative rather than await an opponent's move is crucial. By attacking first, you immediately force him on to the defensive and the aim of effective swordsmanship is to keep him there by relentlessly raining blows from all angles. Ideally, there must be no pause in this onslaught for that would enable the opponent to launch a counter-attack and thereby seize the initiative. Of course, Liechtenauer did consider what was to be done by a swordsman who has been forced on to the defensive, and his principal recommendation was to avoid parrying but rather to use a so-called Master Cut (*Meisterhau*) to deflect the attacking blade in such a way that one's own sword hits the opponent. A purely defensive stance was not to Liechtenauer's taste, and he rejected the policy of waiting to see what an enemy would do. That was a short route to death.[78]

This primacy of attack, evident in all the German combat manuals and their derivatives such as Fiore de' Liberi's *Flos duellatorum*, remained the basis of swordsmanship for a majority of renaissance masters elsewhere in Europe. Monte's fencing with both two-hand and single-hand sword was extremely aggressive; he recommended attacks which were swift and relentless and which, in the majority of cases, culminated with the use of point rather than edge; and, like Liechtenauer, he advocated cuts which might be instantaneously converted into thrusts.[79] He also stressed that no guard is completely safe and that those engaged in arms, or who seek to teach others, are repeatedly thrown into confusion when their guard proves inadequate. Fighters should, in fact, do the very opposite of staying on the defensive. They should take the attack to their enemy, seek out his exposed parts and give him no time to parry their blows.[80] Manciolino, too, praises those fencers who seek to wound their opponents *in tempo* and who do it with *gratia*; and his essentially pragmatic, deadly view of combat is made clear by his extolling the advantages of short weapons which strike more suddenly and are less easily parried than long weapons. Thus the partisan (a staff weapon with a broad pointed head and cutting edges) is more dangerous than the lance, and the dagger more dangerous than the sword. Altoni writes that 'defence is comprised by attack' and di Grassi defines the art of fencing as nothing other than knowing how to 'strike with advantage, and defend with safetie'. Di Grassi also points out that 'he that is neerest, hitteth soonest' and from this infers that 'a man may reap this profit, that seeing the enemies sword farr off, aloft and readie to strike, he may first strike the enemie, before he himselfe be striken'. If one is obliged to ward off a blow, then he especially approves defensive strokes which may, like Liechtenauer's *Meisterhau*, be immediately turned into an attack: 'it is the best waie of all other, because it doth not onely warde, but also in one and the selfesame time, both strike and defend safely'.[81]

It was universally agreed that it was impossible to separate offence and defence, and that 'to use one without the other is not good'.[82] For Marco Docciolini, fencing is the art of skilfully managing arms in order to preserve the safety of our person, and he explains that it consists of two parts (self-defence and injuring the enemy) so intimately connected that giving rules for the one inevitably gives rules for the other.[83] His English contemporary George Hale writes that 'the Science of Defence is an Art Geometricall, wherewith the body is guarded with a single or double weapon, from wrong of the Offender, or the greatest disadvantage of his Offence', adding that there is no surer principle than this: 'that there is no good defence without offence: neither good offence without defending', and he extols rapiers and swords which are able to do both.[84] For dall'Agocchie, the word *schermire* means nothing other than to defend oneself 'with the means to offend one's enemy', and the greater part of the opening section of his treatise is devoted to ways in which the swordsman can ensure that he is the first to strike. Ghisliero also accepts the intimate connection between attack and defence, and insists that 'we shall never simply defend ourselves if, at the same time, we do not attack, because the true defence is to attack; which must be done with resolution, and we should always be the first to deliver the blow'. The swordsman's intention should always be to strike rather than parry.[85]

There were, nevertheless, some dissenting voices. Viggiani, for example, explains that, since the whole art of fencing reduces itself to gaining advantage for oneself and putting the opponent at a disadvantage, it is better to let him make the first move and even aim the first blow because he thereby discommodes both his body and mind.[86] Viggiani's interlocutor is unconvinced because he feels that attacking first puts the opponent on the defensive and thus unable to strike you – an argument concordant with the German long-sword philosophy of preventing your opponent ever taking the initiative. The master does not agree. 'Your argument would be worth something', he says, 'if while one defends oneself one could not also attack: but that is false since there are many defences which can simultaneously be attacks' – a view also in accord with Liechtenauer and his followers.

Viggiani's discussion was evidently a sort of *locus classicus* for it was still being cited in 1619, when Gaiani pondered the same old question and declared it better to take the offensive despite what some masters had written to the contrary 'as did Angelo Viggiani formerly master in Bologna: but admittedly in his time the play was not so strict, nor the thrust so fast, long and strong as is now the case, and to that extent he may have excuse for this error.'[87]

Another master for whom Gaiani might have made excuses was Alfonso Falloppia who, like Viggiani, believed it advantageous to await the opponent's move, arguing that one may easily hit an attacker by a counter thrust.[88] Similarly, the Italian Elizabethan Saviolo warned that, if your opponent is 'a man of judgement and valour', to attack first is extremely hazardous and you may be 'slain or wounded in the counter time, especially if he thrust resolutely'. Equally, if he is not skilful, the more furiously he attacks the more you may gain time and measure and strike at will. On the other hand, Saviolo did not accept the argument advanced by some fencers who were prepared to accept a blow, thinking to 'hit him that shall hit them first'. Defence was paramount. Better by far to defend oneself without injuring the enemy than to allow oneself to be wounded. Yet, when it came to a real fight, even Saviolo had no doubts that you must kill or be killed.[89]

The same is true of Giganti and Capoferro. The former's treatise is introduced by a letter declaring that the sword should be used on only four occasions – for the faith, the Fatherland, self-defence, and the maintaining of honour. This sounds a note of high moral principle but was, in fact, not much of a self-denying ordinance since these four occasions encompassed the greater part of any swordsman's working day; and Giganti devoted his book to illustrating the most lethal techniques possible with a thrusting sword.

More explicitly than Giganti, Capoferro emphasized defence in his definition of fencing and was the first master to understand the true etymology of *la scherma*: 'the end of fencing is self-defence from which, moreover, it takes its name because to fence (*schermire*) does not mean to say anything other than to defend oneself, and fence (*schermo*) and defence are words of the same signification.'[90]

To defend one's life and the safety of one's Fatherland is, he says, the 'prize and excellence of this discipline'. Defence is the principal action in fencing, and no one ought to go on to the offensive, 'if not by way of legitimate defence'. Fencing is an art for effectively defending oneself with the sword; and it is an art because it is 'an assemblage (*ragunanza*) of perpetually true precepts, well ordained, and helpful to Civil Conversation' – by which he means social intercourse.[91] That swordsmanship is in some way a social lubricant is, in itself, a bizarre enough conception and scarcely consonant with what Capoferro has maintained only a couple of pages earlier when he declared that arms are inimical to *la conversation civile*, and argued that well-ordered republics forbid anyone (including nobles)

87. Capoferro's archetypal lunge. 1610, plate 5.

115

88. Calarone displays precision, speed and an unfortunate fowl. 1714, p. 73.

to carry swords or other weapons in time of peace. Subsequently, Capoferro reiterates his view that combatants almost always remain on the defensive and that attack is but a 'last resort to save one's own life'.[92] Yet his actual exposition of practical swordsmanship, like Giganti's treatise, tells a very different story: and here the emphasis placed by both masters upon the lunge is revealing (fig. 87).

The fully extended thrust or lunge – achieving a combination of maximum reach, velocity and accuracy – is the attacking stroke *par excellence* (fig. 88) and, although it has often been asserted that Capoferro and Giganti somehow invented it, we know that for cen-

89. Meyer's fencer lunges at a wall diagram and leaves an instructive footprint. 1600, book II, fol. 61v.

90. An optimistic lunge in Porath, 1693, fig. 23.

turies swordsmen had sought ways to lengthen the reach of their attacks and had, as a consequence, devised techniques which clearly anticipated Capoferro's 'incredible augmentation of the *botta lunga*'. The followers of Liechtenauer had developed a method for 'throwing' the long sword; Monte advocated a method for 'extending the pace as far as is possible' when handling the single sword;[93] Viggiani clearly described and utilized an almost fully developed lunge (his *punta sopramano*);[94] and Agrippa repeatedly illustrated an embryonic lunge – showing the sword hand in supination and the left arm extended backwards as a counterbalance – although the efficacy of the stroke is mitigated by the swordsman's head being turned backwards.[95]

Furthermore, a similar attack was used by Meyer, di Grassi, dall'Agocchie, Falloppia and Ghisliero (fig. 89). None the less, as far as published treatises are concerned, Capoferro's *Gran simulacro* and Giganti's *Scola* (along with Fabris's *Scienza*) are the first which systematically advocate the lunge for all attacks, and the effects are intended to be devastating. The majority of the plates in these works, and in those of their many imitators, show fencers

91. The lost sword, adapted by Heussler from Fabris. 1630, extra plate 12.

92. Lucini –
'Touché'. 1627,
plate 4.

thrusting through an opponent's chest, abdomen, face, head, eyes, neck, mouth or throat
(figs 90–2).[96] The art of defence seems wholly inadequate to stem this relentless tide of
blood and aggression. Yet, for the very reason that attack was so dominant, masters were
committed to teaching not only how to kill an opponent but also how a man may, 'with a
piece of steel, defend his person'; and, in order to communicate these skills, they devised a
number of general principles and several methods of instruction which together form the
subject of Chapter IV.

IV
Sword fighting: vocabulary and taxonomy

'HOW DIFFICULT IT is to be a Master of Fencing!' exclaimed the Roman swordsman Francesco Antonio Marcelli in 1686 as, scarcely able to suppress his
emotion, he pondered the diverse qualities required in a successful teacher. He
agreed with his sixteenth-century predecessor Giovanni dall'Agocchie that a good swordsman must have 'reason, courage, strength, dexterity, knowledge, judgement, and experience', but felt that even these gifts were not enough. However able the practitioner, he
could achieve little as a teacher without *la communicativa*: the ability to communicate, to
make everything clear to a disciple, 'to explain without confusion what it is that he wishes
to make him do'.[1] The entanglements (*imbrogli*), caused by prattling away and crying out
warnings, serve rather to obscure than instruct; and, above all, the master had to 'avoid
imitating those who, passing themselves off as men of skill and learning, spit out certain
maxims and expressions for which, in order to understand them, one requires to be a
member of the Academy della Crusca, or even always to carry Calepino in one's pocket.'[2]
It was much better to adopt those words most commonly used in the profession of arms
and which had been confirmed by both ancient and modern authorities. Trying to introduce new names to ears accustomed to traditional terms 'would be nothing but a nuisance,
a change without profit', and this is why Marcelli had been at pains to avoid the technical
language of philosophy, mathematics and geometry, and had tried to write in a style 'intelligible to all'.[3]

This question of communication was also considered by a Scottish contemporary of
Marcelli, Sir William Hope, but he was more bothered by ignorance than pretentiousness.
As he explained, there are many 'who take upon them the name of Master and pretend to
teach this Art, who have but little Judgement of it'. Whatever practical skills they might
possess, 'yet their communicative Art is a meer Rote'. They have repeated their lessons
throughout seven years of apprenticeship until they are 'so inrooted in them that, put them
off their common jog-trot of Teaching, they are immediately put to a *Nonplus*'. If you ask
them the reasons for what they do, they say that it does not become you to ask questions;
or, if you press them further, they say that that is how they were taught by their own master
who was reputed to be an excellent swordsman.

Again offer but to discourse with them concerning any of the intricat Points belonging
to the Art, and you shall immediately find them either shift the discourse, or tell you

that these Questions you are asking are (*Arcana Gladii*) profound secrets which must not be discoursed of, nor revealed to any, but such as intend to make profession of the Art, although perhaps if put to it, they can give no better satisfaction to the point in question than this *sic dixit Praeceptor*, a mean and ignorant kind of Answer, unbecoming any who pretend to the Name of Master.

This attitude, Hope admits, may be acceptable in a gentleman who intends only to attain a 'superficial practice of the sword' for divertissement or self-defence. But it is wholly unacceptable in masters. However good they may be as practical swordsmen, they are bad instructors if they cannot adequately explain everything that they do, and 'when a man thus contemns Judgement and Reason, he makes use of the Husk and throws away the Kernel'. In any case, the art of fencing has such an 'unexhaustible Treasure of Varieties', that a master unable to make some observations and improvements grounded upon reason must 'needs have a very shallow Brain, and be strangely wedded to his Master's opinions'.[4]

LA COMMUNICATIVA

The problem facing the teacher, admired in hypothesis by Marcelli and Hope, is to a large extent the central issue of my own study. While most masters agreed that there was no substitute for practical demonstration by an instructor, many of them still tried to convey the essentials of their art in books and found, inevitably, that this was a difficult thing to do. Indeed, without some sort of agreed technical vocabulary and taxonomic conventions, it was almost an impossibility. Archibald MacGregor, an eighteenth-century fencing enthusiast, was obliged to confront this matter when publishing a lecture on the *Art of Defence* which he had delivered 'extempore, before respectable audiences, in several towns of Scotland, with universal applause'. MacGregor was bothered because 'it cannot be expected that the reader who was not present at the delivery of it, will understand it so well as those who had the opportunity of seeing the attitude of the body, together with the different weapons then shewn.' After all, 'as plates add life to a treatise on fencing; it must still do more so to see the motions done by manual exercise'.[5] Unfortunately, since all treatises had to be studied by their readers without benefit of the authors' 'motions', how was comprehensibility to be achieved? We have already seen that, from the earliest surviving source onwards, many masters sought to clarify their ideas by using pictorial aids. But, in order to do that, they needed to have ideas in the first place, and all masters – even those who never wrote down their method – would have been forced to express themselves in words so that the pupils in their fencing schools could understand what had to be done. This must have been complicated enough, but it became vastly more so when instructions had to be conveyed at a distance both of space and time.

What was the most effective form of written communication: poetry or prose, dialogue or treatise? Occasionally a master, inspired perhaps by the ancient tradition of didactic poetry, would resort to verse, but the need to twist sense to fit rhyme and rhythm was no more conducive to clarity in the martial arts than it was elsewhere, and the results predictably fell far short of that 'sweet foode of sweetly uttered knowledge' celebrated by Sir Philip Sidney.[6] Nevertheless, rhyme and rhythm can fortify the memory, and the verse portions of MS I.33, for example, were evidently intended as mnemonic aid rather than arcane disguise; while, apart from their dedicatory letters, the treatises of Filippo Vadi and

Spetioli da Fermo, are cast entirely in verse as are the manuscripts of Fiore's *Flos duellato-rum*. Not one of these is notable for clear exposition, but the case of Fiore is especially interesting. The text of the Pisani-Dossi version is cast in neat distichs; whereas the Getty manuscript has much longer descriptions set in verse so bad as to be barely recognizable as such. Yet the tidy distichs do little to illuminate the sense of the illustrations, while the incompetent verse is vastly superior both in comprehensiveness and comprehensibility.

Some masters believed that they could achieve *la communicativa* by mimicking the questions and answers of pupil and teacher. This was the mode favoured by Sir William Hope who, introducing one of his numerous pedagogical effusions, explained that he was 'putting it in a Dialogue, and not in a continued Discourse' because he had tried to find the easiest method 'for to make those of the meanest capacitie understand my meaning (which is no small trouble)' and had settled on the conversational form:

> First, because young beginners, or whoever it be, that are to peruse this treatise, will understand by the scholars' questions, the description of the lessons better than if I had only discoursed of them. Secondly, the scholar in his questions bringeth in many things very pertinently, and useful to the beginner, which had I used any other method, could not have been brought in so much to the purpose. But to tell the truth it is a matter of indifference, for this method I thought best, and therefore made use of it.[7]

This may be the most half-hearted defence of the dialogue form on record; and certainly, notwithstanding the common assumption of a master/pupil relationship by the authors of fencing books towards the reader, relatively few of them adopted a catechestic technique. Viggiani, dall'Agocchie, Lovino, Saviolo, Gaiani and Thibault all tried their hand at dialogue as did Antonio Alfieri who used it, he said, to provide 'for clear understanding of the work and less trouble to him who reads it', and because the dialogue form was the 'most apt to remove doubts'.[8]

The majority of masters thought otherwise and preferred straightforward exposition although, whatever the literary form used, most authors would have agreed with Marcelli that their principal aim was to achieve clarity. It is also evident that they believed it possible to achieve this: first by deducing, from a multiplicity of sword, arm, foot and body movements, some communicable general principles; and then, by analysing particular actions and arranging them in sequences, to form some kind of system. This required both practical expertise and intellectual grasp; and the rarity of such a combination of skills was remarked by Fiore who claimed that, out of a thousand 'so-called masters', you could scarcely find four good scholars; 'and of those four good scholars there will not be one good master'.

Marozzo voiced the same misgiving when he lamented the lack of properly trained and certificated 'Maestri previlegiati'. In his own day, he said, the masters had little science and taught only on the basis of experience – 'they think they have knowledge but do not' – and although they may be good practical swordsmen they are not trained for teaching. Narváez similarly observed that there is a great difference between a master of arms and a mere fencer, 'because the former has to teach scientifically and with provable reasons the causes and effects which arms produce'; and Capoferro complained about masters who, having acquired some practical skill, set themselves to teach others, but 'without foundation or true rule, not realising that having knowledge is very different from teaching it'. It was also necessary, according to La Touche, for a master to be able to convey a grasp of the general principles of combat to his pupils. Yet this was the very thing upon which they bestowed the least trouble, as though 'routine alone' could make a man accomplished in arms. Such teachers do not realize that a perfect comprehension shortens the time required for instruction and ensures that the art is not forgotten and can be taken up again after a period of inactivity.[9]

Certainly all those masters who chose to write down their views were obliged, consciously or unconsciously, to consider the relationships not only between the theory and practice of fencing but also between the language and content of their works; and some believed the task to be well within their capacity. There was no need, wrote Falloppia, for more than seven guards (three for sword alone, one for sword and cape, and three for sword and dagger) which are easily explained and perfectly comprehensible without figures. La Touche, brimful of confidence, declared that although many works on the art of fencing had been published both in France and elsewhere they bore no resemblance to his book which, 'if I am not mistaken, has an order, a clarity, and a depth of knowledge not to be found in any of the others'.[10] Other masters were less sure of their literary expertise, and Marco Docciolini must have expressed the misgivings of many when he explained that while, in his own book, he had tried to describe as clearly as was within his power the rules and methods necessary for the exercise of the sword alone or accompanied by some other arm, he knew that 'having to describe many minutiae and many particular things concerning this art, it is almost impossible to represent it with the clarity that it perhaps demands'.[11]

These issues may be illuminated, somewhat paradoxically, by two examples of unintelligibility. Of these, the first, Johann Liechtenauer's *Art of the Long Sword*, is a seminal work in the history of swordsmanship. The fourteenth-century German master had a thorough grasp of his art, understood how men fought, and had worked out not only general principles of combat but also a method for instructing his disciples. Unfortunately, his work is recorded in gnomic verses of such obscurity that — without the key provided by the comments, elaborations and pictorial representations bequeathed to us by his followers (and their followers) — it would remain for ever enigmatic.[12] This may, in part, be due to the deliberate obfuscation of a master reluctant to cast the pearls of a secret art before swinish uninitiates — although a similar contempt for 'men rustical and of vile condition' did not prevent Filippo di Vadi from trying hard to make his manuscript as clear as possible to 'courtiers, scholars, barons, princes, dukes and kings'.[13] On the other hand, since Liechtenauer's verses appear to have had a mnemonic function, it is not strange that they should be abstruse. One would scarcely remember a mnemonic which did not leave out more than it put in. But beyond that, Liechtenauer's obscurity is also the result of a nomenclature and a system of classification which fail to match the sophistication of the combat techniques they record.

In this respect, the other example of communication failure provides an interesting comparison. The literary remains of English masters of arms at the turn of the fifteenth and sixteenth centuries are exiguous. There is one short text, *The Use of the Two Hand Sworde*, describing different moves in eleven single-sentence 'lessons' and six 'counters', followed by forty-two lines of further explication in verse; and a second, more substantial manuscript which describes fighting techniques in twenty short paragraphs squeezed onto the two sides of a small vellum roll.[14] The existence of these writings can only be due to some desire on the part of the masters to instruct potential readers and, unlike Liechtenauer's verses, they seem not to have been either consciously arcane or elliptical. Face to face, and sword in hand, these men may even have been effective teachers; but they had no conception of what was required to explain the complexities of movement to anybody not physically in their presence. They assume so much knowledge, and use so many unexplained technical terms, that their writings are now barely comprehensible. We stumble at the very 'first fflorysh' with its 'quarter fayre before you'; its 'broken foyne'; and its three 'Rakes' lightly 'Clevyng by thelbowes with a quarter foyne before you wyth both handys and ij quarters affte with ij turnes a downe ryght stroke'. We stagger through thirteen 'Chaces' including 'alle the rowndys', the 'tumblyng chace', the 'Spryng', the 'four poyntes', and the 'gettyng chace'; become entangled in counters such as the 'full spryng' and the 'shorte spryng with fallyng stroke'; and are bemused by a whole series of 'Rabettes', including the 'stopping Rabette', the 'dragonys tayle withe the pendaunte', and the 'duble rabett'. Of course, it is possible to gloss several of the terms and to make informed guesses about others but, even when that has been done, no clear notion of the combat technique can emerge because there are no relevant English texts or pictures which would provide us with the kind of key we have for Liechtenauer. The terminology used by these medieval English masters did not survive in later works and, given the present state of our knowledge, much of their meaning is simply not recoverable.

Yet the basic components of sword combat must have been evident to anyone who considered the matter seriously. The weapon had to be brought into action and held effectively. The swordsman could adopt a variety of stances; move his sword in different ways; attack an opponent with different parts of his blade, from different angles, and aiming at different targets. He could move in various directions, leading with either right or left foot, and adapting his pace according to circumstances. Movements could be performed to lure an opponent into responding in a certain way, thereby giving opportunity for another type of

93. Fiore. The eight basic cuts. c. 1410, fol. 17.

94. Marozzo's wall diagram showing nine cuts. 1536, fol. 48v.

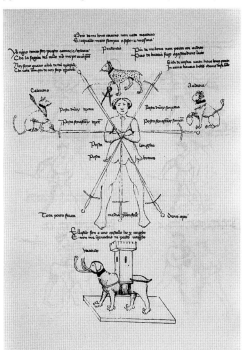

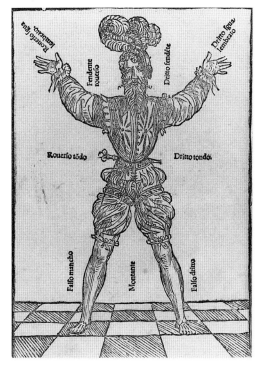

123

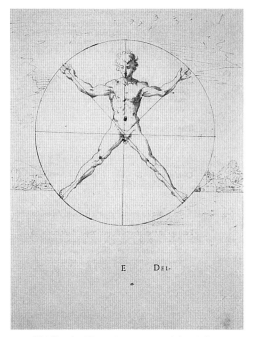

E Del-

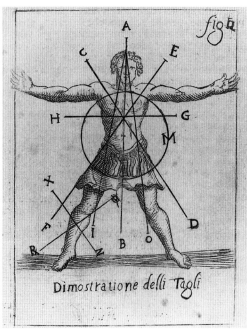

Dimostratione delli Tagli

95. Ghisliero's Vitruvian man, with eight cuts. 1587, p. 33.

96. Another demonstration of the cuts in Marcelli. 1686, p. 124.

97. Pistofilo's cuts for staff weapons. 1621, p. 141.

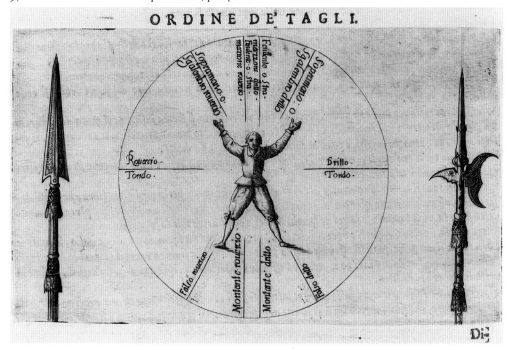

ORDINE DE' TAGLI.

assault. And, of course, when an opponent was himself trying to launch attacks, his blade could be either knocked aside or deflected in such a way as to initiate one's own counter-attack. In other words, there were stances, positions and targets; passes and counter-passes; cuts, thrusts and feints; parries and ripostes. Masters of arms would have understood all this from combat experience and from teaching; and some basic matters, such as the different types of cut possible with a sword, were standardized very quickly. And diagrams illustrating vertical, horizontal and oblique strokes have featured in fencing manuals throughout their history and were also used to clarify the handling of staff weapons (figs 93–7). Yet it took centuries for any uniform method of organizing all this material to develop, and for a generally accepted language of swordsmanship to emerge: while some crucial issues, such as getting the sword into action and gripping it properly, were consistently overlooked.[15] As for the rest, the masters struggled in prose and verse, in dialogue and treatise, with or without pictorial aids, and with varying success, to achieve the elusive goal of *la communicativa*.

EARLY EXPERIMENTS IN THE ART OF EXPLICATION

As has been remarked before, the written record begins in Germany at the turn of the thirteenth and fourteenth centuries with an anonymous Latin treatise on sword and buckler fighting. This work, Royal Armouries MS I.33, stands in splendid isolation although, as common sense and the nature of the text itself suggest, many of its technical terms and part at least of its method must already have been well established. It is, moreover, prophetic in combining several didactic procedures which were to be used, isolated or in combination, in most later works. The author's starting point is to define what he considers to be the most natural positions assumed by men – even those unskilled in the art of fighting – when they take a sword in their hand. He believes that there are seven such *custodiae* or guards which he numbers from 'first' to 'sixth', while to the seventh he gives the German name *Langort* (long point). First guard is with the right arm crossed under the buckler hand, with the buckler pointing outwards and the sword pointing behind and downwards; second is with the buckler held straight out in front of the upper body, and with the sword pointing backwards over the right shoulder; third has the right arm crossed over the buckler and the sword pointing backwards over the left shoulder; fourth is similar to second, with the sword held backwards over the right shoulder, but with the left arm sharply bent at the elbow and with the buckler facing outward. Fifth is a wide open stance (the only one of the series) with the buckler held out straight in front of the body but turned outwards, and the sword held low and far behind the right foot which, again uniquely, is well behind the left foot. The last two *custodiae* differ from the first five by having the sword pointing forward: the sixth with the buckler fully extended but with the right elbow (and therefore the sword) drawn well back; and finally the *Langort* with the buckler extended forward, downward and outward, and the sword held forward and down at an angle of about forty-five degrees. Swordsmanship, the author remarks, is the 'ordering of diverse blows', but the 'kernel' of the art resides in the last guard (*Langort*) in which all actions of the sword find their conclusion;[16] and certainly this posture occurs, either as an initial guard or in answer to some other guard, far more frequently than any other position.[17]

The whole treatise is built around these seven main *custodiae*. The illustration of each posture, precisely as it is shown at the beginning of the treatise, is repeated as a pictograph for each of its occurrences thereafter, sometimes with the swordsman advancing from the right-hand side of the page towards the left, and with his buckler either in profile or with its outer surface presented towards the reader; and sometimes with the guards – and especially the first – shown the other way round (that is the swordsman facing from left to right and with the inside of the buckler, and the hand grasping it, on view). But, whichever way round, the representation of each *custodia* is unvarying and immediately recognizable. All the fighting is broken down into short sequences of varying length; with each key moment of each sequence clarified by drawings of the protagonists (the priest and his pupil) together with a brief running commentary; and with the opening of each new sequence marked by a cross.

The author works systematically through all the guards: eight sequences initiated by a swordsman adopting the first guard; three initiated by the second; four with third; two with fourth; one with sixth; thirteen with seventh, that is *Langort*; four with fifth; and another two with fourth. This series is interrupted by a single reversion to a sequence beginning with first guard, and by an intrusion, into the long *Langort* group, of two movements initiated by the *Vidilpoge* (literally the fiddle-stick) in which the fencer holds his sword more or less at right angles across his outstretched left arm.[18] In the course of the various actions, other movements are introduced and indicated by pictographs which are then added to the repertoire and inserted wherever relevant. These include the *Halbschilt* (half shield) which is a defensive position with both arms extended close together and the sword pointing upwards at approximately forty-five degrees; the *Schiltslac* (shield blow) which is the use of the buckler to strike an opponent's sword and/or buckler to one side, while instantaneously delivering an attack of one's own; the *Krucke* (crutch) in which the sword is held almost vertically, point downward with the buckler turned outward and very close to the sword hand; the *fixura* which is a thrust (not always distinguishable from the *Stich*, another attack with the point), either crossed over or under the buckler or occasionally without crossing the buckler at all; and a special kind of *Langort* in which the buckler is drawn back to the left hip, and the right elbow is advanced but sharply bent so that the sword (held in supination) points down and backwards.[19] There are also two less well-defined terms: *Schutze* (protection), a parry which is inconsistently illustrated; and *Durchtreten* (stepping through) which cannot be distinguished at all because the author never describes leg and foot movements, and his artist shows them throughout in a stylized, unrealistic and undifferentiated manner. Cuts are never defined, though they occur as frequently as the thrust. Again, they are represented by a pictographic stereotype showing the blow delivered forehand to the head or neck: with the sword hand in supination (that is with finger nails on top and thumb to the right) and generally accompanied by the *Schiltslac* to knock aside the opponent's buckler and leave him open to the attack (plates IV–IX).[20]

MS I.33 is noteworthy for several reasons: some positive, some negative. In the first place, much the greater part of the author's meaning is carried by the work of his artist. Without the pictographs, the verbal description of the guards would be inadequate; we would have little understanding of the use of the point; no knowledge whatever of the cuts; and most of the text would be as incomprehensible as the English manuscripts on the two-hand sword. With the pictures, however, these deficiencies are largely remedied; although the failure to indicate accurately any movement below the waist makes it difficult to reconstruct the combat. Another serious deficiency, which the illustrations only partially circumvent, is the lack of any definition of the target area. The direction of every blow has to be worked out by studying the accompanying picture and, in particular, working out the position of the sword hand – a slow, laborious and often uncertain exercise.

98. 'Binding' – a literal
rendition by Lucini,
1627, plate 13.

On the other hand, there are features of considerable historical interest. Perhaps the most striking is the frequency with which the point of the sword is used – especially in sequences beginning with the fourth, fifth or seventh *custodia* – sufficient, of itself, to demonstrate that thrusting was no renaissance discovery dependent upon the development of the rapier. Striking, too, are the manuscript's frequent allusions to *religando* and *mutare gladium* ('binding' and 'exchanging the sword'), terms which survive to the present day, with their meaning virtually unchanged, to indicate sword contact (that is 'engagement' of the opposing blades), or 'change of engagement' where, by passing over or under the opponent's blade, it is engaged in the line opposite to the original position (fig. 98).[21]

One other advanced technical feature which seems quite astonishing (in the light of subsequent profusion and confusion) is the unambiguous identification of guards by allotting to each a single numeral and pictograph: something which did not reappear in fencing manuals until Agrippa developed a similar idea in 1553, and which is still found in the diagrammatic instructions of modern textbooks.[22] Finally, the very use of the term 'guards', to indicate the postures adopted by a swordsman, was to become commonplace throughout the Renaissance even though there was little agreement as to the number of guards, and not every master chose to begin his treatise with them.

The method of communication devised by the author of MS I.33, for all its limitations, is very rational. The method of fighting *seems* considerably less so. Throughout the action, with very rare exceptions, sword and buckler are kept in close proximity even when a blow is being delivered so that the buckler always protects the sword hand. This might well ensure a strong defence, but it would largely nullify the effect of an attack – as is evident from the way in which the majority of both cuts and thrusts are shown being clumsily delivered either under or over the crossed buckler. One result of the artist's scrupulous delineation of hand positions is that one can sometimes discern attitudes of a potentially fatal awkwardness.[23] Also awkward is another feature which might, superficially, be considered very forward looking. This is the way in which the combatants generally lead with the right foot as was to become the norm when fighting with the rapier and later with the small

127

sword. It is not, however, a very comfortable or equilibrious practice when using the sword in such close combination with a shield: and this raises questions concerning both the author's competence and his overall purpose. The constrained sword and buckler fighting taught by the priest to his disciple does not look remotely as efficient as the free-flowing, better balanced techniques later expounded by Talhoffer or Marozzo – although it found its way (perhaps through direct copying) into the compilations of Paulus Hector Mair where about half the postures show the same cramped style.[24] It is just possible that the priest's purpose was simply to record a system of exercises related to, but not the same as, real combat. However, since the great majority of action sequences in MS I.33 culminate with either cuts to the neck or head, or thrusts at the face and abdomen, it seems that the techniques were intended for serious encounters. A mere 'touch on the belly' might not be very debilitating, but being 'penetrated by the sword' in that vulnerable region would be quite another matter.[25] One explanation for the discrepancy would be that, despite their intelligent systematization of words and pictures, neither the author nor his illustrator could devise a way to fill in the inevitable gaps between one isolated frozen gesture and another. In other words there is a limit to what anyone could achieve with permutations of only fifteen stylized poses. Another explanation would be that the author was an indifferent and ineffectual swordsman.

Ineffectuality was not a characteristic of later swordfighting in Germany notwithstanding the fact that, for a long time, the notational methods used by its chroniclers were less sophisticated than those in MS I.33. Johann Liechtenauer's verses, as recorded by Hanko Döbringer, comprise the first surviving work devoted to the use of the long sword. They also include, at the end, the first surviving comments on mounted combat with sword and lance, and on foot combat between armoured warriors using spear, long sword and dagger: but Liechtenauer's main concern was with long sword combat between warriors not wearing armour; and he analysed this, broke it down into what he considered to be its principal components, gave to each posture or blow an evocative name and – if we assume the surviving text to be as he intended – thoroughly disorganized the material. He recognized four *Leger* or basic stances: *Ochs* (Ox) with sword held high and aimed down towards the opponent's face; *Pflug* (Plough) with sword held at waist level but also pointing up at the opponent's face; *Alber* (Fool) with sword held out in front, its point aimed at the ground; and *vom Dach* (from the Roof) with the sword held over the right shoulder and pointing upwards at about forty-five degrees. He distinguished five principal cuts: *Zornhau* (rage cut), diagonally from the right shoulder; *Krumphau* (twisted cut), downwards with the false edge, and effected with crossed or twisted wrists; *Zwerchhau* (side cut), horizontally; *Schielhau* (squint cut), downwards with the false edge at the enemy's shoulder or neck; and *Scheittelhau* (crown cut), vertically downwards and literally aimed at the crown of the head. He identified the counter-attacks suitable against each particular stance or for seizing the initiative from an opponent who strikes first; various parries against cuts and thrusts; different modes of cutting of which the *Abschnieden* or drawing cuts had an especially long future; techniques for getting to close quarters and grappling hand to hand with an opponent; and eight *Winden* which are principally engagements of the blade, including the kind of binding recorded in MS I.33.

Liechtenauer mentions all these matters and more: but he describes them only allusively, if at all; and, as is the case with modern fencing terminology, his meaning was clear only to those who already knew it. It was left to his disciples to draw out his most important ideas many of which have customarily been ascribed to writers of a later and allegedly more sophisticated age of swordsmanship: the division of the sword blade into *Stark und Schwech* (*forte* and *foible*); an acute awareness of the *sentiment du fer*, that is assessing changes in pressure when blades are in contact; the time advantage of point over edge; and even the idea of dividing the body into four areas for purposes of attack.[26] In 1389, Hanko Döbringer explained this last point:

> Here note that Liechtenauer divides a person in four parts, as if he were to draw a line on the body from the crown of the head down between his legs, and another line along the belt horizontally across the body. Thus there are four quarters, a right and a left over the belt, and also under the belt. Thus there are four openings, each of which has particular techniques which are used against it.[27]

The system (even when presented in a disorderly fashion) was comprehensive, intelligent and practical and it is not surprising that Liechtenauer's divisions, headings and nomenclature – amplified and rearranged to make for better understanding – remained the foundation of German swordsmanship until, in the early seventeenth century, the long sword lost its status as the principal German weapon for personal combat. Not only was the tiny original text constantly swollen by annotations and explanations but later masters also relentlessly added to the list of postures and blows so that, although Liechtenauer's original list for the long sword was never superseded, the number of names necessary for understanding the combat grew to a bewildering multiplicity. Furthermore, as was the case with Liechtenauer himself, most teachers were interested in other kinds of fighting besides the use of the long sword. Ott, the Jewish wrestling master of the Habsburgs, for example, prepared a short but very influential treatise on unarmed combat; Lew, another Jew, wrote on fighting in full armour.[28] Andres Liegnitzer displayed his versatility by discoursing on the short sword, sword and buckler, wrestling, and dagger fighting. Martin Hundfeld wrote on the short sword, Sigmund Ringeck on sword and buckler, Johann Lecküchner on the *Messer* or falchion, and Hans Talhoffer on the axe.[29] And such was the appositeness of Liechtenauer's seemingly clumsy terminology that, not only was it possible to adapt it for describing the use of weapons as widely diverse as the falchion and halberd, but it was even found possible to apply it to the new-fangled *Rapier* – as Meyer and his plagiarist, Sutor, were to demonstrate.[30]

The medieval and renaissance German masters also copied each other's works, added their own opinions, incorporated fresh information as they came across it, and included material on judicial duels, tournaments and even analytical studies of arms and armour. The result was a kind of bibliographical snowball, with some of the later collections, such as the spectacular manuscripts commissioned by Paulus Hector Mair, swelling to a monstrous bulk. Mair's fate may, however, have marked the beginning of the end of this process for, to fuel his collecting mania, he was driven to embezzle municipal funds and was hanged for his hobby at Augsburg in 1579.[31]

While some of these masters expanded Liechtenauer's text verbally, others sought to clarify the phases and variations of different types of combat by using illustrations rather than long descriptions. The pictographic method of MS I.33 only reappeared with the advent of printing, and the manuscript manuals never adopted it to elucidate the art of the long sword. But, for the historian, the loss of an easily read notation is more than outweighed by the recording of an abundance of postures, thrusts, cuts and wrestling techniques; by a concern to depict footwork accurately; by proper identification of target areas;

and by the way in which the whole system was firmly set within a coherent, all-embracing combat philosophy. Essentially, the descriptive method boiled down to providing a separate name for every conceivable fighting posture and to illustrating these from a rich repertory of frozen action pictures – a method which long remained the norm not only in Germany but elsewhere in Europe. As a way of conveying information it was, without doubt, cumbersome; and a modern reader might easily conclude that a system of swordsmanship described in this fashion must have been correspondingly inefficient, especially in view of the cannibalism of the German manuscript tradition.[32] Yet any descriptive system of movement, however well conceived, must inevitably be obscure to someone unfamiliar with its conventions. What, for example, would Liechtenauer have made of Léon Bertrand's 'Simple counter-ripostes on compound ripostes', the first of which reads: 'Feint of disengagement – I parry Counter-Quarte and disengage – parry, Sixte (counter-Quarte) and counter-riposte direct'?[33] The truth of the matter is that, considered as a corpus rather than as individual items, the German *Fechtbücher* are not at all obscure and they enable us to recognize that Liechtenauer's opaque verses concealed a martial art of deadly seriousness and efficacy which was sufficiently communicable to have occupied the energies of masters and their pupils for nearly three centuries. The entire system and nomenclature survived intact, though greatly expanded, in Meyer's treatise of 1570; reappeared, digested from Meyer by Sutor, in 1612; gained a new lease of life in 1660 when Meyer was reprinted; and, again in a digested form, was offered as an original scheme by Theodor Verolini in 1679.

An interesting insight into the Liechtenauer tradition, its durability and its limitations, is provided by the first printed German combat manual, Pauernfeindt's *Ritterlicher Kunst der Fechterey* of 1516 and its French translation. As we have already seen, these two books used woodcuts to convey information on postures by using a pictographic technique – one picture per posture, repeated as required.[34] But the differences between the texts are as revealing as their similarities. Pauernfeindt, like all his compatriots, takes Liechtenauer's verses (or a version thereof) as his starting point for discussing the long sword and, like them, he begins each section with a direct quotation from the master which he then expounds with his own sequential account of attacks and counters. He thus gives Liechtenauer's preliminary list of the various divisions of combat; cites the same openings, counters, and stances, *Ochs*, *Phlug*, *Alber*, *vom Dach* (but adding *Hochort*, *Hangendtort* and *Eysenporten*); the techniques for evading an opponent's blade; counters to be used when an opponent attacks first; the principal cuts; engagements or binding with crossed swords; cuts at an opponent's hands; and advice on close grappling, including using the pommel of one's sword.[35] In all, of Liechtenauer's original 211 lines dealing with the long sword, Pauernfeindt cites 166, every one of which is omitted by the author of *La Noble Science* who otherwise renders the sense of the German text with care. Evidently, while the long-sword fighting of the German school was considered well worth translating into French, its idiosyncratic nomenclature (ox, plough, fool, from the roof, rage cut, crown cut, squint cut and so on) was not. The Frenchman's decision is understandable. But fanciful terminology long remained the order of the day: and not only in Germany.

A colourful multiplicity of guards and blows was also characteristic of the early Italian masters, first under German influence and then continuing under its own momentum. In the preface to his *Flos duellatorum*, Fiore de' Liberi da Premariacco tells us that he had studied under German masters in the latter half of the fourteenth century; and much of his work closely resembles the system recorded by Liechtenauer and his disciples. This is apparent in the range of material he discusses; his general approach to swordsmanship; his division of the body to indicate target areas; his recommended postures; his method of combining wrestling and grappling techniques with fencing; his use of *halb-Schwert* techniques for the long sword wielded by armoured combatants;[36] and, more generally, his disordered orderliness. This last characteristic is seen most strikingly in the overall organization of the treatise which deals with a wide variety of fighting: unarmed combat; unarmed man against adversary with dagger; single-handed sword fighting; the use of short thrusting spear against a similar weapon, club or dagger; handling long spears; combat with two-handed swords, first by men without protective armour and then (a shorter section) with armour; axe fighting by armoured men; mounted combat first with short spears and then with swords; footman against mounted troops with lances; then back to foot combat with dagger against sword; and finally a pair of armoured warriors wielding long hammers, one of which is a kind of combination bolas. The arrangement follows precisely the order set forth in Fiore's Prologue or, more properly speaking, his Prologue follows the order already established in the treatise and, although there is some jumping about between topics, the organization is fairly orderly. What is completely orderly and carefully considered is the way in which, within each major section, the pictures of pairs of combatants are preceded by short sequences of single figures demonstrating the principal guards or postures (as in MS I.33), and the target areas for each particular mode of combat. These single figures are crowned to indicate that they are the masters; and, from time to time, similar crowned masters occur in the combat pictures. The whole mode of exposition is, as Fiore himself explains, based upon painted figures each of which is individually glossed. The organization and execution are imperfect, but both have been seriously thought out and, on the whole, achieve a high degree of *la communicativa*. This is especially true of the version of the treatise now in the Getty Museum, where the postures are provided with longer, clearer and more pertinent commentaries.

With regard to sword fighting, Fiore is mainly concerned with the two-hander and, like Liechtenauer, he not only distinguishes sharply between combat where the antagonists wear armour and combat where they do not, but similarly devotes far more space to the latter. He lists seven blows which are applicable to both single and long sword: two *fendenti* or vertical downward cuts from a high position (one from either side); two comparable *sotani*, upward cuts from a low position; two *meçani* or horizontal cuts; and the thrust with the point which he describes, significantly, as being the most effective mode of attack, 'more poisonous than the serpent', and both 'cruel and mortal'.[37] He discusses and illustrates a number of positions, including some half-sword techniques, before dealing with twelve postures or guards – such as the 'wild boar's teeth' and the 'bicorn' – which are first shown individually and then as employed by pairs of swordsmen engaged in combat.[38] Fiore's next section deals with fighting in full armour first with sword and then with polaxe; and his six guards for the armoured swordsman demonstrate a preference, shared by the German masters, for half-sword techniques. Only one of these guards, the 'middle iron gate', shows both hands on the handle: all the others ('serpent', 'true cross', 'chief serpent', 'sagitaria' or 'arrow head'; and 'bastard cross') use one hand on the handle and the other on the blade (figs 99–100).[39]

When, more than eighty years later, towards the end of the fifteenth century, the Pisan master Filippo di Vadi decided to set forth his views on combat, little had changed despite his claim to be writing about a 'new art fashioned according to reason' and not the 'old art' which he cheerfully abandoned to 'our ancients'. Vadi had an elevated if repressive and mercenary view of his art which, he said, 'is the chief of every good' because it enabled cities

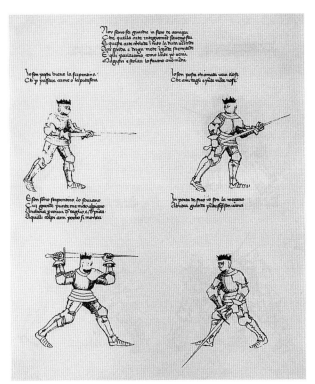

99. A series of half-sword techniques by Fiore. c. 1410, fol. 25.

100. Half-sword techniques by Fiore. c. 1410, fol. 26.

to be retained and people to be restrained, while its skilled professors could achieve fame, favour and wealth. In the event, Vadi's work is scarcely an advance upon Fiore's from which it differs in a few technical details and some of its terminology, but not in its mode of presentation nor in the combat system it describes.[40] Like his predecessor Vadi was primarily, though not exclusively, interested in the two-hand sword used by unarmoured men but added a couple of pages devoted to similar fighting in armour. The target areas into which he divided the body were the same as in Fiore. He listed the same number of blows (six cuts and one thrust); gave a similar, if not identical, series of twelve guards; and followed the same method of distinguishing the master with a crown. He did, it is true, enhance his list with some additional fancy names such as the 'serene leopard' and the 'leopard's tail': but such superficialities do not constitute a 'new art'.

Nor, initially, did things change much with the move from manuscript into print despite the fact that in Italy printing made a far greater impact on the dissemination of material relating to every type of combat (the art of war, the formalities of the duel and the technique of swordsmanship) than anywhere else in Europe; and despite the fact that the first combat manual printed there described a system of sword fighting different from anything which had preceded it.

In 1509, instead of adding to the proliferation of technical terms, Pietro Monte stripped postures and blows down to their barest essentials. He distinguishes only two guards generally adopted by fighters – some have the sword arm high on the right side, others have the sword above the left shoulder 'especially when holding a shield in the left hand' – but he feels that no guard, either in sword fighting or wrestling, is absolutely safe and 'if we wish to shut ourselves up we fall to ruin'.[41] He concedes that descending blows have greater force than ascending blows but still considers the latter to be more effective; and, while he discusses the uses of both *manudextri* (blows from right to left) and *manusinistri* (from left to right), he favours the latter since they do not leave the swordsman uncovered.[42]

Monte, in effect, regards only three attacking strokes as of primary importance: two oblique rising cuts from either right or left, and the thrust or point (*stocchata vel puncta*) which is the most effective of all and may not only be directed from either side but also from a high or low position 'just like the long lance'.[43] These cuts and thrusts are almost invariably used in swift combinations of two or three strokes. As the swordsman advances he delivers one or both of the cuts, and then follows immediately with the thrust 'to finish'. Monte also explains how to throw two ascending cuts, both from the right-hand side (one after the other, the first with left foot forward, the second with right foot forward) and then 'instantaneously' to make the thrust. He also discusses another combination of three blows of which the first is a feint to provoke the enemy, the second actually wounds him, and the third is preparatory for a further attack.

Like his predecessors, Monte sees no fundamental difference between single and two-handed sword fighting except that it is easier to feint with the lighter weapon; but, unlike other masters, he bases his entire system upon feints. His cuts are intended primarily to force an opponent to defend the threatened part of his body and thus leave the real target uncovered – 'making as if to hit the enemy's hand or face, and in exactly one time to strike the leg; or to threaten the lower part and direct a blow at the head' – a technique which can be applied as effectively from the left side as from the right.[44] He likes to keep opponents guessing at all times, explaining that 'it is good to dissimulate with the feet and hands, for if we remain fixed they can easily injure us'. Moreover, when we move into action from a wholly static stance our intentions are easily read; but 'if we temporize as to which part we are moving, they do not know for certain what decision we are going to take'.[45] Monte, like Liechtenauer, especially likes movements in which a cut from either side is instantaneously converted into a thrust, and the phrases which recur throughout his discussion of every kind of fighting are 'in one time', 'at the same instant', 'at the same time', 'without an interval', and 'without cessation of time'. Cuts and thrusts must follow one upon the other without pause; the emphasis is always on speed, aggression and deception. And everything is kept as simple and as economical as possible.

Monte's views on swordsmanship, as expressed in his *Collectanea*, were ignored. Their undeniable originality was obscured by the author's poorly organized jumble of chapters in which he jumps backwards and forwards between general observations on either the two-hand or single-hand sword, discussions of the sword in combination with dagger or cloak, the use of various staff arms, and the techniques for fighting against men in and out of armour. Constant movement and feinting may not only confound an opposing swordsman; it can also unsettle a reader, especially one struggling with the repellent typography of Scinzenzeler the Milanese printer. Monte's fate was also determined by his decision to publish in a bad Latin translation rather than in his original Spanish or in the Italian of his adopted land; and by his insistence on burying everything within a rambling, though not wholly irrelevant, discourse on humours and temperaments. Furthermore, judging by the sometimes equivocal (and always subordinate) role allotted to feints by other masters, it is unlikely that a system based upon these deceptive movements would have had a wide appeal. On the other hand, since we know that Monte taught Galeazzo da Sanseverino and other prominent Italian courtiers and that, according to Castiglione, he was famous as a master, it is odd that his methods made no impact upon his contemporaries – or at least have left no firm record of having done so.

Similarly ignored by posterity was the first native Italian master to appear in print, the Bolognese Antonio Manciolino. His *Opera nova*, providing 'instruction in fighting and fencing with all sorts of arms', is known only in a Venetian edition dated 1531, which claims to be 'newly corrected and printed': but we do not know from what.[46] In the twentieth century Manciolino's reputation, like that of several other masters, has suffered from a blunder by Egerton Castle who dismissed the *Opera nova* as being so concerned with 'picking and deciding quarrels in a gentlemanly manner, that very little actual "fencing" has found its way into his little work'. The pity is that Castle, as his arch enemy Jacopo Gelli gleefully pointed out, had never read Manciolino's book. Had he done so, he could not fail to have been favourably impressed, for it is 'little' merely in format; has almost nothing to say about the sterile subject of 'deciding quarrels'; is unusually well organized; and is densely packed with practical and systematic observations on swordsmanship. It was bad luck for Manciolino that Gelli, his sole modern admirer, also misinterpreted him. The main preoccupation of the *Opera nova* was not combat with sword alone, but with the sword and buckler, either large or small; and the greater part of the treatise (ninety-one pages) deals with these techniques, leaving only thirty-four pages for everything else put together, including just under two pages on the *spada sola*.

Manciolino begins with general observations on swordsmanship including several reminiscent of Monte, such as the perils of the *mandritto*; the usefulness of cultivating ambidexterity; the advantages of practising with weapons heavier than normal; and, with regard to the duel, the advice that if a stronger man has the choice he should weigh down a weaker opponent with heavy armour. The resemblances are fortified by the later chapters of the *Opera nova* which deal with the sword in combination with the large buckler, two swords (one in each hand), the sword on its own or in combination with the cape (one against one and two against two), with the dagger, and with the small round shield; and a concluding section on staff weapons which are 'not of less gracefulness than the aforesaid' and comprise the partisan accompanied by the large round shield or *rotella*, and then partisan, *spiedo*, *ronca*, and thrusting lance on their own. With the exception of the two swords together, these various weapons and combinations are discussed by Monte and, while it is true that several of them occur elsewhere, there is no earlier treatise which combines them all and includes the other observations to which I have already alluded. I am not suggesting that Manciolino was particularly influenced by Monte. Quite the contrary. His own emphasis is on sword and buckler combat to which Monte allotted comparatively little space; he does not discuss the two-hand sword which especially interested Monte; his view of the guards is far more elaborate and forms the basis of his system; and he does not rely upon feints. But there are sufficient affinities to suggest at least the possibility that Manciolino knew the work of his predecessor.

After the introductory general observations on fencing, Manciolino begins with the guards which will 'cast greater light upon the rest of the work'. He lists, names and describes ten of these stances (the high guard, the guards of the head, face, above the arm, below the arm, closed iron gate, open iron gate, iron gate of the wild boar, the high long tail, and closed long tail) and follows these with five principal blows and two others which he considers to be of lesser significance. He then works seriatim through all the guards, treating each possible attack and each counter in strict order and considerable detail. He is methodical and practical but stresses that 'not only should the good fencer make himself skilled at attack and defence, he should moreover give a beautiful form to his blows, mingled with sweet movements of the body' – a markedly Castiglionesque view of mortal combat.[47] None the less, for all its orderliness and aesthetic sense, Manciolino's *Opera nova* was not appreciated. His contemporaries made nothing of it, and neither Pallavicini nor Marcelli included it in their list of historically important works. This may partly be due to the disconcertingly cramped italic typeface in which the book was printed and the fact that its seven feeble illustrations are wholly unrelated to the text – the publisher Nicolò Zoppino simply throwing in anything small and belligerent that he happened to have in stock. A second and not entirely unrelated factor was the publication, barely five years later, of the *Opera nova* by another Bolognese master, Achille Marozzo.

Marozzo's treatise is in some respects inferior to that of Manciolino. It is less neatly organized, more repetitive, and is prodigally productive of guards. But it covers more ground, is better printed, and has the added attraction of eighty-two bold and, in the main, pertinent woodcuts – and these proved decisive. Whereas Manciolino's concise work was never reprinted and never cited, Marozzo's went through another three editions in the sixteenth century and one more in 1615. It was mentioned by Pallavicini and by Marcelli who added that Marozzo's book was worthily reprinted in 1568 when it was 'embellished with beautiful engraved figures, whereas it had first been printed with woodcuts'. As a matter of fact, the engravings are inferior, but it was certainly the profusion of illustrations which provided the excitement and clarification lacking in both Monte and Manciolino.

Marozzo offers a few preliminary remarks on teaching, then begins, like Manciolino, with the techniques of sword and small buckler which he works through systematically, assault by assault – although, as he advises masters, they must limit themselves to matters which are 'good, brief, and useful' to their pupils. Were he himself to put in everything relevant, then a book ten times the size of the present volume would not suffice. There follows a series of short sections made up of tiny chapters on topics familiar to us from Monte and Manciolino:[48] and it is only after this that Marozzo moves on to describe his set of guards which he deems suitable for all the different combinations of weapons thus far mentioned, including either sword or dagger alone. Not only is he describing them, he says, he is also accompanying each with an illustration; and the scholar, who would be examined by his master in these matters, would be expected 'to know all these guards from name to name and from pass to pass, with their parries, and their attacks, that is to say *pro* and *contra*'. Readers, he adds, cannot fail to see that he makes no distinction between guards for all the above mentioned weapons 'because they are one and the same thing', and to save space he is showing each guard once only. Twelve woodcuts follow, each explicated by a paragraph, but there are thirteen guards (the closed iron gate being treated with the open iron gate instead of separately as in Manciolino). Eight of these guards overlap exactly with Manciolino's, five are additions, and two of Manciolino's are missing.[49] Marozzo then gives his little floor plan for teaching foot movements; his wall plan illustrating all the cuts; an illustration and brief discussion of a left-hander fighting a conventional opponent; similar treatment of a man armed with sword and large shield facing staff weapons; and a man on foot armed with sword and cape confronting a mounted swordsman.

The whole of Marozzo's third book is given to the two-hand sword; and his treatment shows in an aggravated form the weakness of a purely descriptive terminology allied to a division of movement which is impressionistic rather than truly analytical. He describes the principal attacks before listing and illustrating seventeen guards which are all

101. Half-sword guard against staff weapons
by Marozzo. 1536, fd. 78v.

classified as either high or low, and none of which is readily distinguishable from blows, either potential or completed. This plethora is by no means the whole story for, as Marozzo admits, there are other guards which he will name but not illustrate because they are too difficult to analyse, and so he merely lists them: the grieving iron gate (*porta di ferro acorata*), the shoulder, the foot, the star, and the elbow. 'Every time', says Marozzo, 'that you parry or are attacked you will always assume one of the above mentioned guards.'[50] And this is the trouble. Many of the guards are obviously only stages of one and the same movement and, as Viggiani was soon to point out, it was possible to break everything up into an infinity of pieces. It is this arbitrariness which makes it pointless to attempt to match the blows and guards of the various masters who have left us a record of their two-hand sword fighting. It is not difficult to find similarities between many of the postures depicted in Fiore, Talhoffer, Dürer, Marozzo and others: but, when all is said and done, the difference between many of the guards is too trifling to merit the dignity of the separate titles which were accorded them. One striking feature of German two-hand sword fighting which is absent from Marozzo is the use of the *halb-Schwert* which was originally a special technique for combat in armour but was later adopted for civilian use. Marozzo does not deal with this technique until, at the end of Book Three, he includes it in his discussion of how to use the two-hand sword against staff weapons. 'Grip the sword', he explains, 'with your left hand near the pommel as is usual, and place your right hand between the great and small guard of your sword' (*tra lelzo grande e piccolo*) – that is the ricasso – and the woodcut illustrating this technique suggests its effectiveness by scattering bits and pieces of staff weapons at the swordsman's feet (fig. 101).

Marozzo's fourth book deals with staff weapons similar to those discussed by Manciolino, but substituting the infantry pike for the lance; and Book Five deals with the judicial combat and duel before moving on to the concluding section which examines how an unarmed man may deal with a dagger-wielding opponent. This part consists of twenty-two *prese* or wrestling techniques all carefully illustrated and described, and of which at least thirteen are identical with (if not copied from) Fiore.[51]

Masters in Italy and Germany found it immensely difficult to break away from the descriptive terminologies they had inherited. Many, indeed, would have seen no reason to make the effort since, apart from imposing a strain on students with poor memories, the system functioned well enough for most practical purposes. Even dall' Agocchie – who was fairly up to date when he published his *Art of Fencing* in 1572 and who remarked that 'many excellent men' had written 'diffusely' on his subject because the art is 'difficult to describe in a way that may be well understood' – remained enmeshed in the old fencing language which he specifically defended. In answer to the questions as to why there were so many names for the guards and why masters sometimes used different terms, the chief interlocutor replies that these names were given by the ancients and subsequently confirmed by the usage of most if not all those who profess the art. They are understood and accepted and, although it is possible to devise other terms, 'to wish to introduce new names to ears accustomed to those already established would be nothing other than a nuisance without profit, and a change to no avail' – words which so appealed to Marcelli a century later that he cited them without acknowledgement.[52] If everyone, continues dall'Agocchie, were to make up his own names, how could these be understood? He therefore follows the accepted terms, 'as we have found them, so shall we leave them'.[53] He is as bad as his word, and it is only necessary to list his terminology for the guards to see how in some ways he was even more confusing than Marozzo upon whom, despite the passage of nearly forty years, he has not improved in this respect. He says that there are only eight important guards, four high and four low, but he then so subdivides and qualifies them that his final tally is fifteen.[54] If, in addition, we bear in mind that many of these guards could be assumed with either right or left foot forward, then the lot of the scholar in such schools of arms seems unenviable.

This kind of luxuriant terminology did not go unchallenged. At about the time that Agrippa was analysing body movement in the 1550s, yet another Bolognese master Angelo Viggiani was trying to rationalize the terminology of swordsmanship and berating fencers who used the old 'bizarre names for guards'. 'Leave off talking about your *code lunghe distese*', he cried, 'your falcons, iron gates open or closed, and such strange fantasies'. He defines guards simply as postures in which one stands 'quietly and commodiously' both for attack or defence; and he observes that, of course, given all the possible directions in which sword and body may be moved, such guards could be regarded as infinite. Masters have identified them according to 'some similitude or effect', giving names such as 'the guard of the Unicorn or guard of the Lion' to the most significant in order to facilitate teaching. But that is school stuff, and Viggiani is not talking about fencing for sport (*per gioco*) but for real fighting when you need to kill your enemy. In such circumstances there are only seven guards – 'three offensive, three defensive, and one general' – which Viggiani not only numbers but also names according to their form, purpose, and quality.[55] Thus a guard is closed (*stretta*) when the point is held in line with the opponent, open (*larga*) when the point is to one side, and high (*alta*) when the hand is above the head; it is offensive when the sword points to the right, or defensive when it points to the left; and it is perfect when it permits the fencer to thrust, or imperfect when he can only cut. The seven guards are clearly illustrated, showing Viggiani's insistence on always leading with the right foot; and all are labelled with their principal characteristics. Thus we have *seconda guardia alta, offensiva, perfetta*; *quarta guardia larga, difensiva, imperfetta*; *quinta guardia stretta, difensiva, perfetta* and so on. The curious thing about Viggiani is that, having arrived at a simple system of numbering his guards, he consistently refers to them thereafter by their full titles which are no less cumbersome than the old 'bizarre' names he condemns.[56]

SWORDS AND COMPASSES

To some masters an altogether different approach to the problem of *la communicativa* had suggested itself. The application of geometry to the notation of movement has been discussed in a previous chapter; but for some masters it was the concept itself (that fencing was a kind of geometric activity in time and space) which proved attractive, for mathematics was an ancient discipline of immense dignity, and claiming an affinity with Euclid must have afforded swordsmen immense gratification. The truth of the matter, though, is that few early masters knew enough about mathematics to progress beyond using it as a figure of speech. Thus Filippo Vadi's first chapter extols fencing as a 'true science and not an art'; compares the infinite divisions of geometry with the measures, blows, and paces of swordsmanship; and declares that 'from geometry fencing is born'. But of applied mathematical knowledge there is nothing either in his exposition of combat or in his illustrations – just as there is nothing of the music which provides his next metaphor.[57] The same is true of the more sophisticated Viggiani who, like many other renaissance authors, feels obliged to justify his profession by weighing the relative merits of arms and letters. His best argument in favour of arms is the fact that they are always the last and most effective mode of settling any dispute: but he has a more intellectual card up his sleeve. 'Movement and time', he says, 'are the two greatest foundations of all natural things; and what art or faculty has greater need of time and motion than the art of war?' Mathematics, he continues, concerns types of quantity. Quantity has three dimensions or spatial elements, that is to say length, width and depth; and these, in turn, comprise six principles of site or position – 'up and down, the ends of the length of a man; right and left, the extremes of his width; before and behind, the extremes of solidity and profundity'. And, he adds triumphantly, we find all these in the sword and in every other weapon which has a point; and we can see them in figures of geometry such as the triangle, square, pentagon, hexagon, circle and the other 'almost infinite figures all of which you may find in the sword'. At least you could find them were it not for the fact, Viggiani confesses, that it would take too long to demonstrate everything and that it is 'also perhaps not meet for our intention'.[58] Significantly, all this vapour is prefaced by Viggiani with a parenthetical acknowledgement that the mathematical sciences are not his main profession.

The gulf between what some masters felt about mathematics and their ability to apply it was unwittingly revealed by Giovanni Battista Gaiani who stressed the need for a master to have 'good letters' and a sufficient knowledge of the science of mathematics, especially of geometry 'whereupon almost the whole art is based, in respect of lines, angles, circles, points, and measures'. Yet when the scholar in Gaiani's dialogue expresses puzzlement over why there should be such diversity in the art of fencing which is, after all, based upon mathematics 'which holds first place amongst certainties', the master explains that this is due to the complexity of the actions involved. The interrelation between oneself and an adversary results in so many diverse blows and movements that things will need to be done which the master has never taught and which can only be acquired by constant practice. Gaiani, despite his conviction that a knowledge of mathematics was relevant to the fencing master, could not demonstrate how this might actually be applied. Or perhaps he did not even try.[59]

One genuine mathematician who did try was Camillo Agrippa and, like other later masters who were serious about applying mathematics to sword play, as opposed merely to enjoying prestige by association, he was attempting to do two different things simultaneously. One task was to use geometry to achieve an intellectual grasp of the general principles underlying the movements of swordsmen in action: and this was an area where Agrippa proved to be a successful innovator both in reducing, to four logical postures designated by number alone, the guards required for a clear exposition of fencing, and in demonstrating (rather than merely assuming) the efficacy of a kind of embryonic lunge.[60] The other task was to use geometry not only to establish general principles but also as a descriptive and explanatory technique; and here, for all his talk of 'points, lines, tempi, measures and suchlike', and the fanciful geometrical figures with which his treatise begins, Agrippa was less effective.

Gearing geometrical diagrams and terminology to an exposition of practical fencing was the task to which Spanish masters, and those influenced by Spanish theories, applied themselves with a devotion bordering on the obsessive and with results which were often little more than exercises in opacity ranging from the verbosity of Carranza who used too few diagrams and the imprecision of Narváez who used poor ones, to the labyrinthine notation of Lorenz de Rada who used a great many, most of them incomprehensible. Yet their enthusiasm was not unproductive although, curiously, the most successful advocates of Spanish theories were non-Spanish masters like Ghisliero who was the first author to apply Carranza's ideas systematically. Ghisliero used mathematical language and diagrams to produce a generally unambiguous exposition of fencing techniques which, in more favourable circumstances, would have exerted wider influence.[61] But, as a geometric exposition of combat, his ingenious treatise was later dwarfed by the labours of Thibault and the team of artists who translated the French master's ideas into images. For Thibault mathematics really was the key to both understanding and explaining swordsmanship. He acknowledged that there were plenty of fighters who acquired speed of body and arm by continual exercise without understanding what they were doing, and without any true and solid theory. Comparing their fencing to the true art of handling weapons was like comparing a 'manual of mechanical works with the inventions of mathematics', for the mechanicals were content to obtain only 'the effect of their intention, even should this be by chance', whereas the mathematicals 'approve nothing which is not founded upon infallible rules'. Thibault has been ridiculed for his elevated and complex view of the art of fencing: but when one takes the trouble to examine his book it reveals him not as a pedant but as a practical teacher seeking out the best method for explaining to his pupils how they should perform. He repeatedly acknowledges the difference between theory and practice and demonstrates that he understands that difference; but he also recognizes that the best teaching must be based upon a clear grasp of principles and that sword exercises, to be effective, must be rational and not merely a chore to be performed by rote.[62]

Ironically, because the style of swordsmanship it advocated was soon to be outmoded everywhere but in Spain, Thibault's *Académie* has come to be regarded more as a massive bibliographical sepulchre than as a serious contribution to the art of fencing. It was rarely cited by later masters[63] and was even ignored by the widely read Morsicato Pallavicini who, steeped as he was in the theories of Carranza and Narváez, might well have admired Thibault's exegetical virtuosity even though he himself never aspired to an elaborate movement notation. He, too, was convinced of the relevance of mathematics not only to the practice of fencing but also to its elucidation, and he used this relationship to substantiate his own lofty view of the dignity of his profession. The real extent of his mathematical knowledge is, of course, another matter. He enjoyed writing about iscoceles triangles as though they embodied some profound secret of swordsmanship, but the majority of his geometrical propositions, along with his references to Euclid, are derived directly from Carranza and Narváez. On the rare occasions when he refers to a corroborative source it turns out to be something like Gregorius Reisch's *Margarita phylosophica* which was about as basic and old-fashioned a school textbook as could be found.[64] But it was probably sufficient for the author's needs and it is doubtful whether a fencing master would have required a profound knowledge of quantitative science.

Certainly mathematical genius was no guarantee of sound fencing practice. When Adrien Baillet was preparing his life of René Descartes (who was, we may assume, the intellectual superior of most fencing masters), he found, among the great man's manuscripts, a little treatise touching the manner of using arms, entitled *The Art of Fencing* in which the 'greater part of the lessons were drawn from his own experience'. Baillet noted that, having spoken in general about the quality of the sword and the way in which it was to be used, Descartes had divided his work into two parts of which the first showed how one may secure oneself against all an adversary's efforts and gain the advantage either at *mesure longue* or at *mesure courte*; while, in the second, Descartes examined how 'having entered *en mesure courte* one could infallibly gain the victory'. However, Baillet observed laconically, in order to achieve this happy result the mathematician had postulated 'two men of equal size, equal strength, and using equal weapons, leaving to another occasion what has to be done in case of inequality'.[65] The treatise has never been found, but Baillet's description suggests that, however much admirers of Descartes might regret its disappearance, it has been no loss to the art of fencing. As La Touche later pointed out, 'if all men were of the same size, if they all had legs and arms of the same proportion with the body and sinews equally supple, and the swords of the same length, one could find a way to calculate the measure approximately'. Sadly, he continued, it is impossible to say precisely how far one must advance to gain 'la mesure' or how far to retreat in order to break with the opposition, because everybody is different.[66] Girard Thibault had grasped this essential truth more than forty years earlier. 'To overcome an adversary', he wrote, 'some sort of advantage is necessary; and to have the advantage there must be inequality, it being impossible that between equal things, in as much as they are equal, there should be any great advantage'. The whole intention of Thibault's work was to use mathematics to explain how such inequalities could be exploited in practice, and in this respect at least he was a more realistic mathematician than Descartes.

RECURRENT AND UNRESOLVED PROBLEMS

Despite all the attempts to characterize, analyse and systematize sword-fighting, there still remained not only the obstinate imponderability of incommensurate bodies but also issues which were resolved not by the masters themselves but by evolutionary forces such as changes in the art of war and in civilian fashion. And there were some issues which were never resolved at all.

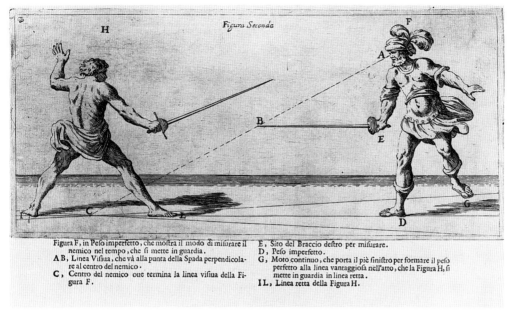

Figura F, in Pefo imperfetto, che moftra il modo di mifurare il
   nemico nel tempo, che fi mette in guardia.
A B, Linea Vifiua, che và alla punta della Spada perpendicola-
   re al centro del nemico.
C, Centro del nemico oue termina la linea vifiua della Figura F.

E, Sito del Braccio deftro per mifurare.
D, Pefo imperfetto.
G, Moto continuo, che porta il piè finiftro per formare il pefo
   perfetto alla linea vantaggiofa nell'atto, che la Figura H, fi
   mette in guardia in linea retta.
I L, Linea retta della Figura H.

102. Senesio shows the line of vision through one's own sword point. 1660, fig. 2.

What, for example, should a swordsman watch when engaged in serious combat? Surely not the point of his own sword, as Alessandro Senesio seemed to suggest (fig. 102).[67] Should he keep his eye on the opponent's sword, point, or hilt, on his whole body, arm, wrist, hand, or face?[68] Some thought it possible to read a man's intentions by watching his eyes, but this found little favour since it was apparent that an enemy might look you full in the face and cut your leg, or look at your foot and strike your head; and it did not pass unnoticed that an adversary with cross-eyes would render the technique wholly futile.[69] Marco Docciolini, who reviewed most of these possibilities, recommended keeping an eye on the point of the opposing sword 'whence the first injury must come', for this would provide a much better idea of the manner in which an enemy was likely to strike.[70] This idea, too, was disputed and the masters never stopped worrying about the issue. Nor did they ever agree a solution. Similarly inconclusive were their views on the value of the feint: simulating an attack in order to elicit a parry, and then immediately striking at another part of the body. 'Beholde a fencer', wrote Guazzo, 'who making at his enimies head, striketh him on the legge.'[71] All masters recognized that feints were widely used and had, therefore, to be understood. Many thought them essential; and, as we have seen, one, Pietro Monte, even built his fencing system almost entirely upon them. Others thought them harmful in yielding a time advantage to the opponent and would have nothing to do with them; and Pallavicini, while considering them useful, compared them to false arguments in logic which, once exposed, would inevitably ruin the perpetrator.[72] In marked contrast to all this uncertainty was the accord with which the masters responded to another recurrent problem. Were there special techniques to deal with a left-hander, and was the left-hander, in his turn, obliged to fence differently from a more conventional adversary? Here most masters felt, like both Monte and Marozzo, that there were no fundamental differences in technique, and that the only difficulty arose from the fact that left-handers were fewer in number and therefore had more experience of right-handers than vice versa.[73] 'Did I not tell you', Saviolo

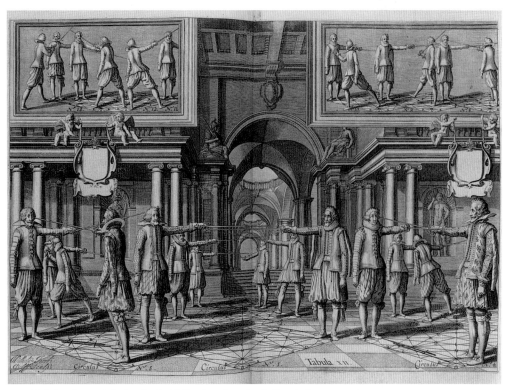

103. Left-hander v. right-hander in Thibault. 1630, book II, tabula 12.

reminds his pupil, 'that the lefte hand had no advantage of the right, nor the right to the lefte? onelye use and knowledge giveth the better either to the right or the lefte.' Thibault accepts this but, more realistically, also accepts that the left-hander must inevitably have the advantage of 'continual use' which can only be countered by trying to gain as much similar experience as possible (figs 103–4). For all these reassurances, it remained common for fencers to feel apprehensive when facing left-handers, and La Touche believed that this was due solely to the failure of teachers to prepare their pupils adequately, which they could easily do by sometimes taking the sword in the left hand to demonstrate that this poses no special threat.[74]

Technical matters like these were regularly debated by the masters most of whom felt obliged to say something about everything. Yet there were two major issues – one historical, the other practical – on which the majority of them remained silent. The precise definition of the art of fencing was something which never troubled medieval and renaissance masters though it has bothered historians who want to establish the origins of what they refer to as *scientific fencing*, by which they mean modern sword play – with the emphasis on play. It took centuries before the words *fencing, Fechten, escrime, esgrima, scrimia, scherma* and so on, came to indicate exclusively the use of the single sword without any other weapon or defence. Many medieval masters taught such fighting, but it was only one of several martial arts in their repertory and never the most important. They generally accorded primacy to the long sword: and the use of that, as we have seen, was anything but unscientific. Early sixteenth-century treatises, too, allow little space to the single sword. Manciolino praised it as an especially convenient weapon because, whereas one may not always have dagger, buckler or cape, 'one can always have the *spada sola*': but he still concentrated

142

104. Detail of fig. 103.

on sword and buckler fighting.[75] In the latter part of the sixteenth century there was a distinct change of emphasis as the long sword, outside Germany, lost ground to the rapier especially when the latter was accompanied with a dagger. As Saviolo explains to his pupil, there is a wide diversity among teachers, some of whom start their scholars off with rapier and dagger, some with rapier and buckler, and others with rapier alone. His own preference is to begin with the rapier alone because noblemen, knights, gentlemen and soldiers wear it 'as being more proper and fit to be worne then other weapons'.[76] This is not much of an argument and, as it turns out, Saviolo spends more time on the rapier/dagger combination than on rapier alone.

With few exceptions, the later renaissance masters gave the greater part of their attention to sword and dagger – though the origins of this style of combat are themselves obscure. In his *Duello*, first printed in the 1470s, Paris de Puteo tells of a challenge issued in Italy by two foreign knights (*doi Cavallieri oltramontani*) to fight using only sword and dagger, and without wearing defensive armour. Several knights protested and the combat was forbidden by the local ruler, but it is not clear whether the objection concerned the weapons or the lack of protective armour. Nor do we know whether the knights intended to use the weapons consecutively or concurrently. And the fact that the disputants were *oltramontani* suggests that the practice may simply have been alien to Italians of the late fifteenth century.[77] Around 1510 there certainly was a sword and dagger duel between Azevedo and Saincte Croix in which the Spaniard fought with sword in right hand and dagger in left; and Dürer's *Fechtbuch* of 1512 includes three illustrations of combats between a man using falchion and dagger against falchion alone, although it is impossible to say whether or not this reflects any kind of actuality.[78] Thereafter, the combination became increasingly dominant, and as late as 1619 it was still possible for a master to imply that this particular combination comprised the whole art of fencing.[79] Nor did the use of increasingly long cut and thrust rapiers encourage men to abandon supplementary arms. The laconic Falloppia gives primacy to *la spada sola*, but he pays almost as much attention to sword with dagger; Ghisliero's fencing system is based on the sword/dagger combination; and Docciolini, who defines fencing as 'the art of well managing arms', devotes less than half his treatise to *la spada sola*. The famous Fabris not only describes all the traditional combinations of sword with dagger, cloak, or buckler but for good measure also throws in the wrestling, pommel jabs and other all-in fighting techniques favoured by masters of a much earlier era. Giganti explains that he is confining himself in his 'first book' to two sorts of arms, that is the sword alone and the sword in combination with dagger; and he begins with the sword, 'in as much that this is the weapon most common and accustomed', claiming that anyone who knows how to handle a sword will know how to handle all other types of weapon. In fact, this occupies less than half his text and, of his forty-two illustrations, the first nineteen deal with sword alone, including six where the fighter uses his left hand to grip or deflect the opponent, and the rest illustrate sword with dagger. His promised second book never materialized, but his work was partially supplemented by Capoferro who also has forty-two plates of which seventeen show sword alone, including four using the left hand to grip or deflect; two for sword and cloak; two for sword and round shield; and twenty-one for sword and dagger.

The one master who was bitterly critical of the dagger disliked it for social, not professional, reasons. Nobles, said the acidulous Frenchman François Dancie in 1623, never carry such a weapon. Having a poniard at one's side is appropriate more to 'un vilain et sanguinaire' than to gentlemen who only use a dagger when it is assigned in a duel. The sword, by contrast, marks the most elevated members of society. It is 'the finest plume of a great man, without which he cannot be distinguished from a financier, merchant, or burgess, whom the abuse of our times permits to be as well-dressed as he'. It is nothing other than the sword worn on its own 'that makes the single nobleman recognized amidst a thousand plebeians who are dressed as well as he'. One might think this compliment sufficiently maladroit, but its dubiety is enhanced by the fact that Dancie's treatise allots considerably more space to techniques for sword and dagger than for the *espée seule*.[80]

As far as I know, Sainct Didier and Viggiani were the first masters to limit their writings to the sword alone, and Thibault the first to declare categorically not only that the sword was self-sufficient but also that it had the advantage of other weapons including the sword/dagger combination, and the two-hander. He even suggested a method whereby the determined swordsman might deal with a musketeer: though here honesty compelled him to admit that success was doubtful.[81] Even forty years later, the autonomy of the sword was still not wholly accepted by masters. *La spada sola* was extolled by Pallavicini in his

Scherma illustrata (1670) as a weapon sufficient of itself for both attack and defence and the book dealt with nothing else. Three years later, however, he published a second volume (just as heavily documented as the first) given over to the sword/dagger combination and to a lengthy treatment of the sword paired with cape or buckler.[82] By Pallavicini's day the rapier, with its accessories, was being superseded by the small sword; and the fashionable French masters were concentrating upon the sword alone – eliminating daggers, cloaks and bucklers, and drastically reducing the role of the left hand and other wrestling tricks.[83] But elsewhere the utility of such techniques, even with the small sword, was still appreciated and they continued in vogue. German manuals in the eighteenth century placed much emphasis on all-in fighting; and we even find the use of dagger, cloak and lantern noted and illustrated in Angelo's *School of Arms* whence they found their way (under 'Escrime') into the greatest monument of Enlightenment scholarship, Diderot and D'Alembert's *L'Encyclopédie* where they are treated as techniques characteristic of Italian and Spanish fencing.[84]

One theme which one might think would have occupied the attention of any master concerned with teaching pupils how to survive in a world of sudden, murderous affrays is the technique of drawing the sword from its scabbard and bringing it into action. The ability to get at an opponent in the shortest possible time could be as critical to the swordsman's longevity as a fast draw is supposed to have been in the case of the western gun-slinger, yet few medieval and renaissance masters gave this matter more than a cursory nod. Some Japanese masters regarded drawing the sword as an art in its own right; but in sixteenth-century Europe only Giovanni Antonio Lovino devoted much thought to the problem and he himself poses something of a riddle. He begins his treatise by remarking that he has observed 'the common use or rather, to say better, the abuse, of the mode of putting one's hand to the sword, not so much by idiots who profess arms as by those who have written divers volumes on this science'. In fact, the identity of these writers is a mystery. The only early authority to refer to drawing the sword was Pietro Monte and he, in fact, anticipates Lovino by advising that the fighter must advance his left foot adding, characteristically, that the sword must be aimed 'with great ostentation' at the opponent's head while simultaneously turning it downward.[85] The draw was not analysed by Pauernfeindt, Manciolino, Marozzo, Agrippa or dall'Agocchie, while Sainct Didier, who does begin his sequence of postures with a brief account of bringing the sword into action, shows one fencer standing with feet together, the other leading slightly with the right foot, and explains neither. (See Chapter II, fig. 47.) It is just possible that a remark of Viggiani's – that it was natural for fencers to lead with the right side – may have prompted Lovino to complain that all these idiots are moved by a 'certain natural inclination' to perform the essential preliminary act of drawing the sword with the right foot forward, thereby failing to take into account that the 'perfection of this science consists primarily in neither incurring danger nor in losing time'.[86] If a man stands right foot forward as he draws his sword he not only loses a hand's breadth of distance – 'con disavantaggio di un palmo di spada' – but is also in danger of having his arm seized by his adversary. By contrast, if he stands left foot forward, holding the scabbard steady with the left hand, not only are these disadvantages avoided but he can withdraw the sword more easily from its sheath and, at the same instant, take up his guard without loss of time and without conceding time to his opponent.

This was a crucial issue and it is hard to understand why it was so generally avoided. Unlike the short sword and small sword, the long and unwieldy rapier must have been incredibly difficult to get into action: yet some of the most famous and most highly praised authorities in the history of renaissance swordsmanship, such as Fabris and Giganti, have nothing to say on the subject. Presumably, judging from their illustrations, they envisaged fencers dashing about in the nude, scabbardless, and obliged, therefore, to carry sword in hand at all times. Capoferro, who does devote a short chapter to the 'Method for putting hand to the sword', has his normally nude, furiously lunging fencers fully clad in the first picture so that they can wear a scabbard.[87] (See Chapter II, fig. 34.) Thus the gentleman on the left can be seen drawing his sword in precisely the posture, left foot forward, recommended by Lovino and still favoured well into the eighteenth century when it was engraved and repeated in the various editions and versions of Domenico Angelo's *L'École des armes*.[88] Despite this, Capoferro's accompanying text is vague and unhelpful; and the moment that their naked swords are out of the scabbards so his fencers are out of their clothes.

As is the case with many other technical aspects of swordsmanship, by far the fullest analysis of the art of drawing the sword was provided by Girard Thibault in his *Académie de l'espée*.[89] Thibault rightly points out that this, the very first action of combat, is of greater importance than is generally appreciated and that ignorance of the correct method has caused considerable inconvenience to some fencers who have been caught so unawares by their adversaries that their swords have been rendered useless. The remedy is to know how to draw the sword dexterously so that we are hindered neither by ourselves nor by our enemies; and Thibault recommends two methods for bringing the sword into action – one when advancing and the other when retreating. The first is appropriate when the opponent is at a reasonable distance but is so clearly threatening us that we are bound to look to our defence. In such circumstances, to retreat merely encourages him to take the initiative and it is better to advance 'to receive him with a spirited resolution'. Having taken two, three or even four paces forward, the swordsman is advised to seize his scabbard with the left hand close to the guard and the hanger, while moving forward with the left foot; and then, as the foot touches the ground, to take hold of the sword with the right hand, hooking the index finger around the outer quillon of the guard. Continuing to step forward, raising the right foot a little higher than when taking an ordinary step, he must strengthen the grip of his left hand to keep the scabbard firm and low so that it does not move forward. The whole of the right side should be lifted, especially the arm, and the sword should, in fact, be drawn by the finger hooked about the quillon and not by the hand which must retain only a loose grip until the blade is out of the scabbard. All this will ensure that the sword is pulled out more easily: 'in such a way that in this action, the foot, the hands both left and right, the shoulder, the arm and, in sum, all the limbs give each other mutual assistance'. Quite the opposite happens to those who keep their right foot on the ground, for it is impossible in such circumstances to avoid inconvenience.

Once the sword is drawn in the correct manner, Thibault continues, the right foot should momentarily be kept raised in order to facilitate the actions which are to follow: 'which is exactly what the figure represents; for you see that his right foot is still raised high and the sword is barely out of the scabbard'. (See Chapter II, fig. 64.) During that 'pause of the right foot', the swordsman should tighten the grip of his right hand and, turning the wrist, raise the sword blade through a semicircle until it is above the right shoulder, at about the height (and by the side) of the head: with the point backward and the pommel forward, and the arm a little bent, 'as is seen in the figure'. The sword is then brought around, from high to low, in a backhander, while the right foot is on the ground and the left is moving forward.

Continue to bring arm and sword in front of the breast, so that the footstep and the descent of the sword finish at the same instant, placing the foot on the ground and letting the extended arm descend together with the sword next to the right thigh, turning at the same time the inner quillon inwards and putting the thumb against it. Thus you will have the sword in hand according to the manner of our practice and all your actions will be prompt, gallant, comely, and suitable always for stepping forward without any interruption.

Thibault now turns his attention to the method of drawing while moving backwards because it often happens, when in company, that a situation arises where one is forced to put hand to one's weapons: and this may be very difficult where the company is so close together that one cannot easily move and defend oneself. In such circumstances one is obliged to draw the sword while moving back 'as is shown here by the four following figures, E.F.G.H. which are the opposite of the four preceding'. Here one may begin the retreat with either foot but the grip of both left hand on the scabbard and of the right hand and index finger on the sword hilt, are as previously set out; the draw again begins as the left foot moves; and the whole action is exactly the same except that it is executed while stepping backwards. Thibault concedes that the actions he describes will seem at first very difficult or even impossible to carry out, 'on account of so many little points to observe in so short a time'. But practice will show that, on the contrary, all these things are really 'natural and easy'.

However one may assess the merits of Thibault's fighting system, there should be no doubt about the superiority of his bibliographical and literary methods nor about his skill in relating theory to practice. His reputation among historians of fencing has always been so dismal that it is worth stressing once again his many virtues: the clarity of his verbal descriptions; the precision with which these are related to his illustrations; his understanding of the psychology of combat (as in the recommendation of moving forward against an oncoming aggressor); and the essential practicality of his instructions which are designed to meet as many eventualities as possible. If it really were possible to teach swordsmanship by means of a printed book, then Thibault was the man to do it for he had the gift of *la communicativa* in abundance. It was his misfortune to be communicating, in French, an art that was dying in France.

V
Staff weapons

THROUGHOUT THE MIDDLE Ages and the Renaissance swords were the most highly regarded of all weapons and, after daggers or knives, were the most portable and widely used. But vying with the sword for popularity, though not in esteem, was the family of staff weapons which offered a great variety of forms, each with its own domain – both in terms of practical use and social status (fig. 105). The wooden staff, of varied length and generally shod at each end with a metal ferrule, was a potent civilian weapon, widely used especially by travellers and country dwellers; hafted weapons with blades, spikes and hooks (or spike alone) – such as halberds, partisans, bills and pikes – enjoyed a long period of success on the battlefields of Europe where they enabled foot soldiers to deal effectively with cavalry opposition; while, at the other end of the social scale, the polaxe was a chivalric weapon which assumed a passing primacy during the fifteenth century among armoured knights fighting within the lists. Yet, despite their diversity and widespread use, staff weapons never received anything like the volume of literary attention which masters of arms bestowed upon the sword – just as they have rarely aroused much interest among historians. In the latter case, the lack of enthusiasm is understandable because the problems posed by the chaotic inconsistency of nomenclature (both early and modern), the multiformity of surviving weapons, and the fact that so few have their original staves, all render scholarly assessment difficult.[1] The masters' reticence is less easily explained: but the fact remains that, with some notable exceptions, their written treatments of fighting with staff weapons tend to be both brief and imprecise and generally convey an impression that the material has been included more for completeness's sake than from conviction. Certainly there was little attempt to reduce such fighting to scientific principles. Particularly indicative of this indifference is Camillo Agrippa's *Trattato*. As we know, Agrippa was enthusiastic about the application of geometry to sword fighting and to the devising of methods for facilitating understanding by means of annotated illustrations. Yet his tiny chapter on staff weapons could scarcely have been more perfunctory so that, when he refers back to it as a demonstration of how to use the two-hand sword (which is itself dismissed as too crude for serious analysis) it is impossible to avoid the conclusion that he rather despised them.[2]

Implicit in Agrippa's handling of the subject are two important assumptions. One is that somehow staff weapons and two-handed swords are not really suitable for a gentleman: an attitude later made explicit by Falloppia when he scorned them as unchivalric and fit only for those engaged in premeditated violence.[3] The other assumption – that there was a technique common to all staff weapons – was shared by several other masters. Andre Paurnfeindt, for example, in 1516, opens his section on quarterstaff combat with the bald

105. Lucini's warriors
advance with pike and
halberd. 1627, plate 2.

statement that it is a fountain-head (*ein Ursprung*) for the handling of all similar hafted weapons. Half a century later di Grassi prefaced his discussion of the 'weapons of the Staffe' – bill (*roncha*), partisan (*pertesanone*), halberd (*allabarda*) and *spiedo*[4] – with the remark that many readers might consider it strange that he was dealing with all four weapons together, as though they were all handled in one and the same manner. But this is precisely his contention. Skill with one, he declares, 'helpeth a man to the knowledge of all the rest'.[5] Certainly, with regard to their advantages and disadvantages, staff weapons were easy to assess. Their length, if pitted against a shorter arm, could be used to keep an opponent at a distance, and they were capable of delivering extremely powerful blows and thrusts. On the other hand, their length and weight meant that they were not suitable for carrying around in built-up areas and would, in any case, have been difficult to wield in a narrow street; while, more generally, their cuts – though weighty – were comparatively slow and easy to anticipate.

Fighting with staff weapons was taught by masters the length and breadth of Europe: yet our knowledge of the techniques involved – though rich – is incredibly uneven. It was usual, in German *Fechtbücher*, to devote some space to such combats and the tradition can be traced from its first brief appearance in Hanko Döbringer's manuscript in 1389 through to the latter half of the seventeenth century.[6] Talhoffer, in the mid-fifteenth century, deals only with spear (or staff) and polaxe; and in 1516 Paurnfeindt has a section on the quarterstaff, which was plagiarized a few years later by Egenolff. Meyer's comprehensive *Fechtbuch* of 1570 discusses and illustrates combat with quarterstaff, halberd and pike; and his plagiarist Sutor elects to write only on the first two weapons, while throwing in a short paragraph on the flail to show individuality. As late as 1660, Meyer was still deemed sufficiently relevant to prompt a third edition, and shortly afterwards Pascha applied his strip-cartoon technique to the handling of the pike alone. In Italy, too, though more sporadically, both spear and axe occur in treatises ranging from early fifteenth-century personal violence to courtly and balletic posturing with wooden simulacra two hundred years later; and the bill, partisan, halberd and *spiedo* feature in several sixteenth-century texts. By contrast, until the pike-drill manuals of the seventeenth century, there are no French treatises on the technique of combat with staff weapons other than a fifteenth-century manuscript on

149

106. A synchronized pike movement in Pistofilo. 1621, p. 111, fig. 76.

axe-fighting and a translation of Paurnfeindt in 1538. In England it was not until 1599 that staff weapons were seriously discussed by a native master; and, Monte excepted, none of the Spanish masters bothered to write about them.

One thing which is apparent from the available material is that, over a period of more than two centuries, despite changes in the configuration and size of the blades, there was little change (let alone evolution) in the handling of staff weapons for personal combat. What did develop was an increasing awareness of their military effectiveness when used in massed formation by the Swiss – first with halberds and then with pikes – and by Spanish, German and other troops. In view of this it is curious that, despite constant asseverations that their teaching had a direct military application, most masters of arms persistently treated staff weapons in terms of single combat and it was left to the military specialists of the early seventeenth century to evolve the rigorous systematization of handling pikes *en masse* and synchronously which is recorded and illustrated in their manuals (fig. 106). The stereotyped routine of the drill yard scarcely appealed to the masters, who always preferred the more personal encounters of street, tavern and duelling field. Earlier, however, fighting in the lists had also interested them and, as far as 'weapons of the staff' were concerned, it was the polaxe – the most individualistic and the least militarily useful – which especially stirred their imagination and impelled their pens. Outside the confines of the lists, the polaxe was not an effective weapon, for, unlike two-hand and bastard swords, they are not well balanced. Their insufficiency is attested by the many accounts of fifteenth-century combats in which knights battered each other unmercifully – denting, puncturing and even knocking bits off each other's armour, yet eventually emerging unscathed and often not even out of breath.[7] This suggests that armour was effective, and that axes were not.[8] But they did offer knights scope for brilliant display, as in a famous combat between Portuguese and French knights in 1415; and some of the early masters of arms also found it a sympathetic subject (fig. 107).[9]

Tem en ces iours fut faict a Sainct odou lhostel du Roy de hors
paris vng champ de trois portugalons · Ce staf sauoir le pmier
Le seigneur de alueron · Le second messire iehan de cousalle
Cheualier · Et le tiers messire pierre cousalle contre trois

107. A sixteenth-century Monstrelet MS showing an axe combat between Portuguese and French knights. Bibliothèque Nationale Paris, MS. Fr. 20,360, fol. 303v.

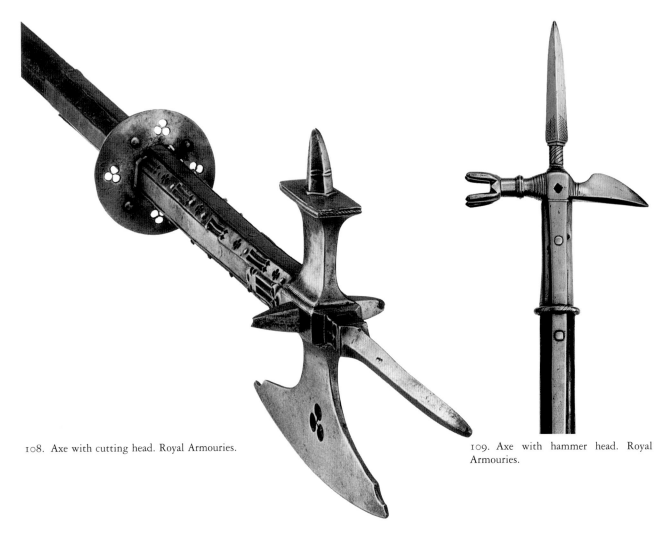

108. Axe with cutting head. Royal Armouries.

109. Axe with hammer head. Royal Armouries.

AXE FIGHTING

Skill in handling the sword was, in the opinion of most masters, the foundation for all the other martial arts; and even those who wrote favourably about staff weapons tended to agree. However, a different view was expressed by the anonymous fifteenth-century author of a treatise, *Le Jeu de la hache*, who believed that fighting with 'light lance, dagger, great sword and small sword' all depended upon knowledge of axe play. His position was undoubtedly tendentious, but there was sufficient similarity between the handling of different staff weapons to make an examination of *Le Jeu de la hache* especially worthwhile despite the fact that the manuscript exerted no influence whatsoever. It was intended as a presentation copy to some unknown prince or dignitary, but there is no record of it until it is mentioned in an inventory of François I's library at Blois, when the books were transferred to Fontainebleau in 1544. Thereafter it remained buried among the French royal manuscripts until it made its way into what is now the Bibliothèque Nationale and it has scarcely been consulted since.[10] Yet it is an important treatise partly because it is the only work ever devoted exclusively to axe combat; partly because it is written with an unusual clarity of style; and, even more remarkably, partly because it is the only surviving martial arts treatise of any sort written and conceived in French prior to Sainct Didier's *Traicté* of 1573.

Before considering the text of *Le Jeu* and related works, it is worth remarking on the nature of the axe envisaged by their authors, since it is not at all what modern readers would expect. Roughly speaking, there are two principal types of polaxe: those bearing an axe blade with a cutting edge, and those with a hammer head – the former balanced at the back with a hammer, spike or curved fluke; the latter by spike or fluke (figs 108–9). Generally, the top of the haft terminates in a long metal spike, either rectangular in section or shaped like a spearhead or thick dagger blade. The bottom end of the haft would normally be protected by a metal ferrule which, if sufficiently developed and sharpened, would amount to what was sometimes referred to as the 'under blade' (*dague dessoubz*). The metal head would be fixed to the haft by strong pyramidal bolts often projecting to such an extent that they constituted transverse spikes so that, whether viewed sectionally, or from the front or the side, the head would appear cruciform. As was normal with staff weapons, long steel bands (known as straps or *languets*) would run down the haft from the head, sometimes on two sides and sometimes on all four, intended both to strengthen the structure and to prevent the haft from being severed. Frequently, a metal rondelle would be attached to these *languets* at roughly a third of the way down the haft to protect the hands; and some axes were also fitted near the bottom of the haft with a thick leather strap or ring – presumably to stop the weapon from flying through, and out of, the hands when the axe was wielded long.

With few exceptions, detailed narratives of axe fighting date from the middle of the fifteenth century and are Burgundian in origin. Of these, only the descriptions of Olivier de la Marche give an impression of accurate reporting, and even he uses an inconsistent terminology. What is significant, though, is the fact that on only one occasion does Olivier specifically refer to a *taillant* – an axe with a cutting edge.[11] The curved fluke or *bec de faucon* also appears rarely in his accounts of combat: but he frequently mentions the use of the hammer head, thrusts with the top spike, and (most frequently of all) thrusts, blows or parries with the butt-end of the axe. Olivier is a good analyst of axe fighting; but the author of *Le Jeu* is even better, and his terminology is impressively consistent. At no point does he refer to a *taillant* or cutting edge but, instead, the head of the axe has a hammer (*mail*) balanced by a curved fluke (*bec de faucon*), and surmounted at the top of the haft with a dagger-like spike (*dague*). The intersection of the head and haft is referred to as the cross (*la croix*) which is, in turn, sometimes distinguished from the transverse spikes (*la croisée*). The lower end of the haft is, with few exceptions, indicated by the word *queue*; while the term 'half axe' (*demy hache*) specifies the centre of the haft between the two hands, and its use in combat is much the same as the half-sword techniques common with two-hand and bastard swords.

Obviously, these features do not constitute an axe in the modern sense of the word but rather form what is often termed a 'pole hammer' or 'bec de faucon'. Nevertheless, 'la hache' in *Le Jeu* is essentially the same weapon as that described as 'la azza' by Fiore de' Liberi; as 'der axst' by Talhoffer; as 'aza' by Filippo di Vadi; and as 'aza vel tricuspis' by Pietro Monte. The only differences are that Fiore's illustrations show a spike at the bottom of the haft which is also described by Monte, but is never mentioned in *Le Jeu*, while Talhoffer, who only occasionally shows a point at the lower end of the haft, depicts a straight spike opposite the hammer head instead of a curved *bec de faucon*.[12]

As with swords, the masters were generally cavalier with regard to the dimensions of the weapons they discussed, and the style and size of polaxes seem to have been matters of individual taste. On this issue, *Le Jeu* is silent; but Monte, in 1509, declares that the axe, up to its hammer head, should be 'one hand' longer than the man using it. If to this we add the length of the *dague* at the top and the spike at the *queue* then something well over six feet would have been in order, while an overall length of nearly eight feet would not have seemed extraordinary for an exceptionally tall man such as Henry VIII. In 1627, Pistofilo – describing the gimcrack axes of his own day, with the *martello* made of wood but painted like gold, silver or shining steel 'so that it should more closely approximate to reality' – says that the haft should be 'tre braccia' in length, which is the height of a 'giusto Cavaliere'. Later he states with approval that it has become normal in his own day to use an axe four 'braccia' in length, which he considers both better in appearance and more effective in combat: although it is difficult to see that painted wooden axes would ever have been particularly fearsome.[13] Certainly some illustrations, including those in Fiore, Talhoffer and *Freydal*, tend to confirm that polaxes were generally about the length of the knight wielding them. But there is no consistency in this matter, and other illustrations suggest lengths intermediate between this and the much shorter one-handed axe or hatchet.

The tone, quality and precision of *Le Jeu* all suggest that it is the work of a professional master of arms, well versed in the practical instruction of knightly pupils, and especially concerned with preparing them for judicial combat in the lists. This is made apparent in his opening remarks where, after declaring the primacy of axe combat, he addresses his reader as one of two champions, 'called on the field of battle, whether to the death or otherwise, whether you may be appellant or defendant'. On leaving his pavilion the knight must recommend himself to God, make the sign of the cross, and 'march upright, with a good and valorous countenance'; he must gaze at the other end of the field to seek out his adversary; and is enjoined, when gazing upon him, to 'take in a measured manner a proud courage in yourself to fight valiantly as is becoming'. The need for a bold and confident demeanour when approaching an enemy was constantly stressed by experts in the martial arts. Ghisliero, for example, advising his warrior on drawing the sword from its scabbard, has nothing to say about technique but stresses instead how advantageous it is to 'clench the fist, grind the teeth, and open the eyes wide to show our fierce visage'. More specifically with reference to axe combat of a sort – that is the gentle mutual patting of seventeenth-century Italian courtiers – even Pistofilo recommends the knight to take up his weapon with a great flourish and signs of defiance, waving it about and transferring it from hand to hand, to demonstrate mastery and ease.

Le Jeu is altogether more serious. It is in two sections: the first and main part dealing with combat between two right-handers; the second on how a right-hander should cope with a left-handed adversary. Throughout the work great care is taken to group together, in a logical sequence, different modes of attack – whether swings or openings with the *croix*, *queue* or *dague* – and to accompany these with various possible parries, counter-attacks and counter-ripostes. There are also clear descriptions of feints and distracting moves. When, for example, you aim a blow at your opponent's head you must take care that, should you miss, your axe does not pass beyond him, 'because that would be dangerous'; and immediately this blow has been accomplished, 'you must make a feint of having another go at his head so that he covers himself high – whereupon you can give him one on the knee with the *bec de faucon*'. In general, *Le Jeu* advocates ceaseless thrusting at the opponent's foot, hand or face, 'so that he does not find your axe at all still, and you can, wholly at your own initiative, make any opening'. This unremitting attack is reminiscent of Liechtenauer's recommendation for the long sword, where an adversary should never be given the slightest opportunity to seize the initiative and go on the attack himself. In short, concludes the author of *Le Jeu*, 'you must frequently attack him with jabs at the face and at the feet to make him lose his composure'.

One of the most impressive features of the treatise is the consistency of its terminology not only for the parts of the axe but also for the categorization of movements and positions. The author repeatedly reminds his pupil to be *en garde*, in the modern sense of being in a position from which he may equally initiate an attack or defend himself; and the *garde* is often qualified by the part of the axe with which the knight leads, whether *queue*, *dague* or, occasionally, *croix*. Of these, the author specifically recommends the *queue* as the most advantageous and there is a heavy reliance on this part of the axe both for attack and defence.[14] It is referred to more than three times as often as the *dague*; while the *mail* and *bec de faucon* (which we might regard as the business end of the weapon) are rarely used. Counters or parries are sometimes described as a cover (*couverte*) or as an 'undoing' (*deffaite*), and the act of successful parrying is indicated by the verb 'to undo' (*deffaire*): but these terms are, on the whole, not differentiated and are used less exactly than the verbs *tourner* and *destourner* which are used for the turning aside of the opponent's axe. Modes of attack are denoted by the words *entrée* and *prinse* which, though not markedly differentiated, indicate an 'opening' or a 'move'.

With regard to specific strokes, *Le Jeu* is very exact and decisive. It distinguishes sharply between the *estocq* which is a thrust or jab; the *tour de bras* which is a big swinging 'round arm' blow; and the *coup* which usually indicates a blow delivered sideways – that is, what would be a cut with an edged weapon. Sometimes *coup* is the generic term for a particular kind of stroke such as the knee stroke (*coup de genou*); and sometimes, suitably qualified, it shows the mode of delivery as, for example, the back hander (*coup darrière main*). Frequently, too, the axe fighter has to *boutter* or deliver a *boutte*; and in the majority of cases this action is associated with the *demy hache* position when it indicates a sharp push against a part of the opponent's weapon or body with which one's axe is already in contact. Much less usual is the instruction *pousser*, as when heaving hard against an opponent's armpit; or the exhortation to deliver a *bonne secousse* or sudden jolt. The opposite movement, that is a tug or pull – as when one has hooked the *bec de faucon* behind the opponent's neck – is naturally indicated by the verb 'to pull' (*tirer*); though, again, the word is also used in its other less specific sense of delivering a blow of any sort.

The principal characteristics of the fighting method advocated in *Le Jeu* are constant motion and ceaseless attacks often preceded by feints to draw the opponent's guard; a heavy emphasis on thrusting, especially with the *queue* of the axe and from a low position upwards; the regular deployment of *demy hache* techniques both for attack and defence; and a selective use of the *bec de faucon* to hook and pull at an opponent's body or his axe. Given the lack of any generally accepted conventions or terminology, the language of *Le Jeu* is remarkably unambiguous and effectively describes a coherent practical system much of which may be confirmed from other early writing on axe combat.

Fiore, for example, who devotes only a short section of his *Flos duellatorum* to axe fighting, begins with a sequence of postures analogous to those he recommends for the sword and follows this with a short group of combats (figs 110–12). There are several discrepancies between the version published by Novati and the Getty manuscript; and the latter is not only more detailed, but has two supplementary postures and five extra fight pictures. These extra illustrations include two with a weapon which, though still called an

110. Fiore's sequence of axe combats. *c.* 1410, fol. 27.

111. Axe combats. Fiore, *c.* 1410, fol. 27v.

112. Axe combats. Fiore, *c.* 1410, fol. 28.

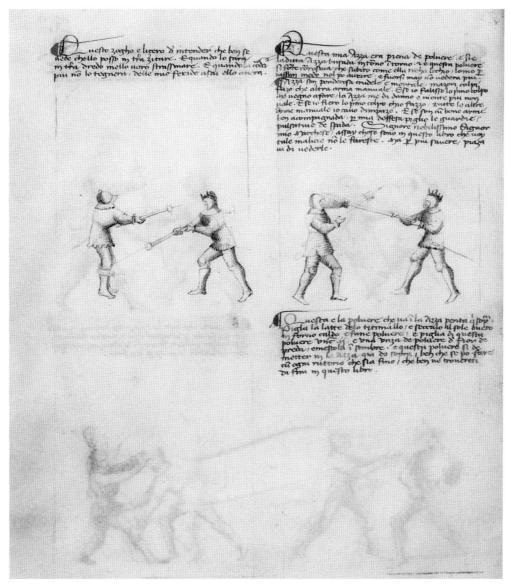

azza, looks more like a sledgehammer and describes itself as 'heavy, cruel, and mortal' and as delivering 'greater blows than other manual arms'. This is not a contention one would care to test, although the strokes would inevitably have been slow and, as Fiore himself points out, if you missed the target you would be likely to damage yourself. This would have been especially true of one of these axes – an extraordinary invention in which the axe head has been hollowed out and the cavity filled with a powder consisting of two ounces of 'the milk of the spurge (*titimallo*) dried in the sun or in a hot oven', and one ounce of powdered *fior de preda*. This is 'so strong and corrosive that, the moment it touches the eye, the man cannot stand it in any way and will see no more' (fig. 113).[15] Such bizarreries apart, Fiore, like the author of *Le Jeu*, attaches great importance to thrusting with the spikes at either end of the haft, even to the extent of using the left hand to force open the opponent's visor while jabbing the *dague* into his face. On the other hand, possibly due to the brevity of Fiore's survey, there is less specific concern with the *demy hache* technique which features so prominently in *Le Jeu*. There is also a marked contrast between the treatises in their treatment of hand-to-hand grappling. Fiore is ready to resort to wrestling tricks such as thrusting the axe between an opponent's legs while forcing his head back with one's left hand; grasping his right arm under the armpit with one's left hand; taking the opportunity, when his hands are spread widely apart, to seize his axe in the centre; and, when the axes have been abandoned, to attempt a leg pick-up. In *Le Jeu*, however, despite many more postures and moves, grappling occurs only once – when a hand under the crutch is recommended to counter a push beneath the armpit.[16]

Greater illumination is provided by the German master Talhoffer in the various versions of his *Fechtbuch* for, although he does include hand-to-hand grappling which does not feature in *Le Jeu*, his system of axe fighting makes similar use of thrusting and of the *demy hache*. However, the most interesting parallels are to be found in Talhoffer's drawings which often seem designed specifically to elucidate not only his own exiguous (or non-existent) text but also to illustrate *Le Jeu* itself.[17] Where, for example, *Le Jeu* deals with a downward swinging blow, explaining how 'you can take it on your *demy hache* as high as your arms can be extended', we can find the manoeuvre clearly depicted in Talhoffer.[18] Where *Le Jeu* explains that – when an opponent thrusts the *queue* of his axe between your thighs and tries to lift you – 'you must stick your axe into the middle of his chest, and he will not be able to do it to you', Talhoffer shows how this is done.[19] Again, if you have aimed a blow at the opponent's knee with your *bec de faucon* and it passes behind the kneecap, *Le Jeu* explains that 'you must pull him toward you, to drag him to the ground', and Talhoffer illustrates this precisely.[20] Similar reciprocity is evident when Talhoffer seems to be illustrating *Le Jeu*'s advice that, if you can hook the *bec de faucon* around your opponent's neck, you may pull him towards you and 'see whether you can overthrow him'; or the suggestion that, if he comes at you with his face forward, 'you can jab at his face with the *queue* of your axe, or at his foot which has no protection' – that is, it is left unguarded.[21] There is, of course, no question of any direct relationship between these two masters. The point is simply that the techniques of German and Burgundian axe fighting were so much alike that the illustrations of one fit well with the text of the other, and it is noteworthy that Pietro Monte later remarked that 'the French especially, and very many Germans, play with the axe'.[22]

Monte published his own short treatment of axe fighting in his *Collectanea* of 1509, and it is reminiscent of *Le Jeu*, with an emphasis on the *calx* (that is the 'heel' or *queue*) which, says Monte, is swifter of delivery; on thrusting rather than swinging; on the efficacy of thrusts from low to high; and on 'half-axe' skills. However, the use of this weapon, if not the basic techniques involved, was becoming outmoded both for serious challenges in settlement of a dispute and for flashy displays as a courtly entertainment. It is true that the Emperor Maximilian is depicted, in his autobiographical *Freydal*, wielding an axe (which has a cutting head instead of a hammer) and prodding with the *dague* at an opponent whom he has already felled (plate XI). But we should not make too much of this because, in *Freydal*, Maximilian is to be seen beating up the opposition with virtually every weapon known to man, including the short hammer and targe, short staff, *Ahlspiess*, *Langspiess*, bastard sword, mace and targe, scimitar, two-hand sword, dagger, sword and large shield, thrusting spear, and flail (plate XII).[23] Inevitably, Henry VIII, too, tried his hand at 'the fyght with battail axes' in a foot combat at Greenwich in October 1510, when he battled against a German named Gyot, 'a talle man, and a good man of armes'. But it is possible that Henry was put out of countenance because Sir Edward Howard subsequently fought the same German and knocked him to the ground.[24] Whatever the reason, the king does not seem to have enjoyed the experience because there is no other record of an axe combat among his many subsequent feats of arms. Perhaps it was simply regarded as old-fashioned since, in the lists, the new trend was for fighting at the barriers with sword or thrusting spear. Moreover, the success of halberds, bills and pikes on the field of battle was becoming widely known both through practical experience and, soon, through the publications of influential military writers. There were better staff weapons than the polaxe for chastizing one's enemies.

OTHER 'WEAPONS OF THE STAFFE'

At the beginning of the fifteenth century, Maestro Fiore devoted only two sections of his compendium of the martial arts to the use of staff weapons on foot. One, as we have seen, dealt with the axe; the other with the spear or short lance.[25] There were certainly other staff weapons in use at the time, but Fiore did not feel obliged to write about them. Nor did the late fifteenth-century master Filippo di Vadi following, at a great distance, in Fiore's footsteps. In 1509, however, Pietro Monte (who always had war as well as single combat in mind) thought it necessary to cover a greater variety of arms. His terminology is not always clear and his arrangement of chapters is more than usually disorganized but, with minor modifications, his choice of weapons became the norm for several masters – though whether by coincidence or influence, it is impossible to say. Besides the axe, he discusses the thrusting spear; the long spear or pike; the partisan held in the right hand with a large round shield worn on the left arm; the partisan used two-handed; and the bill, halberd, and *spiedo*.[26] The length of the partisan he describes as being 'a little longer than a man can reach with his hand raised', with a blade rather like that of the old broad sword though somewhat shorter and wider, and with a cutting edge on both sides. The *rhonca* or bill is, he observes, similar to the partisan but with transverse spikes and a stronger thrusting point; and he makes the interesting observation that the bill and the halberd differ little in their technique which he regards as intermediary between partisan and axe.[27]

Monte's successors, Manciolino and Marozzo, discuss similar weapons though with certain modifications: Manciolino does not discuss the halberd at all; Marozzo mentions it only as requiring much the same technique as the bill and lance; and both drop the polaxe from their repertory.[28] Manciolino introduces *larte delle hastate* – which is the concluding section of his book – by pointing out that these weapons are of no less beauty and utility than the sword (and its various accompaniments) which he has already examined. His treatment is straightforward, and his advice for all hafted weapons is to keep the hands well apart and to open proceedings with the left foot forward when using partisan or *spiedo*, and with the right foot forward with bill or lance. One odd piece of advice concerns the partisan where, says Manciolino, the knuckles of both hands should face upwards (fig. 114). This was not unusual for staff fighting and *demi-hache* techniques, but it seems unnecessarily cumbersome as a basic posture for a hafted weapon with a wide blade, and is clearly not favoured by Marozzo who shows the hands using a more comfortable grip (fig. 115). Manciolino strongly recommends feints, and most of his attacks are delivered as thrusts. He suggests that, when fighting with a *spiedo* against a man similarly armed (*Spiedo contra Spiedo*) but stronger than yourself, you should first tie up his blade with the wings (*le ali*) of your

114. Lucini shows a desperate half-staff defence with the halberd. 1627, plate 18.

115. Marozzo's advance with the partisan. 1536, fol. 83.

116. Marozzo's stance with the *spiedo*. 1536, fol. 86v.

117. Marozzo shows how to lead with the butt of the bill. 1536, fol. 88v.

own, force it over to your left side and then thrust into his exposed flank. It sounds an effective move, but is easier said than done since the stronger man is more likely to work the trick on you. In general, Manciolino has little doubt about the advantages of hafted weapons over shorter arms such as swords and daggers, and of the lance (which is the longest of all) over the partisan, bill or *spiedo*. And his book concludes resoundingly with a sentence which would have won general, if not unqualified, approval from most medieval and renaissance masters: 'with all the hastate arms there is but one proper way to strike, and that is with the point'.

Marozzo is largely in agreement with all this but he shows a more acute awareness of the special qualities of each weapon and of their differences as well as their similarities. Nor does he forget that most staff weapons have an edged blade. Like Manciolino, he considers the thrust far more important than the cut; but he does recommend using the edge when a suitable opportunity presents itself, especially with the bill. He shares Manciolino's enthusiasm for feints and even goes so far as to suggest that, when fighting with the *spiedo*, it is a good idea deliberately to leave oneself exposed so that the opponent is encouraged to attack first (fig. 116). With regard to the partisan used in conjunction with the *rotella*, he strongly recommends that the shield should always guard one's grip on the staff so that the opponent cannot see the right hand at all. It is also important to await an attack rather than to open hostilities because, with this particular combination of weapon and shield, there are only two blows possible, thrusting with the point from above or below: 'and those who would deliver other blows without the point would be without reason and would have little practical effect'. This observation might well be made of Marozzo's entire section on partisan with *rotella* which must have been an awkward combination and probably his soundest advice is to drop the shield altogether and wield the partisan with both hands. For the partisan on its own Marozzo suggests a grip and stance which allows thrusts both with the point and with the butt end of the weapon, and he particularly stresses that one's left hand should never leave the haft.

Of all the staff weapons Marozzo clearly regards the bill (*roncha*), with its comparatively slim head and small hook, as the most versatile; and he discusses thrusts both with the point and with the butt or 'heel' (*calzo*), cuts with the edge of the blade, and a judicious use of the hook (*becha*) (fig. 117). Yet in the end he concedes that the bill, halberd and lance are all handled in a uniform fashion; and this statement, even if substantially true, enhances the general air of ineffectuality characterizing both his own and his predecessors' treatment of a subject which seemed to inspire little enthusiasm. Despite the fact that all his illustrations show men in civilian dress, Marozzo envisages fighting with staff weapons as a formal single combat within closed lists, complete with oaths to God and the Virgin Mary, reverences to the Master of the Field, and jockeying for position so that the sun is in the opponent's eyes. The entire conception is erroneous and, in the 1530s, archaic too. Of the use of staff weapons in war, Marozzo tells us nothing.

An altogether more sophisticated analysis was attempted in 1570 by Giacomo di Grassi who not only ignored the cumbersome combination of partisan with *rotella* but was also the first writer to provide an historical framework within which to understand the purpose and characteristics of staff weapons.[29] His discussion begins with the partisan as the 'plainest' of these and the one 'whereupon all the rest depend'. He omits, he says, 'to shewe who was the inventor thereof' (as though he actually knew!) but explains that 'it was found out to no other end, then for that the foot men in the warres, might be able with them to hurt those horsemen (whome they might not reach with their swords) as well with their point as with their edge.' These partisans were, therefore, made large, heavy and of good steel so that they might 'breake the maile and devyde the Iron' and, says di Grassi, this is borne out by examples of the ancient weapons which are so great and well tempered that they are 'of force to cut any other Iron'. In course of time, men tried to perfect this weapon by adding 'two crookes or forkes' (*rampini*) to the base of the head, adjoining the staff. These were curved and sharp with the points towards the enemy so that they provided an additional means of attack as well as serving to prevent hostile blows from sliding down the staff towards the hands. However, in order not to increase the overall weight of the partisan, 'which ought to be apt and commodious to be handled', the size of the metal blade was diminished in proportion to the size of the new 'forkes and defences'. The resultant weapon was the *spiedo* – not 'Javelin' as in I.G.'s translation – which, because of its diminished width of blade and lighter construction is not very effective in delivering edge blows, and depends solely upon thrusts with its three points. Experiments with the basic design continued. Sometimes the defensive hooks were moved from the base of the blade to the middle, and sometimes one of these was replaced on the false edge with a sharp iron point; and so, eventually, there evolved the 'auncient weapon called the Holberd, out of the which, men of our age have dirived and made another kind of Holberd and Bill' (*roncha*).

It was observed that a man with a weapon in his hand, might make

> six motions, that is to saie, one towards the head, one towards the feete, one towardes the right side, one towards the left, one forwards and towards the enimie, the other backward and toward himselfe. Of all the which, five of them might verie well strike, and the last might neither strike nor defend. Therfore, providing that this last motion also should not be idle and unprofitable, they added a hook with the point turned towards the handle, with the which one might verie easily teare armour, and draw perforce men from their horses.

The placing and nature of this hook are regarded as crucial by di Grassi because, he says, on the modern halberd (*allabarda moderna*)[30] it hinders the cutting blade, whereas on the bill the edge is kept longer and the hook itself is sharpened to serve as yet another cutting tool. The former is, therefore, an inferior weapon: its edge is 'not so apt to strike'; and its point is so weak that, 'hitting any hard thing, either it boweth or breaketh'. The *roncha*, on the other hand, is 'the most perfect weapon of all others, because it striketh and hurteth in every one of these six motions, and his defences both cut and prick'.

Unlike Manciolino and Marozzo, di Grassi remains conscious of the relevance of these staff weapons to mass combat as well as to individual fighting, pointing out that partisans, halberds and bills are used to break up pike formations and to 'disorder the battell raye'; and he believes that they are handled by his contemporaries very effectively. The proper method, he says, is to hold the weapon in the middle of the staff, with the 'heel' (*calzo*) in front and kept very low, while the point is near one's own head. Both the 'heel' and the lower half of the staff, below the hand, must be used to guard against thrusts from the opposing pikes or other weapons; and then, having prepared the opening, the soldier must bring his back foot forward a pace and simultaneously 'let fall his weapon as forcibly as he maie, and strike with the edge athwart the Pikes'. Such a blow coming from above, downwards, with so heavy a weapon, should cut asunder not only pikes but also any other strong impediment. In this kind of encounter the *spiedo* is not considered very effective since it is only good for thrusting; but the partisan, which is primarily a heavy cutting tool, is the best means for dealing with pikes.[31]

118. Di Grassi takes his stance with the bill – partisan, *spiedo* and halberd lie strewn on the ground. 1570, p. 104.

Nevertheless, while recognizing the importance of staff weapons on the battlefield, di Grassi remains essentially a master of arms for the individual so that the greater part of his discussion is given over to the handling of the *roncha* and halberd for single combat and he considers them together because – like Monte long before him – he believes that they have the 'self same offence and defence' and treating them separately would involve repetition which 'being superfluous, would breed loathsomenes'. The relationship between all the principal staff weapons is symbolized by di Grassi in his accompanying illustration which shows a man posing with a *roncha* while, at his feet lie a partisan, halberd and *spiedo* (fig. 118).

Di Grassi's fighter must always bear in mind the difficulty of striking with the point and the danger of striking with the edge. In the former case, 'the full course of the point may very easilie be hindered and tyed, by means of so many hookes and forkes which are in the Holberd'; on the other hand, cuts are slower and leave one exposed because, 'by means of his length, it frameth a greater circle, and therein giveth more time to enter under it'. There is some contradiction in di Grassi's discussion of the best stance for the halberd because he recommends holding the point directly towards the opponent, rather than the 'heel', and there is no doubt that simultaneous thrusting would result in the hooks of the blades becoming entangled. If this happens then it is necessary to take a pace towards the opponent; lift up his blade with your own to disengage them; strike home with the 'heele or the blunt end of the Holberd' (which could, with advantage, be fitted with a strong, sharp iron spike); and then, retiring the pace previously advanced, deliver a strong edge blow. If, however, the opponent tries to raise your blade in the same fashion, you must try to move more quickly than he can by taking a step towards him; using the 'heele' to strike at his thigh or belly; and then, changing hands, deliver an edge blow. As was the case with all masters, di Grassi's advice would work as well for one combatant as for the other so that, in the end, the whole conflict resolves itself into a question of speed and opportunity: 'the most subtill consideration of times, without knowledge whereof, there is no man that may safelie beare himself under anie weapon'.

That is the whole doctrine in a nutshell: and di Grassi restates it when he moves on to discuss the pike which is, 'among the weapons of the Staffe, the most plaine, most honorable, and most noble'. Renowned knights and great lords esteem the pike, knowing that in order to handle it well one needs great physical strength, valour, judgement and

> a most subtill and delicate knowledge and consideration of times, and motions, and a readie resolution to strike. These qualities may not happen or be resident in any persons, but in such as are strong of armes and couragious of stomacke. Neither may they procure to get any other advantage in the handling thereof, then to be more quick and resolute both in judgement and hande than their enimie is.

This is incontrovertible but scarcely profound. Any fighter, stronger, quicker, more resolute and of firmer judgement than his opponent, would be an odds-on favourite to win their encounter. But di Grassi has more to offer than platitudes. Explaining that he is deliberately not dealing with the use of the pike in warfare and that his sole concern is with single combat, he offers a number of useful observations. Some men, more concerned with ease and avoiding pain, prefer to hold the pike in the middle; others, 'more strong of arme, but weaker of hart', like to keep as far away from hurt as is possible and so hold the pike near the 'heel' with the greater length of the staff before them. Both methods, he says, are to be rejected: the former because it is too dangerous; the latter because it is too difficult to maintain beyond a short period. The pike is 'a long straight lyne', so that any slight movement at the hand becomes a considerable movement at the point; and the slightest weakness or unsteadiness (almost inevitable when the staff is held for any length of time at its extremity) makes it virtually impossible to deliver a blow where hand and eye intend. Moreover, the fatigue which results from such a grip makes it increasingly difficult to beat off a powerful blow. Thus di Grassi's recommended method is to hold the pike with the rear hand at about an arm's length from the 'heel', and the forehand another arm's length towards the point. The rear hand must be 'steadfast', that is it should hold the pike in a firm grip; and the forehand somewhat loose 'so that the Pike may shift through it to and fro'.

Di Grassi also argues that the longer the weapon the greater the force of its thrust. This does not depend on weight but on the alleged fact that all thrusts with two-handed weapons are essentially circular, with the shoulder as the central pivot and the point of the blade moving along a circumference proportionate to the length of the staff: 'whereby it is manifest, that the Pike, the longer it is, it frameth the greater circle, and consequently is more swifte, and therefore maketh the greater passage'. This is true as far as it goes, but it does not take into account blows delivered with the piston-like action suggested by di Grassi's own favoured grip.

A concise summary of the feints ('Deceites or falses') which may be employed with staff weapons concludes di Grassi's discussion although, on the whole, he is not very enthusiastic about this aspect of the art because, as he explains, long weapons held with two hands move comparatively slowly so that feints, especially when attempted with edge strokes, are easily seen and countered. Therefore, 'the best false that may be practised in the handling

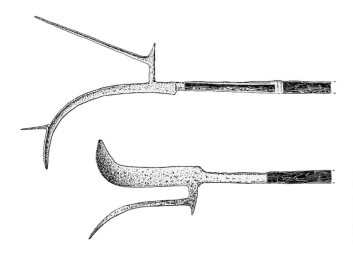

119. The Welsh-hook: George Silver's favourite weapon. Examples in the C.O. Kienbusch Collection, Philadelphia Museum of Art: drawing reproduced by courtesy of Mrs Sarah Blair.

of these weapons, is the false of the thrust', and cuts ought never or seldom to be used, 'except great necessitie constrain'.

Di Grassi's book was published in an English version in 1594. Executed by a certain 'I.G. gentleman', and introduced by Thomas Churchyard, this is a serviceable translation of an intelligent treatise and was, in fact, the first book on the martial arts printed in English. Five years later George Silver, furious at the success of Italian teachers in London and more especially at the publication of Saviolo's treatise on the rapier, burst into print with his own *Paradoxes of Defence* which includes an important section on staff weapons, often congruent with di Grassi, but showing no evidence that Silver had read his predecessor's work. Silver was an independent thinker and a forceful writer but his literary style was as explosive as his temperament, so that reading him tends to be a bewildering experience. He never defines technical terms, repeats himself frequently, contradicts himself intermittently and is constant only in ambiguity. Yet his treatment of staff weapons, both in the *Paradoxes* and in his later *Bref Instructions*, is full of valuable insights and, to a far greater extent than di Grassi, assesses the merits of different arms in varying contexts and draws an especially sharp distinction between 'private and publike fight'.[32]

Once disentangled, his exposition of hafted weapons in the *Paradoxes* falls into three discrete if untidy sections in each of which the arms themselves are divided into three main categories. The first group comprises 'weapons of weight', such as the battle-axe, halberd and 'Blacke-bill'.[33] The second Silver describes as arms of 'perfect length' and includes the partisan and glaive, the 'short staffe' (by which he means the quarterstaff), and the 'Forrest-bill' which he also refers to as the 'Welch hooke'. The identity of this last weapon, which has only recently been established by Claude Blair,[34] is significant because Silver deems it the finest of all – that is until he later contradicts himself when enthusing about the 'short staffe'. It is, in fact, the bizarre weapon (with a long scythe-like blade, and a short right-angled spur at the back carrying a long vertical spike) which was called simply a 'sickle' (*faucille*) by Charles Buttin, 'Forest bill' or *roncola* by Mario Troso, and – erroneously – 'guisarme' by generations of scholars misled by Samuel Rush Meyrick (fig. 119).[35] Silver's third group of staff weapons are those he considers to be 'above the perfect length', such as the 'long Staffe, Morris Pike, or Javelin'.[36]

The first task is to determine the 'perfect length' of those weapons susceptible to such a calculation, and in order to do this a man must stand upright, hold the staff in his left hand, reach with the right hand as high as possible, and finally add to that the length required by both hands in order to wield the weapon comfortably.[37] This, Silver says, will commonly give a length of about eight or nine feet which is suitable for most men because 'in any weapon where the hands may be removed, and at libertie, to make the weapon longer or shorter in fight at his pleasure, a foot of the staffe behind the backmost hand doth no harme'. Certainly these arms should not be shorter because, in that case, other staff weapons greater than the 'perfect length' would have a decisive advantage over them. As far as 'weapons of weight' are concerned, Silver declares that, although there is no fixed length, they should not be longer than five or six feet because they would then be too heavy to manage; and he reminds us that they are weapons for war and battle, 'when men are joined close together, may thrust, and strike sound blowes, with great force both strong and quick'. Finally, for two-hand weapons longer than these, such as the long staff and Morris pike, there is no 'just length' at all: and we know from surviving examples that, although the pike was often about eighteen feet in length, it could be anything from between sixteen to twenty-two feet.

Silver next provides an original comparative statement on the effectiveness of these three groups. All the 'weapons of weight' are handled in one and the same fashion and are superior to the sword either alone or with any of its accompanying aids such as buckler, target or dagger. Arms of 'perfect length' are superior not only to all other weapons but even to attacks by two men armed with swords and daggers. And weapons 'above the perfect length' are effective against all else apart from the previous group. They are, however, vulnerable to attacks by two swordsmen, 'because they are too long to thrust, strike and turne speedily; and by reason of the large distance, one of the Sword and Dagger-men will get behind him'. Finally, says Silver, the 'Welch hooke or Forrest bill, hath advantage against all maner of weapons whatsoever' except in the press of battle when a variety of weapons is being used among multitudes of men and horses. In such circumstances the sword and target, battle-axe, black bill and halberd are more effective. The situation is summarized by Silver:

> The Morris Pike defendeth the battell from both horse and man, much better than can the short staffe, long staffe, or Forrest bill. Againe, the Battel-axe, the Halbard, the Blacke-bill, the two hand sword, and Sword and Target, amongst armed men and troopes, when men are come together, by reason of their weights, shortnesse and great forces, do much more offend the enemies, and are then much better weapons, than is the short staffe, the long Staffe, or Forrest bill.

The greater part of Silver's final chapters on staff weapons largely repeat, elaborate, and occasionally contradict what he has already said, but they also include an encomium of the short staff. A man so armed is able to cope easily with any 'Weapons of weight' because, with his 'nimbleness and length', he can cut and thrust much more swiftly than the battle-axe, 'Blacke-bill' and halberd; and he can fight safely by reason of 'his judgement, distance and time'. Even when confronted by the long Morris pike, the short staff, with its superior agility and strength, has the advantage; while, if attacked by two sword-and-dagger men, the short-staff man may then reap the profit of his superior reach. In the latter case, he need only take one large pace either to attack or retreat, whereas his opponents must take at least four which is 'too great a number with their feet, and too short in distance to offend the Staffe-man'. Similarly, if one of his opponents tries to get behind him while the other keeps

120. Staff fighting in Meyer, 1600, book III, fol. 22.

him occupied in front, he can easily frustrate them: 'by reason of the small number of his feet, for by a verie small turning of his feet, as it were in the Center point of a wheele, the other two to keepe their distance, are driven to runne twentie foote for one, as it were upon the uttermost part or circle of the wheele.' Silver has enormous confidence in the short staff, even arguing that it is not much inferior to the Forest bill despite the latter's being more 'offensive'. Indeed, if the bill man is not especially skilful then the short staff will triumph: for it is, says Silver, 'most commonly the best weapon of all other'. This seems categorical enough: but, just when the reader has decided to invest in a quarterstaff, he finds that Silver has added a short note to the effect that, in the dark of night, the short staff must yield to the pike. 'Thus endeth the vantages of weapons', says Silver, leaving his more cautious readers with the feeling that they had best carry about one of everything.[38]

Enthusiasm for the quarterstaff was not unusual. The weapon had always been favoured by the German masters; the Emperor Maximilian I was a skilled practitioner; Paulus Hector Mair allotted it a generous space in his collections; and Meyer was an influential advocate of its practice (fig. 120, plate XIII). In England, Silver's younger contemporary, the no less irascible master, Joseph Swetnam, 'the Woman-Hater', was even more convinced that the quarterstaff (especially when equipped with a spike) was superior to any other hafted weapon – not only to the halberd, partisan and glaive but also to the dreaded 'Welche-hooke' itself.[39] The trouble with all these other arms, in Swetnam's view, is that they are top-heavy so that, when a man is defending against a feint, 'the head of his weapon will so over-carrie him by reason of the weight, that hee cannot command him nimbly backe againe'. Indeed, says Swetnam: 'without cunning or skill, the Welche-hooke, and these other weapons are more fearefull unto the ignorant, but hee that is cunning in the false play and slippes, belonging unto the Staffe may with a false thrust or with slipping his blow endanger any other, being weaponed with any other of these weapons aforesaid.'[40] Like Silver, however, Swetnam is not convinced that the staff is effective in dealing with an assault on a dark night. One method the staff man may employ is to attempt a 'high guard'; and another, if the staff is long enough, is to stand the enemy off with the point. But, if those fail, there is always a third alternative which is simply 'to trust to thy heeles'. Swetnam may have been tetchy and boastful, but he was also a realist.[41]

A BLOODLESS EPILOGUE: FIGHTING AT THE BARRIERS

Knights, of course, in their battles, could not trust to their heels without incurring the scorn of their peers. None the less, as these warriors gradually metamorphosed into courtiers, they too leavened their valour with discretion. Elimination of risk within the lists was a characteristic of chivalric combats which were increasingly hedged around with a variety of safety measures to protect the performers from injury. The introduction of the tilt had proved effective in reducing the perils of jousting and, towards the end of the fifteenth century, foot combats were similarly emasculated by the introduction of the *barriers* – the name given to an encounter fought over a fence, gate or other obstacle.[42] The purpose was similar to that of the tilt in mounted lance-play: the bar prevented knights from crashing into each other; by limiting valid strokes to those given above the obstacle, it greatly diminished the area to be defended; and, by compelling the adversaries to keep at a certain distance, it reduced the variety of blows which might be delivered and lessened their sting.

In the early days of fighting at the barriers, when the rules were less rigorously applied, it was still possible to inflict real damage. In one of the first recorded contests of this kind, forming part of a tournament organized by Bayard at Aire in 1494, the barrier itself was only waist high which left a good expanse of knight to aim at and plenty of room to swing in. Bayard, during the axe combat, delivered such a blow to his opponent's ear that the recipient staggered and fell to his knees, whereupon the 'good Chevalier' rushed around from behind the barrier and forced the dazed knight to kiss the earth 'whether he would or no'.[43] A few years later this would have been regarded as a flagrant breach of etiquette: but Bayard was not reprimanded and might, in any case, have pleaded unfamiliarity with the new-fangled contest. Even twenty years later knights could still get to grips with an obnoxious opponent as at the *barriers* held at Paris in 1514 to celebrate the marriage of Henry VIII's sister Mary and Louis XII. The French, anxious to embarrass their English guests, introduced a German giant to beat up the Duke of Suffolk but the plan went awry when Suffolk, in no way inhibited by the intervening barrier, 'by pure strength tooke hym about the necke, and pomeled so about the hed that the bloud yssued out of his nose'.[44]

Gradually, though, the pastime became distanced from the all-in fighting which had characterized earlier, barrier-free, fifteenth-century foot combats. Precautions multiplied and knights were expressly forbidden either to touch the bar or to take hold of an opponent's weapon. Instead of a military exercise the contest was becoming a social game, and on one convivial occasion at Brussels an English observer was obliged to remark that 'some took more hurt with the cups than at the barriers with cutting of the sword'.[45] For men who were serious about their fighting, combat at the barriers – as it evolved in the sixteenth and early seventeenth centuries – was merely an effete and pointless show. Brantôme, for example, when praising a bloody and mortal encounter which had taken place between two captains just before the Battle of Ceresole in 1544, is moved to contrast their bravery and skill with 'an infinity of our knights of the Court whom one has seen, and still sees, in combats at the barrier'. Out of a hundred such knights one will not find a dozen who strike home correctly at the visor, cheek or forehead. The rest hit just anywhere, so that their blows land mostly on their opponent's neck, stomach, or shoulders, which is neither beautiful nor what is required of the exercise.[46] Some years later, the Spanish authority Narváez has some sarcastic comments on fighting at the barriers which, in his view, had been reduced to such a state that even women and children could try it as a game and entertainment and could perform nearly as well as the men. Indeed, sneers Narváez, a master of arms must needs be astonished at the weakness of the lances used in this exercise and disgusted at the posturing of the combatants who are so afraid of attack that they keep close to the barrier for protection and even collude one with another to make a good impression: saying quietly that 'there is to be some give and take'. Worse still, these men ignore the fundamental principles of the art of fighting sword against sword, and hack away with no more skill than would be exercised by 'an uncouth peasant or a cart driver from La Mancha'.[47]

Combat at the barriers was generally, though not invariably, waged with pikes, two-hand swords, or puncheon staves designed for thrusting: but, since the possibilities for manoeuvre and effective use of any weapon were so circumscribed, the activity inspired little theoretical writing; and it is especially curious that the first extended treatment was not by a professional master but by a soldier, Federico Ghisliero, and that, despite his military background, he was far more concerned with fine appearances at the barriers than with serious fighting.[48] All chivalric exercises, he says, are designed to demonstrate agility, skill and strength in a spectacle which represents the similitude of a real feat of arms; and he intends to discuss single combat first with 'push of the pike' and then with the sword, before concluding with the 'pell mell' (la folla) when all the knights contend at once. Even when fought with rebated weapons such exercises must imitate 'the truth', although knights should never go to extremes. Their movements should be natural, 'as much with all the body as with the parts thereof, and this always without any affectation'. Ghisliero subjects the phases of combat to an elaborate analysis, characteristically divided and subdivided into a series of static postures each illustrated by a drawing, and the knight is exhorted to ensure that his paces are 'neither great nor small, but natural'; that his deportment must be graceful yet lively, 'so that he does not look like a statue'; and that, in his various movements, he must always avoid the 'error of extremes'. The general attitude towards combat in the lists is reminiscent of Castiglione's Il Cortegiano; and both text and drawings convey a sense not of real knightly endeavour but rather of the kind of balletic display later to be immortalized in the flashy pike virtuosity of Antonio Vezzani (fig. 121).[49]

As a matter of fact, this balletic and Castiglionesque emphasis characterizes all discussions of the barriers, and never more explicitly than in Antonino Ansalone's Il Cavaliere of 1629, a treatise which encapsulates the whole process of the 'mutation from warrior to ceremonial puppet'.[50] Ansalone, writing of combat at the barriers with the pike – in this case a flimsy lath designed to snap rather than penetrate – notes that it is of no small profit

121. Vezzani's balletic exercises with the pike. 1688, p. 61.

to the knight to know how to dance because, 'as said the Count Baldassare Castiglione, one must observe a certain majesty tempered with graciousness, and an airy sweetness of movement, with time and measure', and the knight is enjoined to avoid excessive speed and complicated steps which go beyond decorum. Worse follows. The sword for combat at the barriers must not be 'too heavy'; indeed it must be light. The object is to strike the crest of one's opponent's helm, and the sword must never touch the bar. Only horizontal blows are permitted, either forehand or backhand, and even here, Ansalone concedes, there are those who 'through weakness of arm, not being able to hold the weight of the sword easily in the hand, are obliged to deliver short blows'.

Bartolomeo Sereno, whose thoughts on the barriers had been published in 1610, did not make such allowance for knights too delicate to hold their swords aloft: but he had his own fastidious limits. He makes no attempt at a detailed analysis of combat techniques at the barriers. Handling the pike and the sword interest him less than ensuring that his courtly readers will have the right kind of fanciful *imprese*, suitable assistants and a fine appearance; that they will observe the correct etiquette for every stage of the spectacle; and that they will pay due reverence to the ladies present. Above all else, says Sereno – concluding his discussion of the barriers with the same courtly dictum which had so affected Ghisliero – knights must shun affectation. He does, however, make one practical observation. In combat at the barriers, he observes, the knight can only be attacked above the waist so that any armour worn below that height is superfluous and only serves to hinder that agility which is the principal aim of all contestants. This was, in fact, the general rule, and there are illustrations of barriers in the latter half of the sixteenth century where we may see knights protected from the waist up but, from there on down, clad only in hose or breeches.[51] And this brings Sereno to a matter of supreme importance. In recent years, he complains, the introduction of great breeches (*calzone*) has quite driven out the use of hose (*calza*). Nevertheless, he exhorts the knight to eschew this new-fangled fashion.

Adorn the unarmed part with noble hose of fine appearance, rather than with great breeches. Because the proportion and the strength of the leg is very much better seen with hose than with great breeches which completely cover the firmest part, that is the thigh, and when worn with armour make an ugly sight – and that is something which ought to be avoided on an occasion where spruceness and gentle bearing must be displayed.

It is interesting to speculate what Sereno's more rugged contemporaries, such as Fabris, Giganti and Capoferro, made of all this. But one thing is to be noted. Sereno does go on to say a few words about the armour that should be worn to protect the parts above the elegant, leg-flattering *calza*, whereas few masters of arms showed the slightest interest in that sort of thing because protective garb was largely irrelevant to their purposes.[52]

Armour was, however, *de rigueur* not only for foot combat within the lists but also for mounted combat with sword and lance – that is for those modes of fighting which for a long period were the province of a privileged military caste. Before turning to these specifically chivalric martial arts of western Europe, I shall therefore discuss the sources available to those renaissance and medieval warriors who might have wished for the advice on arms and armour which the majority of the masters denied them. However, before doing that, it is necessary to examine one other area of personal combat which was taught by masters throughout Europe, and was practised at every level of the social hierarchy whether the antagonists were clad in defensive armour or not. No medieval or renaissance fighting man was completely educated without acquiring some skill in the use of his bare hands, dagger or knife.

VI

Bare hands, daggers and knives

A CCORDING TO PAUSANIAS in the fifth century BC, wrestling originated when the King of Eleusis, Cercyon – who had the unpleasant habit of fighting strangers, defeating them, and putting them to death – met his match when Theseus overcame him by skill. Before Theseus, we are given to understand, 'men used in wrestling only size and strength of body'; but Theseus was 'the first to discover the art of wrestling, and through him afterwards was established the teaching of the art'.[1] The ancient Egyptians, whose wrestling frescoes antedate Pausanias by some fifteen centuries, might well have disputed this tale: but the fact remains that the devising and communicating of skills enabling an unarmed man to overthrow or kill a stronger enemy have always been valued by martial peoples. If Theseus had not had the technique to vanquish Cercyon then Cercyon would have killed Theseus. The issues at stake were as uncomplicated as when, in the introduction to his *All-in Fighting*, a training manual for troops on active service in the Second World War, Captain W.E. Fairbairn explained that most of his methods were 'drastic in the extreme'. They recognized no accepted rules; were not intended to provide amusement for spectators; and were solely for use 'in these dangerous times as part of our national preparedness against our enemies'.[2] Fairbairn drew a sharp distinction between combat sports such as boxing and wrestling and the kind of fighting he proposed – a distinction which should be borne in mind because it was recognized and acted upon by many medieval and renaissance masters of arms.[3]

In modern times – at least until very recently when sport has become a kind of surrogate warfare – there has been a clear line of demarcation between gymnasium and arena on the one hand and battlefield on the other. In the Middle Ages and Renaissance the demarcation also existed but was less marked. Wrestling was certainly a popular recreation, spectator sport, and exercise: and the schools of arms may well have provided instruction for these purposes. But the use of bare hands (or 'empty hand' skills as current jargon would have it) was more consistently taught for its relevance to real combat, especially in street or tavern brawls, either on its own or in conjunction with various weapons. In fact, a distinguishing feature of medieval and renaissance personal combat was the combination of two interrelated and legitimate assumptions: first that *prese* (close quarter tricks) could be used, and might often prove decisive, when fighting with swords or with staff weapons; and, equally, that unarmed combat could be effective against an armed assailant. It was only slowly, and very unevenly, that these assumptions were discarded; and some masters recognized that this was an unfortunate development. The chief complaint levelled by the Elizabethan George Silver against the fencing schools of his own day was that their concentration on fancy play had resulted in a failure to prepare students for the business of serious fighting and that these 'Schoolemen' would remain ineffectual as long as instruction in close combat was forbidden to them. As well as handling the sword they needed to learn 'their Closes and Gripes'; they needed to know how to use 'the hilts', daggers and bucklers; and they had to master 'Wrastlings', and be ready to strike with 'the foote or knee in the Coddes'.[4]

Silver was, in fact, advocating 'all-in fighting' or 'unarmed combat', and these terms will be used to describe the techniques taught by the masters to enable a man to use his bare hands to disable or kill an enemy or to deal effectively with an armed adversary. The word 'wrestling' will be reserved mainly to indicate systematic fighting which was fought according to conventions and mutually agreed rules and which, however adaptable for use in a rough house, was devised principally as an exercise or sport. These terms can never be mutually exclusive, for both wrestling and all-in fighting are, obviously, forms of unarmed combat while many wrestling techniques may be applied in mortal encounters. The verbal distinction is merely a convenience and was not made by the early masters who used whatever words were current in their own language for the art of wrestling – *luctatio*, *lutte*, *lotta*, *abraçare*, *lucha*, *ringen*, *ringkampf* and so on – to indicate all types of unarmed combat, regardless of whether their prime purpose was salutiferous, sporting, or homicidal.

THE STATUS OF WRESTLING AND UNARMED COMBAT

The status of wrestling and unarmed combat has always been uncertain. In every age there have been those who regard hand-to-hand grappling as a valuable exercise and as an important training for warriors, and others for whom it is a brutal and useless pastime.[5] When, in 1768, Baron von Bielfeld came to write about the mental benefits of physical exercise he remarked that, since man's natural lot is to live amongst his fellows, one must acquire not only social skills such as dancing and riding, but also the ability to defend oneself against enemies.[6] According to Bielfeld, legislators have provided in their academies and universities instruction in those arts which cannot be mastered without physical dexterity; and his list of these (dancing, riding, fencing, leaping, wrestling, swimming, shooting and games of address) demonstrates the enduring legacy of Baldassare Castiglione and of more remote writers.[7] Bielfeld regards all these activities favourably: all, that is, apart from wrestling. However highly the ancients may have regarded this exercise, Bielfeld could find nothing left in his own day but 'the cruel and disgusting remains of it among the English'. Violent and dangerous, it was so repugnant to humanity that 'a wrestler by profession, and a spectator who is pleased with such encounters, are commonly two persons equally despicable'.

Bielfeld's distaste is certainly a far cry from *Il Cortegiano* where – in addition to dancing, riding, fencing, leaping, swimming and shooting – the ideal all-rounder was advised to acquire knowledge of wrestling because it could be of great service in foot combat with all weapons. Galeazzo da Sanseverino had been especially praised by Castiglione for practising 'wrestling, vaulting, and handling sundry kinds of weapons' under the guidance of the supreme master, Pietro Monte.[8] And Monte himself regarded wrestling as the foundation of all combat skills. Nevertheless, despite such endorsements, specific advocacy of wrestling was rare among educationalists of the early sixteenth century. Luther noted that it developed the body and helped to maintain good health, but otherwise had nothing to say on the subject.[9] The erudite soldier-turned-cleric, Celio Calcagnini, included it in the long list of exercises he considered necessary to prepare the upper-class Italian youth of the early sixteenth century for military activity; and in England Sir Thomas Elyot was convinced that wrestling was an excellent training for youngsters, provided that contestants were properly graded for strength and that 'the place be softe, that in fallinge theyr bodies be nat brused'. Arguing that the exercise may be useful in battle when a warrior breaks or loses his weapon and is obliged to fight hand-to-hand, Elyot makes the further point that through skill a weak man may defeat a stronger adversary – a selling point for the martial arts which has retained its potency from classical times to the present day.[10]

On the other hand, Elyot's contemporary, Zwingli, while including wrestling among the exercises for 'ingenious youth', warned that it should only seldom be used 'because often times it turneth into earnest'; and this was an opinion which apparently prevailed amongst educationalists.[11] By 1581, only a year after the last Tudor edition of Elyot's *The Boke named The Governour*, the knowledgeable and broad-minded schoolmaster Richard Mulcaster reported that wrestling was no longer being recommended by physicians or greatly practised: 'it seemeth not to be much set by, being contemned by the most, and cared for but by the meanest'. Yet the ancients, as he pointed out, had recognized that it helped prepare athletes for other sports, contributed to training for soldiers and 'in the bodye wrought strength, and made it better breathed'. Accordingly, while avoiding the 'catching pancraticall kinde of wrastling, which used all kindes of hould', along with other methods 'which continuance hath rejected, and custome refused', Mulcaster recommends two forms of 'upright' wrestling – that is standing combat as opposed to ground wrestling. One of these he calls 'vehement' which 'taketh awaie fatnesse, puffes, and swellinges'. It also 'maketh the breath firme and strong, the bodie sound and brawnie, it tightes the sinews, and backes all the naturall operations'. The other wrestling mode is more gentle, encourages muscular development and is 'therfore verie commodious for such as be upon the recoverie after sicknesse, as a kinde of motion, which without any danger bringeth strength and stowtnesse'. In general, Mulcaster regards these strictly limited forms of wrestling as beneficial although he warns off those suffering from certain physical disabilities, 'for either bursting some conduit, or stopping some windcourse'. He declares that 'weake kidneis and wearie loynes' do better to remain spectators rather than contestants; and further cautions, 'if weake legges become wrastlers, of their owne perill be it, for they do it without warrant'.[12]

Among the warrior class, it is no easier to trace any consistent opinion regarding the value and propriety of wrestling than it is among the learned. Early in the fourteenth century, the youthful Bertrand Du Guesclin's wrestling escapades were regarded by his guardians as reprehensible: but it is not clear whether their wrath was caused by the activity itself or by the fact that Bertrand was disporting himself with the lower orders.[13] Wrestling is mentioned neither in the lengthy description of Boucicaut's physical training nor in that of Don Pero Niño; and in the mid-fifteenth century the wrestling episode in Anthoine de la Sale's *Le Petit Jehan de Saintré* suggests that such skills were, at least from an idealized viewpoint, regarded as somehow unchivalric.[14] Yet during the fifteenth and sixteenth centuries, knights were not averse to using throws, trips and holds when fighting on foot within the lists. That famous chronicler of European chivalry, Olivier de la Marche, describing an axe combat in Scotland and praising Hervé de Meriadet as one of the most redoubtable knights of his time, notes his strength, agility, coolness and dexterity 'in arms and in wrestling'.[15]

There is even evidence for the chivalric acceptability of all-in fighting at the highest social level of all. When, as part of his massive autobiography, the Emperor Maximilian I commissioned his tournament and masque book, *Freydal*, one of the activities depicted comprised a series of varied foot combats between pairs of combatants of whom the emperor himself is always one. He is also always victorious. Untrammelled by modern notions of fair play, he regularly stands on opponents' feet, kicks their knees, or stamps on their calf muscles, while belabouring them with whatever weapon happens to be the choice of the day. He is also to be seen punching an unfortunate rival in the face; heaving another by the arm over his shoulder; or, having dropped his glaive, wrestling furiously with yet one more victim doomed to an inevitable defeat.[16] The emperor could not have blazoned forth his all-in fighting ability more blatantly (plate XIV). Similarly, the companions of the distinguished Bohemian traveller Leo von Rozmital were proud of their wrestling skills and took every opportunity to display them before the European princes whom they visited; and wrestling matches often enlivened state occasions when not only specialist bruisers would try to demonstrate national superiority but members of the higher echelons of society might also sometimes be involved.[17]

Fleuranges' story about Henry VIII's disastrous attempt to throw François I at the Field of Cloth of Gold has the ring of truth, despite the lack of supporting evidence; while his assertion that the French king was 'un fort bon luiteur' sufficiently testifies to the respectability of such skill, at least among his compatriots.[18] We have already seen how the duellist, des Guerres, had been trained as a wrestler and applied his knowledge in mortal combat; and we know, too, that Brantôme, who admired La Chataigneraie's prowess, particularly noted that as far as wrestling was concerned there was no Breton who could beat him – remarkable praise since the Bretons were regarded as the finest wrestlers in France.[19]

Elsewhere Brantôme informs us that wrestling was part of the martial education arranged by Charles de Cossé, Comte de Brissac, for his son Timoléon. Not only was Timoléon instructed in the handling of arms – first by a Milanese named Jule, and then by a Bordeaux master named Aymart who, 'having lived for ten years in Italy, had no equal' – but he was also taught wrestling by a Ferrarese called Colle with such success that the youth, despite his slender build and modest strength, was able to throw to the ground adversaries bigger, taller and more robust than he. Colle had come to the French court especially to exhibit his skills the like of which – 'without wishing to offend the Bretons', interpolates Brantôme – had never been seen, for he threw everyone he encountered.[20] Brantôme is always an unreliable witness but, if there is anything at all in this story, it suggests that the French nobility took their wrestling seriously. And even more indicative of this high status is the fact that, when the distinguished general François de la Noue advocated the establishment of a series of military academies throughout France in the 1580s, he included wrestling in the syllabus of practical exercises because it made a person 'more robust and agile'.[21]

In England, although Sir Humphrey Gilbert made no specific provision for unarmed combat in his scheme for an academy in London, he did expect his master of defence to instruct pupils in 'the gripe of the dagger' and we know that many such masters used wrestling tricks as part of their fighting system. Wrestling is not mentioned in the several other schemes for military academies which were being mooted at this period and while masters of fence may well have included unarmed combat in their lessons, it does seem that the appropriateness of wrestling for the upper classes was in doubt; and in 1622, when Henry Peacham came to write about 'throwing and wrestling', he held them to be 'exercises not so well beseeming Nobility, but rather soldiers in a Campe, or a Princes guard'.

On the other hand, his contemporary Lord Herbert of Cherbury, who had received much of his martial education in France, approved of wrestling along with leaping and vaulting, 'they being all of them qualities of great use'.[22]

Towards the end of the seventeenth century, the great philosopher John Locke was even more enthusiastic. When considering the benefits of fencing, Locke wrote that it seemed to him 'a good exercise for health, but dangerous to the life', because those who think that they have learnt to use their swords are more likely to engage in quarrels – where a moderate skill in fencing rather exposes them to the sword of their enemy than secures them from it. The reason for this is that

> a man of courage, who cannot fence at all, and therefore will put all upon one thrust, and not stand parrying, has the odds against a moderate fencer, especially if he has skill in wrestling. And therefore, if any provision be to be made against such accidents, and a man be to prepare his son for duels, I had much rather mine should be a good wrestler, than an ordinary fencer; which is the most a gentleman can attain to in it, unless he will be constantly in the fencing school, and every day exercising.[23]

MEDIEVAL AND RENAISSANCE TRADITIONS

Whatever the theoretical status of wrestling among the learned and knightly classes, it is obvious from surviving treatises that, up to the early seventeenth century and even beyond, many masters of arms recognized the advantages bestowed upon their pupils by the physical exercise of wrestling – in order to develop agility, strength and dexterity – and by practising unarmed combat to use against the assaults of an armed assailant or in any other mortal affray.

Learned men such as Elyot and Mulcaster could cite ancient authorities on the therapeutic value of wrestling: but there was, in fact, nothing to be learnt from educationalists such as Clement of Alexandria or from physicians such as Galen about the techniques of combat. Similarly, classical poets and historians might be scoured for scraps of information about different types of fighting and about the social milieu within which these took place, but none of this would enable anyone without prior practical knowledge to execute more than the simplest combat procedures. In this respect, Mercurialis's pioneering work on gymnastics is instructive for, although his short chapter on ancient wrestling refers to eight classical authors, the information derived from them is primarily philological.[24] It was only with the increased availability of ancient pictorial records – and especially the discovery of the wrestling sequences in Egyptian tomb paintings – that scholars were able to arrive at an understanding of the subject sufficiently detailed to justify Hugh F. Leonard's opinion that there was nothing in catch-as-catch-can technique which could not be satisfactorily illustrated from such remote sources.[25]

It must, however, be remembered that none of this evidence was available to the early masters of arms who were obliged to systematize wrestling and unarmed combat solely on the basis of their own observation and experience. Yet several of them accomplished the task with remarkable thoroughness and skill, and their treatises enable us to see that they were conversant with many fundamental aspects of unarmed combat such as the practical application of leverage, balance and the use of an opponent's momentum. However, it was not until 1713 that there was a serious, if ineffectual, attempt to relate mathematics and wrestling, when Sir Thomas Parkyns prefaced his explanation of 'how useful wrestling is to a Gentleman in Fencing' with a ten-page quotation from Mandey and Moxon's *Mechanick Powers* to demonstrate the principles of the lever, steelyard and hammer.[26] As well as exhibiting a pragmatic grasp of general principles, the early masters also employed a wide variety of locks, bars, trips, kicks, punches, gouges, throws and strangleholds, many of which are still used by all-in wrestlers; and their attacks with hand, elbow, foot, knee and head, directed at pressure points and to vulnerable areas of the body, are closely akin to the all-in fighting taught by Captain Fairbairn and to the *Atemi-waza* of oriental fighting systems which are now, ironically, better known in the West than those of the European masters.

The techniques of close combat in medieval and renaissance Europe were sophisticated, effective and violent; and they were recorded despite the lack of any established vocabulary or taxonomy – obstacles which have continued to thwart writers on this topic. At the end of the nineteenth century, Leonard lamented that 'the terminology of wrestling is both meager and confusing' and that 'the same movement has different names in different styles of wrestling, and the same movement in the same style of wrestling is often differently designated in different localities'. Confusion still prevailed in 1968 when Thompson Clayton prepared his *Handbook of Wrestling Terms* in an attempt to sort out the differences in nomenclature which, as he complained, made it almost impossible for a coach in one area to understand a colleague from another and which rendered 'potentially valuable material' in journals well nigh useless.[27] Since then the problem has been exacerbated by the increased popularity of oriental systems (both for sport and for serious combat) shrouded in the exotic and esoteric language which undoubtedly forms part of their attraction. The European masters had to contend with similar regional differences of style and technique together with the fact that not only was there no common vocabulary but often, apart from German and Spanish, no specialized vocabulary at all. It was for this reason that Monte began his *Collectanea* (1509) with a *Vocabulorum expositio* to explain that he was retaining his original Spanish terms, especially in relation to wrestling, simply because there were no equivalents in Latin.

The surviving source materials relating to wrestling and unarmed combat are extremely patchy, both chronologically and geographically, and cannot be moulded into a shapely narrative. It is, however, possible at least to begin at the beginning. With regard to unarmed combat, dagger fighting and the application of wrestling techniques to fencing, the earliest extant systematic treatment by a medieval master is that contained in the versions of Fiore de' Liberi's *Flos duellatorum* – a work written by an Italian and dedicated to an Italian prince, but almost certainly influenced by the German masters with whom Fiore had studied.[28] As the author himself points out in the manuscript now preserved at the Getty Museum, his emphasis throughout is on deadly encounters and on inflicting injuries 'in the most painful and dangerous places, that is to say in the eyes, the nose, the point of the chin, and the flanks'. The version published by Novati similarly mentions attacks to the 'most dangerous places', but refers specifically only to 'dislocating and breaking arms and legs'.[29] Fiore's distribution of material and the amount of space he allots to each aspect of combat are suggestive. There are twenty annotated illustrations of wrestling or all-in fighting; four on the use of the baton; ninety on knife combat and unarmed combat against a knife (the longest single section of the treatise); sixty on the two-hand sword; eighteen on the single-hander; twenty-two on the two-hander wielded by armoured knights; sixteen on the axe; five on spear and staff; nine on dagger against sword; and forty-three on all types of mounted combat.[30] Bearing in mind that a substantial proportion of the armed encounters (including those on horseback) involve the use of unarmed combat tricks, then it becomes apparent that 'empty hand' techniques comprise the fundamental element of Fiore's system. To think of his *Flos duellatorum* primarily as a treatise on swordsmanship is a serious mistake. As he himself explains, the book is simply about 'the art of fighting man to man' – *de conbatere a corpo a corpo*.[31]

Fiore begins with wrestling which, he says, may be practised either for 'recreation' or in 'anger', the latter being when one is fighting for one's life and using 'every deceit, falsity and cruelty that can be committed'. It is important, he says, to be able to assess the power, skill and age of an opponent, and to possess many qualities of one's own:

> that is to say, strength, speed; knowledge of advantageous tricks; knowing how to apply fractures (*roture*) in order to break arms and legs; skill in applying locks (*ligadure*) so that an opponent is no longer able to defend himself nor able to recover his liberty; knowing how to inflict injuries in the most dangerous places; also knowing how to throw someone to the ground without danger to onself; also knowing how to dislocate arms and legs in diverse ways.[32]

Four basic wrestling stances are illustrated, each given a name akin to some of those subsequently used for postures with the sword: *posta longa*, *dente di zenghiar*, *porta di ferro* and *posta frontale*. Then come sixteen pairs of combatants whose activities could be construed as either for 'solace' or 'love' only by contending sadists and masochists. Their manoeuvres include a variety of leg pick-ups; attacks to the pressure points of the throat (the sterno-cleido-mastoid muscle and carotid artery); pushing up into the face with the heel of the hand while clawing the eyes with finger tips; an arm crush or lever for breaking an opponent's arm at the elbow; and the application of one's right thumb to the maxillary hinge just below the opponent's left ear which, Fiore correctly observes, will inflict 'so much pain that you will throw him to the ground without doubt'. There is also a double nelson, guaranteed by Fiore to snap the enemy's spine; a chop to the throat equally certain to cause 'grief and pain'; and a knee driven into his testicles which is likely to afford you some 'advantage', even though here – as in the majority of these attacks – a defence and counter attack is noted (figs 122–6).[33] Only one procedure in this section is assigned a specific name. This is the *gambarola*, a kind of side chancery combined with a hip throw, which is not commended by Fiore who reluctantly suggests that, if you must try it out, force and speed are essential.[34] Then, as a kind of appendix to this group, there are two examples of the use of the *bastonçello* or small baton: in one instance placed cross-hands behind the opponent's neck; in the other thrust between his legs while striking up at his Adam's apple with the fork of your left hand – a blow which now, six centuries later, would be knowingly classified as an *atemi-waza* and prized as a fiendish oriental innovation. Finally, the Getty manuscript has two extra illustrations for this section, showing a seated master using his baton to parry first an upward knife thrust and then, with his legs nonchalantly crossed, a downward stab from a dagger.

The next section deals with how an unarmed man may cope with a dagger attack, and how to oppose knife with knife. In the Getty manuscript, this is prefaced by annotated illustrations showing five primary postures or 'guards': three of which are considered useful for fighting both in armour and without armour because they afford maximum reach and cover, and two which restrict the reach and are therefore less reliable when one is unprotected. It is, incidentally, interesting to note that one of the latter is the cross-arm defence familiar to karate enthusiasts. For dagger fighting, Fiore greatly prefers that the weapon

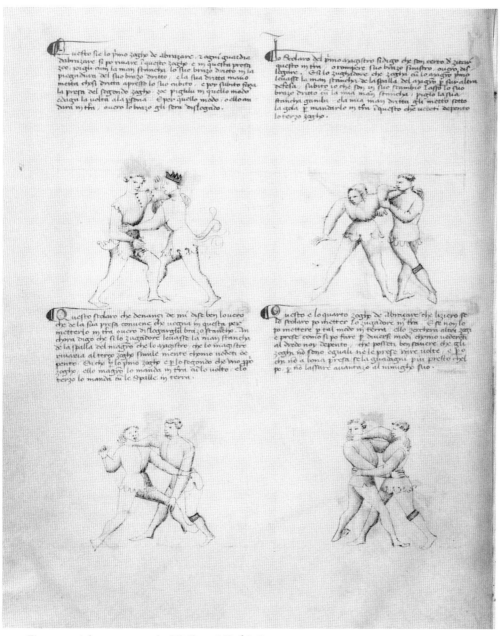

122. Fiore, top right, an arm crush, J.P. Getty MS. fol. 8v.

should be held in the forward grip, with the blade above the hand like a sword, because this gives cover 'from below and above, and every part'. It is, therefore, perverse of Fiore that most of the attacks shown subsequently are with the less flexible reverse grip, blade below hand. There is also a preliminary illustration to demonstrate the dagger's principal targets which comprise more or less the entire upper anatomy. A prosopopoeic caption declares, 'I am the noble weapon called the dagger . . . He who understands my malice and my art/ of every subtle combat has good part . . . No man can prevail against my cruel

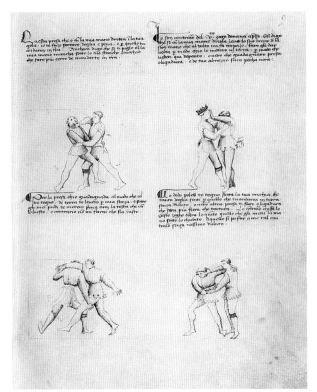

123. Fiore. Top right, heel of hand in face, fingers in eyes; bottom right, thumb on pressure point of throat. J.P. Getty MS. fol. 9.

124. Fiore. Bottom left, a double nelson; top right, the *Gambarola*; bottom right, a knee in the testicles. J.P. Getty MS. fol. 9v.

125. Fiore. Top right, leg pick-up; bottom right, thumbs in eye-balls. J.P. Getty M.S. fol. 10.

126. Fiore. Half-sword techniques for strangling or otherwise disabling an opponent. J.P. Getty MS. fol. 31v.

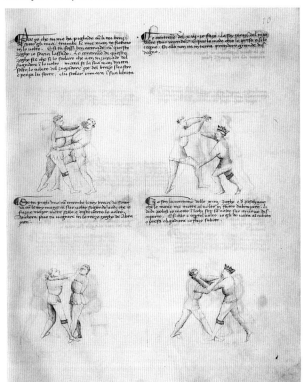

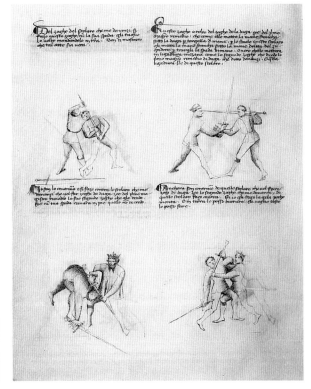

combat': a view shared by Captain Fairbairn who remarked laconically that 'it is admitted by recognized authorities that for an entirely unarmed man there is no certain defence against a knife'.[35]

Despite this perennial drawback, Fiore devotes a substantial part of his work to demonstrating how a dagger attack may be foiled by an unarmed combatant whose success is, indeed, so uniform as to suggest that possession of a dagger constitutes a positive disadvantage. The majority of the counters involve seizing the opponent's dagger hand by the wrist before dislocating or breaking his arm and they would, therefore, depend for their efficacy upon lightning fast reflexes honed by incessant practice. They also presuppose a compliant or lethargic adversary. Many of Fiore's blocking and disarming techniques are similar not only to those of later medieval and renaissance masters but also to methods advocated in modern manuals of self-defence: although he shows none of the kicks which often feature in the latter.[36] In fact, the only kicks advocated in the *Flos duellatorum* (one to the shin or just below the knee-cap, the other to the testicles) are in the section on the two-hand sword. Otherwise, the all-in methods which accompany fighting with two-hander, single sword, axe, or dagger against sword either involve gripping, pushing or parrying with the left hand, or the application of half-sword techniques to tie-up or strangle an opponent (fig. 126). And this kind of thing, despite the misgivings of later courtly fencing masters and modern fencing historians, remained an important feature of real fighting. The immensely influential Salvator Fabris examined the application of all-in fighting techniques to fencing, and his ideas and illustrations were still in vogue at the end of the seventeenth century.[37] Even in Spain, where it might be thought that mathematical and philosophical speculation had eliminated such sordid realities, wrestling tricks were still taught by the masters – as is well illustrated in an early seventeenth-century manuscript treatise by Pedro de Heredia, 'cavalry captain and member of the war council of the King of Spain'.[38] One of Heredia's recommendations strongly resembles the hip throw described in Captain Fairbairn's *All-in Fighting*; while others use an outstretched backward arm leverage across the throat similar to the *Obiotoshi* of judo (plates XV–XVII).

Certainly, the German masters had no purist inhibitions about the use of bare hands. Of the seventy or more surviving German *Fechtbücher* from the late fourteenth to the early seventeenth centuries, at least forty-seven manuscripts and nine printed books include material specifically on wrestling, unarmed combat and/or dagger fighting; and practically the entire corpus deploys wrestling techniques when dealing with fighting with sword and staff weapons. The majority of these texts are variant versions and adaptations of perhaps only a dozen works which are, themselves, rarely wholly independent: but together they comprise a consistent and formidable system.[39]

Of Liechtenauer's wrestling method, we know nothing apart from a few cryptic lines transcribed by Hanko Döbringer: but it is likely to have been similar to that outlined in the treatise written by his follower Ott, the Jewish wrestling master to the dukes of Austria. This text is itself roughly contemporaneous with and (apart from its failure to use illustrations) similar to, Fiore's *Flos duellatorum* both in the style of fighting portrayed and in its methodical procedure whereby each attack is followed by a relevant counter. In common with other early masters, Ott does not linger over generalities, although he does stress that there are three essentials for all forms of wrestling – skill, speed and the precise application of strength – and that, of these, speed is the most important in order 'not to give the opponent time to defend himself'. Ott further advises a wrestler to base his approach to every combat on the perceived strength of his adversary. Thus, in a fight against a weaker man it is advantageous to attack first when your speed will prove decisive. If he is your equal, you must start action the moment that he does, and seek to make him lose his balance; but, if he is stronger, you should allow him to make the first move and go for the back of his knees or hamstrings.

The frequency of such attacks to the hamstrings is a striking feature of Ott's method as is his recommendation of leg pick-ups and a number of other techniques designed to throw an opponent off balance. Many of these tricks recur much later in catch-as-catch-can wrestling: but Ott also advocates more drastic measures such as his defence against a man applying a bear hug around your body when you must, 'with your two thumbs press his eyes, or his jaws, or his throat, and he will be compelled to let you go'. If, on the other hand, he tries this trick on you, then you must strike him in the throat just below the jaw, force him back violently, grasp him behind the knee, 'and you will certainly turn him upside down'. Such blows to the throat, accompanied by a tug at the hamstrings, evidently appealed to Ott who repeats the move on at least three more occasions while also recommending thrusting a hand between the opponent's legs and lifting him on high; stamping on his ankle bone; breaking his arm; thrusting an elbow into his throat; and good straightforward throttling. This was not a textbook for the faint-hearted.

Ott's treatment of wrestling was soon accepted as an authoritative text; and it was copied by other masters who augmented it with tricks of their own devising, and added illustrations to provide further illumination. The earliest surviving text of Ott's *Ringbuch* is that incorporated by Hans Talhoffer in the earliest manuscript of his own *Fechtbuch* where, although not illustrated, it is immediately followed by a complementary series of crude drawings which are only approximately and intermittently relevant to Ott.[40] Each subsequent Talhoffer manuscript incorporates his own contributions to all-in fighting, including counters to knife attacks, and wrestling tricks for use with various weapons. Many of his methods live on in commando-style combat, free-style wrestling and the so-called oriental martial arts; and anybody who had graduated in Talhoffer's course would undoubtedly have been a difficult proposition in a rough house. In addition to a wide range of conventional wrestling manoeuvres, such a pupil would have been equipped with a formidable arsenal of assorted brutalities: two or three types of back-breaker; the hair hold, double nelson and kick to the inside of the thigh just above the knee; the forearm smash to the throat; and the elbow jab to the radial nerve on the outer surface of the forearm.[41]

The fighting system was an effective one but the techniques for recording it were seriously deficient. Talhoffer and the majority of his fifteenth-century German colleagues generally failed to describe adequately how a fighter was to achieve any particular manoeuvre. They also experienced the utmost difficulty in matching words and pictures. Frequently, the latter were superior to the former and the artist's contribution might deliberately be allowed to carry the bulk of a master's meaning. One sees this time and again in Talhoffer's manuscripts. There is, for example, considerable ambiguity in the meaning of the 'little hook' (*das Hecklin*) which shows a wrestler applying both a side chancery hold to the opponent's head and a grapevine (in which a leg is intertwined around one of the opponent's). Without knowing from a subsequent illustration that the title applies to the second hold, we might remain mystified.[42] Then a bare caption, 'This is called a hedging-around (*beschulsz*)', is accompanied by an unmistakable representation of a double nelson, but we are not told how to apply it, and without the picture, we should not even know which hold is indicated. The caption then adds that, in order to escape from this hold, we must break the adversary's fingers, but we are neither informed nor shown how this might

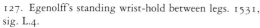

127. Egenolff's standing wrist-hold between legs. 1531, sig. L.4.

128. Erhart's standing wrist-hold between legs. 1533, fol. 110v.

be effected. Something called the 'boys' wrestle' (*Buben Ringen*) proves to be a stomach throw; and, in order to counter this, it is necessary – having been thrown – to fall so that your knee is driven into the aggressor's genitalia. Again, we see this dramatically accomplished: but it is the picture that explains what is happening, not the text.[43] Sometimes the illustrations claim to be sequential as, for example, an 'arm twist', designed to bring the opponent's limb between his own legs (it is what Leonard terms a 'standing wrist hold between the legs' and was clearly a favourite manoeuvre), which we see first in its initial phase and then, immediately after, in its finished form. 'Here', says the caption, 'he has completed the deed described.' But nothing *has* been described and, without prior experience of the trick, there would be no way of knowing how to proceed from the first to the second position.[44] The same is true of the 'trap' (*der Trapp*) which is not further described but proves to be what is known, in catch-as-catch-can wrestling, as the drag hold – with the opponent's right arm held, at both wrist and just above the elbow, by one's left and right hands respectively.[45] The next illustration is supposed to develop from the 'trap' and shows the opponent held in a reverse chancery hold: but it is impossible to learn, either from text or illustration, how one might get him there.[46]

The lack of a sophisticated command of relating words and pictures resulted in far too heavy a dependence on the work of artists; and this was a tendency in many German manuscripts, not only when dealing with wrestling but also with other forms of combat. The captions might be reduced to only a few words or might even be omitted altogether as, for instance, by the Augsburg master Gregor Erhart several of whose drawings are so similar to Hans Weiditz's superior woodcuts (published by Egenolff a couple of years earlier) as to suggest a direct relationship. Erhart confidently relied upon the clarity of his own artwork to convey his meaning when compiling the wrestling section of his *Fechtbuch* in 1533. His confidence was misplaced, and some of his postures are inextricable: although it is only fair to say that it is easy enough to recognize two types of back-breaker, a standing wristhold between the legs, and a complex variation on the arm lift and crutch hold (figs 127–31).[47] By contrast, when early in the sixteenth century, Albrecht Dürer – an artist capable of infinitely greater clarity – had been moved to compile a personal synthesis of combat styles and techniques, he did not eschew words.[48] Instead, he based his work principally upon one of the more meticulously annotated fifteenth-century *Fechtbücher*

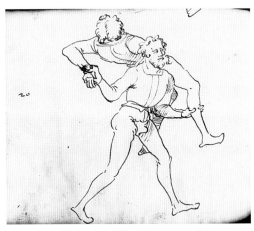

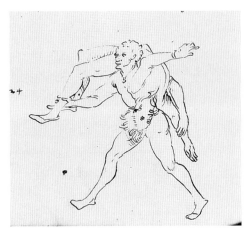

129. One of Erhart's backbreakers. 1533, fol. 104v.

130. Another of Erhart's backbreakers. 1533, fol. 108v.

(Augsburg Codex Wallerstein I.6.4°.2), and followed his source faithfully both with regard to text and illustrations while, inevitably, transmuting the latter from artistic dross to a series of master drawings.[49]

In general, however, our knowledge of unarmed combat in medieval and renaissance Germany depends more on the accumulation of a massive dossier of overlapping evidence than on the clarity of any single treatise. Similar holds, throws and trips recur throughout the different manuscripts. Sometimes they are obviously copied one from another; sometimes they illustrate different stages of a similar manoeuvre; and sometimes they give the impression of the same idea having been arrived at independently. It would, of course, be possible – given sufficient space and time – to collate all the evidence: but here I can merely suggest the general atmosphere of affinity by comparing Dürer's work with another manuscript deriving either from the same, or from a common source. This is the hitherto unnoticed early sixteenth-century *Fechtbuch* in the R.L. Scott Library, which has a series of amateurish but delightful illustrations.[50] If, for example, an opponent attempts to throw you over his head, the Scott manuscript advises that you immediately 'grasp him with both hands around the body, as shown in the drawing, and press him firmly to the ground and stretch your legs firmly apart behind him; in this way he cannot beat you but will fall on his face' (fig. 132, plate XVIII). Dürer's text is almost identical and the relationship between the illustrations is unmistakable as is again the case when both manuscripts describe a leg-hold and sit-back – 'when you are in such a position that one of your opponent's feet is between your own feet, grasp that leg and pull it up: he will then fall on his back as shown' (fig. 133, plate XIX). Similarly, both texts explain that, in order to escape from someone

131. Egenolff's version of the same backbreaker. 1531, sig. L.3v.

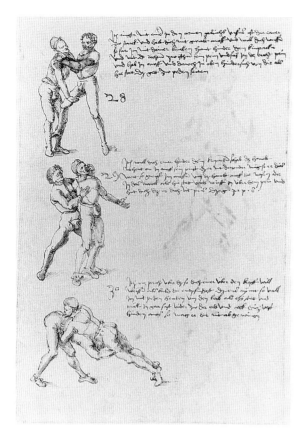

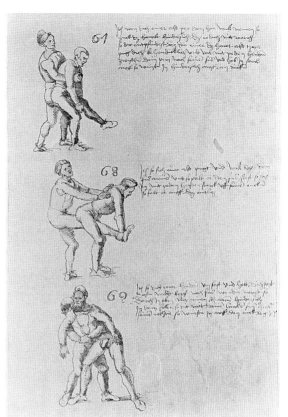

132. How to thwart an opponent's attempt to throw you over his head. Dürer (No. 30). *Fechtbuch*, plate 10. (Cf. plate XVIII below)

133. Leg-pick at an earlier stage in Dürer (No. 67). *Fechtbuch*, plate 23. (Cf. plate XIX below)

134. How to strike down at an adversary who grabs ones jerkin from the front. Dürer (No. 102). *Fechtbuch*, plate 34. (Cf. plate XX below)

135. Breaking a bear's hug, Dürer (No. 99). *Fechtbuch*, plate 33. (Cf. plate XXI below)

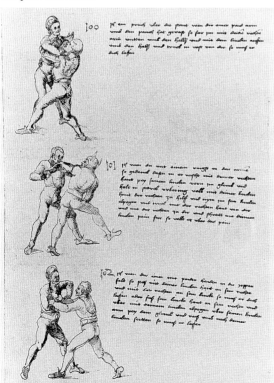

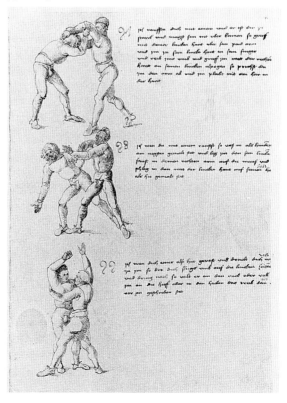

136. Marozzo's 'Second Hold' (mislabelled as 'Tertia'). 1536, fol. 127v.

137. Marozzo's 'Fourth Hold'. 1536, fol. 129v.

who has grasped your jerkin from the front, you must strike his right hand with your right and his left hand with your left, 'and you will be free of him'.[51] Again the drawings are obviously related, although in the Scott the attacker seems intent on tickling his opponent into submission (fig. 134, plate XX). Also in the tickling vein is the Scott version of a bear hug in which the attacker's fingers curl tantalizingly while the escapee indulges in a Spanish dance. And here, at least, Dürer's drawing is scarcely more informative (fig. 135, plate XXI).

When the earlier Codex Wallerstein is added to the equation, two valuable points emerge from the juxtaposition of such different sources. Despite the naivety of the illustrations in the Scott and Wallerstein manuscripts – which would, admittedly, be quite inadequate on their own – they do yield sense in association with their texts and, more than that, they even manage to clarify the words. Then, when Dürer's version is taken into consideration, the whole group becomes fully intelligible as an exposition of a fighting system.

Later masters continued to collect, compile, or commission manuscripts. Some of these are extremely elaborate and of great artistic merit, and it is extraordinary that drawings, such as those executed by Jorg Breu for Paulus Hector Mair, still go largely unheeded by art historians. But, as far as I can see, unarmed combat itself, as recorded in these later collections, shows little development in sophistication or style.[52]

WRESTLING AND THE ADVENT OF PRINTING

The art of printing which proved so enticing to the masters of arms for publicizing their skills with sword and dagger, did not have the same allure with regard to unarmed combat, and the printed literature of wrestling is frustratingly scanty and resistant to orderly dis-

138. Marozzo's 'Fifth Hold'. 1536, fol. 130v.   139. Marozzo's stomach throw. 1536, fol. 144v.

cussion. The Italians, who produced many books on fencing and duelling, never published anything significant on unarmed combat apart from Book Five of Achille Marozzo's *Opera nova* of 1536 which was so frequently reprinted that perhaps no one else felt obliged to write anything further. Unfortunately, Marozzo confines himself solely to ways of dealing with an attacker wielding a dagger – a skill, he says, necessary to men in those times 'for the conservation of their life'. His text is lucid, as are the accompanying woodcuts. His method, too, is well conceived for foiling attacks 'sopra mano', by which he confusingly means stabs from above, with the blade actually held *under* the hand; and, of the twenty-two *prese* discussed and illustrated in the text, only six concern the more deadly thrust with the blade held forward above the hand.[53] We have already encountered this concentration on downward stabbing attacks in Fiore' *Flos duellatorum*, and it is not surprising to find that most of Marozzo's *prese* derive, directly or indirectly, from that prescient source.[54] What is surprising is that, despite the continued use and documentation of wrestling tricks in fighting with weapons – even in the geometrical Camillo Agrippa – there are no further noteworthy Italian discussions of unarmed combat (figs 136–40).[55]

The German printed wrestling book does have at least some semblance of a history which begins with a group of three very slim illustrated volumes dealing with wrestling primarily as a sporting skill. All are versions of a block-book (produced, possibly as early as 1490, by the Landshut woodcutter and printer Hans Wurm) of which only one copy is known to survive. It lacks a title page but otherwise offers a complete series of twenty-two coloured woodcuts, each accompanied by a brief caption, showing pairs of wrestlers in vigorous action, but only two moves suggest serious violence – one an arm-lever which could break the limb to which it is applied, the other something looking suspiciously like the beginning of a back-breaker.[56] The majority of the pictures involve the hook with the leg (*den*

140. Lucini's stomach throw. 1627, plate 20.

Hacken) to unbalance, and ultimately to throw, an opponent, together with a number of side-chancery holds and hip throws which are all sound wrestling procedures but unlikely to prove dangerous to an experienced adversary. The tiny book would not be very effective as a teach-yourself manual, yet it obviously caught other printers' imaginations for it was twice plagiarized, once with exactly the same blocks, and once with the whole series recut. It was also adapted and partially copied into a contemporary manuscript as a treatise on 'Wrestling in the Little Pit' (*Ringen im Grüblein*), and this curious term, though not used in the printed books, confirms the connection with sport rather than all-in fighting.[57] The *Grüblein* was literally a little pit – a small, very shallow hollow – in which one combatant was obliged to keep a foot (rather like a base in rounders) while his opponent tried to force him out of it. According to the wrestling master Fabian von Auerswald, it was an archaic sport in which the man outside the pit was obliged to hop on one leg, presumably to even up the contest: 'It calls for great skill, and is enjoyable to watch'.[58]

Von Auerswald's own wrestling treatise was published at Wittemberg in 1539 when the author was already well into his seventy-seventh year, and it presents a different style of combat and a different approach from those normally found in the traditional *Fechtbücher*. More concerned with wrestling as an exercise and spectator sport (as is suggested by his inclusion of the *Grüblein*) than as a potentially lethal system of unarmed combat, he sometimes comments on the social acceptability of his various moves. A struggle to achieve a hip-throw, for instance, is deemed 'right convivial' (*fein Gesseliglich*);[59] whereas, when describing a drag hold, he writes 'With my left arm I grab under his right elbow and pull him towards me. Then he begins to bend. When he bends, I let my left hand slip into his right fist. This produces a terrible dislocation which is very painful. This is something for rough folk and is not convivial.' We may well concede that it certainly would not be convivial: but, for that matter, neither would the zeal with which von Auerswald wrings his long-suffering opponent by the testicles; grabs him 'between the cheeks of his arse' (*seine Arsbacken*); dislocates or breaks his arm with a hammerlock or arm crush; or breaks his fingers by compressing them with one hand while applying torsion to the wrist with the other.[60] None the less, while some of his techniques could be dangerous, it is undeniable that von Auerswald's attitude is essentially agonistic rather than agonizing, and his intention to demonstrate the triumph of skill over mere strength is symbolized by the fact that

188

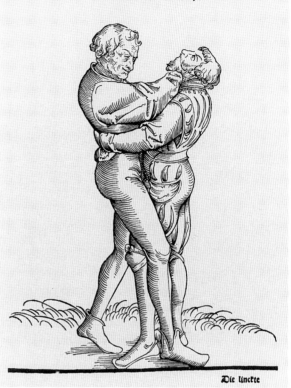

Der Wistback.

141. Auerswald talks here about tugging the opponent's left hand with one's own left hand. But that is certainly not what is being tugged. 1539, sig. A.6.

142. Auerswald's answer to the bear's hug: right hand under the opponent's chin, right leg behind his left knee; and 'this exercise can be done from left or right'. 1539, sig. C.6v.

he – the aged master, bony-faced and seamed with wrinkles – is consistently portrayed out-manoeuvring his youthful, smooth-skinned opponent. Von Auerswald's wrestling system is sophisticated; and so, too, is his exposition. His holds, throws and counters are grouped into logical sequences. His text is concise, though too dependent upon undefined technical terms for complete clarity; and he has the inestimable advantage of an artist, Lucas Cranach the Younger, who plainly understood wrestling, was an expert draughtsman and a virtuoso of the woodcut (figs 141–2).[61]

The only other manuals printed in Germany at this period are more akin to the old manuscript collections than to the monographs of Wurm and von Auerswald. Pauernfeindt (1516) deals with various modes of combat including the use of the dagger, but has no section specifically on unarmed combat and merely shows a couple of grappling techniques to be used in conjunction with the long sword, including the perennial testicle mangler (fig. 143).[62] On the other hand, Der altenn Fechter, first published by Christian Egenolff around 1531 and frequently reissued, included short sections on unarmed combat and dagger fighting, offering a characteristic mixture of conventional wrestling tricks mingled

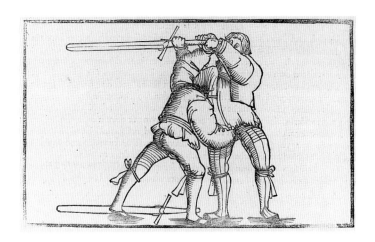

143. Pauernfeindt's version of
an old favourite. sig. F.4v.

with head butts, back breakers and strangleholds.[63] The arrangement is the customary
description of separate attacks each followed by a relevant counter; the woodcuts are by the
masterly Hans Weiditz; and there is nothing remotely 'convivial' about any of it.[64]

After this little flurry of activity in the German printing presses, treatises specifically
devoted to wrestling disappear although, judging from the woodcuts in Joachim Meyer's
Kunst des Fechtens (1570), unarmed combat must still have loomed large in the German
schools of arms. The top of the title page of this famous work is piled up with swords while,
along the bottom there is a scene of long sword and long staff fighting. Contrasting with
these there is, on either side, a view of Hercules in action. On the left, he is poised to club
a prostrate Antaeus who, since he derives his strength from the earth, lives to fight again
on the other side of the page where Hercules is about to lift him and crush him to death
in a bear hug (fig. 144). There could scarcely be a warmer endorsement of the efficacy of
wrestling and, although Meyer does not have a separate discussion of the art, he does have
an important section on dagger fighting practised by warriors using a *Dolch* in the form of
a large, blunted, wooden bodkin;[65] and wrestling, with many traditional holds and throws,
is often shown in the background of the composite scenes devoted to other kinds of fighting (fig. 145). Meyer's book was reprinted in 1600, yet only twelve years later, when Sutor
came to publish his version, bare-hand grappling was vestigial and confined to his last two
illustrations of long-sword fighting.[66]

The subsequent history of unarmed combat in German-speaking lands is obscure for
there was no detailed treatment of wrestling until Pascha in 1657.[67] However, his interest
in the subject cannot have been as unusual as it seems since many masters continued to recommend wrestling tricks in combination with sword fighting well into the eighteenth
century. Some, like Johann Andreas Schmidt, included an extended treatment of all-in fighting as an integral part of their work; and at least one, Theodor Verolini, plagiarized a complete foreign treatise to fill in the lacuna in his own.[68] In England and France, both countries
noted for wrestlers of great strength and skill, there were neither manuscripts nor printed
books on the subject until the Renaissance (however we may choose to define that term)
was long since dead and buried. But there remain for consideration the works of two masters
– one Dutch, the other Spanish – who wrote what are, historically speaking, the most important treatises on unarmed combat ever printed.

144. Hercules and Antaeus fight it out on Meyer's allegorical title page. 1570.

145. Dagger and wrestling practice in Meyer. 1600, book III, fol. 11v.

In many ways, the finest of all wrestling books – and deservedly the most famous – was the treatise by Nicolaes Petter and Romein de Hooghe, first published in 1674 and reprinted several times thereafter, including one complete and unacknowledged plagiarism.[69] The title page of this work, like so many others in the history of the martial arts, makes very ambitious claims.

> The Academy of the admirable Art of Wrestling. Showing in a very exact manner not only the extraordinary strength of Man, but also the marvellous movements, the singular usage, and the suppleness of the principal parts and members of the human body. With clear and homely instruction how one can on all occasions surely and adroitly repel all sorts of affronts and attacks. Represented in seventy-one copper-plate engravings which are very fine and which have been designed by the Celebrated and Famous Mr. Romein de Hoogue.

For once, though, the promises are fulfilled. It is true that there are only a few manoeuvres in this work which may not be found, at least embryonically, in one or the other of its predecessors, even as far back as Fiore and Talhoffer. Yet the combination of Petter's lucid verbal descriptions, quite devoid of technical jargon, and the meticulous violence of de Hooghe's engravings (which make even Dürer's drawings seem gentle by comparison) elevates the treatise to a position of solitary eminence. It is, perhaps, unique in combining an effective system of unarmed combat with an exposition from which it really would be possible to learn. It is, moreover, intensely dramatic. When one of de Hooghe's bruisers twists an arm, wrist or leg, treads on a calf or hamstring, pushes his thumb under a nose, or breaks an arm, the victim's agony is almost palpable.

The general conception underlying Petter's *Academy* is set out in a 'Preface' by an anonymous admirer who remarks that, while such an art is based upon experience, constant practice and theoretical knowledge, it is also necessary that there should be 'Teaching' to disseminate the skill which would otherwise perish with the man who invented it. From this point of view, he continues, Nicolaes Petter has never had an equal in discovering the techniques by which one can defend oneself against all sorts of assaults, 'against blows of foot and fist, and even against knife strokes'. His expertise was so highly esteemed that he was asked to set forth the art 'in the most clear manner' for the public benefit, and he therefore sought out the great artist Romein de Hooghe so that his book should be 'perfect in all its parts'.

The volume is a model of clarity, for de Hooghe's illustrations and Petter's text dovetail perfectly despite the perennial problems posed by the art of wrestling for its interpreters. The ancient Egyptian artists at Beni Hasan had found a partial solution by showing contrasting black and white antagonists, but medieval and renaissance masters did not hit upon so simple a method.[70] Fiore tried to distinguish between master and pupil by bestowing a crown, far too intermittently, upon the former; the artist for the Wallerstein manuscript, with only a few lapses, gave one wrestler fair hair, and the other, dark. Dürer, in his adaptation of that manuscript, generally (but not invariably) provided one wrestler with a kind of coif or hairnet; and von Auerswald had himself depicted throughout as the clean-shaven, aged but successful master, while his pupil was a bearded young man – a formula which certainly differentiates between the combatants but does not always find an answering clarity in the text. Petter clarifies his account partly by having his various combatants wear different garments and partly by using consistently a simple alphabetical reference system reminiscent of Camillo Agrippa's famous treatise.[71]

> In order that no one can make a mistake over the wrestlers, one will find them distinguished and marked by the letters A and B, B and C, and so on; and, since variety gives pleasure, A is sometimes the victor, and sometimes B. The different clothing worn by the wrestlers in the engravings sufficiently distinguishes them in so far as one sees in each part some different additions whereby people of good taste cannot be at all misled.

The treatise is arranged in thirteen sections each devoted to a particular mode of attack or defence. These, in turn, are broken down into several sequential movements each of which is allotted a separate number and illustration which are cross-referenced using the letters of the alphabet assigned to the combatants. De Hooghe's engravings are unambiguous despite the fact that, inevitably, they can only show key moments of an action more fully described in Petter's text.[72] Throughout, the treatise follows the method already established in Fiore's time whereby each attack is answered by a possible counter which is itself countered by yet another trick – the wrestling equivalent of a dialectician's questions, answers, rejoinders and rebuttals.[73]

The first two sections deal at length with blows to the chest and how to counter them; and some of the punishment meted out is severe. In the second section, for example, after B has hurled his assailant C to the ground with a stomach throw, he grasps one of C's feet – his right hand over the toes, his left near the heel – 'and he twists the foot of C with so much violence that he seems to wish to tear it into pieces, which can cause C extreme pain and rob him of much of his strength'. In an attempt to break this excruciating hold, C kicks out at his tormentor's left hand to loosen its grip but is answered by an attack to the throat and right arm. He comes back with a thumb hold, forcing B to fall, and then grasps him by the hair to twist him to the ground.[74]

The third section opens with D escaping from a bear hug attempted by C. The method is to place the left hand behind the assailant's right arm, while pushing his head back by thrusting with the right thumb under his nose, and hooking the right leg behind his left. Although, in fact, a thrust under the nose would be likely to end C's involvement in this and any other fight permanently, he struggles on gallantly to the end of the sequence of six further illustrations despite having his arm almost broken and ending up in the grip of a dislocating arm lever.[75] Seizing an opponent's hair from behind and throwing him over the shoulders is the subject of the next part in which, despite D's successful execution of this move, E 'does not tarry an instant on the ground, but picks himself up and grasps D behind his sleeve or arm, and taking D's right wrist with his right hand forces the arm inwards; and placing his left foot on D's right hamstring, he thus forces him to fall, although the plate does not show him as having fallen'.[76] Various kinds of grip form the theme of the fifth sequence of five postures culminating with an exchange in which F – having fallen after a failed attempt to destroy E by aiming a blow 'with all his strength' to the nape of his neck – still contrives to throw him with a risky combination of ankle pick-up combined with a knee driven into the buttocks.[77] The next two sequences show how to apply an arm lever or trip an attacker who has grasped the breast of one's jacket; and the eighth explains methods to overcome attacks with the fist.

The ninth part is rather problematic in that it purports to show how a wrestler may seize and carry his antagonist wherever he wishes – a mode of wrestling which 'is not less marvellous than charming' and, says Petter, 'gives to the spectators one of the most agreeable divertissements when it is put into practice'. That is why he enjoins his readers to pay special attention to the illustration of a trick which he has himself often used.[78] The difficulty here is that this remark obviously refers to the combat as a spectator sport which, while just conceivably compatible with what appears to be a prototype of the aeroplane whirl sometimes favoured by modern all-in wrestlers, is not the impression conveyed elsewhere by the controlled ferocity of this treatise: certainly not in the tenth section which explains how to combat attacks to the throat by, for example, a right-hander to the solar plexus; nor the eleventh which provides some suitably extreme methods for meting out disaster to a knife-wielding assassin; nor even in the last two parts which deal, respectively, merely with head butts to the belly and testicles, and a selection of shoulder throws and trips.

In view of Petter's evident expertise, it is curious that his section on coping with a knife attack is not as complete as one might expect. The necessity for instruction on this matter was recognized by all the medieval masters and by many of their successors, and Petter has a similar assessment of the peril itself for, he says, there are determined ruffians whose brains are so inflamed that they cannot be calmed down by reason, and who believe that even the slightest disagreement must be terminated by recourse to the knife, 'in which there is very great danger'. As we have already seen, there is a strong relationship between the techniques recommended by Fiore, the German masters and Marozzo for an unarmed man to deal with a knife attack. But Petter's methods differ considerably from those of his predecessors and he makes no attempt at comprehensiveness. He is unique in showing how to step on the assailant's foot while simultaneously punching him in the face (although it must be remembered that the Emperor Maximilian I favoured a similar method in the lists), or how to prevent a man from even drawing his knife. He also depicts tricks for breaking the enemy's knife hand; forcing him to wound himself; and disarming him with a kick (figs 146–55). But, for all the dynamism of the illustrations, the treatment is surprisingly curtailed when compared with that of Fiore or Marozzo even though, unlike his predecessors, Petter does not take the easy option but deals mainly with knife thrusts from a dagger held foward, above the hand.

That minor reservation apart, we may (with only the slightest historical licence) regard Petter and de Hooghe's *Academy* as the summation of the art of wrestling in the Renaissance. At the other end of the printing history of wrestling, the earliest treatise – with the possible exception of the experimental and rudimentary block book published by Hans Wurm – is that incorporated by Pietro Monte in his study of the qualities of men, *De dignoscendis hominibus*. This appeared at Milan in 1492 and was soon afterwards rendered into Italian by an enthusiast who, by discreetly remaining silent about his source, contrived to suggest that the translation was an original work.[79] This was not so: but Monte's treatment itself could scarcely have been more unusual for, although there were earlier manuals of wrestling, no one had attempted to analyse the general principles underlying unarmed combat – one of the tasks Monte set himself. Nor did anyone attempt it again. And that is why I have chosen to end this chapter at the beginning.

A few years later, Monte returned to the subject in his *Collectanea* – setting it within what might appear to be a more suitable context of physical exercise, martial arts and war – but omitting a number of interesting general observations, and reorganizing the material to its disadvantage. There are, however, three underlying assumptions common to both discussions. First is the practical consideration that, because Latin is wholly inadequate to explain wrestling procedures, the various manoeuvres – 'which we call *Magnas* in

146. The first move.

146–55. The ten ways described by Petter and de Hooghe for an unarmed man to deal with a dagger attack. 1674, pp. 55–64.

147. The second move.

148. The third move.

149. The fourth move.

150. The fifth move.

151. The sixth move.

152. The seventh move.

153. The eighth move.

154. The ninth move.

155. The tenth move.

the Spanish idiom' – are, in fact, to be given their Spanish names.[80] The second assumption is that wrestling is the foundation of all other exercises since it develops the strength and agility required in military games and, more particularly, because it teaches warriors how to fall correctly when engaged in real combat.[81] The third assumption – that a balanced temperament is the prime requisite of success – is central to Monte's entire approach to physical training and explains why he so repeatedly discourses upon the Galenic complexions. He feels that an understanding of the melancholic, sanguine, phlegmatic and choleric humours, along with all their combinations and permutations, must lead to an understanding of their relationship to both psychological and somatic types, and that this, in turn, enables a master to devise systematic exercises for the body to meet the needs of different qualities of men.

Specifically with regard to wrestling, Monte considers that a well-tempered athlete will have the ability to refrain from impetuous attacks; to move with appropriate speed and just measure; to anticipate and counter his opponent's movements; to understand where he himself is most vulnerable and, conversely, where his adversary may be most easily injured. In the *De dignoscendis hominibus*, after introductory remarks of this kind, Monte offers more general advice concerning movement and on attack and defence. For example, he advocates taking short steps on the tips of one's toes, with the feet pointing slightly outwards; and he stresses that it is equally important to watch the opponent's behaviour in this respect because one sees by experience that the whole success of an attack or defence may depend upon the slightest variation of foot movement. He also suggests weighing up an opponent before deciding upon one's own fight pattern, and recommends awaiting the impetus and fury of an attack rather than hurling oneself into the fray, because this kind of recklessness has often caused the downfall even of those who were physically stronger than their adversaries.

197

One point emphasized by Monte is the need to be light on one's feet and to maintain suppleness. This conviction is fundamental to his theory of exercise; and later, in his *Collectanea*, he criticizes both ancient and modern authorities on physical education who have, he believes, concentrated too much on heavy muscularity rather than on producing bodies that are straight, well proportioned and without stiffness. It is for the same reason that he disapproves of painters who show the human form with stiff, contorted and too heavily muscled limbs. Such figures are 'in a certain sense monstrous' and jar one's feeling for decorum. Muscles should be smooth and supple, not 'knotty and hilly'; and the human body achieves less by brute force than by skilful control and ease of action.[82] Similarly, in his introductory remarks on wrestling in the *De dignoscendis*, Monte notes the paradox whereby stiffness renders a man more easily lifted. 'When we wish to carry two things of equal size', he remarks, 'one of iron and the other of feathers, wool or cotton, it is, in fact, the former which is easier to lift because of its rigidity and compactness'. These observations are followed by a long sequence of attacks, counter attacks and special ruses, many of them designated by appropriate Spanish terms which are glossed by Gonzalo de Ayora, the young soldier-scholar who translated Monte's original Spanish text into humanistic Latin.[83] This, incidentally, is another reason to pay special heed to Monte's work. We know, with certainty, that there was a powerful tradition of wrestling in fifteenth-century Spain, with a well-developed and consistent technical vocabulary, but the details of this tradition can now be recovered only from Monte's writings.[84]

The first of these Spanish moves, discussed by Monte, is the *rotatio* which, he says, is more frequently and securely used than all the other tricks of this art. According to Ayora's gloss, it is a kind of trip in which one of our feet is placed between the opponent's legs, and the other high against his shin as we push with our arms; and Monte advises us that it is essential to keep our feet only moderately far apart for it is dangerous to have them either too close together or too spread out. A sort of golden mean – not too little, not too much – is Monte's ideal in this as in much else. The successful wrestler must always be in a position which enables him to move in or break away without the slightest delay; but if the feet are badly placed it becomes necessary to waste time making two separate movements either to mount an attack or attempt a defence. All approach work should be swift and without any obvious show of force so that the opponent never has time to prepare a counter. In other words we must not telegraph our intentions. Monte also recommends that the *rotatio* and similar actions, whether launched from the front or behind, should be aimed at the top of the opponent's shin or behind his knee.

There are other attacks which constantly appear in the wrestling system described in the *De dignoscendis* and the *Collectanea*. The *sacaligna*, for example – a word literally meaning a kind of hooked staff or harpoon – is a hooking movement directed to the back of the knee; and the *mediana* is a trip involving wrapping one leg around one of the opponent's, 'in the manner of a snake' – probably akin to the *Haken*, later illustrated in von Auerswald, and to the grapevine commonly used in modern wrestling. The *descaderada* or *disclunata* – in which 'when the contestants are almost back to back, the enemy is lifted up with the buttocks and arms and is thrown flat on the ground' – is the cross-buttock familiar to all catch-as-catch-can wrestlers. Whatever the attack undertaken, Monte insists that it be carried out with ease of movement (*solutione*) and with all possible strength and speed because without these qualities nothing can be achieved, no matter how agile a man may be. On the other hand, if the wrestler does have these qualities, then his opponent will simply not have time to counter the attack – precisely the point made by the

German master Ott in the few general observations with which he had preceded his own treatise.

Attacks such as *rotatio*, *sacaligna*, *mediana* and *disclunata* may be applied equally well on either flank: but Monte regrets that to write about every possible aspect of this art would occupy far too much space. Therefore, while he will discuss most of the important tricks or ruses used by wrestlers, he intends to confine himself only to what is absolutely necessary concerning defensive moves. He then works, fairly systematically and very comprehensively, through a series of wrestling tricks – showing how they may be combined in groups – before describing a number of counter attacks, or ways to escape from the throws and holds already considered. The lack of illustrations was, and remains, a major defect of the treatise: but Monte's descriptions are as clear and concise as words and the ambiguity intrinsic to the Latin language could make them.

What distinguishes Monte from other early writers on wrestling is his willingness to confront the more general issues arising from the technical intricacies of physical combat. He ponders, for example, the advantages and disadvantages of size, strength and weight, and the problems posed by different locations and types of ground. With regard to stature, he considers that when one is confronted by an opponent larger than oneself it is a good idea to get inside his guard whereas with a smaller man it is better to keep at a distance where you can reach him, but where he cannot hurt you. Very tall, heavily built men generally find it advantageous to wrestle in the nude because, while they can get a purchase on the bodies of slender opponents, those opponents cannot do the same to them. Conversely, of course, should these large men remain clothed, then slim wrestlers would have a better chance against them. As far as terrain is concerned, Monte advises against tackling an unskilled but physically powerful adversary on wet, soft ground, because there is always a chance that your feet may slip, while the heavier man may stand firm and be difficult to throw without tremendous effort. Similarly, places where there is running water and where the ground is covered with little stones should be avoided because you could easily come to grief if, as you raise one foot when attacking, the other shoots away from you. In short: poor conditions favour brute strength and disadvantage those who gain their victories more by art than by force so that, without doubt, those who have both strength and skill should always fight in the best possible conditions where the random effects of chance are minimized and where real ability may prevail. Monte is not impressed by mere physical force and he is constantly at pains, here and elsewhere in his writings, to stress the importance of measure and balance. Ever the advocate of speed, grace and poise, he recommends these qualities in a short chapter devoted to the different complexions of men, their capacity for wrestling, and the practical value of being able to recognize each type. The sanguine man, for instance, tends to be very furious at the start of a combat but soon wears himself out, so that it is sensible to brace oneself to withstand his initial onslaught and be ready to overwhelm him when his energy flags. The phlegmatic type, however, tends to be rather weak and slow in the early stages of a contest, so it is best to attack him very suddenly to catch him unawares.

The treatise on wrestling in the *De dignoscendis* ends with a chapter which not only demonstrates Monte's ability to use his knowledge of specific technical skills to explore wider issues but is also remarkable for being organized on a comparative basis which, however dubious the authenticity of its information, certainly demonstrates the author's imaginative view of diversity. From the multiplicity of rules and traditions which existed in different lands, Monte tries to derive some norms of behaviour – some universal laws of wrestling – and his agonistic orientation is shown in several observations and recommendations. He notes that in Brittany it is necessary to throw an opponent on to his back, while in Spain, Portugal, Sicily and most of Italy a fall is not conceded if a wrestler spontaneously touches the ground with hand and knee – a rule which, not surprisingly, often caused controversy. His own preference, though, is that a fall should be awarded when any part of an opponent's body, other than his feet, has touched the ground; and he argues strongly that contests should always be decided on the best of three falls (which has remained the norm to the present day) because, on the one hand, a single fall may be gained by chance and, on the other, continuing beyond three falls may allow for the triumph of stamina over skill. Monte is also very particular about clothing, or the lack of it. Apparel for wrestling should be neither too loose nor too tight and, although in some places it is the custom to wrestle nude, Monte considers this unseemly, dishonourable and impractical. For him the faculty of wrestling must always be associated with the art of arms; and in a real battle there is little point in fighting naked which, he remarks laconically, 'leaves us much exposed to danger'. This is perhaps the only general issue where Monte's thinking is ambivalent for, although he is explicit that wrestling is not merely a sport but is also an exercise relevant to real battle, he nevertheless stresses that attacks on certain areas – 'such as the genitals, mouth, nostrils, eyes, hair and throat' – are generally regarded as shameful and dangerous. This, of course, is true: but Monte was perfectly well aware that the requirements of battle are not identical with those of sport, and that competitive wrestling is not the same as all-in fighting. The tension between the two in his own mind becomes apparent when he discusses the technique, 'permitted in Germany, Hungary, Bohemia and Poland', of grasping the lower limbs with the hands. He is not happy about this style of wrestling but notes that, in the various countries to which he has just alluded, anything is accepted as licit if it enables you to defeat your opponent; and, as a pragmatic man of action, he confesses that he is himself reluctant to condemn anything which leads to victory.

Despite that concession, Monte cannot approve of what is now generally termed ground wrestling because he believes that to fight with hands and feet on the ground is to behave 'like four-footed beasts', whereas nature has made man to stand upright with his head held high to emphasize the rule of reason over brute force.[85] This view of man's upright posture as an expression of human dignity had been a standard argument among the learned from Lactantius (in the fourth century) onwards and was used by Monte's contemporary the philosopher Marsilio Ficino who might, none the less, have been startled to see it cited as justification for a particular style of wrestling.[86] Monte suggests that ground wrestling was customary in the various central European lands he has just mentioned and this raises a slight doubt about the validity of his confident pronouncements on wrestling systems other than those of Spain and Italy. He does, it is true, note an unlikely type of fighting in Great Britain – where the contestants try to strangle one another with a neckerchief – which can, in fact, be verified for England from medieval iconographic sources and for Germany from an early seventeenth-century manuscript.[87] But ground wrestling occurs very rarely in the surviving Germanic combat manuals and, when it does, it tends to be the final stage of a murderous encounter (fig. 156).[88] It is unlikely that Monte's dislike for this aspect of wrestling was really due to a concern for human dignity but was more probably the result of an intuitive grasp of the truth which Captain Fairbairn made explicit in 1942 when he deliberately excluded ground wrestling from his all-in fighting system, 'because it takes years of practice to become proficient, even in dealing with one opponent', while to attempt it in time of war, 'when one is not unlikely to be attacked by two or more opponents, cannot

156. Ground wrestling. A nasty conclusion in Erhart's treatise. 1533, fol. 91v.

be recommended'.[89] Monte came up with the wrong reason but still found the right answer.

Thanks to Castiglione, Monte's fame as a wrestling master still enjoys a tenuous immortality. Nevertheless, for Galeazzo da Sanseverino and Monte's other courtly pupils, unarmed combat would have been a relatively minor part of their martial education – minor, that is, in comparison with what they would have regarded as their speciality. For they were knights. If they fought within the lists on foot, they would do so wearing the bespoke armour which bespoke their lofty status. If they went to war they expected to fight mainly on horseback, again encased in made-to-measure armour. They prided themselves on their traditional chivalric skills which were using lance and sword in mounted combat; and they practised these techniques in the lists by jousting and tourneying. Despite the interest shown by Fiore and the fifteenth-century German masters, writing about chivalric combats became increasingly a specialist concern. The majority of later professional masters of arms – at least in their published treatises – tended to concentrate upon the kinds of martial arts I have already discussed and, even when they did consider mounted combat, they had little to say about arms and armour. In these respects Monte was exceptional for not only was he as much concerned with fighting on horseback as on foot but he also interested himself in the relevant equipment. He is thus a bridge – notionally rather than historically – between the masters who dealt principally with the use of sword and staff weapons on foot and those who were more interested in fighting on horseback. Equally he is a bridge, as we shall see in the next chapter, between medieval and modern attempts to systematize knowledge of arms and armour.

VII

Arms and armour

IF MODERN SCHOLARS, in the course of their work, should be unlucky enough to stumble across a reference to some daunting piece of armour such as a *Visierbolzen mit Schraubmutter*; or if they are puzzled by an unfamiliar weapon such as a *spiedo friulano*; or if the problem were to present itself the other way round and they cannot remember whether the head is best protected by spaudler, besagew or codpiece, then generally they would know how to find the answers. They might consult the polyglot *Glossarium armorum*, not only for English, French, Italian and German terms but also for Danish and Hungarian; delve into Leguina's massive *Glosario* for Spanish words and phrases; or turn to the writings of acknowledged experts, past and present, in search of the information required.[1]

There are two points to be observed here. The first is simply that nowadays there are people who sometimes need that kind of information, however unlikely they may be to fight in the lists either on foot or on horseback. The second point is that there are experts who produce books on arms and armour specifically designed to help the less well informed find their way about the bewildering labyrinth of technicalities. These books are arranged chronologically or thematically; they are indexed and illustrated; and they are usually provided with copious annotation and glossaries. Their systematic erudition descends, in a direct line, from the pioneering work of late eighteenth-century and early nineteenth-century scholars and the results may be found in specialist libraries. But things were not always so straightforward.[2] For several centuries, there was little academic interest in problems relating to arms and armour and little inclination on the part of those who had first-hand practical knowledge about the subject to put pen to paper.

This kind of difficulty is familiar to historians. Where objects or customs are commonplace, it is unusual for contemporaries to explain what they are for. Indeed, they are likely to be as impatient as the anonymous fifteenth-century armour expert who – in his discussion of articulated arm defences – replied to a hypothetical questioner: 'if you ask me of what pieces they are made, I reply to you that there is no need for me to declare it more particularly, because all the world knows it, and it is so much in use that it would only make me lose words and time'.[3]

Obviously, the most important sources for the study of arms and armour are the surviving artefacts themselves, but it is rare for objects to be wholly self-explanatory; and much the same may be said of iconographic evidence. Pictures of armed figures abound, but only a tiny minority were devised to explain the technicalities of armour construction and, like the artefacts themselves, they convey most to those who already know most. This is even the case with the pattern books prepared by armourers and their etchers to record designs of armour, the names of their patrons, and dates of manufacture. Records of this sort are invaluable, but they survive only for a relatively late period in the history of armour and are extremely rare.[4] Moreover, they were designed for professional use and can be regarded as reference works only in a specialized sense.

For a full understanding of the implications, both of artefacts and illustrations, documentary evidence is essential; and the trouble is that the earliest documentary evidence consists, for the most part, not of analytical and expositive treatises, but of inventories and lists. From at least the early fourteenth century onwards, all over Europe, arms and armour occur regularly in the inventories of the possessions of warriors ranging from moderately humble knights to princes, kings and emperors. Such documents are not uncommon, but their principal purpose was to record possessions.[5] They were never intended to provide contemporaries with a kind of encyclopaedic dictionary and, unless furnished with scholarly apparatus, they cannot fulfil that function for the modern researcher.[6] This is also true of other kinds of catalogue such as that drawn up for the shop of the armourer Jean de Vouvray at Tours in 1512; or in the account books of the *Écurie* of François d'Angoulême (soon to be François I), recording armour prepared for the Paris tournament of 1514.[7] The information contained in such records may enable us to resolve many problems of chronology, nomenclature, etymology and comparative costs and values: but they are also dangerously seductive and reductive because scholars working too closely with inventories (glossing an entry in one document by reference to similar entries in others) may tend, like the legendary Ooslum Bird, to fly round in ever-diminishing circles. The process can generate footnotes of imposing bulk but uncertain utility.

The truth of the matter is that, in general, throughout the period when the military caste normally fought wars, mock wars and duels, clad in metal suits, there was little attempt to systematize knowledge either about the ways in which these outfits were constructed and assembled or about the various weapons used against them. Later, when treatises on the art of war developed into a growth industry in renaissance Europe, the complete chivalric panoply was considered by most authors to be as outmoded as the warfare for which it had been designed. Writers were, instead, obsessed with the relevance of ancient models, with issues of morale and morality, with logistics and military arithmetic, fortification and siege warfare, troop formations, and the impact of fire power; and it is not surprising that theorists of this kind were rarely concerned with hand-to-hand fighting or with the nuts and bolts of armed conflict. What is much more curious is the silence of the masters of arms. Their works remain the foundation for our knowledge of the martial arts: yet they rarely felt it necessary to provide information concerning the tools of their own trade. Their reticence concerning defensive armour is readily explicable, since the greater part of their teaching was designed for civilian use; but it is less easy to explain their lack of interest in describing and elucidating 'weapons of percussion and perforation'.[8] Swords, rapiers, daggers and knives flash and clash in almost every paragraph of their books, yet they are seldom defined or described; and crucial details of measurement, weight, shape and construction are, with only a few exceptions, totally ignored.

Brief lists of equipment were, nevertheless, sometimes compiled by non-professionals for reasons other than a desire to provide factual information. Inevitably, in an age when knights were dominant military figures, their paraphernalia proved attractive to writers, and the 'armour of God', in the Epistle of St Paul to the Ephesians, had demonstrated how a wholly arbitrary allegorical interpretation could be imposed upon each piece of chivalric equipment: 'loins girt about with truth'; 'breastplate of righteousness'; 'feet shod with the preparation of the gospel of peace'; 'shield of faith'; 'helmet of salvation'; and 'sword of the Spirit which is the word of God'. Late in the thirteenth century, Ramón Llull devoted a chapter of his *Book of the Order of Chivalry* to just such an allegory. So did Guillaume de Deguileville a few years later, in his *Pilgrimage of the Soul*. And so did Pere March in his late fourteenth-century poem, 'The Knight's Armour'. In all these cases, the meanings attributed to arms and armour were fantastic. The lists do have an undoubted philological and historical value for modern readers: but it is certain that no intelligent contemporary, confronted with an unfamiliar lump of chivalric metal, would have tried to find out about it in any of these texts.[9]

Nor would they have consulted works of fiction, despite the fact that writers of romance also found good copy in the arming of their heroes. Chrestien de Troyes's *Erec*, for example, preparing for combat around about 1170, is armed 'from tip to toe' – though still vulnerable, because the only pieces specifically mentioned are 'iron greaves', 'triple-woven hauberk', ventail, and helmet. By the time that the author of *Sir Gawain and the Green Knight* got around to arming his hero in the latter part of the fourteenth century, the relationship between fiction and fact had become more sophisticated, and Gawain has a better chance of survival. He dons 'dublet', 'crafty capados' (that is a skilfully wrought coif), 'sabatouns', 'quyssewes', 'brace upon his both armes', 'cowters', 'gloves' and 'helme' with viser and 'aventayle', all laced and buckled together.[10]

While Gawain was preparing to fight it out with the Green Knight, real warriors were engaging in judicial combats where practical knowledge was essential. The challenge issued by Pierre Tournemine to Robert de Beaumanoire, for a duel on horseback and on foot at Nantes in 1386, consists largely of a prodigiously detailed list of the equipment to be used. Not only does it name more than forty different parts of defensive armour to be worn by man and horse, but it also provides precise information on the metals from which they were to be fashioned, the materials with which each piece was to be lined or padded, and the ways they were to be fastened together – including mention of every individual strap and buckle, and even of the nails and rivets where required. Each knight was to carry two swords and a dagger and these, too, are strictly prescribed. One sword was to be hung by straps and buckles from the haubergeon, the other from the saddle bow. The blade of the first was to be two and a half feet long, and its grip, including pommel, about thirteen inches; the second, only slightly shorter in the blade, was to be six inches less in the grip. The dagger's blade was to be roughly nine inches in length; and all the weapons were to be openly exhibited before the court so that the measurements could be thoroughly checked. The purpose of a list so comprehensive and so carefully described is unclear. In a judicial combat between significant noblemen, care would always have been taken to ensure equality in every respect, and the obsessively meticulous prescription of arms and armour may simply be legal exactitude carried to extremes. Or perhaps Tournemine was simply hoping to frighten Beaumanoire with a show of martial expertise and a seemingly limitless personal thesaurus of ironmongery. The challenge cannot have been intended by its author as an aid to contemporary seekers after knowledge, but it must have been invaluable as a statement of precedent for similar challenges; and it remains a remarkable resource for scholars.[11]

THE EARLIEST ATTEMPTS AT SYSTEMATIZATION

A purely didactic conception (the idea that it would be useful to systematize information on arms and armour in order to instruct some unknown third party) is perhaps first encountered in a chapter devoted to offensive and defensive arms included in the Old Norse *Speculum regale* written during the thirteenth century. This suggests a comprehensive covering for the knight's mount: 'every part of the horse should be covered, head, loins, breast, belly, and the entire beast, so that no man, even if on foot, shall be able to reach him with deadly weapons'. The knight's apparel is then listed, first for the bottom and then for the top half of his body, from the innermost to the outermost layer: hose of soft linen cloth, coming right up to the breeches-belt; then mail hose high enough to be girded with a double strap; and finally breeches of strong linen on which must be fastened 'knee-pieces made of thick iron with rivets hard as steel'. The upper part of the body should first be clothed in a soft linen *panzara* or gambeson coming down to mid-thigh; and over this an iron *briost biorg* or breast-defence protecting the area from the nipples to the breeches-belt; then two further layers, rendered by one translator as 'a well-made hauberk and over the hauberk a firm gambison', and by another as 'a good byrnie, and over all a good panzar of the same length as the tunic but without sleeves'. The knight must wear a good helm, 'made of tried steel', and a 'good and thick shield suspended from his neck, especially furnished with a strong handle'. He also carries a dagger, two swords (one girded round him, the other hanging at his saddle-bow), and a strong spear pointed with fine steel. The account seems detailed but, in fact, much of the terminology is ambiguous and there is no real attempt to explain how the armour was constructed.[12]

Just as tantalizing is a little document, wedged between notes on falconry and a transcript of Hue de Tabarie's *L'Ordre de chevalerie*, in a long miscellaneous manuscript collection of treatises, poems and sermons compiled by Father William Herebert of Hereford who died in the 1330s.[13] Headed *Modus armandi milites ad torneamentum*, it includes two subdivisions, 'Ad bellum' and 'Ad hastiludia', and is interesting partly because it anticipates later attempts at describing the arming process and partly because, although only 148 words long, it manages to pack in a remarkable amount of confusion.

With regard to war, the anonymous author simply lists *aketoun, plates de Alemayne ou autres*, along with *bone gorgeres, gladius, haches a pik, et cultellus*. He also mentions a shield but notes that it is rarely carried in war because it hinders rather than helps. For mounted lance play (*Ad hastiludia*), only *aketoun, haubert, gambisoun* of silk, steel plates, and *bacyn et galea* are specifically named; and it is for the tourney that the author puts forth his best effort. He thoughtfully recommends that a fire be lit before the knight is stripped to his shirt; and, as in *Sir Gawain and the Green Knight*, advises that the floor be covered with a spread carpet. For reasons which remain undisclosed, the knight combs his hair before his feet are encased in leather shoes and he dons some sort of steel or leather shin guards (*ocreas*) defined by the author in French as *muscylers in tibiis de ascer ou de quyr boily*. Next come *quysons* and *genulers* for thighs and knees respectively; the padded, quilted coat (*aketoun*); and then a *camisia de Chartres et coyfe de Chartres* – both, presumably, in the mail for which Chartres was famous, though why a mail coif should have been donned before the rest of the head defences was probably no more apparent to the author than it is to the modern reader. The ensuing discussion of the headgear does nothing to clarify the matter. The words *coyfe de Chartres* are immediately followed by *et pelvim in qua debet esse cerveylere defendens capud ne contiguetur pelvis cum capite* ('and a basin in which there ought to be a cervellière defending the head lest the basin comes into contact with the head'). This is puzzling because it seems more likely that the *cerveylere* (or skull piece) should go on before the mail *coyfe*. But this would still leave the nature of the interposed *pelvis* (which is presumably the author's Latin rendition of bascinet) wholly mysterious, especially as he elsewhere refers to a *bacyn*. It must be made of metal, for otherwise there would be no need to protect the head from banging against it; and that, in turn, would mean that the *cervelière* must have been some sort of arming cap. The problem here is twofold: first that, as far as I have been able to ascertain, nobody else used the word *pelvis* for the bascinet; second, that all other uses of *cervelière* suggest that it was itself a metal cap and would not, therefore, appreciably soften the impact of another piece of metal headgear.

Oblivious of these complexities, the knight now puts on a hauberk, over which he wears a leather defence, itself surmounted by a surcoat decorated with his coat of arms. This seems fairly straightforward until we recall that, since he is already supposed to be wearing a quilted coat and a mail shirt, he would now have five substantial layers of body protection – unless the *lorica* is made of leather and is, in fact, the *quyree*. Drooping beneath this dead weight of armour, he is further confused by having to put on a gauntlet for his right hand or gauntlets of whalebone (*gayne payns ou gayns de baleyne*). The author does not explain the choice between one special gauntlet and two ordinary ones.[14] Nor does he comment on the weapons, *sa espeye, i.gladius et flagellum*, which the knight now takes up; and this is a pity because, although the spear and sword are straightforward, a flail would have been an eccentric item for any tourney.[15] Finally, there is another attempt at arming the head. *Et galeam i.heame*, says the text, which might mean that the knight dons a bascinet covered by a helm, were it not for the fact that he is already wearing three other items of headgear. He is at last ready for the combat but seems too encumbered to achieve much when he gets there.

This text is worth dwelling on because it typifies the ambiguities and uncertainties facing anybody who attempted to provide a systematic treatment of material for which the terminology remained unsettled and which, in any case, he did not fully comprehend. As so often with secular subjects in an age when most of the writing was done by clerics, we should not expect too much in the way of clarity. None the less, another religious author, the eminent Catalan Franciscan friar and theologian, Francesc Eiximenis, managed rather better than Herebert. His *Dotzè del Chrestià* (*The Twelve Apostles of Christ*), written late in the fourteenth century, includes a brief chapter entitled 'The arms which knights bear at the present time', which demonstrates that Eiximenis did, at least, know the names of more than twenty-four pieces of armour and weapons and understood what they were for.[16] Despite this, his chapter was not conceived as a work of reference, and it no more started a trend than did the obscure mini-treatise transcribed by Herebert.

Then, between 1434 and 1458, there were several attempts to describe arms and armour, not as a literary or allegorical exercise, nor as a list of equipment for some specific occasion, but as serious exposition of a complex technical subject. And this suggests a newly perceived need. The first of these discussions occurs in a short English treatise of the 'Poyntes of Worship in Armes' by one John Hill who describes himself as 'armorier and sergeant in th' Office of Armoryes with Kynges Henry the 4th and Henry the 5th'.[17] Hill, as Claude Blair has pointed out, was an important official – in fact head of the royal armouries.[18] Moreover, when he describes the preparations for a 'bataille of Treason' fought in the lists before the monarch, he writes with established expertise since he had been involved in providing armour and arms for John Upton in a famous combat fought against John Doune at Smithfield in January 1430.[19] His treatise is extremely concise but manages to list more than fifteen parts of the knight's armour for a judicial combat on foot. The suit is of greater complexity than the one described in Herebert's notes a century earlier, but even more significant is the detailed way in which the professional armourer explains both how the pieces are joined together and the order in which they are to be put on.

In this respect it is worth comparing Hill's treatise with another English text, *Howe a man shall be armyd at his ease when he schal fighte on foote*. The two are to a certain extent complementary for, while both describe the process of putting on armour in similar terms, *Howe a man shall be armyd* has more detail on the materials with which the pieces are to be tied together, particularly the arming points under the arm. These must be made of 'fyne twyne suche as men make stryngis for crossebowes and they must be trussid small and poyntid as poyntis', and they must also be waxed with 'cordeweneris coode [pitch or cobbler's wax], and than they woll neythir recche nor breke'. Some sort of authorial relationship between Hill's treatise and *Howe a man shall be armyd* has been suggested: but we do not know when the latter was written since the two manuscripts in which it survives were both compiled some thirty years after Hill's death. On balance, the similarities are no more than one might expect from any two roughly contemporaneous works summarizing equipment for the same kind of activity.[20] One remarkable feature of the Pierpont Morgan copy of *Howe a man shall be armyd* is that it has an illustration showing the arming of a man who is about to fight on foot. He is standing inside a little hut from which the front has been removed for our benefit, and he is being helped by a kneeling attendant. The knight's lower limbs have already been fitted with sabatons, greaves and cuisses, and a mail breech is being adjusted as we watch. On a trestle table at the left side of the hut, the rest of his equipment is laid out: the tonlette, with the breast and back plates to which it has already been attached; vambraces and cowters for the elbows; a rerebrace for the right arm, and another with besagew for the left; gauntlets for right and left hand (*gaigne pain* and *manifer*); and at the far end, to be put on last, the bascinet with visor and neck lames. Behind the table stand a polaxe and a kind of glaive, while behind them, leaning against the wall, is a shadowy outline which may be the knight's sword.[21]

Despite the undoubted value of these English records, they are less impressive than some French manuscript treatises written in the middle decades of the fifteenth century. The most celebrated of these, though not the earliest, is René d'Anjou's *Traictié de la forme et devis d'ung tournoy* which sets out to describe how a tourney should be organized 'at the court or elsewhere in some region of France when princes wish to hold one'. The form, says René, is based principally upon the practice of the Germans, but he has also taken into account the habits of Flanders and Brabant, together with ancient fashions formerly followed in France, 'as I have found in writings' – an early instance of antiquarian research into the history of the tournament. The treatise is mainly concerned with ceremonial but does include a section on arms and armour which, like the tourney itself, is based upon Germanic models. Several de luxe copies of this manuscript were executed, so that René's discussion of arms would have enjoyed a modest circulation amongst those who were probably already conversant with much of the information it contained.[22] There is also a less elaborate, more workmanlike late fifteenth-century copy in the R.L. Scott Collection, which omits all the scenes both of ceremonial and of the action within the lists, but includes careful drawings of the arms and armour.

René's written descriptions are very clear but, instead of dealing with armour in the order in which it would have been put on, and beginning therefore with the sabatons for the feet (as did earlier texts), he begins at the more spectacular end with the *timbre* or crest surmounting the helm which, with its barred metal faceguard, is clearly in the style of a German *Kolbenturnierhelm* (fig. 157).[23] He then moves down to the armour for body, arms and hands; digresses on the special mace and sword for tourneying; returns to the legs and feet which, he says, are to be protected in similar fashion to the armour worn in war; and

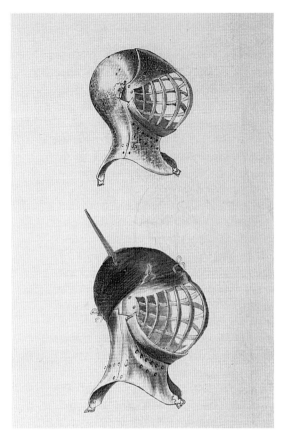

157. Heaulme for the tourney as prescribed by René d'Anjou. Scott MS., fol. 11.

158. René's experimental cuirasse 'pertuissée'. Scott MS. fol. 12.

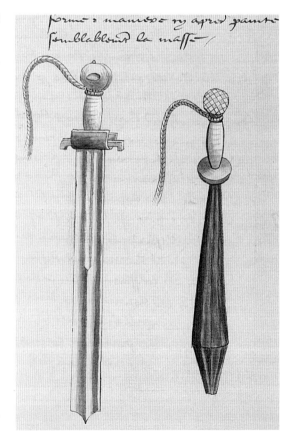

159. René's sword and mace for the tourney. Scott MS. fol. 14.

concludes with the *cotte d'armes*. René strongly recommends that the cuirass should be ample enough to allow room within for an arming doublet (*pourpoint*) of some 'three fingers in thickness at the shoulders'. This undergarment must protect the knight's arms right up to the neck and must similarly cover his back, 'because the blows of maces and swords fall more readily on those places than on others'.

The cuirass itself is René's most remarkable invention. He describes it as *pertuisée* – that is perforated with holes – 'in the best and most fitting fashion and manner that can be for the said tourney', and in the accompanying illustration it is depicted as though both breast-plate and backplate are fashioned from Gruyère cheese (fig. 158). Without doubt such per-forations would have lightened the armour considerably and would also have allowed ample circulation of air without risking penetration by the blunted tourneying weapons. The idea is also mentioned in a contemporary treatise on feats of arms by Antoine de la Sale. His brief description of armour includes what must have been a cuirass (despite being called *la cote d'armes*) since its recommended weight is between ten and twelve pounds. The breast-plate is to be pierced with 'great losenges or round apertures' (*toute percée de grans losenges ou pertruis reons*), in order to give 'the greatly exercised body wind and air'.[24] We do not know whether any armourer ever made this ingenious and practical piece; but certainly no *cuirasse pertuisée* has thus far come to light.

René provides a circumstantial account of the two weapons to be used in a tourney – a broad, blunted sword and a wooden club which he refers to as a *masse*.

Concerning the measure and fashion of the swords and maces, there is not much to say except for the width and length of the blade (*la lumelle*), for it must be four fingers wide so that it cannot pass through the sight of the helm, and must have the two edges one finger in thickness. And so that it should not be too heavy, it must be very much hol-lowed out in the centre and . . .[25] from the quillons (*la croisée*) to the tip; and the quil-lons must be only long enough to guard against a blow which by chance slides down the length of the sword to the fingers. And the whole sword ought to be as long as the arm and hand of he who carries it, and the mace should be similar. And the said mace must have a little rondel well fixed in front of the hand to guard it. And one can, if one so wishes, attach the sword or mace around the arm or waistband with a thin chain, plait or cord, so that if it slips from the hand it can be recovered without falling to the ground.

As far as the sword pommel is concerned, René leaves that to the particular fancy of each knight: but he stresses that, on the eve of the tourney, the judges must check the 'fatness of the maces and the weight of the swords' and brand them (*signées d'ung fer chaud*) to ensure that they are not of 'an outrageous weight or length'. The tourneying mace and sword are depicted in the various manuscripts of René's treatise, and we can see that the sword has a strongly marked fuller (a hollowed-out groove) running for nearly half the length of the blade. Additional features, not mentioned in the text, are also revealed. The mace is, in fact, a heavy wooden club, octagonal in section; while the sword is shown with a short tri-angular tip and a flat hand guard rather like a rudimentary cup hilt curling upwards from the quillons (fig. 159).[26]

Technically, the illustrations in the *Livre des tournois* constitute the work's most impor-tant feature. 'In order the better to explain it to you', says René, 'here below will be depicted one piece after another as they should be'; and there follow the crest, bascinet and helm; the armour for body and arms, broken up into their main components in a way which antici-pates the pattern books of late sixteenth-century armourers; the tourneying sword and mace;

and the padded protection attached to the saddle bow to cover the horse's breast. These, together with the representations of various stages of the ceremonial and combats, certainly make things 'better understood' and they were first reproduced as engravings by Marc Vulson, Sieur de la Colombière, in *Le Vray Théâtre d'honneur* in 1648 where the arms and armour are incorporated into a decorative border around a scene depicting the lists immediately prior to combat. They have been republished many times since, but familiarity should not obscure the originality of René's achievement. There were, as we have already seen, many earlier treatises describing and illustrating the techniques of personal combat. There were also a number of manuscripts showing primitive artillery and infernal machines. But, as far as we know, the *Livre des tournois* is the first work in which anyone had thought to use visual aids to clarify a written description of chivalric armour and weaponry – or rather it is the first one to survive.

Roughly contemporary with René are two manuscript treatises known to us only in copies of lost texts which, as is clear from internal evidence, had originally been illustrated.[27] One of these, written by a certain Merlin de Cordebeuf, is entitled *L'ordonnance et matière des chevaliers errans* and aspires to reconstruct the equipment of an earlier age of chivalry, 'to amuse the lords, princes, knights and squires of this realm'. The little work may have been devised for some specific court festival in which knights were to play out a story from romance; but, whatever the truth of the matter, the future tense used throughout – 'they shall be made in the most ancient fashion that they can be made' – and its generally hortatory tone suggest that it was intended to provide a model.[28] When, for example, Merlin describes armour for legs and feet, he observes that it should be 'made of mail chausses or *flandresques* cut so as to appear more aged and better to resemble the ancient fashion'.[29] Then, when discussing the helm, he refers to 'the form and manner which is painted here below'. Sadly, in the surviving copy, it is not.

Similarly lacking its illustration is the other treatise, an anonymous description of the equipment used by the French in 1446 both for war ('tant à pied comme à cheval') and for jousts. Judging by the author's introductory comments, his original intention had been a good deal more ambitious for he promises to provide a survey of male and female civilian costume in France along with an account of the dances currently used in festivities. In the event – since he opted for the now absent illustration, painted 'in order to avoid prolixity and the boredom of words' – all that we have is a patchy verbal description of military garb. It begins with a brief general statement of the complete 'harnois blanc' or suit of polished steel worn by men-at-arms in battle ('that is to say close cuirass, vambrace, great gardbrace, leg harness, gauntlets, salade with visor, and a little bevor which only covers the chin'), and continues with comments upon protection for the head, arms and legs. Nothing is said about the chest, lower abdomen, thighs and feet.[30] References to the defensive armour worn by archers and other foot soldiers are cursory; and a discussion of weaponry is unremarkable apart from mention of an unidentified type of sword, the *feuilles de Catheloigne*, and the information that archers are to carry two-handed swords 'as sharp as razors'. Things improve considerably when the author moves on to jousting arms and armour, where he is prepared to enlarge upon construction and methods of fastening so that knights may add or subtract the various pieces as suits their fancy. Again he works down from the head, providing several valuable details *en route*, such as the holes on the right side of the helm to facilitate hearing and furnish additional vision;[31] the method whereby the shield is attached to the cuirass; and the armour for hand and arm. The defence for the right shoulder, he tells us, is constructed of plates to which is attached a *rondelle* (a circular steel disk) which 'rises and falls when one wishes to place the lance in its rest'. In other words, this is the laminated pauldron known in English as a spaudler, together with a mobile besagew designed to protect the armpit.

Having got as far as the arms and hands, the author seems suddenly to have lost interest. Remarking that it is customary to wear leg armour for jousting in the kingdom of France, he then refuses to 'divulge in so public a manner' any further details. Yet he has no such inhibitions when dealing with the jousting lance which, he reveals, should be thirteen feet (or thirteen-and-a-half feet) in length 'between *grappe* and *rochet*'. The *rochet* (also known as the *coronal*) was the rebated lance head fitted with blunt points with 'between each of the three points a space of two-and-a half or three inches at most'; and the *grappe* was a form of *arrêt de la lance*, that is the padded collar behind the hand hold, designed to engage with the rest attached to the breastplate. These *grappes*, the author explains, are 'full of little sharp points like little diamonds, of a fatness like little hazel nuts, which come to a stop within the cross of the rest – made of wood or lead – so that the said points cannot penetrate, whereby the said lance holds the blow in such a way that it must break into pieces'.[32] There follows a short note on the *ronde* or vamplate, the funnel-shaped guard on the staff of the lance, fitted to protect the hand. This was often completely circular but here the author states that it need not go all the way round; and the inside, towards the hand, is to be lined with flock stuffed between two pieces of leather. And, apart from some concluding remarks on the duties of the jouster's attendant, the treatise has nothing more to say.

PIETRO MONTE

This is how things stood at the beginning of the sixteenth century with regard to reference works on arms and armour: a small and inaccessible supply meeting what was, presumably, an equally small demand. Then something strange happened. In 1509 Giovan'Angelo Scinzenzeler published Pietro Monte's *Collectanea* with its account of all kinds of exercise relevant to military activity; and, unlike other masters of arms before and after him, in the course of his disquisitions on combat, Monte felt it necessary to provide readers with systematic information on arms and armour for war, jousts, tourneying and foot combats. This mini-treatise, embedded within the *Collectanea*, is the first printed reference work ever devoted to the subject and was to remain the most comprehensive treatment prior to the publication of Francis Grose's *Treatise of Ancient Armour and Weapons* 280 years later.

The *Collectanea* appeared at a crucial moment in the history of the relationship between personal combat, arms and armour, and the art of war. In another of his books, the *De singulari certamine* – which is devoted to the laws and traditions of single combat[33] – Monte attacks private duels fought between men in civilian dress. 'Such challenges', he continues, 'are laughable' and, as far as he is concerned, the only acceptable duels are properly regulated judicial combats in which the opponents are dressed in appropriate armour. Anything else betrays the law and is against all decent military custom. Yet Monte's outburst itself suggests that the chivalric duel in full armour, fought after long preparation, under strict regulations, and amidst solemn ceremony, was already on its way out.

That is one reason why Monte's interest in the use of armour for personal combat is historically significant. Another is the fact that his work came at a critical period in the history of the art of war. New military organizations were being established and new weaponry deployed, so that the efficiency of body armour was being severely tested by the arquebus. New tactics were being evolved: and the role of the heavy cavalry was being called into question not only by theoreticians such as Machiavelli but also in practice on the battle-fields of Italy. It was wholly fortuitous that, at this moment, Monte should arrive on the scene and feel it necessary to describe contemporary arms and armour.

As in the case of wrestling and fencing, Monte offers a general survey of his procedure in the 'Vocabulorum expositio' which begins the whole work, again explaining that he is obliged to use contemporary words because, for many items, there is simply no Latin term available. He then briefly summarizes the equipment required for single combat both on foot and on horse; but his main discussion of armour comes in Book Two of the *Collectanea*, after the various types of fighting have been described.

All defensive armour, says Monte, should have three qualities (lightness, security and freedom of movement) which are, unfortunately, rarely encountered together. Armour gen-erally weighs too much, hinders movement, and is not even safe because it leaves too many places exposed. On the other hand, he concedes, in his own time much better armour is being made than hitherto – and made, moreover, throughout Europe where new pieces and new modes are being devised every day. He therefore works his way through the panoply, naming and describing *en route* more than seventy terms relating to armour: separate pieces, materials used in manufacture and lining, and the buckles, latchets and straps which connect the parts together.

He treats of the arming doublet, its ideal dimensions and the nature of its manufacture: explaining that it should be lined with silk and should cover the groins completely, protect the back and be 'well hollowed out above the buttock-bones' – though in such a way that it does not impede movement. He has a chapter on different sorts of military footwear in mail, and how they are to be laced; and another on the use of mail to protect the arms and especially the armpits – where the sleeves must be very strong, spacious and covered with soft leather so that movement is easy and the arms can be stretched without effort. Gloves (*chirotheca*) should be made with palms of leather or cloth but the left hand should have a mail border on the inside of the palm to facilitate grasping an opponent's weapon. These gloves should be flexible so that the warrior can throw a spear comfortably and, more impor-tant, so that he can retain a firm grip on his sword for a long time. It is for this reason that Monte does not approve of closed gauntlets (*manuthecae clausae*) which quickly tire the hand. This is an interesting practical point because, superficially, it might seem that having the hand locked over the sword grip would make it easier to retain hold: but Monte had probably experienced the numbness and cramp which inevitably afflicts any limb which cannot move about freely and be flexed from time to time.

He is meticulous on leg armour – with chapters on the *schinella* (the greave for the lower leg) and *coxottus* (all the parts that constitute the cuisse for the upper leg, including pro-tection for the knee) – explaining that the front of these pieces should be made stronger than the back since they are the parts which normally receive an adversary's blows; and, as usual, stressing the need to retain as much flexibility of movement as possible.[34]

He has two chapters on the composition of the *thorax* or breastplate, in which he differentiates between those designed for mounted lance combat and those for use on foot, especially for axe fighting. Again he argues that the front of the piece should be made stronger than the back, 'for, beyond the first encounter of the lance, no other point can do as much damage, with the exception of the crossbow or other type of guns (*bombardorum*)'; and notes that it is customary to wear a *supra pectus*, that is a placate or over-breastplate.

On the other hand, in keeping with his general wish to combine flexibility with effective defence, he favours a light backplate because it is possible to avoid the first blow from a lance quite easily as long as we hold our horse in such a way that we can gain the enemy's back as he passes. He does not consider what would happen to you were the enemy to gain your back instead: but it was an assumption common to most masters of arms that their textbooks were unavailable to your opponents. In view of this manoeuvre, Monte even considers that one might leave off the placate altogether, although he does recommend the carrying of a small metal shield 'light in use but sufficiently large in circumference' to protect the left side.

Several chapters are devoted to various types of head armour, and here Monte's vocabulary is not as clearly defined as one would wish. He has a lengthy discussion 'De casside vel galea' which, he says, is commonly called *almettus*. Like other parts of the body defences, the helmet is to be less thick at the back, and, says Monte, it is to be raised up in a kind of bump above the ears and must have openings so that we can hear properly: 'because if we cannot hear, and the ears are compressed, and all the senses are engrossed, then a man has little understanding of what is being done, and very quickly weakens'. There is a separate examination of the structure of the visor which is designed to facilitate both breathing and vision while still affording adequate protection; and a description of what Monte calls the inner *cassis secreta* or *subtilissima* which protects the head from the force of a blow on the outer metal helmet. A very long chapter is devoted to the *baveria*, and another *de baveria sive barbutio* designed for use with lighter armour – and here Monte's identification of the bevor with the barbute is noteworthy since the terms were regarded as synonymous only in Hispanic sources.[35]

Turning to protection for the arms, Monte points out that special attention must be paid to the upper arm and armpit because the former is struck frequently in combat, while the latter is a favourite target for the thrust both with staff weapons and sword. In his chapter on shoulder armour (*De spaldatiis sive scapulatiis*), Monte is critical of the most common form which covers the entire shoulder with large, heavy overlapping plates. These are cumbersome, imposing 'weight without utility', and are inferior to the shoulder defences made of small plates, which are used by the Germans. Monte also describes the besagew (using the Spanish term *luneta*) which is a small mobile plate attached to the upper arm with leather straps. It protects the armpit and 'is not an impediment to the arm, nor in running or wielding the lance'. There is a chapter on the gauntlet (*manupla ferrea*), and another describing the manuple designed specifically for the left hand, reinforced in the palm like the left glove. The various latchets or ties whereby one piece of armour is joined to another are given attention before Monte describes the *fimbria* of the lorica. This, he says, is what, in the vulgar idiom, 'we call the fald', and it covers the buttocks.

If we bear in mind that, in addition to the material gathered together in this section of the *Collectanea*, there are also chapters elsewhere dealing with armour worn in the lists and, in particular, the jousting breastplate and helm; others dealing with the different kinds of saddle suitable for light cavalry, heavy cavalry, and jousting; and still more chapters explaining the handling of different swords, daggers, and staff weapons – then we will begin to grasp the magnitude of Monte's achievement. He had even pondered the practicalities of armour manufacture and the tempering process. As he explains, if you want to combine lightness with security, then you must obtain the best possible iron and steel which was originally to be found in Innsbruck in Germany, where the masters tested their products with bolts from the crossbow. It was commonly believed that this high quality was due to some virtue in the local water: but Monte reckons that any cold water would have done, and that the superlative results were achieved solely by skill in the tempering process. Indeed, the Germans made such excellent steel that they even considered making their breastplates resistant to the arquebus – a 'type of small cannon', as he puts it – and this reference to proofing armour against firearms is, as far as I know, the earliest by roughly half a century.[36] Moreover, the fact that Monte describes the process as having taken place well in the past suggests that the technique may have been practised long before the end of the fifteenth century. The Innsbruck masters, he also remarks, were the first to discover the secret of hammering armour when it had already cooled off: although Italy, he believes, is now producing armour virtually as good as the German. He continues:

> During the time in which I was composing this work, Duke Sigismund of Austria, Galeazzo da Sanseverino and Claude de Vauldray of the Burgundian nation, were busy seeking after different types of armour. Before then almost all men of arms were armed in one and the same manner, especially with regard to defensive armour (*de armis indutivis*).[37] These three illustrious men invented many new armours appertaining as much to foot soldiers as to cavalry, and not so much diverse as very useful.

This passage tells us something about the composition of the *Collectanea*, because Sigismund died in 1496. If, therefore, Monte had been writing the book in his day, it had been lying around for many years before the author decided to publish it. More generally significant are the references to the three innovators none of whom has, to my knowledge, been recognized as such by historians, though surviving armours made for Sigismund and Claude de Vauldray are very well known. Furthermore, Monte insists that Sigismund must rank as the foremost of all innovators, with Galeazzo da Sanseverino in second place: and this raises at least the possibility that much of what we now think of as Maximiliana might well have been Sigismundiana.[38]

Every page of Monte's work teems with the practical detail which can only be garnered by experience. He is constantly giving useful tips to his reader. It is, for example, a good idea for those who have need to walk abroad at night while fully armed to cover the armour of the upper body with hide in order not to be visible. In general, light armour is better than heavy armour because it is more pliant, and enables the wearer to dodge blows. In heavy armour, speedy movement is difficult because 'if we bend the body, the armour's weight is over that part so that we may easily fall or receive some hurt'. In the tourney (that is mounted fencing) it is a good idea to fight with the visor raised. This helps breathing and vision and is rarely dangerous – though it is better not to try it when jousting! Make sure, when being measured for your cuirass and arming doublet, to allow plenty of room because, when the cuirass is too tight 'every blow affords great discomfort, just as when we wear new and tight shoes on the feet, if we should stumble, we feel great pain. And if the shoe is wide it better protects the foot. But in jousting it is necessary that the doublet should be fortified to such an extent that it fills the cuirass everywhere, for the flexibility of the doublet sustains the greater part of the impact.' Similarly, if, when wearing your jousting helm, you tend to be dazed by the percussion of a blow, then why not bind your forehead with bandages soaked in the white of egg and vinegar so that the head cannot come into direct contact with any part of the helm? Or perhaps you might consider putting some wax in the front of the helm so that your head remains untroubled by the noise or clangour of the blow – *fremitus seu clangor*.

In addition to his comments on defensive armour, Monte has much to say about offensive arms: though here he is far less systematic. In his opening discussion of technical vocabulary he describes the polaxe, partisan and bill but, rather than having a separate section on weapons, he treats them when describing their practical use. Thus he gives another generic account of the polaxe at the beginning of his first long chapter on the technique of axe fighting, but repeats suggestions concerning its length in a later chapter particularly relevant to the way it is to be handled. Similarly, he writes about the various kinds of staff weapon for foot combat – the medium-sized *ginetta*, the *lancea longa* and the *spetum* – when discussing the appropriate techniques for wielding them, and has some chapters on sword construction in the middle of observations on fencing.[39]

The *Collectanea* is packed with information, so that anyone wishing to find out what some odd word meant (or discover what covered which bit of the anatomy, or learn how one part fitted onto another) could at last go to one reference book and look it all up – or at least they could if they were fortunate enough to own a copy. Yet it was never reprinted or issued in a vernacular version. A Spanish translation and paraphrase of selected chapters, including most of those concerning armour, still survives in manuscript: but, that apart, there is nothing to suggest that anybody realized what Monte had accomplished.[40] This is a strange state of affairs because the *Collectanea* is not merely remarkable. It is unique.

ARMS AND ARMOUR STUDIES AFTER MONTE

After Monte's pioneering work, no equally comprehensive treatment of arms and armour was published until the late eighteenth century, although Louis de Gaya's little *Traité des armes* of 1678 is noteworthy as a concise, illustrated handbook of weapons which was plagiarized by Manesson Mallet and Gabriel Daniel.[41] In only one respect can it be said that Monte was surpassed during the Renaissance – in a massively elaborate manuscript compilation by the Augsburg painter, Jeremias Schemel.[42] A monument of synthesized learning, Schemel's work was completed some time after 21 February 1568 (the date of the last event mentioned in the text)[43] and deals with the training of horses, their saddlery, furniture and armour; with veterinary medicine; with judicial and chivalric duels; and with the history of tournaments in Germany. The combat material is not original but is adapted from earlier *Fechtbuch* traditions. The tournament history is similarly based on earlier work, notably the various manifestations of Georg Rüxner and *his* antecedents; and, with regard to Schemel's observations on horses and horsemanship, his constant use of Italianisms suggests that he has been influenced by the works of Italian riding masters available to him in print.[44] However, it is in other respects that Schemel offers something special. His text is profusely illustrated throughout, but never more strikingly than in the section devoted to the arms and armour designed specifically for each kind of combat both in the lists and on the field of battle. As has often been remarked about German tournaments of the late fifteenth century and onwards, there was a proliferation of modes of contest which were often differentiated only by variations in the armour used. And it is in his elucidation of these that Schemel excels with some of the most extraordinary surviving illustrations of armour construction. Each type of course is explained in detailed pictures where we first see the armour in an exploded diagram showing everything dismantled for display, even down to the bolts used to hold different parts together. Then, on the facing page, Schemel shows the knight wearing the whole suit reconstructed; and here, at least, even Monte cannot compete (plates XXII–XXIII).

There is nothing else in the sixteenth century to compare with the achievements of Monte and Schemel, but there are two valuable Spanish treatments of defensive armour. The earlier of these is a chapter entitled, 'How a Harness should be made', included in a short treatise on chivalric combat published in 1548 by Juan Quixada de Reayo.[45] Apart from a few comments on individual fighting in battle, Quixada was primarily concerned with mounted lance play in the lists and his comments on armour are brief but pertinent.[46] To achieve perfection, he says, the first thing is that the metal from which it is fashioned must be composed of two parts of iron and one of steel – an enigmatic statement which must refer to the mixing of the billet prior to forging the sheet of metal.[47] The greaves should be long in their lower part, 'for they will look better thus'; the upper part should be of some 'suitable' but unspecified length; and they should be thick because they will inevitably get muddy and need a good deal of cleaning. They are not to be open at the bottom, but should have a little hole through which the rowell of the spur (*el rodete del espuela*) may pass. Quixada adds that, in war, half greaves with mail shoes are used, and 'cuisses and half cuisses'. The pair of plates (which form the cuirass) should be made of several pieces, light and well fitted to the body; the fauld similarly well fitting and not loose; the tassets (*escarçelas*), made of three or four pieces for flexibility, should be lined with cloth; and the *arrêt de cuirasse* must be curved upwards and short rather than long. The rerebraces have to be made with turning joints (*los braçales han de ser de torno*); the elbow guard or cowter (*guarda*) such as to cover the arm well; and the shoulder pieces or pauldrons (*guardabraços*) of good make – the right 'with its bars' (*el derecho con sus barras*), and the left somewhat thicker. The armet has to fit the head properly; have enough room for a full lining; and is to be reinforced at the back with a rondel (*con su barascudo detrás*). When wearing it, the knight must still be able to eat and drink. The cheek pieces opposite the ears should be pierced with five little holes forming a cross and, at this point, the lining should be cut away on the inside in a round hole matching the ear 'to enable you to hear clearly what is said to you'. The visor should be wide below in order to cover the cheek pieces of the armet and there should also be a half-bevor with its aventail of mail (*alpartaz de malla*). The gauntlets should be somewhat wide, yet well fitting, and lined with leather. The pair of plates 'must have their skirts of mail, and in war it is necessary to wear mail gussets because they are advantageous'. Curiously, Quixada, who has not thus far mentioned horse armour, suddenly ends this sentence with a complete non sequitur – 'and a shaffron' (*y testera*) – before turning his attention to reinforcing pieces for jousting armour.

These 'double pieces' should be thick (*gruessas*), and they are eight in number: the placate (*bolante*); tasset (*escarçelón*); waist piece (*guardabarriga* – literally belly-guard); the grand guard (*la gran pieça*) or reinforcing piece for the left shoulder, which must be so made that it offers nothing upon which the opposing lance may bite; the reinforcing bevor (*el baverón*); the visor (*la vista*) which again must not present any hold for the lance; the great elbow guard (*la sobreguarda*) which must be large in order to cover the arm well; and finally the over gauntlet for the left hand (*sobremanopla*).

With regard to fixing the grand guard, Quixada is very circumstantial. It must be secured by a bolt (*clavo*) with a round head below the arm piece (*el guarda braço*), and that bolt must be 'well rebated so that the lance cannot gain a purchase on it'. It is also necessary that it should be attached with two leather straps, one of which has a buckle. The elbow guard, too, must be fixed by a bolt with rebated head to limit the effect of a lance blow. Yet, despite all this detail, Quixada remains unimpressed by such examples of the armourers' art.

> These reinforced (*encampronados*)[48] suits are very handsome but I have seen not a single good thing for those who have jousted in them: for in my time I have seen many deaths occur through striking the sight of the helm. First the son of the Count of Oñate in the house of the Queen; Don Luis Osorio at Tafalla in Navarre; and at Saragossa, Don Gaspar, son of the Count of Sastago, and Geronimo D'Ansa. All these I have seen killed by the encounter, and more than I write down. I never jousted *encampronado* because I always found myself comfortable with the Castillian mode. Each one can joust as seems best to him.[49]

About forty years after Quixada's publication, Luis Zapata (epic poet and self-styled jousting expert) set down his own views on the armour necessary for that exercise, dealing more with matters of style than with technicalities. In the first place, he prefers armour to be new because, just 'like a cape or smock', it can become old-fashioned; and he likes it to be gilded. It is also important that armour should be 'just right' (that is tailor-made) for the rider, with the parts fitting together properly at all the joints, and lined with thin leather to stop them clanging together, 'since it is most unseemly for a jouster to move about in armour, rattling like kettles' (*como calderas sonando*). The shape of the *çelada* (close helmet) poses problems for the fashion-conscious Zapata: too pointed, and the knight looks like a cockerel; too rounded, and he resembles an owl; but, whatever its shape, it should be 'quilted on the inside so that blows do not resound'. Zapata goes on to describe what he calls the *cabeça* which must mean the *cofia* or *escofia* (a jousting reinforce worn over the helmet to provide extra protection to the skull and the back of the head). This *cabeça* has itself to be lined with taffeta or silk; secured towards the front with two straps; and screwed or tightened near the neck guard so that, during the violent movements of an encounter, the helmet does not fall over the jouster's face.[50] The visor must be secure, small and close to the eyes to provide good vision and, Zapata prays, 'May God guard you from the danger of a splinter entering your visor, for one that is a mere inch or two would be enough to kill a rider'. The breastplate should 'bulge out in good proportion', boosting the jouster's confidence. The *targeta* or small round shield should be of a good shape 'which makes men smart'. Rerebraces should not be wide. The cuirass should fit well at the pelvis, to avoid fatal blows in the side; and sabatons ought to be neither sharply pointed nor wide 'like German shoes', but rounded like a boot. Zapata particularly warns against jousting without leg harness not merely because the knight would then look 'rather like a hunter than a jouster', but because without such protection he could be injured by banging into the tilt or counter lists. He also mentions the need for a cuisse on the right thigh to accommodate the lance – an indication that the weapon may be carried into the lists with the butt supported on the thigh rather than sitting in its leather pouch.[51] But, for Zapata, the most important part of armour with regard to jousting is the rest affixed to the right side of the breastplate. It should be sited neither too far towards the front nor towards the back of the breastplate. If too low down, then 'a thousand flourishes with the lance may be made and they will all be ugly'. If too high, then it is simply impossible to couch the lance properly: but he does think that it is better, on the whole, that it should be slightly higher than lower (*un poco alto el ristre que bajo*).[52]

Joust and tourney excepted, the relevance of armour to any close personal combat was considered sufficiently slight by renaissance masters of arms to justify their passing it over in silence. Moreover, despite the fact that soldiers (and especially cavalry) still wore defensive armour on the battlefield, the majority of military writers tended towards brevity when dealing with the topic.[53] Concision is not necessarily to be equated with ignorance, but the fact remains that, with regard to armour, many renaissance texts are more notable for their shortcomings than for their virtues. Even Niccoló Machiavelli – the most frequently copied of all renaissance military theorists – when comparing Roman military equipment with its modern counterpart, was less technically secure than Polybius, his classical source and was, in any case, only interested in foot soldiers.[54] He saw little merit in cavalry beyond the usefulness of light horse in skirmishing, scouting, and the pursuit of fleeing enemies. In heavy cavalry he saw no merit at all.

It was unlikely that any author without a strong belief in the continuing value of mounted troops would bother to write seriously about modern armour. This was certainly the case with Raymond de Beccarie de Pavie Sieur de Fourquevaux who expressed some enthusiasm for heavy cavalry in his French adaptation of Machiavelli's *Arte della guerra*. De Fourquevaux follows his Italian source in describing the Roman infantry but adds a substantial chapter on the *gendarmerie* whose equipment remains essentially chivalric: sabatons, greaves, cuirasse and tassets, gorget, armet and bevor, gauntlets, vambrace, gussets and pauldrons.[55] The reason, says De Fourquevaux, he is setting all this down is because the *gendarmerie* of his own day are no more adequately armed than light cavalry: and this, in his opinion, is a grave error for, whereas the purpose of light horse is swift movement, the *gendarmerie* are 'ordained to stand firm, not to run here and there'. They should accordingly be weighed down with a heavy harness and, to support all this, they must have strong, great horses fully barded. Their offensive weapons should be an arming sword, an *estoc* on one side of the saddle bow, a mace on the other, and a lance which should be 'fat and very long'. Light cavalry, on the other hand, wear less armour (though not all that much less), dispense with the *estoc* and carry a lighter lance. This is more informative than Machiavelli, but not markedly so; and it is, perhaps, significant that – whereas De Fourquevaux and Machiavelli were the best-known renaissance writers on the art of war – the only sixteenth-century military treatise which did include a comprehensive discussion of arms and armour is, by comparison, very obscure. Cesare d'Evoli's *Delle ordinanze et battaglie* was first published in 1583; was reprinted three years later in an augmented edition; but has rarely been cited since.[56]

D'Evoli's interest in military equipment was both practical and analytic. The purpose of the soldier, he writes, 'is not merely to fight, but to fight well and in good order'; and, since perfection in battle requires that troops should be well armed, his first chapter is devoted to their equipment. It opens in a business-like if somewhat chaotic fashion:

> The arms used in war, and commonly praised by all the most understanding men for use in battles are pikes, corslets, thrusting swords (*stocchi*), swords, daggers, muskets, arqebuses, pistols, morions, lances, iron maces and hammers. Arms used by many nations for battles, but not commonly praised by all, are breastplates (*piastre*), mail shirts, staff weapons, lancegays (*zagaglie*), targets, two-hand swords, scimitars, throwing-spears (*dardi*), arbalests, bows, slings, and round shields (*rotelle*).

This list is noteworthy for its concentration upon offensive weapons rather than on defensive armour, and it soon becomes apparent that this is no accident or oversight. D'Evoli has little confidence in the effectiveness of body defences in the face of modern projectile arms or even against staff weapons. He considers each item in turn, and his comments are emphatically not those of an armchair soldier. Pikes, he says, should be at least fifteen feet in length, but the longer the better; and if any troops are to wear corslets in these days when firearms are more common than lances, then it would be as well for them to be *di tempra molle* – which I take to mean tempered in such a way as to avoid excessive brittleness. But even then d'Evoli regards them as unsatisfactory and points out that their excessive weight disables soldiers who should not be overloaded with iron. *Stocchi* are designed to wound more with point than edge and should, therefore, neither bend easily nor have fullers in the middle. Similarly, infantry swords should be 'rather short than long' in order to facilitate close combat, and they should be such as to wound with both point and edge. The swords of the light cavalry and men at arms should be even shorter, 'so that they neither hinder handling, mounting and dismounting'; and daggers, besides a strong and sharp point, should have a keen edge so that in close combat an opponent cannot seize it with his hand. D'Evoli spends little time on individual pieces of armour, but one of the few items he does single out for discussion is the morion worn by arquebusiers. This head piece should be of *tempra molle*, again because it is more often a defence against the arquebus than against the pike, and is used generally in siege and trench warfare where the head is the only part of the body likely to be frequently exposed.

Lances are more to d'Evoli's taste and he comments upon the weakness of the hollow type (*vote dentro*) favoured by the Hungarians who make them in this fashion in order to reduce their weight. However, since this causes them to break easily at every encounter, they are not to be recommended. In fact, d'Evoli observes, if any good has ever been seen in such lances, it has come about not from their perfection but rather through the imperfection of opposing armour and especially of wooden shields. He also discusses the habit of tying the butt of the lance to the saddle bow with a leather strap – a trick which he criticizes as harmful because every movement of the horse's shoulders is thereby transmitted to the lance which, as a result, cannot be held firmly and must strike uncertainly. He concedes that these lances are of great length and that this would, in itself, be a good thing were it not for the other disadvantages; and he argues that it is difficult to achieve mastery using this system because it is the horse, not the man, who carries the lance. On the other hand, he praises Italian lances because they can be controlled and placed easily in the rest; have greater penetration; can be carried with firmness; and are more certain in striking home. Moreover, because they are solid and not hollow, they do not shatter so easily.

Iron maces and hammers do not greatly concern d'Evoli who merely notes that there is no fixed weight to be assigned to them and that 'they must be more or less heavy according to how much the greater or lesser is the strength of the man who wields them'. Defensive armour in general is summarily dismissed – whether plate or mail. Indeed d'Evoli insists that both are imperfect because they fail to resist the very weapons most commonly used to attack them, arquebuses, pistols, pikes, lances, hammers, lancegays, staff weapons in general, bows and arbalests. He does, however, allow that 'the arquebusiers should not give up their mail arm defences because, coming to close combat, these help a good deal against sword blows', and mail is similarly useful to the cavalry since it covers parts which would otherwise remain unprotected.

Weighing the relative merits of various staff weapons as compared with the pike, d'Evoli notes that weapons such as *spiedi*, axes, *ronchi* and halberds have been widely praised in some quarters on the grounds that, in close combat, they can cut the stave of the pike; while it has also been asserted that the fork or cross piece of these weapons can be used to push the pike up and down. 'With all due respect,' says d'Evoli, employing the time-honoured formula which indicates a total lack of that commodity, 'I do not know with what reason that can be affirmed'. These staff weapons are themselves no slight encumbrance at close quarters while, as for cutting the pike staff, that is plainly ridiculous. If they are kept at a distance by the length of the pike then, 'I do not know with what dexterity or art the soldier can cut it'. On the other hand, if they get closer they would lose time by having to wait to cut the staff rather than set about wounding the enemy; and, in any case, once soldiers get to close quarters they must resort to sword and dagger. Nor does d'Evoli give any credence to the idea that it is possible to push the pike up and down with the cross piece of these staff weapons: 'As good fencers well know, this action is so difficult to execute that it is rarely achieved in an action of pike against staff weapon. And if the professors of the art cannot always succeed, so much less should one credit that it can be done by infantrymen recruited by the sound of the drum and as ignorant as can be of the art of fencing.'

D'Evoli next moves on to evaluate the lancegay which was a light spear, sometimes with a sharpened steel tip at each end. In his view this is essentially a missile weapon used by the Moors who certainly handle it dexterously enough. Yet he cannot recommend it as a field weapon because it requires so much room for manoeuvre that it is unsuitable for closely knit battle formations where the space within which each soldier can move is severely restricted.[57] The evolution of military tactics in the sixteenth century required men to stand together rather than to act as dispersed individuals, and clearly this was something which d'Evoli fully understood.

Other common items of defence and offence are similarly subjected to critical scrutiny and generally fail the test. For example, although d'Evoli believes that the small round shield known as the *rotella* is a useful defence for infantry against pike, he is unimpressed by the cavalry's *targa* or wooden shield. The latter has to be secured to the man using it with a leather strap and buckles so entangling him that he is no longer free to move about quickly. Moreover, because the *targa* is made of wood, the metal tip of a lance strikes it full on rather than slipping off safely to one side or another. Worse still, it defends only one side of the body, leaving the rest unprotected, and 'if by any mischance the horse should fall, the man would find himself so tangled up that he would scarcely be able to rise again'. For these reasons, d'Evoli jeers, if it is at all possible to provide other kinds of defence, then it is much better to leave the employment of these shields to the enemy than to arm one's own battalions with them.

Even two-hand swords earn d'Evoli's disapproval. He considers them to be less effective than is generally assumed because, if kept at a distance, they cannot stand effectively against pikes, while in the press of close combat they are simply too unwieldy. For the scimitar, 'commonly used by some nations', he has nothing but contempt. Its quillons are unpro-tected (*hanno le guardie scoverte*). It handles badly, and it is no good for thrusting. Throwing spears, arbalests and bows all come in for equally hostile criticism since to use any of these antiquated weapons in the age of the arquebus would be sheer folly although, unexpectedly, d'Evoli sees some virtue in the sling because it can cause considerable damage when used to hurl artificial fire amongst enemy formations.

There follows what was almost obligatory in treatises on the art of war – an assessment of the most suitable arms for different kinds of troops. D'Evoli would equip infantry with corslets – that is a half armour for the upper half of the body – pikes, swords, daggers, muskets, arquebuses, morions and mail sleeves. Men at arms and light cavalry would have their 'accustomed armour with their lances, thrusting swords, iron maces, hammers, and such like'; and the arquebusiers would have 'long arquebuses to shoot at a distance', morions, swords, daggers and mail sleeves. Of greater (though wholly negative) importance to d'Evoli are the armour and weaponry of the 'Ferraruoli' or light-armed mounted pistoleers whose equipment he uses as an object lesson in ineptitude. Their close helmet (*celata*) or morion, cuisses and pistols are fine enough, but the rest of their arms and apparel are so poor that, 'if anyone should wish to represent the opposite of a well-armed man, he ought to be armed *alla ferrarola*'. In the first place, the swords that all these troops carry have poorly designed quillons and grips; they do not fit comfortably in the hand; and their blades are so narrow that they are 'more suitable for beating wool than for cutting through armour'. Their daggers are badly made and lack penetrative power. Their defensive armour, too, is inadequate. D'Evoli cannot understand why they prefer mail sleeves to plate defences for the arm; considers that their pauldrons are so ill fitting that they hinder the delivery of blows with the sword; and notes that their mail faulds and leg armour not only hinder running but make even walking difficult. And so the sorry inventory continues. Their saddles are as ill-fashioned and as uncomfortable as the rest of their equipment while their stirrups 'are so badly formed that, besides tiring the feet more than any other type, through being insufficiently wide and flat underneath, they furthermore leave the feet completely exposed and unprotected'.

Then, after his scathing survey of armour, and as if to deliver the *coup de grace*, d'Evoli concludes with a few comments on military adornment. He feels that this is apropos because the 'wisest men' have affirmed that plumes, colours, gold decoration and other apparent vanities count for a great deal since they dismay the majority of soldiers who are unaccustomed to such things and lack fortitude. He compares this to 'obnoxious metamorphoses' more befitting 'abominable pigs than valiant men'.[58] Those who paint the face, neck, ears and hands with filthy materials in order to demonstrate their ferocity, end up being 'despised and scorned instead of being feared'.

It is not easy to evaluate this jaundiced view of defensive armour but, in these closing years of the sixteenth century, other practical military men were similarly critical. Sir Roger Williams, whose trenchant views were based upon wide experience gained in the Low Countries, provides an acute assessment of contemporary practice in his *Briefe Discourse of Warre* (1590). Like d'Evoli, he discusses the arming, both defensive and offensive, of various types of soldiery and is especially sceptical about the value of heavy lancers. It is useless, he argues, for their horses to be covered with armour because 'all squadrons of Pikes be lined with Musketiers or Calivers; the lesser of both pearceth any arming that horses use to carry'. Moreover, even if the horseman's breast plate, head piece, two lames of his pauldrons and two or three of his tassets are 'light pistol proof', and all the rest, 'I meane his tases, cuisses, pouldrons, vambraces and gauntlets, bee also so light as you can devise', it will still prove an unserviceably heavy load.[59] Another English military man, Humfrey Barwick, was even more succinct. Barwick was a keen advocate of firearms and believed that the arquebus, musket and pistol had changed warfare to such an extent that 'now by reason of the force of weapons, neither horse nor man is able to beare armours sufficient to defend their bodies from death'.[60]

160. Cavalryman's equipment as displayed by Melzo. 1611, plate 2.

Of the next generation of military writers, only those specifically concerned with cavalry warfare – such as Melzo, della Croce, Basta and Wallhausen – devoted much attention to defensive armour and, if less overtly critical than d'Evoli, they confined their remarks to the essential equipment of the various types of mounted troops, often illustrated by diagrams to facilitate a reader's comprehension (figs 160–1). John Cruso, the best-known English follower of these continental masters, is a perfect example of an approach which had, by 1632, become stereotyped.[61] 'As the ends and employment of the Cavallrie', says Cruso, 'are divers and severall, so there is a diversitie necessarily required in their persons, arms, and horses'; whereupon he describes in succession the arming of a lancer, cuirassier, arquebusier and dragoon. Lancers are no longer the old-fashioned men at arms, completely encased in metal from head to toe, as recommended by De Fourquevaux: but they remain, in theory, the principal shock weapon on the battlefield. In practice, however, Cruso believes that they require too much training and that the cost of their horses is excessive. Their arming was 'first invented to pierce and divide a grosse body, and therefore requires force and velocitie for the shock'; and the lancer's armour, as listed and illustrated in Cruso, is similar to that of his chivalric antecedents except that it stops at the knee and has to be both pistol proof and 'calliver proof (by addition of the placcate)'. None the less, Cruso makes it clear that, by his time, the lancer had largely been superseded by the pistol-carrying cuirassier, a kind of mounted warrior recently invented 'onely by discharging the lancier of his lance'.

While military men related arms and armour to the cavalry warfare of their own time,

222

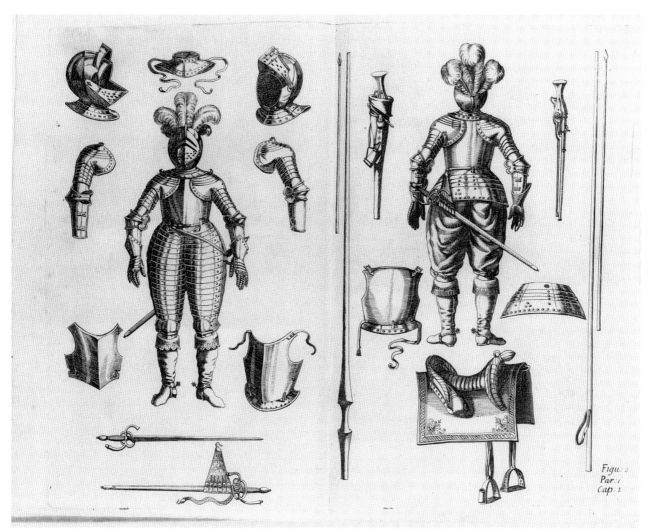

161. Cavalryman's equipment according to Wallhausen. 1634, plate 2.

other minds were approaching the same problem from a very different direction. Wholly erudite and historical, this approach had been initiated by the fifteenth-century antiquary Flavio Biondo whose concern to reconstruct Roman institutions (military as well as civil) in order that they might serve as a model for contemporary society was given greater political impetus and urgency by Machiavelli. The handsome folio volume devoted by Guil- laume du Choul (1557) to Roman military discipline, with its illustrations of soldiers, assorted helmets, encampments and sieges, made the Roman army more immediately acces- sible and intelligible to its renaissance admirers; and, at the end of the sixteenth century, Justus Lipsius, in his *De militia Romana* provided an especially elaborate description, heavily illustrated and stiff with annotation.[62] Throughout the Renaissance and well into the sev- enteenth century it was commonly, though not invariably, assumed that an understanding of ancient military practice was relevant to modern warfare; and this conviction was shared not only by fifteenth-century humanists and later armchair soldiers but also by outstanding generals such as Prince Maurice of Nassau and Gustavus Adolphus. The researches of classical scholars were, therefore, widely regarded as a serious contribution to the art of war.

By contrast, medieval military institutions aroused little enthusiasm, and the earliest writers on chivalry were concerned almost entirely with the origins of heralds and heraldry and with the chivalric orders which still exerted some political and social influence. The deeds of Arthurian and other romantic heroes continued, it is true, to thrill a large lay audience, and the activities of real knights were regularly retailed by chroniclers and historians; but, whatever inspiration may have been derived from them, nobody believed that they had any direct bearing upon the techniques of current military practice.[63] It was not until the very end of the sixteenth century that anyone attempted to examine chivalric warfare and the arms and armour employed therein; and the idiosyncracies of that examination are revealing. In 1600 the historian Claude Fauchet published his *Origines des chevaliers, armoiries, et heraux* which included a substantial section on French military ordinances and equipment.[64] It was said of Fauchet that his tediously bad style induced in the young Louis XIII a life-long distaste for reading; and certainly a perusal of the *Origines* does not have the effect of rendering this tale improbable. However, Fauchet's importance lies in the fact that he was the first scholar to treat chivalric warfare as a discrete historical subject. Citing a wide range of sources from ancient historians, through medieval literary figures such as Chrestien de Troyes and Jean de Meung, to chroniclers such as Villani, Monstrelet and Froissart, he surveys the evolution of armour and weaponry from the time of Belisarius's Italian wars, as reported by Procopius in the sixth century, to the reign of Louis XI in the late fifteenth century. He assigns the change from mail to plate armour to about the year 1330, while noting that the ancient Persians had used plate in the time of Ammianus Marcellinus; treats the equipment of infantry and cavalry separately, naming (though not describing) the principal pieces of armour; gives some detail concerning ancient and medieval siege engines; has something to say about the early development of fire power; and notes a variety of staff weapons. Yet, despite his impressive array of information, he is never technical and practical in the manner of the fifteenth-century English and French treatises, or of Monte and Quixada, or even Zapata. Instead his approach is doggedly etymological, as though he feels that the essence of each weapon and each piece of armour can be conveyed only by establishing a credible origin for its name. This preoccupation with etymology was long to remain a hallmark of academic arms and armour studies – especially since some of the most diligent early research in this field was carried out by lexicographers such as Du Cange and d'Aquino.[65]

With late sixteenth-century etymology, research into medieval narrative sources, and the early historiography of chivalry, it may seem that we are wandering somewhat from the martial arts of renaissance Europe. It would be as well, therefore, to note two things. The first is that, in the very year that Fauchet was setting chivalric warfare within an historical perspective and establishing it as matter for academic research, Alessandro Massario was publishing his *Compendio dell'heroica arte di cavalleria* in which he explained the nature of horses and horsemanship, the proper method for fighting duels on horseback, and the techniques of jousting and mounted fencing. He also included a short section on the arms and armour required for such activities but was more concerned with the fighting itself which he treated in the wholly practical manner of Giorgio Basta and other contemporary cavalry experts. The second point to note is that Massario's observations on these topics were sufficiently succinct and informative to attract the anonymous compiler of a handbook entitled the *Avertimenti cavalereschi* which claimed to be 'of the greatest utility to those who would follow the courts of great personages, and of great profit to all those who wish to go to war'. The precepts, attributed to an 'unknown author' were, in fact, copied verbatim from Massario's recommendations for the duel on horseback – not only describing combat techniques but also listing all the traditional weapons (thrusting sword, dagger, lance, axe, mace, hammer and lancegay, augmented with a pistol) together with an almost complete chivalric panoply.[66] The fact that it is a straight, unadorned copy of Massario is interesting enough. The fact that somebody still considered it worthwhile to perpetrate this plagiarism in 1651, half a century after Massario's work (which might itself have been considered old-fashioned when first published), reminds us that, whatever changes were taking place in military theory, hand-to-hand fighting scarcely altered. And it is to mounted combat that I now turn.

ala cause de sa terre de beauuoisis · lequel s'il ne vouloit pris faire · mais la que
stion fut mise par culx deux ensemble · en la voullente et ordonnance du duc de berry
Apres lesquelles besongnes conclues ledit duc de bour son sen retourna en france
et donna conge atous ses gens d'armes · Et depuis par certain moyen que ledit
bury eut auec led̄ Duc Il fut deliure · Alaquelle assemblee et pour y aller sil'en
conte de saint paol mist sus tresgrosse armee · mais en passant parmy paris luy en
fut ordonne de par le roy qui l'allast plus auant · mais sen retourna es frontiés
de toulomoye ou il estoit especiallement comme de par le roy

Comment deux champs de bataille furent promeus lors a faire a paris pur
le roy · de lareuesque de reme qui fut mort · et du concille de pise · Chapp̄ lii

162. A tilt with counterlists. Bibliothèque Nationale, Paris, MS. Fr. 20,360. fol. 138.

VIII

Mounted combat (1): jousting with the heavy lance

THE CHIVALRIC EXERCISE which, above all others, continues to appeal to popular imagination is jousting – when knights, either singly, in pairs or in groups, rode at each other in a lance charge. The heavy cavalry charge of this sort was for several centuries regarded as the principal shock attack of a battle and, although its efficacy has with good reason been challenged by a number of modern historians, it clearly impressed many observers throughout its long history and was taken seriously by at least some military theorists until well into the seventeenth century. After the initial lance charge knights would resort to close fighting on horseback or would dismount and fight on foot and, as was to be the case with combats which mimicked real hand-to-hand fighting, so the hazards of mounted lance play – when undertaken for practice, recreation or spectacle – were increasingly hedged about with safety regulations. Care was taken in the articles under which tournaments were fought not only to ensure that knights wore adequate armour, but also that neither armour nor weapon gave a contestant unfair advantage. Lances were frequently rebated to diminish the chances of piercing armour; and the tilt – a barrier of cloth or, increasingly, of solid wood – was introduced to stop horses from colliding and to increase the angle at which a lance would strike so that it would be more likely to break on impact than to penetrate. An additional measure, less for safety than to ensure correct running by the horses, was the introduction of the counterlists: smaller rails, one at each side of the tilt and parallel to it, creating an alley along which the knight could ride (fig. 162). Tilting was a much safer activity than running without the tilt (known as 'running at large', 'at random', 'al campo aperto', or 'à champ ouvert'); and by the mid-sixteenth century, it had become far the more popular.

The final effect of these two modes of jousting was very different. Without the tilt it was possible for knights to pass much closer together; the angle of attack was more direct and penetrating, especially when, as was sometimes the case, the course was fought with unrebated spears; a knight could, whether by accident or design, hit an opponent's horse much more drastically; or the horses could simply crash into each other (plate XXIV). Early in the seventeenth century, Bartolomeo Sereno described how once, in Naples, he had seen two pairs of knights jousting at large. There had been a head-on collision and all four men were killed. The main difficulty, Sereno continued, was that generally, in trying to avoid such a crash, knights tended to pass at too great a distance, which meant that inevitably their blows were rather feeble.[1] Indeed, we can see, from surviving score cheques, how the standard of lance play in early Tudor England dropped even further from an already undistinguished norm when knights risked an encounter in the open field.[2]

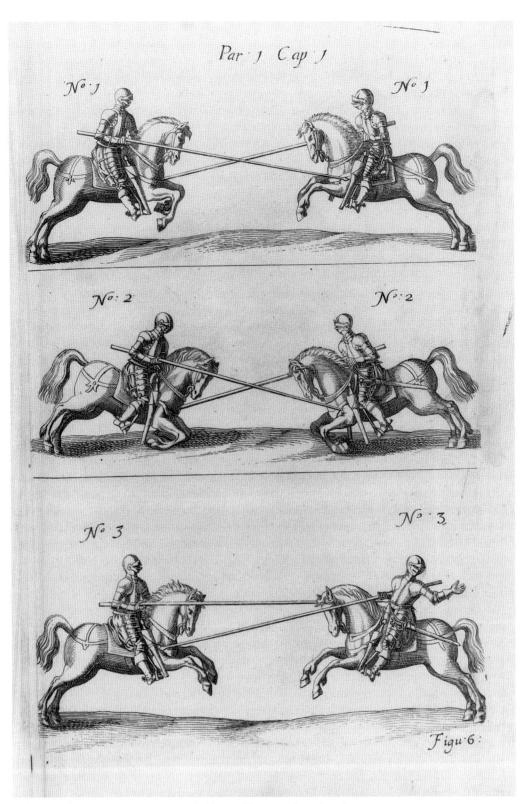

163. Attacking the horse as recommended by Wallhausen. 1634, plate 6.

It is clear that running at large, when properly undertaken, approximated much more exactly than tilting to the real lance charge, though it was still a long way from the brutality of serious combat. In real warfare, said Monte, only fools 'constantly aim their blows against the man and not against the horse, whereas the opposite is done by the wise'.[3] This was the view of most authorities and, a century later, Basta – conceding that mastery of the lance is not easy – advised the knight to cross his lance over his horse's neck, past its left ear; gain the left side of his opponent; and aim, not at the knight, 'who is nowadays too heavily protected', but at the oncoming horse's left shoulder which is a much more vulnerable target than its front.[4] This tactic was also approved by Basta's contemporary critic Wallhausen who includes clear illustrations demonstrating how the cavalryman is to direct his attack at the opposing horse (fig. 163). Nevertheless, despite this fundamental divergence of purpose, the handling of the heavy lance, whether in war or in mock combat, required a basically similar technique which changed little over several centuries, once the general principles of the *projectile vivant* had evolved.[5]

JOUSTING: THE EARLIEST TREATISES

Thursday 11 June 1467 was supposed to be a great day for the fight fanciers of fifteenth-century England. After more than two years of heraldic preliminaries, Lord Scales and the Bastard of Burgundy faced each other in the lists at West Smithfield for the deadly course of running at large with unrebated lances. Trumpets sounded. Heralds proclaimed. The knights charged – and missed each other.[6] Their failure may have been diplomatically expedient, but the records of fifteenth-century tournaments suggest that such ineptitude was not unusual, and it is not difficult to credit Commines's famous observation that, at the battle of Montlhéry in 1465, out of some twelve hundred men at arms there were only fifty who knew how to couch a lance.[7] More than 200 years later, the Italian riding master, Luigi Santa Paulina, expressed disgust at the jousting of his contemporaries; and it was this, together with his recognition that single combat with the heavy lance had become outmoded in modern warfare, which induced him to lay down strict rules for handling the weapon. Lance play had survived only in festivals, he said. Attention was paid merely to beautiful appearances and 'nothing with regard to the safeguard of the body'.[8]

Granted that there always had been incompetent jousters, Santa Paulina still had a point. Perceptive writers on the art of war had long recognized the military inefficacy of the heavy lancer and, by the late seventeenth century, Montecuculli had to admit that, although the lance had once been 'the Queen of weapons for the cavalry', practical considerations had led to its being abandoned. Military desuetude was compounded by academic ignorance. Seventeenth-century historians and philologists were greatly confused by the technical terms relating to armour and lance combat, and their legacy of misinformation constitutes a sorry tale.[9]

If, in the seventeenth century, both scholars and military men experienced difficulties concerning chivalric lance play, then we need to be cautious. Modern reconstructions of jousting, as is the case with other forms of combat, have tended to rely heavily upon three types of evidence – manuscript illustrations, chronicles and armour. But, as we have already seen, they all have drawbacks. Disconnected pictures convey only a rudimentary notion of real combat, and it was a rare artist who had much technical knowledge. Some chroniclers certainly did know what they were talking about and have provided vivid descriptions of fighting. However, their primary concern was narrative, not analytic, and what we can learn from them about the technicalities of jousting approximates to what we might learn about boxing or tennis from a series of well-informed newspaper reports.

This modern analogy prompts another pertinent question. Armour, it must be admitted, became so sophisticated and so specialized that surviving artefacts can tell us a great deal about chivalric practice. Yet, without documentary evidence, even that rich thesaurus would remain largely enigmatic. How far would it be possible to discover the techniques of boxing or tennis if all that survived were a miscellaneous collection of old boxing gloves, balls, rackets, shorts, shoes and athletic supports?

Statements of general principle, rules, regulations and technical analyses by experts are as necessary for the reconstruction of jousting as they would be for any other sport; and, fortunately, such sources are available. As we have seen, from the Renaissance onwards, publication on the martial arts developed into a boom industry; and not only did fencing manuals multiply to satisfy the craving of modern duellists, but treatises on the increasingly obsolete skills of mounted lance play also came into vogue. Sometimes these were incorporated into texts whose main concern was with fencing; sometimes they formed part of treatises on the full range of chivalric activities; or sometimes they appeared in books on horsemanship. Many were written late in the history of jousting but, since mounted lance play changed very little after the evolution of what Buttin has called *le projectile homme-cheval* in the fourteenth century, all these works throw retrospective light on earlier modes of combat. In fact, there were really only a very small number of basic combat skills required for handling the heavy lance and the most important of these involved horsemanship far more than any fighting ability. What the lancer could achieve depended, in large part, upon what he could make his horse do; and it was precisely this point which convinced Monte that mounted single combat was far too dependent upon chance. The lance was a crude, inflexible instrument, so that all the writers concerned with its technique shared the same general conception and merely personalized their account with a few hints, tricks and variations. Obviously, with such limitations, there could be nothing remotely parallel to the contemporary systematization of foot combat and its pictorial representation. A notation was developed for horse ballet in court festivals from the late sixteenth century: but it was a rudimentary track system and had, of course, nothing to do with fighting.

The earliest treatment of jousting technique occurs in a detailed and expert treatise on horsemanship, the *Livro da ensinança de bem cavalgar* (*The book of instruction for good riding*), written about the year 1434 by the Portuguese monarch, Duarte I. Duarte's short reign, from 1433 to 1438, was marked by great literary activity in which the king himself took a leading part, with treatises on the *Loyal counsellor* and on combat, as well as his riding manual. Unfortunately, Duarte's gifts did not extend either to the art of kingship or to the art of war and, politically, his reign was an unmitigated disaster for his Portuguese subjects. On the other hand, historians of riding, hunting and chivalric combat have reason to be grateful to him.[10]

Two long chapters of the *Livro da ensinança* deal, for example, with the ways in which different types of lance may be held.[11] For jousting, the heavy lance is appropriate and is carried into the lists upright supported either on the thigh or in a pouch (*bolsa*) on the saddle bow. As we know from other sources, the latter method was especially popular: though Duarte prefers using as little artificial support as possible.

In order to achieve mastery, the aspiring jouster should begin by exercising on foot with a light lance or wooden staff, always remembering to support its weight not with the fingers but in the palm of the hand. When couching the lance, the beginner should place it under his arm, gripping it as tightly as possible against the chest, while keeping his body straight so that he can breathe easily. The whole movement must be done with a certain little bow of the body or *savoir faire* – an anticipation of the *grazia* later made famous by Castiglione. The movement must also be swift, as this will be the best method when, eventually, the student graduates to the heavy lance. Progress from light to heavy lance must be gradual, to avoid the risk of rupture, backache, headache, or pains in the legs and hands; and only when mastery of the lance has been achieved on foot should the student climb on horse-back to learn his skills there under the tuition of an instructor who can observe his perfor-mance and correct his mistakes.

Practising on foot was still being recommended by later authorities such as Giovanni dall'Agocchie (1572) who maintained that it was easier to learn how to carry the lance, place it in the rest, and lower it *con ragione*, without having a horse getting in the way; and by the famous Antoine de Pluvinel who – although not greatly concerned with combat – heartily approved of practising tilting at the ring on foot, 'because the training one gets carrying one's lance correctly and in various ways, and the judgement of the eye to join adroitly the point of the lance with the ring, can be learned much better on foot than on horseback'.[12] The tradition of training for the joust on foot gives new meaning to those well-known manuscript illustrations of pedestrian lance play which have sometimes been interpreted as merely the lower orders aping their betters. Duarte's remarks on foot prac-tice suggest a different possibility.

Four common weaknesses in jousting technique are diagnosed by Duarte. 'Men may fail', he says, 'through not being able to see; through lack of control of their lances or their horses; or through lack of the will to win'. Interestingly, in view of the common assumption that jousting was a matter of pointing in the right direction and hoping for the best, Duarte's principal concern was that the knight's vision should be unimpeded for, he says, 'accord-ing to our custom I cannot think that anyone who cannot see can joust well'.[13]

Some jousters fail because, without realizing it, they do not have their eyes open at the moment of impact; others, although aware of this weakness, are unable to control it. Some have their vision impeded by a maladjusted helm or shield; others because 'they cannot turn their bodies in the joust to take aim and only turn their eyes within their heads or helms, and, because they are looking forward, fail to see at the moment of encounter'. The best remedy is to have someone at the end of the course who can analyse the jouster's per-formance, 'for one cannot know for sure if one strikes straight'. Involuntary closing of the eyes is very hard to remedy: but an adviser, by pointing out and severely reprimanding this weakness, may induce in the jouster such a feeling of 'displeasure and melancholy' that he will be able to force himself to cure it. This is Duarte's aversion therapy. He is also aware of the psychological effects of success. If the blinking jouster misses because he is striking too late, he should be advised to strike early so that 'if he fails to hit through good vision, he may do so by guessing'. Then, if he happens to succeed, 'the certainty of pleasure may give him the strength to keep his eyes open in jousting'. To correct consistently poor aim, Duarte advises that, when the jouster is armed and mounted, he should take the lance under his arm, holding it at the height at which he intends to strike; place it in such a position that he can see a half or at least a third of it; and keep it in that position until he has run the course. Duarte also has a little tip about fixing the helm so that its sight remains steady. Fasten the helm first at the back and then at the front, he says, for 'in this way the helm stays on more firmly and the sight is more secure'. Finally, on this question of adequate vision, Duarte advises the jouster that, in order to see well at the crucial moment of striking, it is necessary to watch the opponent constantly, keeping the body turned towards him, and turning the face as much as possible so that you see him directly and not out of the corner of the sight of the helm. 'This way', he says, 'is very helpful to get a good view and helps one to joust and to suffer attaints better.'

The second reason for failure is lack of lance control which is itself due to four further weaknesses: being ill-armed or unpractised in wearing armour; having a staff heavier than one's strength warrants; being uncomfortable in the saddle; or having a horse so restless that one cannot keep control of the bridle. The solution to all these problems is self-evident, and Duarte's recommendations of constant practice, sensible choice of weapons and saddlery, and careful training of horses are unexceptionable. There is one detail, however, which is especially revealing. A particular difficulty for jousters was getting their horses to make a correct approach to what Duarte refers to as the *tea*. This word is sometimes translated as the lists, but here it indicates the tilt, as is evident from the relevant passage. Duarte writes:

> I have seen this mistake arise for two causes: one because they have no control of it and let their horses go the length of the *tea* at a distance from it, as I said; and others because they wish to joust with great advantage and come crossways, and arrive so late at the *tea* that the others pass first. In order to guard oneself against these errors one must do as follows: as for the first, when the jouster goes the length of the *tea*, although it seems to him that his horse has gone close enough, he must always turn the horse to the encounter and come as close to the *tea* as he can, because in this way he jousts better and he and his horse will endure encounters much more.[14]

The second error of arriving at the *tea* too late to make contact may be cured by deliberate effort to reach it earlier – even if this means making the opposite error of striking too soon. I dwell on this point because the earliest unequivocal recorded use of the tilt is in Jean Le Févre's account of jousts held in January 1430 at Bruges to celebrate the marriage of the Duke of Burgundy to Isabel of Portugal. He notes that, across the great marketplace, 'there was constructed a single fence of stout timber boards up to the height of the horses' shoulders'. And these jousts, says Le Févre, were 'in the Portuguese fashion' (*à l'usage de Portingal*).[15] The point need not be laboured, although there is some evidence to suggest that the tilt was already customary in Spain as well as in Portugal.[16]

Another aspect of Duarte's treatment of jousting is his recognition of the role of the combatants' 'willpower' (*suas voontades*), and he devotes a couple of chapters to the mental weaknesses which adversely affect performance: being fundamentally unwilling to meet in an encounter; breaking away with fear, as if under compulsion, at the moment of impact; moving the body and the lance restlessly and with haste; and being anxious to have so great an advantage in the joust that often – when such advantage is not forthcoming – the opponent is missed completely.[17] A good deal of Duarte's advice on how to combat these deficiencies is wholly psychological – literally trying to reason oneself out of fear by reflecting on the lack of danger in jousting as compared with the accidents which may occur in the cane game and hunting, let alone in real warfare – and he has some perceptive remarks on the paradoxical need to concentrate hard on staying relaxed. He also makes a shrewd comment on the tendency of some anxious jousters to brace their bodies and to grip their lance so tightly that it wavers and fails to hit the intended target. There are two further practical suggestions. The first – advocating that the lance should be aimed slightly lower than the intended target so that an upward adjustment may be made at the moment of contact – was not favoured by later authorities.[18] The second, by contrast, has remained standard sporting technique even into the late twentieth century. In Duarte's opinion, a jouster's principal object must be to concentrate and keep his eyes fixed on the intended target until he sees the rochet of his lance strike home.

Many of these observations have a modern ring. Nowadays (when sporting contests are commented upon, analysed and replayed in slow motion) we all know the significance of good coaching and motivation, and are aware that a tennis player's serving arm may become tense under psychological pressure, or that golfers have special ways of gripping the putter. We know about failure due to eyes being taken off balls. And we know that, in snooker (the modern lance game), players must keep their eyes glued to the precise spot on the object ball where the cue ball is intended to strike: before, during and even after contact has been made. That Duarte I, King of Portugal (without, as far as we know, either literary models or slow-motion television replays) could make similar comments on jousting more than 560 years ago, argues a man of great practical experience, keen observation and quite remarkable powers of analysis.

Duarte's treatise remained unpublished until 1842; but one of his Spanish associates also wrote about jousting and managed to get into print before the end of the fifteenth century. This was the illustrious Alonso de Cartagena, prelate, politician, poet, philosopher and historian whose translation of Cicero's *Rhetorica* was undertaken at the request of King Duarte, and whose *Doctrinal de los caualleros* was first published at Burgos in 1487, thirty-one years after its author's death. The *Doctrinal* is, as one would expect, largely concerned with the moral obligations of knighthood, but it does include two short chapters on mounted combat: one on tourneying with swords; the other on scoring in the joust.[19]

Alonso recognizes that there is a hierarchy of scoring strokes, so that success depends not merely on the number of lances broken, but also on the quality of the blows. Thus a mere attaint counts less than a single lance broken, while disarming an opponent of his helm counts as two. This, of course, was the standard view: but I do not know the source for Alonso's suggestion that a knight who falls with his horse is less culpable than one who is merely dismounted; and his argument (that in the former case it is the horse's fault and in the latter the knight's) did not find favour with other writers on chivalry. Similarly, it is difficult to interpret Alonso's suggestion that no staff split crosswise (*travesadas*) should count as properly broken; though I imagine that he is distinguishing between lances which break after making contact with the point and those where the lance has broken after striking sideways and without the point making contact – something similar to what a later writer, Quixada de Reayo calls *barrear lança*.[20]

Alonso de Cartagena is a member of an intriguing group of fifteenth-century Spanish clerics who dabbled in military exercises: but his treatment of jousting is very slight.[21] We are certainly on more solid ground with two later discussions, both by experienced soldiers. The first is the passage on mounted combat in Jean de Bueil's *Le Jouvencel* where the veteran is asked to advise on the use of the lance. The prime requisite, he says, is to have a good suit of armour because the lance, which is 'moult subtille', can pass through the smallest opening, and is then merciless. Wielded by the mounted warrior, it is the most dangerous weapon in the world for one cannot shout 'whoa!' to it (*car il n'y a point de holla*). The right arm should be lightly armoured and easy of movement; but the right side of the forearm should have strong and well-wrought protection because the whole force of the lance is felt there and many men have been lost because of this. Like Duarte, he stresses that it is vital to see well, otherwise nothing can be achieved. The knight should keep a cool head; have a loyal and courageous horse with good strength and an easy gait; and he should not try to cut a dash by using fat, huge lances. If he were to hit his opponent low down with such a stave while receiving an answering blow higher up, even from a lighter stave, he would be overturned. A medium-sized, manageable lance will strike more effectively than an unwieldy and heavy lance which can lift the knight who bears it clean out of his saddle. The weight causes a knight to raise his arm and lose his grip so that he cannot deliver a powerful blow. Furthermore, the horse obliged to carry such a burden will move less well. The knight will sit less securely, strike with less force, hold his stave less level, and aim it less accurately than would be the case with a more modest weapon.

Le Jouvencel recalls that, when he himself was young, he had seen a pair of knights jousting and one had struck the other's visor seven times with the point of his lance. Indeed, had not an old warrior – after the second of these blows – warned the knight who was on the receiving end, then Le Jouvencel firmly believes that death would have ensued. The veteran's counsel had been to loosen the fastenings which held the visor to the armet and to fix it with a leather point and with some wax; and it would suffice if it held in place while the horse was at a gallop. Thereafter, although the other jouster continued to strike the visor without fail, it flew off and the lance did not bite. Thus the accurate but unimaginative knight eventually realized that he was wasting his time and would have to aim at another mark. The point of the story, for Le Jouvencel, is that if you notice your opponent repeatedly aiming at one particular spot, then you must try to upset his plan. Similarly, if you yourself constantly try for the same target, but realize that counter-measures are being taken, then you must instantly change your own tactics.[22]

This passage is valuable not merely for its precise recommendation of lances that do not exceed a knight's physical capacity, and its description of the trick with the visor. It also reveals that the jousting knight of the fifteenth century was not a blind, strait-jacketed, muscle-bound lump of iron whose only hope of success with the lance was for his opponent to impale himself thereupon. On the contrary, lightness of movement is stressed, as is the need for clear vision. The ability to aim the lance and to hit a precise target regularly is assumed, as is the technical mastery requisite to alter one's blow at will and to use not only strength to discomfort an adversary, but also skill to outwit him.

The second soldier to leave us some analytical remarks on jousting is Ponç de Menaguerra, a Valencian cavalry officer who served with the royal forces at Perpignan when it was under siege by the French in 1473; and his short work, *Lo cavaller*, was written after Ferdinand's accession in 1479 to the throne of Aragon, and before 1493 when it was printed at Valencia.[23] The greater part of the text is devoted to scoring for the joust but, since Menaguerra makes many nice distinctions between scoring strokes, his remarks are often suggestive both of technique and intentions. He begins by asserting that a jouster who enters the lists with any piece of armour missing cannot win the prize, because it is unacceptable to give 'cause for displeasure in the enjoyment of so magnificent an event'. Moreover, when prizes are awarded for elegance, it is necessary that the judge should observe whether the trappings are uneven or whether the crest is erect and securely fastened.[24] 'No less attention', continues Menaguerra, 'must be paid to the order and movement of the horseman as he enters the lists' along with the way he takes his lance, charges, uses his spurs, sits in the saddle, and how quickly he turns, for he 'must not touch the tilt with the rump of his horse or in any other way'. Faults such as losing the lance when taking it up at the beginning of a course, or losing a stirrup, are penalized at the judge's discretion and may be worth a lance broken to the opposing jouster. There are a number of prohibited attaints, such as hitting the head or neck of the opponent's horse, his saddle bow, bridle hand, thigh or any place below it. A knight making such a foul stroke is barred from receiving the prize that day in order to avoid unpleasantness, 'since through such attaints jousters have died and suffered great injuries, disturbing the cheerfulness of such events'.[25]

It is clear, from Menaguerra's rules, that he expects jousters to begin their course with the lance vertical *en la bossa*, and then to lift it and place it in the rest. Errors might occur at this point, and penalties are recommended for those who place the lance so badly in the rest that the point drops and touches the tilt. Menaguerra places great emphasis on elegance (*les gentilees*) of style, but stresses that this can only affect the award of prizes when jousters are otherwise equal in number of lances broken and attaints.

The relative merits of different blows are meticulously explained; and, in contrast to English practice, breaking a lance on the helm counts no more than any other lance broken 'unless an agreement was made before hand giving the advantage to him who attainted higher'. A horseman who is so wounded that he cannot return to joust is said to be out of the lists:

> On account of the blood shed, the horseman who attainted him wins more than the number of lances which are taken into account for the prize, except the horseman who with or without losing blood is knocked unconscious so that he cannot return to joust, and except a horseman who has fallen with his horse, has lost blood or been wounded in any limb, for they are counted as dead. If a horseman has broken his arm, leg, thigh or collar bone by an attaint, it is judged accordingly, since the attaint that brings the horseman closer to death must be of greater value.[26]

If in attainting, two horsemen fall with their horses, the one who is least hurt and soonest returns to joust wins. This, Menaguerra notes, is according to the custom of the Hungarians and Germans, and follows the style of arms *à outrance*, 'which gives the best to the combatants who emerge from the encounter readier for battle'.[27] In Germany and Hungary, he continues, they count only the attaint in which the horsemen fall; and if two horsemen run good courses and one is unseated as a result of his own lance stroke, then the one who does not attaint wins, 'since such an attaint is not valued for the one who makes it but for the horseman who with such skill shows that he can receive and withstand it'.[28]

Menaguerra gives precise details of the points to be awarded or deducted for the loss of various pieces of armour or horse accoutrements; and the scoring, in his version at least, is so sophisticated that if, for example, a knight's hand strikes the grappe of his lance (*lo gocet de la lança*) and is wounded, 'the blood shed is of no account since the jousting is not ended by it'; or if he is attainted on the vambrace and 'it is so distorted that it cannot be replaced without a hammer, the horseman is out of the lists and it counts as four lances broken'. Similarly, if the helm is removed from the head it is worth ten lances to the one who attaints; but if this causes bleeding from the nose or mouth, on losing a tooth, it is worth twenty lances. On the other hand, leaving a broken piece of lance in the opponent's helm, shield, or any other part of his armour counts for nothing as does the striking of sparks in attaint, because these are normal occurrences in any encounter and do not merit special notice. When a horseman is unseated by an attaint so that he hangs from the saddle bow or stirrups, or falls to the ground, he is declared to be out of the lists and he who unhorses him scores twenty lances broken. Best of all is so to strike an opponent on any licit target that he loses consciousness and cannot return to the joust. This counts for more than all the other incidents which can win the prize, and more than all the lances broken.[29]

Having explained the technicalities of scoring, *Lo cavaller* concludes with a brief 'Scola del junyidor', arguing that skill is all important (*Art és lo mestre*) and that understanding, disposition and natural inclination are the prerequisites of success. Menaguerra particularly comments on how the knight is to arm himself and present himself in the lists, and he provides a concise account of couching the lance: stressing that when it has been lifted from *la bossa* and placed in the rest, in order to exert maximum control and avoid foul strokes, it is to be lowered little by little (*poch a poch*) – a phrase which was to be repeated by jousting masters for at least another two centuries.

Like Ponç de Menaguerra, Pietro Monte was also part of this rich Iberian tradition, although he professed a disdain for single combat on horseback where contestants are placed at the mercy of brute beasts, or where success often depends merely on who is the better armed. In such circumstances, he argued, it is easy for the weak to be protected against the strong, especially when various misfortunes tend to come about because of the horses; whereas in foot combat each man may clearly display his own physical strength. Elsewhere, however, Monte explains how a man of only moderate physique may, by superior art, overcome a very powerful antagonist; and it is not clear where the master's sympathies lay though, on the whole, he admires skill more than brute force and even suggests how it is possible for a man – by adroit horsemanship – to frustrate the attempts of an opponent to bring him to lance conflict.[30]

Despite his preference for fighting on foot, Monte's survey of mounted combat is comprehensive and comprises jousting as well as tourneying; and – although he tends to repeat himself, and sometimes makes observations on lance play while discussing mounted fencing (and vice versa) – on the whole, his presentation is orderly and direct.[31] His first rule is brutal enough. In real warfare, says Monte, provided that you are yourself adequately protected by defensive armour, it is best to aim at the easiest and most vulnerable target. This is undoubtedly the enemy's mount: and the same tactic was still being advocated by later writers on lance combat such as Quixada de Reayo, Ghisliero, Basta and Cruso, none of whom had time for chivalric niceties in serious battle.

Monte, assessing the rival merits of heavy and light armour, is predisposed in favour of the pliancy, agility and ease of dodging blows afforded by the latter – especially on foot, where even a little power may suffice for killing a physically bigger and stronger man. Monte's opinion is especially worth noting because the traditional view that armoured knights were impossibly clumsy and ponderous has been replaced by a fashionable assumption that a suit of armour was rather comfortable sporting attire. Monte knew otherwise. In heavy armour, he says, speedy movement forward and back is scarcely possible 'for if we bend the body, the armour's weight is over that part so that we may easily fall or receive some hurt'. There are similar difficulties on horseback and here the jouster is urged to direct his horse's head towards the adversary and never to await the momentum of the oncoming charge but, on the contrary, always to counter charge.

Not that Monte advocates rash action. He stresses, instead, the value of sensible deliberation: but once a decision has been taken it must be acted upon without hesitation 'so that we may quickly achieve a perfect conclusion'. It is proper always to act prudently, while pursuing our objective 'without hurry but with a determined spirit'. The end of an action must conform to its beginning.

Monte constantly gives tips for the mounted warrior. One of his suggestions applies particularly to tourneying when it is advantageous to fight with the visor raised. This helps breathing and vision and is rarely dangerous although, sensibly, Monte does not recommend it for jousting. Another suggestion concerns the common habit of tying oneself to the saddle – a trick disliked by Monte who points out the dangers which arise if the horse should fall. He also has a great deal to say about the length and weight of different weapons which should always be chosen to conform with one's own physique and strength, although it is sometimes necessary to take into account the arms carried by an opponent. In general, Monte sees considerable advantages in using long weapons and only recommends short heavy weapons for the relatively unskilled. When jousting, it is vital to have a lance which can be managed comfortably so that it can be lifted and placed in the rest without difficulty. None the less, the longer the lance the more effective it will be, 'because we can make contact before the adversary' – an advantage always specifically denied to contestants within the lists.

Monte devotes several chapters to the saddles best suited to different types of combat and assesses opinions concerning their merits.[32] Some people, for instance, recommend that the saddle should slope forward, especially for jousting. Other and 'perhaps better masters' have the opposite opinion and say thus: 'because the shield with the rest of the arms lean forward, if the saddle were to follow in the same direction, anyone would quickly feel fatigue'. Moreover, if the saddle slopes forward, the heavy lance has too little support. It soon wobbles about and falls to the side, 'which would not happen when the saddle slopes back and has a good seat; and in this way they can safely carry arms or burdens, and with little labour'. Monte's point is that, if the arms are themselves heavy, they suffice to pull a man forward especially since it is natural to lean foward at the moment of impact. At all events, for fighting in battle the saddle must slope back, and it should be wide and spacious so that it is possible to avoid blows and 'help ourselves, which is impossible when the saddle is tight and leaning forward'.

The merits of riding short or long for the joust are carefully evaluated, and Monte has no hesitation in recommending the former. 'To ride in the short fashion', he observes, 'is generally found useful; for greater power is found in the legs and for the whole body; and we can carry greater lances.' There are those, he acknowledges, who believe that riding long, 'or with the legs extended', is excellent; but in his opinion, 'it does not have such firmness in it'. It is at this point that Monte defines what he means by the joust and explains how the terminology evolved. The method of running one against one with lances can deservedly be called 'to draw near' (*iustare*) because for things which are equal or without separation we have the designation *iustum*, 'whence *iustus iusta iustum*'. Then also we say adverbially '*iuxta* for one thing resting close to another'. Thus, says Monte, from this exercise of jousting (*iustandi*), 'that is coming close in a direct line, one says jouster (*iustator*), and the operation itself *iusta* or *iustra*'. Du Cange, in his *Glossarium*, might have been more sure of himself on this point had he consulted Monte.[33]

As you would expect of the master who instructed the highly successful jouster, Galeazzo da Sanseverino, Monte's advice on lance handling is wholly practical. He suggests that, when the staff is placed in the rest and directed at the opponent, the skilled jouster must turn not only the weapon but also his body towards the opponent, leading with his right side and so, in effect, extending the length of his lance – a piece of advice subsequently repeated by several later authorities on jousting technique.[34] It is, above all, vital to aim the point of the lance at the oncoming knight and always to adjust aim as the distance diminishes. Those who estimate at the beginning of a course where their lance ought to make contact 'for the most part go astray, because we must constantly direct our lance at the attacker himself, and not towards the place where we think he will come'. As for holding the lance, Monte is clear that, while the arm should be stiff, the hand should not grip the lance tightly 'for then it would vibrate too much' – which is precisely what Duarte had warned against.[35] Also like Duarte, Monte warns against the natural tendency of some jousters to close their eyes when they see the adversary's lance approaching. A cure for this is to practise for several days before a combat by holding the eyes open while being struck on the visor with a lance. Doing this will demonstrate that it is not possible to sustain damage from the metal of a lance through the visor and will inure one to the shock of impact: a process aided, Monte believes, by keeping the mouth open as well as the eyes.

Some authorities, he notes, suggest that it is a good idea to concentrate on the point of one's own lance in order to avoid worrying about that of the opponent: but, very sensibly, this is not a practice he recommends and he returns to the problem in the last of his chapters devoted to mounted combat – a brilliant and prophetic exposition of the relationship between hand and eye.[36] If one wishes to joust 'with understanding' (*cum ratione*), it is essential not only for the knight to be well armed and mounted but, above all, to develop the habit of ensuring that 'the hand is directed by the eye'. When firing a crossbow, catapult, blowpipe, bow or similar instrument, we aim the weapon by means of a sight (*mira*). In much the same way, when jousting, 'we should always look at the opponent in that place where we wish to make contact, and the hand must follow the eye – the lance having been placed in the rest – without being drawn away from that aim.'

Monte's jouster, like Duarte's (and like his modern sporting counterparts) must keep both eyes glued to the precise point which he intends to strike; and I can only assume that, when Lord Scales and the Bastard of Burgundy 'failid bothe unhit', they had, metaphorically speaking, taken their eyes off the ball.

LATER AUTHORITIES

By the time that the next treatise on jousting was published – Juan Quixada de Reayo's *Doctrina del arte de la cavallería* which appeared at Medina del Campo in 1548 – tilting had become the predominant lance exercise and forms Quixada's main preoccupation although, in a concluding chapter on real warfare, he simply tells his knight to strike at the opposing horse's belly.[37] The dominance of tilting did not, however, prevent knights from being slain principally, as Quixada notes, by lances penetrating the sights of their visors. This is a markedly different view from that adopted by Monte who had considered that the dangers of such penetration were slight: but Quixada states that he has himself seen many deaths occur in this way, and names several of the victims. Like Duarte and Monte, Quixada has a good deal to say about saddlery, although his command of language is insufficiently flexible to enable him to convey information with clarity and it is here especially that a reader feels the lack of any explanatory diagrams. Quixada explains that the man at arms must learn from first principles, 'just as the child learns his ABC', and he stresses the need for practice and persistence – 'as the saying goes, practice makes perfect' – and the knight should practise two or three times every week. He advises the knight to sit as upright as possible 'as if standing before the King'; suggests that the saddle bows and saddle cloth should be short to give the impression that the rider has long legs; and recommends Mantuan saddles as the 'best for riding and dismounting from'. The knight should ride 'somewhat short rather than long', seat himself in the saddle 'in the Spanish fashion', and take care to choose a good horse which runs freely (*claro*). Quixada is cautious about using the spurs and especially warns against spurring those horses which, as he puts it, 'on going into an attack, take on new life'. In any case, he adds, a skilled knight will know what is necessary. Jousting skills should, in the first instance, be acquired from only one skilled warrior, 'and not from a number of people', because each person has his own way of doing things and a multiplicity of advice merely causes confusion.

Quixada devotes a chapter specifically to jousting technique, which, though valuable, is marred by tautology and an inept command of language. For example, he explains that, before taking hold of his lance, the knight must check with his second (*padrino*) that *el borne o evilla* is secure. Unfortunately, while *el borne* clearly indicates a lance tip of some sort, the word *evilla* (or *hebilla*) normally means a buckle or clasp, which, in relation to a lance, would make no sense whatever. Leguina, in his *Glosario*, simply listed the words as synonymous; while the Baron de Cosson, in his unpublished notes on Quixada, translated *evilla* as synonymous with *roquete* or *rochet* (that is a rebated metal head) and this is acceptable as consistent with everything else that Quixada writes, although his choice of word remains strange. None the less, Quixada's observation on lance furniture is crucial; as is his insistence that it is the lance-maker's business to ensure that the tip fits snugly on its seat (that is the prepared end of the wooden stave) which should be no more than half the length of the *borne* itself. The metal tip should be driven home with a mallet so that it will remain firm on impact, for if it wobbles even slightly then the lance will not break. Quixada also explains why the judges must ensure that all lances are measured exactly so that they are of equal length. If one stave exceeds another even by the length of a finger, then not only will it break first but it could result in the other lance's not breaking at all.

A sensible practice, mentioned by Quixada, but not generally adopted elsewhere in Europe, is for the lance tips to be smeared with red ochre so that each stroke leaves a mark. At this point in the text it appears that the judges are to appoint somebody to carry out this task, but elsewhere Quixada says that the colouring is the responsibility of the jouster's *padrones*. These *padrones* are clearly more than mere lackeys. Indeed, for Quixada, they serve a function similar to that of the modern sports trainer: checking the players' equipment; scrutinizing and analysing each contest; and correcting flaws. Thus they are expected not only to colour the metal lance tips and check that they are firmly in place, but also to ensure that the gusset of the lance is properly in the rest and that the jouster does not close his eyes at the moment of impact.[38]

As with his fifteenth-century predecessors, there is no question for Quixada that a knight merely starts off in the right direction and hopes for the best. Provided that he watches what he is doing, the jouster should be able to hit whatever he aims at. Indeed, the only reason that a competent knight should ever fail at the tilt is if his horse lets him down. The slightest stumble or dropping to one side, particularly at the moment of impact, spoils the knight's aim by making the lance waver because 'whatever the horse does so too does the rider' and, Quixada notes, a movement of a finger's breadth at the lance rest becomes two palms' width at the lance point. If the lists were so smooth and firm that horses never stumbled then, in Quixada's view, a good man at arms would never give a foul blow; and it is probably for this reason that he recommends the provision of counterlists to help the knight and his mount to avoid swerving.

Quixada's practical hints are, for the most part, very basic. It is important that knights should begin their course simultaneously, and if one has already set off before the other they should both return and try again. The lance is initially supported with the butt end in its *cuxa* (the leather purse attached to the saddle) – a technique also mentioned, though without enthusiasm, by Duarte who uses the term *bolssa*. The lance should then be placed in the rest, aimed across the horse towards the left, and the blow directed either at the opponent's head, grandguard (*gran pieça*), or the rondels covering his shoulder. On no account should the jouster shut his eyes because, in order not to miss his stroke, he must see where his lance is going. Nor should he stare at the oncoming lance 'because it will seem to be heading directly for his eyes'. This is sound advice, although Quixada's own recommendation is itself more than suspect because he considers that if the jouster concentrates his gaze upon the end of his own lance he would be able to hit whatever target he desires. Monte had already considered this technique and had summarily rejected it – and quite rightly because, like a tennis player who keeps his eye on his racquet or a cricketer who concentrates on his bat, a jouster who looked only at the end of his own lance was unlikely to hit anything at all. I can only suppose that Quixada – who was, in fact, an accomplished jouster and was soon to compete successfully at the great tournament for Charles V at Binche – had analysed his own practice erroneously. He would have watched both lance head and oncoming target, like a snooker player whose eyes take in the cue tip, cue ball and then object ball, prior to concentrating on the last of these just before contact.

The rest of Quixada's comments are both ambiguous and controversial. He writes: 'Conviene que el justador ha de engoçetar la lança porque si encuentra y no va engoçetada torna atrás hasta engoçetar y no çeva el borne ni evilla y pierde el encuentro de no romper'. This must mean that when the jouster places his lance in the *arrêt de la cuirasse* (that is the bracket affixed to the right side of the breastplate), he must also ensure that the 'gusset' of the lance – that is the *arrêt de la lance* (the pad around the lance behind the grip) – is firmly in place and ready, on impact, to recoil into the *arrêt de la cuirasse*. If it is not properly positioned then, on impact, the *arrêt de la lance* will slide back before engaging the *arrêt de la cuirasse*, and the metal tip of the lance will fail to bite into the armour. If that should happen then the lance will not break, even though it may strike home. That much is unexceptionable and in accord with other authorities. But there would have been less agreement about Quixada's further advice that, if the jouster breaks his lance, he should not release the remaining fragment until it is taken from him (*y si rompieres no sueltes el troço de la mano hasta que te lo tomen*). It was precisely behaviour of this kind which, within a decade, was to be diagnosed by some observers – though not, perhaps, very convincingly – as the cause of Henri II's death when his tilting opponent, Montgommery, failed to release the broken lance immediately.[39]

Quixada's treatment of the best method for couching the lance is very much along the lines of other authorities. Some jousters, he believes, hold the lance upright until the last moment but, he says, sudden lowering may easily cause the lance to drop too far and result in a foul stroke. His own view, therefore, is that the lance should be placed in its rest at the very beginning of the course and should then be lowered, little by little like the weight of a clock (*poco a poco como pesa de relox*), the great advantage of this method being that it gives the knight time to correct any errors of judgement and even to recover from mishandling the lance. Quixada warns against making an ugly or foul stroke such as striking your opponent on the saddle or even lower, or hitting the tilt; and he notes that there are certain horses which have a tendency to hold their heads high right up to the actual encounter and this sometimes results in the knight's striking their tester.

Three particularly bad habits in lance handling are singled out for criticism. *Barrear lança* is crossing the lance too far on the contact side so that, although it may well be broken, it will not be broken well and will, therefore, be disallowed by the judges.[40] A lance *calada* is one which wavers up and down during the course. And finally the lance *santiguada* (which is literally the act of making the sign of the cross) refers to a side-to-side movement from right to left. All these habits are bad and ugly and, in Quixada's opinion, the expert jouster never commits such errors.

It is illuminating to compare Quixada's account of jousting with that of his fellow Spaniard Luis Zapata who modestly admitted to being one of 'the most experienced and successful' knights in Spain.[41] As was the case with his discussion of armour, Zapata, while not completely ignoring technical issues, seems more concerned with appearances and behavioural stratagems. Thus he insists that the knight choose a horse which has a proud and haughty step and dominates the lists with its very presence, entering 'like a country gentleman, snorting with nostrils wide open'. He also requires that the horse should run 'so level that one could say it were possible to carry a glass of water in the hand' – something which, if ever achieved, would have greatly facilitated the jouster's work. Restricted use of the spurs is another of Zapata's tenets, for he objects to riders whose legs thresh about, kicking at the mount. Apparel both for horse and man is judiciously evaluated and riders are urged to ensure that everything is kept proportionate to stature. A tall horseman must wear a long surcoat, just as a horse with long legs must have long saddle cloths: and, of course, vice versa. Every physiological idiosyncracy must be neutralized, for 'as they say, when nature makes a mistake, let painting put it right'. Zapata also compares the 'loading' of a rider upon his horse with a ship which lists to one side and is rectified when the sailors station themselves on the other.

> The saddle should not be wide for then the horseman's legs would be spread too wide apart; nor should it be slung backwards for this would look ugly and he would be badly harnessed and liable to topple off. It should be such as to let him sit up perfectly straight. He needs a little room to rest when walking and not be so far forward onto the front saddle-tree as to make it look like a travelling bag.

All these factors are, in short, critical to the rider's posture. Indeed, a knight is 'incapable of achieving anything on a poor saddle'. Like Monte and Quixada, Zapata is an advocate of riding short and he recommends that the stirrups should be of a length such as to permit a hand's width between the rider's seat and the saddle itself. Riding long is 'ugly, weak and lamentable'; and, when the jouster first rides about the lists, he must stand up in his stirrups, confident and erect, not 'seated in the saddle with his legs dangling limp like a roasted hen'. Zapata also recommends what dancing masters used to call 'contra-body motion'. The body, he says, should be turned slightly on encounter because movement of this kind looks graceful, showing that the knight is a living body and not merely a piece of iron. Don Diego de Cordoba, he continues, performed most elegantly and with style but, 'for posture in the saddle, no man outclasses my master, King Philip'. This is praise indeed, although somewhat marred by the malicious little postscript: 'he never broke many lances, and that is the absolute truth'.

Zapata's concern with appearances becomes even more evident when he advises a knight about what to do if he 'gets out of breath after many courses, with the fervour of jousting'. The trick here is to stand aside and pretend to be ordering a lackey to lengthen or shorten a stirrup. Or one can say that the *padrino* or armourer is adjusting an item of equipment, 'in the same way that musicians, when they are tired, or when they cannot remember what to play, start to tune up'. As a matter of fact, Zapata confesses, he himself once failed to use this ruse when he got quite out of breath during a tournament at Brussels. He was standing by his horse when up came Don Francisco de Mendoza, son of the Marquis of Mondéjas, with a command from the emperor himself saying that he should carry on jousting or lose whatever advantage he had thus far gained. Unfortunately, he was in no state to obey for some time: the implication being that he would have done better to feign some reason for resting rather than reveal that he was too tired to continue.

Amidst all this Castiglionesque posturing, Zapata does have a few practical observations. He notes, for instance, that lances should be made of pine rather than of ash or beech and should be short, sturdy and rigid, yet light. It is a bad thing to have 'too much wood', because if lances are too heavy and strong, they are useless: 'horses get worn out, riders become disconcerted, and their hands can be broken'. The vamplate, which protects the hand grasping the lance, should be neither very capacious (*cuba*),[42] nor very flat (*plana*), nor very small, but rather middling, 'which is where virtue resides' – a tenet of sound philosophical pedigree but scant precision.

When it comes to actual jousting, Zapata is scarcely more informative. He says, for example, that a knight should begin his course sitting very upright, lance in leather pouch, and body leaning slightly over the lance, 'with much dissimulation' – a cryptic suggestion which is not explicated. Also puzzling is Zapata's remark about the possibly harmful effect of carrying the lance upright on the thigh. He says that if too much weight is applied when the lance is held in this position it can make the thigh bleed, as he himself has experienced. Yet earlier, when discussing jousting armour, he specifically recommended that knights should wear a cuisse on the right thigh 'so that the lance may be accommodated'; and it is difficult to see how, with such protection, the butt of the lance could cause the kind of injury which worries him. His treatment of couching the lance is similarly unclear, although he agrees with Quixada that striking sideways (*el barrear*) is reprehensible, and that the lance should be lowered *poco a poco* in a continuous movement which culminates at the moment when the adversary is struck. There are those, he adds, who lower their lance in one quick movement, 'which is called fishing' (*que llaman pescar*); but this is, in the vast majority of cases, unsuccessful and results in the horse crashing against the tilt, 'and other very disgraceful encounters'.

The manner of lowering the lance was a much discussed topic and, in general, the authorities were agreed that hasty movement was reprehensible. The remarks of Giovanni dall'Agocchie (1572) are especially interesting, and his treatment of jousting is the fullest and most meticulous up to this date.[43] Like several other writers on the martial arts, he was attracted by movement analysis – indeed, to such an extent that his work seems like a caricature of Aristotelian method although this does have the advantage of making his discussion of lance play much better organized and far more detailed than Quixada's. Before dealing with *la prattica* of jousting, he examines *la theorica* which he divides under six heads: good horsemanship; holding and carrying the lance upon the thigh; raising it from the thigh; placing it in the lance rest (that is the *arrêt de la cuirasse*); knowing how to lower it; and finally how to deal with it after making contact.

Skilled horsemanship is, of course, fundamental but dall'Agocchie wastes few words on something which he deems self-evident. Any knight, he says, will know how to ride but, like Quixada and Zapata, he does stress that the knight must sit up straight which is both more handsome, more comfortable and more secure when running with the lance – especially when jousting against a live opponent. At the start of a course, the horse must never be spurred furiously but should be handled *pian piano* so that it approaches the combat more willingly. In any case, too much violence in the charge can cause one to lose the lance – which, from the way dall'Agocchie writes, must have been a common fault. In particular, he warns against giving the horse too much left spur which would cause it to swerve away from the opponent; and he suggests that a timid horse, nervous of the hoof beats of the oncoming rival, might be fitted with bells (*sonagliera*) to hide the sound.

Dall'Agocchie has more to say about carrying the lance which should rest not directly on the thigh but rather between thigh and saddle because, when the jouster is in armour, his harness may otherwise impede his lance handling. The lance itself may be held sloping either to the left or, better still, straight upright with the point inclined slightly forward: and dall'Agocchie's warning, that one's right elbow must be held neither too high nor too low, is a reminder that we are still firmly in Castiglione's Aristotelian world of keeping to the middle way, avoiding extremes, and, above all, doing everything *con bella gratia*. The one serious error is for the jouster to hold his lance sloping to the right because this is not only a very ugly sight but it also gives rise to many mistakes when the moment comes to place the staff in its rest.

Dall'Agocchie's next, rather artificial, division of jousting – the three ways in which the lance may be raised from the thigh – prompts him to some very curious but revealing observations. The knight may either take his lance as he begins the course and place it suddenly in the rest; lift the lance as he begins the course, holding it strongly downwards away from the thigh with the arm held out at length; or he may raise the lance somewhat upwards, grasping it with great strength and with the arm slightly bent so that the point of the lance is directed towards his adversary. Great care must be taken to ensure that the lance does not slope backwards because this is a very ugly sight. All three methods of raising the lance have merit but, in dall'Agocchie's view, the last is the best and most secure for, when the jouster has his arm bent, he can support the lance more easily and couch it more firmly because his fist is closer to the rest. Above all, holding the lance strongly in this way approximates most closely to the practice of real war and 'all things are more beautiful and praiseworthy the closer they approach the truth'.[44]

Dall'Agocchie's interlocutor then asks why it has become so rare for knights to carry the lance *nella borsetta* – that is with the butt resting in the leather purse formerly attached to the saddle for that purpose. The answer is that contemporary lances are more slender and lighter than in the past, while front saddle bows are smaller. The modern lance, when used with the *borsetta*, has a tendency to shake about and can even be broken prematurely. In earlier times, however, the very thick and heavy lances then in vogue were less easily supported on the thigh, while the bigger saddle bows also hindered such a technique. As for the reasons why the heavy lance has been abandoned, dall'Agocchie is clear and informative. Knights no longer seek to unhorse their opponents, as in earlier times, and regard that sort of thing as displeasing. Instead their intention is solely to carry the lance well and to break it with skill, because, 'in making sport, extremes must always be avoided'. This is a perfectly tenable position, but it accords ill with dall'Agocchie's more bellicose noises.

There follows an analysis of three ways in which the lance may be placed in the rest and dall'Agocchie does not favour doing this at the last moment because it generally results in missing the opponent altogether or striking the tilt. On the other hand, couching the lance at the very beginning of the course is equally unsatisfactory because the horse will not yet be settled in its stride and the lance will waver up and down 'which is very ugly to behold'. The best method is for the knight to begin moving the lance only when his horse has got into its stride and then he must ensure that he keeps his fist well forward, turning his hand inwards so that the last knuckle joints of his fingers may be seen facing upwards. This will make it easier to place the lance in the rest. Nor should the *arrêt de la lance* be pushed suddenly against the *arrêt de la cuirasse*, but rather it should be eased 'little by little' during the charge. The interlocutor raises another question about gripping the lance because there are some, he says, who argue that the fist should not be tightly clenched but rather that the hand should be kept somewhat open. This is completely erroneous, retorts dall'Agocchie. Many knights who have used a loose grip have had their hands damaged by the recoil of the lance on impact. It is much better to keep the hand firm in the fashion described. Then all will be well.

When it comes to lowering the lance, dall'Agocchie agrees with most authorities that the knight should avoid either dropping it as soon as it is in the rest or waiting until just before the moment of contact. The movement should be gentle and continuous, giving time for adjustment. The point of the lance should be towards the left so that the opponent is clearly seen and one's eyes should be glued to the sight of his helm. Do this and it is 'almost impossible to run the course without striking'.

The last aspect of *la theorica* of jousting concerns what to do with the lance after an encounter. Dall'Agocchie says that there are only two possibilities: one can either replace the lance on the thigh or, far better, one may hold it point downwards on the right hand side and return it to the thigh only when the horse has come to a halt. What must be avoided at all costs is the common habit of throwing the lance to the ground – something done only by those who do not know the proper method of recovering after a course.

Having completed *la theorica* to his satisfaction, dall'Agocchie then moves on to *la prattica* – the acquisition of mastery by constant exercise. This is first done by the knight's arming himself only with the cuirasse and accustoming himself to carrying a lance and 'placing it securely in the rest without ever looking to see what he is doing' – a necessary skill because, in fact, when wearing his helm he will not be able to see his rest at all. The exercise may be carried out either on horseback or on foot, but – as King Duarte had suggested long before – the latter is preferable for the beginner. Once he can put the lance in its rest automatically, the knight can begin to practise breaking it, either at the quintain or, far more attractive and useful, against a wooden man seated upon a wooden horse like those used for vaulting. These wooden figures must be mounted on a low, four-wheeled cart raised about a foot above the ground and supplied with a rope of about six yards in length:

> and then it will be drawn by a man running as fast as he can for the length of the course, and done in such a way that the wheels turn easily; and so jousting against this said man will be done securely and will make for very fine practice, because this is a fashion very similar to running against an opponent.

Little is known about this jousting device but something very like it was shown among the tournament pictures at the Johanneum in Dresden where, during a court festival in 1566, wooden knights mounted upon wooden horses – attached to low four-wheeled bogies – were drawn along the tilt by ropes; and, a century later, a certain Raphaell Folyarte was awarded a patent in London for a similar mechanical contrivance.[45]

Another practising technique, recommended by dall'Agocchie as particularly effective in preparing a knight for real jousting against an opponent, is the use of the 'lance in two pieces' (*la lancia di due pezzi*) – an invention which, as far as I know, is described in only one other source, and that dependent on dall'Agocchie.[46] According to dall'Agocchie it consisted of the lower part of a lance stave, some four feet in length, the end of which was fitted into a tube of well-soldered, thin metal. This tube was to be at least nine inches in length – one half filled with the end of the half-stave, and the other with six-foot pieces which would have given an overall length of ten feet, which is dall'Agocchie's recommended dimension for the lance. The metal tube was then painted to resemble wood so that the whole thing looked like an ordinary lance. But, of course, it would break very easily and would be far more economical than the normal weapon.

On jousting lances and their dimensions, dall'Agocchie is expansive. He stresses that the distance between the butt of the lance and the grip should not be more than fifteen inches because anything more makes it difficult either to hold the stave or raise it from the thigh. Towards the grip, the butt of the lance should be about six and a half inches in circumference; the *grappella* should be an inch behind the grip; and that part of it which has to recoil against the lance rest should not be more than two-fifths of an inch thick because anything more can impede the lowering of the lance. The lance tip should be made of very fine steel with six teeth opening outwards so that it breaks securely when striking the helm. Excluding the teeth, it should be about an inch long and particularly well tempered so that it can attack the opponent's helm – a piece of armour which is always very hard. As a matter of fact, says dall'Agocchie, it is 'with well-tempered steel that many have gained the prize at jousting'. The vamplate should be eight and a half inches in diameter, about two and a half pounds in weight, and fitted about four inches above the grip. This measurement is critical because, if fitted too high, one's right shoulder is exposed to the opposing lance; but, if fitted too close to the grip, then the edge of the vamplate may touch the cuirasse when making an encounter, or may impede the breaking of the lance.[47]

Dall'Agocchie concludes his discussion of lance play with a brief treatment of the key parts of personal armour relevant to jousting and a few words on the arrangement and dimensions of the lists. The sight of the helm, he says, should be just wide enough to allow a view of the opponent. Indeed, in his opinion, despite what many authorities claim, a jouster can see neither his lance rest nor the left ear of his horse. He cannot even see the point of his lance once it is placed in its rest because it will be obscured by the vamplate, and the opponent will come into view only when one starts to lower the lance. Dall'Agocchie recommends that the left half of the sight of the helm should be closed up for greater security because, as one knows from experience, many have been wounded or killed in the joust by having the opposing lance penetrate this part. As for the bevor (*buffa*), says dall'Agocchie, this should fit right up to the sight of the helm for maximum protection and should be so fashioned that the knight is not forced to turn his head, and therefore his body, away from the adversary – an error which not only offers his left temple as a target but also causes his lance to swing wide and fail to break. Finally, the *arrêt de la cuirasse* should be no more than three inches in length. If it is longer, the arm may strike it as the lance is lowered into place. It should also be bowed or arched (*inarcata*) so that the stave fits securely into it; attached to the right-hand side of the breastplate 'higher rather than lower' (an opinion echoed by Zapata); and, above all, its forward edge must face slightly upwards so that the lance will be more likely to break.

Lance technique continued to interest students of mounted combat – especially when such combat took place within the relative safety of the lists – and, although there was little change in their basic approach to the problem, they did sometimes add interesting detail. Federico Ghisliero, for example, while clearly utilizing dall'Agocchie's treatise and sharing many of the views expressed therein, was even more obsessively preoccupied with

164. Ghisliero' geometrical study of running at the ring. 1587, p. 185.

Aristotelian categorization. Lance play, he says, was invented both to provide recreation and to encourage knights by accustoming them to handling the weapon so that they would be expert when the need arose. It was for this reason that the exercises of running at the ring or quintain and, of course, tilting itself were devised. Since, in his view, running at the ring was the most common, he has decided to concentrate upon that but, he stresses, all these exercises have a single purpose which is to know how to use the lance in the *campo aperto* and in war. He proceeds to divide the stages of lance technique for tilting at the ring into six necessary 'circumstances' (holding the lance on the thigh, raising it from the thigh, placing it in the rest 'handsomely', lowering it in proper time, striking with it as opportunity arises, and dealing with it after the blow has been struck) which are then further subdivided.

There are three different ways in which the lance may be carried on the thigh; six to raise it; four to place it in the rest; four to lower it; astonishingly only one to strike with it; and two to deal with it subsequently. In each case Ghisliero states his own preferences and offers criticism of alternative modes. He disapproves of those who raise the lance by gripping it and holding it away from the body with arm extended (a method he characterizes as *all'Albanese*), or who lift it high and suddenly thrust it into the rest, *alla stradiota*. The method he favours, 'because it is the best', is to raise the lance from the thigh, and then, while relaxing one's grip and supporting the staff with the wrist, direct its point towards the ring, keeping the arm somewhat bent. This makes it easier to place the lance in the rest and is, moreover, 'according to the use of war'. As was Ghisliero's wont, he explicates his argument with an illustration anticipating the diagrams later incorporated in the works of the seventeenth-century French riding masters (fig. 164). Take a straight line from the ring, he says, parallel with the line of the course itself. Then the line through the lance as it penetrates the ring will form an acute angle with the first line – it being the rule that a blow should be struck with the least movement possible. Ghisliero's diagram also shows the *visuale*, that is the sight line which passes over the lance to the point of contact between its point and the ring itself which should be three feet from the *linea della carriera* to the left of the knight as he approaches it, and at a height of some six feet. This accustoms the knight to keeping his lance aimed high and is good practice for tilting against an opponent or even jousting *a campo aperto* where hitting an opponent's head is the best stroke.

Ghisliero's concluding chapter is seemingly designed to incorporate a miscellany of ideas and observations which he could not accommodate elsewhere. He suggests dimensions for the lance more or less in accord with dall'Agocchie; offers various suggestions concerning horse-manship; declares that lance technique should first be practised on foot in order to develop a strong wrist before the knight graduates to horseback and exercises such as running at the ring; recommends the quintain as excellent preparation for tilting against a real opponent; and gives measurements for the lists and counterlists. He also takes from dall'Agocchie the idea of using a lance in two pieces connected by a piece of tubing, in order to moderate the expense of breaking staves while practising. To end his treatise Ghisliero provides two short paragraphs, one on the *campo aperto*, the other on handling the lance in battle. When riding without the tilt, he says, it is important never to spur one's horse on its left side (which would make it shy away from the collision) and to keep one's fist tightly gripped so that the hand is not injured by the impact of the blow. And then comes a devastating coda: 'For the final instruction I say also that when one is running not in play but in earnest, with tempered steel, one must know that in arriving hard by the enemy one has to lean towards the horse to strike it and to do this in as straight a line as possible: one must strike at the left flank or aim to penetrate the haunch which is the least protected part.' Nothing could better demonstrate the military irrelevance of most of what Ghisliero had written about jousting.

LANCE TECHNIQUE IN ACTION

The divorce between real warfare and jousting as sport or spectacle becomes increasingly marked in later chivalric treatises. Bartolomeo Sereno in 1610 devotes thirty-three pages 'to the use of the lance in the joust and in time of war' but, in fact, only two of these concern serious combat and, for the most part, Sereno deals with horses and equestrianism. The horse itself should be speedy, move without being spurred and understand the rider's wish by hints alone. The knight should sit firm and upright in the saddle, without slouching; he should neither look down at his legs nor glance behind him; and, when he begins his charge, he should not beat his horse nor waste time in fancy turns. A knight should never show fear in any action, however arduous or dangerous; and this is why he should fix his eyes on the spot he intends to strike and never stare at the opposing lance-head. To do the latter is a fundamental error because, in such cases, the point always seems to be headed straight at one's face which, in turn, makes one flinch from the anticipated blow, 'which is a most vile and ugly action'.

Particularly interesting is Sereno's detailed handling of what had become, by his time, a jousting axiom. The knight must never turn sideways, nor ever offer any target to the oncoming lance other than his breast. Such bending and twisting is not merely ugly, it is also extremely dangerous. The angle of the approaching stroke is such that, making contact with the breastplate, it will naturally slide across safely; but if it hits one's side it is more likely to penetrate. Moreover, leading with the left side diminishes the length of one's lance by at least four inches and enables your opponent to strike first, 'which always inflicts greater damage'. Sereno does not advocate leading with the right side as did Pietro Monte a century earlier; but he is making a similar general point. Bad lance handling and faulty posture will produce the same effect as running with a shorter lance. And that is potentially disastrous.

Like his predecessors, Sereno has much to say about the importance of beginning the course with the lance point high and then lowering it on approaching the target: though, he exclaims, he does not mean that the lance should be dropped like a cudgel blow (*una bastonata*). At first, the lance is supported on the thigh and inclined somewhat over the horse's right ear – a position in which Sereno appears to differ from most other authorities but which, in fact, is only preparatory to placing the lance in the rest and bringing it around more conventionally across the horse's left ear. At this point the exercise becomes very tricky. Perhaps influenced by Ghisliero, Sereno tries to reduce jousting to a similar geometrical proposition by tracing a notional right-angled triangle between the tip of the lance, the lance rest, and the point of vision through one's visor. But he complicates matters by assuming also a sight line culminating in the mark at which one is aiming – either the opponent's head or any other part of his body. Sereno's timing is equally formalized. His knight is advised to wait until he is between six to three lance-lengths from his enemy and then the whole action (from raising the arm when lifting the lance from the thigh; placing the lance in the rest; lowering it towards the target; and delivering the blow) should be carried out in one continuous movement, so that from the beginning to the end there should be no longer interval than three beats of *canto fermo*. Such smoothness makes the whole delivery more vigorous and gallant. On the other hand, Sereno does not give his jouster much time to perform this complex movement because he recommends that the lance should be placed in its rest as near to the delivery of the blow as possible. This will gain the knight a reputation for being honest and bold, showing not only a resolute spirit, but also such confidence in his own ability that he can give the blow whenever it pleases him to do so. In addition to this, such a stroke, not being foreseen by the other knight, will astonish him greatly and, in consequence, have the greater effect.

Had they been contemporaries, the young Henry VIII might have earned Sereno's approval. That enthusiastic jouster, it was noted in 1511, 'wold nevyr charge him with his spere in the Rest till he came near unto the copyng': but most theoreticians of the joust regarded this technique as flashy and as likely to surprise the jouster himself as his opponent.[48] Sereno himself could do the unexpected. Having virtually completed his analysis of chivalric combat, he suddenly retired into a Benedictine monastery, leaving somebody else to prepare his book for the press. His treatise was by no means the last study of jousting, but later writers added little to the theory of an activity which had already been thoroughly analysed and was now speedily becoming obsolete. Pluvinel (1623), despite acknowledging that the lance 'is a weapon invented to kill men', scarcely bothers to pretend that the lance exercises he describes have any relevance on the battlefield.[49] And in 1629 Antonino Ansalone, who claims that jousting in time of peace is 'an image of war' and who provides a meticulous account of lance technique, shudders at the old *campo aperto* which, he says,

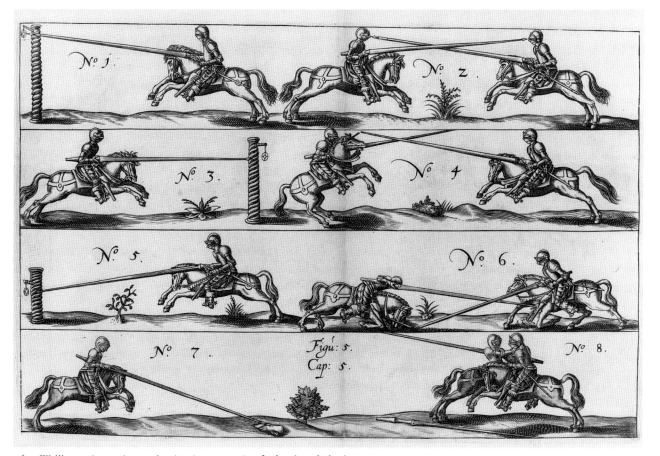

165. Wallhausen's running at the ring in preparation for battle. 1616, plate 5.

originated in Poland and used to be a bloody brawl run with sharp lances. The Polish war-riors were not interested in jousting as entertainment, exercise, or even as a spur to courage, but simply as an excuse to shed blood and lose their lives, 'without reason'. However, in his own more enlightened time, the *campo aperto* is fought with blunted lances or with pistols charged with powder but not lead, 'as a loving entertainment' (*per trattenimento amorevole*); and he even suggests that – in order to avoid the extremes of a collision on one hand or too wide running on the other – it had become customary to mark out the lists with yellow or red sand to serve the same function as tilt and counterlists. Every precaution must be taken to make the spectacle pleasing and to avoid 'ill-omened or tragic perils'.[50]

Ansalone's powder-puff *cavaliere* inhabited a world far removed from the sordid realities of battle but, among his more serious military contemporaries, the wars which filled the closing decades of the sixteenth century and beyond engendered a growing awareness that it had become necessary to formulate new ideas both about cavalry tactics in general and lance technique in particular. Authors such as Melzo, Basta and Wallhausen thought hard about the realities of mounted warfare as it had evolved from the fifteenth to the seven-teenth centuries and, while still considering practice at the ring to be a valuable exercise, they had no time to waste on chivalric games (fig. 165). Earlier writers, working within a different context, had other priorities although, as we have seen, from Monte onwards a clear distinction was drawn between jousting on the battlefield and jousting in the lists,

249

and there is every reason to suppose that this distinction had always been comprehended by realistic warriors.

It is unfortunate, however, that most surviving fifteenth-century narrative sources on lance handling are concerned solely with jousting in the lists, and few writers attempt to treat combat analytically.[51] Many are no more informative on technical matters than are the crude inexactitudes of fiction such as Malory's *Le Morte D'Arthur*; and all suffer from the weaknesses endemic to eye-witness reporting. Two authors are, nevertheless, outstanding for their combination of observation, knowledge and linguistic precision: Olivier de la Marche, whose accounts of Burgundian feats of arms are regularly cited by historians of chivalry; and the less famous, but even more perceptive, Guillaume Leseur who describes several mid-fifteenth-century tournaments in France and Spain where his hero, Gaston de Foix, had competed. From their work, and from corroborative details supplied by lesser reporters, it is possible to confirm, in jousting practice, the basic elements of good and bad lance technique as described by theorists. There are frequent references to carrying the lance upright with the butt resting on the right thigh or in its little leather pouch; placing the lance cleanly in the rest; pointing it across the left shoulder of the horse; and lowering it smoothly during the charge. The physical strenuousness of much early jousting (particularly when undertaken *a campo aperto*) is also well conveyed – with heavy damage regularly done to arms and armour, unhorsing, serious wounding, and occasionally the slaying of knights and horses. Even at the tilt, fatalities and bad injuries are recorded, though such accidents were always rare and became even rarer as the exercise degenerated into a ceremonial breaking of fragile lances. The fashion, and the danger, of using lances beyond one's strength is recorded, as are such habits as empty vaunting with hollow staves, the trick of loosening the visor, and the skill with which some knights could anticipate a blow, even from a mounted lancer, and counter it. The need to provide lances of equal length is a regular concern in the organization of tournaments; while the result of jousting with lances of unequal length is strikingly illustrated by the failure of such an expert as Jacques de Lalaing when his opponent managed to ride against him with a few extra inches of lance up his sleeve.[52]

The importance of properly fixing the lance tip, which had been stressed by Quixada, is attested by jousts in which, despite the fact that the contestants consistently hit each other, the *rochets* did not bite and the lances 'slid' without breaking. Furthermore, the fact that such sliding occurred much more frequently at some tournaments than at others suggests that the quality of the lance-makers varied, or that faulty batches of staves with poorly fitted heads had been supplied. This was an especially troublesome feature in 1455 at the Barcelona tournament where Leseur notes it several times including one particular 'very fine attaint on the gardbrace' struck by Gaston de Foix who, none the less, failed to score 'because his lance slid' without breaking.

Not only was quality control uncertain, but there was also a wide gulf between expert and inexpert jousters and, judging from the number of complete misses recorded for some encounters, the latter often constituted a majority. On the other hand, references to consistent accuracy on the part of certain individuals are sufficiently common to suggest that the exercise could be managed adroitly and that success ultimately did depend more on judgement than on luck. For example, at a joust at Chalons in 1445, one particular knight who ran against Gaston de Foix is described as being not at all a powerful man, 'but a fine rider, skilled man at arms, and very good jouster'. A little earlier in the same year, out of twelve courses run at Nancy in 1445, Jacques de Luxembourg and Monsieur de Janly both broke eight lances; Monsieur de Lochac and Pregent de Coctivi both scored nine; Jacques de Lalaing ten; and Gaston de Foix eleven. But it must be admitted that, at the same tournament, two knights only managed to break six of their twelve lances, while the performance of another who ran twelve courses is passed over without score or comment – a clear implication of incompetence.

Despite the acknowledged skill of some jousters, the extent to which a knight depended upon the quality of his mount is evident from allusions to the way in which horses spoilt contests by swerving, flinching from the encounter, or running wide. Leseur, in particular, has an eye for horseflesh and horsemanship and sometimes pauses to describe the appearance and characteristics of an animal which strikes him as unusually worthy; to dwell on some virtuoso feat of riding; or to remark on the easy posture of his hero in the saddle. He notes the advantage to be gained from ensuring that a steed is adequately prepared before running a course, as when 'my said Monsieur de Foix had his courser already warmed up (*eschauffé*), and he started off more promptly and boldly than on the other occasions'. He is also very observant of the marks left by the impact of the lance head on armour. Sometimes these marks are 'very apparent': even, on one occasion, to the extent that 'the three points of the rochet showed there'. Like the authors of the jousting treatises, Leseur stresses the role played by the knights' seconds especially when warriors were so severely thwacked that they would have been unhorsed had not their attendants rallied round and hastily propped them up in their saddles. Yet, for all their vigilance, there were occasions when both horse and man were knocked to the ground 'all in one heap', beyond the aid of anyone – the sort of thing graphically depicted in the Emperor Maximilian I's tournament book, *Freydal*, where we see knights, steeds and splintered lances crashing down in a confusion of ruins, while attendants dash around vainly trying to put things in order.

Above all else, Guillaume Leseur is noteworthy for preserving what is, perhaps, the most extraordinary episode in the history of jousting and one which finds no place in the chivalric textbooks. This was the feat accomplished by Gaston de Foix in 1445 at Nancy where he had been enjoying himself in the lists; knocking his opponents about; bending their backbones with his buffets (*il luy plier l'echine*); and generally performing wonders. His last course was against a fine jouster and rider, Philippe de Lenoncourt, whose headpiece had an unusually wide sight. Gaston's lance unerringly penetrated this but, miraculously missing Lenoncourt's face, went up into the crown of the helm and lifted the luckless knight clean out of his saddle and over the horse's crupper – leaving him suspended in mid-air. In the entire annals of the joust there is no stranger vision than that of Gaston de Foix riding about the lists with an armoured knight dangling from the end of his lance like a piece of washing. It is an evocation of astonishing physical strength coupled with deadly accuracy. Carrying away a ring with the tip of one's lance was to become a regular chivalric game. But this is the only instance of picking up a whole knight. It is not surprising to learn that Lenoncourt was so bemused that 'he did not know whether he was in heaven or earth'; and it was thought, when the attendants carried him back to his pavilion, that he was dead. However, after large quantities of restorative rose-water and vinegar had been thrown into his face, his heart revived although, the chronicler adds laconically, he jousted no more that day. The extraordinary thing, apart from the incident itself, is that Lenoncourt survived. Yet he was back in the lists less than two years later.[53] Neither his nerve nor his body had been irretrievably broken.

Lenoncourt's unsettling experience reminds us that exercises such as tilting, running at large, running at the ring and other jousts of peace all required that the lance should be

166. Lancer v. foot soldier and other personal combat techniques. Wallhausen. 1616, plate 9.

aimed high. Moreover, the assumption made in most treatises on the use of the heavy lance (certainly all those written in the sixteenth century) is that the mounted warrior would be engaging another mounted warrior behaving in exactly the same way as himself: which was precisely what happened in the lists. On the battlefield, however, the horseman would just as likely be engaging infantry and, in such cases, he would be aiming his lance low (fig. 166). A question therefore arises. Of what use were the techniques described by the authors I have been discussing? They regularly claimed that they were valuable preparation for war and would have agreed with Massario Malatesta that 'every sort of joust and combat has as its end real fighting'.[54] Yet it is impossible to resist the conclusion that the principal value of the skills which knights might acquire from lance play within the lists, resided precisely there – within the lists.[55] But if jousting merely trained knights for their next joust, what, we must now ask, did tourneying accomplish?

IX

Mounted combat (2): cut, thrust, and smash

TOWARDS THE END of the *Doctrina del arte de la cavallería* Quixada de Reayo has a short chapter dealing with mounted combat in time of war. The knight, he says, must begin battle with a lance charge, aiming at the opposing horse's belly. Then, having broken his lance, he must take the *estoque* (that is his thrusting sword), 'secured on the front saddle-tree on the left hand side', and deliver blows to the sight of the opponent's helm and to the weak points of his armour such as the belly and armpits. Next, he must take up the *espada de armas* (that is the sword of arms, for both cut and thrust), fastened around his waist on the left side, and fight on until that, too, is broken whereupon he must seize the hammer fastened to a clip on his belt on the right side and continue battle with that. Finally, when even the hammer has been lost, he must reach behind and draw the dagger carried at his shoulder; and now it will be necessary to grapple with the adversary, trying so to twist his head that he is forced to surrender. And as for killing his horse? Well, says Quixada, there are those who believe that this is an acceptable practice, and he agrees that 'anything is permissible which is to the disadvantage of your opponent'.[1]

Quixada's succinct summary gives a clear idea not only of what must often have taken place on the field of battle but (apart from deliberate attacks on the horse) also within the lists during the tourney or mock combat fought between mounted knights either one against one or in groups. The lance charge would have been succeeded by fighting with swords and other short weapons, such as mace or club, all of which the mounted warrior would be expected to use effectively (figs 167–8). But to what extent could this kind of hand-to-hand combat on horseback ever be subject to systematic analysis? Quixada himself says nothing other than that running with lances 'has to be done on the left hand side, and sword blows have to be done on the right hand side'. His contemporary, Camillo Agrippa, the systematizing mathematician, provided one uninformative illustration of mounted fencing but deliberately avoided discussion of what was obviously an uncertain art. He excused himself on the grounds of his own inadequate skill but it is clear that Agrippa's real reason was that he considered the subject unsuitable for scientific speculation; and the general reticence of most other renaissance masters suggests that they shared this view.[2]

The reasons are not hard to find. Nearly three hundred years later, in an age of almost mystical belief in the efficacy of regular and systematic military drill, René-Julien Chatelain was to declare that, although the principles of fencing on foot could be applied to the handling of the sabre on horseback, not only did this require a great deal of practice but a horse's movements obliged its rider to alter his blows and parries. 'It would be absurd', says

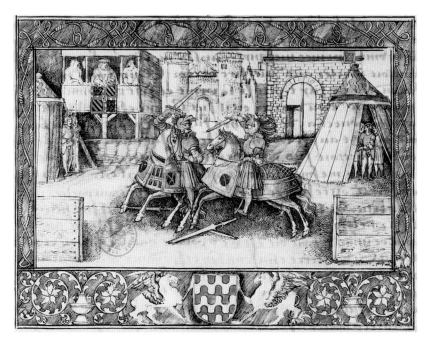

167. A tourney, one against one. Bibliothèque Nationale, Paris. MS. Fr. 20,362, fol. 123.

168. A fourteenth-century melée. Note the two knights using a two-handed grip on their swords. Bibliothèque Nationale, Paris, MS. Fr. 343, fol. 4v.

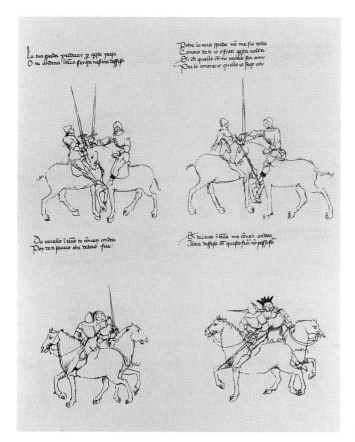

La tua spada perderay p questa presa
O tu andera i tera sença nesuna deffesa

Debe la mia spada nõ me sia tolta
Contra teti io ofato questa uolta
Si ch quello tõ tu uululi far amy
Per lo contrario quello io fazo ati

Da cauallo i tera te conuen andau
Poy te ti fauero che releuo fira

Si del nuto i tera me conuen andau
Altra deffesa di questo fezi nõ poffo fa

169. Mounted wrestling in Fiore. *c.* 1410, fol. 32v.

Chatelain, 'to establish practical rules and principles of fencing in this case.' All the caval-ryman could do was to familiarize himself with his arms and be secure on horseback.[3] This had been, and was to remain, the standard view on mounted sword combat. In the first place, hand-to-hand fighting between mounted warriors inevitably depended more on horsemanship and physical address than on skill with the sword. When, in 1897, towards the end of the long history of cavalry combat, Alessandri and André introduced their manual for sabre fencing on horseback, they began by acknowledging that the principal require-ment for success was control of the horse: 'One can even say that a good horseman, though a poor fencer, would have the advantage over an adversary who was a good fencer but a mediocre horseman'. The authors did stress that a horseman who knew how to handle his sabre would have 'more assurance, more self-confidence, more of the military bearing'.[4] But the impression remains that mounted fencing had more to do with horsemanship than with swordsmanship. It was also unpredictable in that the outcome could be influenced deci-sively by the quality of the mount itself and by an accident such as stumbling – a nega-tion of the fighter's own strength and skill which Monte had so greatly deplored that he even declared that 'no man powerful in the disposition of his limbs ought to fight with another mounted man in single combat, for they are put at the favour of horses or brute animals'.[5] Finally, as a martial activity, mounted sword fighting was severely circumscribed because blows could only be delivered effectively on the swordsman's right-hand side and, as a matter of fact, this was the one type of fencing where being left-handed would have been a positive advantage.

Yet, despite the obvious difficulties, a few medieval and renaissance masters did make sporadic attempts to reduce the activity to some sort of order. In the fourteenth and early fifteenth centuries, Liechtenauer in Germany and Fiore de' Liberi in Italy devoted some space to the use of both sword and light thrusting lance for warriors on horseback. They even paid attention to the awkward and strenuous art of wrestling while seated firmly in one's saddle, and had anticipated the kind of head twisting recommended by Quixada (fig. 169). Around the middle of the fifteenth century, the Jewish master Lew wrote a treatise on mounted sword fighting, and Talhoffer provided an illustrated treatment of the same subject.[6] There are several crude drawings of such combat in the 1459 manuscript of the latter's *Fechtbuch*, while the more sophisticated manuscript of 1467 includes twenty relevant pictures: ten of them showing fencing, four wrestling, two a contest between lance and sword, and four an encounter between lance and crossbow. One odd feature of these illustrations is that, unlike Fiore's warriors, none of the combatants wears armour.[7] In the main, Talhoffer's illustrations, like those of his predecessors, show the horsemen delivering what appear to be cutting strokes, although there is at least one clear thrust to an opponent's face.[8]

It must be admitted, however, that beyond the most rudimentary captions even Talhoffer offers no technical exposition of the various postures; and, as was the case with jousting, the first serious attempt to analyse the specific nature of mounted fencing was in the treatise on horsemanship by Duarte, King of Portugal, who devoted a chapter to the handling of the sword in a tourney.[9] Duarte identifies four ways to strike with a sword when on horseback – cut, reverse, downward blow, and thrust – but considers that, of these, the first two are the best for any rider faced by another mounted opponent. He also recommends utilizing the impetus provided by the horses' movement.

> To give a forceful cut it must be made as the horse approaches and with the body and the arm acting together. I find this very useful in the tourney, because if one strikes when at a standstill and with the arm alone the blow is comparatively weak, whereas if the horse is moving and the body and arm act together it is far stronger. This is my advice to whoever wishes to deliver forceful blows in a tourney: strike almost always on the approach, standing firmly on the legs, the body and arm moving freely, the hand holding the sword tightly, and the blow not just a sideways cut nor straight downwards, but obliquely from high to low.

In a tourney where many knights are engaged it is important, says Duarte, to avoid making short turns and to resist the temptation of following some preconceived plan. In other words, the knight must seize whatever opportunity presents itself, striking wherever advantageous, and, when he has beaten one opponent, 'he must go on to another without bothering to turn until he has gone through the whole field, seeking the places of the most important onlookers'. This method, says Duarte, affords the knight several advantages: he will be more readily observed by the onlookers 'because he is moving around in all parts of the field'; his blows will be stronger because he strikes as he pleases; and neither he nor his horse will be wearied by unnecessary running and turning. 'Because the blows are given at intervals, the arm does not get tired, which is the opposite of what happens to some in a tourney, who suffer by the comings and turnings of the horse, since for every advantage to be gained they must improve their position and, throughout, they and their horses have to work very hard.' Duarte also warns against the example of those who 'stand still to strike' – in other words those who fail to use the horse's momentum – a practice which soon tires the arm and weakens the blow. On the other hand, the reverse stroke is made with the

170. Wallhausen's progression from vaulting horse to real horse. 1616, plate 1.

action of the arm alone, while the downward stroke is used principally against men on foot or animals, and rarely against another mounted adversary. It is necessary, adds Duarte, that when using the downward stroke the knight must be careful not to draw the sword towards himself because he might then easily strike his own foot or horse. The correct technique is to hold the sword firmly and put the whole weight of one's body into the stroke. Finally, Duarte reminds the aspiring warrior that practice is the principal foundation of learning the martial arts, and that, once the proper methods have been thoroughly learnt, they will never be forgotten. Exercises must, of course, be appropriate; and a knight wishing to have a good arm for fencing and for lance play should avoid ball games and especially anything requiring him to throw either very heavy or very light objects, because the essential military skills may easily be lost for others of little importance. Furthermore, inspired by Vegetius, Duarte particularly recommends the Roman custom whereby horsemen not only kept wooden horses in their homes to ensure that they were constantly attuned to the feel of being armed and mounted, but also regularly practised jumping up into their saddles while fully armed so that they did not feel encumbered even when their horse was of great size – a practice still warmly recommended for cavalrymen by Wallhausen in the early seventeenth century (fig. 170).

Duarte's reference to the advantage gained by a knight who constantly moves about – that he will be 'more seen' – reminds us that the tourney was primarily a court spectacle

257

and merely an image of battle in which, like Castiglione's courtier, the knight's principal purpose is to 'draw unto him the eyes of the lookers on as the Adamant stone doth yron'.[10] Nevertheless, throughout his *Ensinança*, Duarte's principal concern was with the practicalities of horsemanship and therefore, whenever appropriate, with the practicalities of mounted combat. By contrast, René d'Anjou, another fifteenth-century prince with literary pretensions, was concerned solely with the preliminaries and ceremonial of tourneying, so that his practical remarks never extend beyond a description of the relevant armour and weaponry, along with the information that neither thrusts nor reverse blows are to be allowed. Such arbitrary limitations would mean that an already rudimentary style of fencing would have been reduced to mere chopping; and, as a matter of fact, if the illustration of a tourney, provided by René, approximates to his practice, this would have been the only stroke possible. The crush of combatants shown in this mêlée would not only have precluded all other blows but it would also have made it impossible to move about in the way described by Duarte. Whatever its merits as a formulary of tournament etiquette and equipment – and in this last respect René's achievement is admirable – the *Livre des tournois* would never have achieved the reputation it has enjoyed among historians were it not for the handsome, oft-reproduced, and largely useless, pictures of combat which enhance its several manuscript manifestations.[11]

Reference to the cramped tourneying depicted in René's treatise raises another technical issue which may conveniently be discussed here. There is scattered evidence suggesting that mounted knights would sometimes use half-sword techniques, that is with both hands on the weapon, to deliver their blows – which was a common enough practice when wielding two-hand swords, bastard swords, or staff weapons. For knights to do this when fighting on horseback is another matter.[12] Given a sufficiently high saddle, and the sort of coagulated mass of men and horses shown in René's *Livre des tournois*, such strokes might be feasible: although no one in René's tourney is attempting them. It is, however, difficult to see that, in any other circumstances, half-sword techniques or, indeed, any two-handed technique would have been effective on horseback. Later writers on mounted fencing insist that control of the reins was of paramount importance and stress that the most dangerous misfortune which could befall a horseman was to have his reins cut by an opponent, because the resulting lack of control meant almost certain death.[13] The control a knight might exercise through his knees and thighs, while engaging in a strenuous combat on the battlefield, would have been negligible; and the difficulty of striking a moving target effectively, using the two-handed grip (with its curtailed reach) while oneself moving about on a horse left largely to its own devices, is self-evident. These things are not impossible and are illustrated in some seemingly authoritative combat manuals – even for handling the lance.[14] Pietro Monte, too, considered the technique seriously when discussing the tourney: and he is an authority to whom one must pay heed. But, beyond the confines of the lists, the use of both hands on the sword seems a fatally flawed technique. (See fig. 168.)

SOME RENAISSANCE AUTHORITIES

Monte's treatment of tourneying and mounted fencing is more concerned with horsemanship and equipment than with weapon handling, but what he has to say about fencing is especially interesting because he is one of the few masters who believed that there was a close relationship between mounted and unmounted swordsmanship and who applied a similar terminology to both. In his view, when it comes to using the sword or *stoccum* on horseback, we should deliver most blows and parries 'exactly as we are accustomed to use on foot'; and, as in his system of fencing, he strongly recommends the use of feints, 'signalling a blow to one side but delivering it to the other'.[15] He repeatedly stresses the advantage of keeping one's horse's head directed towards the opponent and warns against charging too quickly. The sword hand should rest on the front saddle-bow, and the point should always 'look at the adversary'. There are some men who hold their sword firmly above the saddle-bow and then spur their horse fiercely to the attack: 'but this is worth nothing to the wise', because their weapon is easily diverted and we may hit them in the face or anywhere else we may wish.[16]

In addition to the use of the sword, Monte discusses fighting with mace or club and – as a practical belt-and-braces fighter – he recommends carrying two 'so that if we should lose one, the other remains'.[17] The mace should be four palms in length; attached to the arm by a thong so that it does not fly out of the hand when striking rapidly; have a handle sufficient to accommodate both hands in order to deliver two-handed blows which he considers to be much stronger than single-handed; and equipped with a hook (analogous to the *bec de faucon*) in order to grasp an opponent by the neck and drag him from his horse. Monte's enthusiasm for a two-handed attack while on horseback is attested by his awareness of the problem this poses with regard to control of the horse; and he advises that the reins should be attached to one arm with 'something fine and long', so that they cannot fall to the ground over the horse's head. He also has something to say about circumstances in which it would be improper to wound or kill an opponent's horse – presumably in a tourney – and advises that it is still possible to strike the animal on its head with the pommel of a dagger, 'since in this way it cannot be said that the horse would be wounded, and it greatly assists us'.[18] This unchivalric quibble is typical of his recognition that the most effective way to neutralize a rider is to destroy his horse – an attitude also expressed in his discussion of actions appropriate to the relative strength of our mounts. With a horse stronger than the opponent's, we should be able to force him backwards and then, using a *stoccum firmum* which neither bends nor breaks, we may thrust into the rider's throat or under his armpits. Certainly we should be able to knock him out of his saddle. If, on the other hand, we see that his horse is the stronger, then it must be the prime target of our blows and we may club it over the brain and, 'in this fashion if the club is good, and we strike with two hands, the horse will fall'; and he adds, succinctly, 'for when we can kill the horse, it matters little that it is greater than ours'.[19] In fact, says Monte, distilling the essence of life-and-death mounted combat, it is always easy to kill an opponent's horse – and especially so in lance combats when only fools waste time trying to hit their man.

Apart from Quixada's passing reference and Agrippa's few words of exculpation, there is no further discussion of mounted fencing until 1582 when the Spanish master, Jerónimo Carranza, summarized the difficulties attendant upon the art.[20] Carranza was obsessed with the mathematics of fencing and maintained that 'the positions of the arm have their mean and their extremes, just as do the angles and profiles of the body and the positions of the feet'. The same holds true when wielding the sword on horseback although, in that case, it is difficult 'to make the movements of the horse's feet commensurate with the movements of the arm and of the sword'. This problem occurs most obviously when spurring the horse to the attack and Carranza, speaking particularly of the cut, recommends moving the arm prior to urging the horse forward. He further explains that there are three ways of wielding a sword on horseback, and these are quite different from those used on foot because two *motores* (that is the horse and its rider) are involved in each movement. The first posture is to be adopted when the horse is without defensive armour. In such a case, in order both to prevent your adversary from wounding your mount and to block his movements, you should place the point of your sword towards the horse's bit. From this position you can deal easily with all eventualities by raising yourself in the stirrups and pulling slightly on the rein on the left side. The second posture is with the tip of the sword against the right ear of the horse: and here Carranza has a word of praise for the precepts of 'Ludovico Italiano' – an author later referred to by Pacheco de Narváez, Carranza's disciple, but whom I cannot identify.[21] This second way of holding the sword is also suitable when the horse has neck armour because one can parry an adversary's blows and defend the body by turning the horse as occasion demands. The third posture, with sword directed across the horse's neck, also facilitates the blocking of attacks. 'All these postures', says Carranza, 'have their mean of proportion whereby the feints of *la gineta* and *la brida* can be carried out', and he adds that the mean is the 'postura de filo', straight from the arm, while the extremes are with the 'nails upwards and nails downwards' – that is with the hand in supination or pronation.[22]

Although Carranza's mathematical swordsmanship greatly influenced the Bolognese soldier, Federico Ghisliero, the latter did not follow the Spanish master when, in 1587, he devoted a few pages to the subject of mounted fencing.[23] Seeking, as was his habit, to reduce the essentially irreducible to geometrical principles, he informed the swordsman that, when on horseback, it is necessary to gain the 'linea retta', in exactly the same way as when fencing on foot except that the horse may simply be regarded as serving the function of the knight's legs. Figuratively, of course, this may be true but Ghisliero takes no account of the comparatively imprecise control the mounted fencer exercises over these surrogate limbs. Many years later, even Pacheco de Narváez – whose devotion to mathematics quite eclipsed Ghisliero's – jeered at those masters who suggested that the fencer on horseback was as much a master of his own movements as was the fencer on foot. But Ghisliero, unimpeded by such doubt, observes that the horse has a long body, 'formed like a line'. Thus, when it moves sideways, if one extremity is kept stationary, the other extremity describes a circle; and, just as in fencing, when a swordsman gains the 'straight line' by gaining the diameter of the circle, so the same applies on horseback. It is essential that the opponent be approached head on. In such a case, should he linger, then our purpose is served because we can more easily hold the centre with our horse – 'forming a much smaller circumference with our horse than he can with his', and always taking care to keep in the straight line. As is usual with Ghisliero, the correct posture is explained both in words and by an illustration. The sword must be held with the fist in front of the saddle and slanting crossways so that the point is over the horse's left ear, ready for both parrying and for striking. Only two blows are possible on horseback: that is *una punta di sotto* along the length of the horse's neck; and the *riverso* by the same route. All this is illustrated by the accompanying figure in which a line indicates the posture, and a sword the actual blow (fig. 171).

Ghisliero was a noted soldier, but his treatment of mounted fencing, despite its geometrical pretension, is of slight practical value. Certainly it is inferior to the work of two other contemporary Italian military men, Alessandro Massario Malatesta and Giorgio Basta. Massario's *Compendio dell'heroica arte di cavalleria* first appeared in a poorly printed edition at Venice in 1600 and was reissued in a more handsome, but error-strewn version, at Danzig in 1610. The greater part of the book is concerned with advice on horses and riding equipment, but there are some useful observations on hand-to-hand fighting on horseback,

171. Mounted fencing according to Ghisliero. 1587, p. 178.

dealing both with arms and armour and with the technique of single combat.[24] Massario points out that certain weapons, such as the axe, mace and hammer, were no longer much used: but he still has something to say about them. The mace should never be very long and must be heavy and 'comfortable in the hand', and its head may be round, square, or tripartite with points and facets. During combat, this kind of weapon should not be gripped too tightly because that would 'torture the arm and weaken the blow', and forceful down-ward blows are generally the most effective. Axes should be handled similarly, and Massario suggests that those made in the 'fashion of Poland' are the best in that they are well balanced with a quadrate metal spike on one side, which can inflict great damage on armour. The hammer, which has a longer spike, is similarly effective against armour but, as Massario points out, both axes and hammers are used more in personal duels than in other types of fighting because they are neither very handy for striking blows nor easy to retrieve once a blow has been delivered.

With regard to the use of the sword, Massario is one of the few renaissance masters apart from Monte to apply at least some technical fencing terms to mounted combat. The sword, he says, should be suitable for carrying at one's side, solid, two edged, pointed, and neither long nor short, but made after the fashion of the *stocco*. The scabbard should be long, firm and wide so that, when the knight draws the sword with his right hand, he can make it clear his left (that is the bridle) hand. Were the knight to draw his sword by passing his right hand under the bridle hand, he might injure himself or even cut through the reins. Single combat fought without defensive armour is extremely dangerous – truly a *combatti-mento disperato* – and requires great caution and cunning. At the beginning of an encounter you should first try to dodge the opponent in order to gain the advantage; but, if this cannot be done, then you should take your opponent on the outside line, passing your sword over his. Thus, whether he tries a thrust from below (*stoccata*) or from above (*imbroccata*) you may, with a turn of the hand, dash his sword aside and offer your own point to his side or breast: remembering, at the same time, to bend your body slightly at the waist towards the left to avoid his blow. Even if he comes at you with his arm in a very high position (*alto alto*) it is still possible to push his sword to the outside line by turning your hand in that direction, meeting the foible of his blade with your own forte. You may, by twisting the hand, simultaneously also strike at his face with the edge of your sword or cut his arm with a *riverso*, 'as did Monsieur di Fosseùs against Monsieur Sangiusto in the duel fought by them before the gates of Saint Denis; in the which duel Sangiusto was killed'. This, and other circumstantial references to individual combats, suggests the care with which Massario kept abreast of his subject. Fossé and Saint Just fought in Paris in 1593, and according to Vulson de la Colombière, who later described the contest, the latter did indeed ride at his opponent with sword held high and was so badly cut on the arm by Fossé's counter that he dropped his weapon and was then run through the body. Vulson's account, incidentally, gives substance to the constant emphasis on the choice of horse: for he points out that Saint Just's mount had been trained solely for the massed fighting of the battlefield and did not respond correctly in single combat.[25]

The next problem considered by Massario is what to do when an opponent rides at you with his sword held low. The correct counter is to use a similar low guard, parrying the enemy's point on the inside line and offering your own point to his body. If, however, he comes with a high position you must show him your point, keeping your own hand and arm high, sweep his blow aside, and make him dash himself against the point of your sword with his own impetus: 'the which is easily done if you have a secure and accommodating horse under you'. You may also deliver a strong *riverso* at his head, adding power to your stroke by simultaneously turning your horse to the right.

Sententiously, Massario remarks that just as mounted combats have different ends so they are waged in different ways, but always one must remember that such encounters depend on two virtues: 'in the courage of the knight, and in the perfection of the horse'. The mount should always be of good stock and strong, with a good physique and stature; and, if it must exceed in one direction, then a tall horse is better than a low one. This has been found by examples and by continuous testing. A good effect and usefulness are found in tall horses of a good physique, well proportioned, and which have vigour, discipline and obedience – 'the five perfections' necessary for chivalric feats.

Unlike Massario, Giorgio Basta was concerned with cavalry technique solely as it could be applied on the field of battle, and he advised the warrior, whether armed with lance or sword, to aim for the left shoulder of his opponent's horse. His account of mounted swordsmanship is contained in a general discussion of the lancer who, after his lance is lost or broken, will need to resort to the sword.[26] The blade, Basta explains, should be neither too wide nor too narrow, and in length it should be 'a little less than the measure of Spain', with the point 'more round than otherwise' to facilitate its passage through defensive armour.[27] It should be carried tied to the thigh with a strap so that it does not dance about when at a gallop, nor jump from its scabbard, nor move backwards when the hand is put to it. Basta has no time for fancy sword play on horseback because of the distance involved. Indeed, he rejects any attempt at using arm movement, 'as one does when on foot', and recommends instead holding the arm bent, with the sword pushed forward from the thumb

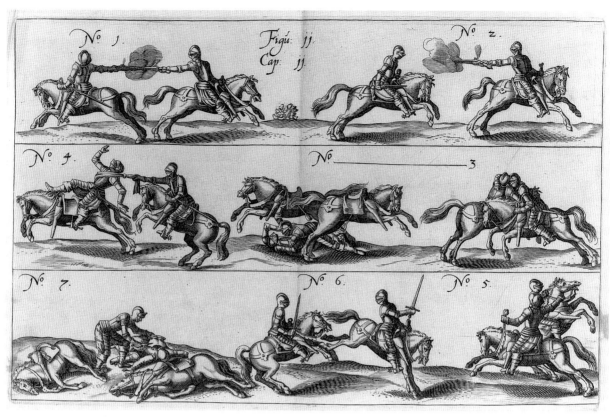

172. A wide range of combat on and off the horse as shown by Wallhausen. 1616, plate 11.

173. A further display by Wallhausen. 1616, plate 6.

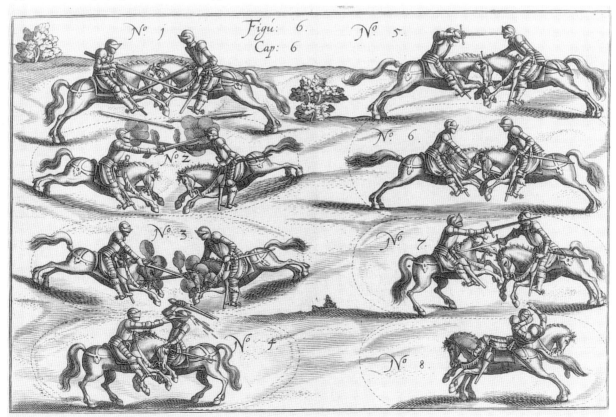

174. Some desperate personal conflicts in Wallhausen. 1616, plate 8.

– 'the point accompanied with the eye' – and then galloping against the foe. For Basta (as for Duarte two centuries earlier and military authorities two centuries later) the important thing was to utilize the momentum of one's mount. He also has one curiously circumstantial piece of advice for the cavalryman intent on striking an opposing horse. It is important, he says, to inflict a wound so deep that the blood cannot issue forth, and this will cause the horse to remain completely immobile – a method taught by Basta's father, Captain Demetrio, to his troops in the Piedmontese wars where they did enormous damage to the opposing cavalry.[28] Basta's work proved popular and not only was it reprinted in Italy, but it was also translated both into Spanish and French. This last version was by Jean Theodore de Bry who also provided a number of engravings to clarify the text. These pictorial aids are not without blemish, and the illustration of mounted fencing – showing the knights reaching awkwardly across the left side of their horses – is particularly unhelpful. Wallhausen, who often disagrees with Basta, shows a good deal more mounted fencing – some of it similarly awkward, some of it more likely to prove effective, and all of it realistically brutal (figs 172–4).[29]

The idea of using the horse's impetus to give force to the sword was similarly stressed by Giovanni Battista Gaiani, a master with Savoyard affiliations but otherwise obscure. In his *Arte di maneggiar la spada* (1619) he advises that the best position for both attack and defence is for the mounted swordsman to rest his sword upon his right thigh with the point held high and directly over his horse's left ear.[30] The principal requisites for victory are to gain the enemy's rear, to prevent him from similarly outmanoeuvring you, to gain his left-hand side, and to be ready to rein the horse quickly for every movement – techniques which

175. Gaining the enemy's crupper, illustrated in Schmidt's cavalry manual. 1797, plate 7.

176. The same manoeuvre but carried out more effectively by approaching the enemy's left side and forcing him to fight across his own horse. Schmidt, 1797, plate 8.

remained standard throughout the history of mounted fencing (figs 175–6). A knight must combine *bravura e la prudenza* – the first to dismay his enemy, and the second to take advantage of so doing – and an opponent must, therefore, be approached at an easy gallop, for it is difficult to handle the sword if one's approach is too *furioso*. A blow from a knight who comes up too fast is easily avoided, while it is equally simple to hit him because his disorderliness will prevent his parrying effectively. Significantly, Gaiani has few observations on sword play itself although, in answer to a doubt as to the efficacy of a cut against an opponent in armour, he does argue that, despite such protection, a knight can be badly wounded – for the impetus provided by the horse's movement adds force to one's blows which can slice off a pauldron or vambrace, or make an opponent lose control of his bridle. Like Duarte, so long before, Gaiani has little confidence in the thrust on horseback; and, while conceding that the point may sometimes be used, he explicitly dismisses it as less reliable than the cut, partly because of the horse's movement and partly because one's sight is frequently obscured.[31]

Indeed, mastery of the sword is clearly secondary to mastery of the horse. Even before mounting, the rider must ensure that every part of his horse's furniture is secure – 'because this is the responsibility of the knight rather than of the stableman' – and Gaiani, stressing the importance of delicate control of the bridle, warns against reliance on spurs, stirrups, legs or spoken command. On no account must the horse be vexed, because flight or unruliness could cost the knight his life. However, if compelled to flee the battlefield, the knight must remember three things: as far as possible to prevent his horse from getting out of breath; to keep any ditch or other obstacle to his left, so that a pursuing enemy is forced to overtake on the right; and to take full advantage of the opportunity presented should that pursuer overrun through ignorance or misjudgement and thereby expose his flank.

To expose one's flank while fencing on horseback was widely regarded as an effective way to commit suicide, and the point was made very forcefully shortly after Gaiani's treatise, when the French riding master, Pierre de la Noue, published a treatise covering a wide range of equestrian issues both in peace and in war, including a chapter on the personal duel fought on horseback with swords.[32] If, says La Noue, you are compelled to fight in such an affair of honour then it is well to remember that, since horses vary from time to time in their humour or condition, it is useful to have two or three mounts from which to choose so that, on the day, you may select the calmest and most obedient to your hand. Once mounted and at the place appointed, you must especially beware of two strokes – the one directed at your horse's nose, and the other intended to cut your reins. These blows are so dangerous that, if successful, they bring certain death. The horse's nose is extremely sensitive and, once injured there, the animal is no longer fit for action. Equally, trying to manage a horse without reins is like a ship's pilot trying to govern a vessel at sea without a rudder. To prevent such disasters a knight can depend solely upon his own judgement, experience and skill. The enemy's intention must be judged by the actions both of his bridle hand and sword hand, which must be watched 'perpetuellement' in order to block his blows or to deliver your own when he is most exposed. La Noue is completely open-minded when considering the best fencing posture for a mounted knight. As far as he is concerned, when it comes to covering oneself with the sword, each fencer must choose whichever guard he thinks best for self-defence. Everyone 'in his own way is naturally inclined more to one than to another, and thus he is ill advised who, born for the *quarte*, is told to hold himself *en seconde* or *en tierce* or *en première*'. All that La Noue will say is that the knight must take care first to keep his bridle hand close to his horse's mane, so that his opponent cannot make him drop the reins, and second to help his horse accomplish the *demie-volte* immediately at the end of the *passade* to avoid 'the death blow' which must inevitably result were the enemy to gain his rear – 'which good knights know'.

Certainly, both Gaiani and La Noue were practical men of the sword, understood the dangers of mounted fencing, and warned against the mistakes which could lead to death. It is, however, unlikely that the enthusiastic Jesuit scribbler, Étienne Binet, would have seen much action or have had any practical experience when he included a short account of the 'Duel à cheval' in his *Essai des merveilles* (1621). Yet Binet, once damned as an author with 'more zeal and piety than talent',[33] had enough sense to see the difference between a real mounted duel fought *à outrance* and the *tournoy de courtoisie*. The former was a horrible, bloody affair; the latter 'nothing more than a princely revel'.

As practised at the later renaissance courts, the tourney seldom put a knight's life at risk. Indeed, the greatest danger which threatened him was to appear ridiculous in the eyes of an audience, as was made clear in 1623 when there appeared the most famous of all riding books, the *Maneige royal* by Antoine de Pluvinel, late riding master to Louis XIII.[34] Pluvinel largely ignores both war and duel. When jousting, the knight's principal opponent was the ring or quintain; while, with regard to fencing, combat is not mentioned, although Crispin van de Pass provides two inaccurate plates illustrating a tourney. Pluvinel's sole concern is with the techniques whereby a rider achieves grace and avoids affectation; and he despises those knights who 'provoke laughter through their bad posture and ridiculous gestures.[35] Such people 'would do better to stay at home than attempt what they do not understand'. The most important element of success is to have a horse which is strong, proportionate to the rider, and which can easily support the weight of armour. It must be patient and vigorous, responsive to every indication given by its rider, and not frightened by the sounds of trumpets, drums, or instruments of war. Without a horse possessing these requisites, the best and most adroit knight in the world would gain nothing but shame. The knight must have a certain liberty in his posture, but without the slightest affectation; must always be straight and 'bien placé' in the saddle; and must avoid extravagant gestures, shouting, or speaking to his horse. Pluvinel accepts that when riding without armour, *en pourpoint*, it is permitted to encourage the horse with the voice; while, in battle, the captain may address his company. But when the knight is participating in a course 'for pleasure' he must on no account speak either to his horse or to his opponent. His sole concern is to perform with grace and thereby earn the applause of the spectators, and the honour and glory due to those who carry themselves worthily.

In the *Maneige royal*, the actual combat is a severely restricted affair. The knights must take their places within the lists, some forty paces apart, their swords held in the posture already indicated by Pluvinel for holding the riding switch. At the sound of the trumpets, they dig their heels in and ride forward, dropping the bridle hand to three fingers above the saddle bow, raising the sword, and passing as close as possible to the adversary. *En passant* they must give a blow – not directly on top of the head for fear that, missing the man, they might wound the horse, but rather towards the left side of the face. Then, when each knight reaches the place whence his opponent started the course, they turn for the second encounter although, if one turns before the other, he must wait so that they can begin together. The action is repeated until the third and final course when, instead of passing, they circle about each other, giving sword blows until they have completed their *troisième volte*. They should thus be facing the direction from which they entered, whither they return *furieusement*. This is how knights 'must fight in great tourneys and triumphs in order that they may be esteemed' for, says Pluvinel, the blows in such encounters are so severe that anyone not adept at receiving them is likely to acquire shame rather than honour. In proof of this he cites the feats of Henri de Montmorency (1534–1614) who, during a tourney at the Bayonne festivities of 1565, knocked a prince over his horse's crupper, and at another festival in Paris knocked 'a lord of quality' (with a big reputation as a horseman) straight out of his saddle. The story may or may not be true: but, significantly, Pluvinel's 'proof' is nearly sixty years out of date.[36]

A valuable account of contemporary French training for the duel on horseback is given by Lord Herbert of Cherbury. Master and pupil, he says, were armed with a 'reasonable riding-rod in our hands, about the length of a sword'. The object was to turn with the right hand to the opponent's left side: 'and he that can do this handsomely, is sure to overcome his adversary, it being impossible to bring his sword about enough to defend himself or offend the assailant'. To get this advantage, 'which they call in French *gagner la crouppe*', it is crucial to be able to make a horse 'to go only sideways until his adversary be past him'. Lord Herbert recommends the works of La Broue and Pluvinel 'excellent masters in that art, of whom I must confess I learned much': although he adds that he learnt more from practical experience than from 'all their precepts'. The comment, while characteristically braggart, is nevertheless suggestive of the artificiality and limitations of the riding schools.[37]

A preoccupation with appearances, grace and the avoidance of affectation is likewise the salient feature of Antonino Ansalone's treatise, *Il cavaliere*, which is the summation of the process whereby the armoured knight was finally transmuted into a courtier. It includes a chapter on the tourney beginning with the assertion that the practice derived from the fifth of the games held in honour of Aeneas's late father.[38] This appeal to antiquity may be intended to add dignity to an activity which, for Ansalone and his contemporaries, had become nothing more than an entertainment in which knights could display skilful horsemanship. Their first concern is to have a totally obedient and responsive mount, and the whole game resides in knowing how to advance, stop and manoeuvre in order to gain the advantage. Ansalone insists, none the less, that the knight must know how to fence in order to gain on his adversary's sword on horseback just as he would on foot, and he issues three special injunctions: that, in the fury of arms, the knight should not dig his heels too forcefully into his horse; that his bridle should be held correctly three fingers above the saddle bow (which was also Pluvinel's recommendation); and that his sword hand should be in a suitable position both to avoid fatigue and be always ready to attack or defend. Full armour, including helm and shield, should be worn; and the sword should be wide, with a good edge, and three palms in length. The action begins with the knights simply trying to outmanoeuvre each other. When they get close enough they may aim blows at each other's heads, but all the time circling in order to gain a winning position which is achieved when one of them brings his horse's head up to the left flank of his opponent's mount. The entire point of this exercise depends on the dexterity of the rider and the agility of his horse, and if either of these is lacking then the action cannot be praiseworthy. Having started his chapter on the tourney with a reference to Virgil, Ansalone ends it with a stanza from Ariosto. Neither allusion has any practical relevance to the art of fencing on horseback, but they accord well both with the courtly tone of Ansalone's treatise (and its Castiglionesque insistence on literary as well as military adroitness), and with the balletic tourneying of his contemporaries.

LATER DISCUSSIONS OF MOUNTED FENCING

By the time that Ansalone published his treatise in 1629, the tourney was falling out of favour, even as a court spectacle, and there was no further detailed treatment. of this outmoded chivalric pastime. Fencing masters, who had rarely devoted much space to the uncertain techniques of mounted swordsmanship, now tended to avoid the subject altogether or merely repeated what had already been said – as when Antonio Alfieri, the obscure relative of a famous master, chose to write on mounted combat by shamelessly copying Gaiani verbatim, differing only in his greater readiness to accept the need to kill an opponent's horse.[39] More interesting was Philibert de la Touche who, in 1670, devoted a chapter to the subject in his *Les Vrays Principes de l'espée seule*. He, too, has little new to say. Indeed he is less analytical than Massario, Gaiani or La Noue: but the long silence of fencing masters gave him the impression that he was undertaking a novel task. He believed that – despite the fame of the French cavalry, and the nation's natural inclination towards mounted combat – it was still worthwhile to provide some precepts on the use of the sword on horseback. While excusing himself from saying anything about riding, La Touche could not suppress a passing regret for the horses of Naples which had formerly been used for war. Now, alas, they were neglected, partly through expense and partly because combatants no longer wore full armour. However, in his opinion, it remained vital to have a big, powerful horse which could break up a crowd, overthrow by its very weight an opponent's mount, and lend extra force to the downward cuts of its rider's sword. Not only should it be strong and courageous, fearing neither 'fire nor iron', it should also be readily manageable for stopping and turning, 'in order to gain the enemy's crupper or for some other intention'. La Touche recommended that the sword itself should have a 'revers' (by which he meant some sort of knuckle guard) to cover the hand, and that it should be attached to the arm by a strong ribbon – neither so loose that you run the risk of losing the weapon, nor so tight as to impede action. It should be held in La Touche's third guard: that is with the arm forward but slightly bent at the elbow and the blade pointing upwards at an angle of about thirty-three degrees. The point, he said, should be between the horse's ears; and the pommel should be beside the hand holding the reins, but a little lower in order to cover the reins and the horse's head. To deliver a stroke, La Touche advised that the enemy should be approached *au petit galop* because, if you go too fast, you cannot judge your opponent's intentions nor can you deceive him and seize the initiative. Rather like his predecessor Massario, La Touche made some attempt to apply his principles of foot fencing to mounted combat but acknowledged that, in the latter case, one's options were severely limited. This restriction was especially apparent in the mêlée where one had 'neither the time nor the freedom' of normal fencing and where adversaries almost always struck simultaneously. So, in the end, La Touche admitted that all one could do was 'to make a few feints before striking, to surprise the enemy, and to hit him either with point or edge'. This is no more illuminating than his suggestion that the three best ways to surprise an opponent are to attack him when he is 'otherwise occupied' during the mêlée; when you can manoeuvre round to his rear; or when you can gain an advantage of time by the speed of your horse. In general, though, La Touche recognizes that there is little opportunity for finesse in mass combat where confusion reigns, and his main advice in these circumstances is reminiscent of Duarte, more than three hundred years earlier:

> In the mêlée one must be aware of everything going on about you, in order to parry or strike to the right and to the left, and to make the sword come and go like a flash of lightning as opportunity and necessity arises without the slightest pause because, being always on the move, your enemies do not have the leisure to keep track of you, to engage you, nor to ward the effect of your blows, which are thereby of greater force and violence.[40]

La Touche was exceptional among fencing masters in that, while primarily concerned with swordsmanship in single combat on foot, he felt the urge to relate his skills to mounted combat in war. For the most part, however, during the seventeenth century mounted fencing was discussed by military writers who invariably repeated the strictly utilitarian precepts of the authoritative Wallhausen and Basta, adorned with perhaps a flourish or two as an assertion of independence. John Cruso is typical.[41] Cruso advises the cuirassier that, when he has fired both pistols and has no time to reload, his next resort is to a 'stiffe and sharp pointed' sword:

> Whereof the best manner of using is to place the pummell of it upon his right thigh, and so with his right hand to direct or raise the point to his mark, higher or lower as occasion serveth: either at the bellie of the adverse horse-man (about the pummell of the saddle) or at his arm pits, or his throat, where if it pierce not, (as it is very like it will not fail, by slipping under the casque) yet meeting with a stay in that part of the bodie, where a man is very weak, and having a sword of a very stiffe blade (as afore-said) it will doubtlesse unhorse him. Being past his enemie, he is to make a back-blow at him, aiming to cut the buckle of his pouldron, whereby he disarmeth one of his arms, &c. Basta highly commendeth the aiming at the enemies sight, and so (by raising the vizures of his casque with the point of the sword) to runne him into the head. But this seemeth not so likely to take effect as that of aiming at the throat; and sometimes (as some casques are made) it would be of no use.

To these suggestions, Cruso adds an important postscript: 'In these and the like exercises the Cuirassier is frequently and diligently to practise himself at some mark, which will render him fit for service when need shall require'. Regular training was obviously desirable and was carefully considered by Basta and Wallhausen in the early seventeenth century;

but it was not until the closing years of the eighteenth century that fencing masters themselves began to make more strenuous efforts to analyse the practice of mounted sword fighting. These authorities, writing in an age of comparative military uniformity, addressed themselves not to knights and courtiers but to cavalrymen on active service, and they believed in the value of regular drill and exercise as the way to improve a recruit's effectiveness. The idea was not in itself unsound, although the excessive stylization of technique could have adverse results, as was pointed out by some nineteenth-century military observers.[42]

Accompanying the demand for regular drill was a commensurate belief in the practical utility of drill books: and for this there was less justification, although the genre of the manual (with its concern to break up sword technique into a readily identifiable sequence of movements, each of which could be described, illustrated and practised *en masse*) itself contributed to the analysis of combat. Despite their misplaced optimism, these texts do have considerable historical value and, while the design of cavalry swords underwent several changes over the centuries, the principles underlying their use scarcely altered, so that this later material – and especially the illustrations which accompanied it – often sheds light on earlier techniques and on the difficulties faced by those few renaissance authors who had tried to articulate some sort of theory.[43]

X
Duels, brawls and battles

S IR THOMAS PARKYNS – philanthropist, student of Isaac Newton, admirer of Moxon's *Mechanical Powers*, and collector of stone coffins – published, in 1713, a treatise on the wrestling system of the 'Cornish Huggers'.[1] It was somewhat diffuse: but what Parkyns lacked in structural sense he made up for in the fervour with which he advocated widespread instruction in wrestling skills, 'in order the more effectually to animate the rising Generation of Bold *Britons*, in the Pursuit of those manly, and martial Delights, which will qualify them for the Defence of their glorious Constitution and Liberties'.[2] Parkyns hardly qualifies as a renaissance master, but his lofty allusions to the military relevance of his book and the part it would play in the defence of the realm were anticipated by those many predecessors who felt obliged to justify their activities on grounds other than, on the one hand, instructing disciples in ways to beat up, cut asunder, or puncture anybody for whom they had conceived a dislike; or, on the other, encouraging courtiers to strike elegant postures and perform rigidly circumscribed evolutions within the lists. Mounted combats in the chivalric mode were the more evidently irrelevant to modern warfare as the effectiveness and, therefore, the role of cavalry changed throughout the period with which this book has been concerned – slowly and unevenly at first, and then at an ever-accelerating tempo. Tourneying, or mounted fencing, lost credibility as serious preparation for war when the number of contestants was reduced, the number of strokes limited, and the amount of protection augmented; while, with regard to mounted lance-play, scarcely anybody after the middle of the fifteenth century regarded the predominant tilting exercise as anything more than an exhibition of equestrian skill and weapon handling which, however useful to a mounted warrior, was only distantly related to the battlefield – and that distance increased rapidly with the passage of time. Contempt for these activities was never more effectively expressed than in Francesco Guicciardini's comment on Galeazzo da Sanseverino, the dedicatee of Monte's *Collectanea* and martial model for Castiglione's *Il Cortegiano*. Describing Galeazzo's dishonourable abandoning of his troops at Alessandria in 1499 and his abject nocturnal flight, the historian simply noted that it showed 'how great difference there was betweene the sport to manage a Courser, and run at tilt and torney with huge Launces (exercises wherein he exceeded most Italians) and the office to be a Captaine of an army'.[3]

The military realities of the various modes of foot combat taught by the masters were, and remain, less clear-cut. Expertise in the martial arts had long been recognized, by those who professed them, as (metaphorically speaking) a two-edged weapon; and swords in particular were susceptible to evil as well as honourable employment. Masters of arms, whose social standing was generally equivocal, naturally stressed the public benefaction of their wares, and di Grassi was expressing a wholly conventional view when he wrote that

> Because this art is a principal member of the *Militarie profession*, which altogether (with learning) is the ornament of all the World, Therefore it ought not to be exercised in Braules and Fraies, as men commonlie practise in everie shire, but as honorable Knights, ought to reserve themselves, and exercise it for the advantage of their Cuntry, the honour of weomen, and conqueringe of Hostes and armies.

That is how the English translator of the *True Art of Defence* rendered the rousing conclusion of the author's original epistle to his reader. The meaning was clear. Skill in handling swords and other weapons was intended for the field of battle in the defence of one's native land, not for private quarrels. Yet, on the very next page, the same translator, in his own 'Advertisement to the curteous reader', praised the book which 'tendeth to no other use, but the defence of man's life and reputation' – which is not at all the same thing and smacks of those very brawls and affrays so despised by di Grassi.[4]

Many masters of arms purported to believe that the transmission of fighting skills suitable for personal violence was merely an unfortunate concomitant to their primary purpose which was to teach men how to fight in the service of their country. On the other hand there were some who openly acknowledged the utility of their work not only in war but also to men engaged in single combat, either formally in a duel or informally in a brawl. Thus dall'Agocchie speedily qualified his categoric opening statement that the art of fencing was the 'principal part of military exercises' with an impassioned panegyric on the courage and skill of men armed with sword alone, fighting without protective armour – in other words, in personal duels.[5]

Vincentio Saviolo, George Silver's *bête noire*, was even more oscillatory. He explained that his book would deal with the managing of rapier and dagger which, though only a small part of the 'arte Militarie', was still a 'most important, excellent, and noble practise thereof'; and he was not impressed by authors who argued that hunting, hawking, wrestling and similar skills were especially relevant to the military profession because they exercised the body or taught a knowledge of terrain. Such recommendations of hunting were certainly a commonplace in literature on the art of war from Xenophon to Monte, Machiavelli and beyond: but, in Saviolo's opinion, practice with rapier and dagger was 'much more rare and excellent than any other Militarie exercise of the bodie, because there is very great and necessarie use thereof, not onely in generall warres, but also in particular combats, and many other accidents'. Furthermore, discords and quarrels frequently arose among soldiers and gentlemen of honour which could not be 'accorded and compounded by lawe, learning, and perswasion' and must be determined instead 'by armes and combat'. This apology for duelling evidently troubled Saviolo and, almost immediately, he insisted that his arts were to be used only for the maintenance of honour and never for the advantage of accomplished bullies.

> For whosoever will followe this profession must flie from rashnes, pride and injurie, and not fall into that foule falt and error which many men incurre, who feeling themselves to be strong of bodie and expert in this science, presuming thereupon, think that they may lawfully offer outrage and injury unto anie man, and with crosse and grosse tearmes and behaviour provoke everie man to fight, as though they were the onely heirs of Mars, and more invincible than Achilles.[6]

Graduates from the schools of violence were unlikely to heed a moral appeal of this kind; and Saviolo had, in fact, identified one of the fundamental social problems posed by the work of the masters. An attack by an armed and murderous assailant in street, tavern, or duelling field was just as perilous as an attack on the field of battle, and civilians were moved, therefore, to carry arms and to learn how they should be handled. Conversely, the murderous assailant might himself have been prompted by the aggressive self-confidence acquired through training with arms. We know that a philosophy of attack rather than defence pervaded the treatises and, presumably, also the schools which instructed generations of enthusiasts in unarmed combat, all-in fighting, and the use of bladed and hafted weapons. Moreover, the whole tendency of this instruction was towards killing or maiming an adversary: and the inculcation of such aggression, together with instruction in deploying it most effectively, is an important aspect of the work of the masters of arms which has been wholly ignored by historians intent on finding sociological explanations for duelling and brawling.[7]

In recent times those concerned with military training for active service have been acutely conscious of the importance of psychological preparation when teaching men the art of killing. As Captain Fairbairn remarked in his manual on unarmed combat and knife fighting, although 'killing with the bare hands at close quarters savours of pure savagery for most people', in a matter of life and death, 'squeamish scruples are out of place'. In war, Fairbairn added, 'your attack can have only two possible objects: either to kill your opponent or to capture him alive'.[8] Renaissance duels and armed affrays were analogous to war; and, to judge from the homicidal pages of the masters and the bloodstained record of personal combats, prisoners were rarely taken.

BRAWLS AND DUELS

The duel – that is a personal combat fought, theoretically at least, according to certain mutually agreed conventions – has always attracted more attention from scholars than informal violence. This is probably because it was always associated with law, theology and debates concerning honour, so that there exists a vast amount of the academic literature on which academic literature feeds. The anarchic nature of assault and battery has, on the other hand, made it less congenial to scholars. But the admiring recitation of variegated homicide in Brantôme's *Discours sur les duels* shows that, during the Renaissance, there was scant difference – other than in degrees of ritualization – between the various modes of personal violence.[9] All combats were characterized by all-in fighting, dirty tricks and strokes to any part of the opposing anatomy. Some encounters have been mentioned elsewhere in this book but, with regard to armed affrays and murderous attacks, one especially graphic account may serve to indicate the martial versatility sometimes required even during an amble on horseback through the streets of a great city. Lord Herbert of Cherbury recounts his experience when Sir John Ayres and four thugs tried to murder him as he rode past 'a place called Scotland Yard, at the hither end of Whitehall'. Ayres was armed with sword and dagger and, without the least warning, says Herbert, 'he ran at me furiously' and 'wounded my horse in the brisket, as far as his sword could enter for the bone'. He then struck the horse in the shoulder which gave Herbert time to draw his own sword, although by now the four lackeys were also attacking his mount which started to kick about so much that they were unable to get near again and Herbert thereupon struck at Ayres with all his force:

but his sword broke within a foot of the hilt when Ayres 'warded the blow both with his sword and dagger'. Herbert now tried to dismount but fell to the ground with one foot still in the stirrup. Ayres dashed up to finish him with a sword thrust, 'when I, finding myself in this danger, did with both my arms reaching at his legs, pull them towards me, till he fell down backwards on his head'. Now Herbert was on his feet and put himself in the 'best posture' he could with his 'poor remnant of a weapon' to deal with a resurgent Ayres and his gang. Herbert rushed at him but he 'knowing my sword had no point, held his sword and dagger over his head, as believing I could strike rather than thrust; which I no sooner perceived but I put a home thrust to the middle of his breast, that I threw him down with so much force, that his head fell first to the ground, and his heels upwards.' The others renewed the assault but Herbert, receiving succour from some onlookers, went for Ayres yet again, thinking that closing with him was the only safe choice. Putting aside a thrust with his left hand, Herbert still received a dagger stab on the right side, 'which ran down my ribs as far as my hip, which I feeling, did with my right elbow force his hand together with the hilt of the dagger so near the upper part of my right side, that I made him leave hold'. Two of Herbert's friends now came to his assistance and pulled out the dagger, enabling the intrepid warrior to smash his enemy on the head and throw him down, whereupon, 'kneeling on the ground, and bestriding him, I struck him as hard as I could with my piece of sword, and wounded him in four several places, and did almost cut off his left hand.' All this while, the thugs continued hacking at Herbert who 'bore off their blows half a dozen times'. Eventually, seeing Ayres in dire straits, they pulled him by his head and shoulders from between Herbert's legs and carried him to safety, leaving their intended victim bloody but triumphant.

Given that Herbert's skill with pen and sword was accompanied by a commensurate vanity, his account may well be exaggerated; but its circumstantiality (in conjunction with the kind of evidence accumulated by Lawrence Stone and other historians) suggests that such bloody encounters were not unusual on the streets of European cities. As with other fight narratives, there is little technical analysis: but the style of the combat is unmistakable. The techniques involved – dealing with unequal odds, left hand parrying, wrestling throws, ruthless battering about the head, stabbings, wards, and a total commitment to death and destruction – are all much the same as those described and illustrated by masters of arms from the late fourteenth century onwards. And, however much such behaviour may later have been frowned upon by academic fencers, similar practices were still being taught long after they are conventionally supposed to have vanished from the sophisticated swordsman's repertory.[10]

At the end of the seventeenth century, Sir William Hope made an interesting distinction between school play and 'sharps', when he drew up an elaborate list of 'Laws to be observed in all fencing-schools'.[11] Among these laws was the prohibition of all thrusts to the face, arms, wrist, thighs and legs. No thrusts should be allowed which were not given to the trunk of the body below the neck and above the 'head-band of the breeches', and within the two shoulders. Similarly, Hope banned the use of the left hand in school play, for 'it not only taketh away a great deal of the variety of play, but it is also noways Graceful'. By contrast, when a man is engaged with 'sharps' he may 'either for his own safety, or to disable his adversary, Thrust at any part of the body', and may also use his left hand. And these more utilitarian techniques, while 'discharged in all publick Assaults', are allowed in private, 'so that the Scholars may know how to perform them, when there shall be a necessity for it'. Even here, whatever limitations were imposed

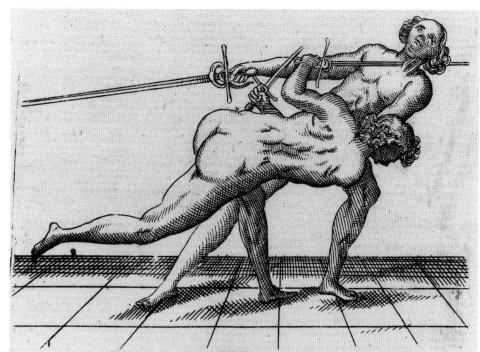

177. Heussler, copying Fabris, illustrates a rushing left-handed attack to the throat. 1615, extra plate 3.

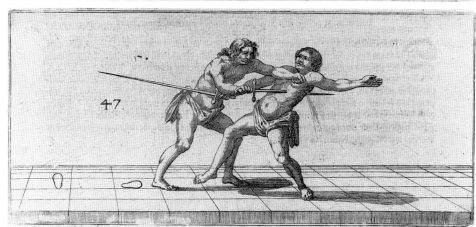

178. Another plagiarism from Fabris, this time by L'Ange. The master's chop to the throat has here been turned into a punch. 1664, plate 47.

179. Yet another Fabris derivative. Porath's lunge and shoulder charge. 1693, plate 22.

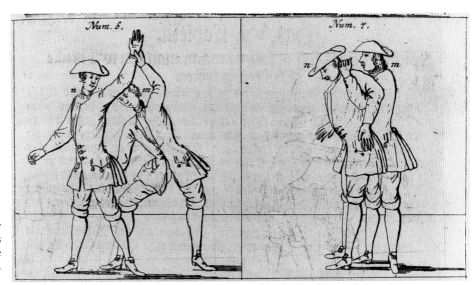

180. Schmidt's first aggressor appears merely to be measuring his opponent for a new jacket: the second applies a double nelson. 1713, p. 317.

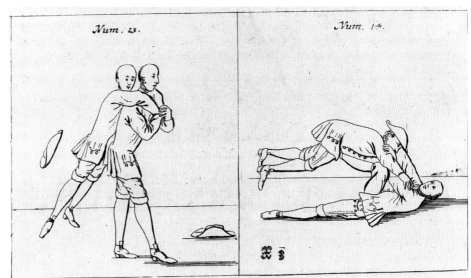

181. Schmidt: beginning a flying mare; then a stomach throw. 1713, p. 325.

182. Schmidt's patent flagon of ale throw; then a leg pick-up. 1713, p. 336.

183. Weischner: how to tread elegantly on a smiling opponent's knee. 1765, plate 28.

184. Weischner with a chancery hold from the rear. 1765, plate 29.

for public exhibitions and group practice, the master was supposed to prepare his pupils for real fighting.

Disarms, grips, throws and left-hand parries were still widely taught throughout Europe, and the German masters, in particular, never seem to have lost their zeal for unarmed combat and for combining all-in fighting with fencing (figs 177–9, plates XXV–XXVIII). The kicking, punching and stabbing antics of the thugs in Heussler and L'Ange, or in the Swedish manual of Porath, do not differ in spirit from those of an earlier age – indeed the greater number of them are based upon the brutalities brilliantly enunciated by Salvator Fabris at the beginning of the seventeenth century (figs 177–9).[12] Andreas Schmidt's treatise of 1713 has wrestling postures familiar to us from the work of Ott and the earliest masters, including a double-nelson, leg pick-up, stomach throw, and a counter to the bearhug which involves gripping the opponent's throat with the left hand and pressing the thumb between his Adam's apple and chin, while clawing his left eye with the right hand. Schmidt also suggests an effective attack with a flagon of ale, which is duly illustrated for the benefit of inexperienced brawlers (figs 180–2). And even the elegant, periwigged smallsword fencers in Weischner's *Ritterliche Fechten* of 1765, with their neat stockings, tight frock coats and lace cuffs, do not balk at twisting an opponent's wrist, treading on his knee, or applying a chancery hold from the rear (figs 183–4).[13]

While informal personal violence is sempiternal, the history of civilian duelling is difficult to trace back beyond the latter years of the fifteenth century when it seems already to have been well established – at least in the Mediterranean lands. The practice was alluded to by Pietro Monte when he expressed contempt for private encounters fought, perhaps, 'in some narrow apartment, with daggers or swords by ruffians in their shirt-sleeves' (*in camisia*). This, said Monte, was not the kind of thing practised by honest soldiers who put on armour for battle. Getting undressed to fight was an impropriety fit only for 'pimps, blasphemers, and shopkeepers'.[14] In Monte's view, the ideal duel involved strong, skilled warriors fighting on foot and in armour. In other words, he admired the chivalric duel of honour within closed lists (fig. 185). Combats of this type – described by fifteenth-century chroniclers, and depicted in gory detail by Talhoffer and other German masters – were still being advocated as ideal in 1648 when La Colombière devoted a large volume to the history and ritual of personal combat and set out his purpose pictorially on the frontispiece (fig.

185. The end of a trial by combat. Bibliothèque Nationale, Paris, MS. Fr. 2258, fol. 23v.

186). La Colombière explains how the engraving compares the excellence and justice of ancient combats within the lists, with the detestable and 'enraged fury' of contemporary duellists. We see a gentleman armed at 'all pieces' – in the fashion employed in times past, 'with the permission of princes or of their parliaments' – treading underfoot an enemy, vanquished and slain. Also depicted are Innocence and Justice, the principal virtues which 'inspired those who had them on their side': Innocence as a naked child holding a pair of scales, and Justice as a woman holding a sword and crowning the victor with laurel. However, in stark contrast, the same plate shows two duellists 'in their shirts (*en chemise*) in the fashion now followed'.

186. The allegorical title page to Vulson *Le vray théâtre d'honneur* demonstrating the difference between the old duel and the new. Both opponents are equally dead. 1648.

One of these is lying dead, pierced by many wounds; the other is accompanied by the Fury, Alecton, who fills him with rage and despair. And instead of receiving some sort of satisfaction and praise for his unhappy victory, he is pursued by the Goddess Minerva – enemy of those who use their valour in such unjust and detestable combats: combats which must be regarded with horror and execration by all those who wish to follow more solid virtue, and who wish to battle only for True Honour.[15]

Such antiquarian zeal for the duel of chivalry had been old-fashioned even in Monte's time when, as Castiglione remarked, the courtier was expected to be adept with the weapons normally used among gentlemen not only in war, where no great subtlety (*sottilità*) was necessary, but also in the combats arising from the frequent quarrels between gentlemen. This not only suggests that, by the first decade of the sixteenth century, duels and affrays were common in Italy but it also distinguishes sharply between fighting in wars (where a refined technique was not required) and fighting personal combats (where it certainly was). This was not at all what the masters of arms cared to hear. But the true nature of their art could not be hidden. Even when Marco Docciolini specifically compared fighting in armour with fighting unencumbered, his own assessment of the relative importance of the two modes of fencing is revealed by the fact that the entire chapter devoted to this issue was barely one page long and declared that fighting without armour was much the more subtle art in that the least error meant death.[16] It is true that Docciolini went on to suggest that, in other respects, the techniques were very much the same; but the infinitesimal space devoted to fighting in armour makes it clear that his interest – after fifty-two years' experience as a professional master – lay in fighting *en chemise*.[17]

That there was neither time nor space for subtlety on the battlefield must have been obvious: but, with the exception of George Silver, few masters admitted this in their published treatises since it would have undermined their assumed role as benefactors to the public weal. In any case, it would have seemed equally obvious to them that physical strength, adroitness at unarmed combat and the confidence that comes from familiarity with the sword and other weapons would all be valuable to men engaged in hand-to-hand combat on the field of battle. Whatever the reason, the task of showing how the geometrical arts learnt in the fencing schools might be applied amidst the press of battle was one which few masters felt obliged to undertake. We have encountered this issue when discussing criticisms of the rapier as a militarily useless weapon; and it is illuminating to approach the more general question of the military relevance of swordsmanship via George Silver, the most vociferous defender of the English sword against its Italianate rivals. Or, to be more precise, we may approach this issue via a late nineteenth-century interpretation of Silver.

When it came to the use of the sword and other personal combat weapons on the battlefield, everything depended on individual strength, stamina and the confidence which can only come with familiarity and psychological preparation. The crucial issues always remained the exact nature of that skill; how confidence was acquired; and how the mind was prepared for killing. In 1898, Captain Cyril Matthey had no doubts about these matters as he completed his edition of the works of George Silver with a powerful plea for the relevance of the Elizabethan master to contemporary warfare. Moreover, although Matthey did not realize it, he was also writing an implicit apologia for the all-in methods of the medieval masters whose works he does not mention and almost certainly did not know.[18]

Noting the similarities between the regulation military sword of his own day and the sword recommended by Silver, Matthey asserted that 'much, if not all, that he has written upon the handling of it in his time may well prove of immense service to those whose lives are at times dependent upon the more or less ready use of their swords'. The problem with the sword instruction of the contemporary English army was that there was little or no distinction between the requirements of the duellist and that of the soldier: and here Matthey put his finger on an issue completely ignored by the evolutionist historians of the art of fencing. He believed it imperative that officers should be instructed in the 'vast distinction that exists between the sabre duel and the sabre fight, shorn of all formality and rules, as he would find it on service, whether against a savage or a civilized enemy'. One especially stupid schoolroom nicety which had found its way into military sword training was the prohibition against attacking or defending any part of the body below the hip. Yet, as Matthey pointed out, what the soldier really needed to know was how to defend himself thoroughly and how to attack an adversary without the inhibiting irrelevancies of complicated parries and movements feasible with the featherweight duelling sabre in the fencing school, but 'utterly impossible with the regulation sword' in a real 'rough and tumble'. What was required was a 'simple common-sense method of *sword-fighting* suitable for service requirements'; a system from which, as far as possible, the advanced 'science' of the sword had been eliminated in order to teach the smallest number and the simplest of parries that 'will protect a man *from head to foot* and the *correct and quickest way* of delivering a cut or thrust, coupled with careful instruction in the judicious use of the left hand in defence, which is now and has long been totally ignored.'

As a matter of fact, not only had the use of the left hand in defence been ignored, it had positively been frowned upon as merely the uncouth practice of an age when people did not understand how their sword was sufficient for *all* purposes. But Matthey knew full well that there were no rules when a man was fighting for his life. It was to counter this sort of myopia that he recommended a careful perusal of Silver's *Bref Instructions* – and especially the 'Gryps' and the ripostes that could be made from them – which not only offered precisely the kind of real fighting system needed to replace the current impractical method but could, moreover, be adapted to suit the modern sword, 'almost without modification'. One feature particularly appealed to Matthey. Silver had grasped the fact that

> the hilt or pommel of the sword (or the butt of any arm) constituted an effectively offensive portion of the weapon if properly handled. A few modern authors, who have written upon bayonet fighting, have taught the use of the rifle-butt, but Silver was, so far as I have been able to ascertain, the first writer to attach any importance to the offensive possibilities of the sword-hilt.

Matthey was correct in his view that schoolroom fencing (with its etiquette, strictly limited targets, protective clothing and ultra-light blades) was useless as a preparation for the all-in violence of battle; but he overestimated Silver's originality in grasping this essential point. Nor did he follow up Silver's own implication that earlier masters had taught a combat style more practical for war than contemporary Italian rapier play.

Indeed they had. Recognition of the effectiveness of the pommel, for example, and of every other part of the sword may be found in the treatises of Hanko Döbringer, Maestro Fiore, Talhoffer and many others. The same is true of the combination of all-in wrestling with sword fighting, the concentration on powerful weapons which could both cut and thrust, and the 'judicious use of the left hand in defence'. The difference between Silver and his medieval predecessors is that he lived in an age when the fashion for single-handed use of increasingly long sword blades dictated an elaborate and artificial style of fighting which was, in turn, ousting more robust weapons from private affrays. How far this fashion ever spread to the battlefield is another matter. Sir John Smythe, it is true, was vehement on the subject. But then he was vehement on most subjects. He attacked these modish 'Rapiers of a yard and a quarter long the blades or more' which, he asserted, were nowadays ignorantly worn by both infantry and cavalry despite the fact that they were impossible to draw 'with any celeritie', and that their blades – 'being so narrow, and of so small substance, and made of a verie hard temper to fight in privat fraies' – broke as soon as they struck armour.[19] If Smythe were correct then the fashion would certainly have been perilous for those adopting it; but the available evidence suggests that military swords in the late sixteenth century and thereafter were cut and thrust weapons of a length, weight and solidity suitable for close combat in war.

The real confusion (as opposed to distinction) between swordsmanship for battle and for duelling arose at a much later period and, I suspect, partly as an indirect result of stereotyped group teaching methods for warfare. Matthey's lamentation concerning the state of army sword training came at the end of the nineteenth century. Forty years earlier, in a succinct treatment of the swordsmanship of the British cavalry, Captain Valentine Baker had observed that, while 'every dragoon should be an expert swordsman', the basic skills were entirely neglected. It was true, he admitted, that there was a prescribed sword exercise, but it was taught more for the purpose of giving the soldier 'a command over, and ease in the use of the weapon, than for any real purpose of attack or defence'. No real swordsman, he jeered, would think of carrying out these prescriptions if actually engaged with an enemy: 'Who would be guilty of so suicidal an act as parrying a real thrust as laid down in the regulations?' Yet that is all that the soldier was taught, and it was natural that he would resort to it when in action. Baker was even more acid when condemning, as simply ridiculous, 'the present theatrical system of attack and defence as carried out in cavalry riding-schools'; and he tells a story about a dragoon at Balaclava who explained how he had been wounded because his Russian opponent did not follow the rules – 'When he came at me, I gave right defence, but the fool gave cut 7, and hit me on the head, and down I went'.[20] The story, Baker admitted, might have been apocryphal but he still felt that it illustrated the folly of the current drill system.

It would be a complex if not impossible task to trace the history of the effectiveness (or otherwise) of weapon drill. Certainly the masters with whom this book has been concerned never believed that their vocation was to provide a set of mechanical exercises enabling a large body of recruits – even the most inept – to execute a few rudimentary flourishes. Yet, with regard to preparation for fighting real battles in real wars, the future of western martial arts lay precisely in facing up to that task so that, while the masters' claims as to the relevance of swordsmanship on the battlefield may be largely discounted, it is still worth considering their work in the context of changing military techniques, theories and the specialist literature which accompanied them.

THE MASTERS AND WAR

Military books of every kind poured from the presses of renaissance Europe in an ever increasing flood and, with regard to the actual disposition, management and training of troops, most writers, and many commanders, were agreed that ancient discipline provided an ideal model. The problem was to translate that ideal from the printed page to the field of battle via the drill yard; and only Maurice of Nassau, in the military reforms he encouraged between 1590 and 1609, was completely successful in using a knowledge of ancient armies, derived from classical sources, to achieve practical results.[21] The growing logistic and technological complexities of warfare; the recruiting and maintenance of large, more or less permanent armies; the importance of artillery and smaller firearms; the elaboration and sophistication of fortification and an emphasis on siege rather than battle; the perceived relevance of drilling and training in groups – all led to an increasing demand for a specialist military education which would produce leaders and captains able to cope with these new factors. The result was that, from the middle of the sixteenth century, schemes for setting up military academies were being mooted throughout Europe. Many of these projects remained figments of their authors' imaginations; some did materialize but perished after a few years of desultory activity; and only a few managed to establish themselves as serious institutions.[22] But, insubstantial or real, ephemeral or longeval, each of these academies made provision for instruction not only in up-to-date theoretical military sciences and mathematics but also in all the old skills of personal combat as recommended both by chivalric and humanistic authors: riding, gymnastics, wrestling, weapon handling in general, and fencing in particular. The masters of arms, it seemed, still had a place in the new scheme of things: but so, too, did teachers of dancing.

The precise role of sword instruction in these academies is difficult to determine but, in practical terms, it was probably only to teach budding young officers how to kill their peers on the duelling field: for the fact remains that, whatever their pretensions and aspirations, the masters of arms had scarcely ever demonstrated just how they were militarily relevant. Extravagantly individualistic themselves, they thought, taught and wrote about individualistic combat. They did not concern themselves with the group discipline demanded, if only theoretically, by troop formations in battle; and neither di Grassi nor Silver (who both remarked that weapons would be handled differently for public and private purposes) attempted a systematic military application of their methods, while their isolated illustrations belong to a world totally different from the drill postures and synchronized movements soon to become commonplace in the military manuals of the seventeenth century. Masters who did treat both warfare and personal combat within a single treatise wrote as though the mere act of juxtaposition constituted a sufficient demonstration of martial pertinence. Thus Giovanni dall'Agocchie, whose work declares itself to be 'necessary to captains, soldiers, and gentlemen', supplemented his discussions of fencing and jousting with a section on military arithmetic (to facilitate the drawing up of troops in battle order) and, in so doing, inevitably achieved an effect of total irrelation. Similarly, when Giovanni Cassani promised on the title page of his *Essercitio militare* to explain 'fencing with the sword and ranging an army for battle', readers might have expected an ingeniously integrated treatment of the two topics: but his three scrappy pages on swordsmanship, followed by another sixty on military arithmetic, do not suggest that the two skills had anything to do with each other – which, of course, they did not.[23]

The examples of dall'Agocchie and Cassani highlight the difficulty of relating mass conflict to the activities of an individual within a group, whether as part of a lance charge, a caracole of pistoleers, or a push of pikes.[24] Indeed, it is evident from the diametrically opposed views of experts on cavalry techniques from the sixteenth to the nineteenth centuries that some problems were intractable and some solutions impractical.[25] That disputatious Elizabethan soldier Sir John Smythe roundly declared that the sword was the 'last weapon of refuge both for horsemen and footmen'; and this was not only true in the sixteenth century but remained so to the latter half of the nineteenth.[26] Nevertheless, the whole thrust of military thinking in the Renaissance and beyond was towards a dehumanized type of warfare where soldiers were not only organized into groups according to specific functions and specialities (which was no novelty), but were also arranged and rearranged according to mathematical tables (which certainly was); and most military writers were concerned with organizational matters, technological innovations, or both. The actual wielding of hand weapons rarely concerned them. They were not masters of arms. And, as far as I know, only one renaissance master, Pietro Monte, had ever seriously attempted to establish a relationship between martial arts and martial service.

Conceived and written in the early years of the wars in Italy, Monte's *Collectanea* consists of three sections. The first two provide a detailed treatment of weapons, armour, physical exercise and every kind of armed and unarmed combat, together with a lengthy analysis of the various types and qualities of men, considered both somatically and temperamentally.

The third section, *De arte militari*, is based upon one of Monte's most cherished beliefs: that knowledge of one art can be applied to the practice of another. He argues that this is especially the case with single combat and the waging of war; and, upon this premise, he ingeniously erects a general view of military affairs which is shaped by (but not especially dependent upon) the classic treatise by Vegetius. Barely a decade later, Machiavelli relied much more heavily on Vegetius when he composed his own *Arte della guerra* in which, like his Roman model, he devoted a brief space to the regions from which troops should be levied, to the question of whether troops from town or country were more apt for war, and to considerations of age and physical appropriateness. Monte had dealt with similar questions but, as a master of arms versed in the teaching of combat skills and as a physical-training specialist concerned with questions of comparative physiology and temperament, he had entered into much greater detail. His examination of human types (however arbitrary the regional, geographical and humoral generalizations may now seem, with 'fleshy and insufficiently agile' Frenchmen, 'slothful' Germans, and 'strongly boned and sinewed' Englishmen), his expertise in systematic physical exercise, his distinction between activities suitable or unsuitable for soldiers, and his knowledge of how men may be accustomed to wearing armour and to handling a wide variety of weapons, all give his work a precision and professionalism far beyond that of Machiavelli's many discussions of military practice.[27]

There are, none the less, affinities between Monte's views on war and some of the ideas expressed in Machiavelli's *Arte della guerra* and *Il principe* which appear to be more than coincidental. Both writers accepted the intrinsic cruelty and immorality of total warfare and understood that Hannibal's success as a general could not be divorced from his cruelty and deceit. Both stressed that, more than other men, the soldier should be devout since his fate was so frequently in the hands of providence. Both extolled the advantages of hunting as an exercise for the military commander and stressed its topographical value in terms independent of Xenophon, the classical source for this notion. And, above all, both were concerned to find ways of dealing with the 'well-nigh invincible' German infantry. How were these transmontane masters of brutal warfare to be defeated on the battlefield? Monte pointed out that, since they had no difficulty in coping either with mounted crossbowmen or with heavy cavalry, a new method had to be devised and he suggested that, first of all, the Germans might be surprised with armoured chariots. This is just the kind of ingenuity that Monte may have picked up from Leonardo da Vinci but, having suggested it, he immediately conceded that these machines would only be effective on level terrain and then probably only once in several years – a prescient observation if one bears in mind the results of the premature use of tanks in the First World War. It was, therefore, necessary in Monte's view to devise some sort of battle order based on the Germans' own strength, yet even more powerful; and he came up with the idea of arming his troops with staff weapons longer than those used by the Germans – although this, in fact, posed as many problems as it solved since the advantage of being able to strike the first blow with the longer pike was offset by the superior agility of the shorter weapon.[28] Monte further suggested that these extra-long pikes should be flanked on one side with arquebuses, catapults and crossbows – that is 'all the machines that can kill or wound at a distance' – and, on the other side, with heavy cavalry. The first seven or eight rows of infantry would be protected by heavy shields; at least half would wear steel plate armour; and their first objective would be to bring the enemy to a halt. Then the missiles and heavy infantry could break their ranks, giving opportunity to hurl in other troops with short swords, who could get among the Germans and rout them so that, finally, once they were in disorder, they would fall easy prey to a heavy cavalry charge.

These recommendations on how to deal with the Germans are very close to those offered by Machiavelli but it is well to remember that Monte was writing several years earlier than the famous Florentine and that he really knew something about the business end of a pike or sword.[29] Unfortunately, it is also true that, whereas Machiavelli's *Il principe* appeared in at least thirty-eight editions, translations and versions during the sixteenth century, and his *Arte della guerra* in some twenty-four versions, Monte's *Collectanea* was never reissued and was never even referred to by later writers. Yet, despite the fact that it was *sui generis*, Monte's comprehensive treatment of the martial arts may serve as a focus for the transition from a medieval to a renaissance view of the techniques of personal combat and for their putative relationship to the art of war in the aftermath of the French invasion of Italy.

In the closing decades of the sixteenth century and the beginning of the seventeenth, the struggle between Spain and the United Provinces in the Low Countries provided a new 'scoole of war' many of whose students were to practise their arts in an even greater struggle which was soon to engulf most of Europe. This period witnessed an explosion of military literature: but one author is especially informative and suggestive. In 1617, John of Nassau-Dillemburg, admirer and disciple of Maurice of Nassau, established in his capital, the Westphalian town of Siegen, an exclusive military school for 'Princes, Counts, Noblemen and the sons of Patricians'. It was, as John Hale has remarked, 'a full-fledged professional military college, the first of its kind in Europe', and its curriculum, designed primarily to produce efficient officers, was comprehensive and practical. It included engineering, fortification, siege warfare and the use of artillery; tactics and mathematics; Latin, French and Italian; marching, battle formations and drill in the 'Netherlandish manner'; and, inevitably, riding and the handling of both bladed and staff weapons.[30]

To direct this school, John of Nassau-Dillemburg invited a man who must have seemed made-to-measure for the post. This was Johann Jacobi von Wallhausen, 'Principal Captain of the Guards, and Captain of the praiseworthy town of Danzig': a seasoned soldier and admirer of Maurice of Nassau; a man consumed with a passion for providing military instruction; and a scholar of vast if erratic erudition who had already published numerous works on the art of war, covering almost every aspect of the subject both topically and historically.[31] His treatise on infantry embraces the handling of musket and pike, the exercise of a company of foot soldiers according to the practice of Maurice of Nassau, the ordering of battles for entire regiments, and the discipline of the Hungarian infantry. His book on cavalry specifically declared that it is necessary to write not for those who already have knowledge of the subject but rather for those who are only beginners, and it not only covers the principal types of mounted soldiery but also includes a dialogue 'on the excellence of the military art' maintaining, largely on the basis of classical authorities, that, 'with the exception of Theology, it surpasses all the other arts and sciences, liberal as much as mechanical'. The cannon and all its appurtenances are dealt with in his treatise on artillery which goes into considerable technical detail and demonstrates how the many variations of trajectory may be deployed in action. And his *Military Manual* deals with troop formations, camps and fortifications; provides a comparative study of Greek, Spartan and Roman military discipline; and concludes with a valuable military vocabulary.[32] He also published an *Alphabetum* or *ABC* for the novice infantryman; and, while director at Siegen, he issued a

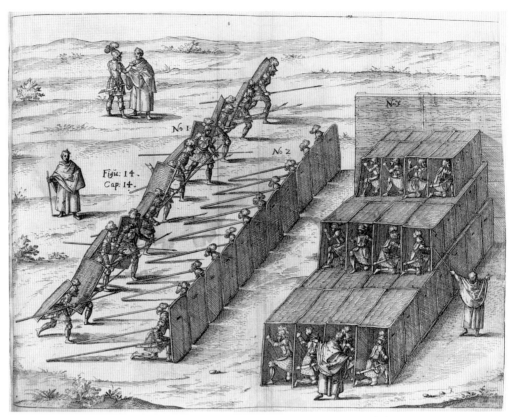

187. The Roman *testudo* as reconstructed by Wallhausen. *De la milice Romaine*, 1616, plate 14.

188. Other Roman techniques realized by Wallhausen. 1616, plate 15.

concise treatise devoted solely to the art of handling the pike, in which he discusses and illustrates 203 separate postures and treats the weapon both on its own and in conjunction with the sword.[33] (See Chapter II, fig. 40.)

As if these labours were insufficient to tax his energies, Wallhausen also engaged in works of translation and annotation. His *Militia Gallica* is a rendering of Louis de Montgommery's *La Milice françoise*, showing his interest in recent writing on the art of war. But no contemporary author could compare with the classical masters, and Wallhausen promised to publish Aelian's *Tactica* in German and French, 'with the most appropriate illustrations for its better understanding'.[34] As far as I know, this never materialized, but another promise was fulfilled. At the end of his book on cavalry Wallhausen had announced a translation of the 'renowned author Flavius Vegetius, to demonstrate the military custom and armament of the ancient Romans with fine figures and illustrations of the same', a work of 'singular importance and curiosity as much for new soldiers as for old and experienced captains'. This duly appeared in the following year, published at Wallhausen's own expense in Frankfurt-am-Main in both a German and French edition, preceded by Wallhausen's exposition elaborating the Roman system of military training. The latter is remarkable principally as the first commentary on Vegetius to be fully illustrated with detailed reconstructions, or rather realizations, of Roman practice intended to serve as a model for contemporary training methods (figs 187–8).[35] But it is also notable for its daring defence of the Roman writer against the hostile criticisms of the illustrious scholar Justus Lipsius whom Wallhausen reprimands for ignorance, declaring that, 'if Lipsius had been as experienced in practical warfare as he was versed in theology, he would not have been so rash and hasty in his judgement'.[36]

Despite his qualifications, Wallhausen did not last long at Siegen. Perhaps his methods were too brutal. As he wrote about recruits who were incompetent at drill, 'whoever will not have it without blows, must learn with blows'.[37] In the event, he was dismissed after only a few months as director; and the whole experiment collapsed even before the death of its founder, John of Nassau, in 1623. Historians have largely overlooked Wallhausen's many publications; and, when not ignored, his work as a military theorist has been decried. His contemporaries, on the other hand, took him seriously and Jean Theodore de Bry wrote, in the dedication of his French translation of the *Art militaire à cheval*, that it was offered to Frederick V, Count Palatine as 'a fruit which derives from the school of this great Maurice of Nassau'. Wallhausen's views were regularly cited and debated by military authors. Several of his German works were translated almost immediately into French. One was published in Dutch; another appeared in a Russian translation; and most went into more than one edition.[38]

We, too, should take him seriously. For one thing, he remains of paramount importance for his consistent and effective use of illustrations to clarify his text. Many military writers, it is true, had recognized the value of both diagrams and pictures as an aid to understanding and, just a few years before Wallhausen began to publish, Jacob de Gheyn had issued a volume with engravings showing, in three series of static postures, a system of drill for caliver, musket and pike.[39] The engravings in De Gheyn have become famous, but they are dead things in comparison with the illustrations in Wallhausen whose works, considered as a corpus, remain in a class of their own.[40] In addition, Wallhausen offers modern readers a perfect focus for the most fundamental military ideas of the early seventeenth century: the relationship between ancients and moderns, theory and practice, academic military education and battle experience, training exercises and real warfare, and the role of personal combat skills within the larger context of battle.

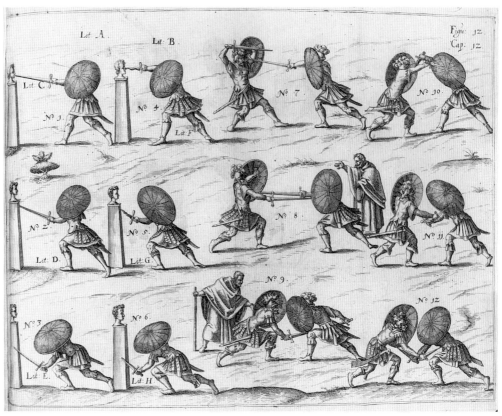

189. Roman infantry training at the post, according to Wallhausen. 1616, plate 12.

190. Wallhausen: mounted sword practice at the ring. 1634, plate 8.

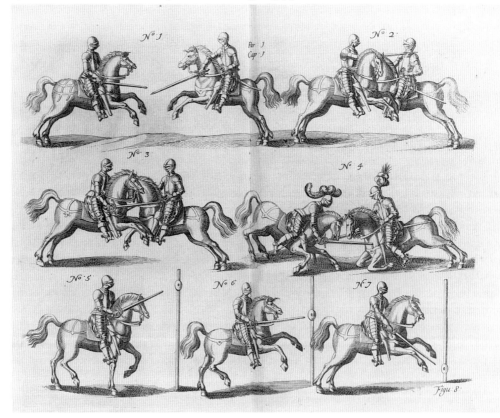

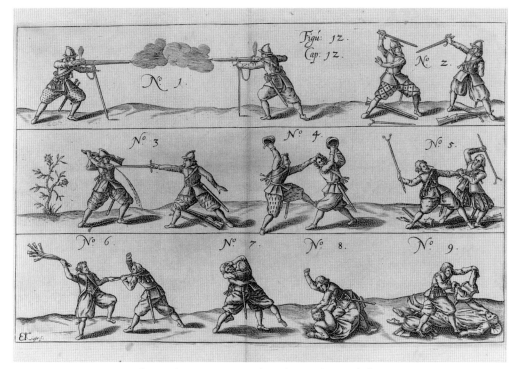

191. Wallhausen: close combat on foot with no holds barred. *Ritterkunst*, 1616, plate 12.

It is, of course, with these last two aspects of Wallhausen's legacy that we are here concerned. He was not a master of arms like Liechtenauer, Fiore, Talhoffer, Marozzo, di Grassi, Capoferro and so many others. Yet, in his books, ideas which never went beyond mere intuition in the work of his predecessors (Monte excepted) are made explicit, described and illustrated. The Roman sword exercises at the post, for example, become suddenly not a topic for scholarly discussion but a practical teaching method – 'very useful not only for soldiers but also for fencers' – from which the pupils may be seen on the page, graduating to fighting with an opponent (fig. 189).[41] The recruit practising vaulting on a wooden horse is, within the confines of a few plates, transmuted into a warrior prepared for every type of mounted combat – not in the lists, but on the field of battle. (See Chapter 9, fig. 170.) The knight who runs with his lance at the ring immediately applies his skill to running at an opponent or, more effectively, at his opponent's horse; and when he has to resort to close combat he batters his enemy with edge, point or pommel, tears him from the saddle, knocks him to the ground and stabs him in the throat. (See Chapter 9 figs 172–4.) He practises tourneying at a post, aiming his sword high, medium and low; and, when faced by an enemy, he wastes no time before running the opposing steed through the chest (fig. 190). When foot soldiers get to close quarters, they exploit a wide repertoire of violence: slashing at each other with their swords; swinging furiously with a caliver butt; tugging at an opponent's hair while braining him with a helmet; battering him with a musket rest; wrestling him to the ground; killing him, and robbing him of his armour. And, when all these things have been taught and practised, they are then shown in action within the context of a battle (figs 191–2).

Wallhausen's vast survey of war relates the activities of each individual soldier to the activities of the army as a whole; or, to put it more accurately perhaps, he shows how the activities of an army are built up from the contributions of individual soldiers. Above all,

192. Wallhausen: all the techniques deployed in battle. *Ritterkunst*, 1616, plate 13.

he tries to instil two essential qualities in the soldier. One is discipline. The other is the killer instinct and the brutality without which it is impossible to survive. The great masters of arms would have approved. Wallhausen's drastic deeds are all foreshadowed in the old *Fechtbücher* and are precisely the kind of 'Closes and Gripes' that the realistic George Silver had recommended. For 'this is the ancient teaching, the perfectest and most best teaching; and without this teaching, there shall never scholler be made able, doe his uttermost, nor fight safe'.[42]

Colour plates

I. Belfin's fencing school as a theatre. 1767, frontispiece.

II. Heredia's case of rapiers. *c.* 1600.

III. Maximilian engages in a combat with daggers. Vienna, Kunsthistorisches Museum, *Freydal*, plate 127.

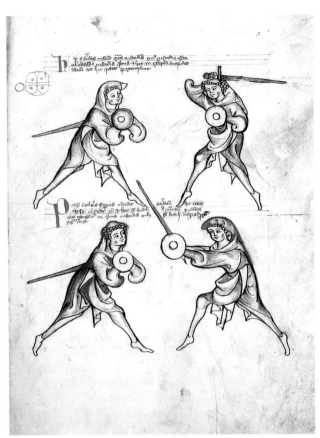

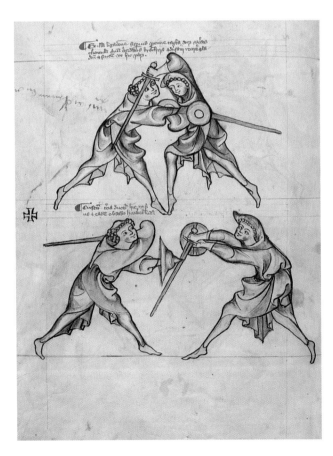

facing page

IV. First Guard, Fourth Guard and *Halbschilt*. Royal Armouries MS., I-33, fol. 29.

V. Second Guard, *Schiltslac*, *Stich*, *Schutz*. Royal Armouries MS., I-33, fol. 19.

VI. Third Guard, *Bind*, *Schutz*. Royal Armouries MS., I-33, fol. 24.

VII. Fifth Guard, special *Langort*, *Bind*. Royal Armouries MS., I-33, fol. 53.

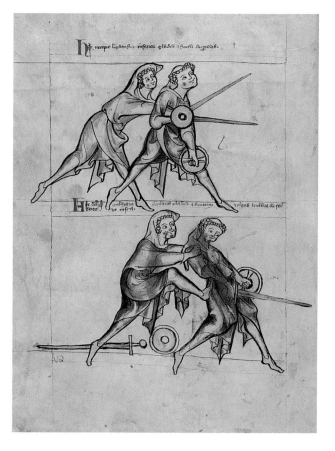

this page

VIII. Sixth Guard and a thrust. Royal Armouriees MS., I-33, fol. 33.

IX. *Langort*, *Bind*, *Stich*. Royal Armouries MS., I-33, fol. 39.

X. A judicious use of the foot. Royal Armouries MS., I-33, fol. 36.

XI. Maximilian triumphs, as always. Vienna, Kunsthistorisches Museum, *Freydal*, plate 254.

XII. Maximilian's dexterity with the flail. Vienna, Kunsthistorisches Museum, *Freydal*, plate 35.

XIII. Maximilian executes a leg pick-up with quarter-staff. Vienna, Kunsthistorisches Museum, *Freydal*, plate 67.

XIV. Maximilian treads on his opponent's knee. Vienna, Kunsthistorisches Museum, *Freydal*, plate 39.

Ceste figure demonstre la lutte que se poult faire a ceulx qui se mettent au prouffit de la garde, cōe est declaré au livre des lecons. fol. 117.

Ceste figure demonstre la lutte que se poult faire ayant paré le coup de l'ennemÿ, lors quil vient de passade, cōe est declaré au livre des lecons fol. 117. art. 1.

Ceste figure demonstre coe la luitte se poinct faire a celluy qui tire de resolution en dehors l'espe de son adversaire, coe est declaré au livre des leçons fol. 117. art 2.

XVII. Heredia's throw over the thigh, effected by a backward chop across the throat. *c.* 1600, fig. 35.

XV. Fencers getting to grips in Heredia's treatise. *c.* 1600, fig. 33.

XVI. Heredia's hip-throw. *c.* 1600, fig. 34.

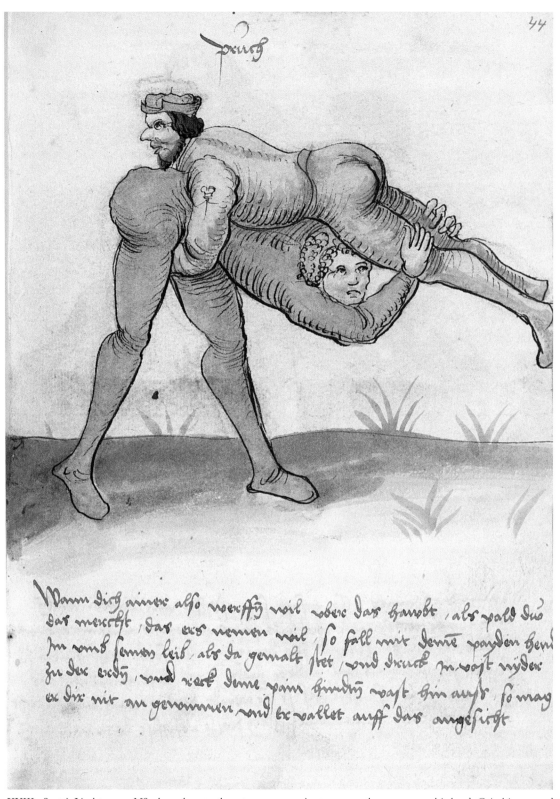

Wann dich ainer also werffz wil ober das haubt, als pald du
das merckst, das er nemen wil so fall mit deine payden hend
zu der erdy, und reck deine pain hindun wast hin auß so mag
er dich nit an genomen und er vallet auff das angesicht

XVIII. Scott's Liechtenauer MS. shows how to thwart an opponent's attempt to throw you over his head. Grip him around the body, press him down and stretch your legs. 'In this way he cannot beat you but will fall on his face.' Fol. 44.

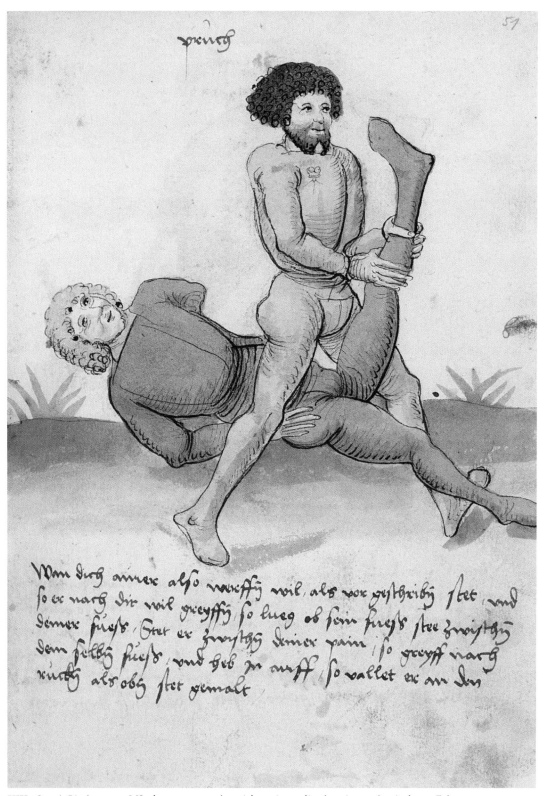

preuch

Wan dich ainer also uarffig wil, als vor geschribn stet, und
so er nach dir wil greyffn so lueg ob sein fueß stee zwischn
deinen fuesn. Stet er zwischn deiner pain so greyff nach
dem selbn fueß, und heb jn auff so vallet er an den
ruck als obn stet gemalt

XIX. Scott's Liechtenauer MS. demonstrates a leg pick-up immediately prior to the sit down. Fol. 51.

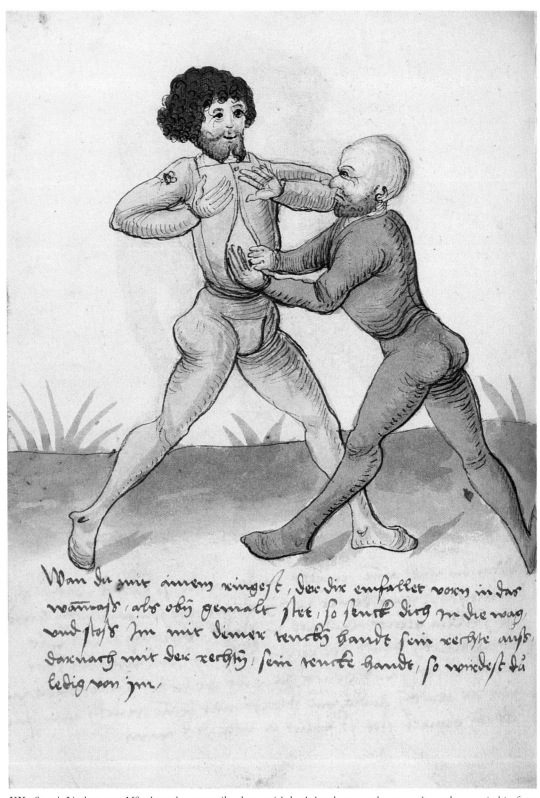

Wan du mit ainem ringest, der dir emfallet vorn in das
wamas, als obg gemalt stet, so senck dich in die wag,
und stost in mit deiner rencke hande sein rechte auf,
darnach mit der rechten, sein rencke hande, so werdest du
ledig von im.

XX. Scott's Liechtenauer MS. shows how to strike down with both hands at an adversary who grabs your jerkin from the front. Fol. 54v.

53

Wan dich ainer hat gefaßt mit paÿdy arme als obṅ gemalt
stet dar du freÿ steest und ſo er dich zu In druckt und haltet
dich vast ſo ſetz dich in die wag und wan dich bedunckt das
du gar wol in der wag ſeyeſt und dein arm in der höhe habeſt
vberking ſo dree dich vor Im und gar starck und vall mit der
tenncken hande Im umb ſein halß und druck Ir damit zu
der erdẏ ſo vallet er gar liederlich

XXI. Breaking a bear's hug according to Scott's Liechtenauer MS., fol. 53.

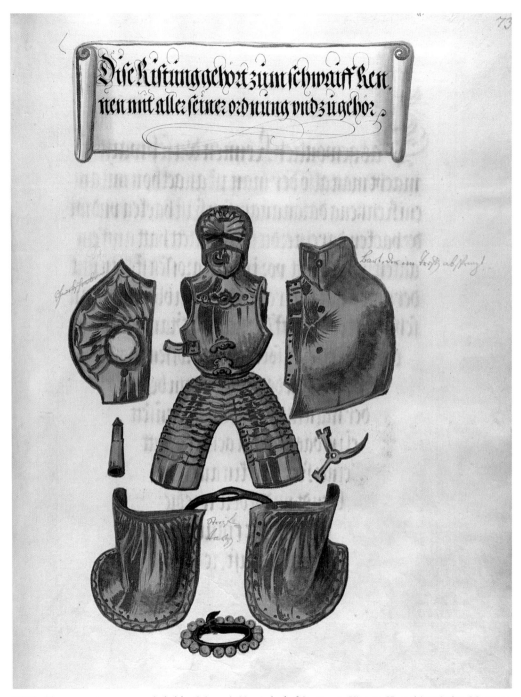

XXII. Tournament armour exploded by Schemel. *Turnierbuch*, fols. 72v-3. Vienna, Kunsthistorisches Museum.

XXIII. The same armour reassembled by Schemel. *Turnierbuch*, fols. 73v-4.

49.

XXIV. The dangers of running at large as seen in *Freydal*. Vienna, Kunsthistorisches Museum, plate 49.

Das ist der text vnd die glos von durch lauffen,
Durch lauff las hangen, mit dem knopf greuff wildu ryngen,
wer gegen dir sterck durch lauff da mit merck Glosa Merck das ist,
wen einer dem andern ein laufft fert er dan auff mit den armen vnd
                                                              auff
wil dich mit sterck vber dringen So far auch, vnd far halt dein
schwert mit der lincken hant pey dem knopf, vber deinem haubt
vnd las dein kling hinden vber deine ruck hangen, vnd lauff mit
                                        rechtn
dem haubt durch vndter seinem arm, vnd spring mit dem rechtn
fuess hinter seinen rechten, vnd mit dem sprung far jm mit dem
rechten arm vorn wol vmb den leib, vnd fass jn alß auff dein
rechte hueff vnd wirff jn fur dich, alß am nächsten gemalt stett

XXV. Scott's Liechtenauer MS. showing how to charge under an oncoming opponent, duck under his right arm, grip
him around the body and then throw him over one's right hip. Fol. 16v.

Das ist ein stuck aber von durchlauffen/
Merck, wen er dich in dem ein lauffen mit dem schwert oben
mit sterck wil über dringen/ so halt dein schwert mit der lin
cken handt pey dem knoff/ und las dein kling über deinen rück
hangen/ und ß laufft mit dem haubt durch under seine rechtn
arm/ und pleib mit dem rechten fues vor seine rechten/ und far
Jm mit dem rechten arm hindten wol umb den leib und far
Jn auff dein rechte huff/ und wirff Jn hinnter dich alß gemalt stett —

XXVI. Scott's Liechtenauer MS. with a similar move, but supposed to work in the opposite direction. It is
feasible, but does not look effective. Fol. 17.

Uber am ringen Ein Schwert

Merck wan In ainem ein lauffs so las d dein schwert aus d der
linckin hant und halt es in der rechtin und far Im mit
dem knopff oben uber sein rechtin arm und zeuch damit
undtrsich und mit der linckin begreiff seinen rechtin
tolpogen und spring mit dem linckin fuß fur sein rechtn
und ruck In also uber den fuß auff dein rechte seytten
als am nachsti da gemelt stet

XXVII. Scott's Liechtenauer MS. showing how to apply pressure on an opponent's right elbow. Fol. 17v.

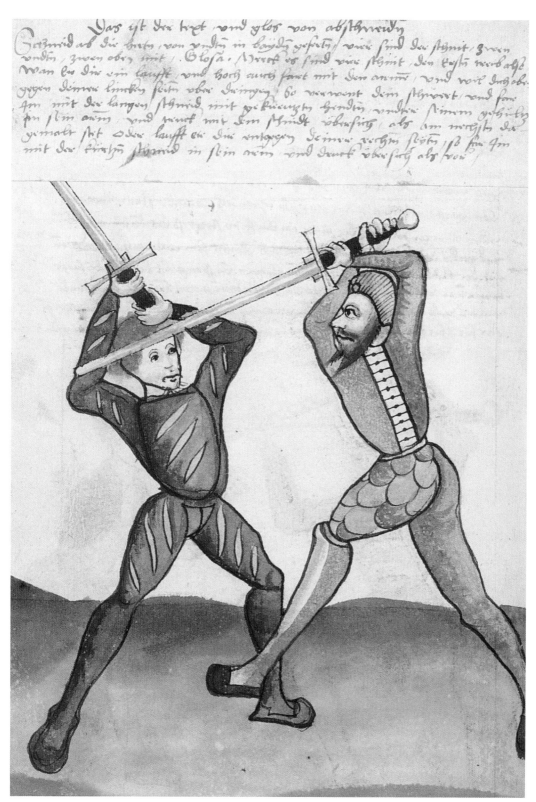

XXVIII. Scott's Liechtenauer MS. The fighter on the left assumes the overhead *Vom Dach* stance, while his opponent is supposed to be attacking with the *Ochs* stance but is hampered by having his left hand attached to his right arm and vice versa. Fol. 19v.

Notes

PREFACE

1 For a short summary of Scott's achievement, see Robert C. Woosnam-Savage,
'Robert Lyons Scott (1871–1939)', *Fifth
Park Lane Arms Fair* (1988), pp. 10–14.
See also Félix Joubert, *Catalogue of the Collection of European Arms and Armour formed
at Greenock by R.L. Scott* (privately published, 1924). Two special numbers of the
Scottish Art Review were devoted to material from the Scott Collection: VI, No. 1
(1956); XII, No. 2 (1969); and some of
the material is described in a brief guide
by J.G. Scott, *European Arms and Armour
at Kelvingrove* (Glasgow, 1980).

2 On the Corble Collection, see Hilde
Peeters and Tom Vanleeuwe, *Archibald
Harrison Corble 1883–1944. His Biography
and Donation to the Catholic University of
Leuven* (Leuven, n.d.). See also Chris
Coppens, ed., *En Garde! Schermen verbeeld.
Schermboeken uit de Corble-collectie, wapens &
attributen* (Leuven, 1998).

INTRODUCTION

1 Thomas Hobbes, *Leviathan, or the Matter,
Forme, & Power of a Commonwealth Ecclesiasticall and Civill* (1651), p. 22.

2 See Sydney Anglo, 'The man who taught
Leonardo darts. Pietro Monte and his
"lost" fencing book', *Antiquaries Journal*,
LXIX (1989), pp. 261–78. Monte
remains something of a mystery. He is
almost certainly the 'Pero Monte' referred
to in a letter from 'Los reyes católicos'
(Ferdinand V of Aragon and Isabel I of
Castile) to Galeazzo da Sanseverino in
January 1496 (*Documentos sobre relaciones
internacionales de los reyes Católicos*, ed.
Antonio de la Torre, Volumen V, 1495–97
(Barcelona, 1965, p. 200) as having supplied them with information; and on the
basis of his having written his treatises in
Castilian (and dealt with Spanish systems
of sword fighting and wrestling), I believe
that he belongs to the rich Iberian tradition of masters of arms – a view long ago
suggested by C.F. Duro, 'Noticias de la
vida y obras de Gonzálo de Ayora y fragmentos de su crónica inédita', *Boletín de
la Real Academia de la Historia*, XVII
(1890), pp. 435–6. Monte has, however,
been identified as the condottiere Pietro
del Monte of the family Marchesi di
Monte Santa Maria by Marie-Madeleine
Fontaine, *Le Condottiere Pietro del Monte
philosophe et écrivain de la Renaissance*
(Geneva-Paris, 1991). In an article,
'Comment Pietro del Monte, condottiere
Italien parlait Espagnol', *Bibliothèque
d'Humanisme et Renaissance*, LIV (1992),
pp. 163–73, Fontaine has suggested why
such a man might have been able to speak
some Spanish. But that is wholly irrelevant. The problem is not whether a contemporary Italian soldier could manage
conversational Spanish but why he should
choose to write several long, technical
treatises in Spanish before having them
translated into Latin. This notion was
dismissed as absurd by Carlo Dionisotti,
'Appunti sulla nobiltà', *Rivista Storica
Italiana*, Anno CI (1989), pp. 302–5. Yet
in a revised version of her article,
reprinted in *Libertés et savoirs du corps*

à la renaissance (Caen, 1993), Fontaine refers to Dionisotti favourably without noticing that he completely rejects her position.

3 *Petri Montij exercitiorum: atque artis militaris collectanea* (Milan, 1509), I, 2.

4 Martial artists such as John Clements, S. Matthew Galas and J. Christoph Amberger, are becoming increasingly concerned with the analysis of historical sources as the articles in *Hammerterz Forum* (edited and produced by Amberger) amply demonstrate.

5 The early history of pistol duelling awaits its historian. Frederick Bryson, *The Sixteenth-Century Italian Duel* (Chicago, 1938), pp. 47, 52, 58–9, cites a few theoretical references to the use of firearms; and François Billacois, *Le Duel dans la société française des XVIᵉ–XVIIᵉ siècles* (Paris, 1986), pp. 105–6, notes some pistol duels (but only one prior to the seventeenth century). Brantôme, in his *Discours des duels*, remarks *en passant* that duelling on horseback with pistols was commonplace, but provides no evidence. On the other hand, his observation that, in such duels, the judges and guards of the field were as likely to be shot as the principals, suggests something about the accuracy of these weapons. Alessandro Massario Malatesta, *Compendio dell'heroica arte di cavalleria* (Venice, 1600), fols 8v–11, refers to single combat on horseback with pistols, but is primarily concerned with war. However, a document of 1657 suggests that, in France, firearms had by then started to make an impact on duels which were fought with 'Swords, Daggers, Knives, and of late Pistols or other Fire-Arms'. See *The Laws of Honor: or, An Account of the Suppression of Duels in France. Extracted out of the French King's Edicts etc.* (1685), p. 90.

CHAPTER I

1 *Select Pleas of the Crown*, ed. F.W. Maitland (Selden Society, 1888), pp. 129–33; *Rotuli litterarum clausarum*, ed. T.D. Hardy (Record Commission, 1833–4), I, pp. 410b, 424.

2 *Rot. litt. claus*, I, p. 88b.

3 V.H. Galbraith, 'The Death of a Champion (1287)', in *Studies in Medieval History Presented to Frederick Maurice Powicke*, ed. R.W. Hunt, W.A. Pantin and R.W. Southern (Oxford, 1948), pp. 283–95.

4 Similar instruction was allowed to litigants in Germany from a very early period. See A. Schultz, *Das höfische Leben zur Zeit der Minnesinger* (Leipzig, 1879), II, p. 134. The armourer, John Hill, in his treatise on judicial combat (1434), refers to the 'counsaille' assigned to each litigant who is 'ordeyned and bounden to teche hym alle maner of fightynge and soteltees of Armes that longeth for a battaile sworne'. See the text printed in Charles ffoulkes, *The Armourer and His Craft from the XIth to the XVIth Century* (1912), p. 172.

5 *Calendar of Letter Books of the City of London*, Letter Book C, fol. 15d.

6 Not only was the process of trial by battle singularly stupid, but the habit of choosing skilled champions made it even more so. As was pointed out in the latter half of the twelfth century, it would have been more sensible to choose decrepit men to make clearer the miracle of God's judgement. See John W. Baldwin, *Masters, Princes and Merchants. The Social Views of Peter the Chanter and his Circle* (Princeton, 1970), I, p. 327.

7 Henry Charles Lea, *Superstition and Force*, 4th edn (Philadelphia, 1892), Lib. II, Cap. vii, pp. 179–98, gives a succinct summary of the role of the champions. For fundamental bibliography, see 'Dei campioni' in Giorgio Enrico Levi, *Il duello giudiziario. Enciclopedia e bibliografia* (Florence, 1932), pp. 132–44.

8 *Select Pleas of the Crown* (1888), pp. 123–7.

9 George Neilson, *Trial by Battle* (Glasgow, 1890), p. 49. The case is referred to in *Henrici de Bracton de legibus et consuetudinibus Angliae*, ed. Sir Travers Twiss (Rolls Series, 1878–83), pp. 516–17.

10 H.T. Riley, ed., *Memorials of London and London Life in the XIIIth, XIVth, and XVth Centuries* (1868), pp. 54, 64, 86–8, 112, 192, 268–9, 325, 371, 453, 491–4.

11 J.D. Aylward, *The English Master of Arms from the Twelfth to the Twentieth Century* (1956), pp. 13–16, 255–6. Many English

masters boasted another, more socially acceptable occupation although it is not clear whether this was a cover or because teaching the martial arts was unremunerative. German masters, who enjoyed higher social esteem than their English counterparts, were often members of another craft. See Karl Wassmannsdorff, *Sechs Fechtschulen der Marxbrüder und Federfechter* (Heidelberg, 1870).

12 On 1496 see J.H. Baker, ed., *The Reports of Sir John Selden*, II (Selden Society, 1978), p. 313. On William Smith's fencing school see Public Record Office MS KB 9/975, m 36. I am grateful to Rhys Robinson for these references.

13 Sir Humphrey Gilbert, *Queene Elizabethes Achademy*, ed. F.J. Furnivall, in *Early English Treatises and Poems on Education, Precedence and Manners in Olden Time* (E.E.T.S., extra series III, 1869), p. 7.

14 Public Record Office MS C 82/770. On the Tudor masters see Aylward (1956), pp. 17–73; Jay P. Anglin, 'The schools of defense in Elizabethan London', *Renaissance Quarterly*, XXXVII (1984). pp. 393–410. On the London masters, see Herbert Berry, ed., *The Noble Science. A Study and Transcription of Sloane MS 2530, Papers of the Masters of Defence of London, Temp. Henry VIII to 1590* (London and Toronto, 1991); and my review of Berry, in *Renaissance Studies*, VII (1993), pp. 317–19.

15 Wassmannsdorff, *Fechtschulen* (1870), p. 1, n. 3; Eduard Winkelmann, *Urkundenbuch der Universität Heidelberg* (Heidelberg, 1886), I, pp. 106–7; Henri Daressy, *Archives des maîtres d'armes de Paris* (Paris, 1888), pp. 12–13, 128; Gabriel Letainturier-Fradin, *Les Joueurs d'épée à travers les siècles* (Paris, n.d.), pp. 74–5; J.B.L. Crevier, *Histoire de l'Université de Paris* (Paris, 1761), VI, pp. 306, 345; VII, p. 73.

16 Alfred Schaer, *Die altdeutschen Fechter und Spielleute* (Strasbourg, 1901), p. 68.

17 'Maestros de armas', *Memorias de la Real Academia Española*, XI (1914), p. 267; José Gestoso y Pérez, *Esgrimidores sevillanos. Documentos inéditos para su historia* (Madrid, 1911), p. 2.

18 Wassmansdorff, *Fechtschulen* (1870); Schaer (1901); Francesco Novati, intro-duction to his edition of Fiore de' Liberi da Premariacco *Flos duellatorum in armis, sine armis, equester, pedester* (Bergamo, 1902); Gestoso y Pérez (1911).

19 Henry, 'Sur l'art de l'escrime en Espagne au Moyen Age', *Revue archéologique*, 1er série, VIe année (1849), pp. 582–93.

20 A late Spanish example of a master's certificate, dated 26 May 1847 is in the Corble Collection at Leuven, 4.C.48. It is for Faustino de Zea and consists of seven card folios, lavishly if crudely illuminated, signed and countersigned, and describes fencing as 'la ciencia filosófica y matemática'.

21 Marozzo (1536), Book II, Cap. 143, *Esordio*.

22 Dall'Agocchie (1572), fols 7v–8. This passage is cited by Pallavicini (1673), in his letter to the reader, where he similarly regrets the passing of old methods of examination.

23 Gaiani (1619), pp. 7–8. On the Spanish system of having masters examined by the 'Maestri Generali', especially in Madrid, see Pallavicini (1670), pp. 15–16 where he refers back to Narváez *La verdadera destrezza*, fol. 25. A similar passage in Marcelli (1686), p. 13, derives (like much else in his work) from Pallavicini.

24 La Curne de Sainte-Palaye, *Dictionnaire de l'ancien langage français* (1875), VII, p. 114; *Bulletin de la Société historique des Archives d'Aunis et de Saintonge* (1888), p. 299.

25 Daressy (1888), pp. 53–83.

26 As well as indicating a concern for standards, this accusation gives substance to Ascham's remark, shortly afterwards, that there were schools of fence in England 'almost in every town'. See *Toxophilus* in *The Whole Works of Roger Ascham*, ed. Giles (1864), II, ii, p. 88.

27 See Claude Chauchadis, *La Loi du duel. Le Code du point d'honneur dans l'Espagne des XVe–XVIIe siècles* (Toulouse, 1997), pp. 263–7.

28 Dancie (1623), pp. 5–6.

29 On playing for prizes in Tudor England, see Aylward (1956), pp. 30–8.

30 *Journal de voyage de Michel de Montaigne*, ed. François Rigolot (Paris, 1992), p. 41.

31 Claude Blair and Ida Delamer, 'The Dublin civic sword', *Proceedings of the*

Royal Irish Academy, LXXXVIII (1988), p. 127.

32 *Hommes illustres et grands capitaines François,* in *Oeuvres complètes de Pierre de Bourdeille Seigneur de Brantôme,* ed. Ludovic Lalanne (Paris, 1873), V, p. 277.

33 E. Fyot, *L'Escrime à Dijon de 1500 à 1911* (Dijon, 1911), pp. 3–5.

34 Sousa Viterbo, *A esgrima em Portugal. Subsidios para a sua história* (Lisbon, 1899), pp. 33–5, 58–62.

35 Sousa Viterbo (1899), pp. 46–8; Joseph Swetnam, *The Schoole of the Noble and Worthy Science of Defence* (1617), sigs. C3v–4.

36 For the Turner/Crichton affair, see Aylward (1956), pp. 36–7, 42–3, 81.

37 Ben Jonson, *The New Inne,* II, v. Blenkinsopps' career was linked with that of John Godwin who, on 30 March 1564, was prohibited by the Cambridge authorities from establishing a fencing school. At that date a certain John Godwin was still only a free scholar, but Godwin crops up again in a letter dated 20 January 1580 from the Mayor and Aldermen of Cambridge to Lord Burghley where he is described (correctly) as a Master of Defence and 'no common fencer'. He had been challenged at six weapons by John Blenkinsopps, but the officials feared that public peace might be disturbed as was usual after such exercises. Godwin had gained the rank of Master in May 1579 a fortnight before Blenkinsopps. See C.H. Cooper, *Annals of Cambridge* (Cambridge, 1843), II, pp. 372–3, V, p. 296; Berry, *The Noble Science* (1991), pp. 17, 32.

38 Fiore de' Liberi, ed. Novati (1902), pp. 18–19.

39 For a list of the seven Parisian masters, extracted from the *Taille* of 1292, see Daressy (1888), p. 126. For the document itself see Hercule J.F. Geraud, *Paris sous Philippe-le-Bel, notamment d'après un manuscrit contenant le rôle de la taille 1292* (Paris, 1837). For the gratuitous Italianization of three of the Parisian masters (as Tomasso, Nicolò, and Filippo) see Gelli, *L'arte* (1906), p. 13.

40 See Wierschin (1965); Hils (1985).

41 For information on the French masters, see Daressy (1888) and Letainturier-Fradin, *Les Joueurs d'épée;* on Spanish masters see Gestoso y Pérez (1911); for the Portuguese see Sousa Viterbo (1899).

42 Pallavicini (1670), p. 10, comments on the fact that there must have been many excellent masters who, because they did not write about their art, have been 'buried in oblivion'. See Chapter 3, pp. 92–4.

43 The handgun practice is, in some ways, the most remarkable feature of this mid-fifteenth-century scene. Nearly a century and a half later, Swanenburgh (fig. 4) shows arquebus practice at Leiden, yet evidence of firearms instruction in the schools is scanty. The masters do not discuss the matter, and only scraps of information survive such as Sir Humphrey Gilbert's suggestion that a master appointed to teach riding, tilting and tourneying should also provide instruction 'to skirmish on horsebacke with pistolles' (*Queene Elizabethes Achademy,* p. 4). In an Act of 1536, soldiers at Calais, 'apt and willing' to learn the 'feat of shooting in a gun', were to receive instruction every Tuesday and Thursday afternoon. And there is a Privy Council letter of July 1541 concerning a certain Bernadyn de Valois appointed to teach various unspecified gentlemen 'to shoot in a gun' (*Letters and Papers of the Reign of Henry VIII,* XVI, p. 467). Such references could easily be multiplied for both England and the Continent. But they would not establish the existence of a regular pedagogic system analogous to that which had long since evolved for close combat.

44 Furthermore, Leiden's *salle d'armes* was situated in the former chapel of the convent. See R.E.O. Ekkart, ed., *Athenae Batavae De Leidse Universiteit/The University of Leiden 1575–1975* (Leiden, 1975), p. 29.

45 Johann Christoph Neyffer and Ludwig Ditzinger, *Illustrissimi Wirtembirgici ducalis novi collegii quod Tubingae quam situm quam studia quam exercitia accurata delineatio* (n.p., n.d. but probably Tübingen, 1600). Three of Ditzinger's engravings (football, the fencing school and tilting at the ring) are reproduced in Peter Kühnst, *Sports. A Cultural History in the Mirror of Art* (Dresden, 1996), p. 60.

46 Johann Andreas Schmidt, *Leib-beschirmende und Fecht-Kunst* (Nuremberg, 1713); Alexander Doyle, *Neue Alamodische Ritterliche Fecht und Schirm-Kunst* (Nuremberg, 1715); G. Belfin, *Abregé de l'exercice des armes*, dated 'à Luxembourg 1767' (manuscript treatise in the Scott Collection). Henry Blackwell, *The Art of Defence* survives only as a series of twenty-four engraved plates with title-page. It was printed, without date, by John King 'att the signe of the Globe in the Poultry', and – according to a manuscript note by Alfred Hutton prefixed to his own copy (now in the National Art Library at the Victoria and Albert Museum) – it comprised 'extra plates' intended by Blackwell for a 'large book on fencing which was never completed'. See also Aylward, (1956), pp. 179–81.

47 Marozzo (1536), II, Caps 144, 145. Marozzo also explains the use of the wall figure, with all the blows indicated by letters, in I, Cap. 1.

48 Silver (1599), pp. 64–5. A century later, Sir William Hope, *The Fencing Master's Advice to his Scholar* (1692), pp. 14–16, described 'How a Fencing School should be Ordered, for the better accommodation of the Scholars'. The room should be well lit, neat, clean, and with chairs so that everyone except the master may be seated. It should be quiet and without distractions; and all shoes and 'Flurets' should be hung out of the way to avoid accidents. In short, the room should be large and pleasant so that scholars may delight in their practice, 'which none can do when they play in a dark and nefty room'.

49 The use of weights parallels, perhaps consciously, Vegetius, *De re militari* (I, 11, 12, 14, 17) where much is made of training with weapons of double weight in order to facilitate handling the real thing. Machiavelli, *Arte della guerra*, II (Feltrinelli ed., p. 372) develops this idea and says that the Romans made their young men train in armour twice as heavy as that used in battle. Monte (1509), II, 53, suggests that, a few days before serious fighting with a normal sword, it is helpful to practise with a much heavier weapon, and the idea occurs in Manci-

olino (1531), fol. 5 and Narváez (1600), fol. 245. Di Grassi (1570), however, in the discussion of exercises at the end of his treatise, disapproves of such practice because it diminishes speed which is all-important.

50 Brantôme (1873), VI, p. 296.

51 Dall'Agocchie (1572), fols. 28v–9; de La Touche (Paris, 1670), II, 7.

52 On the cult of secrecy in Japanese sword play, see Oscar Ratti and Adèle Westbrook, *Secrets of the Samurai. A Survey of the Martial Arts of Feudal Japan* (Rutland, Vermont and Tokyo, 1973), pp. 165–8. However, Miyamoto Musashi, the famous seventeenth-century master swordsman, was critical of the 'indoor' techniques of the exclusive fencing schools. See *A Book of Five Rings*, tr. Victor Harris (1974, reprinted 1977), p. 47.

53 George Hale, *The Private Schoole of Defence. or the Defects of Publique Teachers exactly discovered, by way of Objection and Resolution* (1614), sig. C1v.

54 For Montaigne's comment on Olivier de la Marche, see Pierre Villey, *Les Sources et l'évolution des essais de Montaigne* (Paris, 1933), I, p. 235. Brantôme (1873) p. 240, declares that Olivier was 'fort accomply pour les armes et pour la plume'.

55 See S. Anglo, 'Anglo-Burgundian feats of arms: Smithfield, June 1467', *Guildhall Miscellany*, II (1965), pp. 271–83.

56 See Chapter 4, pp. 143–4.

57 See *La Tresjoyeuse, plaisante et recreative hystoire, composée par le loyal serviteur, des faiz, gestes, triumphes et prouesses du bon chevalier sans paour et sans reproche, le gentil Seigneur de Bayart*, ed. Petitot (Paris, 1820), pp. 112–13; Jean d'Auton, *Chroniques de Louis XII*, ed. R. de Maulde la Clavière (Paris, 1893), III, pp. 121–6; Symphorien Champier, *Les Gestes ensemble la vie du preulx Chevalier Bayard* in M.L. Cimber and F. Danjou, *Archives curieuses de l'histoire de France* (Paris, 1835), sér. 1, ii, pp. 104–5.

58 Even when a narrator not only had martial skill and eloquence but also participated in an affray, technical information remains scanty. See Chapter 10, pp. 273–4.

59 Silver (1599), pp. 65–72.

60 Sir Thomas Overbury, *Characters* in *The Miscellaneous Works in Prose and Verse of*

Sir Thomas Overbury, ed. E.F. Rimbault (1856), pp. 111–12.

61 Although these two books, by Jayme Pons de Perpiñan and Pedro de la Torre, are constantly referred to by bibliographers there is some doubt about their dates (see Novati, p. 107, n. 169), and much more doubt about whether they were printed. Pons is frequently cited by Pacheco de Narváez who unfortunately says only that he wrote 135 years before Carranza which could mean about 1447. However, Pallavicini (1670) states that both Pons and de la Torre had their books *printed* in 1474 and cites the latter with precision (at pp. 10, 27, 36, 42, 54, 74). See Chapter 3, p. 93.

62 Francisco Román, *Tratado de la esgrima con figuras por Francisco Román natural de Carmona* (Seville, 1532). On Román see Enrique de Leguina, *Bibliografía e historia de la esgrima Española* (Madrid, 1904), pp. 39, 107–8; José Gestoso y Pérez (1911), pp. 3, 5–6; 'Maestros de armas' (1914), pp. 268–9.

63 The approximate overall number of surviving printed books relating, wholly or in part, either to sword fighting and its concomitants, to wrestling, or to mounted combat with sword or lance are as follows: up to the year 1620 (and excluding reprints and revised editions of individual titles) there were at least thirty-nine Italian books, twenty-three German, sixteen Spanish, ten French and eight English.

64 Royal Armouries Manuscript I. 33. This manuscript is described by Hils (1985), pp. 84–6, where it is assigned to the early fourteenth century, although Hils cites Lhotsky who suggested a slightly earlier date. It is discussed by Jeffrey L. Singman, 'The medieval swordsman: a thirteenth-century German fencing manuscript', *Royal Armouries Yearbook*, II (1997), pp. 129–36. Singman cites Karl E. Lochner, *Die Entwicklungsphasen der europäische Fechtkunst* (Vienna, 1953), pp. 11–12, to the effect that there was an Italian combat manual by the 'del Serpente brothers' dating from 1295, but Lochner himself gives no evidence. Nor does Ada Bruhn Hoffmeyer in 'From mediaeval sword to renaissance rapier', in *Gladius*, II (1963),

pp. 40–1, where she says that 'As early as 1295 the Italian del Serpente of Milan had written a work on the technique of fencing'. The only contemporary serpent I have so far located in connection with fencing is Phelippe, one of the Parisian masters mentioned in the *Taille* of 1292, who lived in the 'rue de la Serpente'. For further misinformation see Gelli, *L'arte* (1906), p. 13.

65 Heinrich von Gunterrodt, *De veris principiis artis dimicatoriae* (Wittemberg, 1579), sigs C3v–C4v.

66 On Döbringer and Lecküchner, see Hils (1985), pp. 110, 153, 155, 185, 186. The Baron des Guerres chose the bastard sword for his combat against de Fendilles: see Marc Vulson, Sieur de la Colombière, *Le Vray Théâtre d'honneur et de chevalerie, ou le miroir héroïque de la noblesse* (Paris, 1648), II, pp. 439–71; Brantôme, *Discours sur les duels*, in *Oeuvres complètes*, ed. Lalanne, VI, pp. 235–40, 502–3.

67 Anthoine de la Sale, *Le Petit Jehan de Saintré*, Caps 81, 82.

68 On Martínez de Toledo, see Chapter 6, n. 84.

69 Nuremberg, Germanisches National-museum, Codex MS 3227a. The contents are discussed in Wierschin (1965), pp. 31–4; Hils (1985), pp. 104–10.

70 Fiore, ed. Novati (1902), pp. 22, 193. On the manuscripts of this treatise, see Chapter 2, n. 21.

71 Hils (1985), pp. 75–6. Fabian von Auerswald similarly features in his own treatise as does Angelo in his. Thibault, too, appears in his own *Académie de l'espée* but only in the first plate which illustrates how to draw the sword.

72 Combinations of sword with dagger, cape, buckler or small 'rotella di notte' were still being seriously considered as of contemporary value in Pallavicini (1673); and Bondi di Mazo, *La spada maestra* (Venice, 1696), has a solid section on sword and dagger, followed by a brief discussion of sword and cape against sword and *targa*.

73 For an interesting description and pictorial record of a duel fought with the case of rapiers, see Silvio Longhi, *Il duello dipinto di Castiglione del Lago: Pitigliano, 26 maggio 1546* (Cortona, 1995). Another duel with two swords is described in *Les*

Mémoires de Messire Martin du Bellay, ed. Michaud and Poujoulat (Paris, 1838), pp. 466–7. This was fought before the King of France in 1538 between the Seigneurs de Veniers and de Sarzay who managed quite well but, 'at length, like men not greatly accustomed to such weapons, they came to grips, abandoning their swords'.

74 Falloppia (1594), sig. A.2r–v. Sainct Didier (1573) concentrates on the use of sword alone, but it is not clear whether he intended to supplement this with a further treatise on other weapons and combinations.

75 The manuscript is in Vienna, Kunsthistorisches Museum, Kunstkammer Inv. P.5073. It was edited in its entirety, in black and white heliogravure, by Quirin von Leitner, *Freydal des Kaisers Maximilian I. Turniere und Mummereien* (Vienna, 1880–2), where the 255 illustrations are amazingly faithful, especially bearing in mind that they are not photographed from the original manuscript but from specially drawn copies – a labour-intensive procedure which makes the mind boggle.

76 Henry, 'Sur l'art de l'escrime en Espagne', pp. 590–3; José Gestoso y Pérez (1911), pp. 12–13; 'Maestros de armas' (1914), pp. 271–2.

77 *The Diary of Henry Machyn*, ed. J.G. Nichols (1848), p. 250.

78 Sir Humphrey Gilbert, *Queene Elizabethes Achademy* (1869), p. 7. Cf. the weapons in the challenge to the Italian masters of London issued by George Silver and his brother Toby, listed in Silver (1599), p. 66.

79 On military academies, see Chapter 10, pp. 282–3.

80 Barthélemi de Chasseneux, *Catalogus gloriae mundi*, Part XI, Consideratio 52; Mario Muta, *Commentaria . . . in Antiquissimas Consuetudines* (Palermo, 1843), Cap. 72, No. 23; Pallavicini (1670), p. 4.

81 *The Reports of Sir John Selden*, ed. J.H. Baker (Selden Society, 1978), Introduction, pp. 310–14.

82 So-called by Felix Gilbert, 'Machiavelli: the renaissance of the art of war', in *Makers of Modern Strategy*, ed. E.M. Earle (Princeton, 1944).

83 See Anglo, *Machiavelli: A Dissection* (1969), pp. 143–7, 153–5.

84 The practice of archery is first enjoined in the Assize of Arms in 1252. See Stubbs, *Select Charters* (Oxford, 1870), p. 372.

85 Vergerio, 'De ingenuis moribus', tr. W.H. Woodward in *Vittorino da Feltre and Other Humanist Educators* (Cambridge, 1897), p. 115.

86 On Luther, see Carl von Raumer, *Geschichte der Pädagogik* (Berlin, 1843–54), I, pp. 142–3. For Zwingli, see the English translation, *Certeyne preceptes* (1548), sig. C.3v–4.

87 Valerius Maximus, *Romae antiquae descriptio*, II. 3, tr. Samuel Speed (1678).

88 Richard Mulcaster, *Positions*, ed. R.H. Quick (1888), pp. 76–9.

89 Miyamoto Musashi, *A Book of Five Rings*, tr. Victor Harris (1974), p. 17.

90 Fiore, ed. Novati (1902), pp. 194–5.

91 Salvator Fabris, *Scienza e pratica d'arme* (Copenhagen, 1606), sig. A.3v.

92 George Hale, *The Private Schoole of Defence* (1614), sigs A.3v-4; Pallavicini (1670), p. 54.

93 Jean-Baptiste Le Perche, *L'Exercice des armes ou le maniement du fleuret* (Paris, 1676), 'Avertissement au lecteur'.

94 Cf. Captain M.W. Berriman, *The Militiaman's Manual and Sword Play without a Master. Rapier and Broad Sword Exercises copiously explained and illustrated* (New York, 1859). Berryman (also on his title page) modestly describes this effusion as 'the most perfect manual ever placed in a soldier's hand', and as a book 'to be carried in every soldier's knapsack'.

95 Marin Bresciani, *Li trastulli guerrieri* (Brescia, 1668), Cap. 3.

96 *Escrime de chambre. Méthode pour s'exercer, seul, à faire des armes par M. le Commandant E.T.* (Paris, Limoges, n.d.).

97 J.B. Viti, *Taccometro. Machine d'escrime du Prof. Gioberti* (n.p., n.d.). This curious pamphlet is in the Corble Collection, at the Catholic University of Leuven.

98 Germanisches Nationalmuseum, Nuremberg, Codex MS 3227a, fol. 15v. I must thank S. Matthew Galas for providing a selection of notes and translations from this important manuscript.

99 Monte (1509), I, 2. Unlike the man, mocked by James Howell, *Instructions for*

Forreine Travell (1642), p. 2, 'who thought to bee a good Fencer, by looking on Agrippa's book–postures only'. In the second edition (1650), after 'Agrippa's', the author has updated his allusion by adding 'or Don Lius [*sic*] de Nervius'.

100 Saviolo (1595), sig. H1v.

101 Viggiani (1575), fol. 52v–3. The author had died some twenty-three years prior to the publication.

102 These terms, *spada da giuoco* and *spada da filo* are self-explanatory. But Viggiani also uses the term *spada da marra* (that is literally with a sort of mattock or fluke) for the rebated sword. In an inventory of 1543, drawn up for the Gonzagas, there are references to 'lame da spada da gioco'. See James G. Mann, 'The lost armoury of the Gonzagas, part II', *Archaeological Journal*, C (1945), pp. 120–1 where Mann misleadingly translates the term as blades for 'fencing swords'. Both sharp and rebated swords were equally for 'fencing', but the meaning of that word was notably different from what was current in the twentieth century. On the other hand, things were obviously changing even in the Renaissance. From examples given by Leguina, *Glosario* (1912), pp. 390, 429, 431–2, it is clear that in late sixteenth-century Spain, the *spada da marra* was recognized as an Italian equivalent to the *spada negra* which was a blunted sword with a button and itself synonymous with the *espada de esgrima*. This issue, which is more than a mere question of semantics, is discussed by Pallavicini (1673), 'A chi legge'.

103 The crucial difference between fighting with protective garments and rebated weapons on the one hand and with what earlier masters referred to as 'sharps' on the other, has been commented upon by J. Christoph Amberger, 'Fear! The role of angst in single combat', *Hammerterz Forum. The International Newsletter for the Fencing Collector* (Spring/Summer 1996), pp. 17–19, 31.

104 Castle (1885), p. 7.

105 Sebastiano Fausto, *Duello* (Venice, 1560), p. 6; Bernardo Sacco, *De Italicorum rerum varietate et elegantia* (Pavia, 1565), fol. 97v.

106 Saviolo (1595), pp. 11–12.

107 Brantôme (1873), p. 269.

108 Hale, *The Private Schoole of Defence* (1614), sigs. A5v, C6. Cf. Monsieur J. Olivier, *Fencing Familiarized, or a New Treatise on the Art of Sword Play* (1771), p. xlviii, who recommends fencing as providing men with the 'faculty of defence whether it be of their honour or of their life' when either of these is threatened by 'disagreeable accident or attacked by those turbulents and dangerous persons whose correction is of service to Society in general'.

109 Gaiani (1619), p. 1; Castiglione, *Il Cortegiano*, I, xx.

110 P.L. Hughes and J.F. Larkin, *Tudor Royal Proclamations* (New Haven and London, 1969), II, Nos 432, 493. See also Nos 542, 601, 646.

111 William Harrison, *A Description of England*, originally printed as an introduction to Raphael Holinshed, *Chronicles* (1577) and reprinted several times thereafter. The relevant chapter 'Of armour and munition' is Book II, Cap. 12 of that first edition. In Elizabethan England, a military man might consider himself unarmed if only bearing a sword and dagger: see E.M. Tenison, *Elizabethan England* (Leamington, 1932–51), I, p. 178; XI, p. 475. It is also curious that, in contemporary illustrated books of costume such as those compiled by Caspar Rutz or Cesare Vecelli, the 'plebei adolescentis in Anglia habitus' prances along with sword and buckler at his side. Nevertheless, Harrison was certainly wrong in assuming that carrying bladed weapons was an English idiosyncracy.

112 Bibliothèque Nationale MS Espagnol 60 is a collection of edicts, proclamations and public cries, both in print and manuscript, relating to life in Valencia from the mid-1570s to the early seventeenth century. As well as matters of public safety it includes material on taverns, gaming houses, the food trade, the horse trade, hunting, travellers, vagabonds, bandits, brigands, beggars, blasphemers, coiners, the registration of aliens, prosecution of criminals, and the expulsion of the Moriscoes.

113 Ghisliero (1587), pp. 30–1. Cf. Pallavicini (1670), p. 31, where he advises teachers to ensure that their pupils understand the difference between school fight-

ing and street fighting. In the former they can keep their feet wide apart; in the latter they must keep them closer together because of the poor terrain and muddy and stony surfaces.

114 Di Grassi (tr. 1594), sig. D4r–v.

115 See Chapter 10, pp. 273–7.

116 Marozzo (1536), II, p. 143, *Esordio*.

117 Pallavicini (1670), pp. 16, 28–9.

118 See Chapter 4, pp. 122–3.

119 Monte (1509), I, 1.

120 In fact, according to Lomazzo, Leonardo was asked by a Milanese master of arms, Gentile de' Borri, to illustrate a work for him, but the outcome is not known. See Giovanni Paolo Lomazzo, *Trattato dell'arte della pittura, scoltura ed architettura* in *Scritti sulle arti*, ed. R.P. Ciardi (Florence, 1974), pp. 334–6.

CHAPTER II

1 Francesco Ferdinando Alfieri, *Lo spadone* (Padua, 1653). For other works by Alfieri, see Jacopo Gelli, *Bibliografia generale della scherma* (Milan, 1906). Carl Thimm, *A Complete Bibliography of Fencing and Duelling* (London, 1896) also lists Alfieri's works: but his transcription of Italian titles is often eccentric.

2 Francesco di Lorenzo Altoni, 'Trattato dell'armi intitolato monomachia' (this is the title heading of the 'Proemio'; the first chapter is headed 'Trattato della arte di scherma'), Biblioteca Nazionale, Florence, MS II.iii.315, fol. 4. Cf. Flaminio della Croce, *L'essercitio della cavalleria et d'altre materie* (Antwerp, 1625), sig. b.2, where he considers that the primary purpose of illustrations is to give pleasure to readers.

3 Falloppia (1584), sig. A.iiv.

4 Dancie (1623), p. 83. Liancour (1686), does use plates, each showing two pairs of fencers, but points out (at p. 6) that 'because the quantity of principles would demand too great a number' he has contented himself with including only the main postures and representing therein the greater part of what he has to say.

5 Zachary Wylde, *The English Master of Defence* (York, 1711), sig. A.2v; A. Lonnergan, *The Fencer's Guide* (1771), pp.

vii–viii; Joseph Roland, *The Amateur of Fencing, or a Treatise on the Art of Sword Defence* (1809), pp. xxx–xxxii. Despite Lonnergan's objections, he includes a folding plate showing footprints in a primitive track system. However, since this is bound opposite the page to which it refers (p. 252) but is labelled 'to face page 254' – and since the text 'the scheme for the Backsword explained' (p. 252) should elucidate the diagram, but does not – it is possible to understand Lonnergan's doubts about visual aids.

6 The value of pictorial aids was most neatly expressed by the pedagogue Captain Robaglia who wrote that it is with the image that 'the eye begins, the brain continues, and the body executes': *L'Escrime ou le jeu d'épée enseigné par l'image* (Paris, 1893), p. v.

7 K. Keele, 'Leonardo da Vinci's anatomical drawings at Windsor', *Studi Vinciani*, II (1954), pp. 76–85.

8 See E.H. Gombrich, *Symbolic Images. Studies in the Art of the Renaissance* (1972).

9 E.H. Gombrich, *Art and Illusion* (Washington, DC, 1960), pp. 227–9.

10 Otto Pächt, *The Rise of Pictorial Narrative in Twelfth-Century England* (Oxford, 1962), p. 15. Beamount Newhall, *History of Photography* (1982), p. 117, quotes from the *Foreign Quarterly Review* (1839), pp. 213–18 to the effect that moving objects 'can never be delineated without the aid of memory'.

11 Fabritio Caroso, *Nobiltà di dame* (Venice, 1600). There is an English translation and edition by Julia Sutton and F. Marian Walker (Oxford, 1986). On the relative uselessness of isolated images, see Sharon Fermor, 'On the question of pictorial "evidence" for fifteenth-century dance technique', *Dance Research. The Journal of the Society for Dance Research*, V, ii (1987), pp. 18–32.

12 See E.H. Gombrich, 'Pictorial instructions', in Horace Barlow, Colin Blakemore, Miranda Weston-Smith, eds, *Images and Understanding* (Cambridge, 1990), pp. 26–45, 372.

13 Jacob de Gheyn, *The Exercise of Armes for Calivres, Muskettes, and Pikes* (The Hague, 1607). See M.J.D. Cockle, *A Bibliography of Military Books up to 1642* (1900), Item

79. For other early drill books, see Cockle, Items 89, 97, 142, 738–43.

14 Nelson Goodman, *Languages of Art. An Approach to a Theory of Symbols* (London, 1969), pp. 211–12.

15 Gilbert Austin, *Chironomia: A Treatise of Rhetorical Delivery* (1806), pp. 293, 366–7, *et passim*.

16 See Ann Hutchinson Guest, *Dance Notation: The Process of Recording Movement on Paper* (New York, 1984); Martine Kahane, Josselin Le Bourhis and Laurence Louppe, *L'Ecriture de la danse* (Bibliothèque Nationale, Paris, 1993).

17 Thoinot Arbeau, *Orchésographie* (Lengres, 1588). My references are to the translation by Mary Stewart Evans (New York, 1948). On early dance notation, see Mark Franko, *The Dancing Body in Renaissance Choreography* (Birmingham, Alabama, 1986), pp. 2–12, 79–83.

18 Arbeau (1948), p. 79.

19 On Egyptian wrestling, see Percy E. Newberry, *Beni Hasan* (1903–4); Helmut Wilsdorf, *Ringkampf im alten Ägypten* (Würzburg, 1939); Walter Wreszinski, *Atlas zur altaegyptischen Kulturgeschichte* (Leipzig, 1923), II, Plates 169–79; H.A. Groenewegen-Frankfort, *Arrest and Movement* (1951), pp. 131 ff., fig. 32a,b.

20 Royal Armouries MS I.33. See Chapter 1, p. 22 and Chapter 4, pp. 125–8.

21 Maestro Fiore de' Liberi da Premariacco, *Flos duellatorum in armis, sine armis, equester, pedester*. It exists in various forms of which the best known is the Pisani-Dossi manuscript edited by Francesco Novati (Bergamo, 1902). There were also two manuscripts listed in an early inventory of the Estense Library at Ferrara – but the whereabouts of these and the Pisani-Dossi are not now known. A very incomplete copy is in the Pierpont Morgan Library, New York, Morgan 383; but by far the best version (originally Phillipps MS 4204) is at the Getty Museum in Los Angeles.

22 *Freydal des Kaisers Maximilian I. Turniere und Mummerein*, ed. Quirin von Leitner (Vienna, 1880–2).

23 Filippo di Vadi's *De arte gladiatoria dimicandi*, written between 1482 and 1487, though different in artistic style, is similar to Fiore's work in content, combat technique and pictorial method, including the master's distinguishing crown. See p. 339 n. 40.

24 On the German fencing manuscripts, see G. Hergsell, *Talhoffers Fechtbuch aus dem Jahre 1467* (Prague, 1887); Karl Wassmannsdorff, *Aufschlüsse über Fechthandschriften und gedruckte Fechtbücher des 16. und 17. Jahrhunderts* (Berlin, 1888); Wierschin (1965); Hils (1985).

25 Both Wierschin, p. 23, and Hils, pp. 30–32, believed that Gregor Erhart's manuscript had been lost, which (to all intents and purposes) it was, after Scott purchased it for his collection in 1935. On Erhart, see the article in Thieme-Becker, X, pp. 597–8. On Ettenhard, see Martin Fernández de Navarette, *Biblioteca maritima española* (1851), I, pp. 456–8; D.L. D'Orvenipe (Pedro Vindel), *Armas y desafíos. Bibliografía de la esgrima y el duelo* (Madrid, 1911), pp. 16–19.

26 *Albrecht Dürers Fechtbuch*, ed. Friedrich Dörnhoffer, *Jahrbuch der Kunsthistorischen Sammlungen des Allerhöchsten Kaiserhauses*, XXVII, Pt ii (Vienna, 1909).

27 Andre Pauernfeindt, *Ergrundung Ritterlicher Kunst der Fechterey* (Vienna, 1516). On the bibliography of this and other early German printed texts, see Hellmuth Helwig, 'Die deutschen Fechtbücher. Eine bibliographische Übersicht', in *Börsenblatt für den deutschen Büchhandel, Frankfurter Ausgabe Nr. 55* (Frankfurt, 1966), pp. 1407–16. The French version of Pauernfeindt is *La Noble Science des joueurs d'espée* (Antwerp, 1538) in which the woodcuts are a close imitation of the German originals but with a little decoration added to some of the costumes. The cuts in the French version are marginally more crude and are arranged in a slightly different order. Pauernfeindt is the first printed fencing manual, but it was preceded by a small group of wrestling books which are discussed in Chapter 6, pp. 187–8.

28 In fact there are only twenty-one pictures because one combination is repeated (sigs B.2v, D.4v).

29 Pauernfeindt (1516), sig. G.4v. *La Noble Science* (1538) translates the text concerning this encounter correctly but forgets

to use the block of the man wielding the long sword.

30 Johannes Lecküchner, *Der altenn Fechter* (Frankfurt-am-Main, 1531). See Wassmannsdorff (1888), pp. 23–30; Helwig (1966), p. 1409; Hils (1985), pp. 183–6.

31 On Weiditz, see Campbell Dodgson, *Catalogue of Early German and Flemish Prints Preserved in the Department of Prints and Drawings in the British Museum* (London, 1911), II, pp. 139–86.

32 Fabian von Auerswald, *Ringer Kunst* (Wittenberg, 1539); facsimile edition by G.A. Schmidt, with an introduction by K. Wassmannsdorff (Leipzig, 1869); facsimile edition with essays by G. Witt, G. Wonneberger and W. Schade (Leipzig, 1988). See Chapter 6, pp. 188–9.

33 On Francisco Román, see Chapter 1, n. 62.

34 See the entry on Marozzo's *Opera nova* in Ruth Mortimer, ed., *Harvard College Library Department of Printing and Graphic Arts. Catalogue of Books and Manuscripts. Italian 16th Century Books* (Cambridge, Mass, 1974), II, No. 287.

35 Plates from Marozzo, possibly from the Venice 1550 edition, are used in Giuseppe Colombani, *L'arte maestra* (Venice, 1711).

36 André Desbordes, *Discours de la théorie et la pratique et de l'excellence des armes* (Nancy, 1610); Pallavicini (1670), p. 10. Egerton Castle regarded Agrippa's geometrical pretensions favourably; Jacopo Gelli deemed them relatively unimportant.

37 Dancie (1623), pp. 83–4.

38 In conception this is not dissimilar to the pictographic method used in MS I. 33, but the relationship between words and pictures is far more sophisticated.

39 The illustrations in the first edition of Agrippa have been attributed, at various times, to Leonardo da Vinci or (marginally less impossible) to Michelangelo who was at least still alive in 1553.

40 Gelli, *L'arte* (1906), pp. 79–85 prints several plates from Agrippa with incorrect captions.

41 Agrippa (1568), sig. *2r.

42 Agrippa (1553), fol. 2r–v.

43 Gelli, *Bibliografia*, p. 10.

44 Joachim Meyer, *Gründtliche Beschreibung der freyen Ritterlichen unnd Adelichen kunst des Fechtens* (Strasbourg, 1570); Jacob Sutor, *New Künstliches Fechtbuch* (Frankfurt-am-Main, 1612); Theodor Verolini, *Der Kunstliche Fechter* (Würzburg, 1679).

45 The Italian books without illustrations are dall'Agocchie (1572), Falloppia (1584), and Docciolini (1601). Of the German fencing books only Gunterrodt (1579) is without illustrations, and it is hardly a combat manual.

46 Saviolo (1595), sig. B2.

47 Nicoletto Giganti, *Scola overo teatro* (Venice, 1606). For the German/French edition (Frankfurt, 1619), the plates have been re-engraved very faithfully but without the panache of Fialetti's originals. Thirteen of Giganti's plates are reproduced in Gelli, *L'arte* (1906).

48 Some seventy of Fabris's plates are reproduced by Arthur Wise, *The Art and History of Personal Combat* (Greenwich, Connecticut, 1972).

49 Fabris (1606), p. 25.

50 Capoferro (1610). This first edition is 1610, but the armorial engraving on the verso of the title page has, on the base of the pedestal on the left, 'Anno 1609'. Jacopo Gelli, in the second edition of his *Bibliografia*, maintained that there was an earlier version of Capoferro and, in *L'arte* (1906), p. 103, declared that it had been published in Bologna in 1600: but his opinion was based upon a misunderstanding of a set of detached plates from the 1629 edition. A feature of the work which should be noted here is its use of an alphabet system, similar to Agrippa's, to indicate six principal guards. These letters recur throughout the text and illustrations.

51 On Raffaello Schiaminossi, see Sue Welsh Reed and Richard Wallace, eds, *Italian Etchers of the Renaissance and Baroque* (Museum of Fine Arts, Boston, Mass., 1989), pp. 214–15. Gelli reproduces thirteen plates, and Wise thirty-nine from the first edition of Capoferro's work.

52 On Franz Brun, see Heino Maedebach, ed., *Die Fechtkunst 1500–1900 Grafik und Waffen. Katalog* (Coburg, 1968), Nos 102–13. The German MS referred to was offered for sale to R.L. Scott in 1935. Terms could not be agreed; and I only know of the work from the

correspondence and sample photographs in the Scott Collection.

53 On the 1629 edition of Capoferro, see Artemisia Calcagni Abrami and Lucia Chimirri, eds, *Incisioni toscani del Seicento al servizio del libro illustrato* (Biblioteca Nazionale Centrale, Florence, 1987), Nos 6–8.

54 *Gran simulacro dell'arte e dell'uso della scherma. Dal Capitelli ridotto in questa forma* (n.p., 1632). This title is from the Library of Congress copy. The Scott copy lacks the title page.

55 Wilhelm Schöffer, *Gründtliche und eigentliche Beschreibung der freyen Adelichen und Ritterlichen Fechtkunst im einfachen Rappir und im Rappir und Dolch etc.* (Marburg, 1620). See Helwig (1966), p. 1411.

56 On Pascha's works, see Thimm, pp. 218–19; Helwig (1966), p. 1412.

57 Johann Jacobi von Wallhausen, *Künstlicher Piquen Handlung* (Hanau, 1617). A horizontal strip method for conveying fencing information was later adopted by Jacques Dierickx, *Traité et théorie d'escrime* (Brussels, 1849), but it is a very simple affair in comparison with either Pascha or Wallhausen.

58 *The Literary Works of Leonardo da Vinci*, ed. J.P. Richter (3rd edn, London, 1969), I, pp. 304–5, Plate XXXI, No. 1.

59 Arbeau (1948), p. 37.

60 See John Hale, 'A humanistic visual aid. The military diagram in the Renaissance', *Renaissance Studies*, II, ii (October 1988), pp. 280–98.

61 *The Arte of Warre* tr. Peter Whitehorne (1560), reprinted in *The Tudor Translations* (1905), p. 234.

62 Hale, 'A humanistic visual aid', p. 283. Flaminio della Croce, *L'essercitio della cavalleria et d'altre materie* (Antwerp, 1625), sig. b.2, stresses that *his* illustrations are 'useful' – not 'vain and superfluous' or intended merely to 'please the eyes'.

63 William Patten, *The Expedition into Scotlande of the most woorthely fortunate prince Edward, Duke of Somerset* (1548).

64 For examples, see Mario Savorgnano, *Arte militare terrestre e maritima* (Venice, 1599); Ludovico Melzo, *Regole militari sopra il governo e servitio particolare della cavalleria* (Antwerp, 1611); Herman Hugo, *De militia equestri antiqua et nova ad Phillipum IV. Libri quinque* (Antwerp, 1630).

65 Francesco Altoni, *Trattato*, Biblioteca Nazionale, Florence, MS II.iii.315, fols 10–13v.

66 Fabris (1606), 'A lettori'.

67 Giganti (1606), 'Alli sig. lettori'. This introductory essay runs from sig. a.4 to b.3v. Many years earlier, Angelo Viggiani (or Vizani), in his *Trattato dello schermo* (1575), had also suggested that every kind of geometrical figure was involved in sword-play, but made no use of geometry either in his text or illustrations.

68 Giacomo di Grassi, *Ragione di adoprar sicuramente l'arme si da offesa come da difesa* (Venice, 1570). There was an English version, *Giacomo di Grassi, his true Arte of defence, etc.* (London, 1594), the plates of which offer an agonizing demonstration of the incompetence of English book illustration at that period.

69 Georges Dubois, *Essai sur le traité d'escrime de Saint Didier publié en 1573* (Chartres, 1918).

70 The figures without their numbers are Nos. 61–8. Sutor, *New Künstliches Fechtbuch* (1612), occasionally shows numerals (and even more occasionally footprints), but they are used in an ineffectual and desultory fashion.

71 Silver (1599), p. 14.

72 Geronimo Sánchez de Carranza, *Libro que trata de la philosophía de las armas y de su destreza de la aggresión y defensión christiana* (Lisbon, 1582). On Carranza, see Leguina, *Bibliografía* (1904), pp. 51–3; Orvenipe (1911), pp. 1–2.

73 Carranza (1582), fol. 28.

74 *Ibid.*, fols. 147v–8.

75 On Ghisliero, see Anglo, 'Sixteenth-century Italian drawings in Federico Ghisliero's *Regole di molti cavagliereschi essercitii*', *Apollo* (November 1994), pp. 29–36.

76 With regard to radial and circumferential fencing, it is worth noting that the pragmatic and effective fighter, Donald McBane, *The Expert Sword-Man's Companion* (Glasgow, 1728), p. 9, very much approves of trying to move round an opponent.

77 For the application of mathematics to the elucidation of leaping and tumbling, and for a debate concerning the validity of this approach, see Arcangelo Tuccaro, *Trois dialogues de l'exercice de sauter et voltiger en l'air* (Paris, 1599), especially at fols. 67v–77, 83r–v, 95–6v, 107v–9, 114v–15v, 120, 125, 126, 138v–40.

78 Docciolini (1601), p. 9.

79 On Narváez, see Leguina, *Bibliografía* (1904), pp. 91–8; Orvenipe (1911), pp. 3–7.

80 Luis Pacheco de Narváez, *Advertencias para la enseñanza de la filosofía y destreza de las armas, assí a pie, como a cavallo* (Pamplona, 1642), reprinted in D.L. Orvenipe, *Antiquos tratados de esgrima (siglo XVII)* (Madrid, 1898), p. 129.

81 Cf. Narváez's overhead views with the fencing analysis devised by Georges Dubois, Maître d'Armes de l'Opéra Comique, *L'escrime de duel. Une technique* (Paris, 1913), where the illustrations are similar, but figurative rather than diagrammatic and much easier to follow.

82 Marcelli (1686); Bondi di Mazo da Venetia, *La spada maestra* (Venice, 1696). The strange opening illustration to Bondi's book is scarcely related to the rest of his illustrations which, like Marcelli's, are figurative. In England, where Narváez was so well known, the Spanish diagrammatic legacy was almost non-existent. There are, however, illustrations reminiscent of Narváez in a fragment in the British Library (Harleian MS 5219) entitled 'The mathematical demonstration of the sorde' from a work, dated 1676, by Henry Cavendish, Marquis (and subsequently Duke) of Newcastle. Newcastle's complete treatise is in Harleian MS 4206 where the 'Mathematical demonstration' is announced at fol. 9.

83 On Quevedo and Narváez, see Leguina, *Bibliografía* (1904), pp. 22–8; Claude Chauchadis, *La Loi du duel. Le code du point d'honneur dans l'Espagne des XVIe–XVIIe siècles* (Toulouse, 1997), pp. 263–7.

84 Quevedo, *Historia de la vida del Buscón llamado don Pablos*, I. viii.

85 *Compendio dell'armi de Caramogi d'Antonio Francesco Lucini. In Firenze A°. MDCXXVII*. These have been reproduced from sheets in the Bibliothèque Nationale (but in a tiny format, in the wrong order and mixed up with unrelated engravings), in F. Viatte, 'Allegorical and burlesque subjects by Stefano Della Bella', *Master Drawings*, XV, 4 (1977), 362, figs 10–12. Lucini was a pupil of della Bella.

86 Arsène Vigeant, *Ma collection d'escrime* (Paris, 1892), lists, under the heading 'Albums anciens d'escrime', a work he entitles *Guerriers, rodomonts, spadassins, matamores*, a series of twenty-four rectangular engravings, 'peu connues', which he attributes to Callot about the year 1615. I have not been able to find this series and wonder whether it was, in fact, an untitled set of Lucini's *Compendio*.

87 Bibliothèque Nationale MS Espagnol 443. Don Juan de la Rocha's *Discurso sobre la nobleza, antigüedad y necesidad de la destreza de las armas* is only about 6,000 words in length but covers the history of human conflict since the creation, the history of arms and armour, and the relationship between the celestial and terrestrial worlds, along with remarks on the elements, planets, zodiacal signs, mathematics, architecture, navigation and geography. It does not, however, offer any information on fencing.

88 Girard Thibault, *Academie de l'espée* (Leyden, 1630). The production of this masterpiece merits a full bibliographical essay, but, as far as I know, such a work does not exist.

89 Apart from Crispin van de Pass the Younger, Thibault's engravers were David Bailly, Julius Caesar Boëtius, Scheltius à Bolswert, Willem Delff, Johann Gelle, Petter Isselburg, Nicolaes Lastman, Adrian Mathan, Egbert van Panderen, Crispin van den Queboorn, Salomon Saurius, Pieter Serwouters, Andreas Stock.

90 Antoine de Pluvinel, *Le Maneige royal* (Paris, 1623). An English translation by Hilda Nelson (London, 1989) includes all the plates. Unfortunately, these are reproduced from a facsimile (Leipzig, 1969) of the German edition (Braunschweig, 1626).

91 Castle (1885), p. 127.

92 Johannes Georg Bruchius, *Grondige Beschryvinge van der Edele ende Ridderlijke Scherm-ofte Wapen-Konste* (Leyden, 1671), sig. *3r–v.

93 Thibault (1630), I, Tableau I, p. 3; Tableau IV, p. 9.

94 Castle (1885), p. 124, pours scorn on the centricity of the navel and upon 'the most artificial postulata' of Thibault's theory of human proportions, without realizing that, for good or ill, they are based upon Dürer.

95 Thibault (1630), I, Tableau II. It is impossible to determine which edition of the Dürer was known to Thibault or was used by his artists as their source. Pallavicini (1673), pp. 2–3, also makes much of the proportions of the human body, referring both to Dürer and to Vitruvius.

96 Castle (1885), p. 122.

97 Thibault (1630), 'Advertissement sur la consideration des figures de ce livre'.

98 Thibault (1630), I. Tableau I, p. 22.

99 Agustin de Lara, *Cornucopia numerosa* (Madrid 1675); Miguel Pérez de Mendoza, *Resumen de la verdadera destreza de las armas* (Madrid, 1675); Francesco Antonio de Ettenhard, *Compendio de los fundamentos de la verdadera destreza y filosofía de las armas* (Madrid, 1675). The Spanish masters in Italy were, of course, propagating an identical system of fencing and explicating it in the same geometrical fashion as can be seen, for example, in Pedro Texedo, *Escuela de principiantes y promptuario de questiones en la philosofía de la berdadera destreç de las armas* (Naples, 1678) which comprised a text in both Spanish and Italian.

100 On Rada's extensive writings, see Leguina, *Bibliografía* (1904), pp. 75–9; Orvenipe (1911), pp. 10–13.

101 Francisco Lorenz de Rada, *Nobleza de la espada* (Madrid, 1705).

102 Cf. Narváez, *Nueva sciencia, y filosofía de la Destreza de las armas, su teorica y práctica* (Madrid, 1672), fol. 26.

103 Cf. Aristotle, *De anima*, III, 7.

104 Rada, *Nobleza* (1705), II, pp. 147–56, and Plate 3; Ghisliero (1587), pp. 93–108.

105 Rada's diagrammatic representation of the sword blades is obviously based upon that of Narváez (1600). The system is explained in *Nobleza* (1705), II, pp. 207–10, and Plate 11.

106 A valuable later work which uses mathematics to *explain* sword movements diagrammatically is by the young naval officer, John McArthur, *The Army and Navy Gentleman's Companion* (1781) in which he 'endeavoured to fix the most essential movements in Fencing upon a basis of incontrovertible principles, by devising the plan of constructing mathematical figures for the farther illustration of the various lessons on the parades' (p. ix). For McArthur's remarkable career, see Aylward, *The English Master of Arms* (1956), pp. 203–6; *Dictionary of National Biography*, XII, pp. 402–4.

107 The issue was well summarized by R.A. Lidstone, *Fencing. A Practical Treatise on Foil, Épée, Sabre* (1952), p. xviii:

> To illustrate a book whose theme is action is no easy task, and when technical correctness is of the first importance the difficulty is doubled ... it must be remembered that a drawing can only show a position, or indicate a movement, as it should be made under one particular set of circumstances which necessarily govern the action. These circumstances may vary to such an extent that a movement can quite well be made correctly though differently on two successive occasions.

CHAPTER III

1 Pallavicini (1670), 'L'autore a chi legge'. Pallavicini also provides a separate chapter on 'The nobility of the art of fencing', pp. 8–9. References to the nobility of the sword are commonplace and scarcely worth noting.

2 In the introduction to *The Book of the Sword* (1884), Richard Burton wrote that 'the history of the sword is the history of humanity'; and even if this is not strictly true it cannot be denied that swords and, by implication, swordsmanship have a long history. The weapons of the ancient world are copiously if unevenly documented, but our knowledge of the use of those weapons in classical times is exiguous.

3 Germanisches Nationalmuseum, Nuremberg, MS 3227a, fols. 13v–14. Cited in Hils (1985), p. 107.

4 Heinrich von Gunterrodt (1579), sig. C2v–3, citing the twelfth-century Danish chronicler, Saxo Grammaticus, lib. 6.

5 Gunterrodt (1579), sig. C3–E2, the manuscript is now Royal Armouries MS I.33.

6 Narváez's predecessor, Carranza (1582), fol. 96v, offers nothing on the history of his art apart from a short list of Seville masters.

7 See, for example, D. Gómez Arias de Porres, *Resumen de la verdadera destreza en el maneio de la espada* (Salamanca, 1667), who refers not only to Carranza and Narváez but also to Pons, de la Torre, Monte and di Grassi.

8 Pallavicini here cites Capoferro (1610), pp. 4–5, who had referred to Ninus and to the translation of empires.

9 Pallavicini refers to scholars such as Jean Ravisius-Textor, Polidore Vergil, Luigi Contarini, Pedro Mexia, Vincenzo Bruno, Bonaventura Pistofilo (himself a master), and Wolfgang Lazius.

10 The whole question has been fruitlessly debated. Gelli, *L'arte* (1906) in particular, was anxious to deny that anyone preceded the Italian masters in anything whatsoever. See his *L'arte*, pp. 46–7, where, amongst much else, he confuses Carranza and Narváez.

11 Narváez mentions all these masters, and all were Spanish – even Pietro Monte.

12 Of this group, only Antonio Marchini remains mysterious. Pallavicini (1670) refers to him (with a folio reference) at p. 36; quotes from his work at p. 47; and again refers to him in *La seconda parte* (1673). But I have not located the book.

13 In addition to the works listed in his historical chapter, Pallavicini (1670) refers to Carmona (p. 29), Giganti (p. 32) and Pistofilo (p. 47). In his *Seconda parte* he also includes many references to Docciolini (1601) and refers scathingly to 'il moderno Autore della Scherma Siciliana' who is Giuseppe Villardita, *La scherma siciliana ridotta in compendio* (Palermo, 1670). Marcelli (1686), includes a brief history of fencing, based upon Pallavicini, with the same wrong dates and additional mistakes and flourishes. He makes a show of supplying some titles and printers' names – given in Pallavicini (1673) – mentions Viggiani; still omits Manci-

olino; and adds further works for the seventeenth century: Francesco Alfieri, Senesio, Mattei, the first part of Pallavicini's book, and 'per ultimo nel 1680 stampò Michel Pérez Spagnolo' which must be something by Miguel Pérez de Mendoza y Quijada although none of his books appeared in 1680. Most interesting is Marcelli's reference to a work by Jacques Descars 'Francese', printed in 1568, which dealt not only with fencing but also with musket, pike and military evolutions, and was 'adorned with figures, and printed in folio'. This is sufficiently circumstantial to ring true: but the book has not been identified, and the fact that Costantino Calarone, *Scienza prattica* (Rome, 1714), pp. 13–14, includes 'Ioquez de Scar' in his alphabetical list of masters, is no help at all. The only French work in folio containing this kind of material is de Lostelnau, *Le Mareschal de bataille. Contenant le maniement des armes* (Paris, 1647).

14 See Gordon Warner and Donn F. Draeger, *Japanese Swordsmanship. Technique and Practice* (New York and Tokyo, 1982), pp. 79–94; Howard Reid and Michael Croucher, *The Way of the Warrior. The Paradox of the Martial Arts* (1995), pp. 118–51.

15 This theory was, in fact, first advanced by Giovan' Battista Gaiani, *Arte di maneggiar la spada a piedi et a cavallo* (Loano, 1619), p. 4, where the *Maestro* is asked why the Roman gladiators were deemed 'vile persons and shameful'. He replies that, before the coming of the Goths into Italy, people did not carry arms in the city in times of peace; nor did they settle private injuries by duelling. These practices were introduced by the barbarians; permitted only to 'knights and counts'; and forbidden to the lower orders. Thus only nobles carried arms and 'in particular the sword and dagger'; which, in turn, led to the 'artificial use of those arms, which today is called the Art of Fencing whereby a man, in encounters, may with reason defend himself and offend the enemy with the arms of the knight'. For Gaiani the art of fencing was defined as the use of sword *and* dagger; its origin could be traced to the barbarian occupation of Italy; and it

derived solely from a change in civilian customs.

16 The best-known medieval sword and buckler men are Chaucer's Miller and the university students Alleyn and John. See also G.R. Owst, *Literature and Pulpit in Medieval England* (Oxford, 1961), p. 277, for John Myrc's satirical portrait of the priest who wears a long sword and ornamented dagger to show himself 'bold and austere'. An early reference (738) to the wearing of swords by civilians is in the *Gesta Abbatum Fontanellensium*, reprimanding secular clergy for going about girded with short sword (*semispatium*) and military cloak (*sagum*): see Georg Heinrich Pertz, *Monumenta Germaniae Historica . . . Scriptorum* (Hanover, 1829), II, p. 284, For other examples, see Bertha M. Marti, *The Spanish College at Bologna in the Fourteenth Century* (Philadelphia, 1966), pp. 328–31; H. Denifle, *Chartularium Universitatis Parisiensis* (Paris, 1899), I, pp. 138, 481–2, 540–1; M. Fournier, *Les Statuts et privileges des universités françaises* (Paris, 1890), I, pp. 73–6, 105–7, 453; II, pp. 28–30, 50, 141.

17 The best general study remains H. Seitz, *Blankwaffen. Geschichte und Typentwicklung im europäischen Kulturbereich* (Brunswick, 1965, 1968); and the best specific treatment is A.V.B Norman, *The Rapier and Small Sword, 1460–1820* (London, Melbourne and New York, 1980).

18 Monte (1509), II, 61.

19 Viggiani (1575), fol. 54. The date of this edition has confused historians, even those who have realized that the author died long before publication. The book has two dedications the second of which is addressed by Angelo Viggiani to Maximilian, King of Bohemia; whereas the first (by the master's brother Battista) is addressed to Maximilian, now King of the Romans. Battista points out that Angelo had died before his treatise could be published and that only now, fifteen years later, was his intention being fulfilled. Calculation, based on the year of publication, would place Angelo's death in 1560. However, a manuscript in the Osterreichische Nationalbibliothek (Codex Vindob. 10723) proves to be a beautifully executed presentation copy –

with Battista's dedication dated 10 October 1567 and Angelo's dated 15 May 1551. Thus the master died in 1552 and his work clearly precedes Agrippa as well as di Grassi and dall'Agocchie. Moreover, the manuscript not only has original drawings for all the subsequent published copperplates but also includes other drawings (a pictorial title page and two pairs of swordsmen) which never found their way into either the first printed edition or the second edited by Zacharia Cavalcabo (1588). I am preparing a study of the relationship between the versions of Viggiani's work.

20 Ghisliero (1587), pp. 18, 47.

21 The presentation copy of Silver's manuscript (British Library Additional MS 34,192) illustrates this posture at fol. 23 with an elegantly executed pen-and-ink drawing. In the printed version this is transformed into a crude woodcut.

22 Silver (1599), sigs E1, E2v–3, F1.

23 *Ibid.*, sig. E3.

24 Filippo Vadi, *Liber de arte gladiatoria dimicandi*, Biblioteca Nazionale di Roma, fondo Vittorio Emmanuele, MS 1342: partly edited by Carlo Bascetta, in *Sport e giuochi. Trattati e scritti dal XV al XVIII secolo* (Milan, 1978), I, pp. 146–83. The treatment of the two-hand sword is printed at pp. 157–8 with the illustration at Plate LXXIII. Bascetta, p. 157 n. 9, mistakenly glosses *la ferruzza* as 'the iron of the hilt' (*il ferro dell'elsa*).

25 Agrippa (1553), fol. 61v; Rodríguez del Canto's *El discípulo instruido* is cited by Leguina, *Glosario* (1912), p. 389 under *Espada de dos manos, montante, ó mandoble*. Some sample dimensions and illustrations of two-hand swords are given in Blair and Delamer (1988), pp. 124–7.

26 See A.V.B. Norman, *Wallace Collection Catalogues. European Arms and Armour Supplement* (1986), p. 116.

27 The illustrations in both versions are of limited value because the blocks are often repeated regardless of the sense of the text. Lexicographers recognized that distinctions had to be made but, on the whole, failed to understand them. Cotgrave's definition of *espadon* as 'A short two-handed sword' is acceptable. Less so is his rendering of *espée bastarde* as 'A short

sword; or a sword that is not long ynough', which turns the word *bastard* into an adverse criticism. Florio is even less helpful, defining *spadone* as 'a long, or two-hand sword', and *spada a due mani* as 'a two-handed sword' – which are not wrong, but merely inadequate.

28 Bibliothèque Nationale, MS Italien 959, Plates LIII, LIV, LV. On Lovino, see n. 67, pp. 335–6.

29 *Halb-Schwert* or half-sword techniques (both with two-hand sword and bastard sword) were practised throughout Europe and may be seen, for example, in Fiore, Talhoffer and Pauernfeindt. Two particularly interesting anonymous manuscripts, devoted to foot combat in armour and concentrating almost entirely on the *Halb-Schwert*, are in Vienna – Kunsthistorisches Museum, P. 5013 (dating from about 1430), and Oster-reichische Nationalbibliothek, Codex Vindob. 11093 (mid-fifteenth century).

30 Thibault (1630), I, Tableau I, pp. 14–15.

31 Capoferro (1610), p. 7. Cf. Ghisliero (1587), n. 20 above.

32 Thibault (1630), I, Tableau II, pp. 5–6.

33 Scholarly concentration on the hilt is understandable in view of the difficulty of dating blades which, in any case, frequently do not belong to their present hilts. Blades, too, tended to be mass-produced in a number of centres of excellence, whereas hilts were more individually crafted.

34 A.V.B. Norman, *The Rapier and Small-Sword* (1980), pp. 19–31, refers to most of the available evidence, and reviews some of the theories concerning the origin of the word *rapier*. He strongly inclines to Claude Blair's view that the key is to be found in the Spanish *espada ropera* and the development of the fashion for using a sword with civilian dress.

35 Gunterrodt (1579), sig. D3r-v, glosses the Latin *framea* as *rappier* without explaining why. Johann Georg Wachter, *Glossarium Germanicum* (Leipzig, 1737) defines the rapier as a very sharp sword, deriving from *schrappier* (a razor or *scarificator*) and from *schrappen* (to scrape), and he traces its origins back to the fourth book of *Saxo Grammaticus* where King Waramundus has a sword of extraordinary

sharpness called 'Skrep'. Hence all such swords were subsequently called *schrepper* and ultimately *rapier*. Wachter's etymology has not found favour.

36 Dresden, Sächsische Landesbibliothek MS C.94, fols 137–161v; Munich, Bayerische Staatsbibliothek MS icon.393, Bd.2, fols 2v, 52–82v; Vienna, Osterreichische Nationalbibliothek, Codex Vindob. 10826, fols 122–9.

37 Giles Duwes, *An introductorie for to lerne to rede to pronounce, and to speke Frenche trewly* (1533?).

38 See A.V.B. Norman *The Rapier and Small-Sword* (1980), pp. 19–20 for these terms in inventories. Coupled with their extreme rarity, the fact that the masters do not use these words throws doubt on the Spanish origins of the *rapier* which are otherwise plausible.

39 Brantôme, *Oeuvres complètes* (1864–82), VI, pp. 258–9.

40 Bibliothèque Nationale MS Espagnol 60. On this volume see Chapter 1, p. 36, n. 112.

41 Hughes and Larkin, *Tudor Royal Proclamations* (1969), II, pp. 74, 191, 282, 462.

42 I must thank Barry Scrase, our erudite gardener, for elucidating this matter of the 'grain of barley' which had puzzled me. When he explained that the barley grain has a distinctive needle-like awn, it became clear that the term was used ('vulgarmente' as is noted in the proclamation of 28 June 1575) to indicate a blade terminating in a long, thin, sharp point with a needle-like section.

43 Little has been written about prohibited arms, but Claude Blair has recommended Charles Buttin, 'Les Armes prohibées en Savoie sous les royales constitutions', *Revue Savoisienne. Publication périodique de la Société Florimontane* (37ᵉ Année), 1896, pp. 111–29. Though mainly concerned with the eighteenth century, Buttin shows that, at least from the sixteenth century, the authorities in Savoy were trying to ban knives with very narrow blades of a triangular or similar section.

44 On the relationship between Florio and Saviolo, see Sergio Rossi, 'Vincentio Saviolo his practise (1595): a problem of authorship', in *England and the Continental*

Renaissance. Essays in Honour of J.B. Trapp, ed. E. Chaney and P. Mack (Woodbridge, 1990), pp. 165–75.

45 Cotgrave does better with other swords: *Espée d'armes* ('Espée de chevalier, or Estoc d'armes'); *Espée de chevalier* ('A sharpe, and broad sword, of a reasonable length, and plaine-hilted, having but onely one crosse-barre'); *Espée Hunisque* ('A kind of Scimiter'); *Espée rabatue* ('a foile'); *Estoc d'armes* ('A kind of strong, sharp, and short horseman's sword, broad at the handle (where it hath but one barre for defence) and narrowing to the point-wards'; *Fauchon* ('A Fauchion, Curtleax, or Hangar').

46 *Rhomphaea* was, in classical Latin, a missile weapon, but it later came to indicate a sword which, like the missile, did its work with the point.

47 It is unfortunate that it was not until 1678 that anyone thought to illustrate the current range of swords: doubly unfortunate in that the work, the Sieur de Gaya's *Traité des armes*, is a moderately crude compilation. It was published in a facsimile edition by Charles ffoulkes (Oxford, 1911) and shows the 'Épée de rencontre à la Françoise'; 'Épée à la Suisse'; 'Estoc, ou longue épée à lame étroite, telle qu'on portoit il n'y a pas encore trente ans'; 'Épée à l'Espagnole'; 'Braquemart, Couteau, ou Coutre épée'.

48 In Marozzo the two-hand sword has a very long handle and a clearly marked ricasso or blunted section of blade below the grip and quillons. Agrippa has only one illustration of the two-hand sword which is almost as tall as the man who poses beside it. Meyer's *Schwert* is what, in modern terminology, would now be called a 'long bastard sword' in comparison with Talhoffer's which would be a 'short bastard sword'.

49 Castle (1885), pp. 45–6; Gelli, *L'arte* (1906), p. 87. Gelli's attitude towards Castle underwent a dramatic change. In his *Bibliografia generale della scherma* (Milan, 1895), pp. 487–9, Gelli lavished praise on Castle's *Schools and Masters of Fence* which, he said, demonstrated an 'enviable cleverness', and constituted a complete history 'critical and anecdotal, written with a profound knowledge of fencing and according to rational and just criteria'. However, by the time he came to write *L'arte*, Gelli had either read Castle's work more carefully or had discovered the poor opinion enjoyed by his own *Bibliografia* in England. Whatever the reason, he omitted no opportunity (real or imaginary) to castigate Castle's mistakes. Many of his criticisms were justified: but his own work (despite its continuing value) remains a model of slovenly scholarship.

50 Both Castle and Gelli make much of the distinction, in Viggiani and dall' Agocchie, between upward and downward thrusts delivered from both right and left. But these were already carefully differentiated and illustrated in medieval German treatises, and they are also analysed by Monte (1509), II, 19–21. See Chapter 4, p. 133.

51 When the habit of carrying a sword was ousted by the umbrella and walking stick, the use of these implements as weapons was discussed in a number of treatises, including *Anti-Pugilism* (1790) and J.S. Duncan, *Hints to the Bearers of Walking-sticks and Umbrellas* (1809). The stick was also recognized as an effective weapon, especially for thrusting, in commando textbooks of the Second World War.

52 I believe that the first critic to object to the unhistorical method of nineteenth-century historians was Georges Dubois in his short but brilliant *Essai* on Sainct Didier (1918), where he points out that the fencing systems employed by renaissance masters *necessarily* derived from the long and heavy swords of the period.

53 Captain Frank Brinkley, *Japan, its History, Arts, and Literature* (Boston, 1903–4) is useful but has remained too long a staple for westerners dealing with the history of Japanese fencing. For example, the constant reference to the 'sixteen cuts', in modern western texts, clearly derives from Brinkley, II, p. 142. He was not necessarily wrong: but it does emphasize how little we, in the West, know about the history (as opposed to the comparatively recent practice) of Japanese martial arts. For a sensibly inconclusive assessment of an East/West confrontation, see John Clements, 'Heroic fantasy: Katana vs Rapier', *Hammerterz Forum* (Spring/Summer 1997), pp. 23–4.

54 It is also likely that the Samurai's sword would cut through the rapier blade. On the art of drawing the sword, see Warner and Draeger (1982), pp. 50–8; Oscar Ratti and Adèle Westbrook, *Secrets of the Samurai. A Survey of the Martial Arts of Feudal Japan* (Rutland, Vermont and Tokyo, 1973), pp. 275–81.

55 Swetnam (1617), pp. 171–3, 184. For a critique of Swetnam's work, see Aylward (1956), pp. 79–85.

56 Thibault (1630), I, Tableaux IX, X, XI.

57 Serious comparison between German long-sword fighting and Japanese fencing was, I believe, first raised by G. Panconcelli-Calzia in a short monograph, *Das Fechten mit alten Waffen* (Göttingen, 1925), pp. 13–15. The idea has been further explored by S. Matthew Galas, 'Kindred spirits. The art of the sword in Germany and Japan', *Journal of Asian Martial Arts*, VI (1997), pp. 20–46.

58 A question does, however, arise from the illustrations in Talhoffer and other German manuals, concerning the sharpness of the long sword and falchions. On occasions these swords are shown as cutting deeply: yet the bare-handed grasp of the blade, especially when involving rapid movement and the shock of impact, would seem almost impossible unless the edge were very blunt indeed. For bare hands used on the blade see Dürer's drawings of 1512, reproduced by Dörnhöffer (1909), plates 41–5, 54–7, 65–6.

59 Silver (1599), pp. 23–5.

60 Another anti-evolutionist aspect of fencing history which has not been explored is the extent to which archaic fencing books retained popularity and exerted influence – especially in Germany. Meyer (1570) was reprinted in 1660 and copied by Verolini in 1679; Viggiani was reprinted in 1688. Narváez (1600) continued to dominate Spanish fencing until well into the eighteenth century; Fabris (1606) was reprinted together with a German translation in 1677 and 1713, and was heavily raided by several late seventeenth-century masters; while Heussler (1615), who based his work on Fabris and Capoferro, was still being reprinted in 1716–17.

61 Vegetius, *De re militari*, I, 11, 12. For a concise survey of the transmission of

Vegetius, see G.A. Lester, *The Earliest English Translation of Vegetius' De Re Militari, ed. from Oxford MS Bodl. Douce 291* (Heidelberg, 1988).

62 See Chapter 10, p. 289, for Wallhausen's reference to this exercise.

63 Dionysius of Halicarnassus, XIV, 9–10. See *The Roman Antiquities of Dionysius of Halicarnassus*, tr. Edward Spelman, revised by Ernest Cary (Loeb Library, 1937–40), pp. 269–77. Cf. later Roman sword technique as described by Polybius, *The Histories*, II, 33. In 223 BC the Gauls were still slashing away wildly 'which is the peculiar and only stroke of the Gauls as their swords have no points'; while the Romans, continuing 'to thrust with their swords which did not bend, the points being very effective', slew the greater part of the opposing army.

64 Germanisches Nationalmuseum, Nuremberg, MS 3227a, fols 13v–14, 19–19v. The quotations from this manuscript are drawn from material generously supplied by S. Matthew Galas. In 1408, an English translator of Vegetius interpolated a passage of great interest within this context of medieval swordsmanship. Vegetius, when discussing training at the post, makes a merely general allusion to edge and point. But the translator, elaborating this, explains that the thrust is to be used to wound an enemy in his side or 'forbody'; that the cut is to be directed against head, arm, or legs; and that it is necessary for the soldier to be instructed 'now to lepe in on his enemye with his strook and now to flee bakward fro his enemyes strook'. See Lester (1988), pp. 98–9.

65 Bibliothèque Nationale, Paris, MS Italien 959, Plates XXVIII, XXIX. See n. 67 below.

66 Ghisliero (1587), pp. 31–2. Docciolini (1601), p. 45, said much the same thing. The point was more secure, 'because cuts have to travel further and go more slowly, so that the guard is not firm and the posture is disordered, whence there are greater dangers'.

67 This *Ragionamento* is appended to the magnificently illustrated fencing treatise, offered by Lovino to Henri III. This work in the Bibliothèque Nationale is well

known to scholars from a publication edited in 1909 by Henri Omont who reproduced the surviving sixty-five illustrations together with what appear to be the Dedication and Lovino's comments on each picture. In fact, Omont omitted a section of the Dedication together with about 95 per cent of Lovino's explicatory text and the whole of the *Ragionamento*. As a result, scholars think that they know Lovino's work, but do not; and it has never received the attention it deserves.

68 The single swords depicted in Lovino's manuscript are, apart from their comparatively simple hilt, similar to those shown in Liancour (1686) who suggests (p. 3) that the sword should be about thirty inches, and certainly no more than thirty-six inches, in length.

69 Capoferro (1610), p. 23; Gaiani (1619), p. 34.

70 Thibault (1630), I, Tableau XIV. Another seventeenth-century master who equivocated was Francesco Alfieri in *La scherma* (Padua, 1640), pp. 58–60. He notes that swordsmen generally argue that thrusts are far better than cuts for the reason that they are more likely to inflict a fatal wound: but he is not entirely satisfied because cuts from a short, broad sword delivered by a powerful arm 'are as much to be feared as thrusts'. No, he says, there are other reasons for the superiority of the point, and proceeds to advance much the same argument as his predecessors.

71 La Touche (1670), II, 8. Cf. di Grassi, discussed above, p. 112.

72 Pallavicini (1670), p. 14.

73 The debate is a good example of massive erudition deployed to little purpose. The protagonists were Holger Jacobsen, Fritz C. Skaar and Ada Bruhn who fought their battle in the pages of the *Vaabenhistoriske Aarboger*, IV (1943). I am grateful to Claude Blair for supplying copies of this material.

74 Di Grassi (1594 edn), sig. D2v.

75 See, for example, Christine de Pisan, tr. William Caxton, *The Book of Fayttes of Armes and of Chyvalrye*, ed. A.T.P. Byles (E.E.T.S., 1932), p. 31.

76 Di Grassi (1594 edn), sigs D3r–v, E3r–v, F1, Aa3v–4.

77 Miyamoto Musashi, *A Book of Five Rings*, tr. Victor Harris (1974), p. 59.

78 Wierschner (1965), p. 33, citing the 1389 manuscript at Nuremberg, Germanisches Nationalmuseum, Codex MS 3227a, fol. 32. See also Galas, 'Kindred spirits', pp. 32–4.

79 Monte (1509), II, 21.

80 *Ibid.*, II, 45.

81 Manciolino (1531), fol. 6; Altoni, fol. 10; di Grassi (1594 edn), sig. E4r–v. Dall'Agocchie (1572), p. 29, gives, as the first of five *tempi* for striking your enemy, the moment when you have parried one of his blows. On Liechtenauer's *Meisterhau*, see Galas, 'Kindred spirits', p. 33.

82 Mercurio Spetioli da Fermo, *Capitolo di schermire et cavalcare* (Bologna, 1577), sig. A2v.

83 Docciolini (1601), p. 6.

84 George Hale (1614), sigs B2v, B8.

85 Ghisliero (1587), pp. 31, 34.

86 Viggiani (1575), fol. 62r–v. Cf. the treatise by the Bolognese master, Girolamo Cavalcabo. It has always been assumed that this latter text was lost and survived only in translations: but the Italian original (or a copy thereof) is in the Bibliothèque Nationale (MS Italien 1527), entitled *Nobilissimo discorso intorno il schermo di spada e pugnale, et di spada, e altre utilissime instruttioni pertinenti in esso schermo e conveniente ad'ogni nobile et honorato cavaliere*. It was also thought that the French translation by the Seigneur de Villamont was first published at Rouen in 1609: but an earlier edition, *Traicté ou instruction pour tirer des armes, de l'excellent Scrimeur Hyeronimo Calvacabo, Bolognois, Avec un discours pour tirer de l'espée seule, fait par le deffunct Paternostrier de Rome* (Rouen, 1597), is preserved in the Corble Collection at Leuven. A German translation of the French version was published by Conrad von Einsidell at Leipzig (1611) and at Jena (1612). In MS Italien 1527, fols 20v–2, Cavalcabo maintains that it is advantageous to wait and provoke an enemy into the first attack because he will thus expose his body by holding his weapons (sword and dagger) 'apart', and will also be physically 'discommoded', whereas he who waits is never discommoded.

87 Gaiani (1619), p. 24. This passage was used verbatim but without acknowledgement by Antonio Alfieri, *Quesiti del cavaliero instrutto nell'arte dello schermo. Con le risposte del suo maestro. Opera utile e curiosa divisa in tre parti* (Padua, 1644), pp. 27–36.

88 Falloppia (1584), sig. A.4r–v.

89 George Silver regarded Saviolo's method as defective precisely because, in his view, the Italian 'did not teach Defence but offence'. The proof of this, said Silver, was the frequency with which those who practised the Italian method generally slew each other. See Silver's 'Bref instructions upon my paradoxes of defence', in *The Works of George Silver*, ed. C.G.R. Matthey (1898), pp. 78–9.

90 Capoferro (1610), p. 1. On etymology, see Schaer, *Die altdeutschen Fechter* (1901), pp. 32–41.

91 Capoferro is, of course, using the term in the all-embracing sense of manners, behaviour, and social intercourse popularized by Stefano Guazzo's *La civil conversatione* (Brescia, 1574).

92 Capoferro (1610), pp. 1–6. Pallavicini (1670), pp. 56–7, repeats Capoferro's definition of the word *Scherma* but adds that there is no better defence than attacking one's enemy.

93 Monte (1509), II, 20.

94 On Viggiani's lunge, see Castle (1885), p. 66. Gelli, *L'arte* (1906), pp. 98–9, in a characteristic attempt to denigrate Castle, foolishly belittles Viggiani.

95 In Agrippa the relevant posture is marked throughout his treatise with the letter 'I'.

96 Fatal thrusts account for thirty-two of Capoferro's forty-two plates, and thirty-three of Giganti's forty-two. Because Fabris includes a large number of intermediate postures, it is less easy to categorize them: but it still true to say that a substantial majority of his 190 illustrations show lethal thrusts.

CHAPTER IV

1 Marcelli (1686), p. 14. The citation from dall'Agocchie (1572), fol. 6 is correctly given, but Marcelli does not acknowledge a more striking borrowing which I cite at the end of the paragraph.

2 The Accademia della Crusca, devoted to the purification of the Italian language, had been founded in 1582 and had published its great *Vocabulario* in 1612. The first edition of Ambrogio Calepino's Latin-Italian dictionary appeared in 1502 and was subsequently enlarged and much reprinted.

3 See Marcelli's introductory 'L'autore a chi legge', sig. a3v–4. Cf. Liancour (1686), p. 5, who stresses that the principles of the single sword demand not so much 'la politesse' of language but rather clarity of expression and simple terms, and asks his reader 'to seek here utility rather than pleasure'. Many masters made similar claims.

4 Sir William Hope, *The Fencing-Master's Advice to his Scholar: or a Few Directions for the More Regular Assaulting in Schools* (Edinburgh, 1692), pp. 27–32.

5 Archibald MacGregor, *MacGregor's Lecture on the Art of Defence* (Paisley, 1791), pp. 1, 67.

6 Sir Philip Sidney, *An apologie for poetrie* in G. Gregory Smith, *Elizabethan Critical Essays* (1904), I, p. 158. For a late example of the genre, see P.F.M. L'Homandie, *La Xiphomanie ou l'art de l'escrime, poème didactique en quatre chants* (Angoulême, 1821).

7 Sir William Hope, *The Scots Fencing-Master or Compleat Small-Sword-Man* (Edinburgh, 1687), sigs. *2v–3.

8 Antonio Alfieri, *Quesiti* (1644), 'Introduttione al dialogo'.

9 La Touche (1670), fol. 9.

10 *Ibid.*, Dedication.

11 Docciolini (1601), p. 114. Cf. Fiore, ed. Novati (1902), p. 195; Marozzo (1536), II,143; Narvàez (1600), fol. 24; Capoferro (1610), fol. 29.

12 Versions of Liechtenauer's text are printed in Wierschin (1965), pp. 87–97, 167–73; and in *Talhoffer* (1443), pp. 19–23.

13 Philippo di Vadi, *De arte gladiatoria dimicandi*, in Bascetta (1978), pp. 151–2.

14 The first manuscript is British Library, Harleian MS 3542, fols. 82–5, and is well known in the transcription published by Hutton, *The Sword and the Centuries* (1901), pp. 36–40. The vellum roll is British Library, Additional MS 39,564, and has never been published. Also in the British Library (Cottonian MS

Titus A. xxv, fols 105r–v) is a fragment of a late fifteenth-century text concerning *Strokes off ij hand swerde*. This is too tiny to do more than confirm the use of the terms 'Rownde', 'Quarter', 'Rake' and 'Double Rake'.

15 See pp. 145–7.

16 MS I. 33, pp. 1–2. The manuscript has been given a modern pagination which is used by Jeffrey L. Singman in his forthcoming edition of the text, and I follow this throughout.

17 *Ibid.*, pp. 33–52, for the sequences based upon the guard of *Langort* or some variation of it.

18 *Ibid.*, pp. 43–5.

19 This particular *Langort* is a curiosity. It is introduced at p. 46 – 'Here the priest adopts his special guard, that is to say Langort' (*custodiam specificatam videlicet langort*) – and a very awkward posture it is, having nothing of the 'long point' about it. It recurs at pp. 48–9, 51–3, 59–61. There is also, on one occasion, a high (*superior*) *Langort* (p. 41).

20 There are only three significant exceptions to this view of the cut: at p. 18, where the scholar delivers a backhand cut with his hand in pronation to the back of the priest's neck; and at p. 42 and p. 62 where similar cuts are delivered from the fencer at the right-hand side of the page.

21 The German terms *Anbinden* and *Binden*, with the same meaning, occur in the later *Fechtbuch* manuscripts, and the Italian *ligadura* is used by Fiore de' Liberi.

22 Pauernfeindt (1516) uses crude pictographs but not in the systematic and sophisticated manner of Agrippa.

23 See for example, MS I. 33, pp. 50–2.

24 See, for example, Osterreichische Nationalbibliothek, Codex Vindob. 10826, fols 130–48v.

25 MS.I.33, p. 45: 'fingitur super ventrem sive penetratur gladio'.

26 The only study in English of Liechtenauer's work and its implications is S. Matthew Galas, 'Johannes Liechtenauer. The father of German swordsmanship', *Journal of the Society of American Fight Directors* (1998) which is similar to, though with a different emphasis from, the same author's 'Kindred spirits' (1997). Galas's case for Liechtenauer's swords-

manship is cogent but his rearrangement of the material (for the sake of clarity), and his knowledge of the later commentaries, make the original verse seem more coherent than it really is.

27 Hanko Döbringer, in Germanisches Nationalmuseum, Codex MS 3227a, fol. 25, translated by S. Matthew Galas.

28 A book on Jewish fencing by P.E. Christfals, *Jüdische Fechtschule* (Enderes, 1760) sounds intriguing, but I have never seen a copy.

29 *Messer* does not necessarily always indicate a falchion; and in the Talhoffer manuscripts it is represented variously.

30 Sutor, *New Künstliches Fechtbuch* (1612), sometimes regarded as the last work in the old tradition, was dismissed by Wassmannsdorff (1888), p. 20, as a 'deplorable plagiarism of Joachim Meyer and others'. Bibliographically speaking, the last important publication within the Liechtenauer tradition was the third edition of Joachim Meyer's *Gründtliche Beschreibung* (Augsburg, 1660), although this was itself abridged in Theodor Verolini, *Der Künstlicher Fechter* (1679).

31 On Mair's career, see Hils (1985), pp. 197–201. The compendia themselves suggest that Mair was an obsessive completist. Gathered from every available source of conventional information, both in manuscript and print, they are augmented with more exotic fighting techniques – such as the handling of scythes, sickles and 'rustic staves' (*fuste agreste* or *Bauernstangen*) which look like tree trunks. Each mode of combat is broken down into a series of individual postures: with each illustration introduced by a short title in German and Latin, and followed by a similar bilingual explication. Finally, each section concludes with a short treatise, again in German and Latin, summarizing the system.

32 These German texts are no more obscure than Miyamoto Musashi's similarly conceived account of Japanese swordsmanship with its plethora of colourful, metaphoric technical terms which mask a highly efficient combat system.

33 Léon Bertrand, *The Fencer's Companion* (Aldershot, 1934) p. 45.

34 See Chapter 2, p. 46.

35 Pauernfeindt transcribes Liechtenauer's verses as prose and rearranges the original order: 'Der zorn Haw' (sig. A.3); 'Das ist der Text' (sig. A.4); 'Die vier Blossen' (sig. B.1); 'Der Zwerchaw' (sig. B.2); 'von verseczen' (sig. B.3); 'Die vier leger' (sig. B.4); 'von Überlauffen' (sig. C.1); 'von Durchwechslen' and 'von Zucken' (sig. C.2); 'von Nachraysen' (sig. C.3); 'Der Schilhaw' (sig. C.4); 'Der Schaittelhaw', 'von Durchlauffen', and 'von Sprechfenster' (sig. D.1); 'von Zwayen hengen' and 'von Hende trucken' (sig. D.2); 'von Durchlauffen' partially repeated (sig. D.3). Each of these passages introduces Pauernfeindt's own elaborations. At the end of the material which may be said to derive ultimately from Liechtenauer, and before moving on to half-sword techniques, Pauernfeindt (sig. E.4v) cites Liechtenauer's concluding verses. *Der altenn Fechter* (1531) reproduces all this material on the long sword, both Liechtenauer's verse and Pauernfeindt's glosses, together with Pauernfeindt's text on fighting with staves, dagger and buckler; but it has an altogether different treatment by 'Hans Lebkommer' (that is Lecküchner) on the *Messerfechten* and devotes a long section to wrestling which was not treated by Pauernfeindt.

36 The German masters contemporary with Fiore similarly confined the use of *halb-Schwert* techniques principally to armoured warriors: but by the mid-fifteenth century the technique was being applied to swordsmen without defensive armour.

37 Fiore, ed. Novati (1902), pp. 142–3, 204–5; Getty MS, fol. 24.

38 Fiore, ed. Novati (1902), pp. 152–5, 208–9; Getty MS, fols 24v–6v. They are arranged in pairs, one counter to the other: but not all of these postures recur in the subsequent combat scenes and, when they do, are not pictographic as in MS I.33.

39 Fiore, ed. Novati (1902), pp. 167–70, 212; Getty MS, fols 34v–7.

40 There is a succinct summary of the relationship between Fiore and Vadi in Bascetta (1978), II, pp. 146–50, although Bascetta overstates what he sees as original elements in Vadi such as his rec-

ommendation of thrusts, bindings and feints which were all techniques well-known to earlier German masters and, indeed, to Fiore himself.

41 Monte (1509), II, 45.

42 *Ibid.*, II, 47.

43 *Ibid.*, II, 19–21. Such distinctions between types of thrust were mistakenly regarded, by Castle and Gelli, as later innovations. See Chapter 3, n. 50.

44 *Ibid.*, II, 20, 48.

45 *Ibid.*, II, 46.

46 Manciolino, *Opera nova . . . novamente corretta e stampata* (1531).

47 *Ibid.*, fols 19v–20.

48 The chapters deal with sword and dagger; dagger alone; dagger and cape; sword and cape; two swords; sword and large buckler; sword alone; sword and *rotella*; and two sections on the sword and *targa* or square shield.

49 Marozzo (1536), II, 137–43. Castle (1885), pp. 35–44, gives a summary of these guards; and Gelli, *L'arte* (1906) pp. 76–85, a much better account of the work as a whole, comparing it not only with Manciolino but also Fiore de' Liberi.

50 Marozzo (1536), III, 170.

51 See Chapter 6, p. 345 n. 54.

52 Cf, above, p. 119.

53 Dall'Agocchie (1572), p. 11.

54 Dall'Agocchie's main guards are: *porta di ferro, porta di ferro cinghiale, porta di ferro stretta, porta di ferro larga, coda lunga stretta, coda lunga larga, coda lunga distesa, coda lunga alta, guardia d'alicorno, guardia di testa, guardia di faccia, guardia d'entrare, guardia alta, guardia con la spada sopra il braccio sinistro, guardia di sotto.*

55 Viggiani (1575), fol. 59v.

56 Viggiani also shows the guards and the cuts in diagrammatic 'trees' which are more confusing than the text they are intended to elucidate.

57 Vadi in Bascetta (1978), II, pp. 155–6.

58 Viggiani (1575), fols 11r–v. Like Vadi, Viggiani moves on to music: but he does not linger.

59 Gaiani (1619), pp. 8, 10–12. See Chapter 2, pp. 89–90.

60 Despite the obvious advantages of Agrippa's system, reference to the guards by number alone was not much taken up until Cavalcabo simplified the whole

1111111

11111111111

business in his 'Nobilissimo discorso' (Bib. Nat. MS Italien 1527) and in the published translations which followed. See Chapter 3, n. 86.

61 On Ghisliero, see Chapter 2, pp. 68–71.

62 Cf. La Touche (1670), fol. 9.

63 Authors who did refer favourably to Thibault were Lorenz de Rada and Bruchius. See Chapter 2, p. 76, and n. 92.

64 Gregorius Reisch, *Aepitoma omnis phylosophiae alias Margarita phylosophica* (Strasbourg, 1504). There were many later editions of this work including an Italian translation by G.P. Gallucci (Venice, 1599).

65 Adrien Baillet, *La Vie de Monsieur Des-Cartes* (Paris, 1691), p. 407.

66 La Touche (1670), fol. 36.

67 Alessandro Senesio, *Il vero maneggio di spada* (Bologna, 1660), fig. 2.

68 Fencers were variously advised to watch the opponent's sword (Vadi, Falloppia and Ghisliero); his sword hand (Manciolino, Agrippa and Capoferro); his dagger hand (Marozzo); his sword point (Lord Herbert of Cherbury); his right arm (Pallavicini); wrist, point and eyes (Donald McBane).

69 Henry Blackwell (1702), pp. 27–8; MacGregor (1791), p. 56.

70 Docciolini (1601), pp. 48–9, noted that the slightest movement of the hand in any direction 'will make the point travel so far that you will not be able to judge it in any way'. Watching the opposing sword point was also recommended by Lord Herbert of Cherbury and by Captain John Godfrey (1747), p. 2, where it is noted that the sword point is much nearer to your eye and thus every minute motion is more perceptible; 'and as the arm and wrist are the mechanical causes of it, they must answer to the effect, and that effect is nearer to your ken than the cause. And this I take to be a mathematicall proof.'

71 Stefano Guazzo, *La civil conversatione* (Brescia, 1574), tr. George Pettie, ed. Sir E. Sullivan (1925), I, p. 86.

72 Typical of those who dislike feints are di Grassi who thinks them only really effective when fighting with the case of rapiers; Ghisliero who says that men may pay for feints with their lives; Docciolini who thinks they are used only by those without much science; and Capoferro who

says that they are vain. Dall'Agocchie and Falloppia have mixed feelings. Fabris and Pallavicini think they are good but dangerous; and Lovino advocates them, saying that 'he who does not know how to feint well and to defend himself against feints, has little understanding of this our science'.

73 The great boxer Jimmy Wilde, *The Art of Boxing* (London, n.d.), pp. 50–6, did not consider that the left-handed boxer posed any special difficulty: 'if there is any awkwardness for you, it should be just as awkward for him, except perhaps that he is a little more accustomed to the sort of opposition he encounters'.

74 La Touche (1670), preface. Cf. Marozzo (1536), II, 150; Saviolo (1595), sig. N.1. Falloppia (1584), sig. E.3, dismisses the whole question with contempt: 'there being no difference between them other than one of relation', a view shared much later by Marcelli (1686), Part II, p. 96. Cavalcabo, on the other hand, deemed the matter sufficiently important to warrant one of the longer chapters of his short treatise because, as he points out, the conventional fencer is obliged to do everything the wrong way round: see Bib. Nat. MS Italien 1527, fols. 29v–32v.

75 Manciolino (1531), fol. 5r–v. Dall'Agocchie also has the highest regard for the sword alone but does not consider it exclusively.

76 Saviolo (1595), sig. D.1v–2.

77 Paris de Puteo, *Duello* (Naples, 1476–77), IV, iii.

78 For Azevedo and Saincte Croix see *Le Loyal Serviteur*, ed. Petitot, pp. 244–5; for the Dürer, see Dörnhöffer's edition, Plate 64.

79 Gaiani (1619), p. 4. On the use of sword and dagger see Leonid Tarassuk, 'Some Notes on Parrying Daggers and Poniards', *Metropolitan Museum Journal*, XII (1978), pp. 33–54, which, despite minor errors, is an excellent study.

80 Dancie (1623), pp. 73–4.

81 Thibault (1630), II, Tableau 13.

82 As Pallavicini points out in his preliminary letter to the reader, some masters, when publishing a treatise, have promised a further volume but, unlike him, they have failed to deliver. The sad thing is

1

1

that critical comment has always been confined to his first book, while the second has been ignored.

83 La Touche (1670) dismisses all books written prior to his own because they have become useless due to changes in arms and armour.

84 See Chapter 10, pp. 274–7.

85 Monte (1509), II, 49. 'Characteristically' is appropriate here because, as so often, he recommends a feint.

86 See Viggiani (1575), p. 66, for the idea that it is natural to lead with the right side.

87 Capoferro's fencers are naturally also clad for his two illustrations of sword and cloak fighting.

88 Domenico Angelo, *L'École des armes, avec l'explication général des principales attitudes et positions concernant l'escrime* (1763). On this text and its various editions, see J.D. Aylward, *The House of Angelo* (1953), pp. 40–53, 208. Angelo's arch critic Danet shows the draw with right foot forward as condemned by Lovino.

89 Thibault (1630), I, Tableau II.

CHAPTER V

1 On staff weapons, see the long series of articles by Charles Buttin on 'Les armes de hast' which appeared in the *Bulletin Trimestriel de la Société des Amis du Musée de l'Armée* (Paris, 1936–52); and Mario Troso, *Le armi in asta delle fanterie Europee (1000–1500)* (Novara, 1988). These authorities are sometimes irreconcilable. Staff weapons and the principal modes of handling them are more or less universal. See, for example, Roald Knutsen, *Japanese Polearms* (1963), pp. 75–84; Ratti and Westbrook, *Secrets of the Samurai* (1973), pp. 241–53.

2 Agrippa (1553), II, 23, 24.

3 Falloppia (1584), sig. A.ii.

4 There was (and still is) no English word for *spiedo* as a staff weapon and, although it has sometimes been identified with the *corsèque*, there seems little point in rendering the Italian term with a French approximation. See n. 26 below.

5 Paurnfeindt (1516), sig. I, 2; di Grassi (1594 edn), sig. O.4v; di Grassi (1570), pp. 99–100.

6 Nuremberg, Germanisches National-museum, Cod. MS 3227a, fol. 78; see Hils (1985), p. 105.

7 For an excellent survey of foot combat within the lists, see Claude Gaier, 'Technique des combats singuliers d'après les auteurs "bourguignons" du XVe siècle', *Le Moyen Age*, No. 3–4 (1985), pp. 415–57; No. 1 (1986), pp. 5–40. Viscount Dillon, 'Barriers and foot combats', *Archaeological Journal*, LXI (1904), pp. 276–308, is informative but chaotic.

8 There are exceptions such as the fight between the Earl of Warwick and Pandolfo Malatesta when the latter is supposed to have been 'sore wounded' in the left shoulder. See *Pageant of the Birth Life and Death of Richard Beauchamp Earl of Warwick KG 1389–1439*, ed. Viscount Dillon and W.H. St John Hope (1914), Plate XIV.

9 The combat between three Portuguese and three French knights is mentioned by Monstrelet (I, 134) and more fully described by Saint-Remy, *Chronique*, ed. F. Morand (Paris, 1876–81), I, pp. 208–10.

10 For the text of the manuscript, with annotated translation, see Anglo 'Le Jeu de la hache. A fifteenth-century treatise on the technique of chivalric axe combat', *Archaeologia*, CIX (1991), pp. 112–28.

11 Olivier de la Marche, *Mémoires* (1883–8), II, p. 125.

12 Axes with a cutting edge instead of hammer are shown in a neatly drawn mid-fifteenth-century *Fechtbuch* manuscript – Osterreichische Nationalbibliothek, Codex Vindob. 11093, fols 37v–9v.

13 Bonaventura Pistofilo, *Il torneo* (Bologna, 1627), pp. 59–60, 247, 257–8.

14 *Le Jeu*, para. 65.

15 I do not know what the *fior de preda* is, but *Titimalo* is defined by Florio as 'Milk-thistle, Sea-lectuce or Wolfes-milke, or as some say Spurge-hearbe'. As Barry Scrase, a horticulturist, has pointed out to me, many varieties of spurge (or euphorbia) are common in the Mediterranean and are notorious for their inflammatory effect on the mucous membranes.

16 *Le Jeu*, para. 58.

17 For a fuller listing of these parallels, see *Ibid.*, notes 33, 34–7, 38–40, 43, 45–51, 55–6, 58, 61.

18 *Ibid.*, para. 12.

19 *Ibid.*, para. 71.

20 *Ibid.*, para. 22.

21 *Ibid.*, paras. 39, 43.

22 Monte (1509), II, 13.

23 The flail, which was very much a peasant weapon, makes only an occasional appearance in the German manuscripts. Each of Paulus Hector Mair's three major compilations includes carefully annotated sections on combat with flails as well as with other agricultural weapons such as sickles and scythes. See Vienna, Osterreichische Nationalbibliothek, Codex Vindob. 10826, fols. 1–12v; Munich, Bayerische Staatsbibliothek, MS icon.393, Vol.I, fols 203–34v; Dresden, Sächsische Landesbibliothek, MS Dresd. C.93, fols 212–42v.

24 Edward Halle, *Chronicle*, ed. H. Ellis (1809), p. 515.

25 Although broadly speaking the two principal versions of Fiore's treatise are in accord, the Getty Manuscript (as usual) has greater detail and extra illustrations. It also shows the combatants wearing full armour for most of the lance fighting.

26 I have translated *Spetum* (in Monte) by the Italian term *spiedo* (as in Manciolino, Marozzo, and di Grassi). Both *spetum* and *spiedo* mean literally a roasting spit – deriving, perhaps, from the tripartite head. The weapon is identified with the *corsèque* by ffoulkes, Buttin, Laking and Troso: and, although there is no unequivocal sixteenth-century source for this identification, Jean Nicot in his *Thrésor de la langue françoise tant ancienne que moderne* (Paris, 1606), p. 153, defines *une corsèque* as 'une javeline ayant le fer longuet et larget à deux oreillons, *Hastile Corsicum*'. 'I.G. gentleman' renders di Grassi's *spiedo* simply as 'javelin' – which is clearly wrong.

27 Monte (1509), I,1; II, 40.

28 Monte labels these staff weapons as the *lancea* 'commonly called the *ginetta*', *lancea longa* or *picha*, *partesana et rotella*, *partesana*, *roncha*, *alabarda*, and *spetum*. Manciolino discusses the partisan with and without *rotella*, the *spiedo*, *roncha* and spear; Marozzo discusses the partisan with and without *rotella*, the pike or *lancioto*, the *spiedo*, and the *roncha*.

29 As elsewhere in this book, quotations from di Grassi are based on the English translation by 'I.G. gentleman' (1594) who, though fairly accurate, still has several misleading errors which have been corrected *en route*. He also offers a number of felicities of which the choice one is his rendering of an original Italian recommendation – to deliver a blow with the buckler on the snout (*nel mostaccio*) – as 'he may with his buckler give the enimie, the *mustachio* in the face'. This coinage is at sig. K.2v in the translation, while the source is di Grassi (1570), p. 65.

30 I.G., misreading *moderna* as *mediana*, translates this as the 'middle or meane Holbert', although subsequently he gives it correctly.

31 This idea that the shorter staff weapons could cut through a pike was later ridiculed by Cesare d'Evoli. See Chapter 7, p. 220.

32 The *Bref Instructions*, which remained in manuscript until they were edited by Matthey in 1898, supplement the general observations of the *Paradoxes* with a more detailed analysis of individual moves and counters with all weapons.

33 The term 'Black-bill', although common in Silver's time, has not been clearly identified by modern scholars. As a comparatively short-hafted weapon 'of weight', it clearly does not correspond to di Grassi's agile *roncha*.

34 Claude Blair, 'Welsh bills, glaives, and hooks', *Journal of the Arms and Armour Society*, XVI, No. 2 (March 1999), pp. 71–85.

35 See Charles Buttin, *Bulletin Trimestriel de la Société des Amis de la Musée de l'Armée*, XLVI (March 1937), pp. 108–9; Mario Troso, *Le armi in asta* (1988), pp. 121, 259.

36 The 'Morris pike' is simply the normal, long military pike. 'Long Staffe' and 'Javelin' remain unclear.

37 This is roughly what Monte had suggested ninety years earlier.

38 Silver (1599), p. 44. The virtues of the quarterstaff were most strikingly portrayed in a pamphlet by the adventurer Richard Peeke, *Three to one: being, an English-Spanish combat, performed by a westerne gentleman, of Tavystoke* (1626), in which the author describes how, in the presence of the Duke of Medina Sidonia

and other Spanish dignitaries, he fought successfully against three Spanish sword-and-dagger men, 'at once' – killing one and disarming the others. Significantly, the fatal blow was delivered with the butt end of his staff, 'where the iron pike was'.

39 Swetnam (1617) has been largely ignored except by Aylward (1956), pp. 79–85. He is better known for *The Araignement of Lewde, idle, froward, and unconstant women* (1615), a heavy-handed joke which earned him the sobriquet 'Swetnam the Woman-hater' among his contemporaries and the attention of feminists in the late twentieth century. Another fencing master with a grudge against the ladies was Zachary Wylde who, when attacking the fashion of writing prefaces to 'every little Treatise', observed that they, 'oftentimes like Womens Faces, are found the most promising and inviting Part of the whole Piece'. See Wylde, *The English Master of Defence* (York, 1711), sig. A.2r–v.

40 Swetnam (1617), pp. 144–5.

41 *Ibid.*, p. 139.

42 A forerunner of this activity may be found in the unlikely setting of a subterranean military operation at the siege of Melun in 1420. The English, mining under the fortifications, ran into the French counter-terminers. A strong, breast-high timber beam was erected between the two sides and, illuminated by torchlight, fighting across the barrier soon became a regular activity. See Jean Juvenal des Ursins, *Histoire de Charles VI, Roy de France*, ed. Michaud and Poujoulat (1836), pp. 559–60. I do not know when the barrier was introduced for foot combats in the lists. An early example is at Sandricourt in 1493, but it is unlikely that there were no prior experiments. For remarks on the barriers, see Dillon (1904), pp. 299–306; Anglo, *Great Tournament Roll* (1968), pp. 43–4; Anglo, *Spectacle* (1969), pp. 155–6.

43 *Le Loyal Serviteur* (1820), p. 63.

44 Halle (1809), pp. 571–2.

45 *The Lisle Letters*, ed. M. St C. Byrne (1983), V, No. 1109a.

46 Brantôme (1873), I, p. 234.

47 Narváez, *Advertencias* (1642), in Orvenipe (1898), pp. 278–81.

48 Ghisliero (1587), pp. 153–72.

49 Antonio Vezzani, *L'esercizio accademico di picca* (Parma, 1688), which shows sequences of postures clarified by dotted lines indicating movements of feet and pike.

50 The phrase is my own, from 'The courtier. The Renaissance and changing ideals', in A.G. Dickens, ed., *The Courts of Europe* (1977), p. 41.

51 See, for example, the view of a barriers combat in Vienna, engraved by Hans Lautensack in 1560, reproduced in the exhibition catalogue, *Die Fechtkunst 1500–1900 Grafik Waffen*, ed. Heino Maedebach (Coburg, 1968), Plate 1; the barriers at Brussels in 1569 engraved by Franz Hogenberg, reproduced in Dillon, 'Barriers' (1904), plate opposite p. 304; and the 'Barriers' tapestry reproduced in Frances Yates, *The Valois Tapestries* (1959), Plate III.

52 Bartolomeo Sereno, *Trattati del uso della lancia a cavallo, del combattere a piede, alla sbarra et dell' imprese et inventioni cavalieresche* (Naples, 1610), pp. 91–151. Another relevant work is Giovan' Battista Gaiani, *Discorso del tornear a piedi* (Genoa, 1619), which is similarly concerned with appearances.

CHAPTER VI

1 Pausanias, *Attica*, XXXIX, 3 (Loeb Library, I, p. 209). The earliest wrestling treatise so far discovered is a Greek papyrus fragment of the first or second century AD. See M.B. Poliakoff, *Studies in the Terminology of the Greek Combat Sports* (Meisenheim, 1986), pp. 161–72, and his *Combat Sports in the Ancient World* (New Haven and London, 1987), pp. 51–3.

2 W.E. Fairbairn, *All-in Fighting* (1942), p. 7.

3 Many teachers have recognized that combat skills, acquired in exercise and sport, must be regarded and applied differently when fighting for one's life. Emile André, founder of the journal *L'Escrime Française*, for example, draws this distinction sharply throughout his *Manuel de boxe et de canne* (Paris, n.d.), and includes a section on 'Coups de lutte et ruses diverses pour le combat réel'.

4 Silver (1599), p. 25.

5 The issue was discussed by Plato: but the *locus classicus* for the debate is Lucian's *Anacharsis*.

6 Baron Jacob Friedrich von Bielfeld, *L'Érudition universelle* (Berlin, 1768); English translation, *The Elements of Universal Education* (1770), III, pp. 359–61.

7 The link with Castiglione is obvious, but already in the twelfth century Pedro Alfonso had listed knightly activities, including riding, swimming, archery and hunting. He also included chess and pugilism with the cestus (*cestibus certare*) which seem odd. See *Disciplina clericalis*, ed. and tr. A.G. Palencia (Madrid, 1948), p. 19.

8 *Il Cortegiano*, I, 21, 25. Castiglione's inclusion of wrestling as a necessary skill for the courtier is repeated, along with most of his other ideas, in Louis Guyon, *Les Diverses Leçons* (Paris, 1604).

9 Carl von Raumer, tr. H. Barnard, *German Schools and Pedagogy* (1861), II, p. 190.

10 Celio Calcagnini's funeral oration for Antonio Constabile, *Opera aliquot* (Basle, 1554), p. 514; Sir Thomas Elyot, *The Boke named The Governour* (1531), fol. 63v – a passage included, almost verbatim, in James Cleland, *The Institution of a Young Noble Man* (Oxford, 1607), p. 220.

11 Ulrich Zwingli, *Praeceptiones* (Basle, 1523); tr. *Certeyne preceptes* (1548), sig. C. 3v–4.

12 Richard Mulcaster, *Positions* (1581), ed. R.H. Quick (1888), pp. 76–7.

13 *Anciens mémoires du XIVe siècle sur Bertrand du Guesclin* (1836–9), ed. Michaud and Poujoulat, pp. 439–40.

14 *Le Livre des faicts du Mareschal de Boucicaut*, I, 5–7; *Le Victorial*, I. 24. On Jehan de Saintré's wrestling bout see Chapter 1, p. 23.

15 Olivier de la Marche, II, p. 108. Most of the foot combats described by Olivier and the other Burgundian chroniclers, especially those involving Jacques de Lalaing, include hand-to-hand grappling.

16 Maximilian I, *Freydal*, Plates 39, 99, 131, 139, 143, 163, 171, 198, 202, 226.

17 *The Travels of Leo von Rozmital*, ed. M. Letts (1957), pp. 36–7, 93–5, 138. For examples of wrestling exhibitions see as follows: for 1474, Pietro Spino, *Historia della vita dell'eccellentissimo Bartolomeo Coglione* (Venice, 1569), p. 218; for 1507, d'Auton, IV, p. 328; for 1519, Prost (1872), p. 245; for 1520, Anglo, *Spectacle* (1969), pp. 154–5; for 1532, Ellis, *Original Letters*, ser. 3, II, pp. 217–21.

18 Maréchal de Fleuranges, *Les Mémoires*, ed. Michaud and Poujoulat, p. 71.

19 See Chapter 1, pp. 22–3; Brantôme, *Oeuvres*, ed. Lalanne, VI, p. 273.

20 Brantôme, *Oeuvres*, VI, pp. 140–1.

21 François de la Noue, *Discours politiques et militaires* (Basle, 1587), 'Discours', V. See the edition by F.E. Sutcliffe (Geneva, 1967), pp. 153–4.

22 Sir Humphrey Gilbert (1869), p. 7; Henry Peacham, *The Compleat Gentleman* (1622), Cap. XVI; Edward Herbert, first Lord Herbert of Cherbury, *The Autobiography*, ed. Sidney Lee (1906), pp. 41–2.

23 John Locke, 'Some thoughts concerning education' (1693) in *The Works of John Locke* (1812), IX, pp. 192–3.

24 Hieronymus Mercurialis, *Artis gymnasticae libri sex* (Venice, 1569), II, viii. The authorities cited are Galen, Plutarch, Pollux, Plato, Aristotle, Martial, Suetonius and Hippocrates.

25 Hugh F. Leonard, *A Hand-Book of Wrestling* (New York, 1897), Chapter I. Leonard's information on ancient wrestling came from an unspecified edition of Sir J.G. Wilkinson, *Manners and Customs of the Ancient Egyptians*. For a concise, annotated modern survey, see Poliakoff, *Combat Sports* (1987).

26 Sir Thomas Parkyns, *Progymnasmata. The Inn-Play: or, Cornish-Hugg Wrestler* (1713), pp. 22–33. V. Mandey and J. Moxon, *The Mechanick Powers* was published in 1696 and again in 1709, but Parkyns drew few precise connections between the material quoted and his own description of wrestling.

27 Thompson Clayton, *A Handbook of Wrestling Terms and Holds* (South Brunswick, New York, London, 1968), 'Foreword'.

28 Chronologically, Fiore's work had been preceded by the brief remarks on Liechtenauer's wrestling system in Hanko Döbringer's manuscript of 1389. See Hils (1985), pp. 104–5.

29 Getty MS, fol. 3v; Novati (1902), p. 194.

30 There are discrepancies between the versions but I have given the totals of the Getty MS, which is slightly fuller than Novati's.

31 Fiore, ed. Novati (1902), p. 194.

32 Getty MS, fol. 3v. In Novati, p. 195, the distinction is between *amore* and *ira* rather than *solaço* and *ira*.

33 For the arm crush see Getty MS, fol. 8v; Novati, p. 126. For the double nelson and *lo zinachio in coglioni*, see Getty MS, fol. 9v; Novati, p. 127. A much clearer illustration of the double nelson is in *Talhoffer* (1467), Plate 200.

34 Getty MS, fol. 9v; Novati, p. 127.

35 Fairbairn (1942), p. 94.

36 See, for example, Mikonosuke Kawaishi, *My Method of Self Defence*, tr. E.J. Harrison (London, 1957); Dennis Rovere, *Chinese Military Police: Knife, Baton and Weapon Techniques* (Calgary, Canada, 1996).

37 Fabris (1606), 'Second Book, Third and Last Part. Treatise on wrestling, seizures of the sword, hurlings of the cape, and laws of the dagger'. See figs 177–9.

38 The manuscript, Pedro de Heredia's *Traité des armes*, is in the Scott Collection in Glasgow. A Spanish manuscript of Heredia, *Tratado de las armas* (described as sixteenth-century) is noted by Leguina, *Bibliografía* (1904), p. 71, without further reference. The Scott manuscript is in French and has fifty-four watercolour drawings (the same number as listed in Leguina).

39 In addition to a few anonymous masters, the treatises by Ott, Andreas Liegnitzer, Hans Talhoffer, Sigmund Ringeck, Paulus Kal, Jorg Wilhalm, Hans Czynner and Fabian von Auerswald have at least some claim to originality. Hils has carefully worked out the overall relationship between the manuscripts at his disposal (which constitute the great majority): but his study is necessarily more bibliographical than martial. The standard work on early German wrestling is Karl Wassmannsdorff, *Die Ringkunst des deutschen Mittelalters* (Leipzig, 1870).

40 The text is in *Talhoffer (1443)*, pp. 29–34; the drawings are at Plates 126–60. Hils (1985), p. 63, states that Ott's text in this manuscript is followed by an illustrated version: but this suggests a closer, more consistent relationship between text and pictures than really exists.

41 *Talhoffer (1443)*, Plate 136; *Talhoffer (1467)*, Plates 200, 201, 210, 215, 220.

42 *Talhoffer (1467)*, Plates 198, 216.

43 *Ibid.*, Plates 200, 207.

44 *Ibid.*, Plate 212. This hold, with a much longer but still unsatisfactory explanation, appears in Fiore, Getty MS, fol. 20v. Cf. Leonard (1897), pp. 52–3.

45 In von Auerswald (1539), a drag hold is shown at fol. 19v, but has no special name; while *Der Trapp*, at fol. 9, is something quite different and akin to a hip throw. Cf. Leonard (1897), pp. 72–3.

46 *Talhoffer (1467)*, Plate 213.

47 Gregor Erhart's manuscript was long thought to be lost after its last public sighting – listed in a sale catalogue of Karl and Faber in May 1935 as noted by Wierschin (1965), p. 23 and Hils (1985), pp. 32–5. It was, in fact, purchased by R.L. Scott and remains in the Scott Collection. It was once the property of the fatally acquisitive Paulus Hector Mair who notes on fol. 3 that he received the book from the Cutler, Leonhard Zolinger, in 1560.

48 Tradition attributes to Dürer more than an academic interest in combat. For a slate relief showing him engaged in a duel with an unknown opponent, see Wilhelm Waetzoldt, *Dürer and his Times* (London, 1950), p. 24 and plate opposite p. 9.

49 Dürer's source was the Augsburg Codex Wallerstein I.6.4°.2, and both manuscripts were published in a masterly edition by Friedrich Dörnhöffer.

50 See plates XVIII–XXI, XXV–XXVIII.

51 The Scott manuscript mistranscribes this and refers twice to the right hand against right hand.

52 A fine illustration by Jorg Breu of a sickle fight is reproduced in Anthony Hobson, *Great Libraries* (1970), pp. 138–9.

53 The six thrusts along with eight of the downward stabs, and the corresponding *prese*, are illustrated and discussed in Alfred Hutton, *Cold Steel* (1889), pp. 198–229.

54 Cf. for example: Marozzo's *Presa* I with Fiore (Getty MS) fol. 13; *Presa* II with Getty MS, fol. 14v and Novati, p. 132; *Presa* III with Getty MS, fol. 16v and

Novati, p. 136; *Presa* IV with Getty MS, fol. 15v and Novati, p. 134; *Presa* V with Getty MS, fol. 16v and Novati, p. 136; *Presa* VI with Getty MS, fol. 18 and Novati, p. 139; *Presa* IX with Getty MS, fol. 15v and Novati, p. 134; *Presa* X with Getty MS, fol. 12v and Novati, p. 129; *Presa* XIII with Getty MS, fol. 40 and Novati, p. 137; *Presa* XVI with Getty MS, fol. 40v and Novati p. 138; *Presa* XXI with Getty MS, fol. 17 and Novati, p. 139; *Presa* XXII with Getty MS, fol. 13 and Novati, p. 130.

55 Agrippa (1553), fols. 56r–v, shows a couple of wrestling tricks; and there are a few relevant remarks in Torquato d'Alessandri, *Il cavalier compito* (Viterbo, 1609), pp. 90–5. An appreciation of the value of wrestling endured, as in Pallavicini (1670), pp. 44–5, where he discusses the relative importance of strength and dexterity and explains how the Roman wrestling master taught weak pupils to overcome the strong:

> At the beginning of the wrestling bout the weak remain vigilant in getting to know the *tempo* of their opponent, and seizing the movement of the strong man, with dexterity they throw him to the ground; whence dexterity is superior to force, and thus it is in fencing; and it is necessary to have a good eye, spirit, dexterity of arm, and nimbleness of legs.

56 Hans Wurm (*Ringerbuch*). The work was first described by Sotzmann in *Serapeum* (1844), pp. 33–44. The arm lever is at fol. 2, the incipient back breaker at fol. 2v.

57 All three printed versions are transcribed and reproduced in black and white by Helmut Minkowski, *Das Ringen im Grüblein. Ein spätmittelalterliche Form des deutschen Leibringens* (Stuttgart, 1963) with an excellent introduction and notes dealing with cognate manuscript material. There is also a coloured reproduction of Wurm's edition by Hans Bleibrunner, *Das Landshuter Ringerbuch* (Munich, 1969) which does not take Minkowski's work into account. On Hans Wurm, see Campbell Dodgson (1911), II, pp. 263–5.

58 Eight *Grüblein* woodcuts form an appendix to the seventy-seven wrestling postures which constitute the main part of von Auerswald's treatise.

59 Von Auerswald (1539), fol. 15v. He calls this throw 'the Two Hips' (*Die zwo Hüffe*).

60 *Ibid.*, fols. 6, 21, 25v, 27v, 28, 34v, 35.

61 Von Auerswald's work is one of the few combat treatises to have attracted attention. In the essays appended to the facsimile edition by Witt, Wonneberger and Schade (Leipzig, 1988) all the relevant literature is discussed. There is also a summary (at pp. 8–9) of von Auerswald's wrestling terms: but it is incomplete and not helpful technically.

62 Pauernfeindt (1516), sig. K2r–v. 'Wringing' the testicles was the method whereby Reynard the Fox gained an unexpected victory in his duel with Sir Isegrim the Wolf; and H.C. Lea, *Superstition and Force*, 4th edition (Philadelphia, 1892), p. 179 refers to an early twelfth-century wager of battle in which the victor triumphed by pulling off his opponent's testicles.

63 Egenolff includes Pauernfeindt (unacknowledged) on the long sword, staff and dagger fighting; Leküchner on the *Messer* (acknowledged); and Ringeck (unacknowledged and via Pauernfeindt) on sword and buckler. I have not yet identified his source for unarmed combat.

64 In a reversal of his own procedure (manuscript to printed book), Egenolff's work, along with Dürer's, was copied in an early seventeenth-century manuscript now in Wrocław, on which see Dörnhoffer (1909), pp. XXIV–XXXIII, and Hils (1985), pp. 44–6. Weiditz's woodcuts for Egenolff were also copied in the wrestling sections of Paulus Hector Mair's compendia as, for example, in Osterreichische Nationalbibliothek, Codex Vindob. 10826, fol. 70 (derived from Weiditz's *Gurgel werffen*), fol. 70v (*Uberachsel stürtzen*), fol. 71 (*An kopff stellen*), fol. 71v (*Hin tragen*), fol. 72v (*Gefangen nemen*). Ten out of the total of seventeen wrestling woodcuts by Weiditz, and all six on dagger fighting, are reproduced in Arthur Wise, *The Art and History of Personal Combat* (Greenwich, Connecticut, 1971), pp. 211, 232–4.

65 Practice with the wooden bodkin had featured in the manuscript collections of Paulus Hector Mair (1542).

66 Sutor, *New Künstliches Fechtbuch* (1612), pp. 18–19.

67 Johann Georg Pascha, *Kurze Unterrichtung belangend die Pique, die Fahne, den Jäger-stock, das Voltesiren, das Ringen, das Fechten auf den Stoss und Hieb, und endlich das Trincieren verferrtigts* (Wittenberg, 1657).

68 On Schmidt see Chapter 10, pp. 276–7. See also the following note.

69 Petter's work was issued three times in Amsterdam (1674); once in Mompel-garten (1675); once in Leiden (1712); and once, in a reduced size, in an edition by Karl Wassmannsdorff (Heidelberg, 1887). The German version and illustrations were also reproduced complete (but badly engraved and ill printed) by Theodor Verolini in his *Der Künstliche Fechter* (Würzburg, 1679).

70 The system adopted by Arnold Umbach and Warren R. Johnson, *Successful Wrestling* (1953), actually echoed, consciously or otherwise, the contrasts used at Beni Hasan; and the method has been regularly used ever since in textbooks on wrestling, judo and other martial arts.

71 In the classic work by H. Irving Hancock and Katsuma Higashi, *The Complete Kano Jiu-Jitsu* (New York and London, 1905), the master is differentiated throughout by his black belt. Also see Chapter 2, pp. 46–7.

72 See for example, Petter and Hooghe, p. 17, No. 5; p. 18, No. 6; p. 65, No. 1.

73 This methodical procedure was to remain the norm for all serious wrestling manuals and reached its high point in Leonard (1897) in which, as the author explains at p. 31, the pictures illustrate not only every hold, lock, trip and throw used in catch-as-catch-can but also the various guards and methods to escape from them, while 'the text opposite each picture traces and describes each position there illustrated, from its inception to the fall which would result'. Hancock and Higashi adopt a similar method for the 505 postures in their *Complete Kano Jiu-Jitsu*.

74 Petter and Hooghe, pp. 13–18 (Part II, Nos 1–6).

75 *Ibid.*, pp. 19–25 (Part III, Nos 1–7).

76 *Ibid.*, pp. 26–9 (Part IV, Nos 1–4).

77 *Ibid.*, pp. 30–4 (Part V, Nos 1–5).

78 *Ibid.*, Part IX, Introduction, p. 48 (Part IX, No. 2).

79 This Italian version was edited from the manuscript at Modena (MS, Estense T.VII.25) by Carlo Bascetta, *Sport e giuochi* (1978), I, pp. 297–340. Bascetta can hardly be criticized for missing the derivation from Monte, and he provides an excellent text and commentary. See Anglo, 'The man who taught Leonardo darts', *Antiquaries Journal*, LXIX (1989), p. 263.

80 Monte (1509), I, 1.

81 *Ibid.*, II, 83.

82 *Ibid.*, II, 1.

83 On Ayora and Monte see Anglo (1989), pp. 262–5 and the sources cited therein. Concerning the relationship between Monte's text and Ayora's comments, M.-M. Fontaine (1992), pp. 166–7, misses the point of Ayora's commentary which is to gloss (for non-Spaniards) the Hispanicisms constantly used by Monte in his treatment (written in Spanish) of a wrestling system which is itself wholly Spanish.

84 The existence of a Spanish tradition is attested by the allegorical wrestling match between Poverty and Fortune in Alfonso Martínez's *Arçipreste de Talavera*, written in the mid-fifteenth century. This combat is full of the technical wrestling terms later used by Monte and would hardly have been used by a poet-priest had he not thought them familiar to his readers. See the edition by Mario Penna (Turin, 1955), pp. XLIII–XLVI.

85 Monte would not, therefore, have approved of catch-as-catch-can which involves a great deal of ground wrestling. See for example, Leonard (1897), Umbach and Johnson (1953), and Thompson Clayton (1968).

86 For examples of the argument, including Ficino, see Charles Trinkaus, *In Our Image and Likeness. Humanity and Divinity in Italian Renaissance Thought* (1970), pp. 181, 190–1, 204, 213, 221, 232, 474–5. For Lactantius, see his *Divine Institutes* in *The Works of Lactantius*, tr. William Fletcher (Edinburgh, 1871), I, p. 449.

87 For England, see Graeme Kent, *A Pictorial History of Wrestling* (1968), p. 100. The German manuscript referred to is Osterrreichische Nationalbibliothek Codex Vindob. 10799. This very large format *Fechtbuch* is dated 1623 and is entirely pictorial. It is, in the main, dependent on earlier, readily-identifiable manuscript traditions including that represented by Augsburg Codex Wallerstein I.6.4°.2 (see above n. 49), but it includes a remarkable section (fols 141–3) in which almost nude wrestlers strangle each other with looped kerchieves. The contests are extremely violent and several of the wrestlers have blood gushing from nose and mouth.

88 For examples see *Talhoffer (1443)*, Plates 68–71; *Talhoffer (1459)*, Plates 63, 79–81; *Talhoffer (1467)*, Plates 189, 202, 297; Wallerstein MS fol. 72v; Egenolff (1531), fol. 46; Erhart MS (1533), fol. 91v. Codex Vindob. 10799 (1623) has rather more ground wrestling than usual – for example, at fols. 115, 121, 122, 123, 127, 128.

89 Some medieval masters recognized the problem of being attacked by more than one adversary, and tried to suggest ways to deal with it. For examples see Fiore, ed. Novati (1902), p. 187; Getty MS, fol. 33; Wallerstein MS, fols. 71–3; *Talhoffer (1467)*, Plates 240–1.

CHAPTER VII

1 *Glossarium armorum*, ed. C. Blair, V. Norman, O. Gamber and others (Graz, 1972); Leguina, *Glosario* (1912).

2 Even now things are not wholly straightforward. One is still faced not only with a variety of terms in different languages but also with changing nomenclature within any one language and, inevitably, disagreement between experts.

3 René de Belleval, *Du costume militaire des Français en 1446* (Paris, 1866), pp. 2–3.

4 See the *Almain Armourers' Album. Selections from an Original Manuscript in Victoria and Albert Museum, South Kensington*, ed. Viscount Dillon (1905); Charlotte Becher, Ortwin Gamber, Walter Irtenkauf, *Das Stuttgarter Harnisch-Musterbuch 1548–63*

(Vienna, 1980). The earliest album of which we have knowledge, the *Thun-Tetschen Sketchbook*, recording the work of Lorenz Helmschmied, disappeared during the Second World War and is now known only from photographs. See Ortwin Gamber, 'Die Turnierharnisch zur Zeit König Maximilians I und das Thunsche Skizzenbuch', *Jahrbuch*, LIII (1957), pp. 33–70. Tangentially relevant are the sketch books of Filippo Orsini at the Victoria and Albert Museum and at Wolfenbüttel. See J.F. Hayward, 'Filippo Orsini, designer, and Caremolo Modrone, armourer, of Mantua', in *Waffen- und Kostümkunde*, XXIV (1982), pp. 1–16, 87–102.

5 Fernand de Mély and Edmund Bishop, *Bibliographie générale des inventaires imprimées* (Paris, 1892–5), includes references to all relevant inventories printed up to their time. See also my Bibliography under: Francis M. Kelly, 'A knight's armour of the early fourteenth century, being the inventory of Raoul de Nesle'; E. de Prelle de la Nieppe, 'L'Inventaire de l'armurerie de Guillaume III comte de Hainaut en 1358'; L.F. Salzman, 'Property of the Earl of Arundel, 1397'; Viscount Dillon and W.H. St John Hope, 'Inventory of the Goods and Chattels belonging to Thomas, Duke of Gloucester (1397)'; J.G. Mann, 'The lost armoury of the Gonzagas'; Mario Scalini, 'The weapons of Lorenzo de Medici'; F.H. Cripps-Day, *An Inventory of the Armour of Charles V*.

6 A partial exception is the illuminated inventory of the Emperor Charles V (in the Royal Armoury at Madrid), where the illustrations of the armour, with their various reinforcing or exchange pieces, themselves constitute a kind of visual encyclopaedia. See Conde Valencia de Don Juan, 'Bildinventar der Waffen, Rüstungen, Gewänder und Standarten Karl V in der Armeria Real zu Madrid', *Jahrbuch*, X (1889), XI (1890). A few illustrations are reproduced in Antonio Domínguez Ortiz, Concha Herrero Carretero and José A. Godoy, eds, *Resplendence of the Spanish Monarchy* (New York, 1991), pp. 108, 110, 118, 138. Another illuminated armour inventory is that for the Archduke Ferdinand of Tyrol, on which

see August Grosz and Bruno Thomas, *Katalog der Waffensammlung in der Neuen Burg Schausammlung* (Vienna, 1936), VII/86/4.

7 See J.-B. Giraud, *Documents pour servir à l'histoire de l'armement au moyen âge et à la renaissance* (Lyon, 1895, 1899), I, pp. 167–78; II, pp. 9–59.

8 This phrase can be found in Aylward (1956), p. 35.

9 Ramón Llull, *Ordre de cavayleria*, Cap. VI; Guillaume de Deguileville, *Le Pèlerinage de vie humaine*, ed. J.J. Stürzinger (Roxburghe Club, 1893), pp. 119 ff.; Pere March, *L'arnès del cavaller* – but note that this is a modern title of convenience, according to Marti de Riquer, *L'arnès del cavaller. Armes i armadures catalanes medievals* (Barcelona, 1968), p. 74.

10 Chrestien de Troyes *Erec et Enide*, verses 547–746; *Sir Gawain and the Green Knight*, ed. Sir Israel Gollancz (E.E.T.S. Oxford, 1940), lines 566–89.

11 The document is printed in Gui Alexis de Lobineau, *Histoire de Bretagne* (Paris, 1707), II, cols 663–77. A challenge of 1309 (col. 1639) also provides a list of equipment but less detailed. Including such lists became common practice in later challenges. See Riquer (1968), pp. 191–206; Frederick Bryson, *The Sixteenth-Century Italian Duel* (Chicago, 1938), pp. 44–54.

12 Two translations of the text have been conflated here: *The King's Mirror (Speculum Regale – Konungs Skuusjá)*, tr. Laurence Marcellus Larson (New York, 1917), pp. 217–20; John Hewitt, *Ancient Armour and Weapons in Europe from the Period of the Northern Nations to the End of the Thirteenth Century* (Oxford and London, 1855), pp. 109–11.

13 Additional MS 46919, fols 86v–7, printed by P. Meyer, 'Notice et extraits du MS 8336 de la bibliothèque de Sir Th. Phillips à Cheltenham', *Romania*, XIII (1884), p. 530.

14 In the French manuscript of 1446, referred to below, there is reference to 'ung petit gantellet lequel se appelle gaignepin' which is assigned to be worn on the right hand: but it is impossible to say how this relates to the *gayne payns* and gauntlets of whalebone in Herebert.

15 As with most of these early records, it is sometimes difficult to understand the author's meaning or even to be sure that he himself knew what he meant. There is no ambiguity, however, about the *flagellum* which R. Barber and Juliet Barker, *The Tournament* (Woodbridge, 1989), pp. 153–4, mistakenly gloss as a whip.

16 On the *Dotzè del Chrestià*, see Riquer (1968), pp. 73–91.

17 John Hill's treatise survives only in seventeenth-century copies. One version (Bodleian Library, Ashmolean MS 856) is printed in *Illustrations of Ancient State and Chivalry*, ed. W.H. Black (Roxburghe Club, 1840), pp. 876–83, and in Charles ffoulkes, *The Armourer and his Craft* (1912), pp. 173–6; the other (in the Library of Lincoln's Inn) is printed in L.O. Pike, *A History of Crime in England* (1873), I, pp. 389–92.

18 I am grateful to Claude Blair for allowing me to see his notes on John Hill for his forthcoming work on the Armourers and Brasiers Company.

19 See George Neilson, *Trial by Combat* (1890), p. 199.

20 On the manuscripts, see G.A. Lester, *Sir John Paston's 'Grete Boke'* (Woodbridge, 1984), pp. 84–5. One version (now Pierpont Morgan Library MS 775) was edited in Viscount Dillon, 'On a manuscript collection of ordinances of chivalry of the fifteenth century, belonging to Lord Hastings', *Archaeologia*, LVII (1900), pp. 43–4. Dillon also prints another fifteenth-century text, the *Abilment for the Justes of the Pees*, which merely lists equipment for mounted lance combat without descriptions. Cf. Lester, *op.cit.*, pp. 86–7. Both Blair and Lester suggest a possible relationship between Hill's treatise and *Howe a Man Shall be Armyd*.

21 The whole drawing is reproduced in Dillon, 'On a manuscript collection . . .' Plate VII. Riquer (1968), fig. 215, reproduces the central section (with the table, knight and attendant), showing the detail more clearly, though the ambiguities of the drawing itself are irremediable. The glaive-like weapon is obscure: but for some possible relations, see the *Candeliere* and *Vouge francese* in Mario Troso, *Le armi in asta* (Novara, 1988), pp. 128, 130.

22 The *Traictié* was published by Marc Vulson, Sieur de la Colombière, *Le Vray Théâtre d'honneur* (Paris, 1648), I, pp. 49–80; included in the *Oeuvres complètes du roi René d'Anjou*, ed. Comte de Quatre-barbes, (Angers, 1845–6) II; edited, from an inferior version, in *Verve* (Paris, 1946); and issued in a new edition by the Bibliothèque Nationale. Jean-Pierre Reverseau, 'L'Habit de guerre des Français en 1446', *Gazette des Beaux Arts*, XCIII (1979), p. 198 n. 5, suggests that the *Traité* is 'falsely attributed to King René', but elsewhere writes as though René were the author.

23 On armour for the *Kolbenturnier* see Bruno Thomas and Ortwin Gamber, *Katalog der Leibrüstkammer, Waffensammlung*, I (1976), pp. 101–2, Plates 38, 39.

24 Antoine de la Sale, *Des anciens Tournois et faictz d'armes* in Bernard Prost, *Traités du duel judiciare, relations de pas d'armes et tournois* (Paris, 1872), p. 210. La Sale's helm, 'barred with iron', is similar to the one depicted by René.

25 The following words, here italicized, are omitted in the translation because their meaning is not clear: 'elle doibt estre vuidée par le meilleu *et mosse devant et toute d'une venue se bien pou non* depuis la croisée jusques au bout'.

26 These features of the sword can also be seen in the pictures of tourneying which illustrate the more elaborate manuscripts of the *Livre des tournois*. A.V.B. Norman suggested that it was almost certainly made of leather.

27 Bibliothèque Nationale MS fonds français, 1997, which consists of four items: a version of Antoine de la Sale's *Des Anciens Tournois et faictz d'armes*, superior to that published by Prost; a copy of La Sale's verses, *La journée d'onneur et de prouesse*; and the two treatises on armour. The text of the first treatise on armour was published, with copious annotation, by René de Belleval, *Du Costume Militaire des Français en 1446* (Paris, 1866). Belleval apparently owned another copy of this manuscript which, like that in the Bibliothèque Nationale, he dated at around 1460. The text was reprinted from Belleval by F.H. Cripps-Day, *The History of the Tournament in England and France* (1918), Appendix IX,

and re-edited with a valuable new commentary by Jean-Pierre Reverseau, *Gazette des Beaux Arts* (1979), pp. 179–98. Merlin de Cordebeuf's work was published without commentary by Belleval as a note to his principal text, but has never been reprinted.

28 Tournaments based upon romantic literary themes were well established long before the fifteenth century and have often been commented upon. We also know that in Provence at least there was an association of knights errant who deliberately wore armour of an earlier age. See C. Beard, 'Genuine or forgery? The Rufford Abbey panel', *Connoisseur*, LXXXVI (1930), p. 85.

29 The *flandresque* is a form of protection for the lower leg, made of leather reinforced with metal scales.

30 Reverseau suggests that this is due to the contemporary French attitude which regarded protection of the limbs as more important than protection of the torso (Reverseau, 1979, p. 181). However, since the author does subsequently discuss body armour for the joust, the omission is more likely to be a simple oversight.

31 Cf. Quixada de Reayo on sight and hearing. See p. 216.

32 The fullest treatment of the evolution and structure of lances and of the armour worn when using them is François Buttin, 'La Lance et l'arrêt de cuirasse', *Archaeologia*, XCIX (1965), pp. 77–178.

33 *Petri Montij de singulari certamine siue dissensione: deque veterum, recentiorum ritu ad Carolum Hyspaniarum principem & Burgundie Archiducem libri tres* (Milan, 1509). This text is *not* about the techniques of personal combat as M.-M. Fontaine (1992), p. 165, n. 4, implies. There is a great difference between a *fencing* book and a *duelling* book.

34 Monte's term, *coxottus*, is a neologism related to the Latin *coxa* or thigh, but even more akin to the Spanish word for greave, *quijote* or *quixote*.

35 See Riquer (1968), pp. 129–32.

36 Charles Buttin, 'Notes sur les armures à l'épreuve', *Revue Savoisienne* (1901), has a remarkable collection of sources relating to armour proofing, but his earliest reference is dated 1568.

37 Fontaine (1992), p. 166, criticizes my translation of the phrase *De armis indutivis* as 'arms of peace' which was derived from *indutiae* (a truce) and related to 'jousts of peace'. She suggests a derivation from *induere* (to put on an article of clothing, in this case armour) which makes better sense, although Monte generally prefers the term *arma defensibilia*.

38 On the Innsbruck armourers during Sigismund's reign, see Bruno Thomas and Ortwin Gamber, *Die Innsbrucker Plattnerkunst*, catalogue of the exhibition held at the Ferdinandeum, Innsbruck (June–September 1954), pp. 17–20, 51–61. See also the comments by Meinrad Pizzinini in Gert Ammann, ed., *Die Herzog und sein Taler. Erzherzog Sigmund der Münzreich. Politik, Münzwesen, Kunst*, catalogue of the exhibition held in the Ferdinandeum, Innsbruck (June–September 1986), pp. 16–21.

39 Monte (1509), II, 54–6.

40 Real Biblioteca, Madrid, Escorial MS A.IV.23, fols. 1–52v.

41 Louis de Gaya, *Traité des armes* (Paris, 1678); Alain Manesson Mallet, *Les Travaux de Mars, ou l'art de la guerre* (Paris, 1685), III; Gabriel Daniel, *Histoire de la milice Françoise* (Paris, 1721).

42 Two copies of Schemel's work are in the Herzog August Bibliothek, Wolfenbüttel: MS 1.6.3 and MS 5 Blankenberg. Another version is in Vienna, Kunsthistorisches Museum, Kunstkammer Inv. P. 5247. See Ortwin Gamber, 'Die Harnischgarnitur', *Livrustkammaren* (Stockholm), VII (1955–7).

43 The last tournament described by Schemel is that organized on 21 February 1568 to celebrate the wedding of Duke William of Bavaria.

44 See F.W. Huth, *Works on Horses and Equitation. A Bibliographical Record of Hippology* (1887, repr. Hildesheim, New York, 1981), pp. 7–8.

45 Juan Quixada de Reayo, *Doctrina del arte de la cavallería* (Medina del Campo, 1548). There is now a modern critical edition by Noel Fallows, *Un texto inédito sobre la caballería del renacimiento español. Doctrina del arte de la cauallería de Don Juan Quijada de Reayo* (Liverpool, 1996). I am grateful to Dr Fallows for having provided me

with a typescript of his work prior to its publication.

46 For Quixada's account of jousting technique, see Chapter 8, pp. 238–41.

47 This is the view expressed by the Colchester-based armourer, Christopher Dobson with whom this reference has been discussed.

48 From *encombronar*, to strengthen something with iron.

49 These unfortunate jousters are identified by Noel Fallows in the edition referred to in n. 45.

50 For general remarks on the *cofia* and *escofia* see Leguina *Glosario* (1912), pp. 245–7. Sir Guy Francis Laking, *A Record of European Arms and Armour* (1920–2), IV, p. 122, reproduces an example which incorporates the straps mentioned by Zapata.

51 Cf. Zapata's further comments discussed in Chapter 8, pp. 241–2.

52 Cf. dall'Agocchie below, Chapter 8, pp. 243–5.

53 A typical example, from 1477, is the treatise, *Governo et exercitio de la militia* by Orso degli Orsini, in the Bibliothèque Nationale, MS Italien 958, which has only a short discussion of arms and armour at fols. 10v–11v. On this treatise, see Piero Pieri, 'Il "governo et exercitio de la militia" di Orso degli Orsini e i "Memoriali" di Diomede Carafa', *Archivio storico per le provincie napoletane*, XIX (1933), pp. 99–179.

54 Machiavelli, *Arte della guerra* (Florence, 1521), II; Polybius, *The Histories*, VI, 19–26.

55 Raymond de Beccarie de Pavie, Sieur de Fourquevaux, *Les Instructions sur le faict de la guerre* (Paris, 1548), fol. 24v. Cf. the translation by Paul Ive, *Instructions for the Warres* (1589), p. 61.

56 Cesare d'Evoli, *Delle ordinanze et battaglie del Signor Cesare d'Evoli Napolitano* (Rome, 1586). An earlier edition of 1583 is mentioned in Mariano Ayala, *Bibliografia militare italiana* (Turin, 1854).

57 Cf. Alessandro Massario Malatesta, *Compendio dell'heroica arte di cavalleria* (Venice, 1600), fol. 10, noting that the lancegay may have one point or two (that is a sharpened tip at both ends) and can be effective either as a missile or as a hand weapon

when a knight is surrounded by enemies, 'striking with it both in front and behind'.

58 Armour decorated with gold and silver, elaborate plumage, and other fancy falderals had been similarly scorned a century earlier by Orso degli Orsini who, dismissing them as nothing but a superfluous expense, recommended merely sufficient adornment to enable easy identification. Bibliothèque Nationale MS Italien 958, fols 10v–11.

59 *The Works of Sir Roger Williams*, ed. John X. Evans (Oxford, 1972), pp. cxii–cxxiii, 28–41.

60 Humfrey Barwick, *A Breefe Discourse, Concerning the force and effect of all manuall weapons of fire* (?1594), sig. B.2v.

61 John Cruso, *Militarie Instructions for the Cavallrie* (Cambridge, 1632), pp. 28–31. Cruso's work was reprinted with an introduction by Brigadier Peter Young (Kineton, 1972). It must be stressed that cavalry specialists rarely agreed on the comparative efficacy of different types of mounted troops.

62 Guillaume du Choul, *Discours sur la castramentation et discipline militaire des Romains, des bains et antiques exercitations* (Lyons, 1557); Justus Lipsius, *De militia Romana libri quinque* (Antwerp, 1596). Jacob Lydius, *Syntagma sacrum de re militari* (Dordrecht, 1698), Plate between pp. 62, 63, reproduces, without acknowledgement, nine of the ten helmets engraved in Du Choul, *Discours*, fols 49v–50.

63 For the continuing popularity of romance, see Richard Cooper, '"Nostre histoire renouvelée": the reception of the romances of chivalry in renaissance France (with bibliography)', in S. Anglo, ed., *Chivalry in the Renaissance* (Woodbridge, 1990), pp. 175–238.

64 Claude Fauchet, *Origines des chevaliers, armoiries et heraux. Ensemble de l'ordonnance, armes, et instruments desquel les François ont anciennement usé en leurs guerres* (Paris, 1600), fols 32–60.

65 Charles Dufresne, Sieur Du Cange, *Glossarium ad scriptores mediae et infimae latinitatis* (Paris, 1678); Carlo d'Aquino, *Lexicon militaris* (Rome, 1724).

66 *Avertimenti cavalereschi usati da prencipi e signori, per ben cavalcare, e difendersi à* *cavallo armato, e disarmato, con la spada, ò pistola così in guerra, come in Campagna, ò passegiando per la città* (Padua, 1651).

CHAPTER VIII

1 On Sereno see, pp. 170–1, 247–8.

2 Sydney Anglo, *The Great Tournament Roll* (1968), pp. 38–9.

3 Monte (1509), II, 66, 74.

4 Giorgio Basta, *Il governo della cavalleria leggiera* (Frankfurt, 1612), p. 46.

5 See François Buttin, 'La lance et l'arrêt de cuirasse', *Archaeologia*, XCIX (1965). For earlier lance techniques, see Victoria Cirlot, 'Techniques guerrières en Catalogne féodale: le maniement de la lance', *Cahiers de Civilisation Médiévale*, XXVIII (1985), pp. 35–42; Jean Flori, 'Encore l'usage de la lance . . . la technique du combat chevaleresque vers l'an 1100', *Cahiers de Civilisation Médiévale*, XXXI (1988), pp. 213–40.

6 Sydney Anglo, 'Anglo-Burgundian feats of arms: Smithfield, June 1467', *Guildhall Miscellany*, II (1965), pp. 271–83.

7 For examples of ineptitude, see Buttin (1965), pp. 117–18.

8 Luigi Santa Paulina, *L'arte del cavallo* (Padua, 1696), pp. 181–93.

9 Buttin (1965), pp. 83–90, 115–17, 121–2.

10 Duarte's two principal surviving works were first edited by J.I. Roquete (Paris, 1842). There are modern editions by Joseph M. Piel: *Leal conselheiro* (Lisbon, 1942), and *Livro da ensinança de bem cavalgar toda sela* (Lisbon, 1944). My references are to this last edition. The manuscript treatise on combat was listed by Leguina, *Bibliografía* (1904), p. 59, but its present location is unknown.

11 Duarte, *Livro*, pp. 74–81.

12 Dall'Agocchie (1572), fol. 62v–3; Antoine de Pluvinel *Maneige royal*. This quotation is from the English version of Pluvinel by Hilda Nelson (London, 1989) p. 140. Cf. Ghisliero (1587), p. 188. On the history of training for the joust, see the well documented study by Lucien Clare, *La Quintaine, la course de bague et le jeu des têtes* (Paris, 1983).

13 Duarte, *Livro*, pp. 82–3.

14 *Ibid.*, p. 88.

15 *Chronique de Jean Le Févre Seigneur de Saint-Remy*, ed. François Morand (Paris, 1876–81), II, p. 170.

16 Guttiere Diaz de Gámez, *Le Victorial. Chronique de Don Pedro Niño*, ed. and tr. the Comte Albert de Circourt and the Comte de Puymaigre (Paris, 1867), pp. 348–55, describes a joust in Paris about the year 1405, specifically stating that French knights joust in a fashion different from the Spanish. The French 'joust without tilt after the fashion of war' (*Justan sin tela, a manera de guerra*) and the account shows that this results in knights crashing into each other.

17 Duarte, *Livro*, p. 96.

18 *Ibid.*, p. 100.

19 Alonso de Cartagena, *Doctrinal de los caualleros* (Burgos, 1487), III, Cap. 5. For an exhaustive examination of the text and its history, see Noel Fallows, *The Chivalric Vision of Alfonso de Cartagena: Study and Edition of the Doctrinal de los caualleros* (Newark, Delaware, 1995).

20 Cf. pp. 240–1.

21 See Ruy Sánchez de Arévalo, successively Bishop of Oviedo, Zamora, Calahorra and Palencia, *Verjel de los príncipes*, ed. F.R. de Uhagón (Madrid, 1900), pp. xvi, 78; Alfonso Martínez de Toledo, chaplain to Juan II, *Arçipreste de Talavera*, ed. Mario Penna (Turin, 1955), pp. XLIII–XLVI, 212–18.

22 *Le Jouvencel par Jean de Bueil*, ed. C. Favre and L. Lecestre (Paris, 1887–9), II, pp. 100–1.

23 Ponç de Menaguerra, *Lo cavaller* (Valencia, 1493). The text has been edited by Pere Bohigas Belaguer in his *Tractats de cavalleria* (Barcelona, 1947), pp. 177–95. See also Palau y Dulcet, No. 162774.

24 *Lo cavaller*, Cap. II.

25 *Ibid.*, Cap. XXX.

26 *Ibid.*, Cap. XIII.

27 *Ibid.*, Cap. XV.

28 *Ibid.*, Cap. XVI.

29 *Ibid.*, Caps. XVIII, XIX, XXI, XXIII, XXIV.

30 Monte (1509), II, 82.

31 *Ibid.*, II, 76–83.

32 *Ibid.*, II, 88–91.

33 *Ibid.*, II, 92.

34 *Ibid.*, II, 102. Cf. pp. 248, 354 n. 50.

35 *Ibid.*, II, 93.

36 *Ibid.*, II, 103.

37 Quixada's work has been edited and annotated by Noel Fallows (1996). See Chapter 7, n. 45.

38 Cf. the anonymous treatise on French military equipment in 1446, ed. Belleval (1866), p. 12 where the final paragraph deals with the jouster's 'bon serviteur' who has three principal responsibilities for his master even prior to handing him his lance before each course. First, he must check that the knight has not lost any piece of armour in the previous encounter. Second, he must see whether he has been in any way dazed or injured by a blow. And third, he must keep watch to see whether there is an opponent in the lists with lance in rest, ready to joust against his master: 'so that his said master does not have to wait too long, with his lance in the rest, without running a course; or so that he does not run his course in vain without an opponent coming against him'.

39 On Henri II's injury and death, see C.D. O'Malley and J.B. de C.M. Saunders, 'The "relation" of Andreas Vesalius on the Death of Henry II of France', *Journal of the History of Medicine and Allied Sciences*, III (1948), pp. 197–213.

40 This may be what Alonso de Cartagena meant by lances broken *travesadas*.

41 Luis Zapata, 'Miscelánea', in *Memorial histórico español: colección de documentos, opúsculos y antigüedades*, XI (Madrid: Real Academia Española, 1859), pp. 212–18. This has been reprinted with annotations in Noel Fallows's edition of Quixada.

42 *Cuba* is literally a wine cask.

43 Dall'Agocchie (1572), fols. 58v–66.

44 *Ibid.*, fol. 60.

45 The Dresden painting is described in R.C. Clephan. *The Tournament*, pp. 90–91. Folyarte's patent is listed in Bennet Woodcroft, *Alphabetical Index of Patentees of Inventions* (London, 1854; reprinted London, 1969), p. 193. See also Charles ffoulkes, *The Armouries at the Tower of London* (1916), I, p. 26. There is an excellent German manuscript illustration of a joust (1570) between knights mounted on wheeled wooden horses, reproduced in *Das Grosse Buch der Turniere . . . Die*

Bilderhandshrift des Codex Rossianus 711 im besitz der Biblioteca Apostolica Vaticana, ed. Lotte Kurras (Stuttgart, Zürich, 1996), Commentary, p. 104.

46 Apart from dall'Agocchie, only Ghisliero (who clearly copies his predecessor) writes about *la lancia di due pezzi*. So far I have found no other source describing this special lance and none of the arms and armour specialists consulted knows of any surviving examples although, at a much later period in Sweden, there were lances with detachable tips used for the quintain. See Lena Rangström, ed., *Riddarlek och Tornerspel, Catalogue of the Tournament Exhibition* (Stockholm, 1992), Nos 269, 270, 273–6, 301, and p. 429.

47 On the lance and its dimensions, cf. the anonymous French text of 1446 in Belleval (1866), pp. 11–12, 73–6.

48 A.H. Thomas and I.D. Thornley, *The Great Chronicle of London* (1938), p. 373.

49 Antoine Pluvinel, *Maneige royal* (Paris. 1627), pp. 171–6.

50 Antonino Ansalone, *Il cavaliere descritto in tre libri* (Messina, 1629), pp. 61–83. Ansalone repeats the old admonition against twisting to the right and recommends, instead, a slight turn to the left in order to gain a few inches on the opponent's lance.

51 For Burgundian sources on chivalric combat, including jousting, see Claude Gaier (1985, 1986). Evelyne van den Neste, *Tournois, joutes, pas d'armes dans les villes de Flandre à la fin du moyen age* (Paris, 1996), contrives not to mention combat techniques but, at pp. 213–332, provides a valuable 'Chronologie des tournois (1300–1500)'.

52 This is noted by Olivier de la Marche, *Mémoires*, ed. Beaune and d'Arbaumont, II, p. 102. Most of what follows in my summary is drawn from the *Histoire de Gaston IV, Comte de Foix par Guillaume Leseur*, ed. Henri Courteault (Paris, 1893–6), I, pp. 150–93, II, pp. 43–59.

53 Lenoncourt jousted at Tours in January 1447. See Leseur, I, p. 197.

54 Alessandro Massario Malatesta, *Compendio dell'heroica arte di cavalleria* (Padua, 1600), fols 12v–13, although he adds, significantly, that knights are better armed with pistols than with lances. To use mounted

pistoleers must, at this period, have seemed a soft option and they certainly became popular, although soon condemned by Wallhausen. It was only in the middle of the nineteenth century that the invention of the revolver really turned mounted pistoleers into worthwhile warriors. Their uselessness in the seventeenth century must have been prodigious. See Valentine Baker, *The British Cavalry. With remarks on its practical organization* (1858), pp. 30–32.

55 This view has been cogently argued by Carroll Gillmor, 'Practical chivalry: the training of horses for tournaments and warfare', *Studies in Medieval and Renaissance History*, New Series, XIII (1992), pp. 5–29.

CHAPTER IX

1 On Quixada, see Chapters 7 and 8, pp. 216–17, 238–42.

2 Agrippa (1553), fol. 62. Alessandro Massario Malatesta (1600), sig+3v, refers to Agrippa's 'promise' to treat this subject and suggests that he had failed because of its intrinsic difficulty and the novelties constantly being introduced into it.

3 René-Julien Chatelain, *Le Guide des officiers de cavalerie* (Paris, 1817), pp. 76–83.

4 A. Alessandri and E. André, *L'Escrime du sabre à cheval* (Paris, 1897), pp. 7–9.

5 Monte (1509), II, 82.

6 On Lew's work, see Hils (1985), pp. 32–3.

7 *Talhoffer (1467)*, plates 251–70.

8 *Ibid.*, plate 254.

9 Duarte, *Livro da ensinança*, ed. Piel (1944), pp. 113–17.

10 Castiglione, *Il Cortegiano*, II, 8.

11 Cf. Chapter 7, pp. 207–10.

12 For a fifteenth-century illustration of a *Kolbenturnier* within tiny circular lists, in which knights wield their clubs two-handed overhead, see Ortwin Gamber, 'Ritterspiel und Turnierrüstung im Spätmittelalter', in *Das Ritterliche Turnier im Mittelalter*, ed. Josef Fleckenstein (Göttingen, 1985), figure 7. The German *Kolbenturnier* with a wooden mace was a sporting version of serious combat. See William H. Jackson, 'Tournaments and the Germanic

chivalric *renovatio*. Tournament discipline and the myth of origins' in *Chivalry in the Renaissance*, ed. Sydney Anglo (Woodbridge, 1990), pp. 80–81.

13 See Gaiani and La Noue, below pp. 265–6.

14 In Jeremias Schemel's *Turnierbuch* (Kunsthistorische Museum, Vienna, Kunstkammer Inv. P.5247). fols 120v–9, 134v–5, knights are shown using a two-hand grip on lances, and there are similar illustrations in Paulus Hector Mair's compendia as, for example, in Osterreichische Nationalbibliothek, Codex Vindob. 10826, fols 293–5v.

15 Monte (1509), II, 67, 70.

16 *Ibid.*, II, 69.

17 *Ibid.*, II, 72.

18 *Ibid.*, II, 73.

19 *Ibid.*, II, 74.

20 Carranza (1582), fols 157v–8.

21 The only Italian Ludovico who was an authority on cavalry was Melzo. But his *Regole militari sopra il governo e servitio particolare della cavalleria* was not published until 1611. Cf. the reference to 'Ludovico' amongst the 'extranjeros' in Narváez, *Advertencias*, para. 217, where it *could* indicate Melzo.

22 The two different styles of horsemanship to which Duarte refers were chiefly characterized by riding short (*a la gineta*) or long (*a la brida*).

23 Ghisliero (1587), pp. 176–9.

24 Massario Malatesta (1600), fols 8v–14v.

25 Marc Vulson, Sieur de la Colombière, *Le Vray Théâtre d'honneur* (Paris, 1648), II, pp. 481–6.

26 Giorgio Basta, *Il governo della cavalleria leggiera* (Venice, 1612), pp. 45–6.

27 Basta does not explain what he means by 'the measure of Spain'.

28 This passage, including what Captain Demetrio did in Piedmont, is used without acknowledgement by Ansalone at the end of his own bloodless *Il cavaliere* (1629).

29 See Chapter 10, pp. 287–90.

30 Gaiani, *Arte di maneggiar la spada a piedi et a cavallo* (Loano, 1619), pp. 84–91.

31 It is interesting that, though little concerned with mounted fencing, Capoferro (1609), p. 23 does stress that on horseback the cut is superior to the thrust.

32 Pierre de la Noue, *La Cavalerie françoise et italienne* (Lyon, 1621), pp. 155–7.

33 Binet is so described in the *Biographie universelle, ancienne e moderne* (Paris, 1811–28), IV, p. 499.

34 Antoine de Pluvinel, *Maneige royal* (Paris, 1623). The references here are to the edition of Paris, 1627.

35 Pluvinel (1627), pp. 178–83.

36 Montmorency's deeds are referred to by Edward Lord Herbert of Cherbury in his *Autobiography*, ed. Lee (1906), p. 40, where both feats are wrongly supposed to have been accomplished at one tourney. He cites as his source Labroue 'in his book of horsemanship': and in fact the story is given in Salomon La Broue, *Second livre des preceptes de cavalerice françois* (Paris, 1612), Cap. 18, pp. 40–1, but more accurately.

37 Lord Herbert of Cherbury, *Autobiography*, ed. Lee, pp. 39–40.

38 Ansalone (1629), pp. 84–6.

39 Antonio Alfieri, *Quesiti del cavaliero instrutto nell'arte dello schermo* (Padua, 1644), pp. 96–147.

40 La Touche (1670), II, ix.

41 John Cruso, *Militarie Instructions for the Cavallrie* (Cambridge, 1632), p. 42.

42 See Chapter 10, p. 282.

43 For a history of mounted fencing see General Durfort's sketchy introduction to the French translation of Schmidt, *Instruction pour la cavalerie, sur le maniement le plus avantageux du sabre* (Paris, 1828), pp. I–CCCXL. From a considerable volume of publications on cavalry fencing, the following are especially worth noting: the original edition of Schmidt, *Lehrbuch für die Kavallerie zum vortheilhaften Gebrauch des Säbels* (Berlin, 1797); Andres Pedro Olmeda de la Cuesta, *Tratado de esgrima de lanza uso de esta arma contra sable y espada de caballería* (Cadiz, 1812); A. Muller, *Théorie sur l'escrime à cheval* (Paris, 1816); Chatelain, referred to above n. 3; *A Self-Instructor of the new system of Cavalry and Infantry Sword Exercises* (Manchester, 1822); Giuseppe Weiss, *Istruzione sulla scherma a cavallo* (Naples, 1829); Henry Angelo, *Instructions for the Sword Exercise* (1835); Le Capitaine Dérué, *Nouvelle méthode d'escrime à cheval* (Paris, 1885).

CHAPTER X

1 On Parkyns, see Thomas Seccombe's article in the *Dictionary of National Biography*.

2 Parkyns (1713), pp. 12–13.

3 Francesco Guicciardini, *Storia d'Italia*, IV, ix, quoted in Fenton's translation (1579), p. 175. It has been pointed out that Galeazzo's limitations as a commander were widely recognized by his contemporaries and that Guicciardini's sneer is not a comment on the widening gap between the tiltyard and the battlefield but rather on the fact that skills in weapon handling do not compensate for poor military judgement. But this is precisely my point: Guicciardini recognizes that the individual skills displayed in the lists were simply irrelevant.

4 Di Grassi (1594 ed.), sigs 4v, 1.

5 Dall'Agocchie (1572), fols 3, 12v.

6 Saviolo (1595), sig. B1v–2.

7 I raised the issue in an article, 'How to kill a man at your ease: fencing books and the duelling ethic', in Anglo, *Chivalry in the Renaissance* (1990), pp. 1–12. The philosopher, John Locke, recognized the problem when he noted that the acquisition of skill with the sword made men 'apt to engage in quarrels' and to be 'more touchy than needs, on points of honour, and slight or no provocations'. See Chapter 6, n. 23.

8 W.E. Fairbairn, *All-In Fighting* (1942), p. 8.

9 Lawrence Stone, *The Crisis of the Aristocracy 1558–1641* (Oxford, 1965), pp. 223–50, has much valuable information on English affrays, murders and duels: but he does not mention the violence necessarily inculcated by the martial artists.

10 The left-hand parry, for example, used throughout the sixteenth century, was illustrated by Angelo in the eighteenth century and popularized thence in the *Encyclopédie*. It still figures in the manual by the younger La Boëssière, *Traité de l'art des armes* (Paris, 1818), Plates 17, 19, 20.

11 Sir William Hope, *The Fencing-Master's Advice to his Scholar* (Edinburgh, 1692), pp. 20–3.

12 Sebastian Heussler, *Neu Künstlicher Fechtbuch* (Nuremberg, 1615 and later editions); Daniel L'Ange, *Deutliche und Gründliche Erklärung der Adelichen und Ritterlichen freyen Fechtkunst* (Heidelberg, 1664); Diederich Porath, *Palaestra Suecana* (Stockholm, 1693).

13 Johann Andreas Schmidt, *Leibbeschirmende und Feinden Trotz bietende Fecht-Kunst* (Nuremberg, 1713); Siegmund Carl Friedrich Weischner, *Die Ritterliche Geschicklichkeit im Fechten* (Weimar, 1765).

14 Monte, *De singulari certamine sive dissensione* (Milan, 1509), sig. A.6v.

15 La Colombière, *Le Vray Théâtre* (1648), II, frontispiece and 'Explication'.

16 Docciolini (1601), Cap. 21, 'Sopra l'Armato', pp. 113–14. A similar point was made by Giovanni Pietro Gorio, *Arte di adoprar la spada* (Milan, 1682), pp. 27–30, where he argues that the art of fencing is completely different from other arts in that whereas in the latter it is possible to correct mistakes, in the former retribution immediately ensues.

17 Docciolini mentions his fifty-two years' experience at sig. A.2.

18 Cyril G.R. Matthey, ed., *The Works of George Silver* (1898), 'Introduction'. Matthey was not only a scholar and soldier but was also one of the great collectors of fencing books and the catalogue of his library is a valuable reference work in its own right. The collection was dispersed at his death and several volumes made their way into the R.L. Scott Collection.

19 Sir John Smythe, *Certain Discourses* (1590), fol. 4. This attitude was not peculiar to England. In Spain, too, the authorities inveighed against the fashion for exaggeratedly long, thin *estoques* designed only for murdering civilians and 'useless for the war'. See Chapters 1 and 3, pp. 36, 100.

20 Valentine Baker, *The British Cavalry* (1858), p. 59.

21 See John Bingham, *The Tactiks of Aelian, or art of embattailing an army after the Grecian manner* (1616).

22 John Hale, 'The military education of the officer class in early modern Europe', in *Cultural Aspects of the Italian Renaissance: Essays in Honour of Paul Oskar Kristeller*, ed. Cecil Clough (Manchester, 1976), pp. 440–61; and his 'Military academies on the Venetian terrafirma in the early sev-

enteenth century', *Studi Veneziani*, XV (1973), pp. 273–95.

23 Giovanni Alberto Cassani, *Essercitio militare, il quale dispone l'huomo à vera cognitione del scrimire di Spada, e dell'ordinare l'essercito à battaglia* (Naples, 1603).

24 The caracole was a cavalry manoeuvre developed in the latter half of the sixteenth century to combat squares of pikemen by riding at them in successive lines, firing pistols at them, and then wheeling off to the rear in order to reload. As an attempt to adapt new technology to the battlefield, it became very popular and was especially espoused by La Noue. Theoretically, it might have been effective but, in practice, it proved an abject failure because, as Sir Roger Williams justly observed,

> out of a hundred pistolers, twentie nor scarce tenne at the most doo neither charge pistoll, nor enter a squadron as they should, but commonlie and lightly alwaies they discharge their pistols, eight and five score off, and so wheele about.

See Sir Roger Williams, *Works*, ed. J.X. Evans (Oxford, 1972), pp. 33–5. It is not surprising that Gustavus Adolphus (a commander who believed in aggression) banned the manoeuvre. On the other hand, the caracole was ideally suited for equestrian festivals during the seventeenth century and knights, riding about on a level surface, discharging their pistols at dummies who did not fire back, made a great noise. But the exercise was even less demanding than tilting – and possessed about as much significance as preparation for battle.

25 The contradictory views of La Noue, Roger Williams, Ghisliero, Basta, Melzo and Wallhausen on the use of lance and/or pistols and/or swords were still being echoed by Nolan, Beamish, Baker and Dennison in the mid-nineteenth century. For a brief survey of aspects of the latter debate, see Hubert Moyse Bartlett, *Louis Edward Nolan and his Influence on the British Cavalry* (1971).

26 Smythe, *Certain Discourses* (1590), sig. 3v.

27 Conversely, Monte does not attempt to consider the political role of the army which was Machiavelli's primary concern in every one of his major works and his great contribution to political thinking.

28 Hans Delbrück, tr. Walter J. Renfroe, Jr, *History of the Art of War* (1985), IV, pp. 53–7, comments on pike length, but does not mention Monte.

29 For references, see Anglo, 'The man who taught Leonardo darts', pp. 271–2.

30 On the academy at Siegen see, Max Jahns, *Geschichte der Kriegswissenschaften, vornehmlich in Deutschland* (Munich, 1889–91), II, pp. 1026–9; Hale, 'Military education', pp. 444–5. There is also a Berlin dissertation by L. Plathner, *Graf Johann von Nassau und die erste Kriegschule* (1913), which I have not seen.

31 See Max Jahns (1889), II, pp. 873–4, 930–3, 987–9, 1017–21; Cockle, *Bibliography of Military Books* (1900), Nos. 621, 622, 685, 735, 739, 740; Max Trippenbach, 'Johann Jacobi-Tautphoeus von Wallhausen, der erste deutsche Militärschriftsteller (1580–1627)', *Hanauisches Magazin* (1937).

32 Wallhausen had announced in the address to his reader, in *Kriegskunst zu Fuss* (Oppenheim, 1615), a master plan to restore the military arts to the light in a series of eight separate books. He fulfilled a large part of this plan but published other works which were creative deviations from it.

33 Wallhausen, *Künstliche Piquen Handlung* (Hanau, 1617) in which he describes himself as head and director of the 'Kriegs und Ritterschulen zu Siegen'.

34 Wallhausen, *De la milice romaine, premier partie* (1616), p. 71.

35 Earlier illustrated editions of Vegetius merely provide fantastic adaptations of woodcuts from Valturius's fifteenth-century treatise and have no independent value.

36 This is especially important because, throughout the Middle Ages and Renaissance, Vegetius had been accepted as the supreme authority for the Roman art of war, and it was Lipsius who had challenged that supremacy.

37 Delbrück, IV, p. 253.

38 For a useful though incomplete list of Wallhausen's publications, see *The National Union Catalog Pre–1956 Imprints*.

39 Jacob de Gheyn, *The Exercise of Armes for Calivres, Muskettes, and Pikes after the Ordre of His Excellence Maurits Prince of Orange* (The Hague, 1607). See Cockle (1900), No. 79.

40 The famous engraver Jean Theodore de Bry was intimately concerned with the translation and publication of the French versions of Wallhausen's texts, but he is specifically credited only with the engravings A. B. C. D. as appears from the author's letter to his reader in *L'Art Militaire pour l'infanterie* (1615), sig. 4.

41 In 1563 Giovanni Maria Memmo had suggested a similar training routine, based on Vegetius's text, for Venetian citizens, but nothing came of it. See Hale, 'Military education', p. 453. It is curious, given Wallhausen's interest in real fighting, that he should repeat Vegetius's statement on using the point rather than the edge as though it were authoritative. See the *Romanische Kriegskunst*, Chapter XII. And cf. above Chapter 3, p. 108.

42 Silver, *Paradoxes*, p. 25.

Bibliography

This bibliography is confined solely to manuscripts and printed sources cited in this book. If a source has not been specifically referred to in the text or notes then it is not included here.

MANUSCRIPTS

1 Augsburg
Universitätsbibliothek
Codex Wallerstein I.6.4°.2: anonymous *Fechtbuch*.

2 Dresden
Sächsische Landesbibliothek
MS Dresd. C.93 and C.94: two-volume collection of a wide range of combat materials, compiled by Paulus Hector Mair and illustrated by Jörg Breu the Younger.

3 Florence
Biblioteca Nazionale
MS II.iii.315: Francesco di Lorenzo Altoni, *Trattato dell'armi intitolato monomachia*. (This is the title heading the 'Proemio'; the first chapter is headed 'Trattato della arte di scherma'.).

4 Glasgow
Scott Collection
René d'Anjou, *Traictié de la forme et devis d'ung tournoy* (late fifteenth-century copy of section on arms and armour).

Fecht und Ringerbuch (c. 1508), collection of texts by Liechtenauer, Emring, Andres Juden, Ott, Hundfeld, Liegnitzer.

Gregor Erhart, *Fechtbuch* (1533).

Don Pedro de Heredia, *Traité des armes* (c. 1600).

Desbordes, André, *Discours de la théorie et de la pratique et de l'excellence des armes* (1610), modern copy.

G. Belfin, *Abregé de l'exercice des armes. Necéssaire à la jeunesse de savoir, pour pouvoir se deffendre avec son espée* (Luxembourg, 1767).

Fechtbuch (sixteenth century), collection of eight photographs from an unidentified German manuscript offered for sale by E.P. Goldschmidt and Company, October 1935.

5 Leeds
Royal Armouries
MS I.33: sword and buckler manual.

6 Leuven
Corble Collection
MS 4.C.48: Master's certificate of Faustino de Zea (1847).

7 London
British Library
Additional MS 34,192: the presentation copy of George Silver's manuscript.

Additional MS 39,564: vellum roll of exercises with the two-hand sword.

Additional MS 46919, fols 86v–7: *Modus armandi milites*.

Cottonian MS Titus A. xxv, fols 105r–v: *The strokes off ij hand swerde* (fragment).

Harleian MS 3542, fols 82–5: *The use of the two hand sworde*.

Harleian MS 4206: treatise on fencing by Henry Cavendish, Marquis (and then Duke) of Newcastle.

Harleian MS 5219: *Mathematical demonstration of the sorde* by Henry Cavendish – a fragment of the preceding manuscript.

Sloane MS 376: George Silver's *Bref instructions*.

Public Record Office

C 82/770: Bill concerning the masters of defence.

KB 9/975, m 36: On William Smith's sword-playing house.

8 Los Angeles
Getty Museum
MS Ludwig XV. 13: the best version of Fiore de' Liberi's treatise (originally Phillipps MS 4204).

9 Madrid
Real Biblioteca
Escorial MS A.IV.23, fols 1–52v: *Ejercicios de las armas*, a Spanish translation of sections of Monte's *Collectanea*.

10 Munich
Bayerische Staatsbibliothek
MS icon.393: collection of Paulus Hector Mair.

11 New York
Pierpont Morgan Library
MS Morgan 383: a version of Fiore de' Liberi's treatise.

MS Morgan 775: ordinances of chivalry (formerly belonging to Lord Hastings).

12 Nuremberg
Germanisches Nationalmuseum
Codex ms. 3227a: Hanko Döbringer/Liechtenauer.

13 Oxford
Bodleian Library
Ashmolean MS 856: Hill's treatise on armour.

14 Paris
Bibliothèque Nationale
MS Espagnol 60: edicts relating to Valencia.

MS Espagnol 443: Don Juan de la Rocha's *Discurso sobre la nobleza, antigüedad y necessidad de la destreza de las armas*.

MS fonds français, 343: *L'Histoire du S. graal*.

MS fonds français, 1236: Philibert de la Touche, *Les Vrayes Principes de l'espée seule*.

MS fonds français, 1996: *Le Jeu de la hache*.

MS fonds français, 1997: Antoine de la Sale's *Des anciens tournois et faicts d'armes* and *La journée d'onneur et de prouesse*; and two treatises on armour.

MS fonds français, 20,362: Monstrelet's chronicles.

MS fonds français, 2258: *Cérémonies du gage de bataille*.

MS Italien 958: Orso degli Orsini, *Governo et exercitio de la militia*.

MS Italien 959: Giovanni Antonio Lovino, *Modo di cacciare mano all spada* and *Ragionamento sopra la scienza dell' arme*.

MS Italien 1527: Girolamo Cavalcabo, *Nobilissimo discorso intorno il schermo di spada e pugnale, et di spada, e altre utilissime instruttioni pertinenti in esso schermo, e conveniente ad'ogni nobile et honorato cavaliere. Dell'Eccellente Scrimitore Signor Girolomo Cavalcabo Bolognese.*

15 Rome
Biblioteca Nazionale
Fondo Vittorio Emmanuele, MS 1342: Filippo Vadi, *Liber de arte gladiatoria dimicandi* (partly edited in Bascetta).

16 Vienna
Kunsthistorisches Museum
P.5012: Peter Falkner, *Fechtbuch*.

P.5013: anonymous treatise on foot combat.

Kunstkammer Inv. P.5073: *Freydal*.

Kunstkammer Inv. P.5247: Jeremias Schemel, *Turnierbuch*.

Osterreichische Nationalbibliothek
Codex Vindob. 10723: presentation copy of Angelo Viggiani's, *Trattato dello schermo* with the editor's dedication dated 10 October 1567, and the author's dedication dated 15 May 1551.

Codex Vindob. 10799: anonymous *Fechtbuch* dated 1623.

Codex Vindob. 10825 and 10826: two-volume collection compiled by Paulus Hector Mair. Its contents are almost the same as in Mair's other collection (MS Dresd. C.93 and C.94) but with texts in both German and Latin.

Codex Vindob. 11093: mid-fifteenth-century *Fechtbuch* (illustrations without text) largely, though not exclusively, concerned with the long sword.

17 Wolfenbüttel
Herzog August Bibliothek

MS 1.6.3: Jeremias Schemel, *Turnierbuch*.

MS 5 Blankenberg: another version of Schemel.

PRINTED SOURCES

Unless otherwise stated, place of publication is London.

Agocchie, Giovanni dall', *Dell'arte di scrimia libri tre* (Venice, 1572).

Agrippa, Camillo, *Trattato di scientia d'arme, con un dialogo di filosofia* (Rome, 1553).

Alfieri, Antonio, *Quesiti del cavaliero instrutto nell'arte dello schermo. Con le risposte del suo maestro. Opera utile e curiosa divisa in tre parti* (Padua, 1644).

Alfieri, Francesco Ferdinando, *La scherma* (Padua, 1640).

Alfieri, Francesco Ferdinando, *Lo spadone. Dove si mostra per via di figure il maneggio e l'uso di esso* (Padua, 1653).

Alessandri, A. and André, E., *L'Escrime du sabre à cheval* (Paris, 1897).

Alessandri, Torquato d', *Il cavalier compito* (Viterbo, 1609).

Alfonso, Pedro, *Disciplina clericalis*, ed. and tr. A.G. Palencia (Madrid, 1948).

Amberger, J. Christoph, 'Fear! The role of angst in single combat', *Hammerterz Forum. The International Newsletter for the Fencing Collector* (Spring/Summer 1996).

Ammann, Gert, ed., *Die Herzog und sein Taler. Erzherzog Sigmund der Münzreich. Politik, Münzwesen, Kunst*, Catalogue of the exhibition held in the Ferdinandeum, Innsbruck (June–September 1986).

André, Emile, *Manuel de boxe et de canne. Ouvrage contenant un chapitre complémentaire sur les coups de lutte et des ruses diverses utiles pour la défensive dans la rue* (Paris, n.d.).

Angelo, Domenico, *L'École des armes, avec l'explication général des principales attitudes et positions concernant l'escrime* (1763).

Angelo, Henry, *Instructions for the Sword Exercise* (1835).

Anglin, Jay P., 'The schools of defence in Elizabethan London', *Renaissance Quarterly*, XXXVII (1984), pp. 393–410.

Anglo, Sydney, 'Anglo-Burgundian feats of arms: Smithfield, June 1467', *Guildhall Miscellany*, II (1965), pp. 271–83.

Anglo, Sydney, *The Great Tournament Roll of Westminster* (Oxford, 1968).

Anglo, Sydney, *Machiavelli: A Dissection* (1969).

Anglo, Sydney, *Spectacle, Pageantry and Early Tudor Policy* (Oxford, 1969).

Anglo, Sydney, 'The courtier. The Renaissance and changing ideals', in A.G. Dickens, ed., *The Courts of Europe* (1977).

Anglo, Sydney, 'How to win at tournaments: the technique of chivalric combat', *Antiquaries Journal*, LXVIII (1988), pp. 248–64.

Anglo, Sydney, 'The man who taught Leonardo darts', *Antiquaries Journal*, LXIX (1989), pp. 261–78.

Anglo, Sydney, 'How to kill a man at your ease: fencing books and the duelling ethic', in S. Anglo, ed., *Chivalry in the Renaissance* (Woodbridge, 1990), pp. 1–12.

Anglo, Sydney, '*Le Jeu de la hache*. A fifteenth-century treatise on the technique of chivalric axe combat', *Archaeologia*, CIX (1991), pp. 112–28.

Anglo, Sydney, Review of Berry's *The Noble Science*, *Renaissance Studies*, VII (1993), pp. 317–19.

Anglo, Sydney, 'Sixteenth-century Italian drawings in Federico Ghisliero's *Regole di molti cavagliereschi essercitii*', *Apollo* (November 1994), pp. 29–36.

Ansalone, Antonino, *Il cavaliere descritto in tre libri* (Messina, 1629).

Anti-pugilism or the science of defence exemplified (1790).

Aquino, Carlo d', *Lexicon militaris* (Rome, 1724).

Arbeau, Thoinot (pseud. for Jean Tabourot), *Orchésographie. et traicté en forme de diaologue, par lequel toutes personnes peuvent facilement apprendre & practiquer l'honneste exercice des dances* (Lengres, 1588). There is an English translation by Mary Stewart Evans (New York, 1948).

Ascham, Roger, *The Whole Works of Roger Ascham*, ed. Giles (1864).

Auerswald, Fabian von, *Ringer Kunst* (Wittenberg, 1539); facsimile edn by G.A. Schmidt, with an introduction by K. Wassmannsdorff (Leipzig, 1869); facsimile edn with essays by G. Witt, G. Wonneberger and W. Schade (Leipzig, 1988).

Austin, Gilbert, *Chironomia: A Treatise of Rhetorical Delivery* (1806).

Auton, Jean d', *Chroniques de Louis XII*, ed. R. de Maulde la Clavière (Paris, 1893).

Avertimenti cavalereschi usati da prencipi e signori, per ben cavalcare, e difendersi à cavallo armato, e disarmato, con la spada, ò pistola così in guerra, come in campagna, ò passegiando per la città (Padua, 1651).

Ayala, Mariano, *Bibliografia Militare Italiana* (Turin, 1854).

Aylward, J.D., *The House of Angelo* (1953).

Aylward, J.D., *The English Master of Arms from the Twelfth to the Twentieth Century* (1956).

Baillet, Adrien, *La Vie de Monsieur Des-Cartes* (Paris, 1691).

Baker, J.H., ed., *The Reports of Sir John Spelman* (Selden Society, 1978).

Baker, Valentine, *The British Cavalry. With remarks on its practical organization* (1858).

Baldwin, John W., *Masters, Princes and Merchants. The Social Views of Peter the Chanter and his Circle* (Princeton, 1970).

Barber, R. and Barker, Juliet, *The Tournament* (Woodbridge, 1989).

Bartlett, Hubert Moyse, *Louis Edward Nolan and his Influence on the British Cavalry* (1971).

Barwick, Humfrey, *A Breefe Discourse, concerning the force and effect of all manuall weapons of fire* (1594?).

Bascetta, Carlo, *Sport e giuochi. Trattati e scritti dal XV al XVIII secolo* (Milan, 1978).

Basta, Giorgio, *Il governo della cavalleria leggiera* (Venice, 1612).

Bayard, *La Tresjoyeuse, plaisante et recreative hystoire, composée par le Loyal Serviteur, des faiz, gestes, triumphes et prouesses du bon chevalier sans paour et sans reproche, le gentil Seigneur de Bayart*, ed. Petitot (Paris, 1820).

Beamish, N.L., *The Uses and Application of Cavalry in War* (1855).

Beard, C., 'Genuine or forgery? The Rufford Abbey panel', *The Connoisseur*, LXXXVI (1930), p. 85.

Becher, Charlotte, Gamber, Ortwin and Irtenkauf, Walter, *Das Stuttgarter Harnisch-Musterbuch 1548–1563* (Vienna, 1980).

Belleval, René de, *Du Costume Militaire des Français en 1446* (Paris, 1866).

Berriman, Captain M.W., *The Militiaman's Manual and Sword Play without a Master. Rapier and Broad Sword Exercises copiously explained and illustrated* (New York, 1859).

Berry, Herbert, ed., *The Noble Science. A Study and Transcription of Sloane MS 2530, Papers of the Masters of Defence of London, Temp. Henry VIII to 1590* (London and Toronto, 1991).

Bertrand, Léon, *The Fencer's Companion* (Aldershot, 1934).

Bielfeld, Baron Jacob Friedrich von, *L'Érudition universelle* (Berlin, 1768); English translation, *The Elements of Universal Education* (1770).

Billacois, François, *Le Duel dans la société française des XVIᵉ–XVIIᵉ siècles* (Paris, 1986).

Binet, Étienne, *Essai sur les merveilles de la nature* (Paris, 1621).

Bingham, John, *The Tactiks of Aelian Or art of embattling an army after the Grecian manner* (1616).

Biographie universelle, ancienne et moderne (Paris, 1811–28).

Blackwell, Henry, *The English Fencing Master, or the Compleat Tutor of the Small-Sword* (1702).

Blackwell, Henry, *The Art of Defence in which the several sorts of Guards, Passes, and Disarmes &c are represented by proper Figures with their respective Explications* (n.d.).

Blair, Claude, *European Armour circa 1066 to circa 1700* (1958).

Blair, Claude and Delamer, Ida, 'The Dublin civic sword', *Proceedings of the Royal Irish Academy*, LXXXVIII (1988).

Blair, Claude, 'Welsh bills, glaives, and hooks', *Journal of the Arms and Armour Society*, XVI, No. 2 (March 1999), pp. 71–85.

Bleibrunner, Hans, *Das Landshuter Ringerbuch* (Munich, 1969).

Bohigas Belaguer, Pere, *Tractats de cavalleria* (Barcelona, 1947).

Bondi di Mazo da Venetia, *La spada maestra. Libro dove si trattano i vantaggi della nobilissima professione della scherma, si del caminare, girare e ritirarsi, come del ferire sicuramente e difendersi* (Venice, 1696).

Boucicaut, *Le Livre des faicts du Mareschal de Boucicaut* ed. Michaud and Poujoulat (Paris, 1836).

Bracton, Henry, *Henrici de Bracton de legibus et consuetudinibus angliae*, ed. Sir Travers Twiss (Rolls Series, 1878–83).

Brantôme, *Oeuvres complètes de Pierre de Bourdeille Seigneur de Brantôme*, ed. Ludovic Lalanne (Paris, 1873).

Bresciani, Marin, *Li trastulli guerrieri* (Brescia, 1668).

Brinkley, Captain Frank, *Japan, its History, Arts, and Literature* (Boston, 1903–4).

Bruchius, Johannes Georgius, *Grondige Beschryvinge van der Edele ende Ridderlijcke Scherm-ofte Wapen-Konste* (Leyden, 1671).

Bryson, Frederick, *The Sixteenth-Century Italian Duel* (Chicago, 1938).

Bueil, Jean de, *Le Jouvencel par Jean de Bueil*, ed. C. Favre and L. Lecestre (Paris, 1887–9).

Bulletin de la Société historique des Archives d'Aunis et de Saintonge (1888).

Burton, Richard, *The Book of the Sword* (1884).

Buttin, Charles, 'Les Armes prohibées en Savoie sous les royales constitutions', *Revue Savoisienne. Publication périodique de la Société Florimontane* (37e Année), 1896, pp. 111–29.

Buttin, Charles, 'Notes sur les armures à l'épreuve', *Revue Savoisienne* (1901), pp. 5–99.

Buttin, Charles, 'Les Armes de hast', *Bulletin Trimestriel de la Société des Amis du Musée de l'Armée* (Paris, 1936–52).

Buttin, François, 'La Lance et l'arrêt de cuirasse', *Archaeologia*, XCIX (1965), pp. 77–178.

Calarone, Costantino, *Scienza prattica* (Rome, 1714).

Calcagni Abrami, Artemisia and Chimirri, Lucia, eds, *Incisioni toscani del seicento al servizio del libro illustrato* (Florence, 1987).

Calcagnini, Celio, *Opera aliquot* (Basle, 1554).

Calendar of Letter Books of the City of London, ed. R.R. Sharpe (1899–1912).

Canto, Rodríguez del, *El discípulo instruido* is cited by Leguina, *Glosario* (1912), p. 389.

Capitelli, Bernardino, *Gran simulacro dell'arte e dell'uso della scherma. Dal Capitelli ridotto in questa forma* (n.p., 1632).

Capoferro, Ridolfo, *Gran simulacro dell'arte e dell'uso della scherma* (Siena, 1610; 2nd edn, 1629).

Caroso, Fabritio, *Nobiltà di dame* (Venice, 1600): English translation and edition, Julia Sutton and F. Marian Walker (Oxford, 1986).

Carranza, Geronimo Sánchez de, *Libro que trata de la philosophía de las armas y de su destreza de la aggresión y defensión christiana* (Lisbon, 1582).

Cartagena, Alonso de, *Doctrinal de los caualleros* (Burgos, 1487). See also Fallows (1995).

Cassani, Giovanni Alberto, *Essercitio militare, il quale dispone l'huomo à vera cognitione del scrimire di spada, e dell'ordinare l'essercito à battaglia* (Naples, 1603).

Castiglione, Baldassare, *Libro del cortegiano* (Venice, 1528).

Castle, Egerton, *Schools and Masters of Fence* (1885, reprinted 1969).

Cavalcabo, Girolamo and Paternostrier, tr. Monsieur de Villamont, *Traicté ou instruction pour tirer des armes, de l'excellent scrimeur Hyeronyme Calvacabo, Bolognois. Avec un discours pour tirer de l'espée seule, fait par le deffunct Paternostrier de Rome* (Rouen, 1597).

Champier, Symphorien, 'Les Gestes ensemble la vie du preulx Chevalier Bayard' in M.L. Cimber and F. Danjou, *Archives curieuses de l'histoire de France* (Paris, 1835), sér. 1, ii.

Chasseneux, Barthélemi de, *Catalogus gloriae mundi* (Lyon, 1546).

Chatelain, René-Julien, *Le Guide des officiers de cavalerie* (Paris, 1817).

Chauchadis, Claude, *La Loi du duel. Le code du point d'honneur dans l'Espagne des XVe–XVIIe siècles* (Toulouse, 1997).

Chrestien de Troyes, *Erec et Enide*, ed. M. Roques (Paris, 1952).

Christfals, P.E., *Jüdische Fechtschule* (Enderes, 1760).

Christine de Pisan, tr. William Caxton, *The Book of Fayttes of Armes and of Chyvalrye*, ed. A.T.P. Byles (E.E.T.S., 1932).

Cirlot, Victoria, 'Techniques guerrières en Catalogne féodale: le maniement de la lance', *Cahiers de Civilisation Médiévale*, XXVIII (1985), pp. 35–42.

Clare, Lucien, *La Quintaine, la course de bague et le jeu des têtes* (Paris, 1983).

Clayton, Thompson, *A Handbook of Wrestling Terms and Holds* (South Brunswick, New York, London, 1968).

Cleland, James, *The Institution of a Young Noble Man* (Oxford, 1607).

Clements, John, 'Heroic fantasy: Katana vs Rapier', *Hammerterz Forum* (Spring/Summer 1997).

Clephan, R.C., *The Tournament* (1919).

Cockle, M.J.D., *A Bibliography of Military Books up to 1642* (1900).

Colombani, Giuseppe, *L'arte maestra* (Venice, 1711).

Cooper, C.H., *Annals of Cambridge* (Cambridge, 1843).

Cooper, Richard, ' "Nostre histoire renouvelée": the reception of the romances of chivalry in renaissance France (with bibliography)', in S. Anglo, ed., *Chivalry in the Renaissance* (Woodbridge, 1990), pp. 175–238.

Coppens, Chris, ed., *En Garde! Schermen verbeeld. Schermboeken uit de Corble-collectie, wapens & attributen* (Leuven, 1998).

Cotgrave, Randle, *A Dictionarie of the French and English Tongues* (1611).

Crevier, J.B.L., *Histoire de l'Université de Paris* (Paris, 1761).

Cripps-Day, F.H., *The History of the Tournament in England and France* (1918).

Cripps-Day, F.H., *Fragmenta Armamentaria*, II, Part V, *An Inventory of the Armour of Charles V*, (Frome, 1951), an edition and translation of the so-called *Relación de Valladolid*.

Croce, Flaminio della, *L'essercitio della cavalleria ed'altre materie* (Antwerp, 1625).

Cruso, John, *Militarie Instructions for the Cavallrie* (Cambridge, 1632), reprinted with introduction by Brigadier Peter Young (Kineton, 1972).

Dancie, François, *L'Espée de combat, ou l'usage de la tire des armes* (Tulle, 1623).

Daniel, Gabriel, *Histoire de la milice françoise* (Paris, 1721).

Daressy, Henri, *Archives des maîtres d'armes de Paris* (Paris, 1888).

Deguileville, Guillaume de, *Le pèlerinage de vie humaine*, ed. J.J. Stürzinger (Roxburghe Club, 1893).

Delbrück, Hans, tr. Walter J. Renfroe, Jr, *History of the Art of War* (1985).

Denifle, Henricus, *Chartularium Universitatis Parisiensis* (Paris, 1899).

Dérué, Le Capitaine, *Nouvelle méthode d'escrime à cheval* (Paris, 1885).

Desbordes, André, *Discours de la théorie de la pratique et de l'excellence des armes* (Nancy, 1610).

Diaz de Gámez, Guttiere, *Le Victorial. Chronique de Don Pedro Niño*, ed. and tr. the Comte Albert de Circourt and the Comte de Puymaigre (Paris, 1867).

Diderot, Denis and d'Alembert, J. Le Rond, *Encyclopédie ou Dictionnaire raisonné des sciences, des arts et des métiers* (Paris, 1751–77).

Dierickx, Jacques, *Traité et théorie d'escrime* (Brussels, 1849).

Dillon, Viscount, 'On a manuscript collection of ordinances of chivalry of the fifteenth century, belonging to Lord Hastings', *Archaeologia*, LVII (1900), pp. 43–4.

Dillon, Viscount, 'Barriers and foot combats', *Archaeological Journal*, LXI (1904), pp. 276–308.

Dillon, Viscount, ed., *Almain Armourers' Album. Selections from an Original Manuscript in Victoria and Albert Museum, South Kensington* (1905).

Dillon, Viscount and St John Hope, W.H., 'Inventory of the goods and chattels belonging to Thomas, Duke of Gloucester (1397)', *Archaeological Journal*, LIV (1897), pp. 275–308.

Dillon, Viscount and St John Hope, W.H., eds, *Pageant of the Birth Life and Death of Richard Beauchamp Earl of Warwick KG 1389–1439* (1914).

Dionisotti, Carlo, 'Appunti sulla nobiltà', *Rivista Storica Italiana*, Anno CI (1989), pp. 302–5.

Dionysius of Halicarnassus, *The Roman Antiquities of Dionysius of Halicarnassus*, tr. Edward Spelman, revised Ernest Cary (Loeb Library, 1937–40).

Docciolini, Marco, *Trattato in materia di scherma* (Florence, 1601).

Documentos sobre relaciones internacionales de los reyes católicos, ed. Antonio de la Torre, volumen V, 1495–7 (Barcelona, 1965).

Dodgson, Campbell, *Catalogue of Early German and Flemish Prints Preserved in the Department of Prints and Drawings in the British Museum* (1911).

Dörnhöffer, Friedrich, 'Albrecht Dürer's Fechtbuch', in *Jahrbuch der Kunsthistorischen Samm-*

lungen des Allerhöchsten Kaiserhauses, XXVII (1907–9).

Doyle, Alexander, *Neue Alamodische Ritterliche Fecht und Schirm-Kunst* (Nuremberg, 1715).

Duarte, King of Portugal, ed. Joseph M. Piel, *Leal conselheiro* (Lisbon, 1942).

Duarte, King of Portugal, ed. Joseph M. Piel, *Livro da ensinança de bem cavalgar toda sela que fez El-Rey Dom Eduarte de Portugal e do Algarve e Senhor de Centa* (Lisbon, 1944).

Du Bellay, Martin, *Les Mémoires de Messire Martin du Bellay*, ed. Michaud and Poujoulat (Paris, 1838).

Dubois, Georges, Maître d'Armes de l'Opéra Comique, *L'Escrime de duel. Une technique* (Paris, 1913).

Dubois, Georges, *Essai sur le traité d'escrime de Saint Didier publié en 1573* (Chartres, 1918).

Du Cange, Charles Dufresne, Sieur, *Glossarium ad scriptores mediae et infimae latinitatis* (Paris, 1678).

Du Choul, Guillaume, *Discours sur la castramentation et discipline militaire des Romains, des bains et antiques exercitations* (Lyons, 1557).

Du Guesclin *see* Guesclin.

Duncan, J.S., *Hints to the Bearers of Walking-Sticks and Umbrellas* (1809).

Dürer, Albrecht, *Vier Bücher von menschlicher Proportion* (Nuremberg, 1528).

Dürer, Albrecht, *Fechtbuch*, see Dörnhöffer.

Durfort, General, 'Introduction' to the French translation of Schmidt, *Instruction pour la cavalerie* (Paris, 1828).

Duro, C.F., 'Noticias de la vida y obras de Gonzálo de Ayora y fragmentos de su crónica inédita', *Boletín de la Real Academia de la Historia*, XVII (1890), pp. 433–46.

Duwes, Giles, *An introductorie for to lerne to rede to pronounce, and to speke Frenche trewly* (1533?).

Egenolff, Christian, see Lecküchner.

Ekkart, R.E.O., ed., *Athenae Batavae De Leidse Universiteit/The University of Leiden 1575–1975* (Leiden, 1975).

Ellis, Henry, ed., *Original Letters Illustrative of English History* (1824, 1827, 1846).

Elyot, Sir Thomas, *The Boke named The Governour* (1531).

Ettenhard, Francesco Antonio de, *Compendio de los fundamentos de la verdadera destreza y filosofía de las armas* (Madrid, 1675).

Evoli, Cesare d', *Delle ordinanze et battaglie del Signor Cesare d'Evoli Napolitano* (Rome, 1583, reprinted 1586).

Fabris, Salvator, *Scienza e pratica d'arme* (Copenhagen, 1606).

Fairbairn, W.E., *All-in Fighting* (1942).

Falloppia, Alfonso, *Nuovo et brieve modo di schermire* (Bergamo, 1584).

Fallows, Noel, *The Chivalric Vision of Alfonso de Cartagena: Study and Edition of the Doctrinal de los caualleros* (Newark, Delaware, 1995).

Fallows, Noel, *Un texto inédito sobre la caballería del renacimiento español. Doctrina del arte de la cauallería de Juan Quijada de Reayo* (Liverpool, 1996).

Fauchet, Claude, *Origines des chevaliers, armoiries et heraux. Ensemble de l'ordonnance, armes, et instruments desquels les François ont anciennement usé en leurs guerres* (Paris, 1600).

Fausto, Sebastiano, *Duello* (Venice, 1560).

Die Fechtkunst 1500–1900 Grafik Waffen, ed. Heino Maedebach (Coburg, 1968).

Fermor, Sharon, 'On the question of pictorial "evidence" for fifteenth-century dance technique', *Dance Research. The Journal of the Society for Dance Research*, V. ii (1987), pp. 18–32.

ffoulkes, Charles, *The Armourer and His Craft from the XIth to the XVIth Century* (1912).

ffoulkes, Charles, *The Armouries at the Tower of London* (1916).

Fiore de' Liberi da Premariacco, *Flos duellatorum in armis, sine armis, equester, pedester*, ed. Francesco Novati (Bergamo, 1902). This is the lost Pisani-Dossi manuscript.

Fleuranges, Maréchal de, *Les Mémoires*, ed. Michaud and Poujoulat (Paris, 1838).

Flori, Jean, 'Encore l'usage de la lance . . . La technique du combat chevaleresque vers l'an 1100', *Cahiers de Civilisation Médiévale*, XXXI (1988), pp. 213–40.

Florio, John, *Queen Anna's World of Words* (1611).

Fontaine, Marie-Madeleine, *Le Condottiere Pietro del Monte philosophe et écrivain de la renaissance* (Geneva/Paris, 1991).

Fontaine, Marie-Madeleine, 'Comment Pietro del Monte, condottiere Italien, parlait Espagnol', *Bibliothèque d'Humanisme et Renaissance*, LIV (1992), pp. 163–73.

Fournier, M., *Les Statuts et privilèges des universités françaises* (Paris, 1890).

Fourquevaux, Raymond de Beccarie de Pavie Sieur de, *Les Instructions sur le faict de la guerre* (Paris, 1548), tr. Paul Ive, *Instructions for the Warres* (1589).

Franko, Mark, *The Dancing Body in Renaissance Choreography* (Birmingham, Alabama, 1986).

Fyot, E., *L'Escrime à Dijon de 1500 à 1911* (Dijon, 1911).

Gaiani, Giovan' Battista, *Arte di maneggiar la spada a piedi et a cavallo* (Loano, 1619).

Gaiani, Giovan' Battista, *Discorso del tornear a piedi* (Genoa, 1619).

Gaier, Claude, 'Technique des combats singuliers d'après les auteurs "bourguignons" du XVe siècle', *Le Moyen Age*, (1985), pp. 415–57; (1986), pp. 5–40.

Galas, S. Matthew, 'Kindred spirits. The art of the sword in Germany and Japan', *Journal of Asian Martial Arts*, VI (1997), pp. 20–46.

Galas, S. Matthew, 'Johannes Liechtenauer. The father of German swordsmanship', *Journal of the Society of American Fight Directors* (1998).

Galbraith, V.H., 'The Death of a Champion (1287)', in *Studies in Medieval History presented to Frederick Maurice Powicke*, ed. R.W. Hunt, W.A. Pantin and R.W. Southern (Oxford, 1948), pp. 283–95.

Gamber, Ortwin, 'Die Harnischgarnitur', *Livrustkammaren* (Stockholm), VII (1955–7).

Gamber, Ortwin, 'Die Turnierharnisch zur Zeit König Maximilians I und das Thunsche Skizzenbuch', *Jahrbuch der Kunsthistorischen Sammlungen in Wien*, LIII (1957), pp. 33–70.

Gamber, Ortwin, 'Ritterspiel und Turnierrüstung im Spätmittelalter', in *Das Ritterliche Turnier im Mittelalter*, ed. Josef Fleckenstein (Göttingen, 1985).

Sir Gawain and the Green Knight, ed. Sir Israel Gollancz (E.E.T.S., Oxford, 1940).

Gaya, Louis de, *Traité des armes, des machines de guerre, des feux d'artifices, des enseignes et des instruments militaires anciens et modernes* (Paris, 1678), edited in facsimile by Charles ffoulkes (Oxford, 1911).

Gelli, Jacopo, *Bibliografia generale della scherma* (Milan, 1890).

Gelli, Jacopo, *L'arte dell'armi in Italia* (Bergamo, 1906).

Geraud, Hercule J.F., *Paris sous Philippe-le-Bel, notamment d'après un manuscrit contenant le rôle de la taille 1292* (Paris, 1837).

Gesta Abbatum Fontanellensium in Georg Heinrich Pertz, *Monumenta Germaniae Historica . . . Scriptorum*, II (Hanover, 1829).

Gestoso y Pérez, José, *Esgrimidores sevillanos. Documentos inéditos para su historia* (Madrid, 1911).

Gheyn, Jacob de, *The Exercise of Armes for Calivres, Muskettes, and Pikes after the Ordre of his Excellence Maurits Prince of Orange Counte of Nassau etc.* (The Hague, 1607).

Ghisliero, Federico, *Regole di molti cavagliereschi essercitii* (Parma, 1587).

Giganti, Nicoletto, *Scola overo teatro nel qual sono rappresentate diverse maniere e modi di parare e di ferire di spada sola, e di spada e pugnale* (Venice, 1606).

Gilbert, Felix, 'Machiavelli: the renaissance of the art of war', in *Makers of Modern Strategy*, ed. E.M. Earle (Princeton, 1944).

Gilbert, Sir Humphrey, *Queene Elizabethes Achademy*, ed. F.J. Furnivall, in *Early English Treatises and Poems on Education, Precedence and Manners in Olden Time* (E.E.T.S., extra series VIII, 1869).

Gillmor, Caroll, 'Practical chivalry: the training of horses for tournaments and warfare', *Studies in Medieval and Renaissance History*, New Series, XIII (1992), pp. 5–29.

Giovannini, Francesco, *Il ballo. Balli d'oggi* (Milan, 1914).

Giraud, J.-B., *Documents pour servir à l'histoire de l'armement au moyen âge et à la renaissance* (Lyons, 1895, 1899).

Glossarium armorum. Arma Defensiva, by C. Blair, V. Norman, O. Gamber and others (Graz, 1972).

Godfrey, Captain John, *A Treatise upon the useful Science of Defence* (1747).

Gombrich, E.H., *Art and Illusion* (Washington, DC, 1960).

Gombrich, E.H., *Symbolic Images. Studies in the Art of the Renaissance* (1972).

Gombrich, E.H., 'Pictorial instructions', in Horace Barlow, Colin Blakemore, Miranda Weston-Smith, eds, *Images and Understanding* (Cambridge, 1990), pp. 26–45, 372.

Goodman, Nelson, *Languages of Art. An Approach to a Theory of Symbols* (1969).

Gorio, Giovanni Pietro, *Arte di adoprar la spada* (Milan, 1682).

Grassi, Giacomo di, *Ragione di adoprar sicuramente l'arme si da offesa come da difesa: con un trattato dell'inganno et con un modo di essercitarsi da se stesso per acquistare forza, giudicio et prestezza* (Venice, 1570); English tr. *Giacomo di Grassi, his true Arte of defence, etc.* (1594).

Groenewegen-Frankfort, H.A., *Arrest and Movement* (1951).

Das Grosse Buch der Turniere . . . Die Bilderhandschrift des Codex Rossianus 711 im besitz der Biblioteca Apostolica Vaticana, ed. Lotte Kurras (Stuttgart, Zürich, 1996).

Grosz, August and Thomas, Bruno, *Katalog der Waffensammlung in der Neuen Burg Schausammlung* (Vienna, 1936).

Guazzo, Stefano, *La civil conversatione* (Brescia, 1574): tr. George Pettie, ed. Sir E. Sullivan (1925).

Guesclin, *Anciens mémoires du XIVe siècle sur Bertrand du Guesclin*, ed. Michaud and Poujoulat (Paris, 1836).

Guest, Ann Hutchinson, *Dance Notation: The Process of Recording Movement on Paper* (New York, 1984).

Guicciardini, Francesco, *Storia d'Italia*, tr. G. Fenton (1579).

Guillaume de Deguileville, *see* Deguileville.

Gunterrodt, Heinrich von, *De veris principiis artis dimicatoriae* (Wittemberg, 1579).

Guyon, Louis, *Les diverses leçons* (Lyons, 1604).

Hale, George, *The Private Schoole of Defence. Or the Defects of Publique Teachers exactly discovered, by way of Objection and Resolution* (1614).

Hale, John, 'Military academies on the Venetian terrafirma in the early seventeenth century', *Studi Veneziani*, XV (1973), pp. 273–95.

Hale, John, 'The military education of the officer class in early modern Europe', in *Cultural Aspects of the Italian Renaissance: Essays in Honour of Paul Oskar Kristeller*, ed. Cecil Clough (Manchester, 1976), pp. 440–61.

Hale, John, 'A humanistic visual aid. The military diagram in the Renaissance', *Renaissance Studies*, II. ii (October 1988), pp. 280–98.

Halle, Edward, *Chronicle*, ed. H. Ellis (1809).

Hancock, H. Irving and Higashi, Katsuma, *The Complete Kano Jiu-Jitsu* (New York and London, 1905).

Harrison, William, *A Description of England*, originally printed as an introduction to Raphael Holinshed, *Chronicles* (1577).

Hayward, J.F., 'Filippo Orsini, designer, and Caremolo Modrone, armourer, of Mantua', in *Waffen- und Kostümkunde*, XXIV (1982), pp. 1–16, 87–102.

Helwig, Hellmuth, 'Die deutschen Fechtbücher. Eine bibliographische Übersicht', in *Börsenblatt für den deutschen Büchhandel, Frankfurter Ausgabe Nr. 55* (Frankfurt-am-Main, 1966), pp. 1407–16.

Henry, 'Sur l'art de l'escrime en Espagne au Moyen Age', *Revue Archéologique*, 1er série, VIe année (1849), pp. 582–93.

Herbert, Edward, first Lord Herbert of Cherbury, *The Autobiography*, ed. Sidney Lee (1906).

Hergsell, Gustave, see Talhoffer.

Heussler, Sebastian, *Neu Künstlich Fechtbuch* (Nuremberg, 1615).

Hewitt, John, *Ancient Armour and Weapons in Europe from the Period of the Northern Nations to the End of the Thirteenth Century* (Oxford and London, 1855).

Hils, Hans-Peter, *Meister Johann Liechtenauers Kunst des langen Schwertes* (Frankfurt-am-Main, Bern, New York, 1985).

Hobbes, Thomas, *Leviathan, or the Matter, Forme, & Power of a Commonwealth Ecclesiasticall and Civill* (1651).

Hobson, Anthony, *Great Libraries* (1970).

Hoffmeyer, Ada Bruhn, 'From mediaeval sword to renaissance rapier', *Gladius*, II (1963).

Hope, Sir William, *The Scots Fencing-Master or Compleat Small-Sword-Man* (Edinburgh, 1687).

Hope, Sir William, *The Fencing-Master's Advice to his Scholar: or a Few Directions for the more regular assaulting in Schools* (Edinburgh, 1692).

Howell, James, *Instructions for forreine Travell* (1642).

Hughes, P.L. and Larkin, J.F., *Tudor Royal Proclamations* (New Haven and London, 1969).

Hugo, Herman, *De militia equestri antiqua et nova ad Phillipum IV. Libri quinque* (Antwerp, 1630).

Huth, F.W., *Works on Horses and Equitation. A Bibliographical Record of Hippology* (London, 1887; reprinted Hildesheim, New York, 1981).

Hutton, Alfred, *Cold Steel* (1889).

Hutton, Alfred, *Old Sword-Play* (1892).

Hutton, Alfred, *The Sword and the Centuries* (1901).

Illustrations of Ancient State and Chivalry, ed. W.H. Black (Roxburghe Club, 1840).

Jackson, William H., 'Tournaments and the Germanic chivalric renovatio. Tournament discipline and the myth of origins' in S. Anglo, ed., *Chivalry in the Renaissance* (Woodbridge, 1990), pp. 77–91.

Jacobsen, Holger, Skaar, Fritz C. and Bruhn, Ada, *Vaabenhistoriske Aarbøger*, IV (1943).

Jahns, Max, *Geschichte der Kriegswissenschaften, vornehmlich in Deutschland* (Munich, 1889–91).

Jonson, Ben, *The New Inne* (1631).

Joubert, Félix, *Catalogue of the Collection of European Arms and Armour formed at Greenock by R.L. Scott* (privately published, 1924).

Juvenal des Ursins, Jean, *Histoire de Charles VI, roy de France*, ed. Michaud and Poujoulat (Paris, 1836).

Kahane, Martine, Le Bourhis, Josseline and Louppe, Laurence, *L'Écriture de la danse* (Paris, 1993).

Kawaishi, Mikonosuke, *My Method of Self Defence*, tr. E.J. Harrison (1957).

Keele, K., 'Leonardo da Vinci's anatomical drawings at Windsor', *Studi Vinciani*, II (1954), pp. 76–85.

Kelly, Francis M., 'A knight's armour of the early fourteenth century, being the inventory of Raoul de Nesle', *Burlington Magazine* (1904), pp. 457–70.

Kent, Graeme, *A Pictorial History of Wrestling* (Feltham, 1968).

The King's Mirror (Speculum Regale – Konungs Skuggsjá), tr. Laurence Marcellus Larson (New York, 1917).

Knutsen, Roald, *Japanese Polearms* (1963).

Kühnst, Peter, *Sports. A Cultural History in the Mirror of Art* (Dresden, 1996).

La Boëssière, *Traité de l'art des armes* (Paris, 1818).

La Broue, Salomon, *Second livre des preceptes de cavalrice françois* (Paris, 1602).

La Colombière *see* Vulson.

Lactantius, *Divine Institutes* in *The Works of Lactantius*, tr. William Fletcher (Edinburgh, 1871).

La Curne de Sainte-Palaye, J.B., *Dictionnaire de l'ancien langage français* (Paris, 1875).

Laking, Sir Guy Francis, *A Record of European Arms and Armour* (1920–2).

L'Ange, Daniel, *Deutliche und Gründliche Erklärung der Adelichen und Ritterlichen freyen Fechtkunst* (Heidelberg, 1664).

La Noue, François de, *Discours politiques et militaires* (Basle, 1587), ed. F.E. Sutcliffe (Geneva, 1967).

Lara, Agustín de, *Cornucopia numerosa, alphabeto breve de principios assentados, y rudimentos conocidos de la verdadera filosofía, y destreza de las armas. Colegidos de las obras de Don Luis Pacheco de Narváez, príncipe de esta ciencia* (Madrid, 1675).

La Sale, Antoine de, *Des Anciens Tournois et faictz d'armes* in Prost, *Traités* (Paris, 1872).

La Sale, Antoine de, *Le Petit Jehan de Saintré*, tr. I. Gray (1931).

La Touche, Philibert de, *Les Vrayes Principes de l'espée seule* (Paris, 1670).

The Laws of Honor: or an Account of the Suppression of Duels in France. Extracted out of the King's Edicts etc. (1685).

Lea, Henry Charles, *Superstition and Force*, 4th edition (Philadelphia, 1892).

Lecküchner, Johannes, *Der altenn Fechter an fengliche Kunst mit samt verborgenen heymicheytten, Kämpffens, Ringens, Werffens &c.* (Frankfurt-am-Main, 1531).

Leguina, Enrique de, *Bibliografía e historia de la esgrima española* (Madrid, 1904).

Leguina, Enrique de, *Glosario de voces de armería* (Madrid, 1912).

Leonard, Hugh F., *A Hand-Book of Wrestling* (New York, 1897).

Leonardo da Vinci, *The Literary Works of Leonardo da Vinci*, ed. J.P. Richter, 3rd edn (1969).

Le Perche, Jean-Baptiste, *L'Exercice des armes ou le maniement du fleuret* (Paris, 1676).

Leseur, Guillaume, *Histoire de Gaston IV, Comte de Foix par Guillaume Leseur*, ed. Henri Courteault (Paris, 1893–6).

Lester, G.A., *Sir John Paston's 'Grete Boke'* (Woodbridge, 1984).

Lester, G.A., *The Earliest English Translation of Vegetius' De Re Militari, ed. from Oxford MS Bodl. Douce 291* (Heidelberg, 1988).

Letainturier-Fradin, Gabriel, *Les Joueurs d'épée à travers les siècles* (Paris, n.d.).

Letters and Papers, Foreign and Domestic of the Reign of Henry VIII, ed. J.S. Brewer, R.H. Brodie and J. Gairdner (1862–1932).

Levi, Giorgio Enrico, *Il duello giudiziario. Enciclopedia e bibliografia* (Florence, 1932).

L'Homandie, P.F.M., *La Xiphomanie ou l'art de l'escrime, poème didactique en quatre chants* (Angoulême, 1821).

Liancour, André Wernesson de, *Le Maistre d'armes, ou l'exercice de l'espée seule dans sa perfection* (Paris, 1686).

Lidstone, R.A., *Fencing. A Practical Treatise on Foil, Épée, Sabre* (1952).

Lipsius, Justus, *De militia Romana libri quinque* (Antwerp, 1596).

The Lisle Letters, ed. Muriel St Clare Byrne (Chicago and London, 1983).

Llull, Ramón, *Llibre de l'Orde de Cavalleria*, ed. Marina Gustà (Barcelona, 1981).

Lobineau, Gui Alexis de, *Histoire de Bretagne* (Paris, 1707).

Lochner, Karl E., *Die Entwicklungsphasen der europäische Fechtkunst* (Vienna, 1953).

Lochner, Karl E., *Waffenkunde für Sportfechter und Waffenliebhaber* (Vienna, 1960).

Locke, John, *Some thoughts concerning education* (1693) in *The Works of John Locke* (1812), IX, pp. 1–205.

Lomazzo, Giovanni Paolo, *Trattato dell'arte della pittura, scoltura ed architettura* in *Scritti sulle arti*, ed. R.P. Ciardi (Florence, 1974).

Longhi, Silvio, *Il duello dipinto di Castiglione del Lago: Pitigliano, 26 maggio 1546* (Cortona, 1995).

Lonnergan, A., *The Fencer's Guide* (1771).

Lostelnau, – de, *Le Mareschal de bataille. Contenant le maniement des armes* (Paris, 1647).

Lucini, Antonio Francesco, *Compendio dell'armi de Caramogi d'Antonio Francesco Lucini. In Firenze A°. MDCXXVII* (Florence, 1627).

Lydius, Jacob, *Syntagma sacrum de re militari* (Dordrecht, 1698).

McArthur, John, *The Army and Navy Gentleman's Companion; or A New and Complete Treatise on the Theory and Practice of Fencing* (1781).

McBane, Donald, *The Expert Sword-Man's Companion* (Glasgow, 1728).

MacGregor, Archibald, *MacGregor's Lecture on the Art of Defence* (Paisley, 1791).

Machiavelli, Niccolò, *Arte della guerra* (Florence, 1521), tr. Peter Whitehorne, *The Arte of Warre* (1560), reprinted in *The Tudor Translations* (1905).

Machyn, Henry, *The Diary of Henry Machyn*, ed. J.G. Nichols (1848).

Maedebach, Heino, *see Die Fechkunst*.

'Maestros de armas', *Memorias de la Real Academia Española*, XI (1914).

Manciolino, Antonio, *Opera nova, dove li sono tutti li documenti & vantaggi che si ponno havere nel mestier de l'armi d'ogni sorte novamente corretta & stampata* (Venice, 1531).

Mandey, V. and Moxon, J., *The Mechanick Powers* (1696).

Manesson Mallet, Alain, *Les Travaux de Mars, ou l'art de la guerre* (Paris, 1685).

Mann, J.G., 'The lost armoury of the Gonzagas', *Archaeological Journal*, XCV (1939), pp. 239–336; *Ibid.*, C (1945), pp. 16–127.

Marcelli, Francesco Antonio, *Regole della scherma* (Rome, 1686).

March, Pere, 'L'arnès del cavaller', ed. Lluís Faraudo de Saint-Germain, *Recull de textes catalans antichs*, XV (Barcelona, 1910).

Marche, Olivier de la, *Mémoires*, ed. H. Beaune and J. d'Arbaumont (Paris, 1883–8).

Marozzo, Achille, *Opera nova. Chiamata duello, o vero fiore dell'armi de singulari abattimenti offensivi et diffensivi . . . con le figure che dimostrano con l'armi in mano tutti gli effetti et guardie possano far etc.* (Modena, 1536).

Marti, Bertha M., *The Spanish College at Bologna in the Fourteenth Century* (Philadelphia, 1966).

Martínez de Toledo, Alfonso, Chaplain to Juan II, *Arçipreste de Talavera*, ed. Mario Penna (Turin, 1955).

Massario Malatesta, Alessandro, *Compendio dell'heroica arte di cavalleria* (Venice, 1600).

Matthey, Cyril G.R., ed., *The Works of George Silver* (1898).

Matthey, Cyril G.R., *Catalogue of Works on Fencing, Duelling, and Allied Subjects forming the Private Collection of Captain C.G.R. Matthey* (1900).

369

Maximilian I, Emperor, *Freydal des Kaisers Maximilian I. Turniere und Mummereien*, ed. Quirin von Leitner (Vienna, 1880–2).

Mély Fernand de, and Bishop, Edmund, *Bibliographie générale des inventaires imprimées* (Paris, 1892–5).

Melzo, Ludovico, *Regole militari sopra il governo e servitio particolare della cavalleria* (Antwerp, 1611).

Mendoza, Miguel Pérez de, *Resumen de la verdadera destreza de las armas* (Madrid, 1675).

Mercurialis, Hieronymus, *Artis gymnasticae libri sex* (Venice, 1569).

Meyer, Joachim, *Gründtliche Beschreibung der freyen Ritterlichen unnd Adelichen kunst des Fechtens* (Strasbourg, 1570, reprinted 1600).

Meyer, P., 'Notice et extraits du MS 8336 de la bibliothèque de Sir Th. Phillips à Cheltenham', *Romania*, XIII (1884), p. 530.

Michaud, J.F. and Poujoulat, J.J.P., *Nouvelle Collection des mémoires pour servir à l'histoire de France* (Paris, 1836–9).

Minkowski, Helmut, *Das Ringen im Grüblein. Ein spätmittelalterliche Form des deutschen Leibringens* (Stuttgart, 1963).

Montaigne, Michel de, *Journal de voyage de Michel de Montaigne*, ed. François Rigolot (Paris, 1992).

Monte, Pietro, *De dignoscendis hominibus* (Milan, 1492).

Monte, Pietro, *Petri Montii exercitiorum, atque artis militaris collectanea in tris libros distincta* (Milan, 1509).

Monte, Pietro, *Petri Montij de singulari certamine siue dissensione: deque veterum, recentiorum ritu ad Carolum Hyspaniarum principem & Burgundie Archiducem libri tres* (Milan, 1509).

Mortimer, Ruth, ed., *Harvard College Library. Department of Printing and Graphic Arts. Catalog of Books and Manuscripts. Italian 16th Century Books* (Cambridge, Mass., 1974).

Mulcaster, Richard, *Positions wherin those primitive circumstances be examined, which are necessarie for the training up of children, either for skill in their booke, or health in their bodie* (1581), ed. R.H. Quick (1888).

Muller, A., *Théorie sur l'escrime à cheval* (Paris, 1816).

Musashi, Miyamoto, *A Book of Five Rings*, tr. Victor Harris (London, 1974, reprinted 1977).

Muta, Mario, *Commentaria . . . in Antiquissimas Consuetudines* (Palermo, 1843).

Narváez, Luis Pacheco de, *Libro de las grandezas de la espada, en que se declaran muchos secretos del que compuso el Comendador Geronimo de Carrança. En el qual cada uno se podrá licionar y deprender a solas, sin tener necessidad de maestro que le enseñe* (Madrid, 1600).

Narváez, Luis Pacheco de, *Advertencias para la enseñanza de la filosofía y destreza de las armas, así a pie, como a cavallo* (Pamplona, 1642), repr. in D.L. Orvenipe, *Antiquos tratados de esgrima (siglo XVII)* (Madrid, 1898).

Narváez, Luis Pacheco de, *Nueva sciencia, y filosofía de la destreza de las armas, su teórica y práctica* (Madrid, 1672).

Navarette, Martín Fernández de, *Biblioteca marítima española* (Madrid, 1851).

Neilson, George, *Trial by Battle* (Glasgow, 1890).

Neste, Evelyne van den, *Tournois, joutes, pas d'armes dans les villes de Flandre à la fin du moyen age* (Paris, 1996).

Newberry, Percy E., *Beni Hasan* (1903–4).

Newhall, Beamont, *History of Photography* (1982).

Neyffer, Johann Christoph and Ditzinger, Ludwig, *Illustrissimi Wirtembirgici ducalis novi collegii quod Tubingae quam situm quam studia quam exercitia accurata delineatio* (n.p., n.d. but probably Tübingen, 1600).

Nicot, Jean, *Thresor de la langue françoise tant ancienne que moderne* (Paris, 1606).

Nolan, L.E., *Cavalry: Its History and Tactics* (1853).

Norman, A.V.B., *The Rapier and Small Sword, 1460–1820* (London, Melbourne and New York, 1980).

Norman, A.V.B., *Wallace Collection Catalogues. European Arms and Armour Supplement* (1986).

Noue, Pierre de la, *La Cavalerie françoise et italienne* (Lyons, 1621).

Noveli, Nicolás Rodrigo, *Crisol especulativo, demostrativo o práctico mathemático de la destreza* (Madrid, 1731).

Olivier, J., *Fencing Familiarized, or a New Treatise on the Art of Sword Play* (1771).

Olmeda de la Cuesta, Andres Pedro, *Tratado de esgrima de lanza uso de esta arma contra sable y espada de caballería* (Cadiz, 1812).

O'Malley, C.D. and Saunders, J.B. de C.M., 'The "Relation" of Andreas Vesalius on the death of Henry II of France', *Journal of the History of Medicine and Allied Sciences*, III (1948), pp. 197–213.

Ortiz, Antonio Domínguez, Carretero, Concha Herrero and Godoy, José A., eds, *Resplendence of the Spanish Monarchy. Renaissance Tapestries and Armor from the Patrimonio Nacional* (New York, 1991).

Omont, Henri, ed., *Traité d'escrime de G.A. Lovino* (Paris, 1909).

Orvenipe, D.L. d'(Pedro Vindel), *Armas y desafíos. Bibliografía de la esgrima y el duelo* (Madrid, 1911).

Overbury, Sir Thomas, *Characters* in *The Miscellaneous Works in Prose and Verse of Sir Thomas Overbury*, ed. E.F. Rimbault (1856).

Owst, G.R., *Literature and Pulpit in Medieval England* (Oxford, 1961).

Pächt, Otto, *The Rise of Pictorial Narrative in Twelfth-Century England* (Oxford, 1962).

Palau y Dulcet, Antonio, *Manual del librero hispano-americano* (Barcelona, 1948–87).

Pallavicini, Giuseppe Morsicato, *La scherma illustrata* (Palermo, 1670).

Pallavicini, Giuseppe Morsicato, *La seconda parte della scherma illustrata* (Palermo, 1673).

Panconcelli-Calzia, G., *Das Fechten mit alten Waffen* (Göttingen, 1925).

Parkyns, Sir Thomas, *Progymnasmata. The Inn-Play: or, Cornish-Hugg Wrestler* (1713).

Pascha, Johann Georg, *Kurze Unterrichtung belangend die Pique, die Fahne, den Jägerstock, das Voltesiren, das Ringen, das Fechten auf den Stoss und Hieb, und endlich das Trincieren verferrtigts* (Wittenberg, 1657).

Pascha, Johann Georg, *Kurze Anleitung des Fechtens auf den Stoss und Hieb* (Frankfurt-am-Main, 1661).

Pascha, Johann Georg, *Kurze iedoch Deutliche Beschreibung handlend Vom Fechten auf den Stoss und Hieb* (Halle, 1664).

Patten, William, *The Expedition into Scotlande of the most woorthely fortunate prince Edward, Duke of Somerset* (1548).

Pauernfeindt, Andre, *Ergrundung Ritterlicher kunst der Fechterey durch Andre paurnfeindt Freyfechter czu Wienn in Osterreich, nach klerlicher begreiffung und kurczlicher verstendnusz* (Vienna, 1516).

Pauernfeindt, Andre, *La Noble Science des joueurs d'espée* (Antwerp, 1538).

Pausanias, *Description of Greece*, tr. W.H.S. Jones (Loeb Library, 1959–65).

Peacham, Henry, *The Compleat Gentleman* (1622).

Peeke, Richard, *Three to one: being, an English-Spanish combat, performed by a westerne gentleman, of Tavystoke in Devonshire, with an English quarterstaff, against three Spaniards at once with rapiers and poniards* (1626).

Peeters, Hilde and Vanleeuwe, Tom, *Archibald Harrison Corble 1883–1944. His Biography and Donation to the Catholic University of Leuven* (Leuven, n.d.).

Petter, Nicolaes and Hooghe, Romein de, *Der künstlicher Ringer* (Amsterdam, 1674).

Petter, Nicolaes and Hooghe, Romein de, *Ring-Kunst vom Jahre 1674*, ed. Karl Wassmannsdorff (Heidelberg, 1887).

Pieri, Piero, 'Il "Governo et exercitio de la militia" di Orso degli Orsini e i "memoriali" di Diomede Carafa', *Archivio storico per le provincie napoletane*, XIX (1933), pp. 99–179.

Pike, L.O., *A History of Crime in England* (1873).

Pistofilo, Bonaventura, *Oplomachia* (Siena, 1621).

Pistofilo, Bonaventura, *Il Torneo* (Bologna, 1627).

Pluvinel, Antoine de, *Le Maneige royal* (Paris, 1623), another editon (Paris, 1627); English tr. Hilda Nelson (1989).

Poliakoff, M.B., *Studies in the Terminology of the Greek Combat Sports* (Meisenheim, 1986).

Poliakoff, M.B., *Combat Sports in the Ancient World* (New Haven and London, 1987).

Polybius, *The Histories*, tr. W.R. Paton (Loeb Library, 1960).

Ponç de Menaguerra, *Lo cavaller* (Valencia, 1493), see Bohigas Belaguer.

Porath, Diederich, *Palaestra Suecana* (Stockholm, 1693).

Porres, D. Gómez Arias de, *Resumen de la verdadera destreza en el maneio de la espada* (Salamanca, 1667).

Prelle de la Nieppe, E. de, 'L'Inventaire de l'armurerie de Guillaume III comte de Hainaut en 1358', *Annales de la Société Archéologique de l'arrondissement de Nivelles*, VII (1900).

Prost, Bernard, ed., *Traités du duel judiciare, relations de pas d'armes et tournois* (Paris, 1872).

Puteo, Paris de, *Duello* (Naples, 1476–7).

Quevedo y Villeqas, *Historia de la vida del Buscón llamado don Pablos* (Valencia, 1627).

Quixada de Reayo, Juan, *Doctrina del arte de la cavallería* (Medina del Campo, 1548). There is now a modern critical edition by Noel Fallows (1996).

Rada, Francisco Lorenz de, *Respuesta filosófica y matemática* (Madrid, 1695).

Rada, Francisco Lorenz de, *Nobleza de la espada, cuyo esplendor se expressa en tres libros, segun ciencia, arte y experiencia* (Madrid, 1705).

Rangström, Lena, ed., *Riddarlek och Tornerspel. Tournaments and the Dream of Chivalry, Catalogue of the Tournament Exhibition* (Stockholm, 1992).

Ratti, Oscar and Westbrook, Adèle, *Secrets of the Samurai. A Survey of the Martial Arts of Feudal Japan* (Rutland, Vermont and Tokyo, 1973).

Raumer, Carl von, *Geschichte der Pädagogik* (Berlin, 1843–54), tr. H. Barnard, *German Schools and Pedagogy* (1861).

Reed, Sue Welsh and Wallace, Richard, eds *Italian Etchers of the Renaissance and Baroque* (Boston, Mass., 1989).

Reid, Howard and Croucher, Michael, *The Way of the Warrior. The Paradox of the Martial Arts* (1995).

Reisch, Gregorius, *Aepitoma omnis phylosophiae alias Margarita phylosophica* (Strasbourg, 1504).

René d'Anjou, *Oeuvres complètes du roi René d'Anjou*, ed. Comte de Quatrebarbes (Angers, 1845–6).

Reverseau, Jean-Pierre, 'L'Habit de guerre des Français en 1446', *Gazette des Beaux Arts*, XCIII (1979), pp. 179–98.

Riley, H.T., ed., *Memorials of London and London Life in the XIIIth, XIVth, and XVth Centuries* (1868).

Riquer, Marti de, *L'arnès del cavaller. Armes i armadures catalanes medievals* (Barcelona, 1968).

Robaglia, Le Capitaine, *L'Escrime ou le jeu d'épée enseigné par l'image à l'usage des enfants et des adolescents sans crainte d'accidents et sans dépenses* (Paris, 1893).

Roland, Joseph, *The Amateur of Fencing, or a Treatise on the Art of Sword Defence* (1809).

Román, Francisco, *Tratado de la esgrima con figuras por Francisco Román natural de Carmona* (Seville, 1532) – a lost treatise.

Rossi, Sergio, 'Vincentio Saviolo his practice (1595): a problem of authorship', in *England and the Continental Renaissance. Essays in Honour of J.B. Trapp*, ed. E. Chaney and P. Mack (Woodbridge, 1990), pp. 165–75.

Rotuli litterarum clausarum, ed. T.D. Hardy (Record Commission, 1833–4).

Rovere, Dennis, *Chinese Military Police: Knife, Baton and Weapon Techniques* (Calgary, Canada, 1996).

Rowlandson, Thomas, *Hungarian and Highland Broadsword* (1799).

Rozmital, *The Travels of Leo of Rozmital*, tr. and ed. by M. Letts (Cambridge, 1957).

Sacco, Bernardo, *De Italicarum rerum varietate et elegantia libri X* (Pavia, 1565).

Sainct Didier, Henri de, *Traicté contenant les secrets du premier livre de l'espée seule, mère de toutes armes. Qui sont espée, dague, cappe, targue, bouclier, rondelle, l'espée à deux mains & les deux espées, avec ses pourtraictures etc.* (Paris, 1573); facsimile reproduction (Paris, 1907).

Saint-Remy, Seigneur de, *Chronique de Jean Le Févre Seigneur de Saint-Remy*, ed. François Morand (Paris, 1876–81).

Salzman, L.F., 'Property of the Earl of Arundel, 1397', *Sussex Archaeological Collections*, XCI (1953), pp. 32–52.

Sánchez de Arévalo, Ruy, successively Bishop of Oviedo, Zamora, Calahorra and Palencia, *Verjel de los príncipes . . . códice del siglo XV*, ed. F.R. de Uhagón (Madrid, 1900).

Santa Paulina, Luigi, *L'arte del cavallo* (Padua, 1696).

Saviolo, Vincentio, *Vincentio Saviolo his Practise, in Two Bookes* (1595).

Savorgnano, Mario, *Arte militare terrestre e maritima* (Venice, 1599).

Saxo Grammaticus, *Gesta Danorum*, ed. J. Olrik and H. Raeder (Copenhagen, 1931–7).

Scalini, Mario, 'The weapons of Lorenzo de Medici. An examination of the inventory of the Medici palace in Florence drawn up upon the death of Lorenzo the Magnificent in 1492', *Art, Arms, and Armour*, ed. Robert Held (Chicago, 1979), pp. 12–29.

Schaer, Alfred, *Die altdeutschen Fechter und Spielleute* (Strasbourg, 1901).

Schmidt, Johann Andreas, *Leib-beschirmende und Feinden Trotz bietende Fecht-Kunst* (Nuremberg, 1713).

Schmidt, Cavalry officer, *Lehrbuch für die Kavallerie zum vortheilhaften Gebrauch des Säbels* (Berlin, 1797).

Schmidt, Cavalry officer, tr. General Durfort, *Instruction pour la cavalerie, sur le maniement le plus avantageux du sabre* (Paris, 1828).

Schöffer, Wilhelm, *Gründtliche und eigentliche Beschreibung der freyen Adelichen und Ritterlichen Fechtkunst im einfachen Rappir und im Rappir und Dolch etc.* (Marburg, 1620).

Schultz, Alwyn, *Das höfische Leben zur Zeit der Minnesinger* (Leipzig, 1879).

Scott, J.G., *European Arms and Armour at Kelvingrove* (Glasgow, 1980).

Seitz, H., *Blankwaffen. Geschichte und Typentwicklung im europäischen Kulturbereich* (Brunswick, 1965, 1968).

Select Pleas of the Crown, ed. F.W. Maitland (Selden Society, 1888).

A Self-Instructor of the New System of Cavalry and Infantry Sword Exercises (Manchester, 1822).

Senesio, Alessandro, *Il vero maneggio di spada* (Bologna, 1660).

Sereno, Bartolomeo, *Trattati del uso della lancia a cavallo, del combattere a piede, alla sbarra et dell' imprese et inventioni cavalieresche* (Naples, 1610).

Sidney, Sir Philip, *An apologie for poetrie* in G. Gregory Smith, *Elizabethan Critical Essays* (1904).

Silver, George, *Paradoxes of Defence* (1599).

Silver, George, *Bref instructions upon my paradoxes of defence*, ed. C.G.R. Matthey in *The Works of George Silver* (1898).

Singman, Jeffrey L., 'The medieval swordsman: a thirteenth-century German fencing manuscript', *Royal Armouries Yearbook*, II (1997), pp. 129–36.

Smythe, Sir John, *Certain Discourses* (1590).

Sotzmann, 'Ueber ein unbekanntes xylographisches Ringerbuch', *Serapeum. Zeitschrift für Bibliothekwissenschaft, Handschriftenkunde und ältere Litteratur*, III (1844), pp. 33–44.

Spetioli da Fermo, Mercurio, *Capitolo di schermire et cavalcare* (Bologna, 1577).

Spino, Pietro, *Historia della vita dell'eccellentissimo Bartolomeo Coglione* (Venice, 1569).

Stone, Lawrence, *The Crisis of the Aristocracy 1558–1641* (Oxford, 1965).

Stubbs, William, *Select Charters* (Oxford, 1870).

Sutor, Jacob, *New Künstliches Fechtbuch* (Frankfurt, 1612).

Swetnam, Joseph, *The Araignement of Lewde, Idle, Froward, and Unconstant Women* (1615).

Swetnam, Joseph, *The Schoole of the Noble and Worthy Science of Defence* (1617).

T., Le Commandant E., *Escrime de chambre. Méthode pour s'exercer, seul, à faire des armes par M. le Commandant E.T.* (Paris, Limoges, n.d.).

Talhoffer, Hans, *Fechtbuch aus dem Jahre 1467*, ed. G. Hergsell (Prague, 1887).

Talhoffer, Hans, *Fechtbuch (Gothaer Codex) aus dem Jahre 1443*, ed. G. Hergsell (Prague, 1889).

Talhoffer, Hans, *Fechtbuch (Ambraser Codex) aus dem Jahre 1459*, ed. G. Hergsell (Prague, 1889).

Tarassuk, Leonid, 'Some notes on parrying daggers and poniards', *Metropolitan Museum Journal*, XII (1978), pp. 33–54.

Tavernier, Adolphe, *Amateurs et salles d'armes de Paris* (Paris, 1886).

Tenison, E.M., *Elizabethan England* (Leamington, 1932–51).

Texedo, Pedro, *Escuela de principiantes y promptuario de questiones en la philosofía de la berdadera destreça de las armas* (Naples, 1678).

Thibault, Girard, *Académie de l'espée, ou se demonstrent par reigles mathematiques, sur le fondement d'un cercle mysterieux, la théorie et pratique des vrais et iusqu'a present incognus secrets du maniement des armes a pied et a cheval* (Leyden, 1630).

Thieme, Ulrich and Becker, Felix, *Algemeines Lexikon der bildenden Künstler* (Leipzig, 1907–50).

Thimm, Carl, *A Complete Bibliography of Fencing and Duelling* (1896).

Thomas, A.H., and Thornley, I.D., *The Great Chronicle of London* (1938).

Thomas, Bruno and Gamber, Ortwin, *Die Innsbrucker Plattnerkunst*, Catalogue of the exhibition held at the Ferdinandeum, Innsbruck (June–September 1954).

Thomas, Bruno and Gamber, Ortwin, *Katalog de Leibrüstkammer, Waffensammlung*, I (Vienna, 1976).

Trinkaus, Charles, *'In Our Image and Likeness'. Humanity and Divinity in Italian Renaissance Thought* (1970).

Trippenbach, Max, 'Johann Jacobi-Tautphoeus von Wallhausen, der erste deutsche Militärschriftsteller (1580–1627)', *Hanauisches Magazin* (1937).

Troso, Mario, *Le armi in asta delle fanterie Europee (1000–1500)* (Novara, 1988).

Tuccaro, Arcangelo, *Trois dialogues de l'exercice de sauter, et voltiger en l'air. Avec les figures qui servent à la parfaicte demonstration et intelligence dudict art* (Paris, 1599).

Umbach, Arnold and Johnson, Warren R., *Successful Wrestling* (St Louis, 1953).

Valencia de Don Juan, Conde, 'Bildinventar der Waffen, Rüstungen, Gewänder und Standarten Karl V in der Armeria Real zu Madrid', *Jahrbuch des Kunsthistorischen Sammlungen des allerhöchsten Kaiserhauses in Wien*, X (1889), XI (1890).

Valerius Maximus, *Romae antiquae descriptio*, tr. Samuel Speed (1678).

Vecelli, Cesare, *Degli habiti antichi et moderni* (Venice, 1590).

Vegetius, Flavius Renatus, *Epitoma rei militaris*, ed. C. Lang (Leipzig, 1885).

Vergerio, Pietro Paulo, *De ingenuis moribus* (Rome, 1475?).

Verolini, Theodor, *Der Künstliche Fechter* (Würzburg, 1679).

Vezzani, Antonio, *L'esercizio accademico di picca* (Parma, 1688).

Viatte, F., 'Allegorical and burlesque subjects by Stefano della Bella', *Master Drawings*, XV, 4 (1977).

Vigeant, Arsène, *Ma collection d'escrime* (Paris, 1892).

Viggiani, Angelo, *Lo schermo* (Venice, 1575) but actually completed before May 1551.

Villardita, Giuseppe, *La scherma siciliana ridotta in compendio* (Palermo, 1670).

Villey, Pierre, *Les Sources et l'évolution des essais de Montaigne* (Paris, 1933).

Viterbo, Sousa, *A esgrima em Portugal. Subsidios para a sua história* (Lisbon, 1899).

Viti, J.B., *Taccometro. Machine d'escrime du Prof. Gioberti* (n.p., n.d.).

Vulson, Marc, Sieur de la Colombière, *Le Vray Théâtre d'honneur et de chevalerie, ou le miroir héroique de la noblesse* (Paris, 1648).

Wachter, Johann Georg, *Glossarium Germanicum* (Leipzig, 1737).

Waetzoldt, Wilhelm, *Dürer and his Times* (1950).

Wallhausen, Johann Jacobi von, *ABC der Soldaten zu Fuss* (Frankfurt-am-Main, 1615).

Wallhausen, Johann Jacobi von, *Kriegskunst zu Fuss* (Oppenheim, 1615).

Wallhausen, Johann Jacobi von, tr. de Bry, *L'Art militaire pour l'infanterie* (Oppenheim, 1615).

Wallhausen, Johann Jacobi von, tr. de Bry, *Art militaire à cheval* (Frankfurt-am-Main, 1616).

Wallhausen, Johann Jacobi von, tr. de Bry, *De la milice romaine, Premier partie* (Frankfurt-am-Main, 1616).

Wallhausen, Johann Jacobi von, *Kriegskunst zu Pferd* (Frankfurt-am-Main, 1616).

Wallhausen, Johann Jacobi von, *Kriegsmanual* (Hanau, 1616).

Wallhausen, Johann Jacobi von, *Ritterkunst* (Frankfurt, 1616).

Wallhausen, Johann Jacobi von, *Romanische Kriegskunst* (Frankfurt-am-Main, 1616).

Wallhausen, Johann Jacobi von, *Künstliche Piquen Handlung* (Hanau, 1617).

Wallhausen, Johann Jacobi von, *Kriegs-Kunst zu Pferd* (Frankfurt-am-Main, 1634).

Warner, Gordon and Draeger, Donn F., *Japanese Swordsmanship. Technique and Practice* (New York and Tokyo, 1982).

Wassmannsdorff, Karl, *Die Ringkunst des deutschen Mittelalters* (Leipzig, 1870).

Wassmannsdorff, Karl, *Sechs Fechtschulen der Marxbrüder und Federfechter* (Heidelberg, 1870).

Wassmannsdorff, Karl, *Auffschlüsse über Fechthandschriften und gedruckte Fechtbücher des 16. und 17. Jahrhunderts* (Berlin, 1888).

Weischner, Siegmund Carl Friedrich, *Die Ritterliche Geschicklichkeit im Fechten* (Weimar, 1765).

Weiss, Giuseppe, *Istruzione sulla scherma a cavallo* (Naples, 1829).

Wierschin, Martin, *Meister Johann Liechtenauers Kunst des Fechtens* (Munich, 1965).

Wilde, Jimmy, *The Art of Boxing* (n.d.).

Wilkinson, Sir J.G., *Manners and Customs of the Ancient Egyptians* (1878).

Williams, Sir Roger, *The Works of Sir Roger Williams*, ed. John X. Evans (Oxford, 1972).

Wilsdorf, Helmut, *Ringkampf im alten Ägypten* (Würzburg, 1939).

Winkelmann, Eduard, *Urkundenbuch der Universität Heidelberg* (Heidelberg, 1886).

Wise, Arthur, *The Art and History of Personal Combat* (Greenwich, Connecticut, 1972).

Woodcroft, Bennet, *Alphabetical Index of Patentees of Inventions* (1854; reprinted 1969).

Woodward, W.H., *Vittorino da Feltre and Other Humanist Educators* (Cambridge, 1897).

Woosnam-Savage, Robert C., 'Robert Lyons Scott (1871–1939)', *Fifth Park Lane Arms Fair* (1988), pp. 10–14.

Wreszinski, Walter, *Atlas zur altaegyptischen Kultergeschichte* (Leipzig, 1923).

Wurm, Hans, *Ringerbuch* (*c.*1490) *see* Minkowski (1963) and Bleibrunner (1969).

Wylde, Zachary, *The English Master of Defence* (York, 1711).

Yates, Frances, *The Valois Tapestries* (1959).

Zapata, Luis, *Miscelánea*, in *Memorial histórico español: colección de documentos, opúsculos y antigüedades*, XI (Madrid: Real Academia Española, 1859), pp. 212–18. See also Quixada.

Zwingli, Ulrich, *Quo pacto ingenui adolescentes formandi sint praeceptiones* (Basle, 1523), English translation, *Certeyne preceptes* (1548).

Index

vocabulary and language of, 39, 119–25, 128, 134, 136–8
See also all-in fighting, combat, fencing, jousting, tourneying, wrestling
Martinez de Toledo, Alfonso, 23, 347 n. 84
Marxbrüder, 92
Mary Tudor, marriage to Louis XII, 168
Massario Malatesta, Alessandro, 224–5, 252, 260–2, 268, 269, 318 n. 5 (Introduction), 351 n. 57, 354 n. 54
Masters of arms, Chapter I, *passim*, 203, 271–3
  English, 10
  examination system of, 9–11
  ignorance of, 119–20
  medieval German, 109
  practice and teaching of, 121–2
  purpose of, 30–9
  qualities necessary for, 39
Matthey, Captain Cyril, 280–2, 356 n. 18
Maurice of Nassau, 224, 282, 285, 287
Maximilian I, Emperor, 2, 167, 175, 194, 251, 295, 298–301
Maximilian I, *Freydal* of, 27, 45, 46, 154, 158, 175, 251, 323 n. 75; *fig. 20; plates III, XI–XIV, XXIV*
Mayrick, Samuel Rush, 165
McArthur, John, writer on fencing, 330 n. 106
McBane, Donald, writer on fencing, 328 n. 76
Mecklenburg, Duke of, 92
Medina Sidonia, Duke of, 342 n. 38
Melzo, Ludovico, writer on cavalry, 222, 249; *fig. 160*
Memmo, Giovanni Maria, 358 n. 41
Mendoza, Don Francisco de, 242
Mendoza y Quixada, Miguel Perez de, master of arms, 82, 83; *fig. 70*
Mercurialis, Hieronymous, writer on gymnastics, 176
Mercury, 17
Meriadet, Hervé de, axe-fighter, 174
Messer, 102
Meung, Jean de, 224
Meyer, Joachim, master of arms, 12–14, 16, 17, 51–2, 54, 65, 92, 93, 94, 102, 116–17, 129, 130, 149, 167, 190–1; *figs 1, 9, 89, 120, 144, 145*
Michelangelo, 48, 327 n. 39
Military equipment, 221, 222, 223; *fig. 161*
Military institutions, ancient and medieval, 223–4
Minerva, 17, 279; *fig. 186*
Modus armandi milites ad torneamentum, 205–6
Monstrelet, Engeurrand de, 224
Montaigne, Michel de, 11, 19
Monte, Pietro, 1–4, 22, 26, 29, 33–4, 39, 93, 95, 109, 113, 117, 132–4, 141, 145, 150, 153–4, 158–9, 163, 173, 177, 194–201, 211–15, 224, 229, 230, 236–8, 240–1, 248–9, 255, 258–9, 271–2, 277, 279, 283–5, 289, 317–18 n. 2 (Introduction), 320 n. 49, 334 n. 50, 357 n. 27
Montecuculli, Raimondo, 229
Montgommery, Gabriel de, kills Henri II in joust, 240
Montgommery, Louis de, military writer, 287
Montlhéry, Battle of, 229

Montmorency, Henri de, tourneying skill of, 267
Morales, Juan de, master of arms, 27
Mourao, Antonio, master of arms, 11
Moxon, J., 177
Mulcaster, Richard, 29, 174, 176
Musashi, Miayamoto, Japanese master swordsman, 30, 112, 321 n. 52, 338 n. 32
Music and harmonic proportions, 87
Muta, Mario, jurist, 28
Myrc, John, 332 n. 16

Nancy, joust at (1445), 250–1
Narváez, Luis Pacheco de, master of arms, 10, 71–3, 78, 82, 84, 86, 88, 92, 93, 121, 139, 140, 169, 260; *figs 14–15, 58*
Nassau-Dillemburg, John of, 285, 287
Newhall, Beaumont, 325 n. 10
Nicolas, master of arms, 12
Nicot, Jean, 101
Niklaus of Toblem, master of arms, 23
Niño, Don Pero, 174
Ninus, King of Assyria, 92
Noah's ark, 56
Norman, A.V.B., 99
Notation, Chapter II, *passim*
  dance, 44, 89–90
  fencing, limitations of, 88–90
  pictographs as, 125–7, 129
  rhetoric, 43–4
Noue, Pierre de la, writer on horsemanship, 265–6, 268
Novati, Francesco, 103, 155. *See also* Fiore de'Liberi
Nuremburg, masters of arms of, 9

Olivier, Monsieur J., master of arms, 324 n. 108
Oñate, Count of, killed in joust, 217
Orozco, Marcus, engraver, 82
Orsini, Orso degli, military writer, 351 n. 53, 352 n. 58
Osorio, Don Luis, killed in joust, 217
Ott the Jew, wrestling master, 23, 129, 181–2
Overbury, Sir Thomas, 21–2
Ovid, 92

Pächt, Otto, 41
Padrini, role in tournaments, 239, 251, 353 n. 38
Pallavicini, Giuseppe Morsicato, master of arms, 28, 30, 38–9, 48, 52, 91–4, 110–11, 135, 140–1, 144–5, 324 n. 113, 330 n. 95, 331 n. 13, 337 n. 92, 340 n. 82, 346 n. 55; *fig. 28*
Palum, sword exercise at the, 108; *fig. 189*
Paris, masters of arms at, 8–10
Parkyns, Sir Thomas, 176–7, 271
Partisan, 159–65
Pascha, Johann Georg, master of arms, 58–60, 149–50; *fig. 39*
Patten, William, military writer, 62
Pauernfeindt, Andre, master of arms, 46, 97 130, 145, 148–9, 189, 190, 326 n. 27, 338 n. 22, 339 n. 35; *fig. 143*
Pauernfeindt, French translation of, 150
Pausanias, 172
Peacham, Henry, 175–6
Pecour, Louis Guillaume, choreographer, 89